Introduction to

Java

Programming

with JBuilder 3

Y. Daniel Liang
Purdue University at Fort Wayne
Department of Computer Science

━━━ *An Alan R. Apt Book* ━━━

Prentice Hall
Upper Saddle River, New Jersey 07458
http://www.prenhall.com

Library of Congress Cataloging-in-Publication Data

Liang, Y. Daniel.
  Introduction to Java programming with JBuilder3 / Y. Daniel Liang.
      p.   cm.
    ISBN 0-13-086911-2
    1. Java (Computer program language)   2. JBuilder.   I. Title
  QA76.73.J38 L53 2000
  005.13'3—dc21   99-053385
                                                                              CIP

Editor-in-chief: *Marcia Horton*
Publisher: *Alan R. Apt*
Project manager: *Ana Arias Terry*
Editorial assistant: *Toni Holm*
Marketing manager: *Jennie Burger*
Production editor: *Pine Tree Composition*
Executive managing editor: *Vince O'Brien*
Managing editor: *David A. George*
Art director: *Heather Scott*
Cover design: *John Christiana*
Manufacturing manager: *Trudy Pisciotti*
Manufacturing buyer: *Beth Sturla*
Assistant vice president of production and manufacturing: *David W. Riccardi*

 © 2000 by Prentice-Hall, Inc.
Upper Saddle River, New Jersey

The author and publisher of this book have used their best efforts in preparing
this book. These efforts include the development, research, and testing of the
theories to determine their effectiveness.

Printed in the United States of America
10   9   8   7   6   5   4   3   2   1

ISBN 0-13-086911-2

Prentice-Hall International (UK) Limited, *London*
Prentice-Hall of Australia Pty. Limited, *Sydney*
Prentice-Hall Canada Inc., *Toronto*
Prentice-Hall Hispanoamericana, S.A., *Mexico*
Prentice-Hall of India Private Limited, *New Delhi*
Prentice-Hall of Japan, Inc., *Tokyo*
Pearson Education Asia Pte. Ltd., *Singapore*
Editora Prentice-Hall do Brasil, Ltda., *Rio de Janeiro*

ABOUT THE AUTHOR

Y. Daniel Liang has B.S. and M.S. degrees in computer science from Fudan University in Shanghai and a Ph.D. degree in computer science from the University of Oklahoma. He is the author of four Java books. He has published numerous papers in international journals and has taught Java courses nationally and internationally. He has consulted in the areas of algorithm design, client/server computing, and database management.

Dr. Liang is currently an associate professor in the Department of Computer Science at Purdue University at Fort Wayne, where he twice received the Excellence in Research Award from the School of Engineering, Technology, and Computer Science. He can be reached via the Internet at **liangjava@yahoo.com**.

ACKNOWLEDGMENTS

This book has benefited from the second edition of my *Introduction to Java Programming*. I would like to acknowledge the following people who helped produce the *Introduction to Java Programming* text: Hao Wu, Michael Willig, Russell Minnich, Balaram Nair, Ben Stonebraker, C-Y Tang, Bertrand I-P Lin, Mike Sunderman, Fen English, B-J Kim, James Silver, Mark Temte, Bob Sanders, Marta Partington, Tom Cirtin, Songlin Qiu, Tim Tate, Carolyn Linn, Alfonso Hermida, Nathan Clement, Eric Miller, Chris Barrick, John Etchison, Louisa Klucznik, Angela Denny, Randy Haubner, Robin Drake, Betsy Brown, and Susan Kindel.

For this edition, I would like to thank Alan Apt, Ana Terry, and Toni Holm, and their colleagues at Prentice Hall for organizing and managing this project, and thank Patty Donovan, Robert Milch, and Dan Boilard, and their colleagues at Pine Tree Composition for helping to produce the book.

As always, I am indebted to my wife, Samantha, for love, support, and encouragement.

To Samantha, Michael, and Michelle

INTRODUCTION

To the Instructor

There are three popular strategies in teaching Java. The first is to mix Java applets and graphics programming with object-oriented programming concepts. The second is to introduce object-oriented programming from the start. The third strategy is a step-by-step approach, first laying a sound foundation on programming elements, control structures, and methods, and then moving on to graphical user interface, applets, internationalization, multimedia, I/O, and networking.

The first strategy, starting with GUI and applets, seems attractive, but requires substantial knowledge of OOP and a good understanding of the Java event-handling model; thus, students may never fully understand what they are doing. The second strategy is based on the notion that the objects should be introduced first because Java is an object-oriented programming language. This notion, however, does not strike a chord with students. From the more than 20 Java courses I have taught, I have concluded that introducing primary data types, control structures, and methods prepares students to learn object-oriented programming. Therefore, this text adopts the third strategy, first proceeding at a steady pace through all the necessary and important basic concepts, then quickly moving to object-oriented programming, and then to using the object-oriented approach to build interesting GUI applications and applets with multimedia and networking.

Although this book is primarily intended for freshman programming courses, it can also be used in teaching Java as a second language, or for a short training course for experienced programmers. The book contains more material than can be covered in a single semester for freshmen. You can skip all the optional topics and cover the first 10 chapters, and use the remaining chapters as time permits.

The Instructor's Manual on CD-ROM is available for instructors of this book. It contains the following resources:

■ Lecture notes with suggested teaching strategies and activities.

■ Microsoft PowerPoint slides for lectures.

■ Answers to chapter reviews.

■ Solutions to programming exercises.

■ Over 400 multiple-choice and true-or-false questions and answers covering all of the chapters in sequence,

To obtain the Instructor's Manual, contact your Prentice-Hall sales representative.

Pedagogical Features of This Book

Introduction to Java Programming with JBuilder 3 uses the following elements to get the most out of the material:

- **Objectives** lists what students should have learned from the chapter. This will help them to determine whether they have met these objectives after completing the chapter.

- **Introduction** opens the discussion with a brief overview of what to expect from the chapter.

- Programming concepts are taught by representative **Examples**, carefully chosen and presented in an easy-to-follow style. Each example is described, and includes the source code, a sample run, and an example review. The source code of the examples is contained in the companion CD-ROM.

  Each program is complete and ready to be compiled and executed. The sample run of the program is captured from the screen to give students live presentation of the example. Reading these examples is much like entering and running them on a computer.

- **Chapter Summary** reviews the important subjects that students should understand and remember. It also reinforces the key concepts they have learned in the chapter.

- **Chapter Review** helps students to track progress and evaluate learning.

- **Programming Exercises** at the end of each chapter provide students with opportunities to apply the skills on their own. The trick of learning programming is practice, practice, and practice. To that end, the book provides a large number of exercises.

- **Notes**, **Tips**, and **Cautions** are inserted throughout the text to offer valuable advice and insight on important aspects of program development.

NOTE
Provides additional information on the subject and reinforces important concepts.

TIP
Teaches good programming style and practice.

CAUTION
Helps students steer away from the pitfalls of programming errors.

What's New in this Edition

This book expands and improves upon the second edition of *Introduction to Java Programming*. The major changes are as follows:

- All the AWT user-interface components are replaced with state-of-the-art Swing components, which improves all the chapters after Chapter 8, "Getting Started with Graphics Programming."

- JBuilder is introduced throughout the book rather than clustered in one or two chapters. This incremental approach makes learning JBuilder easy, because its new features are covered in relation to the topics in each chapter.

- Chapter 12, "Internationalization," is an entirely new chapter added to introduce the development Java programs for international audiences.

- A new appendix, G, titled "Rapid Java Application Development Using JBuilder," was added to demonstrate rapid Java application development using JBuilder.

- Several new case studies are provided to give more examples of such programming fundamentals as writing loops.

- Nonessential sections are marked optional and can be skipped without affecting the student's understanding of later chapters. These sections cover such topics as recursion, event adapters, anonymous inner classes, advanced layout managers, and resource bundles.

To the Student

There is nothing more important to the future of computing than the Internet. There is nothing more exciting on the Internet than Java. A revolutionary programming language developed by Sun Microsystems, Java has become the de facto standard for cross-platform applications and programming on the World Wide Web since its inception in May 1995.

Before Java, the Web was used primarily for viewing static information on the Internet using HTML, a script language for document layout and for linking documents over the Internet. Java programs can be embedded in an HTML page and downloaded by Web browsers to bring live animation and interactive applications to Web clients.

Java is a full-featured, general-purpose programming language that is capable of developing robust, mission-critical applications. In the last three years, Java has gained enormous popularity and has quickly become the most popular and successful programming language. Today, Java is used not only for Web programming, but to develop standalone applications. Many companies that once considered Java to be more hype than substance are now using it to create distributed applications accessed by customers and partners across the Internet. For every new project being developed today, companies are asking how they can use Java to make their work easier.

Java's Design and Advantages

Java is an object-oriented programming language. Object-oriented programming is a favored programming approach that has replaced traditional procedure-based programming techniques. An object-oriented language uses abstraction, encapsulation, inheritance, and polymorphism to provide great flexibility, modularity, and reusability for developing software.

Java is platform-independent. Its programs can run on any machine with any operating system that supports the Java Virtual Machine, a software component that interprets Java instructions and carries out associated actions.

Java is distributed. Networking is inherently built-in. Simultaneous processing can occur on multiple computers on the Internet. Writing network programs is treated as simple data input and output.

Java is multithreaded. Multithreading is the capability of a program to perform several tasks simultaneously; for example, a program can download a video file while playing the video at the same time. Multithreading is particularly useful in graphical user interfaces (GUI) and network programming. Multithread programming is smoothly integrated in Java. In other languages, you have to call procedures that are specific to the operating system to enable multithreading.

Java is secure. Computers become vulnerable when they are connected with other computers. Viruses and malicious programs can damage your computer. Java is designed with multiple layers of security that ensure proper access of private data and restrict access to disk files.

Java's Versatility

Stimulated by the promise of writing programs once and running them anywhere, the computer industry has given Java its unqualified endorsement. IBM, Sun, Apple, and many other vendors are working to integrate the Java Virtual Machine with their operating systems so that Java programs can run directly and efficiently on the native machine. Java programs are not restricted to full-featured computers, but also run on consumer electronics and appliances.

Java has the potential to unite existing legacy applications written on different platforms so that they can run together. Because it is seen as a universal front end for the enterprise database, the leading database companies, IBM, Oracle, Sybase, and Informix, have extended their commitment to Java by integrating it into their products. Oracle, for example, plans to enable native Java applications to run on its server and to deliver a complete set of Java-based development tools supporting the integration of current applications with the Web.

Learning Java

The key to developing software is to apply the concept of abstraction in the design and implementation of the software project. The overriding objective of this book is, therefore, to teach you how to use many levels of abstraction to solve problems, and how to see problems in small and in large.

My students were the inspiration for this book. I learned to teach programming from them, and they told me they wanted a book that used easy-to-follow examples to explain programming concepts. In the summer of 1996, I was looking for a Java text. There were many reference books on the market, and several books that had been converted from C and C++ texts, but I could not find the kind of book I was looking for. As a result, the idea of writing a book that would use good examples to teach basic Java concepts was born.

This book covers the major topics in Java programming, including programming structures, methods, objects, classes, inheritance, graphics programming, applets, exception handling, internationalization, multithreading, multimedia, I/O, and networking. Students new to object-oriented programming will need some time to become familiar with the concept of objects and classes. Once students master the principles, programming in Java is easy and productive. Students who know object-oriented programming languages like C++ and Smalltalk will find it easier to learn Java. In fact, Java is simpler than C++ and Smalltalk in many respects.

The book is completely based on Java 2, and the graphics examples are built using Swing components. The source code for all the examples in the text can be found in the companion CD-ROM. The companion CD-ROM also contains JBuilder 3 University Edition.

Learning Java with JBuilder

You can use Java 2 SDK to write Java programs. Java 2 SDK (formerly known as JDK) consists of a set of separate programs, such as compiler and interpreter, each of which is invoked from a command line. Besides Java 2 SDK, there are more than a dozen Java development tools on the market today, including JBuilder, Visual J++, and Visual Café. These tools support an *integrated development environment* (IDE) for rapidly developing Java programs. Editing, compiling, building, debugging, and online help are integrated in one graphical user interface. Using these tools effectively will greatly increase your programming productivity.

The overriding objective of this book is to introduce the concepts and practice of Java programming. To facilitate developing and managing Java programs, the book is aided by JBuilder. With a tool like JBuilder, students can not only develop Java programs more productively, but can also learn Java programming more effectively.

JBuilder is a premier Java development tool for developing Java programs produced by Borland. Borland products are known to be "best of breed" in the Rapid Application Development tool market. Over the years, it has led the charge in creating visual development tools like Delphi and C++ Builder. Inprise is now leading the way in Java development tools with JBuilder. JBuilder is endorsed by major information technology companies like IBM, which also makes its own Java IDE tool, *VisualAge for Java*.

JBuilder is easy to learn and easy to use. The JBuilder development team worked hard to simplify the user interface and make it easy to navigate through the programs, projects, classes, packages, and code elements. As a result, JBuilder has fewer windows than Microsoft Visual J++ and Symantec Visual Café. This makes JBuilder an ideal tool for beginners and for students who have little programming experience.

JBuilder is an indispensable, powerful tool that boosts your programming productivity. It may take a while to become familiar with it, but the time you invest will pay off in the long run. This text takes an incremental approach to facilitate learning JBuilder. Programming with JBuilder is introduced throughout the book to help you gradually adapt to using it.

My *Rapid Java Application Development Using JBuilder 3*, which introduces many advanced Java features, including JavaBeans, model-view architectures, advanced Swing components, database programming, and distributed programming is now available. This book is also published by Prentice Hall.

Organization of this Book

This book is divided into four parts that, taken together, form a comprehensive introductory course on Java programming. Because knowledge is cumulative, the early chapters provide the conceptual basis for understanding Java and guide students through simple examples and exercises; subsequent chapters progressively present Java programming in detail and culminate in teaching the development of comprehensive Java applications. The appendixes contain a mixed bag of topics that include an HTML tutorial.

Part I: Fundamentals of Java Programming

The book's first part is a stepping stone to prepare you to embark on the journey of learning Java. You will start to know Java, and learn how to write simple Java programs with primitive data types, control structures, and methods.

Chapter 1, "Introduction to Java and JBuilder 3," gives an overview of the major features of Java: object-oriented programming, platform-independence, Java bytecode, security, performance, multithreading, and networking. This chapter also introduces JBuilder and uses it to create, compile, and run Java applications and applets. Simple examples of writing applications and applets are provided, along with a brief anatomy of programming structures.

Chapter 2, "Java Building Elements," introduces primitive data types, operators, and expressions. Important topics include identifiers, variables, constants, assignment statements, primitive data types, operators, and shortcut operators. Java programming style and documentation are also addressed. You will learn how to run Java programs from the command line, get online help from JBuilder, and customize JBuilder IDE options.

Chapter 3, "Control Structures," introduces decision and repetition statements. Java decision statements include various forms of `if` statements, the `switch` statement, and the shortcut `if` statement. Repetition statements include the `for` loop, the `while` loop, and the `do` loop. The keywords `break` and `continue` are discussed. You will learn how to manage Java projects in JBuilder.

Chapter 4, "Methods," introduces method creation, calling methods, passing parameters, returning values, method overloading, and recursion. Applying the concept of abstraction is the key to developing software. The concept of method abstraction in problem-solving is also introduced. Various JBuilder commands in the Search, View, Build, and Run menus are discussed.

Part II: Object-Oriented Programming

In the book's second part, object-oriented programming is introduced. Java is a class-centric, object-oriented programming language that uses abstraction, encapsulation, inheritance, and polymorphism to provide great flexibility, modularity, and reusability for developing software. You will learn programming with objects and classes, arrays and strings, and class inheritance.

Chapter 5, "Programming with Objects and Classes," begins with objects and classes. The important topics include defining classes, creating objects, using constructors, passing objects to methods, instance, and class variables, and instance and class methods. Many examples are provided to demonstrate the power of the object-oriented programming approach. Students will learn the benefits (abstraction, encapsulation, and modularity) of object-oriented programming from these examples. There are more than 500 predefined Java classes grouped in several packages. Starting with this chapter, students will gradually learn how to use Java classes to develop their own programs. The `Math` class for performing basic math operations is introduced. You will learn how to use the wizards in the JBuilder Object Gallery to generate program templates.

Chapter 6, "Arrays and Strings," explores two important structures: arrays for processing data in lists and tables, and strings using the `String`, `StringBuffer`, and `StringTokenizer` classes. Java treats arrays as objects. Unlike the many high-level languages that treat strings as a special kind of array, it does not relate strings to arrays. Java uses strings and arrays quite differently. You will also learn how to use JBuilder to debug programs.

Chapter 7, "Class Inheritance," teaches how to extend an existing class and modify it as needed. Inheritance is an extremely powerful programming technique that further extends software reusability. Java programs are all built by extending predefined Java classes. The major topics include defining subclasses, using the keywords `super` and `this`, using the modifiers `protected`, `final` and `abstract`, and casting objects and interfaces. This chapter introduces the `Object` class, which is the root of all Java classes. You will learn primitive data type wrapper classes to encapsulate primitive data type values in objects, as well as how to use the Implement Interface Wizard and Override Methods Wizard in JBuilder.

Part III: Graphics Programming

In this part Java graphics programming is introduced. Major topics include event-driven programming, creating graphical user interfaces, and writing applets. You will learn the architecture of Java graphics programming API and use the user interface components to develop graphics applications and applets.

Chapter 8, "Getting Started with Graphics Programming," introduces the concepts of Java graphics programming using the Swing components. Topics include the graphics class hierarchy, event-driven programming, frames, panels, and simple layout managers (`FlowLayout`, `GridLayout`, and `BorderLayout`). This chapter also introduces drawing geometric figures in the graphics context. You will learn how to use the JBuilder Application Wizard to create Java applications.

Chapter 9, "Creating User Interfaces," introduces the user interface components: buttons, labels, text fields, text areas, combo boxes, check boxes, radio buttons, message dialogs, menus, scrollbars, scroll panes, and tabbed panes. Today's client/server and Web-based applications use a graphical user interface (GUI, pronounced "goo-ee"). Java has a rich set of classes to help you build GUIs.

Chapter 10, "Applets and Advanced Graphics," takes an in-depth look at applets, and discusses applet behaviors and the relationship of applets to other AWT and Swing classes. Applets are a special kind of Java class that can be executed from the Web browser. Students will learn how to convert applications to applets, and vice versa, and how to run programs both as applications and as applets. This chapter also introduces two advanced layout mangers (`CardLayout` and `GridBagLayout`) and the use of no layout. Advanced examples on handling mouse and keyboard events are also provided. You will learn to create applets using the JBuilder Applet Wizard, and learn to use the Deployment Wizard to create archive files for deploying Java applications and applets.

Part IV: Developing Comprehensive Projects

This part is devoted to several advanced features of Java programming. You will learn how to use these features to develop comprehensive programs; for example, using exception handling to make your program robust, using internationalization to create Java projects for international audiences, using multithreading to make your program more responsive and interactive, incorporating sound and images to make your program user friendly, using input and output to manage and process a large quantity of data, and creating client/server applications with Java networking support.

Chapter 11, "Exception Handling," teaches students how to define exceptions, throw exceptions, and handle exceptions so that programs can continue to run or terminate gracefully in the event of runtime errors. The chapter discusses predefined exception classes, and gives examples of creating user-defined exception classes.

Chapter 12, "Internationalization," introduces the development of Java programs for international audiences. You will learn how to format date, numbers, currencies, and percentages for different regions, countries, and languages. You will also learn how to use resource bundles to define which images and strings are used by a component depending on the locale and preferences of the user.

Chapter 13, "Multithreading," introduces threads, which enable the running of multiple tasks simultaneously in one program. Students will learn how to use the Thread class and the Runnable interface to launch separate threads. The chapter also discusses thread states, thread priority, thread groups, and the synchronization of conflicting threads.

Chapter 14, "Multimedia," teaches how to incorporate sound and images to bring live animation to Java programs. Various techniques for smoothing animation are introduced.

Chapter 15, "Input and Output," introduces input and output streams. Students will learn the class structures of I/O streams, byte and character streams, file I/O streams, data I/O streams, print streams, delimited I/O, random file access, and interactive I/O.

Chapter 16, "Networking," introduces network programming. Students will learn the concept of network communication, stream sockets, client/server programming, and reading data files from the Web server.

Appendixes

This part covers a mixed bag of topics. Appendix A lists Java keywords. Appendix B gives tables of ASCII characters and their associated codes in decimal and in hex. Appendix C shows the operator precedence. Appendix D summarizes Java modifiers and their usage. Appendix E introduces HTML basics. Appendix F provides information for using the companion CD-ROM. Appendix G introduces rapid Java application development using JBuilder. Finally, Appendix H provides a glossary of key terms found in the text.

What's on the Companion CD-ROM?

The companion CD-ROM contains JBuilder 3 University Edition, and the source code for all the examples in the text. Please refer to Appendix F, "Using the Companion CD-ROM," for instructions on installing JBuilder 3 and using the example source code.

CONTENTS AT A GLANCE

TABLE OF CONTENTS

FUNDAMENTALS
OF JAVA PROGRAMMING

By now you have heard a lot about Java and are anxious to start writing Java programs. The first part of this book is a stepping stone to prepare you to embark on the journey of learning Java with JBuilder. You will begin to know Java and learn how to write simple Java programs with primitive data types, control structures, and methods.

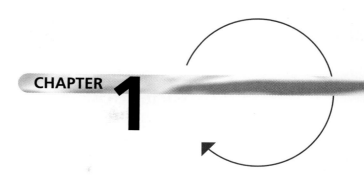

CHAPTER 1

INTRODUCTION TO JAVA AND JBUILDER 3

Objectives

- Learn about Java and its history.
- Understand the relationship between Java and the World Wide Web.
- Become familiar with JBuilder 3.
- Know how to create Java projects, compile and run Java programs with JBuilder 3.
- Understand the Java environment.
- Write a simple Java application.
- Write a simple Java applet.

3

Introduction

Java, a new and exciting programming language, seems to be everywhere! There are Java books in your local bookstore. All the major newspapers and magazines are running articles about Java. You can't read a computer magazine without seeing the magic word *Java*. Why is Java so hot? Java is important because it enables the user to deploy applications on the Internet. The future of computing will be greatly influenced by the Internet, and Java promises to remain a big part of that future. Java is *the* Internet programming language.

You are about to begin an exciting journey, learning a powerful programming language. Java is cross-platform, object-oriented, network-based, and multimedia-ready. After its inception in May 1995, Java quickly became a mature language for deploying mission-critical applications. This chapter begins with a brief history of Java and its programming features, followed by simple examples of Java applications and applets.

The History of Java

Java was developed by a team led by James Gosling at Sun Microsystems, a company best known for its workstations. Originally called Oak, Java was designed in 1991 for use in embedded consumer electronic applications. In 1995 it was re-designed for developing Internet applications and renamed Java. Java programs can be embedded in HTML pages and downloaded by Web browsers to bring live animation and interaction to Web clients.

The power of Java is not limited to Web applications. Java is a general-purpose programming language. It has full programming features and can be used to develop standalone applications. Java is inherently object-oriented. Although many object-oriented languages began strictly as procedural languages, Java was designed to be object-oriented from the start. Object-oriented programming (OOP) is currently a popular programming approach that replaces traditional procedural programming techniques.

NOTE

One of the central issues in software development is how to reuse code. Object-oriented programming provides great flexibility, modularity, clarity, and reusability through method abstraction, class abstraction, and class inheritance—all of which you'll learn about in this book.

Characteristics of Java

Java has gained enormous popularity. It is the language for networking and controlling smart appliances and futuristic devices, and is seen as a universal front end for enterprise databases. Java's rapid ascent and wide acceptance can be traced to its design and programming features, particularly its promise that you can write a program once and run it anywhere. As stated in the Java language white paper by Sun,

Java is *simple, object-oriented, distributed, interpreted, robust, secure, architecture-neutral, portable, high-performance, multithreaded,* and *dynamic.* Let's analyze these often-used buzzwords.

Java is Simple

No language is simple, but Java is a bit easier than the popular object-oriented programming language C++, which was the dominant software-development language before Java. Java is partially modeled on C++, but greatly simplified and improved. For instance, pointers and multiple inheritance often make programming complicated. Java replaced multiple inheritance in C++ with a language construct called an *interface*, and eliminated pointers.

Java uses automatic memory allocation and garbage collection, whereas C++ requires the programmer to allocate memory and to collect garbage. Also, the number of language constructs is small for such a powerful language. The clean syntax makes Java programs easy to write and read. Some people refer to Java as "C++−−" because it is like C++, but with more functionality and fewer negative aspects.

Java is Object-Oriented

Object-oriented programming models the real world. Everything in the world can be modeled as an object. A circle is an object, a person is an object, and a window's icon is an object. Even a mortgage can be perceived as an object. A Java program is called object-oriented because programming in Java is centered on creating objects, manipulating objects, and making objects work together.

An object has *properties* and *behaviors*. Properties are described by using *data*, and behaviors are defined by using *methods*. Objects are defined by using classes in Java. A class is like a template for the objects. An object is a concrete realization of a class description. The process of creating an object of the class is called *instantiation*. For example, you can define the class `Circle` by which to model all `Circle` objects (see Figure 1.1), with `radius` as the property and `findArea` as the method to find the area of the circle. You can create a `Circle` object by instantiating the class with a particular radius. You can create a circle with radius 2, and another circle with radius 5. You can then find the area of the respective circles by using the `findArea()` method.

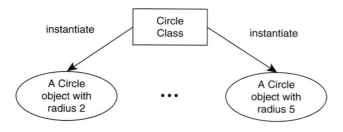

Figure 1.1 *Two* `Circle` *objects with radii 2 and 5 were created from the* `Circle` *class.*

A Java program consists of one or more classes. Classes are arranged in a treelike hierarchy, so that a child class can inherit properties and behaviors from its parent class. Java comes with an extensive set of predefined classes grouped in packages. You can use them in your programs.

Object-oriented programming provides great flexibility, modularity, and reusability. For years, object-oriented technology was perceived as elitist, requiring substantial investments in training and infrastructure. Java has helped object-oriented technology enter the mainstream of computing. Java has a simple, clean structure that makes it easy to write and read programs. Java programs are very *expressive* in terms of applications and designs.

Java is Distributed

Distributed computing involves several computers on a network working together. Java is designed to make distributed computing easy. Networking capability is inherently integrated into Java. Writing network programs in Java is like sending and receiving data to and from a file. For example, Figure 1.2 shows three programs running on three different systems; the three programs communicate with each other to perform a joint task.

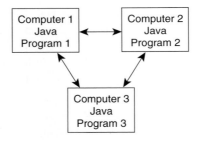

Figure 1.2 *Java programs can run on different systems that work together.*

Java is Interpreted

You need an interpreter to run Java programs. Programs are compiled into Java Virtual Machine code called *bytecode*. The bytecode is machine-independent and can run on any machine that has a Java interpreter.

Usually, a compiler translates a high-level language program to machine code. The code can only run on the native machine. If you run the program on other machines, it has to be recompiled on the native machine. For instance, if you compile a C program in Windows, the executable code generated by the compiler can only run on the Windows platform. With Java, you compile the source code once, and the bytecode generated by a Java compiler can run on any platform. *Java programs do not need to be recompiled on a target machine.*

Java is Robust

Robust means *reliable*. No programming languages can ensure complete reliability. Java puts a lot of emphasis on early checking for possible errors, because Java compilers can detect many problems that would first show up at execution time in other languages. Java does not use certain types of programming constructs in other languages that are prone to errors. It does not support pointers, for example, which eliminates the possibility of overwriting memory and corrupting data.

Java has a runtime exception-handling feature to provide programming support for robustness. Java can catch and respond to an exceptional situation so that the program can continue its normal execution and terminate gracefully when a runtime error occurs.

Java is Secure

As an Internet programming language, Java is used in a networked and distributed environment. If you download a Java applet (a special kind of program) and run it on your computer, it will not damage your system, because Java implements several security mechanisms to protect your system from being damaged by stray programs. The security is based on the premise that *nothing should be trusted*.

There is no absolute security, however. Security bugs have recently been discovered in Java, but they are subtle and few, and have been addressed.

NOTE
A computer security team at Princeton University maintains a Web site devoted to Java security issues. You can find new security bugs and fixes at **www.cs.princeton.edu/sip/**.

Java is Architecture-Neutral

The most remarkable feature of Java is that it is *architecture-neutral*, also known as platform-independent. You can write one program that will run on any platform with a Java Virtual Machine. The major OS vendors have adopted the Java Virtual Machine, and soon Java will run on all machines.

Java's initial success lies in its Web programming capability. You can run Java applets from a Web browser, but Java is for more than just writing Web applets. You can also run standalone Java applications directly from operating systems by using a Java interpreter. Today, software vendors usually develop multiple versions of the same product to run on different platforms (Windows, OS/2, Macintosh, and various UNIX, IBM AS/400, and IBM mainframes). Using Java, developers need to write only one version to run on all of the platforms.

Java is Portable

Java programs are very portable because they can be run on any platform without being recompiled. Moreover, there are no platform-specific features in the Java language specification. In some languages, such as Ada, the largest integer varies on different platforms. But in Java, the size of the integer is the same on every platform, as is the behavior of arithmetic. This fixed size for numbers makes the program portable.

The Java environment itself is portable to new hardware and operating systems. In fact, the Java compiler itself is written in Java.

Java's Performance

Java's performance is often criticized because the execution of the bytecode is never as fast as in a compiled language, such as C++. Since Java is interpreted, the bytecode is not directly executed by the system, but instead is run through the interpreter. However, the speed is more than adequate for most interactive applications, where the CPU is often idle, waiting for input or for data from other sources.

CPU speed has increased dramatically in the past few years, and this trend is likely to continue. There are many ways to improve performance. If you used the earlier Sun Java Virtual Machine (JVM), you will certainly notice that Java is slow. However, new JVMs from Borland, Microsoft, and Symantec are 10 or even 20 times faster than the first Sun JVM. These new JVMs use the technology known as just-in-time compilation. They compile bytecode into native machine code, store the native code, and reinvoke the native code when its bytecode is repeatedly executed. Sun recently unveiled the Java HotSpot Performance Engine, which includes a compiler for optimizing the frequently used code. The HotSpot Performance Engine can be plugged into a JVM to dramatically boost its performance. Thus speed will continue to improve over time.

NOTE

IBM has formed a joint lab with Sun and Netscape to improve Java performance. IBM is one of the strongest and most influential supporters of Java. IBM views Java as a glue that unifies different platforms and applications.

Java is Multithreaded

Multithreading is a program's capability to perform several tasks simultaneously—for example, downloading a video file while playing the video. Multithread programming is smoothly integrated in Java. In other languages, you have to call operating-system-specific procedures to enable multithreading.

Multithreading is particularly useful in graphical user interface (GUI) and network programming. In GUI programming, there are many things going on at the same time. A user can listen to an audio recording while surfing a Web page. In network programming, a server can serve multiple clients at the same time. Multithreading is a necessity in visual and network programming.

Java is Dynamic

Java was designed to adapt to an evolving environment. You can freely add new methods and properties in a class without affecting their clients. For example, in the `Circle` class, you can add a new data property to indicate the color of the circle, and a new method to obtain the circumference of the circle. The original client program that uses the `Circle` class remains the same. Also at runtime, Java loads classes as they are needed.

Java and the World Wide Web

The World Wide Web is an electronic information repository that can be accessed on the Internet from anywhere in the world. You can book a hotel room, buy an airline ticket, register for a college course, download *The New York Times*, chat with friends, and listen to live radio using the Web. There are countless activities you can do on the Internet. In today's world, a lot of people spend a lot of their computer time surfing the Web for fun and profit.

The Internet is the infrastructure of the WWW. The Internet has been around for more than thirty years, but has only recently become popular. The colorful World Wide Web is the major reason for its popularity.

The primary authoring language for the Web is Hypertext Markup Language (HTML). HTML is a markup language: a simple language for document layout, linking documents on the Internet, and bringing images, sound, and video alive on the Web. However, it cannot interact with the user except through simple forms. Web pages in HTML essentially are static and flat.

Java programs can run from a Web browser. Because Java is a full-blown programming language, you can make your program responsive and interactive with the user. Java programs that run from a Web page are called *applets*. Applets use a modern graphical user interface, including buttons, text fields, text areas, option buttons, and so on. Applets can respond to user events, such as mouse movements and keystrokes.

Figure 1.3 shows an applet in an HTML page, and Figure 1.4 shows the HTML source. The source contains an applet tag, and the applet tag specifies the Java applet. The HTML source can be seen by choosing View, HTML Source from the Web Browser.

NOTE

For a demonstration of Java applets, visit **www.javasoft.com/applets/**. This site contains a rich Java resource.

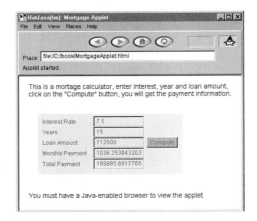

Figure 1.3   *A Java applet for computing a mortgage is embedded in an HTML page. The user can find the mortgage payment by using this applet.*

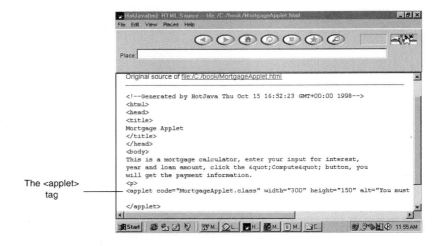

Figure 1.4   *The HTML source that contains the applet shows the tag specifying the Java applet.*

The Java Language Specification

Computer languages have strict usage rules. You must follow the rules when writing programs in order for them to be understood by the computer. Sun Microsystems, the originator of Java, intends to keep control of it for a good reason: to prevent the language from losing its unified standards. The complete reference on Java standards can be found in *Java Language Specification* by James Gosling, Bill Joy, and Guy Steele (Addison-Wesley, 1996). The book is accessible online in JBuilder Help.

The specification is a technical definition of the language, including syntax, structures, and the *application programmer interface* (API), which contains predefined classes. The language is still rapidly evolving. At the JavaSoft Web site (**www. javasoft.com**), you can view the latest version and updates of the language. Sun maintains online documentation for API and language specification.

Sun releases each version of Java with a Java Development Toolkit known as JDK, a primitive command-line tool set that includes a compiler, an interpreter, and the Applet Viewer, as well as other useful utilities.

Although the letters stand for "Java Development Toolkit," JDK is not only a toolkit consisting of the compiler, the interpreter, and the Java run-time environment; it is also a Java language standard. This book is compliant with JDK 1.2, which was a substantial enhancement to JDK 1.1. In turn, JDK 1.1 benefited from significant improvements over the previous version, JDK 1.0.

NOTE

Sun announced the Java 2 name in December 1998, just as it released JDK 1.2. Java 2 is the overarching brand that applies to the latest Java technology. JDK 1.2 is the first version of the Java development toolkit that supports the Java 2 technology. Recently, Sun renamed JDK 1.2 as Java 2 SDK. The current version of Java 2 SDK is v 1.2.2. Since most Java programmers are familiar with the name JDK, this book uses the terms Java SDK and JDK interchangeably.

Java Development Tools and JBuilder

JDK consists of a set of separate programs, each of which is invoked from a command line. Besides JDK, there are more than a dozen Java development packages on the market today. The major development tools are:

> JBuilder by Borland (**www.borland.com**)
> Visual J++ by Microsoft (**www.microsoft.com**)
> Visual Café by Symantec (**www.symantec.com**)
> JFactory by Rouge Wave (**www.rougewave.com**)
> Sun Java Workshop (**www.javasoft.com**)
> Visual Age for Java by IBM (**www.ibm.com**)

These tools provide an *integrated development environment* (IDE) for developing Java programs. The basic functions of these tools are very similar. Editing, compiling, building, debugging, and online help are integrated in one graphical user interface. Just enter source code in one window, or open an existing file in a window, then click a button, menu item, or function key to compile the source code. The use of development tools makes it easy and productive to develop Java programs. This book introduces Java programming with JBuilder 3.

JBuilder 3 is easy to learn and easy to use. The JBuilder development team made a significant effort to simplify the user interface and make it easy to navigate through the programs, projects, classes, packages, and code elements. As a result, JBuilder has fewer windows than Microsoft Visual J++ and Symantec Visual Café. This makes JBuilder an ideal tool for beginners and for students who have little programming experience. If you are interested in Visual J++, please refer to my *Introduction to Java Programming Using Microsoft Visual J++ 6*, published by Prentice-Hall.

JBuilder 3, released in May 1999 by Borland, is a premier Java development tool for developing Java programs. Borland products are known to be "best of breed" in the Rapid Application Development tool market. Over the years, Borland has led the charge to create visual development tools like Delphi and C++ Builder. Borland is leading the way in Java development tools with JBuilder. JBuilder delivers 100% pure Java code and is one of the most popular Java tools used by professional Java developers. JBuilder is endorsed by major information technology companies like IBM, which also makes its own Java IDE tool, *VisualAge for Java*.

JBuilder 3 is available in four versions: JBuilder University Edition, JBuilder Standard, JBuilder Professional, and JBuilder Enterprise.

- The University Edition is ideal for students to learn the basics of Java programming without the need to create JavaBeans and use visual design tools. The University Edition is free for educational use and included in the companion CD-ROM. This book teaches Java programming with JBuilder 3 University Edition.

- JBuilder Standard is a lean package that contains all the essential components for developing Java applications and applets. It is a perfect development tool for Java beginners who want to learn and explore Java visual design capabilities.

- JBuilder Professional contains the components in JBuilder Standard, plus Java Database Connectivity (JDBC) to help develop database clients.

- JBuilder Enterprise contains all the components in JBuilder Professional, plus support for creating distributed applications using CORBA.

Getting Started with JBuilder 3

Assume you have successfully installed JBuilder University Edition on your machine. Start JBuilder from the Windows Start button, selecting Programs, Borland JBuilder 3 University, JBuilder 3. The main JBuilder user interface appears, as shown in Figure 1.5. If you don't see the Welcome project, choose Welcome Project (Sample) from the Help menu.

NOTE

I recommend that you install JBuilder 3 with the default options. The default installation options will enable you to install the projects in this book and run them without modifications. For information on installing JBuilder 3 and using the examples, please refer to Appendix F, "Using the Companion CD-ROM."

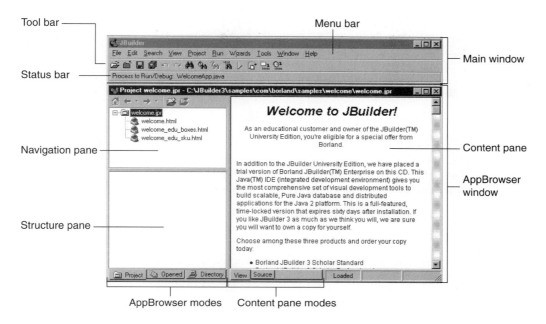

Figure 1.5   *The JBuilder user interface consists of the main window and the AppBrowser window.*

The user interface primarily consists of the main window and the AppBrowser window. The main window is at the top of the screen when you start JBuilder. The main window serves as the development control center, consisting of the main menu bar, the toolbar, and the status bar. The AppBrowser window (below the main window) is used to perform all the usual development functions, such as creating and editing programs, designing user interfaces, compiling and running program, and debugging programs.

NOTE

JBuilder Standard Edition, JBuilder Professional Edition, and JBuilder Enterprise edition also contain the Component palette in the main window. The Component palette contains the components for Rapid Application Development. For a demonstration of rapid Java application development using JBuilder 3, see Appendix G, "Rapid Java Application Development Using JBuilder."

The Main Window

The main window consists of the menu bar, the toolbar, and the status bar. The menu bar is similar to that of other Windows applications and provides most of the commands you need to use JBuilder, including those for creating programs, editing programs, compiling, running, and debugging programs. The menu items are enabled and disabled in response to the current context.

The tool bar provides buttons for several frequently used commands on the menu bar. Clicking a toolbar is faster than using the menu bar. For some commands, you also can use function keys or keyboard shortcuts. For example, you can save a file in three ways:

- Select File, Save from the menu bar.
- Click the "save" toolbar button ■.
- Use the keyboard shortcut Ctrl+S.

TIP

You can display a label, known as *ToolTip*, for a button by pointing the mouse to the button without clicking.

The status bar displays a message to alert users of the operation status, such as file saved for the Save file command and compilation successful for the Compilation command.

The AppBrowser Window

Traditional IDE tools use many windows to accommodate various development tasks, such as editing, debugging, and browsing information. As a result, finding the window you need is often difficult. Because it is easy to get lost, beginners may be intimidated. For this reason, some new programmers prefer to use separate utilities, such as the JDK command line tools, for developing programs.

Borland is aware of the usability problem and has made significant efforts to simply the JBuilder user interface. JBuilder introduces the AppBrowser window, which enables you to explore, edit, design, and debug projects all in one unified window.

An AppBrowser window contains three panes (see Figure 1.5): the Navigation pane (upper left), the Content pane (right side), and the Structure pane (bottom left).

The Navigation Pane

The Navigation pane shows a list of one or more files. In the case of the Project browser, you will see the project (.jpr) file first. Attached to that is a list of the files in the project. The list can include .java, .html, text, or image files. You can select a file in the Navigation pane by clicking it. The Content pane and the Structure pane display information about the selected file. As you select different files in the Navigation pane, each one will be represented in the Content and Structure panes.

The Navigation pane shown in Figure 1.5 contains three HTML files. You can add new files into the project using the Add button ■. The Add button is located above the Navigation pane, as shown in Figure 1.7. For example, you can add a Java source file named WelcomeFrame.java into the project as follows:

1. Click the Add button to display the Open dialog box shown in Figure 1.6.

2. Open WelcomeFrame.java. You will see WelcomeFrame.java in the Navigation pane, as shown in Figure 1.7.

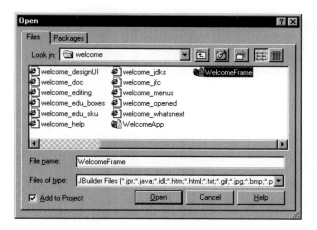

Figure 1.6   *The Open dialog box enables you to open an existing file.*

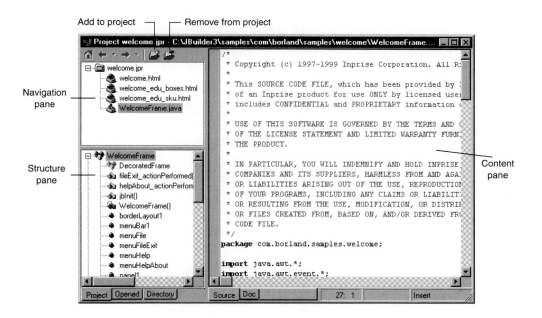

Figure 1.7   *The AppBrowser Window shows WelcomeFrame.java.*

The three tabs (Project, Opened, and Directory) below the Structure pane allow you to navigate through the project, the opened files, and files in the directory, respectively. For example, if you choose the Directory tab, you will see the directories in the Navigation pane (see Figure 1.8).

Click the Directory tab

Figure 1.8 *Choosing the Directory tab enables you to navigate through the directories and files.*

If you choose the Project tab, you will see five buttons above the Navigation pane enabled (see Figure 1.7). You can see the tool tip of the button by pointing the mouse on the button. The first three buttons are for navigating through the browser, and the last two are for adding files to the project or removing files from the project.

The Content Pane

The Content pane displays the detailed content of the file selected in the Navigation pane. The editor or viewer used is determined by the file's extension. If you click the WelcomeFrame.java file in the Navigation pane, for example, you will see two tabs (Source and Doc) on the bottom of the Content pane (see Figure 1.7). If you select the Source tab, you will see the JBuilder Java Source Code Editor. This is a full-featured, syntax-highlighted programming editor.

If you select welcome_edu_boxes.html in the Navigation pane, you will see the Content pane become an HTML browser. If you choose the Source tab, you can view and edit the HTML code in the Content pane, as shown in Figure 1.9. You can also view the image files in the Content pane. To view an image file, first use the Add button to add it to the project if it is not in the Navigation pane, and choose the image file in the Navigation pane to view the image in the Content pane. Figure 1.10 shows the image for the file btn_tutorials.gif.

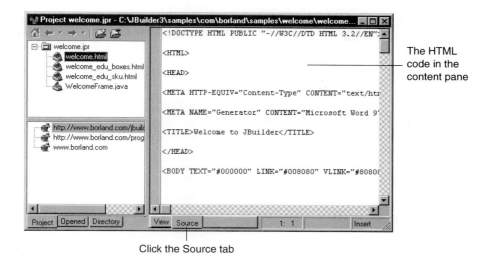

The HTML code in the content pane

Click the Source tab

Figure 1.9 *You can edit HTML files in the Content pane of the AppBrowser.*

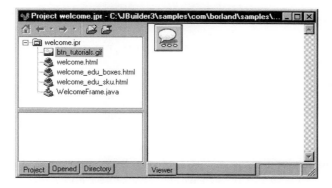

Figure 1.10 *You can view image files in the Content pane.*

The Structure Pane

The Structure pane displays the structural information about the files you selected in the Navigation pane. All the items displayed in the Structure pane are in the form of a hierarchical indexed list. The + symbol in front of an item indicates that it contains subitems. You can see the subitems by clicking on the + symbol.

You also can use the Structure pane as a quick navigational tool to the various structural elements in the file. If you select the WelcomeFrame.java file, for example, you see classes, variables, and methods in the Structure pane (see Figure 1.7). If you then click on any of those elements in the Structure pane, the Content pane will move to and highlight it in the source code.

If you click on the menuFile item in the Structure pane, as shown in Figure 1.11, the Content pane moves to and highlights the statement that defines the menuFile data field. This provides a much faster way to browse and find the elements of a .java file than scrolling through it.

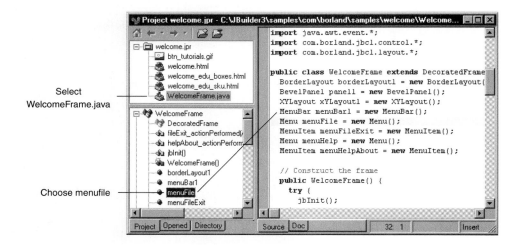

Figure 1.11 *You can cruise through the source code from the Structure pane.*

Creating a Project

A project is like a holder that ties all the files together. The information about each JBuilder project is stored in a project file with a .jpr file extension. The project file contains a list of all the files and project settings and properties. JBuilder uses this information to load and save all the files in the project and compile and run the programs. In this book, I will create a project for each chapter, put all files of the project in a folder called Chapter1, Chapter2, and so on, and place the folder under c:\jbBook. The following steps are for setting default project properties.

1. Choose Tools, Default Project Properties from the main menu bar to display the Default Project Properties dialog box, as shown in Figure 1.12.

2. Replace both the source root directory and the output root directory with c:\jbBook.

3. Click OK to close the window.

These settings are the default for the new projects created henceforth in this book. To create a new project for holding the programs in Chapter 1, use the Project Wizard as follows.

1. Choose File, New Project to bring up the Project Wizard dialog box, as shown in Figure 1.13.

2. Replace "untitled1" by "Chapter1" in the File field.

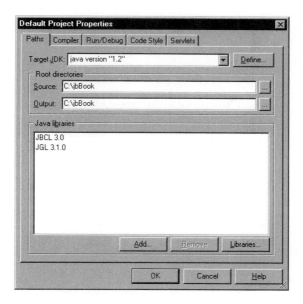

Figure 1.12   *The Path page of the Project Properties dialog box enables you to set the source root directory and output root directory.*

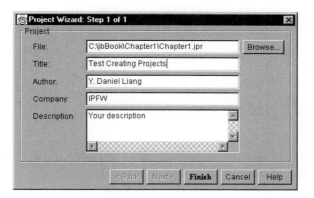

Figure 1.13   *The Project Wizard dialog box enables you to specify the project file with other optional information.*

3. Fill in the title, author, company, and description fields. These optional fields provide a description for the project.

4. Click Finish. The new project is displayed in a new AppBrowser, as shown in Figure 1.14.

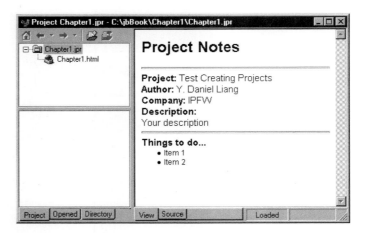

Figure 1.14   *Each project has an independent AppBrowser window.*

NOTE

The Project Wizard created the project file (.jpr) and an HTML file (.html) and placed these files in c:\jbBook\Chapter1. You cannot edit the project file manually; it is modified automatically, however, whenever you add or remove files from the project or set project options. The HTML file contains default project information. You can edit this to record any pertinent information about the project that you want to display. The contents of this file always display in the Source pane when the project file is selected, even if you remove the file from the project. Appendix E, "An HTML Tutorial," introduces writing HTML documents.

CAUTION

Creating a project is a preliminary step before developing Java programs. Creating projects incorrectly is a common problem for new JBuilder users, which could lead to frustrating mistakes. I recommend you to create projects following a persistent pattern with each project placed in a separate directory and group all the project directories under a root directory. Suppose the root directory is JohnDoe. Use the following steps to create your Project1:

1. Choose File, New Project to display the Project Wizard. Type C:\JohnDoe\Project1\Project1.jpr in the File field. Click Finish to close the wizard.

2. Choose Project, Properties to display the Project Properties dialog box. Set both Source and Output path to C:\JohnDoe.

You will learn how to create Java applications and applets in the following sections.

Java Applications

There are two types of Java programs: *applications* and *applets*. Applications are standalone programs, such as any program written using high-level languages. Applications can be executed from any computer with a Java interpreter and are ideal for developing standalone applications. Applets are special kinds of Java programs that can run directly from a Web browser. Applets are suitable for deploying Web projects.

Let's begin with a simple Java application program that displays the message "Welcome to Java!" on the console.

Example 1.1 A Simple Application

This program shows how to write a simple Java application and demonstrates the compilation and execution of an application.

```
// Welcome.java: A simple Java application to print Welcome to Java
package Chapter1;

public class Welcome
{
  // Main method
  public static void main(String[] args)
  {
    System.out.println("Welcome to Java!");
  }
}
```

Example Review

In this program, `println("Welcome to Java!")` is actually the statement that prints the message. So why do you use the other statements in the program? Computer languages have rigid styles and strict syntax, and you need to write code that the Java compiler understands.

Every Java program must have at least one class. Each class begins with a class declaration that defines data and methods for the class. In this example, the class name is `Welcome`.

The statement `package Chapter1` tells the compiler to store the bytecode in the Chapter1 folder.

The class contains a method called `main`. The `main()` method in this program contains the `println` statement. The `main()` method is invoked by the interpreter.

Creating a Java Program

There are many ways to create a Java program in JBuilder. This book will show you how to use various wizards to create certain types of Java programs. In this section, you will first learn how to create Java programs without using wizards.

The following are the steps to create a Java program for Example 1.1:

1. Click the Add to project button (see Figure 1.14) above the Navigation pane of the AppBrowser for project Chapter1.jpr. You will see the Open dialog box, as shown in Figure 1.15.

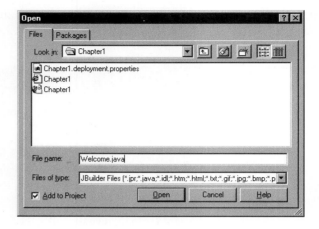

Figure 1.15   *The Open dialog box allows you to open files from a file directory or a package or to create a new file.*

2. On the File page of the File Open dialog box, type Welcome.java in the File name field and click Open. By convention, Java program source files must end with the extension .java. You should see Welcome.java added to the project and currently selected in the Navigation pane.

3. Type Example 1.1 in the Content pane, as shown in Figure 1.16.

4. Select File, Save All to save all your work. You should see a confirmation message in the status bar that indicates the files are saved.

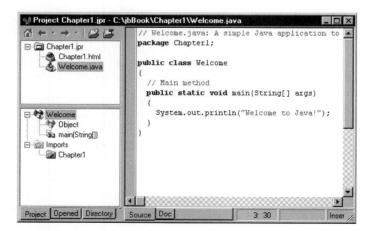

Figure 1.16   *The program Welcome is typed in the Content pane.*

■■■ **NOTE**

As you type, watch two things happen:

■ The code completion assistance may automatically come up to give you suggestions for completing the code. For instance, when you type a dot (.) after System and pause for a second, JBuilder displays a popup menu with suggestions to complete the code, as shown in Figure 1.17. You can then select from the menu to complete the code.

■ The structural information of the program appears in the Structure pane as you type. For example, when you type the first-line package Chapter1, Chapter1 appears under the node Imports in the Structure pane.

■■■ **CAUTION**

Java source programs are case-sensitive. It would be wrong, for example, to replace main in the program with Main. Program file names are case-sensitive on UNIX and generally not case-sensitive on PCs, but file names are case-sensitive in JBuilder.

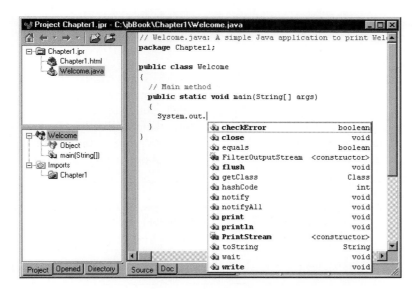

Figure 1.17   *The Code Insight popup menu is automatically displayed to help you complete the code.*

Compiling a Java Program

To execute the program, you have to compile it first, using one of the following methods. (Be sure that Welcome.java is selected in the Navigation page.)

■ Select Build, Make "Welcome.java" from the menu bar.

■ Click the Make toolbar button 🔳.

■ Point to Welcome.java in the Navigation pane, right-click the mouse button to display a popup menu (see Figure 1.18), and choose Make from the menu.

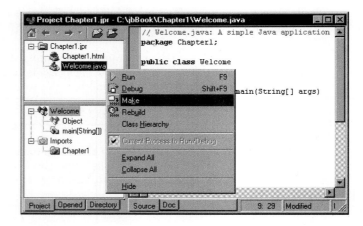

Figure 1.18   *Point the mouse to the file in the Navigation pane and right-click it to display a popup menu that contains the commands for processing the file.*

The compilation status is displayed on the status bar. If there are no syntax errors, the compiler generates a file named Welcome.class. This file is called the *bytecode*, as shown in Figure 1.19. The bytecode is similar to machine instructions, but is architecture-neutral and can run on any platform that has the Java interpreter and runtime environment. This is one of Java's primary advantages: Java bytecode can run on a variety of hardware platforms and operating systems.

■ **NOTE**
The bytecode is stored in Output root directory + Package Name. Therefore, Welcome.class is stored in c:\jbBook\Chapter1, since the Output root directory is set to c:\jbBook (see Figure 1.12) and the package name is Chapter1.

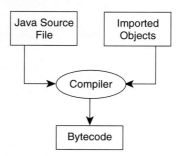

Figure 1.19   *The source code of a Java program is compiled into bytecode.*

Executing a Java Application

To run Welcome.class, use one of the following methods. (Make sure that Welcome.java is selected in the Navigation pane.)

■ Select Run, Run "Welcome.java" from the main menu.

■ Click the Run toolbar button 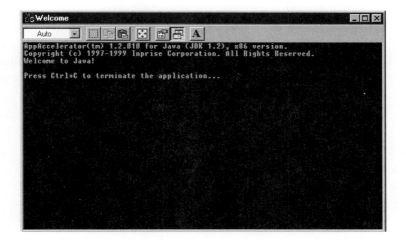.

■ Point to Welcome.java in the Navigation pane and right-click the mouse button to display a popup menu. Choose Run from the popup menu.

NOTE

The Run command invokes the Compile command if the program is not compiled or was modified after the last compilation.

When this program executes, JBuilder launches a DOS window to display the output, as shown in Figure 1.20. When the program finishes, press Ctrl+C to close the DOS window.

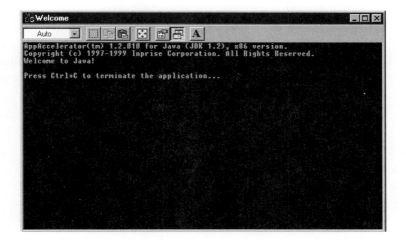

Figure 1.20 *The execution result is shown in the DOS window.*

NOTE

If the DOS window is closed when the program terminates, uncheck "Close Console Window on exit" in the Run/Debug page of the Project Properties dialog box.

TIP

To close an AppBrowser window, choose File, Close from the main menu bar. To close all the AppBrowser windows, choose File, Close All. To exit JBuilder, choose File, Exit.

Anatomy of the Application Program

The application program in Example 1.1 has the following components:

Comments
Reserved words
Modifiers
Statements
Blocks
Classes
Methods
The `main()` method

To build a program, you need to understand these basic elements. The following sections explain each of them.

Comments

The first line in the program is a *comment* that documents what the program is and how it is constructed. Comments help programmers or users to communicate and understand the program. Comments are not programming statements and are ignored by the compiler. In Java, comments are preceded by two slashes (`//`) in a line, or enclosed between `/*` and `*/` in multiple lines. When the compiler sees `//`, it ignores all text after `//` in the same line. When it sees `/*`, it scans for the next `*/` and ignores any text between `/*` and `*/`.

Here are examples of the two types of comments:

```
// This application program prints Welcome to Java!

/* This application program prints Welcome to Java! */
```

Reserved Words

Reserved words or *keywords* are words that have specific meanings to the compiler and cannot be used for other purposes in the program. For example, when the compiler sees the word `class`, it understands that the word after `class` is the name of the class. Other reserved words in Example 1.1 are `public`, `static`, and `void`.

TIP

Because Java is case-sensitive, `class` is a reserved word, but `Class` is not. For clarity and readability, it would be best to avoid using reserved words in other forms. (See Appendix A, "Java Keywords.")

Modifiers

Java uses certain reserved words called *modifiers* that specify the properties of the data, methods, and classes, and how they can be used. Examples of modifiers are `public` and `static`. Other modifiers are `private`, `final`, `abstract`, and `protected`.

A `public` data, method, and class can be accessed by other programs. A `private` data or method cannot be accessed by other programs. Modifiers are discussed further in Chapter 5, "Programming with Objects and Classes."

Statements

A *statement* represents an action or a sequence of actions. The statement `println("Welcome to Java!")` in the program in Example 1.1 is a statement to display the greeting "Welcome to Java!" Every statement ends with a semicolon (;) in Java.

The following lines of code are statements:

```
x = 5;

x = x + 5;
```

The first statement assigns 5 to the variable x, and the second adds 5 to the variable x.

Blocks

The braces in the program form a *block* structure that groups statements together. The use of blocks helps the compiler to identify components of the program. In Java, each block begins with an open brace ({) and ends with a closing brace (}). Blocks can be *nested*—that is, one block can be placed within another.

The following code contains two blocks. The inner block is nested within the outer block.

```
{
  x = 5;
  x = x + 5;
  if (x > 6)
  { x = x - 1;  }
}
```

Classes

The *class* is the essential Java construct. A class is a template or blueprint for objects. To program in Java, you must understand classes and be able to write and use them. The mystery of the class will continue to be unveiled throughout this book. For now, though, understand that a program is defined by using one or more classes. Every Java program has at least one class, and programs are contained inside a class definition enclosed in blocks. The class can contain data declarations and method declarations.

NOTE
Each class in Java is compiled into a separate bytecode file with the extension .class.

Methods

What does `System.out.println` mean? It is a *method*: a collection of statements that performs a sequence of operations to display a message on the console. `println` is predefined as part of the standard Java language. It can be used even without fully understanding the details of how it works. It is used by invoking a calling statement with arguments. The arguments are enclosed in parentheses. In this case, the argument is `"Welcome to Java!"`. You can call the same `println()` method with a different argument to print a different message.

The `main()` method

You can create your own method. Each Java application must have a user-declared `main()` method that defines where the program begins. The `main()` method provides the control of program flow. The `main()` method looks like this:

```
public static void main(String[] args)
{
   // statements;
}
```

Java Applets

Applications and applets share many common programming features, although they differ slightly in some aspects. For example, every application must have a main method that contains the first sequence of instructions to be executed. The Java interpreter begins the execution of the application from the `main()` method.

Java applets, on the other hand, do not need a main method. They run within the Web browser environment. Example 1.2 demonstrates the applet that displays the same message, "Welcome to Java!"

Example 1.2 A Simple Applet

This program shows how to write a simple Java applet and demonstrates the compilation and execution of an applet.

```
/* WelcomeApplet.java: A simple Java applet to display Welcome to Java
*/
package Chapter1;

import java.awt.Graphics;

public class WelcomeApplet extends java.applet.Applet
{
   // Draw the message on the applet
   public void paint(Graphics g)
   {
      g.drawString("Welcome to Java!",10,10);
   }
}
```

Example Review

Applets run in a graphical environment. You need to display everything, including text, in graphical mode, and Java provides the `drawString()` method to display text in an applet.

The `drawString("Welcome to Java!", 10, 10)` method draws the string `"Welcome to Java!"` on the line. The baseline of the first character in the string, *W*, is displayed at the location (`10, 10`). The drawing area is measured in pixels, with (`0,0`) in the upper-left corner.

Creating an Applet

You can create and compile an applet the same way you created and compiled an application in the preceding section. JBuilder provides the Applet Wizard that enables you to quickly create templates for the applet and its associated HTML file.

The following are the steps in creating the applet using the Applet Wizard:

1. Open the AppBrowser window for project Chapter1.jpr if it is not opened. To open it, choose File, Reopen to display a submenu consisting of the most recently opened projects and files, as shown in Figure 1.21. Select the project if it is in the menu. Otherwise, choose File, Open to locate and open Chapter1.jpr. The project file is the one with the 🗎 icon.

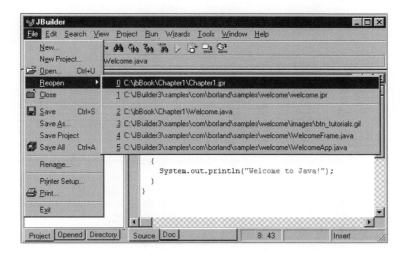

Figure 1.21   *Recently used projects can be reopened by choosing File, Reopen.*

2. Choose File, New to display the New dialog box, as shown in Figure 1.22. The New dialog box is also referred to as *Object Gallery*.

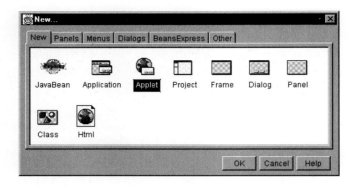

Figure 1.22   *The New dialog box contains wizards for creating various types of Java programs.*

3. Click the Applet icon in the New dialog box to display the Applet Wizard, as shown in Figure 1.23. Type WelcomeApplet.java in the Class field. Click Finish to close the dialog box. JBuilder automatically created WelcomeApplet.java and WelcomeApplet.html, as shown in Figure 1.24.

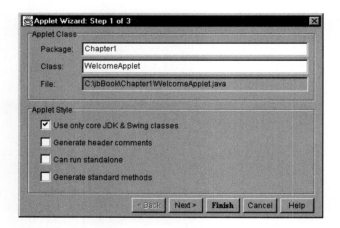

Figure 1.23   *The Applet Wizard enables you to create an applet and its associated HTML file.*

4. WelcomeApplet.java contains a lot of code we are not interested at this time. Therefore, replace the code with Example 1.2.

5. Choose File, Save All to preserve your work.

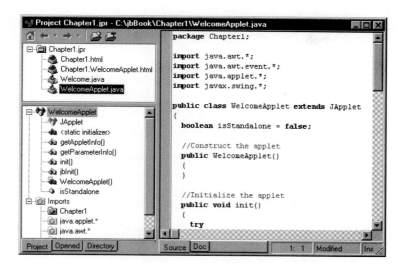

Figure 1.24   *The Applet Wizard generated WelcomeApplet.java and WelcomeApplet.html.*

The HTML file

The WelcomeApplet.html was automatically created by the Applet Wizard, as shown in the Navigation pane in Figure 1.24. HTML is a markup language that presents static documents on the Web. It uses tags to instruct the Web browser how to render a Web page. HTML contains a tag called `<applet>` that incorporates applets into a Web page.

▬ NOTE

The Applet Wizard placed WelcomeApplet.html in the c:\jbBook directory, not in the c:\jbBook\Chapter1 directory.

The HTML file shown below contains a tag to invoke `WelcomeApplet.class`. This file is a simplified version of WelcomeApplet.html generated by the JBuilder Applet Wizard.

```
<html>
<head>
<title>Welcome Java Applet</title>
</head>
<body>
<applet
  code = "Chapter1.WelcomeApplet.class"
  width = 200
  height = 50>
</applet>
</body>
</html>
```

A tag is an instruction to the Web browser. The browser interprets the tag and decides how to display or otherwise treat the subsequent contents of the HTML document. Tags are enclosed in brackets. The first word in a tag is called the *tag name*; it describes the tag's functions. Tags can have additional attributes, sometimes with values after an equals sign, which further define the tag's action. For example, in the following tag, `<applet>` is the tag name, and `code`, `width`, and `height` are the attributes:

```
<applet code="Chapter1.WelcomeApplet.class" width = 100 height = 40>
```

The `width` and `height` attributes specify the rectangular viewing area of the applet.

Most tags have a *start tag* and a corresponding *end tag*. The tag has a specific effect on the region between the start tag and the end tag. For example, `<applet...>...</applet>` tells the browser to display an applet. An end tag is always the start tag's name preceded by a slash.

An HTML document begins with the `<html>` tag, which declares that the document is written with HTML. Each document has two parts, *head* and *body*, defined by `<head>` and `<body>` tags, respectively. The head part contains the document title, using the `<title>` tag and other parameters the browser can use when rendering the document, and the body part contains the actual contents of the document. The header is optional. For more information, refer to Appendix E, "An HTML Tutorial."

Compiling and Viewing Applets

Compile the program by pointing to WelcomeApplet.java in the Navigation pane and right-clicking the mouse button to display a popup menu. Select Make to compile the program in the popup menu. You may have already noticed that the Run command is not available in the popup menu. You use the Java interpreter to run applications, but applets are executed by a Web browser from an HTML file. Applets are embedded in HTML files and run from a Web browser.

You now can use a Web browser to view the applet in c:\jbBook\ WelcomeApplet.html. The result is displayed in Figure 1.25.

Figure 1.25   *The message Welcome to Java! is drawn on the browser.*

Applets can run from a Web browser on any platform. For example, the same applet can run on a Windows-based PC or on a UNIX workstation.

NOTE

Make sure that your Web browser supports JDK 1.1 or above. At the time of this writing, HotJava, Netscape Communicator 4.7, and Internet Explorer 5.0 support JDK 1.1. Other vendors will undoubtedly follow in the near future. To view the applets with the Swing components introduced in Chapter 10, "Applets and Advanced Graphics," you need the Java Plug-In utility installed on top of a Web browser. The Java Plug-In utility is introduced in Chapter 10.

You can also use Java's Applet Viewer to view a Java applet. With this utility, there is no need to start a Web browser. Applet Viewer functions as a browser. It is a valuable utility to test an applet before deploying it on a Web site. To view the applet using the Applet Viewer utility, simply select WelcomeApplet.html in the Navigation pane and click the Run button in the Toolbar. The applet is displayed in Figure 1.26.

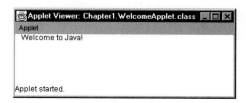

Figure 1.26   *The output of the WelcomeApplet program is running from the Applet Viewer utility as if it were running in a Web browser.*

Anatomy of the Applet Program

Let's take a closer look at the program in Example 1.2 and examine its components: the `import` statement, the `Graphics` class, the `extends` keyword, the `paint()` method, the `drawString()` method, and the class instance. As you have seen, applications and applets have much in common. Indeed, an applet is merely a special kind of Java program with certain characteristics that make it run from a Web browser. The components mentioned here are also used in other Java programs.

The *import* Statement

The first line after the comment is an `import` statement. The `import` statement tells the compiler to include existing Java programs in the current program. In this case, the existing program is `java.awt.Graphics`. You can use the operations in `java.awt.Graphics` in your program rather than rewrite the code. This is an example of software *reusability*; that is, the same program is written once and used by many other people without rewriting it.

Java code is organized into packages and classes. Classes are inside packages, and packages are libraries of Java code that contain all kinds of operations ready for you to import and use. Java provides standard libraries, such as java.awt, that come with the compiler. Users can create their own libraries. Graphics is a class contained in the java.awt package. (See Chapter 5, "Programming with Objects and Classes," for more information.)

Class Instance

The g in the paint() method is called an *instance* for the class Graphics. An instance is a concrete object of the class. g can access the methods defined in Graphics. drawString is a method in Graphics that can now be used in g by a call, such as g.drawString("Draw it", 20, 20). This is exactly the way object-oriented programming works. You can create an instance from a class and invoke the methods in the instance without knowing how the methods are implemented.

The *paint()* method and the Graphics Class

Every applet that displays graphics must have a paint() method that looks like this:

```
public void paint(Graphics g) {...}
```

This method contains drawing methods to tell the Web browser what should be displayed.

Because the Web is a graphical environment, everything—including text—needs to be displayed as a graphic. The Java Graphics class provides operations for drawing objects, such as text strings, lines, rectangles, ovals, arcs, and polygons. The drawing area is a rectangle measured in pixels with (0,0) at its upper-left corner. The following is an example:

```
public void paint(Graphics g)
{
  g.drawLine(10, 10, 50, 30);
  g.drawRect(10, 20, 20, 30);
  g.drawString("Welcome to Java", 30, 10);
}
```

The drawLine() method draws a line from (10, 10) to (50, 30). The drawRect() method draws a rectangle of width 20 and height 30; the upper-left corner of the rectangle is at (10, 20). The drawString() method draws the string "Welcome to Java" at (30, 10). See Figure 1.27 for the drawings.

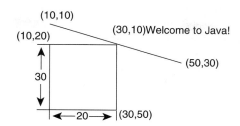

Figure 1.27   *The string* `Welcome to Java!` *is drawn at* `(30, 10)`*; a line is drawn from* `(10, 10)` *to* `(50, 30)`*; and a rectangle is drawn with its upper-left corner at* `(10, 20)` *with width of* `20` *and height of* `30`.

The *extends* Keyword and Class Inheritance

The class definition in Example 1.2 is different from the class definition in Example 1.1; Example 1.2 has an extra keyword, `extends`, which tells the compiler that the class to be defined is an extension of an existing class. In this case, the class `WelcomeApplet` extends the existing class `Applet`. The extended class `WelcomeApplet` inherits all functionality and properties from class `Applet`. This is an example of *inheritance*, another software engineering concept. Inheritance complements and extends software reusability.

`Applet` is a class in the package `java.applet`. You could add the statement `import java.applet.Applet` at the beginning of the program and directly extend `Applet`, as follows:

```
import java.awt.Graphics;
import java.applet.Applet;

public class WelcomeApplet extends Applet
{
  public void paint (Graphics g)
  {
    g.drawString("Welcome to Java!", 10, 10);
  }
}
```

The `import java.applet.Applet` statement imports the `Applet` class so that you can use it in the program without explicitly referencing `Applet` as `java.applet.Applet`.

Applications versus Applets

You probably have many questions, such as whether two programs are needed, one for the application and the other for the applet, or when to use applications and when to use applets. To answer these questions, it is important to understand the similarities and differences between applications and applets.

Although much of the code for applications and applets is the same, there are differences in the code dealing with their running environments. Applications run as standalone programs, as do programs written in any high-level language. Applets, however, must run from inside a Web browser. If your program is not required to run from a Web browser, choose applications. Developing Java applications is slightly faster than developing applets because you do not need to create an HTML file and load it from a Web browser to view the results.

For security reasons, the following limitations are imposed on applets to prevent destructive programs from damaging the system on which the browser is running:

- Applets are not allowed to read from, or write to, the file system of the computer. Otherwise, they could damage the files and spread viruses.

- Applets are not allowed to run any program on the browser's computer. Otherwise, they might call destructive local programs and damage the local system on the user's computer.

- Applets are not allowed to establish connections between the user's computer and another computer, except for the server where the applets are stored. This restriction prevents the applet from connecting the user's computer to another computer without the user's knowledge.

Applications, however, can directly interact with the computer on which they are running without these limitations. Applications can be used to develop fully functional software. In fact, applications can use the same graphical features used for applets, although with applications slightly more effort would be required in order to create the graphical environment.

In general, you can convert a Java applet to run as an application without loss of functionality. However, because of the security limitations imposed on applets, an application cannot always be converted to run as an applet. In Chapter 10, "Applets and Advanced Graphics," you will learn how to convert between applications and applets.

Chapter Summary

In this chapter, you learned about Java and the relationship between Java and the World Wide Web. Java is an Internet programming language, and since its inception in 1995, it has quickly become a premier language for building fully portable Internet applets and applications.

Java is platform-independent, meaning that you can write a program once and run it anywhere. Java is a simple, object-oriented programming language with built-in graphics programming, input and output, exception handling, networking, and multithreading support.

The Java source file ends with the .java extension. Every class is compiled into a separate file called a bytecode that has the same name as the class and ends with the .class extension.

Every Java program is a class definition. The keyword `class` introduces a class definition. The contents of the class are included in a block. A block begins with an open brace (`{`) and ends with a close brace (`}`). The class contains at least one method. A Java application must have a main method. The `main()` method is the entry point where the application program starts when it is executed.

The Java applet always extends the `Applet` class. The keyword `extends` enables new classes to inherit from an existing class. The `import` statement loads classes required for compiling a Java program.

Modifiers are keywords that specify how classes and methods can be accessed. A Java applet must be a `public` class so that a Web browser can access it.

Web browsers control the execution of Java applets. You must create an HTML file with an `<applet>` tag to specify the bytecode file (with the extension .class) for the applet, and the width and the height of the applet viewing area in pixels.

The Web browser calls the `paint()` method to display graphics in the applet's viewing area. The coordinates of the viewing area are measured in pixels with (`0,0`) at the upper-left corner. The `drawString()` method draws a string at a specified location in the viewing area.

You have begun to use JBuilder to create Java applications and applets. You learned how to create projects, create and add files to the project, and compile and run applications and applets.

Chapter Review

1.1. Briefly describe the history of Java.

1.2. Java is object-oriented. What are the advantages of object-oriented programming?

1.3. Can Java run on any machine? What is needed to run Java on a computer?

1.4. What are the input and output of a Java compiler?

1.5. List some Java development tools. Are Visual J++ and JBuilder different languages from Java, or are they dialects or extensions of Java?

1.6. What is the relationship between Java and HTML?

1.7. Explain the concept of keywords. List some Java keywords you learned in this chapter.

1.8. Is Java case-sensitive? What is the case for Java keywords?

1.9. What is the Java source file name extension, and what is the Java bytecode file name extension?

1.10. How do you create a Java project in JBuilder?

1.11. How do you compile a Java program in JBuilder?

1.12. How do you run a Java application in JBuilder?

1.13. How do you create a Java applet in JBuilder?

1.14. Where is the .class file stored after successful compilation in JBuilder?

1.15. What is the purpose of the statement package Chapter1 in the Welcome.java program in Example 1.1?

1.16. What is a comment? What is the syntax for a comment in Java? Is the comment ignored by the compiler?

1.17. What is the statement to display a string on the console?

1.18. Is the following statement correct?

```
System.out.println('Welcome to Java');
```

1.19. What is a block? What is the symbol that encloses a block?

1.20. What is the import statement for?

1.21. What is Graphics, and what is the paint() method?

1.22. What are the differences between applications and applets? How do you run an application, and how do you run an applet? Is the compilation process different for applications and applets?

1.23. What is Applet Viewer?

1.24. Is a lot of work needed to convert between applications and applets?

1.25. List some security restrictions of applets.

Programming Exercises

1.1. Find the Java online JDK documentation at www.javasoft.com, and run samples of Java applets from that site.

1.2. Create a project named Project1. Add a Java program named Welcome-HTML.java in the project. WelcomeHTML.java displays a message "Welcome to HTML" onto the screen. Use the Applet Wizard to create an applet and its associated HTML file to display a message "Welcome to HTML" on the screen.

2

JAVA BUILDING ELEMENTS

Objectives

- Understand variables and constants.
- Write simple Java programs.
- Use assignment statements.
- Use Java primitive data types: `byte`, `short`, `int`, `long`, `float`, `double`, `char`, and `boolean`.
- Use Java operators and write Java expressions.
- Understand the classification of programming errors.
- Become familiar with Java documentation, programming style, and naming conventions.
- Run Java programs from the command line.
- Get online help from JBuilder.
- Customize JBuilder environment options.

39

Introduction

In this chapter, you will be introduced to basic programming elements, such as variables, constants, data types, operators, and expressions, in Java.

To begin, let's look at a simple program that computes the area of a circle. The program reads in the radius of a circle and displays its area. Representing the circle and the area as variables, and using a constant π, the program uses an expression to compute the area.

Writing this program involves designing algorithms and data structures, as well as translating algorithms into programming codes. An algorithm describes how a problem is solved in terms of the actions to be executed, and it specifies the order in which these actions should be executed. Algorithms can help the programmer plan a program before writing it in a programming language. A pseudocode is often used to describe an algorithm.

The algorithm for this program can be described as follows:

1. Read in the radius.

2. Compute the area using the following formula:

        area = radius × radius × π

3. Display the area.

Many of the problems encountered during an introduction to programming course using this text can be described with simple, straightforward algorithms. As your education progresses, and you take courses on data structures, algorithm design, and analysis, you will encounter complex problems that have sophisticated solutions. In order to solve such problems, you will need to design correct, efficient algorithms with appropriate data structures.

Data structures involve data representation and manipulation. Java provides basic data types for representing integers, floats, characters, and Boolean types. Java also supports array and string types as objects. Some of the advanced data structures, such as stacks and hashing, are already supported by Java.

To novice programmers, coding is a daunting task. When you *code*, you translate the algorithm into a programming language understood by the computer. You already know that every Java program begins with a class declaration, in which the keyword `class` is followed by the class name. Assume that you have chosen `ComputeArea` as the class name. The outline of the program would look like this:

```
class ComputeArea
{
  // Data and methods to be given later
}
```

The program needs to read the radius entered by the user from the keyboard. You should consider two important issues next:

■ Reading the radius.

■ Storing the radius in the program.

Let's address the second issue first. How does a computer identify radius and area in the program? To store the radius, the program needs to declare a symbol called *variable,* which represents the radius in the program. Variables are used to store data and computational results in the program.

Choose the descriptive names `radius` for radius and `area` for area. To let the compiler know what `radius` and `area` are, specify their data types, indicating whether they are integer, float, or others. Declare `radius` and `area` as double-precision, floating-point numbers. The program can be expanded as follows:

```
class ComputeArea
{
  // Declare radius and area
  static double radius, area;

  // Method to be given later
}
```

The program declares `radius` and `area` as static variables. The reserved word `static` indicates that `radius` and `area` can be accessed by the `main()` method. Every application must have a main method that controls the execution of the program. The first step is to read in `radius`. Use the method `readDouble()`, which will be defined in the class, to read a `double` value from the keyboard. When this method is executed, the computer waits for the input from the keyboard. You will learn the details of implementing this method in Chapter 15, "Input and Output."

The second step is to compute area; assign the expression `radius*radius*PI` to area, where `PI` is a constant representing the number π.

In the final step, print area on the console by using method `System.out.println()`.

The program is completed in Example 2.1. The result is shown in Figure 2.1.

Example 2.1 Computing the Area of a Circle

This program lets the user enter the radius for a circle and then computes the area. Finally, it displays the area.

```
// ComputeArea.java: Compute the area of a circle
package Chapter2;

import java.io.*;
import java.util.*;

public class ComputeArea
{
  static double radius;
  static double area;
  static final double PI = 3.14159;

  static private StringTokenizer stok;
  static private BufferedReader br
    = new BufferedReader(new InputStreamReader(System.in), 1);
```

continues

```java
// Main method
public static void main(String[] args)
{
  System.out.println("Enter radius");
  radius = readDouble();
  area = radius*radius*PI;
  System.out.println("The area for the circle of radius " +
    radius + " is " + area);
}

// Read a double value from the keyboard
public static double readDouble()
{
  double d = 0;
  try
  {
    String str = br.readLine();
    stok = new StringTokenizer(str);
    d = new Double(stok.nextToken()).doubleValue();
  }
  catch (IOException ex)
  {
    System.out.println(ex);
  }
  return d;
}
}
```

Example Review

As usual, you create a new project using the New Project Wizard. To display the New Project Wizard dialog box, choose File, New Project. Type c:\jbBook\Chapter2 in the File field, and click OK to create a new project for the examples in Chapter 2. Create a source file for Example 2.1 and name the file **ComputeArea.java** in the project Chapter2 Compile and run the program. Sample output is shown in Figure 2.1.

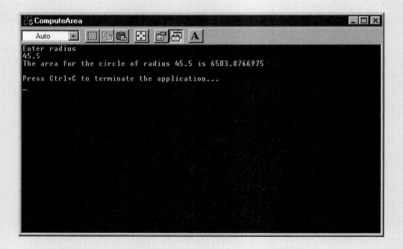

Figure 2.1   *The program receives the radius from the keyboard and displays the area of the circle.*

`System.out.println` is a system-predefined method. It can print strings and numbers. The plus sign (+) in the `System.out.println("The area for the circle of radius " + radius + " is " + area)` statement means to concatenate strings if one of the operands is a string. If both operands are numbers, the + operator adds these two numbers.

Suppose `i` = `1` and `j` = `2`, what is the output of the following statement?

```
System.out.println("i+j is " + i + j);
```

The output is "i+j is 12," because `"i+j is "` is concatenated with `i` first. To force `i + j` to be executed first, enclose `i + j` inside the parentheses.

If you replaced

```
static double radius;
```

with

```
double radius;
```

you would get an error because `main` is always a static method. The static method cannot reference nonstatic variables or methods. You would find the same type of error if you eliminated the word `static` from in front of the method `readDouble()`. You will learn more about method and class modifiers in Chapter 5, "Programming with Objects and Classes."

Identifiers

Just as every entity in the real world is identified by a name, it is necessary to name the things that will be referred to in a program. Programming languages use special symbols called *identifiers* to name such programming entities as variables, constants, methods, classes, and packages. Here are the rules for naming identifiers:

- An identifier must start with a letter, an underscore (_), or a dollar sign ($).

- An identifier cannot contain operators, such as +, −, and so on.

- An identifier cannot be a reserved word. (See Appendix A, "Java Keywords," for a list of reserved words.)

- An identifier cannot be `true`, `false`, or `null`.

- An identifier can be of any length.

For example, `$2`, `Area`, `Char`, `a`, and α (the Greek alpha) are legal identifiers, whereas `2A` and `d+4` are illegal identifiers. Illegal identifiers do not follow the rules. The Java compiler detects illegal identifiers and reports syntax errors.

> ### NOTE
> Java uses the Unicode specification for characters. A letter does not just stand for a letter in the English alphabet. It can be any of the tens of thousands of Unicode letters representing international languages. Therefore, α is a legal identifier.

> ### TIP
> Identifiers are used for naming variables, constants, methods, classes, and packages. Descriptive identifiers make programs easy to read. Since Java is case-sensitive, X and x are two different identifiers.

Variables

Variables are used to store data—input, output, or intermediate data. In the program in Example 2.1, `radius` and `area` were variables of the double-precision, floating-point type. You can assign any float value to `radius` and `area`, and the values of `radius` and `area` can be reassigned. For example, you can write the following code to compute the area for different radii:

```
// Compute the first area
radius = 1.0;
area = radius*radius*3.14159;
System.out.println("The area is " + area + " for radius " + radius);

// Compute the second area
radius = 2.0;
area = radius*radius*3.14159;
System.out.println("The area is " + area + " for radius " + radius);
```

Declaring Variables

Variables are used to represent many different types of data. To use a variable, you need to declare it and tell the compiler the name of the variable as well as what type of data it represents. This is called a *variable declaration*. The syntax to declare a variable is as follows:

```
datatype variableName;
```

The following are examples of variable declarations:

```
int x;           // Declares x to be an integer variable;
double radius;   // Declares radius to be a double variable;
char a;          // Declares a to be a character variable;
```

The examples use data types `int`, `float`, and `char`. You will be introduced to additional data types, such as `byte`, `short`, `long`, `float`, `char`, and `boolean`, in this chapter.

Assignment Statements

Once a variable is declared, you can assign a value to it by using an *assignment statement*. The syntax for the assignment is one of the following formulations:

```
variable = value;
variable = expression;
```

For example, consider the following code:

```
x = 1;            // Assign 1 to x;
radius = 1.0;     // Assign 1.0 to radius;
a = 'A';          // Assign 'A' to a;
```

CAUTION

In an assignment statement, the data type of the variable on the left must be compatible with the data type of the value on the right. For example, x = 1.0 would be illegal because the data type of x is int. You cannot assign a double value (1.0) to an int variable.

The variable name must be on the left. For example, 1 = x would be wrong.

An expression represents a computation involving values, variables, and operators. As an example, consider the following code:

```
area = radius*radius*3.14159;
```

The variable on the left can also be used in the expression on the right, as follows:

```
x = x + 1;
```

In this assignment statement, x + 1 is assigned to x. If x is 1 before the statement is executed, then x becomes 2 after the statement is executed.

CAUTION

The Java assignment statement uses the equals sign (=), not :=, which is often used in other languages.

Declaring and Initializing Variables in One Step

Variables often have initial values. You can declare a variable and initialize it in one step. For example, consider the following code:

```
int x = 1;
```

This is equivalent to the following two statements:

```
int x;
x = 1;
```

CAUTION

A variable must be declared before it can be assigned a value. A variable must be assigned a value before it can be used.

TIP

Whenever possible, declare a variable and assign its initial value in one step. This makes the program easy to read.

Constants

The value of a variable may change during the execution of the program. A constant represents permanent data that never change. In our `ComputeArea` program, `PI` is a constant. If you use it frequently, you don't want to keep typing 3.14159; instead, you can define a constant for π. The following is the syntax for declaring a constant:

```
static final datatype CONSTANTNAME = VALUE;
```

The word `final` is a Java keyword, which means the constant cannot be changed. For example, in the `ComputeArea` program, you defined

```
static final double PI = 3.14159;
```

and then used it in the following computation:

```
area = radius*radius*PI;
```

CAUTION

A constant must be declared and initialized before it can be used. You cannot change the constant value once it is declared.

Numerical Data Types

Every data type has a domain (range) of values. The compiler allocates memory space to store each variable or constant according to its data type. Java provides several primitive data types for numerical values, characters, and Boolean values. In this section, numeric data types are introduced.

Java has six numeric types: four for integers and two for floating-point numbers. Table 2.1 lists the six numeric data types, their domains, and their storage sizes.

TABLE 2.1   Numeric Data Types

Name	Domain	Storage Size
byte	-2^7 to 2^7-1	8-bit signed
short	-2^{15} to $2^{15}-1$	16-bit signed
int	-2^{31} to $2^{31}-1$	32-bit signed
long	-2^{63} to $2^{63}-1$	64-bit signed
float	$-3.4E38$ to $3.4E38$ (6 to 7 significant digits of accuracy)	32-bit IEEE 754
double	$-1.7E308$ to $1.7E308$ (14 to 15 significant digits of accuracy)	64-bit IEEE 754

Standard arithmetic operators for numerical data types include addition (+), subtraction (–), multiplication (*), division (/), and modulus (%). For examples, see the following code:

46

```
int i1 = 34 + 1;          // i1 becomes 35
double d1 = 34.0 - 0.1;   // d1 becomes 33.9
long  i2 = 300*30;        // i2 becomes 90000
double d2 = 1.0/2.0;      // d2 becomes 0.5
int i3 = 1/2;             // i3 becomes 0; Note the result is
                          // the integer part of the division
byte i4 = 20%3;           // i4 becomes 2; Note the result is
                          // the remainder after the division
```

The result of integer division is an integer. For example, 5/2 = 2 instead of 2.5.
The fraction part is truncated.

Numeric Literals

A *literal* is a primitive type value that directly appears in the program. For example,
34, 1,000,000, and 5.0 are literals in the following statements:

```
int i = 34;
long l = 1000000;
double d = 5.0;
```

Floating-point literals are written with a decimal point. By default, a floating-point
literal is treated as a `double` type value. For example, 5.0 is considered a `double`
value, not a `float` value. You can make a number a `float` or a `double` by appending
the letter f, F, d, or D. For example, you can use `100.2f` or `100.2F` for `float` numbers, and `100.2d` or `100.2D` for `double` numbers. A floating-point literal can also be
written in scientific notation; for example, 1.23456e+2, which is equivalent to
123.456.

Shortcut Operators

It is common practice to use the current value of a variable, modify it, and reassign
the results back to the same variable. For example, consider the following code:

```
i = i + 8;
```

This statement is equivalent to

```
i += 8;
```

The += is called a *shortcut operator*. The common shortcut operators are shown in
Table 2.2.

TABLE 2.2   Shortcut Operators

Operator	Example	Equivalent
+=	i+=8	i = i+8
-=	f-=8.0	f = f-8.0
*=	i*=8	i = i*8
/=	i/=8	i = i/8
%=	i%=8	i = i%8

Two more shortcut operators are for incrementing and decrementing a variable by 1. This is handy because that's how much the value often needs to be changed. These two operators are ++ and --. They can be used in prefix or suffix notation. For example:

> x++ is equivalent to x = x+1;
>
> ++x is equivalent to x = x+1;
>
> x-- is equivalent to x = x-1;
>
> --x is equivalent to x = x-1;

Any numeric value can be applied to x. These operators are often used in loop statements. Loop statements are the structures that control how many times an operation or a sequence of operations is performed in succession. This structure and the subject of loop statements are introduced in Chapter 3, "Control Structures." The prefix (++x, --x) and suffix (x++, x--)differ when they occur in the expression. If the operator is prefixed to the variable, the variable is first incremented or decremented by 1, then used in the expression. If the operator is a suffix to the variable, the variable is used in the expression first, then incremented or decremented by 1. Therefore, the prefixes ++x and --x are referred to as the *preincrement operator* and the *predecrement operator*, respectively; and the suffixes x++ and x-- are referred to as the *postincrement operator* and the *postdecrement operator*, respectively. The following code illustrates this:

```
int i=10;
int newNum;
newNum = 10*i++;
```

In this case, i++ is evaluated after the entire expression (newNum = 10*i++) is evaluated. If i++ is replaced by ++i, ++i is evaluated before the entire expression is evaluated. So newNum is 100 for the first case and 110 for the second case. In both cases, i is incremented by 1.

Here is another example:

```
double x = 1.0;
double y = 5.0;
double z = x-- + ++y;
```

After all three lines are executed, y becomes 6.0, z becomes 7.0, and x becomes 0.0.

 TIP

Shortcut operators originally came from C. They were inherited by C++ and adopted by Java. The use of shortcut operators makes expressions short, but it also makes them complex and difficult to read. Avoid using shortcut operators in long expressions that involve many operators.

Numeric Type Conversion

The numerical values of different types are often mixed in computations. Consider the following statements:

```
byte i = 100;
long l = i*3+4;
double f = i*3.1+l/2;
```

Are these statements correct? Java allows binary operations on numerical variables and sometimes on values of different types. When performing a binary operation involving two operands of different types, Java automatically converts the less accurate operand to the type of the more accurate operand. For example, if one operand is int and the other is float, the int operand is converted to float, since float is more accurate than int. If one of the operands is of the type double, the other is converted to double, since double is the most accurate of all the numerical types. Thus, the result of 1/2 is 0, and the result of 1.0/2 is 0.5.

You can always assign a value with less accuracy to a variable with more accuracy, such as assigning a long value to a float value. You cannot, however, assign a value with more accuracy to a variable with less accuracy unless you use *type casting*. Casting is an operation that converts a value of one data type into a value of another data type. The syntax for casting is to give the target type in parentheses, followed by the variable name. For example, see the following code:

```
float f = (float)10.1;
int i = (int)f;
```

In this case, i has a value of 10; the fractional part in f is truncated. Be careful when using casting. Lost information may lead to inaccurate results, as shown in the following example:

```
int i = 10000;
byte s = (short)i;
```

In this example, s becomes 16, which is totally distorted. To ensure correctness, you can test whether the value is in the correct target type range (see Table 2.1) before performing casting.

CAUTION
Casting is necessary if assigning a value of more accuracy to a variable with less accuracy, such as assigning a double value to an int variable. A compilation error would occur if casting were not used in these situations.

Character Data Type

The character data type, char, is used to represent a single character.

A character value is enclosed within single quotation marks. For example, consider the following code:

```
char letter = 'A';
char numChar = '4';
```

The first statement assigns character A to the char variable letter. The second statement assigns numerical character 4 to the char variable numChar. Note the following illegal statement:

```
char numChar = 4;
```

In this statement, 4, a numerical value, cannot be assigned to a character variable.

The char type only represents one character. To represent a string of characters, use the data structure called String. For example, the following line of code declares the message to be a string that has an initial value of "Welcome to Java!"

```
String message = "Welcome to Java!";
```

String is discussed in more detail in Chapter 6, "Arrays and Strings."

CAUTION

A string must be enclosed in quotation marks. A literal character is a single character enclosed in single quotation marks.

Java characters use *Unicode*: a 16-bit encoding scheme established by the Unicode Consortium to support the interchange, processing, and display of written texts in the world's many different languages. (See the Unicode Web site at **www.unicode.org** for more information.) Unicode takes two bytes, expressed in four hexadecimal numbers that run from '\u0000' to '\uFFFF'. Most computers use ASCII code. Unicode includes ASCII code with '\u0000' to '\u00FF' corresponding to the 128 ASCII characters. (See Appendix B, "The ASCII Character Set," for a list of ASCII characters and their decimal and hexadecimal codes.)

In addition to Unicodes, you can use ASCII characters, such as 'X', '1', and '$', in a Java program. Java also allows you to use the escape sequence for special characters, as shown in Table 2.3.

TABLE 2.3   Examples of Special Characters

Character Escape Sequence	ASCII	Unicode
Backspace	\b	\u0008
Tab	\t	\u0009
Linefeed	\n	\u000a
Carriage return	\r	\u000d

The following statements are equivalent:

```
char letter = 'A';
char letter = '\u0041';
```

Both statements assign character A to char variable letter.

You can use casting to convert a character to a numerical code, and vice versa. For example, to obtain the decimal code of a character, use a casting like this:

```
int decimalCode = (int)'0'
```

The variable `decimalCode` becomes `48`.

boolean Data Type

The `boolean` data type comes from Boolean algebra. The domain of the `boolean` type consists of two values: `true` and `false`. For example, the following line of code assigns `true` to the `boolean` variable `lightsOn`.

```
boolean lightsOn = true;
```

The operators associated with Boolean values are comparison operators and Boolean operators. Comparison operators can be used in expressions that result in a Boolean value. Table 2.4 contains a list of the comparison operators.

TABLE 2.4   Comparison Operators

Operator	Name	Example	Answer
<	less than	1 < 2	true
<=	less than or equal to	1 <= 2	true
>	greater than	1 > 2	false
>=	greater than or equal to	1 >= 2	false
==	equal to	1 == 2	false
!=	not equal to	1 != 2	true

CAUTION

The equality comparison operator is two equals signs (==) instead of a single equals sign (=). The latter symbol is for assignment.

Boolean operators operate on Boolean values to result in a new Boolean value. Table 2.5 contains a list of Boolean operators.

TABLE 2.5   Boolean Operators

Operator	Name	Description
!	not	logical negation
&&	and	logical conjunction
||	or	logical disjunction
^	exclusive or	logical exclusion

These operators are demonstrated by using examples. In the examples, the variables `width` and `height` contain the values of 1 and 2, respectively.

Table 2.6 defines the not (!) operator. The not (!) operator negates `true` to `false` and `false` to `true`. For example, `!(width == 3)` is true because `(width == 3)` is `false`.

TABLE 2.6   Truth for Operator !

Operand	!Operand
true	false
false	true

Table 2.7 defines the and (&&) operator. The and (&&) of two Boolean operands is true if and only if both operands are `true`. For example, `(width == 1) && (height > 1)` is true because `(width == 1)` and `(height > 1)` are both `true`.

TABLE 2.7   Truth for Operator &&

Operand1	Operand2	Operand1 && Operand2
false	false	false
false	true	false
true	false	false
true	true	true

Table 2.8 defines the or (¦¦) operator. The or (¦¦) of two Boolean operands is `true` if at least one of the operands is `true`. For example, `(width > 1) || (height > 2)` is `false` because `(width > 1)` and `(height > 2)` are both `false`.

TABLE 2.8   Truth for Operator ¦¦

Operand1	Operand2	Operand1 ¦¦ Operand2
false	false	false
false	true	true
true	false	true
true	true	true

Table 2.9 defines the exclusive or (^) operator. The exclusive or (^) of two Boolean operands is `true` if and only if two operands have different Boolean values. For example, `(width > 1) ^ (height == 2)` is true because `(width > 1)` is `false` and `(height == 2)` is true.

TABLE 2.9   Truth for Operator ^

Operand1	Operand2	Operand1 ^ Operand2
false	false	false
false	true	true
true	false	true
true	true	false

When evaluating p1 && p2, Java first evaluates p1, then evaluates p2 if p1 is true; if p1 is false, p2 is not evaluated. When evaluating p1 ¦¦ p2, Java first evaluates p1, then evaluates p2 if p1 is false; if p1 is true, p2 is not evaluated.

Java also provides the & and ¦ operators. The & operator works identically to the && operator, and the ¦ operator works identically to the ¦¦ operator with one exception—the & and ¦ operators always evaluate both operands. In some rare situations, you can use the & and ¦ operators to guarantee that the right operand is evaluated regardless of whether the left operand is true or false. For example, the expression (width < 2) & (height-- < 2) guarantees that (height-- < 2) is evaluated. Thus, the variable height will be decremented regardless of whether width is less than 2 or not.

TIP

Avoid using the & and ¦ operators. The benefits of the & and ¦ operators are marginal. Using the & and ¦ operators makes the program difficult to read and could cause errors. For example, the expression (x != 0) & (100/x) results in a runtime error if x is 0.

Operator Precedence

Operator precedence determines the order in which expressions are evaluated. Suppose that you have the following expression:

```
3 + 4*4 > 5*(4+3) - i++
```

What is its value? How does the compiler know the execution order of the operators? The expression inside the parentheses is evaluated first. (Parentheses can be nested, in which case the expression in the inner parentheses is executed first.) When evaluating an expression without parentheses, the operators are applied in the order shown in Table 2.10. Table 2.10 contains the operators you have learned in this section. (See Appendix C, "Operator Precedence Chart," for a complete list of Java operators and their precedence.)

TIP

You can use parentheses to force an evaluation order as well as to make a program easy to read.

TABLE 2.10   Operator Precedence Chart

Precedence	*Operator*
Highest Order	casting
	++ and -- (prefix)
	*, /, %
	+, -
	<, <=, >, =>
	==, !=
	&&
	!!
	=, +=, -=, *=, /=, %=
Lowest Order	++ and -- (postfix)

Programming Errors

Programming errors are unavoidable, even for experienced programmers. There are three types of programming errors: *compilation errors*, *runtime errors*, and *logic errors*.

Compilation Errors

Errors that occur during compilation are called *compilation errors* or *syntax errors*. Compilation errors result from errors in code construction, such as mistyping a keyword, omitting some necessary punctuation, or using an opening brace without a corresponding closing brace. These errors are usually easy to detect because the compiler tells you where they are and the reasons for them. For example, compiling the following program results in compilation errors, as shown in Figure 2.2.

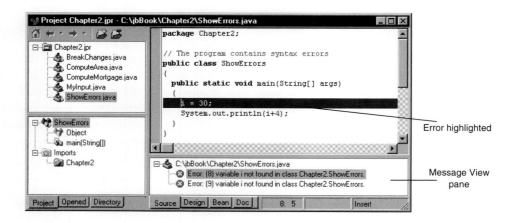

Figure 2.2   *The compiler detects a syntax error: undefined variable* i.

```
package Chapter2;

// The program contains syntax errors
public class ShowErrors
{
  public static void main(String[] args)
  {
    i = 30;
    System.out.println(i+4);
  }
}
```

Both errors are the result of not declaring variable i. Since single errors commonly display multiple lines of compilation errors, it is a good practice to start debugging from the top line and working downward. Fixing errors that occur earlier might fix cascading errors that occur later in the program.

JBuilder makes finding and fixing syntax errors easy. As shown in Figure 2.2, compilation errors are displayed in the Message View pane. Pointing the mouse and clicking on the line that shows the syntax error in the Message View pane leads you to the line that caused the error in the source code.

In general, syntax errors are easy to find and easy to correct because the compiler indicates where the errors came from and why they are there. Finding runtime errors, on the other hand, can be very challenging. You will learn how to use JBuilder debugger to trace the program and find runtime errors in the section "Debugging in JBuilder," in Chapter 6.

Runtime Errors

Runtime errors are errors that cause a program to terminate abnormally. They occur when the application is running and the environment detects an operation that is impossible to carry out. Input error is a good example of a runtime error.

An *input error* occurs when the user enters an unexpected input value that the program cannot handle. For instance, if the program expects to read in a number, but instead the user enters a string, data-type errors occur in the program. To avoid the input error, the program should prompt the user to enter the correct type of values. For instance, the program may display a message, such as "Please enter an integer," before reading an integer from the keyboard.

Another common source of runtime error is division by zero. It occurs when the divisor is zero or is too small, thereby causing overflow.

Logical Errors

Logical errors occur when a program does not perform the way it was intended to. This happens for many different reasons. Logical errors are called *bugs;* the process of finding them is called *debugging*. A popular approach to debugging is to use a combination of methods to narrow down to the part of the program where the bug is situated. Debugging a large program can be a daunting task. Debugging techniques are introduced in Chapter 6.

Programming Style and Documentation

Programming style deals with the appearance of the program. If you were to write an entire program on one line, it would compile and run fine. Doing this would be bad programming style, however, because the program would be hard to read. Programming documentation consists of the explanatory remarks and comments for the program. Programming style and documentation are as important as coding. Good programming style and appropriate documentation reduce the chance for errors and make programs easy to read. Following are some guidelines for Java programming style and documentation.

Appropriate Comments

Include a summary at the beginning of the program to explain what the program does, its key features, its supporting data structures, and any unique techniques it uses. In addition, include comments to introduce each major step in a long program and to explain anything that is difficult to read. It is important to make your comments concise so that you do not crowd the program or make it difficult to read.

■■■ NOTE

In addition to the two comment styles, `//` and `/*`, Java supports a special type of comments, referred to as *javadoc comments*. Javadoc comments begin with `/**` and end with `*/`. Javadoc comments are usually for documenting classes and data and methods. They can be extracted into an HTML file using the Javadoc Wizard from the Wizard menu. You can then display the HTML file by clicking the Doc tab in the Content pane, as shown in Figure 2.3. The Javadoc Wizard is available in the JBuilder 3 Professional Edition and Enterprise Edition, but not available in the JBuilder University Edition.

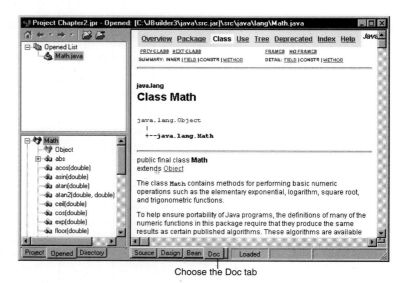

Choose the Doc tab

Figure 2.3 *You can view the documents for the Java files in the Content pane by clicking the Doc tab.*

Naming Conventions

You should choose descriptive names for variables, constants, classes, and methods so that their meanings are straightforward. Names are case-sensitive. The following are the conventions for naming variables, methods, and classes:

- For variables and methods, always use lowercase. If the name consists of several words, concatenate all into one, making the first word lowercase and capitalizing the first letter of each subsequent word in the name; for example, the variables `radius` and `area` and the method `readDouble()`.

- For class names, capitalize the first letter of each word in the name; for example, the class name `ComputeArea`.

- All letters in constants should be capitalized, and underscores should be used between words; for example, the constant `PI` and constant MAX_VALUE.

TIP

It is important to become familiar with naming conventions. Understanding naming conventions will help you to comprehend Java programs. Sticking with the naming conventions makes programmers more willing to accept your program.

Proper Indentation

A consistent indentation style makes your programs clear and easy to read. Indentation can be used to illustrate structural relationships among the program's components or statements. Java can read the program even if all of the statements are in a straight line, but it is easier to read and maintain code that is aligned properly. Indent each subcomponent or statement several spaces more than the structure within which it is nested.

Block Styles

A block is a group of statements surrounded by braces. A block can be written in many ways. The following, for example, are equivalent:

```
public class Test
{
  public static void main(String[] args)
  {
    System.out.println("Block Styles");
  }
}

public class Test {
  public static void main(String[] args) {
    System.out.println("Block Styles");
  }
}
```

The former is referred to as the *next-line* style, and the latter as the *end-of-line* style. In the next-line style, the opening brace and the closing brace are on the same column; thus, it is easy to see the beginning and end of the block. That is why the next-line block style is adopted in this book.

Separate Classes

You will frequently use readDouble to get a double floating-point number from the keyboard. Do you have to code the method readDouble() in every program that invokes readDouble? In Java, you can define a separate class for readDouble so that all of the programs using readDouble can use it without rewriting the code.

Now let's look at a new class called MyInput. This class contains the readDouble() and the readInt() methods for reading a double and an int literal, respectively, from the keyboard.

```java
// MyInput.java: Contain the methods for reading int and double
// values from the keyboard
package Chapter2;

import java.io.*;
import java.util.*;

public class MyInput
{
  static private StringTokenizer stok;
  static private BufferedReader br
    = new BufferedReader(new InputStreamReader(System.in), 1);

  // Read an int value from the keyboard
  public static int readInt()
  {
    int i = 0;
    try
    {
      String str = br.readLine();
      StringTokenizer stok = new StringTokenizer(str);
      i = new Integer(stok.nextToken()).intValue();
    }
    catch (IOException ex)
    {
      System.out.println(ex);
    }
    return i;
  }

  // Read a double value from the keyboard
  public static double readDouble()
  {
    double d = 0;
    try
    {
      String str = br.readLine();
      stok = new StringTokenizer(str);
      d = new Double(stok.nextToken()).doubleValue();
    }
    catch (IOException ex)
    {
      System.out.println(ex);
    }
    return d;
  }
}
```

The following case studies utilize the `MyInput` class.

Case Studies

In the preceding sections, you learned variables, constants, primitive data types, operators, and expressions. You are ready to use them to write interesting programs. This section presents two examples—one for computing mortgage payments, and the other for breaking down a unit of money into its component smaller denominations.

Example 2.2 Computing Mortgages

This example shows you how to write a program that computes mortgage payments. The program will let the user enter the interest rate, year, and loan amount, and then compute the monthly payment and the total payment. Finally, it will display the monthly and total final payments.

The formula to compute the monthly payment is as follows:

$$\frac{\text{principal} \times \text{monthly Interest}}{(1-(1(1+\text{monthly Interest}))^{\text{years} \times 12})}$$

The mortgage calculation program follows, and the output is shown in Figure 2.4.

```java
// ComputeMortgage.java: Compute mortgage payments
package Chapter2;

public class ComputeMortgage
{
  // Main method
  public static void main(String[] args)
  {
    double interestRate;
    int year;
    double loan;

    // Enter monthly interest rate
    System.out.println(
      "Enter yearly interest rate, for example 8.25: ");
    interestRate = MyInput.readDouble()/1200;

    // Enter number of years
    System.out.println(
      "Enter number of years as an integer, for example 5: ");
    year = MyInput.readInt();

    // Enter loan amount
    System.out.println("Enter loan amount, for example 120000.95: ");
    loan = MyInput.readDouble();
```

continues

```
                  // Calculate payment
                  double monthlyPay =
                    loan*interestRate/(1 - (Math.pow(1/(1 + interestRate),
                       year*12)));
                  double totalPay = monthlyPay*year*12;

                  // Display results
                  System.out.println("The monthly pay is " + monthlyPay);
                  System.out.println("The total pay is " + totalPay);
               }
           }
```

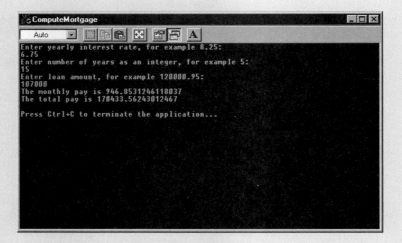

Figure 2.4   *The program receives interest rate, years, and loan amount, then displays the monthly payment and total payment.*

Example Review

The methods defined in the MyInput class are readInt() and readDouble(). They are available for use in this program because MyInput is created in the same project with this program.

The method for computing b^p in the Math class is pow(b, p). The Math class, which comes with the Java runtime system, is available to all Java programs. The Math class is introduced in Chapter 5.

Example 2.3 Changing Money

This example shows you how to write a program that finds the changes for a given amount. The program will let the user enter the decimal amount representing dollars and cents and output a report listing the monetary equivalent in single dollars, quarters, dimes, nickels, and pennies.

The program follows, and the output is shown in Figure 2.5.

```
// BreakChanges.java: Find changes for a given amount
package Chapter2;

public class BreakChanges
{
  // Main method
  public static void main(String[] args)
  {
    double amount; // Amount entered from the keyboard

    // Receive the amount entered from the keyboard
    System.out.println(
      "Enter an amount in integer, for example 11.56");
    amount = MyInput.readDouble();

    int remainingAmount = (int)(amount*100);

    // Find the number of one dollars
    int numOfOneDollars = remainingAmount/100;
    remainingAmount = remainingAmount%100;

    // Find the number of quarters in the remaining amount
    int numOfQuarters = remainingAmount/25;
    remainingAmount = remainingAmount%25;

    // Find the number of dimes in the remaining amount
    int numOfDimes = remainingAmount/10;
    remainingAmount = remainingAmount%10;

    // Find the number of nickels in the remaining amount
    int numOfNickels = remainingAmount/5;
    remainingAmount = remainingAmount%5;

    // Find the number of pennies in the remaining amount
    int numOfPennies = remainingAmount;

    // Display results
    System.out.println("The amount " + amount + " is " +
      numOfOneDollars +
      " dollars, " + numOfQuarters + " quarters, " + numOfDimes +
      " dimes, "
      + numOfNickels + " nickels, and " + numOfPennies + " pennies");
  }
}
```

continues

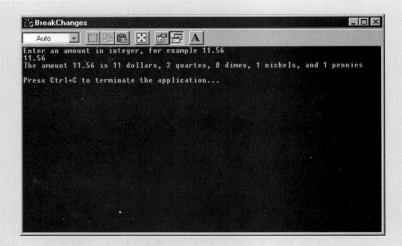

Figure 2.5   *The program receives an amount in decimal and breaks it into singles, quarters, dimes, nickels, and pennies.*

Example Review

The program extracts the maximum number of singles from the total amount and obtains the remaining amount in the variable remainingAmount. It then extracts the maximum number of quarters from remainingAmount and obtains a new remainingAmount. Continuing the same process, the program finds the dimes, nickels, and pennies in the remaining amount.

The variable amount stores the amount entered from the keyboard. This variable is not changed because the amount has to be displayed at the end. So the program introduces the variable remainingAmount to store the changing remainingAmount.

The variable amount is a double decimal representing dollars and cents; it is converted to an int variable remainingAmount, which represents all cents. For instance, if amount is 11.54, then the initial remainingAmount is 1154. The division operator yields the integer part of the division. Thus, 1154/100 is 11. The remainder operator obtains the remainder of the division. Thus, 1154%100 is 54.

One serious problem with this example is the possible loss of precision when casting a double amount to an int remainingAmount. There are two ways to fix the problem. One is to enter the amount as an int value representing cents, and the other is to read the decimal number as a string and extract the dollars part and cents part separately as int values. Processing strings will be introduced in Chapter 6, "Arrays and Strings."

Run Java Applications from the Command Line

So far you have run the programs in JBuilder IDE. You also can run the program standalone directly from the operating system. Here are the steps in running the **ComputeMortgage** application from the DOS prompt.

1. Start a DOS window by clicking the Window's Start button, Programs, MS-DOS Prompt.

2. Type **c:\jBuilder3\bin\setvars.bat c:\jBuilder3** to set the environment variables for running Java programs in the DOS environment.

3. Type **cd c:\jbBook** to change the directory to **c:\jbBook**.

4. Type **java Chapter2.ComputeMortgage** to run the program. A sample run of the output is shown in Figure 2.6.

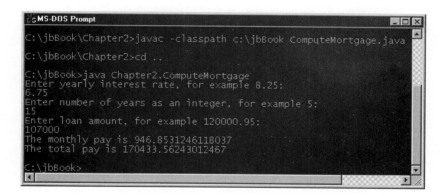

Figure 2.6   *You can run the Java program from the DOS prompt using the java command.*

Insert the following line

```
c:\jBuilder3\bin\setvars.bat c:\jBuilder3
```

in the autoexec.bat file on Windows 95 or Windows 98 to avoid setting the environment variables in Step 2 for every DOS session.

Setting environment variables enables you to use the JDK command-line utilities. The java command invokes the Java interpreter to run the Java bytecode.

NOTE
You can also compile the program using the javac command at the DOS prompt as shown in Figure 2.6, where **-classpath c:\jbBook** specifies the class path to locate MyInput.class that is referenced in ComputeMortgage.

JBuilder's Online Help

JBuilder provides a large number of documents online, giving you a great deal of information on a variety of topics pertaining to the use of JBuilder and Java.

To access online help, choose Help, Help Topics to display JBuilder Help, as shown in Figure 2.7. Alternatively, you can get Help Viewer by pressing F1 with the main menu focused.

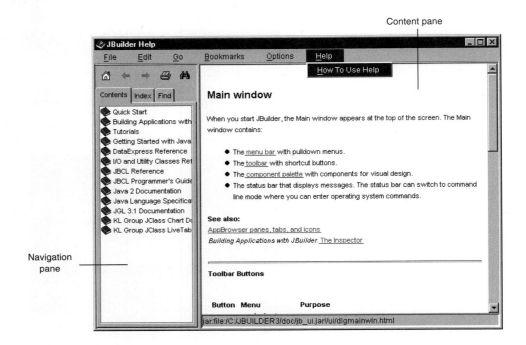

Figure 2.7   *All help documents are displayed in JBuilder Help.*

JBuilder Help behaves like a Web browser and contains the main menus, Navigation pane, and Content pane. From the main menus, you can open a URL from the File menu, add bookmarks from the Bookmarks menu, and get help on using JBuilder Help from the Help menu.

The Navigation pane contains five action buttons on top of the three tabs. The buttons are **Home**, **Previous**, **Next**, **Print**, and **Find in Page**. The Home, Previous, and Next buttons are to go to the first, previous, and next topic in the history list. The Print button prints the document in the Content pane. The Find in Page button enables you to search the current topic.

The three tabs are **Contents**, **Index,** and **Find**. The Contents tab displays available documents. The table of contents of the document is displayed in a tree-like list in the Navigation pane. To view a given topic, select the node in the tree associated with the topic. JBuilder Help displays the document for the topic in the Content pane.

The Index tab shows the index entries for the current document. The Find page shows the combined index entries for all the available documents in JBuilder. To display the index, simply type the first few letters in the entry. As you start typing, the index scrolls, doing an incremental search on the index entries to find the closest match. Select and double-click the index in the entry to display the document for the entry in the Content pane.

TIP

The Help menu is not the only way to get help. There are many ways to get help on a topic when you are using JBuilder. For example, if you want to find out what a particular menu item does, highlight a menu item on a pull-down menu without activating the item and press F1.

JBuilder Environment Options

JBuilder allows you to customize your development environment by changing various environment options. Certain options, such as syntax highlighting, can make your programs easy to read and help you to spot errors.

To set environment options, choose Tools, Environment Options to display the Environment Options dialog box, as shown in Figure 2.8. The dialog box contains five pages: Editor, Display, Colors, AppBrowser, and Code Insight.

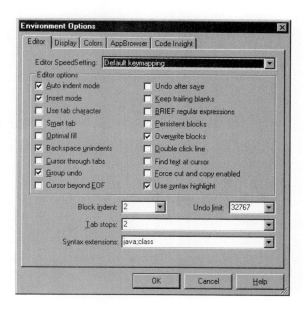

Figure 2.8   *The Environment Options dialog box enables you to set the environment, such as Editor, Display, Colors, AppBrowser, and Code Insight.*

The Editor page enables you to customize editing behavior in the Source pane. You can set the editor's handling of text by using editor options like Auto indent mode, Use tab character, and Use syntax highlight. Checking the Auto indent mode positions the cursor under the first nonblank character of the preceding nonblank line when you press Enter. Checking the Use tab character option inserts a tab character when you press the Tab key instead of using spaces to fill the gap. Checking the Use syntax highlight option sets syntax highlighting preferences. You can use the options on the Colors page of the environment Options dialog box to set the colors for highlighted syntax.

The Display page (see Figure 2.9) enables you to select display and font options and other miscellaneous Editor-related features for the Source pane. You can set the display and file options, such as BRIEF cursor shapes, Create backup file, Preserve line ends, and Zoom to full screen. For example, checking the BRIEF cursor shapes option uses a small bold square for blank spaces and a bold underline for nonblank spaces, checking the Create backup file option creates a file that replaces the first letter of the extension with a tilde (~) when you save the file, and checking the Zoom to full screen maximizes the Source pane to fill the entire screen. When this option is off, the Source pane does not cover the JBuilder Main window when maximized.

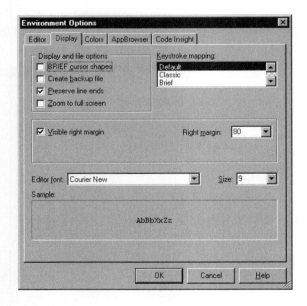

Figure 2.9   *You can customize display, and font options for the Source pane in the Display page of the Environment Options dialog box.*

The Colors page (see Figure 2.10) specifies the colors of the different elements of your code in the Source pane. You can specify foreground and background colors for the elements, such as Comment, Reserved word, String, Symbol, and Error line, in the Element list. The sample code at the bottom of the dialog box shows

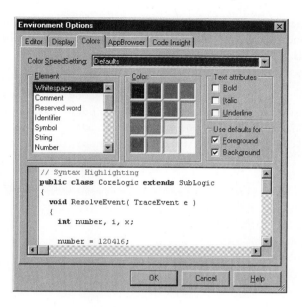

Figure 2.10   *You can customize colors for different elements of the source code.*

how your settings will appear in the Source pane. You must select Use syntax high-light on the Editor page for the setting in the Colors page to be effective.

The AppBrowser page (see Figure 2.11) enables you to configure the behavior of the AppBrowser. You can control how data members and methods are grouped,

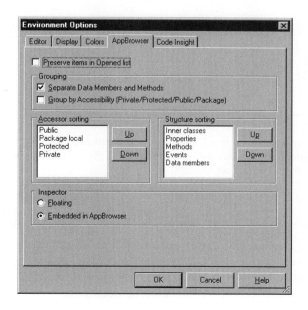

Figure 2.11   *You can customize AppBrowser for grouping data and methods based on access modifiers.*

how accessors, such as public and private, are used to sort the display, how properties, methods, events, and data members are grouped, and how the Inspector is displayed.

The Code Insight page (see Figure 2.12) enables you to configure Code Insight (Code completion assistant). JBuilder's Code Insight enhancements display a context-sensitive popup window within the Editor. Code Insight provides code completion, parameter lists, and tool tip expression evaluation. Code Insight highlights illegal class references and statements that import packages not on the Class Path.

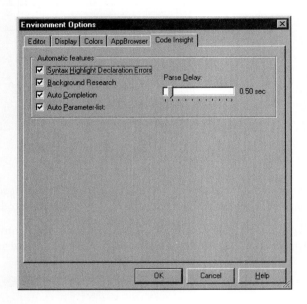

Figure 2.12   *You can specify whether to use Code Insight and how Code Insight is used on the Code Insight page of the Environment Options dialog box.*

TIP
You can restore all the JBuilder environment settings to the default values by deleting the file jbuilder3\bin\jbuilder.ini. When JBuilder is restarted, a new jbuilder.ini file will be created.

Chapter Summary

In this chapter, you learned about data representation, operators, and expressions. These are the fundamental elements needed to construct Java programs. You also learned about programming errors, debugging, and programming styles. These are all important concepts and should be fully understood before you apply them in Java programming.

Identifiers are used for naming programming entities, such as variables, constants, methods, classes, and packages. Variables are symbols that represent data. The value of a variable can be changed with an assignment statement. All variables must be declared with an identifier and a type before they can be used. An initial value must be assigned to the variable before the variable is read (or referenced).

The equals sign (=) is used to assign a value to a variable. The statement with the equals sign is called an assignment statement. When a value is assigned to a variable, it replaces the previous value in the variable, which is destroyed.

A constant is a symbol representing a value in the program that is never changed. Sometimes it is called a constant variable. You cannot assign a new value to a constant.

Java provides four integer types (`byte`, `short`, `int`, `long`) that represent integers of four different sizes, and two floating-point types (`float`, `double`) that represent float numbers of two different sizes. Character type (`char`) represents a single character, and `boolean` type represents a `true` or `false` value. These are called primitive data types. Java's primitive types are portable across all computer platforms. When they are declared, the variables of these types are created and assigned memory space.

Java provides operators for performing numerical operations, such as + (addition), – (subtraction), * (multiplication), / (division), and % (modulus). The integer division (/) yields an integer result. The modulus operator (%) yields the remainder after integer division.

The increment operator (++) and the decrement operator (--) increment or decrement a variable by 1. If the operator is prefixed to the variable, the variable is first incremented or decremented by 1, then used in the expression. If the operator is a suffix to the variable, the variable is first used in the expression, then incremented or decremented by 1.

In a computation involving different types of numerical values, numbers are converted to a unifying type. The unifying type is chosen according to the data type of the operands in the following order: `double`, `float`, `long`, `int`, `short`, `byte`. You can assign a value in a lower order to a variable in a higher order. However, an explicit casting operator must be used if you assign a value of a higher order (for instance, `double`) to a variable of a lower order (for instance, `int`).

The operators in arithmetic expressions are evaluated in the order determined by the rules of operator precedence. Parentheses can be used to force the order of evaluation to occur in any sequence.

You learned how to run Java programs from the DOS windows, how to view help online, and how to customize JBuilder environment options.

Chapter Review

2.1. Are the following identifiers valid?

```
applet, Applet, a++, --a, 4#R, $4, #44, apps
```

2.2. Declare the following:

- An `int` variable with an initial value of `0`.
- A `long` variable with an initial value of `10000`.
- A `float` variable with an initial value of `3.4`.
- A `double` variable with an initial value of `34.45`.
- A `char` variable with an initial value of `4`.
- A `boolean` variable with an initial value of `true`.

2.3. Assume that a = 1 and d = 1.0 and that each expression is independent. What are the results of the following expressions?

```
a = 46/9;
a = 46%9+4*4-2;
a = 45+43%5*(23*3%2);
a = 45+45*50%a--;
a = 45+1+45*50%(--a)
d += 34.23*3+d++
d -= 3.4*(a+5)*d++
a %= 3/a+3;
```

2.4. Find the largest and smallest `byte`, `short`, `int`, `long`, `float`, and `double`. Which of these data type requires the least amount of memory?

2.5. Can different types of numeric values be used together in a computation?

2.6. Describe Unicode and ASCII code.

2.7. Can the following conversions involving casting be allowed? If so, find the converted result. (Write a program to test your results.)

```
char c = 'A';
i = (int)c;

boolean b = true;
i = (int)b;

float f = 1000.34f;
int i = (int)f;

double d = 1000.34;
int i = (int)d;

int i = 1000;
char c = (char)i;

int i = 1000;
boolean b = (boolean)b;
```

2.8. What is the result of 25/4? How would you rewrite the expression if you wanted the quotient to be a floating-point number?

2.9. Are the following statements correct? If so, show the printout.

```
System.out.println("the output for 25/4 is "+ 25/4);
System.out.println("the output for 25/4.0 is "+ 25/4.0);
```

2.10. What does an explicit conversion from a `double` to an `int` do with the fractional part of the double value?

2.11. How would you write the following formula so that it produces a double value?

```
4/3(r + 34)
```

2.12. List six comparison operators.

2.13. Show the result of the following Boolean expressions if the result can be determined.

```
(true) && (3 > 4)
!(x > 0) && (x > 0)
(x > 0) || (x < 0)
(x != 0) || (x == 0)
(x >= 0) || (x < 0)
(x != 1) == !(x = 1)
```

2.14. Write a Boolean expression that evaluates to `true` if the number is between 1 and 100.

2.15. Write a Boolean expression that evaluates `true` if the number is between 1 and 100 or the number is negative.

2.16. Are the following expressions correct?

```
x > y > 0
x = y && y
x /= y
x or y
x and y
(x != 0) |¦ (x = 0)
```

2.17. How do you denote a comment line? How do you denote a comment paragraph?

2.18. Describe compilation errors, runtime errors, and logical errors.

2.19. What are the conventional styles for class names, methods names, constants, and variables? Which of the following items can be a constant, a method, a variable, or a class according to Java naming conventions?

```
MAX_VALUE, Test, read, readInt
```

2.20. What is the quick way to get help document on a menu command in JBuilder?

2.21. How do you set the tab positions in JBuilder?

2.22. How do you change the colors for keywords in the source code editor in JBuilder?

Programming Exercises

2.1. Write a program to convert Fahrenheit to Celsius. The formula for the conversion is as follows:

```
celsius = (5/9)*(fahrenheit-32)
```

Your program reads a Fahrenheit degree in double from the keyboard; it then converts it to Celsius and displays the result on the console.

2.2. Write a program to compute the volume of a cylinder. Your program reads in radius and length, and computes volume using the following formulas:

```
area = radius*radius*π;
volume = area*length;
```

2.3. Write a program to display "Welcome to Java" in large block letters, each letter made up of the same character it represents. The letter should be seven printed lines. For example, *W* is displayed as follows:

Control Structures

Objectives

- Understand the concept of program control.
- Use various decision statements to control the execution of a program.
- Use various loop structures to control the repetition of statements.
- Understand and use the keywords break and continue.
- Manage JBuilder projects.

Introduction

Program control can be defined as specifying the order in which statements are executed in a computer program. The programs that you have written so far execute statements in sequence. Often, however, you are faced with situations in which you must provide alternative steps.

In Chapter 2, "Java Building Elements," if you entered a negative input for `radius` in Example 2.1, "Computing the Area of a Circle," for instance, the program would print an invalid result. If the radius is negative, you don't want the program to compute the area. Like all high-level programming languages, Java provides decision statements that let you choose actions with two or more alternative courses. You can use the decision statements in the following pseudocode to rewrite Example 2.1:

```
if the radius is negative
   the program displays a message indicating a wrong input;
else
   the program computes the area and displays the result;
```

Java supports several variations of decision statements. The three main forms are `if` statements, shortcut `if` statements, and `switch` statements.

Like other high-level programming languages, Java provides loop structures in order to control the repeated execution of statements. Suppose that you needed to print the same message a hundred times. It would be tedious to write the same statement over and over again. Java provides a powerful control structure called a *loop*, which controls how many times an operation or a sequence of operations is performed in succession. Using a loop construct, you can simply tell the computer to print the message a hundred times without actually coding the print statement a hundred times. Java has three basic loop constructs: `for` loops, `while` loops, and `do` loops.

In this chapter, you will learn various decision and loop control structures.

Using *if* Statements

Java has two types of `if` statements: the simple `if` statement and the `if...else` statement. The simple `if` statement executes an action only if the condition is `true`. The actions that the `if...else` statement specifies differ based on whether the condition is `true` or `false`.

The Simple *if* Statement

The syntax for the simple `if` statement is as follows:

```
if (booleanExpression)
{
   statement(s);
}
```

The execution flow chart is shown in Figure 3.1.

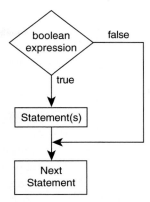

Figure 3.1 *The* if *statement executes the statements if the* boolean *expression evaluates them as* true.

If booleanExpression evaluates as true, the statements inside the block are executed. For example, see the following code:

```
if (radius >= 0)
{
  area = radius*radius*PI;
  System.out.println("The area for the circle of radius " +
    radius + " is " + area);
}
```

If the value of radius is greater than or equal to 0, then the area is computed and the result is displayed; otherwise, the two statements inside the block will not be executed.

CAUTION
The booleanExpression is enclosed in the parentheses for all forms of the if statement.

The curly braces can be omitted if they enclose a single statement. For example:

```
if ((i >= 0) && (i <= 10))
  system.out.println("i is an integer between 0 and 10");
```

The *if . . . else* Statement

The simple if statement takes an action if the specified condition is true. If the condition is false, nothing is done. But what can you do if you want to take alternative actions when the condition is false? You can use the if...else statement. The syntax for this statement is as follows:

```
if (booleanExpression)
{
  statement(s)-for-the-true-case;
}
else
```

```
{
  statement(s)-for-the-false-case;
}
```

The flow chart of the `if...else` statement is shown in Figure 3.2.

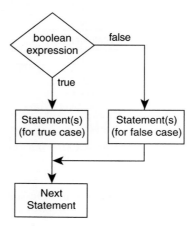

Figure 3.2   *The* `if...else` *statement executes the statements for the* `true` *case if the* `boolean` *expression evaluates them as* `true`; *otherwise, the statements for the* `false` *case are executed.*

If the `booleanExpression` evaluates as `true`, the `statement(s)` for the true case is executed; otherwise, the `statement(s)` for the false case is executed. For example, consider the following code:

```
if (radius >= 0)
{
  area = radius*radius*PI;
  System.out.println("The area for the circle of radius " +
    radius + " is " + area);
}
else
{
  System.out.println("Negative input");
}
```

If `radius >= 0` is true, area is computed and displayed; if it is `false`, the message `"Negative input"` is printed.

As usual, the curly braces can be omitted if there is only one statement within them. The curly braces enclosing the `System.out.println("Negative  input")` statement can therefore be omitted in the previous example.

Nested *if* Statements

The statement inside an `if` or `if...else` statement can be any legal Java statement—including another `if` or `if...else` statement. The inner `if` statement is said to be *nested* inside the outer `if` statement. The inner `if` statement can contain another `if` statement; in fact, there is no limit to the depth of the nesting. Here is an example of a nested `if` statement:

```
if (i > k)
{
  if (j > k)
    System.out.print("i and j are greater than k");
}
else
  System.out.println("i is less than or equal to k");
```

The `if (j > k)` statement is nested inside the `if (i > k)` statement.

A nested `if` statement can be used to implement multiple alternatives. For example, the following statement assigns a letter grade to the variable `grade` according to the score, with multiple alternatives:

```
if (score >= 90.0)
  grade = 'A';
else
  if (score >= 80.0)
    grade = 'B';
  else
    if (score >= 70.0)
      grade = 'C';
    else
      if (score >= 60.0)
        grade = 'D';
      else
        grade = 'F';
```

The execution of this `if` statement proceeds as follows. The first condition (`score >= 90.0`) is tested. If it is `true`, the grade becomes `'A'`. If it is `false`, the second condition (`score >= 80.0`) is tested. If the second condition is `true`, the grade becomes `'B'`. If that condition is `false`, the third condition and (if necessary) the remaining conditions continue to be tested until a condition is met or all of the conditions prove to be `false`. If all of the conditions are `false`, the grade becomes `'F'`. Note that a condition is tested only when all of the conditions that precede it are `false`.

The `if` statement presented above is equivalent to the one that follows:

```
if (score >= 90.0)
  grade = 'A';
else if (score >= 80.0)
  grade = 'B';
else if (score >= 70.0)
  grade = 'C';
else if (score >= 60.0)
  grade = 'D';
else
  grade = 'F';
```

In fact, this is the preferred writing style for multiple alternative `if` statements. This style avoids deep indentation and makes the program easy to read.

Example 3.1 Using Nested *if* Statements

In Example 2.2, "Computing Mortgages," you built a program that reads interest rate, year, and loan amount and computes mortgage payments. In this example, assume that the interest rate depends on the year.

Suppose that you have three different interest rates: 7.25 percent for 7 years, 8.5 percent for 15 years, and 9 percent for 30 years. The program prompts the user to enter a loan amount and the number of years of the loan, then finds the interest rate according to year. The program concludes by displaying the monthly payment amount and the total amount paid. Figure 3.3 shows a sample run of the program.

```java
// TestIfElse.java: Test if-else statements
package Chapter3;

import Chapter2.MyInput;

public class TestIfElse
{
  // Main method
  public static void main(String[] args)
  {
    double interestRate = 0;
    int year;
    double loan;

    // Enter number of years
    System.out.println("Enter number of years:  7, 15 and 30" +
      "only :");
    year = MyInput.readInt();

    // Find interest rate based on year
    if (year == 7)
      interestRate = 7.25/1200;
    else if (year == 15)
      interestRate = 8.50/1200;
    else if (year == 30)
      interestRate = 9.0/1200;
    else
    {
      System.out.println("Wrong year");
      System.exit(0);
    }

    // Enter loan amount
    System.out.println("Enter loan amount, for example 120000.95: ");
    loan = MyInput.readDouble();

    // Compute mortgage
    double monthlyPay =
      loan*interestRate/(1-(Math.pow(1/(1+interestRate), year*12)));
    double totalPay = monthlyPay*year*12;

    // Display results
    System.out.println("The monthly pay is " + monthlyPay);
    System.out.println("The total pay is " + totalPay);
  }
}
```

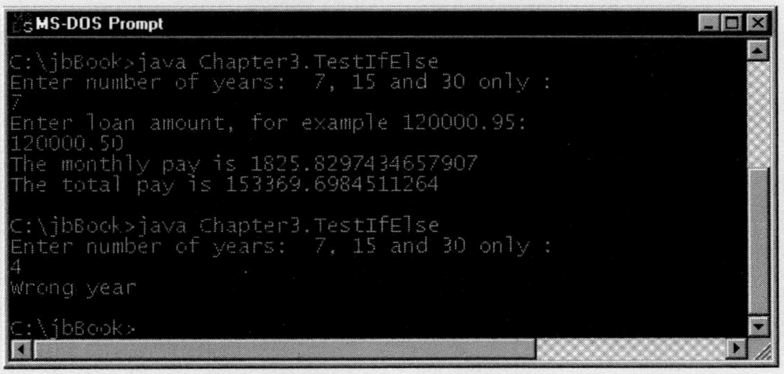

```
MS-DOS Prompt                                          _ □ ×
C:\jbBook>java Chapter3.TestIfElse
Enter number of years:  7, 15 and 30 only :
7
Enter loan amount, for example 120000.95:
120000.50
The monthly pay is 1825.8297434657907
The total pay is 153369.6984511264

C:\jbBook>java Chapter3.TestIfElse
Enter number of years:  7, 15 and 30 only :
4
Wrong year

C:\jbBook>
```

Figure 3.3   *The program in Example 3.1 validates the input year, obtains the interest rate according to the year, receives the loan amount, and displays the monthly payment and the total payment.*

Example Review

The program receives the year and assigns the interest rate: 7.25 percent for 7 years, 8.5 percent for 15 years, and 9 percent for 30 years. If the year value is not 7, 15, or 30, the program displays Wrong Year.

Note that an initial value of 0 is assigned to interestRate. A syntax error would occur if it had no initial value because all of the other statements that assign values to interestRate are within the if statement. The compiler thinks that these statements might not be executed and therefore reports a syntax error.

The import statement makes the class Chapter2.MyInput available for use in this example. In future examples, simply import Chapter2.MyInput if the program needs to read numerical values from the keyboard.

Shortcut *if* Statements

You might want to assign a value to a variable that is restricted by certain conditions. For example, the following statement assigns 1 to y if x is greater than 0, and −1 to y if x is less than or equal to 0.

```
if (x > 0)
   y = 1
else
   y = -1;
```

Alternatively, you can use a shortcut if statement to achieve the same result:

```
y = (x > 0) ? 1 : -1;
```

The shortcut form of the if statement is in a completely different style. There is no explicit if in the statement. The syntax is as follows:

```
variable = booleanExpression ? true-result-expression :
   false-result-expression;
```

This is equivalent to the following:

```
if (booleanExpression)
  variable = true-result-expression;
else
  variable = false-result-expression;
```

NOTE

The shortcut if statement is also known as a *conditional expression*, because it returns a value based on the condition.

TIP

The shortcut if statement originally comes from C. It is unfamiliar to many programmers who do not have a C background. Because the statement is not descriptive, you should avoid using it.

Using *switch* Statements

The if statement in Example 3.1 makes decisions based on a single true or false condition. There are three cases for assigning interest rates, which depend on the year value. To fully account for all cases, nested if statements were used. Clearly, the overuse of the nested if statement makes the program difficult to read. Java provides a switch statement to handle multiple conditions efficiently. You could write the following switch statement to replace the nested if statement in Example 3.1:

```
switch (year)
{
  case 7:  interestRate = 7.25;
           break;
  case 15: interestRate = 8.50;
           break;
  case 30: interestRate = 9.0;
           break;
  default: System.out.println("Wrong number of Years");
}
```

The flow chart of the preceding switch statement is shown in Figure 3.4.

This statement checks to see whether the year matches the value 7, 15, or 30, in that order. If matched, the corresponding statement is executed; if not matched, a message is displayed. Here is the full syntax for the switch statement:

```
switch (switch-expression)
{
  case value1: statement(s)1;
               break;
  case value2: statement(s)2;
               break;
  ...
  case valueN: statement(s)N;
               break;
  default:     statement(s)-for-default;
}
```

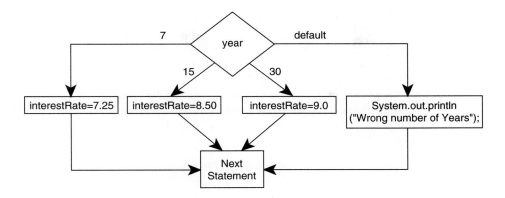

Figure 3.4   *The* switch *statement obtains the interest rate according to the year.*

The switch statement observes these rules:

- The switch-expression must yield a value of char, byte, short, or int type and must always be enclosed in parentheses.

- The value1...valueN must have the same data type as the value of the switch-expression. The resulting statements in the case statement are executed when the value in the case statement matches the value of the switch-expression. (Each case statement is executed in sequential order.)

- The keyword break is optional. The break statement terminates the entire switch statement. If the break statement is not present, the next case statement will be executed.

- The default case, which is optional, can be used to perform actions when none of the specified cases is true. The default case always appears last in the switch block.

CAUTION

Do not forget to use the break statement when one is needed. For example, the following code always displays Wrong Year, regardless of what year is. Suppose year is 15. The statement interestRate = 8.50 is executed, then the statement interestRate = 9.0 is executed, and finally the statement System.out.println("Wrong number of Years") is executed.

```
switch (year)
{
  case 7:  interestRate = 7.25;
  case 15: interestRate = 8.50;
  case 30: interestRate = 9.0;
  default: System.out.println("Wrong number of Years");

}
```

Using Loop Structures

Loops are structures that control repeated executions of a block of statements. The part of the loop that contains the statements to be repeated is called the *loop body*. A one-time execution of a loop body is referred to as an *iteration of the loop*. Each loop contains a loop continue-condition, a Boolean expression that controls the execution of the body. After each iteration, the continue-condition is reevaluated. If the condition is true, the body is repeated. If the condition is false, the loop terminates.

The concept of looping is fundamental to programming. Java provides three types of loop structures: the for loop, the while loop, and the do loop.

The *for* Loop

The for loop is a common type of program loop. It is a construct that causes the loop body to be repeated for a fixed number of times. The syntax of the for loop is as follows:

```
for (control-variable-initializer; continue-condition;
     adjustment-statement)
{
   // Loop-body;
}
```

The flow chart of the loop is shown in Figure 3.5.

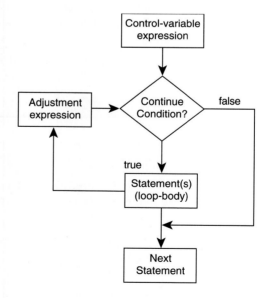

Figure 3.5   *The* for *loop initializes the control variable, executes the statements in the loop body, and then repeatedly evaluates the adjustment expression when the* continue-condition *evaluates as* true.

The loop construct starts with the keyword `for`, followed by the three control elements, which are enclosed by the parentheses, and the loop body, which is inside the curly braces. The control elements, which are separated by semicolons, control how many times the loop body is executed and when the loop terminates. The following `for` loop prints `Welcome to Java!` 100 times:

```
int i;
for (i = 0; i<100; i++)
{
   System.out.println("Welcome to Java!");
}
```

The flow chart of the statement is shown in Figure 3.6.

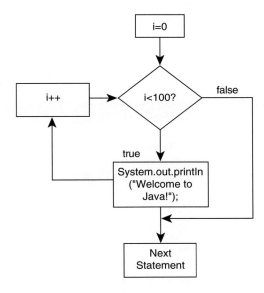

Figure 3.6   *The* `for` *loop initializes* `i` *to* `0`*, executes the* `println` *statement, and then repeatedly evaluates* `i++` *when* `i` *is less than* `100`*.*

The first element, `i = 0`, initializes the control variable, `i`. The control variable tracks how many times the loop body has been executed. The adjustment statement changes the value of the variable.

The next element, `i < 100`, which is the `continue-condition`, is a Boolean expression. The expression is evaluated at the beginning of each iteration. If the `continue-condition` is `true`, execute the loop body. If it is `false`, the loop terminates and the program control turns to the line following the loop.

The adjustment statement, `i++`, is a statement that adjusts the control variable. This statement is executed after each iteration. Usually, an adjustment statement either increments or decrements the control variable. Eventually, the value of the control variable forces the `continue-condition` to become `false`.

The loop control variable can be declared and initialized in the `for` loop. An equivalent statement for the previous example is as follows:

```
for (int i = 0; i<100; i++)
{
  System.out.println("Welcome to Java!");
}
```

If there is only one statement in the loop body, as in this example, the curly braces can be omitted.

NOTE

The three elements in a `for` loop—control-variable-initializer, continue-condition, and adjustment-statement—can be any statement or expression, or can be omitted. So the following statement, which is an infinite loop, is correct.

```
for ( ; ; )
{
}
```

Example 3.2   Using *for* Loops

This example computes the summation of a series, starting with 0.01 and ending with 1.0. The numbers in the series will increment by 0.01, as follows: 0.01+0.02+0.03, and so on. The output of this program appears in Figure 3.7.

```
// TestSum.java: Compute sum = 0.01 + 0.02 + … + 1;
package Chapter3;

import Chapter2.MyInput;
public class TestSum
{
  // Main method
  public static void main(String[] args)
  {
    // Initialize sum
    float sum = 0;

    // Keep adding 0.01 to sum
    for (float i=0.01f; i <= 1.0f ; i = i+0.01f)
      sum += i;

    // Display result
    System.out.println("The summation is " + sum);
  }
}
```

Figure 3.7   *Example 3.2 uses a* `for` *loop to sum a series from 0.01 to 1 in increments of 0.01.*

Example Review

The `for` loop repeatedly adds the control variable `i` to the sum. This variable, which begins with 0.01, is incremented by 0.01 after each iteration. The loop terminates when `i` exceeds 1.0.

The example shows that a control variable can be a `float` type. In fact, it can be any numeric data type.

If you run the program and get a result close to, but not exactly, 50.499985, you probably are using an earlier version of JDK.

You may already have noticed that the answer is not precise. This is because computers have to use a fixed number of bits to represent floating-point numbers; some floating-point numbers cannot be represented exactly. If you change `float` in the program to `double`, you will see a small improvement in precision because a double variable takes 64 bits, whereas a float variable takes 32 bits.

CAUTION

Always use semicolons rather than commas in the `for` loop header to separate the control elements. The use of commas in the `for` loop header is a frequent mistake.

TIP

Do not change the value of the control variable inside the `for` loop, even though it is perfectly legal to do so. Changing the value makes the program difficult to understand and could lead to subtle errors.

Example 3.3 Using Nested *for* Loops

The following program uses nested `for` loops to print a multiplication table. A nested loop is composed of an outer loop and one or more inner loops. Each time the outer loop is repeated, the inner loops are reentered, their loop control parameters are reevaluated, and all required iterations are performed. The output of the program is shown in Figure 3.8.

```
// TestMulTable.java: Display a multiplication table
package Chapter3;

public class TestMulTable
{
  // Main method
  public static void main(String[] args)
  {
    // Display the table heading
    System.out.println("       Multiplication Table");
    System.out.println("------------------------.");
```

continues

```java
    // Display the number title
    System.out.print("  | ");
    for (int j=1; j<=9; j++)
      System.out.print("  " + j);
    System.out.println(" ");

    // Print table body
    for (int i=1; i<=9; i++)
    {
      System.out.print(i+" | ");
      for (int j=1; j<=9; j++)
      {
        // Display the product and align properly
        if (i*j < 10)
          System.out.print("  " + i*j);
        else
          System.out.print(" " + i*j);
      }
      System.out.println(" ");
    }
  }
}
```

Figure 3.8   *Example 3.3 uses nested* for *loops to print a multiplication table.*

Example Review

The program displays a title on the first line, dashes (-) on the second line. The first for loop displays the numbers 1 through 9 on the third line.

The next loop is a nested for loop with the control variable i on the outer loop and j on the inner loop. For each i, the product i*j is displayed on a line in the inner loop, with j being 1, 2, 3, . . . , 9. The if statement in the inner loop is used so that the product will be aligned properly. If the product is a single digit, it is displayed with a space before it.

The *while* Loop

If you know how many times you need to repeat an operation, you can use a for loop to control the repetition of the statements. If the number of repeats is unknown, the for loop cannot help you. Suppose that you need to find the sum of all numbers entered from the keyboard. If you know that the total number is 100, it is easy to use a for loop like this:

```
int sum = 0;
for (int i = 1; i <= 100; i++)
   sum += readInt();
```

Assume that the total number is not specified. However, you do know that you will have all of the numbers when the input is 0—that is, the input 0 signifies the end of the input. You need to use a while loop for this problem. The while loop handles an unspecified number of repetitions. The syntax for the while loop is as follows:

```
while (continue-condition)
{
   // Loop-body;
}
```

The while loop flow chart is shown in Figure 3.9.

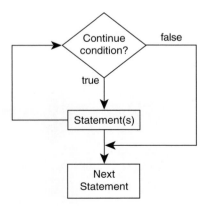

Figure 3.9   *The* while *loop repeatedly executes the statements in the loop body when* continue-condition *evaluates as* true.

The `continue-condition`, a Boolean expression, must appear inside the parentheses. It is always evaluated before the loop body is executed. If its evaluation is `true`, the loop body is executed; if its evaluation is `false`, the entire loop terminates and the program control turns to the statement that follows the `while` loop.

Example 3.4 Using a *while* Loop

This example reads and calculates an unspecified number of integers. The input 0 signifies the end of the input.

The program's sample run is shown in Figure 3.10.

```java
// TestWhile.java: Test the while loop
package Chapter3;

import Chapter2.MyInput;

public class TestWhile
{
  // Main method
  public static void main(String[] args)
  {
    int data;
    int sum = 0;

    // Read an initial data
    System.out.println("Enter an int value");
    data = MyInput.readInt();

    // Keep reading data until the input is 0
    while (data != 0)
    {
      sum += data;

      System.out.println(
        "Enter an int value, the program exits if the input is 0");
      data = MyInput.readInt();
    }

    System.out.println("The sum is "+sum);
  }
}
```

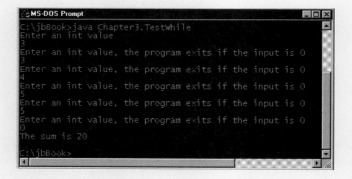

Figure 3.10   *Example 3.4 uses a* while *loop to add an unspecified number of integers.*

Example Review

If data is not 0, it is added to the sum and the next input data is read. If data is 0, the loop body is not executed and the while loop terminates.

Note that if the first input read is 0, the loop body never executes, and the resulting sum is 0.

CAUTION

Ensure that the continue-condition eventually becomes false so that the program will terminate.

TIP

Avoid using floating-point values for equality checking in a loop control. Using them could result in infinite loops because floating-point values are approximations.

The *do* Loop

The do loop is a variation of the while loop. Its syntax is as follows:

```
do
{
  // Loop body;
} while (continue-condition)
```

Its execution flow chart is shown in Figure 3.11.

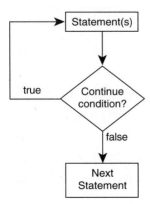

Figure 3.11   *The* do *loop body executes once when* continue-condition *evaluates as* false, *and it executes repeatedly when* continue-condition *evaluates as* true.

The loop body is executed first. Then the continue-condition is evaluated. If the evaluation is true, the loop body is executed again; if it is false, the do loop terminates. The major difference between a while loop and a do loop is the order in which the continue-condition is evaluated and the loop body is executed. The while loop and the do loop have equal expressive power. Sometimes it is more convenient to choose one over the other. For example, you can rewrite Example 3.4 as follows:

```java
// TestDo.java: Test the do loop
package Chapter3;

import Chapter2.MyInput;

public class TestDo
{
  // Main method
  public static void main(String[] args)
  {
    int data;
    int sum = 0;

    do
    {
      data = MyInput.readInt();
      sum += data;
    } while (data != 0);

    System.out.println("The sum is " + sum);
  }
}
```

TIP

The loop body is always executed at least once. I recommend the do loop if you have statements inside the loop that must be executed at least once, as in the case of the do loop in the preceding TestDo program. These statements must appear before the loop as well as inside the loop if you are using a while loop.

Using the Keywords *break* and *continue*

Two statements, break and continue, can be used in loop constructs to provide the loop with additional control:

- **break**—This keyword immediately ends the innermost loop that contains it.

- **continue**—This keyword only ends the current iteration. Program control goes to the next iteration of the loop.

You have already used the keyword break in a switch statement. You can also use break and continue in any of the three kinds of loop constructs.

The diagrams in Figures 3.12 and 3.13 illustrate the work of break and continue in a loop statement.

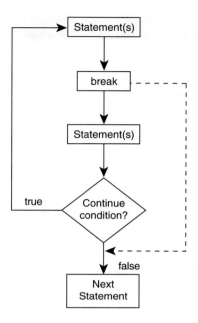

Figure 3.12   *The* break *statement forces its containing loop to exit.*

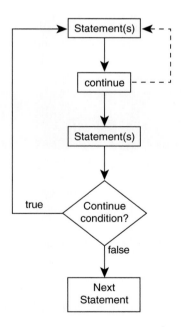

Figure 3.13   *The* continue *statement forces the current iteration of the loop to end.*

Example 3.5 Testing the *break* Statement

In this example, you will see how the break statement affects the results of the following program.

```java
// TestBreak.java: Test the break keyword in the loop
package Chapter3;

public class TestBreak
{
  // Main method
  public static void main(String[] args)
  {
    int sum = 0;
    int item = 0;

    do
    {
      item ++;
      sum += item;
      if (sum >= 6) break;
    } while (item < 5);

    System.out.println("The sum is " + sum);
  }
}
```

Example Review

Without the if statement, this program calculates the sum of the numbers from 1 to 5. But with the if statement, the loop terminates when the sum becomes greater than or equal to 6. The output of the program is shown in Figure 3.14.

Figure 3.14 *The* break *statement in the TestBreak program forces the* do *loop to exit when* sum *is greater than 6.*

If you changed the if statement to the following, the output would resemble that in Figure 3.15:

```java
if (sum == 5) break;
```

In this case, the if condition would never be true. Therefore, the break statement would never be executed.

Figure 3.15   *The* break *statement is not executed in the modified* TestBreak *program because* sum == 5 *cannot be* true.

Example 3.6 Using the *continue* Statement

In this example, you will see the effect of the continue statement on a particular program.

```
// TestContinue.java: Test the continue keyword
package Chapter3;

public class TestContinue
{
  // Main method
  public static void main(String[] args)
  {
    int sum = 0;
    int item = 0;

    do
    {
      item++;
      if (item == 2) continue;
      sum += item;
    } while (item < 5);

    System.out.println("The sum is " + sum);
  }
}
```

Example Review

With the if statement in the program, the continue statement is executed when item becomes 2. The continue statement ends the current iteration so that the rest of the statement in the loop body is not executed; therefore, item is not added to sum when it is 2. The output of the program is shown in Figure 3.16.

continues

Figure 3.16 *The* continue *statement in the* TestContinue *program forces the current iteration to end when* item *equals 2.*

Without the `if` statement in the program, the output would look like Figure 3.17.

Figure 3.17 *The modified* TestContinue *program has no* continue *statement; therefore, every item is added to* sum.

Without the `if` statement, all of the items are added to sum, including when item is 2. Therefore, the result is 15, which is two more than it was with the `if` statement.

 TIP
You can always write a program without using break or continue in a loop.
See Chapter Review Question 3.20.

Case Studies

Control structures are fundamental in programming. The ability to write control statements is an essential part of Java programming. This section presents two additional examples of solving problems using decision statements and loops.

Example 3.7 Finding Sales Amount

You have just started a sales job in a department store. Your pay consists of a base salary and a commission. The base salary is $5000. The following scheme is used to determine the commission rate:

Sales Amount	Commission Rate
$1–$5,000	8 percent
$5,001–10,000	10 percent
10,001 and above	12 percent

Your goal is to earn $30,000 in a year. Write a program to find out the minimum sales that you have to generate in order to make $30,000.

Since your base salary is $5000, you have to make $25,000 on commission to earn $30,000 in a year. What is the sales amount for a $25,000 commission? If you know the sales amount, the commission can be computed as follows:

```
if (salesAmount >= 10001)
  commission = 5000*0.08 + 5000*0.1 + (salesAmount-10000)*0.12;
else if (salesAmount >= 5001)
  commission = 5000*0.08 + (salesAmount-5000)*0.10;
else
  commission = salesAmount*0.08;
```

This suggests that you can try to find the salesAmount to match a given commission through incremental approximation. For salesAmount of $1, find commission. If commission is less than $25,000, increment salesAmount by 1 and find commission again. If commission is less than $25,000, repeat the process until commission is greater than $25,000. This is a tedious job for humans, but it is exactly what a computer is good for. You can write a loop and let a computer execute it with no pain.

The complete program is given below, and a sample run of the program is shown in Figure 3.18.

```
// FindSalesAmount.java: Find the sales amount to get the desired
// commission
package Chapter3;

public class FindSalesAmount
{
  // The commission sought
  final static double COMMISSION_SOUGHT = 25000;

  // Main method
  public static void main(String[] args)
  {
    double commission = 0;
    double salesAmount = 1;

    while (commission < COMMISSION_SOUGHT)
    {
      // Compute commission
      if (salesAmount >= 10001)
        commission = 5000*0.08 + 5000*0.1 + (salesAmount-10000)*0.12;
      else if (salesAmount >= 5001)
        commission = 5000*0.08 + (salesAmount-5000)*0.10;
      else
        commission = salesAmount*0.08;
```

continues

```
        salesAmount++;
      }

      // Display the sales amount
      System.out.println("The sales amount " + salesAmount +
        " is needed to make a commission of $" + COMMISSION_SOUGHT);
    }
  }
```

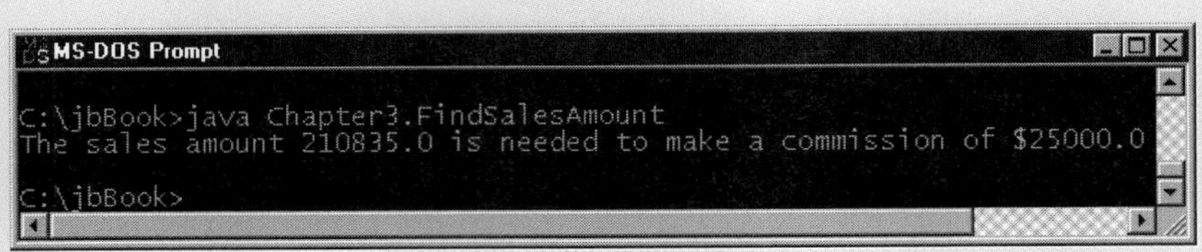

```
MS-DOS Prompt                                              _ □ ×
C:\jbBook>java Chapter3.FindSalesAmount
The sales amount 210835.0 is needed to make a commission of $25000.0

C:\jbBook>
```

Figure 3.18   *The program finds the sales amount for the given commission.*

Example Review

The `while` loop is used to repeatedly compute `commission` for an incremental `salesAmount`. The loop terminates when `commission` is greater than or equal to a constant `COMMISSION_SOUGHT`.

In Exercise 3.10, you will rewrite this program to let the user enter `COMMISSION_SOUGHT` dynamically from the keyboard.

You can improve the performance of this program by using the *binary search* approach. The binary search approach is introduced in Chapter 6, "Arrays and Strings." A rewrite of this program using the binary search is proposed in Exercise 6.9.

Example 3.8 Displaying a Triangle

In this example, you will use nested loops to print the following output:

```
    1
   212
  32123
 4321234
543212345
```

Your program prints five lines. Each line has three parts. The first part consists of the spaces before the numbers, the second part consists of the leading numbers, such as 3 2 1 on line 3, and the last part consists of the ending numbers, such as 2 3 on line 3.

You can use an outer loop to control the lines. At the nth row, there are 5 - n leading spaces, the leading numbers are n, n-1, . . . , 1, and the ending numbers are 2, . . . , n. You can use three separate inner loops to print each part.

The complete program is given below, and a sample run of the program is shown in Figure 3.19.

```java
// PrintTriangle.java: Print a triangle patterm
package Chapter3;

public class PrintTriangle
{
  // Main method
  public static void main(String[] args)
  {
    for (int row = 1; row < 6; row++)
    {
      // Print leading spaces
      for (int column = 1; column < 6 - row; column++)
        System.out.print(" ");

      // Print leading numbers
      for (int num = row; num >= 1; num—)
        System.out.print(num);

      // Print ending numbers
      for (int num = 2; num <= row; num++)
        System.out.print(num);

      // Start a new line
      System.out.println("");
    }
  }
}
```

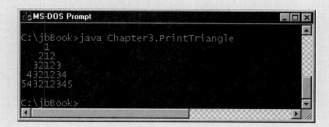

Figure 3.19 *The program uses nested loops to print numbers in a triangle shape.*

Example Review

Printing patterns like this as well as the ones in Exercises 3.4 and 3.5 is my favorite exercise for practicing loop control statements. The key is to understand the pattern and to describe it using loop control variables.

Managing Projects in JBuilder

The IDE tools use a project file to store project information. You cannot edit the project file manually; it is modified automatically, however, whenever you add or remove files from the project or set project options. You can see the project file as a node at the top of the project tree in the Navigation pane (see Figure 1.5). JBuilder uses a Project Properties dialog box for setting project properties and provides a Project Wizard to facilitate creating projects.

Setting Project Properties

JBuilder uses Default Project Properties dialog box to set default environment properties for all the projects. An individual project has its own Project Properties dialog box, which can be used to set project-specific properties.

To display the default Project Properties dialog box, select Project, Default Properties, as shown in Figure 3.20. To display the Project Properties dialog box, select Project, Properties, as shown in Figure 3.21. You can also right-click the project file in the Navigation pane and choose the Properties command to display the Project Properties dialog box.

The Default Project Properties dialog box (Figure 3.20) and the Project Properties dialog box (Figure 3.21) look the same but have different titles. Both dialog boxes contain Paths, Compiler, Code Style, Run/Debug, and Servlets tabs. You can set options in these pages for the current project or the default project, depending on whether the dialog box is for the current project or for the default project. JBuilder Professional and JBuilder Enterprise Edition have more options in the Project Properties dialog box.

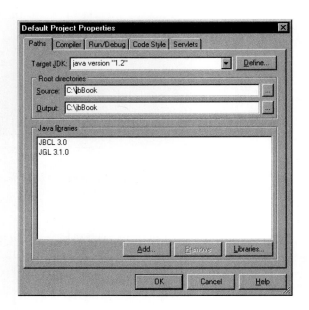

Figure 3.20   *The Default Project Properties dialog box enables you to set default properties to cover all the projects.*

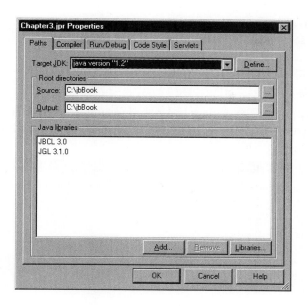

Figure 3.21 *Each project keeps its own project properties.*

The Paths Page

The Paths page of the Project Properties dialog box sets the following options:

- JDK version to compile against.

- Source root directories where the source code is located.

- Output root directory where the compilation output is stored.

- Java libraries to use for compiling and running.

JBuilder can compile and run against JDK 1.1 or JDK 1.2. To set up the list of available JDKs, click the Define button to display the Available JDK Versions dialog box for adding new JDK compilers.

Setting proper paths is necessary for JBuilder to locate the associated files in the right directory for compiling and running the programs in the project. The Source specifies one or more paths (separated with semicolons) for the source file. The Output root directory specifies the path where the compiler places the .class files. Files are placed in a directory tree that is based on the Output root directory and the package name. For example, if the Output root directory is c:\jbBook and the package name is Chapter3 in the source code, the .class file is placed in c:\jbBook\Chapter3.

All the libraries you need for this book have already been taken care of. If you need to add the custom libraries to the project, click the Add button to display a list of available libraries. To remove a library, click the Remove button. To switch the order of libraries, drag-and-drop them. To change the list of available libraries, choose the Libraries button to display the Available Java Libraries dialog.

The Compiler Page

The Compiler page of the Project Properties dialog box (see Figure 3.22) sets compiler options. The options are applied to all the files in the project, as well as to files referenced by these files, stopping at packages that are marked "stable."

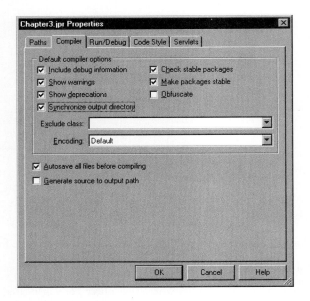

Figure 3.22   *The Compiler page of the Project Properties dialog box sets compiler options for the project.*

The option "Include Debug Information" includes symbolic debug information in the .class file when you compile, make, or rebuild a node. The option "Show Warnings" displays compiler warning messages. The option "Show Deprecations" displays all deprecated classes, methods, properties, events, and variables used in the API. The option "Synchronize output directory" deletes class files on the output path for which you don't have source files before compiling.

The Option "Check Stable Packages" checks files in the packages marked "stable" to see whether they and their imported classes need to be recompiled. This option shortens the edit/recompile cycle by not rechecking stable packages.

The option "Make Package Stable" checks all the classes of a package on the first build and marks the package "stable." If this option is unchecked, only the referenced classes of this package will be compiled, and the package will not be marked "stable." This option should be unchecked when working with partial projects. It is especially useful for working with a library of classes with no source code.

The option "Obfuscate" makes your programs less vulnerable to decompiling. Decompiling means to translate the Java bytecode to Java source code. After decompiling your obfuscated code, the generated source code contains altered symbol names for private symbols.

The "Exclude Class" choice lets you specify that a .class file is excluded from being compiled. The "Encoding" choice menu specifies the encoding that controls how the compiler interprets characters beyond the ASCII character set. If no setting is specified, the default native-encoding converter for the platform is used.

The option "Autosave all files before compiling" automatically saves all files in the project before each compile.

The option "Generate source to output path" is applicable only to RMI (Remote Method Invocation) and IDL (Interface Definition Language) files. These files are used in multi-tier Java applications, which are covered in my *Rapid Java Application Development Using JBuilder 3* text.

The Run/Debug Page

The Run/Debug page of the Project Properties dialog box (see Figure 3.23) lets you enter command-line arguments that can be passed to your application at runtime. You also can use this page to set Debugger options. You can send the output either to the console or to the Execution Log in Console I/O section. You can view the Execution Log by choosing View, Execution Log. If the option "Close Console Window on exit" is selected, the console window is closed when the application's main method is completely executed.

Figure 3.23 *The Run/Debug page of the Project Properties dialog box enables you to set execution and debugging options.*

The Code Style Page

The Code Style page of the Project Properties dialog box (see Figure 3.24) enables you to specify the code style of the program generated by JBuilder.

Figure 3.24   *The Code Style page of the Project Properties dialog box sets the options for the code style of the program generated by JBuilder.*

With the option "End of line" selected, JBuilder will generate the code with opening braces inserted at the end of the line; otherwise, the opening braces are inserted at the beginning of the new line.

In the Event Handling section, you can choose one of the options to tell JBuilder to generate event-handling code using anonymous adapter, standard adapter, or matching the existing style of event-handling code. The adapters are used in the UI designer in JBuilder. For more information on adapters, please refer to Appendix G, "Rapid Java Application Development Using JBuilder 3."

The option "Use Beans.instantiate" tells JBuilder to instantiate objects using `Beans.instantiate()` instead of the new operator. This feature is discussed in my book *Rapid Java Application Development Using JBuilder 3.*

Chapter Summary

Program control is used to specify the order in which statements are to be executed in a program. In this chapter, you learned about two types of control structures: decision control and loop control.

Decision statements are for building decision steps into programs. You learned several forms of decision structures: `if` statements, `if...else` statements, nested `if` statements, `switch` statements, and shortcut `if` statements.

The various `if` statements all use a Boolean expression to make control decisions. Based on the `true` or `false` evaluation of that expression, the statements take one or two possible courses. The `switch` statements make control decisions based on a switch variable that can be of type `char`, `byte`, `short`, or `int`. The shortcut `if` statement is rarely used.

You learned three types of repetition statements: the `for` loop, the `while` loop, and the `do` loop. In designing loops, both the loop control structure and the loop body must be considered.

The `for` loop is generally used to execute a loop body for a predictable number of times; this number is not determined by the loop body. The loop control has three parts. The first part is a control variable, which has an initial value. The second part is the `continue-condition`, which determines whether the loop body is to be executed. The third part is the adjustment statement, which changes the control variable. Loop control variables are usually initialized and changed in the control structure.

The `while` loop control structure contains the `continue-condition`, which is dependent on the loop body. Therefore, the number of repetitions is determined by the loop body. The `while` loop is often used for an unspecified number of repetitions.

The `while` loop checks the `continue-condition` first. If the condition is `true`, the loop body is executed; if it is `false`, the loop terminates. The `do` loop is similar to the `while` loop, except that the `do` loop executes the loop body first and then checks the `continue-condition` to decide whether to continue or to terminate.

You also learned the `break` and `continue` keywords. The `break` keyword immediately ends the innermost loop, which contains the break. The `continue` keyword only ends the current iteration.

You learned how to manage project properties and customize Paths options, Compiler options, Run/Debug options, and Code Style options in the JBuilder Project Properties dialog box.

Chapter Review

3.1. Show the output of the following code, if any:

```
x = 2;
y = 3;
if (x > 2)
  if (y > 2)
  {
    int z = x + y;
    System.out.println("z is " + z);
  }
else
  System.out.println("x is " + x);
```

3.2. Show the output of the following code, if any:

```
x = 3;
y = 2;
if (x > 2)
{
  if (y > 2)
  {
    int z = x + y;
    System.out.println("z is " + z);
  }
}
else
   System.out.println("x is " + x);
```

3.3. Can you convert a switch statement to an equivalent if statement, or vice versa?

3.4. What are the advantages of using the switch statement?

3.5. What data types are required for a switch variable? If the keyword break is not used after a case is processed, what is the next statement to be executed?

3.6. What is y after the following switch statement is executed?

```
x = 3;
switch (x+3)
{
   case 6:  y = 1;
   default: y += 1;
}
```

3.7. Use a switch statement to rewrite the following if statement:

```
if (a == 1)
   x += 5;
else if (a == 2)
   x += 10;
else if (a == 3)
   x += 16;
else if (a == 4)
   x += 34;
```

3.8. What is y after the following statement is executed?

```
x = 0;
y = (x > 0) ? 1 : -1;
```

3.9. Do the following two statements result in the same value in sum?

```
for (int i=0; i<10; ++i)
{  sum += i;   }

for (int i=0; i<10; i++)
{  sum += i;   }
```

3.10. What are the three parts in a for loop control? Write a for loop that will print numbers from 1 to 100.

3.11. What does the following statement do?

```
for (;;)
{
  do something;
}
```

3.12. If a variable is declared in the `for` loop control, can it be used after the loop exits?

3.13. Can you convert a `for` loop to a `while` loop? List the advantages of using `for` loops.

3.14. Convert the following `for` loop statement to a `while` loop and to a `do` loop:

```
long sum = 0;
for (int i=0; i<= 1000; i++)
  sum = sum + i;
```

3.15. How many times is the following loop body repeated? What is the printout of the loop?

```
int i = 1;
while (i < 10)
  if ((i++)%2==0)
    System.out.println(i);
```

3.16. What are the differences between a `while` loop and a `do` loop?

3.17. What is the keyword `break` for? Will the following program terminate? If so, give the output.

```
int balance = 1000;
while (true)
{
  if (balance < 9)
    break;
  balance = balance - 9;
}

System.out.println("balance is " + balance);
```

3.18. What is the keyword `continue` for? Will the following program terminate? If so, give the output.

```
int balance = 1000;
while (true)
{
  if (balance < 9)
    continue;
  balance = balance - 9;
}

System.out.println("balance is " + balance);
```

3.19. Can you always convert a `while` loop into a `for` loop? Convert the following `while` loop into a `for` loop.

```
int i = 1;
int sum = 0;
while (sum < 10000)
{
   sum = sum + i;
   i++;
}
```

3.20. Rewrite the programs `TestBreak` and `TestContinue` without using `break` and `continue` (see Examples 3.5 and 3.6).

3.21. How do you set options to direct the compiler to store .class files on the A drive?

3.22. How do you set options to direct JBuilder to save files before compiling?

3.23. If you want the output to be sent to Execution Log, what should you do?

Programming Exercises

3.1. Write a program that will read an integer and find out whether it is even or odd.

3.2. Write a program that will sort three integers. The integers are entered from the keyboard and stored in variables `num1`, `num2`, and `num3`, respectively. The program sorts the numbers so that `num1` ≤ `num2` ≤ `num3`.

3.3. Write a program that will compute sales commissions using the same scheme as in Example 3.7. Your program reads the sales amount from the keyboard and displays the result on the console.

3.4. Write a nested `for` loop that will print the following output:

```
1
1 2
1 2 3
1 2 3 4
1 2 3 4 5
```

3.5. Write a nested `for` loop that will print the following output:

```
                              1
                          1   2   1
                      1   2   4   2   1
                  1   2   4   8   4   2   1
              1   2   4   8  16   8   4   2   1
          1   2   4   8  16  32  16   8   4   2   1
      1   2   4   8  16  32  64  32  16   8   4   2   1
  1   2   4   8  16  32  64 128  64  32  16   8   4   2   1
```

Hint: Here is the pseudocode solution:

```
for the row from 0 to 7
{
  Pad leading blanks in a row using a loop like this:
  for the column from 1 to 7-row
    System.out.print("   ");

  Print left half of the row for numbers 1, 2, 4, up to
  2row using a look like this:
  for the column from 0 to row
    System.out.print((int)Math.pow(2, column)+"   ");

  Print the right half of the row for numbers
  2row-1, 2row-2, ..., 1 using a loop like this:
  for (int column=row-1; column>=0; col—)
    System.out.print((int)Math.pow(2, column)+"   ");

  Start a new line
  System.out.print('\n');
}
```

The `Math.pow()` method was introduced in Example 2.2. Can you write this program without using this method?

3.6. Write a program that will check whether an input integer is a prime number. (An integer is a prime number if its only divisor is 1 or itself.)

3.7. Write a program that will read an unspecified number of integers and determine how many positive and negative values have been read. Your program ends when the input is 0.

3.8. Write a program that will read integers and will find the total and average of the input values. Your program ends with the input 0.

3.9. Use a `while` loop to find the smallest n such that n^2 is greater than 10,000.

3.10. Rewrite Example 3.7 as follows:

  ■ Use a `for` loop instead of a `while` loop.

  ■ Let the user enter COMMISSION_SOUGHT from the keyboard instead of fixing it as a constant.

3.11. You can approximate π by using the following series:

$$\pi = 4*(1-1/3+1/5-1/7+1/9-1/11+1/13+...)$$

Write a program that will find out how many terms of this series you need to use before you get 3.14159.

CHAPTER 4

METHODS

Objectives

- Understand and use methods.
- Create and invoke methods.
- Understand the role of arguments in a method.
- Use pass by value for primitive type parameters.
- Understand method overloading.
- Understand method abstraction and its use in developing software.
- Become familiar with recursion.
- Know how to use the JBuilder menu commands.

Introduction

In Chapter 2, "Java Building Elements," and Chapter 3, "Control Structures," you learned about methods like `println()`, which is used to print messages, and `readDouble()` and `readInt()`, which are used to read `double` and `int` numbers, respectively. A method is a collection of statements that are grouped together to perform an operation. When you call the method `println()`, for example, the system actually executes several statements in order to display a message on the console.

This chapter introduces many topics that involve or are related to methods. You will learn how to create your own methods with or without return values, invoke a method with or without parameters, overload methods using the same names, write a recursive method that invokes itself, and apply method abstraction in the program design.

Creating a Method

In general, a method has the following structure:

```
modifier returnValueType methodName(list of parameters)
{
   // Method body;
}
```

The method `readDouble()` was created in Chapter 2 to read a double value from the keyboard. Figure 4.1 illustrates the components of this method.

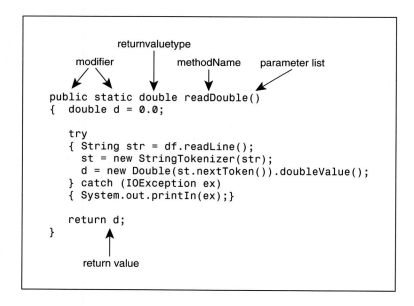

Figure 4.1 *The method* `readDouble()` *has a signature that consists of modifiers, return type, and the method name, which is followed by the method body block.*

The method heading specifies the *modifiers, returning value type, method name,* and *parameters* of the method. The modifier, which can be optional, specifies the *property* of the method and tells the compiler how the method can be called. Modifiers are discussed in more depth in Chapter 5, "Programming with Objects and Classes."

A method may return a value. The `returnValueType` is the data type of the value the method returns. If the method does not return a value, the `returnValueType` is the keyword `void`. For example, the `returnValueType` in the `main()` method is `void`. All methods except constructors require `returnValueType`. For a detailed discussion of constructors, see Chapter 5.

A method can have a list of parameters—*formal parameters*—in the method specification. When a method is called, these formal parameters are replaced by variables or data, which are referred to as *actual parameters*. Parameters are optional. The `readDouble()` method, for example, has no parameters.

The method body contains a collection of statements that define what the method does. Let's take a look at a method created to find which of two integers is larger. This method, named `max()`, has two `int` parameters, `num1` and `num2`, the larger of which is returned by the method.

```
int max(int num1, int num2)
{
  if (num1 > num2)
    return num1;
  else
    return num2;
}
```

This method body simply uses an `if` statement to determine which number is larger and to return the value of that number. The keyword `return` is required for nonvoid methods other than those with a `void` return value type. The return statement can also be used in a void method to simply terminate the method and return to its caller. The method terminates when a `return` statement is executed.

NOTE

In some languages, methods are referred to as *procedures* and *functions*. A method with a return value type is called a *function*; a method with a `void` return value type is called a *procedure*.

CAUTION

You need to declare a data type for each parameter separately. For instance, `int i, j` should be replaced by `int i, int j`.

Calling a Method

How do you know whether a method works? You need to test it by calling it in a test program. There are two ways to call a method; the choice is based on whether the method returns a value or not.

If the method returns a value, a call to the method is usually treated as a value. For example,

```
int larger = max(3, 4);
```

calls `max(3, 4)` and assigns the result of the method to the variable `larger`. Another example of a call that is treated as a value is

```
System.out.println(max(3,4));
```

which prints the return value of the method call `max(3,4)`.

If the method returns `void`, a call to the method must be a statement. For example, the method `println()` returns `void`. The following call is a statement:

```
System.out.println("Welcome to Java!");
```

NOTE

A method with return value can also be invoked as a statement in Java. In this case, the return value is ignored by the caller. In the majority of cases, a call to a method with return value is treated as a value. In some cases, however, the caller is not interested in the return value. For example, many methods in database applications return a Boolean value to indicate whether the operation is successful. You can choose to ignore the return value if you know the operation will always succeed. I recommend, however, that you always treat the call to a method with return value as a value to avoid programming errors.

When a program calls a method, program control is transferred to the called method. A called method returns control to the caller when its return statement is executed or when its method-ending right brace is reached.

The following example gives the complete program used to test the `max()` method.

Example 4.1 Testing the *max()* Method

This example demonstrates how to create a test program for the `max()` method. The program's output is shown in Figure 4.2.

```
// TestMax.java: Demonstrate using methods
package Chapter4;

public class TestMax
{
  // Main method
  public static void main(String[] args)
  {
```

```
        int num1 = 5;
        int num2 = 2;
        int num3 = max(num1, num2);
        System.out.println("The maximum between " + num1 +
          " and " + num2 + " is " + num3);
    }

    // A method for finding a max between two numbers
    static int max(int num1, int num2)
    {
      if (num1 > num2)
        return num1;
      else
        return num2;
    }
}
```

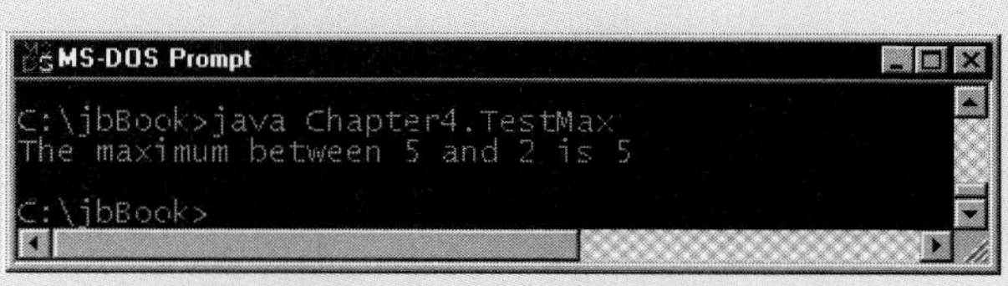

Figure 4.2   *The program invokes* max(5, 2) *in order to discover whether 5 or 2 is the maximum value.*

Example Review

This program contains the main() method and the max() method. The main() method is just like any other method, with one exception: It is invoked by the Java interpreter.

The main() method's heading is always the same, like the one in this example, with modifiers public and static, return type value void, method name main, and parameters String[] args. String[] indicates that args is an array of String, which is addressed in Chapter 6, "Arrays and Strings."

The statements in main() may invoke other methods that are defined in the class that contains the main() method or in other classes. In this example, the main() method invokes max(num1, num2), which is defined in the same class with main().

Passing Parameters

The power of a method is its ability to work with parameters. You can use println() to print any message and max() to find the maximum between any two numbers. When calling a method, you need to provide actual parameters, which must be given in the same order as their respective formal parameters in the method specification. This is known as *the parameter order association*. For example, the following method prints a message n times:

```
void nPrintln(String message, int n)
{
  for (int i=0;  i<n;  i++)
    System.out.println(message);
}
```

You can use nPrintln("Hello", 3) to print "Hello" three times. The
nPrintln("Hello", 3) statement passes the actual string parameter, "Hello", to the
formal parameter, message; passes 3 to n; and prints "Hello" three times. However,
the statement nPrintln(3,"Hello") would be wrong. The data type of 3 does not
match the data type for the first formal parameter, message, nor does the second
parameter, "Hello", match the second formal parameter, n.

■■■ CAUTION
The actual parameters must match the formal parameters in type, order, and
number.

Pass by Value

When invoking a method with a parameter of primitive data type, such as int, the
copy of the value of the actual parameter is passed to the method. This is referred
to as *pass by value*. The actual variable outside the method is not affected, regardless
of the changes made to the formal parameter inside the method. Let's examine an
interesting scenario in the following example, in which the formal parameter is
changed inside the method, but the actual parameter is not affected.

Example 4.2 Testing Pass by Value

The following program shows the effect of passing by value. The output of the
program is shown in Figure 4.3.

```java
// TestPassByValue.java: Demonstate passing values to methods
package Chapter4;

public class TestPassByValue
{
  // Main method
  public static void main(String[] args)
  {
    // Initialize times
    int times = 3;
    System.out.println("Before the call, variable times is "+times);

    // Invoke nPrintln and display times afterwards
    nPrintln("Welcome to Java!", times);
    System.out.println("After the call, variable times is "+times);
  }

  // Method for printing the message n times
  static void nPrintln(String message, int n)
  {
```

```
        while (n > 0)
        {
          System.out.println("n = "+n);
          System.out.println(message);
          n--;
        }
      }
    }
```

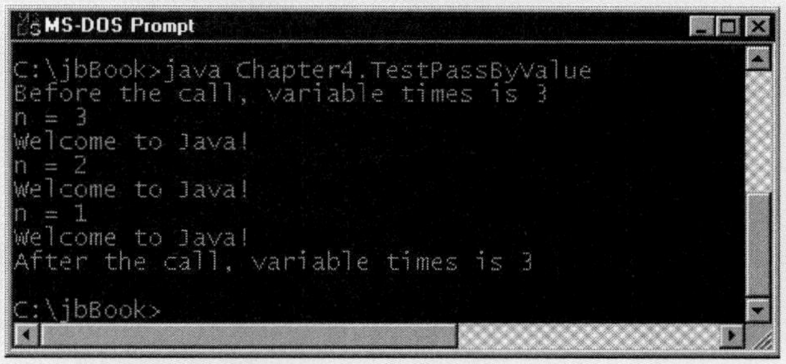

Figure 4.3   *The* times *variable is passed by value to the method* nPrintln(); *therefore,* times *is not changed by the method.*

Example Review

A while loop with a changing formal parameter of n was used to rewrite the nPrintln() method in the previous section. The method nPrintln("Welcome to Java!", times) was then invoked. Before the call, the times variable was 3. Interestingly, after the call, the times variable is still 3. This is because n is a parameter of primitive data type. Java passes the value of times to n. The times variable itself is not affected by the changes made to n inside the method.

Another twist is to change the formal parameter name n in nPrintln() to times. What effect does this have? No change occurs because it does not matter whether the formal parameter and the actual parameter have the same name. The formal parameter represents imaginary data, which does not exist until it is associated with an actual parameter.

See Chapter 5 to learn about another mechanism for passing objects: *pass by reference.*

Overloading Methods

The max() method that was used earlier works only with the int data type. But what if you need to find which of two floating-point numbers has the maximum value? The solution is to create another method with the same name but with different parameters, as shown in the following code:

```java
double max(double num1, double num2)
{
  if (num1 > num2)
    return num1;
  else
    return num2;
}
```

If you call max() with int parameters, the max() method that expects int parameters will be invoked; if you call max() with double parameters, the max() method that expects double parameters will be invoked. This is referred to as *method overloading*; that is, two methods have the same name, but have different parameter profiles. Java runtime system is able to determine which method to invoke based on the number and types of parameters passed to that method.

Example 4.3 Overloading the *max* Method

In the following program, two methods are created. One method finds the maximum integer; the other finds the maximum double. Both methods are named max. The output of the program is shown in Figure 4.4.

```java
// TestMethodOverloading.java: Demonstrate method overloading
package Chapter4;

public class TestMethodOverloading
{
  // Main method
  public static void main(String[] args)
  {
    // Invoke the max method with int parameters
    System.out.println("The maximum between 3 and 4 is "
      + max(3, 4));

    // Invoke the max method with the double parameter
    System.out.println("The maximum between 3.0 and 5.4 is "
      + max(3.0, 5.4));
  }

  // Find the max between two double values
  static double max(double num1, double num2)
  {
    if (num1 > num2)
      return num1;
    else
      return num2;
  }

  // Find the max between two int values
  static int max(int num1, int num2)
  {
    if (num1 > num2)
      return num1;
    else
      return num2;
  }
}
```

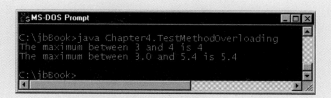

Figure 4.4. *The program invokes two different* max *methods*—max(3, 4) *and* max(3.0, 5.4)—*even though both have the same name.*

Example Review

Two max() methods were created in the same class with different types of parameters—one for finding maximum integers, and the other for finding maximum doubles.

When calling max(3.0, 5.4), the max() method for finding maximum doubles is invoked. When calling max(3, 4), the max() method for finding maximum integers is invoked.

TIP

Overloading methods can make programs clear and more readable. Methods that perform closely related tasks should be given the same name.

Creating Methods in Separate Classes

Thus far in this chapter, the methods in the examples have been placed in the same class in which they were invoked. You can create methods in separate classes so that they can be used by other classes.

Example 4.4 Computing Square Roots

In this example, you will see how to write a program that computes square roots. The square root of a number, num, can be approximated by repeatedly performing a calculation using the following formula:

```
nextGuess = (lastGuess + (num / lastGuess))/2
```

When nextGuess and lastGuess are almost identical, nextGuess is the approximate square root.

The initial guess will be the starting value of lastGuess. If the difference between nextGuess and lastGuess is less than a very small number, such as 0.001, you can claim that nextGuess is the approximate square root of num. The sample output of the following program is shown in Figure 4.5.

continues

117

```
// TestSquareRoot.java: Demonstrate invoking methods from other class
package Chapter4;

public class TestSquareRoot
{
  // Main method
  public static void main(String[] args)
  {
    System.out.println(
      "The square root for 9 is " + SquareRoot.sqrt(9.0));
    System.out.println(
      "The square root for 2000 is " + SquareRoot.sqrt(2000.0));
  }
}

// This class contains sqrt method
class SquareRoot
{
  // Find the square root of the value
  public static double sqrt(double num)
  {
    double nextGuess;
    double lastGuess = 1.0;
    double difference;

    do
    {
      nextGuess = (lastGuess + (num/lastGuess))*0.5;
      difference = nextGuess - lastGuess;
      lastGuess = nextGuess;
      if (difference < 0)
        difference = -difference;
    } while (difference >= 0.001);

    return nextGuess;
  }
}
```

Figure 4.5   *The program invokes the* sqrt() *method in order to compute the square root.*

Example Review

The sqrt() method is defined in the SquareRoot class. To invoke sqrt(), put the class name SquareRoot in front of the sqrt().

The sqrt() method implements the approximation algorithm for finding the square root. In this case, the constant 0.001 is often referred to as error tolerance. The smaller the difference, the better the approximation.

Method Abstraction

The key to developing software is to apply the concept of abstraction. *Method abstraction* is defined as separating a method's use from its implementation. This is referred to as *information hiding*. The client can use a method without knowing how it is implemented. If you decide to change the implementation, the client program will not be affected.

When writing a large program, use the "divide and conquer" strategy to decompose a problem into more manageable sub-problems. You can apply method abstraction to make programs easy to manage. The following example demonstrates method abstraction in software development.

Example 4.5 Illustrating Method Abstraction in Developing a Large Project

In this example, a program is created that displays the calendar for a given month of the year. The program prompts the user to enter the year and the month, and then displays the entire calendar for the month, as shown in Figure 4.6.

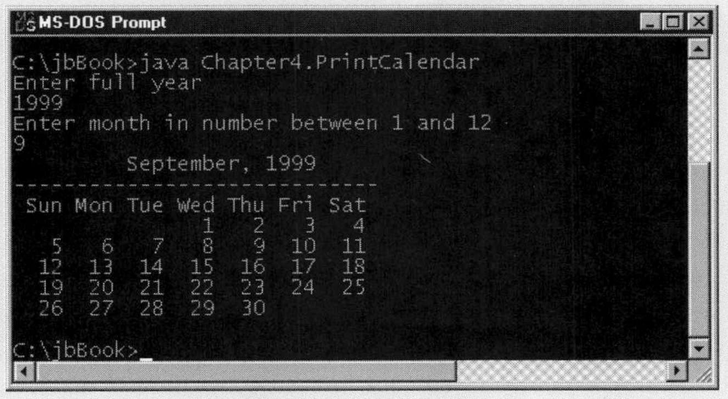

Figure 4.6.   *After prompting the user to enter the year and the month, the program displays the calendar for that month.*

How would you get started on such a program? Would you immediately start coding? Beginning programmers often start by trying to work out the solution to every detail. Although details are important in the final program, concern for detail in the early stages may block the problem-solving process. To make problem solving flow as smoothly as possible, this example begins by using method abstraction to isolate details from design, and only later implements the details.

For this example, the problem is first broken into two subproblems: get input from the user, and print the monthly calendar. At this stage, the creator of the

continues

119

program should be concerned with what the subproblems will achieve but not with the ways in which they will get input and print the calendar for the month. Note the structure chart used to help you visualize the subproblems (see Figure 4.7).

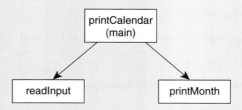

Figure 4.7   *The structure chart shows that the* `printCalendar` *problem is divided into two subproblems:* `readInput` *and* `printMonth`.

You may use `System.out.println()` to display a message to prompt the user for the year and the month. Then, `MyInput.readInt()` can be used to get the input.

In order to print the calendar for a month, you would need to know the day for the first date in the month and the number of days in the month. With this information, you can print the title and body of the calendar. Therefore, the print month problem can be further decomposed into four subproblems: get the start day, get the number of days in the month, print title, and print month body.

How would you get the start day for the first date in a month? There are several ways to find the start day. The simplest approach is to use the `Date` and `Calendar` classes in Chapter 12, "Internationalization." For now, an alternative approach is used. Assume that you know that the start day (`startDay1800 = 3`) for January 1, 1800 is Wednesday. You could compute the total number of days (`totalNumOfDays`) between January 1, 1800, and the first date of the calendar month. The start day for the calendar month is (`totalNumOfDays + startDay1800`) `% 7`.

To compute the total days (`totalNumOfDays`) between January 1, 1800, and the first date of the calendar month, you could find the total number of days between the year 1800 and the calendar year and then figure out the total number of days prior to the calendar in the calendar year. The sum of these two totals is `totalNumOfDays`.

You would also need to know the number of days in a month and in a year. Remember the following:

- January, March, May, July, August, October, and December have 31 days.

- April, June, September, and November have 30 days.

- February has 28 days during a regular year and 29 days during a leap year. A regular year, therefore, contains 365 days, while a leap year contains 366 days.

To determine whether a year is a leap year, use the following condition:

```
if ((year % 400 == 0) || ((year % 4 == 0) && (year % 100 != 0)))
   return true;
else
   return false;
```

To print a title, use `println()` to display three lines, as shown in Figure 4.8.

Figure 4.8 *The calendar title consists of three lines: month and year, a dash line, and the names of the seven days of the week.*

To print a body, you would first pad some space before the start day and then print the lines for every week, as shown for September 1998 (refer to Figure 4.6).

In general, a subproblem corresponds to a method in the implementation, although some are so simple that this is unnecessary. You need to decide which modules to implement as methods and which to combine in other methods. Decisions of this kind should be based on whether the overall program would be easier to read as a result of your choice. In this example, the subproblem `readInput` was implemented in the `main()` method (see Figure 4.9).

When implementing the program, use the "top-down" approach. In other words, implement one method in the structure chart at a time—from the top to the bottom. Use stubs for the methods waiting to be implemented. Implement the `main()` method first and then use a stub for the `printMonth` method. For example, simply let `printMonth` display the year and the month in the stub.

continues

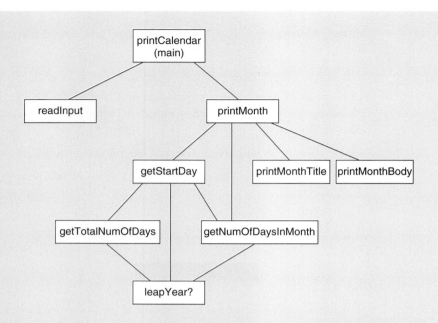

Figure 4.9   *The structure chart shows the hierarchical relationship of the subproblems in the program.*

The sample run of the following program is shown in Figure 4.6.

```java
// PrintCalendar.java: Print a calendar for a given month in a year
package Chapter4;

import Chapter2.MyInput;

public class PrintCalendar
{
  // Main method
  public static void main(String[] args)
  {
    // The user enters year and month
    System.out.println("Enter full year");
    int year = MyInput.readInt();
    System.out.println("Enter month in number between 1 and 12");
    int month = MyInput.readInt();

    // Print calendar for the month of the year
    printMonth(year, month);
  }

  // Print the calendar for a month in a year
  static void printMonth(int year, int month)
  {
    // Get start day of the week for the first date in the month
    int startDay = getStartDay(year, month);

    // Get number of days in the month
    int numOfDaysInMonth = getNumOfDaysInMonth(year, month);
```

```
      // Print headings
      printMonthTitle(year, month);

      // Print body
      printMonthBody(startDay, numOfDaysInMonth);
    }

    // Get the start day of the first day in a month
    static int getStartDay(int year, int month)
    {
      // Get total number of days since 1/1/1800
      int startDay1800 = 3;
      long totalNumOfDays = getTotalNumOfDays(year, month);

      // Return the start day
      return (int)((totalNumOfDays + startDay1800) % 7);
    }

    // Get the total number of days since Jan 1, 1800
    static long getTotalNumOfDays(int year, int month)
    {
      long total = 0;

      // Get the total days from 1800 to year -1
      for (int i = 1800; i < year; i++)
      if (leapYear(i))
        total = total + 366;
      else
        total = total + 365;

      // Add days from Jan to the month prior to the calendar month
      for (int i = 1; i < month; i++)
        total = total + getNumOfDaysInMonth(year, i);

      return total;
    }

    // Get the number of days in a month
    static int getNumOfDaysInMonth(int year, int month)
    {
      if (month == 1 || month==3 || month == 5 || month == 7 ||
        month == 8 || month == 10 || month == 12)
        return 31;

      if (month == 4 || month == 6 || month == 9 || month == 11)
        return 30;

      if (month == 2)
        if (leapYear(year))
          return 29;
        else
          return 28;

      return 0; // If month is incorrect.
    }

    // Determine if it is a leap year
    static boolean leapYear(int year)
    {
      if ((year % 400 == 0) || ((year % 4 == 0) && (year % 100 != 0)))
        return true;
```

continues

```java
      return false;
    }

    // Print month body
    static void printMonthBody(int startDay, int numOfDaysInMonth)
    {
      // Pad space before the first day of the month
      int i = 0;
      for (i = 0; i < startDay; i++)
        System.out.print("    ");

      for (i = 1; i <= numOfDaysInMonth; i++)
      {
        if (i < 10)
          System.out.print("   " + i);
        else
          System.out.print("  " + i);

        if ((i + startDay) % 7 == 0)
          System.out.println();
      }

      System.out.println();
    }

    // Print the month title, i.e. May, 1999
    static void printMonthTitle(int year, int month)
    {
      System.out.println("         "+getMonthName(month)+", "+year);
      System.out.println("——————————————-");
      System.out.println(" Sun Mon Tue Wed Thu Fri Sat");
    }

    // Get the English name for the month
    static String getMonthName(int month)
    {
      String monthName = null;
      switch (month)
      {
        case 1: monthName = "January"; break;
        case 2: monthName = "February"; break;
        case 3: monthName = "March"; break;
        case 4: monthName = "April"; break;
        case 5: monthName = "May"; break;
        case 6: monthName = "June"; break;
        case 7: monthName = "July"; break;
        case 8: monthName = "August"; break;
        case 9: monthName = "September"; break;
        case 10: monthName = "October"; break;
        case 11: monthName = "November"; break;
        case 12: monthName = "December";
      }

      return monthName;
    }
  }
```

Example Review

The program does not validate user input. For instance, if the user enters a month not in the range between 1 and 12, or a year before 1800, the program would display an erroneous calendar. To avoid this error, you can add an `if` statement to check the input before printing the calendar.

This program can print calendars for a month but could easily be modified to print calendars for a whole year. It can only print months after January 1800, but could be modified to trace the day of a month before 1800.

See Chapter 12 to find out how to simplify the program using the `Date` and `Calendar` classes.

NOTE
Method abstraction helps modularize programs in a neat, hierarchical manner. Programs written as collections of concise methods are easier to write, debug, maintain, and modify. This writing style also promotes method reusability.

TIP
When implementing a large program, use the top-down coding approach. Start with the main() method, and code and test one method at a time. Do not write the entire program at once. This approach seems to take more time for coding (because you are compiling and running a program repeatedly), but it actually saves time and makes debugging easier.

Recursion (Optional)

You have seen a method calling another method—that is, a statement contained in the method body calling another method. Can a method call itself? And what happens if it does? This section examines these questions and uses two classic examples to demonstrate recursive programming.

Recursion, a powerful mathematical concept, is the process of a method calling itself, either directly or indirectly. In some cases, using this method enables you to give a natural, straightforward, simple solution to a problem that would otherwise be difficult to solve. Consider the well-known Fibonacci series problem. The Fibonacci series begins with two 1s in succession (1, 1, 2, 3, 5, 8, 13, 21, 34, and so on); each subsequent number is the sum of the preceding two numbers in the series. The series can be recursively defined as follows:

```
fib(1) = 1;
fib(2) = 1;
fib(n) = fib(n-2) + fib(n-1); n > 2
```

The Fibonacci series was originally formulated by Leonardo Fibonacci, a medieval mathematician, to model the growth of the rabbit population. It can be applied in numeric optimization and in various other areas.

How do you find `fib(n)` for a given n? It is easy to find `fib(3)` because you know `fib(1)` and `fib(2)`. Assuming that you know `fib(n-2)` and `fib(n-1)`, `fib(n)` can be obtained immediately. Thus, the problem of computing `fib(n)` is reduced to computing `fib(n-2)` and `fib(n-1)`. When computing `fib(n-2)` and `fib(n-1)`, you apply the idea recursively until n is reduced to 1 or 2.

If you call the method with n=1 or n=2, the method immediately returns the result. The method knows how to solve the simplest case, which is referred to as the *base case* or the *stopping condition*. If you call the method with n>2, the method divides the problem into two subproblems of the same nature. The subproblem is essentially the same as the original problem, but slightly simpler or smaller. Because the subproblem has the same property as the original, you can call the method with a different actual parameter, which is referred to as a *recursive call*.

The recursive algorithm for computing `fib(n)` can be simply described as follows:

```
if ((n==1) || (n==2))
   return 1;
else
   return fib(n-1)+fib(n-2);
```

The recursive call results in many more recursive calls as the method is dividing a subproblem into new subproblems. For a recursive method to terminate, the problem must eventually be reduced to a stopping case. When it reaches a stopping case, the method returns a result to its caller. The caller then performs some computation and returns the result to its own caller. This process continues until the result is passed back to the original caller. The original problem can now be solved by adding the results of the two subproblems.

Example 4.6 Computing Fibonacci Numbers

In this example, a recursive method is written for computing a Fibonacci number `fib(n)`, given index n. The test program prompts the user to enter index n, then calls the method and displays the result.

A sample run of the following program is shown in Figure 4.10.

```java
// TestFibonacci.java: Find a Fibonacci number for a given index
package Chapter4;

import Chapter2.MyInput;

public class TestFibonacci
{
  // Main method
  public static void main(String args[])
  {
    // Read the index
    System.out.println("Enter an index for the Fibonacci number");
    int n = MyInput.readInt();

    // Find and display the Fibonacci number
    System.out.println("Fibonacci number at index " + n +
      " is "+fib(n));
  }
```

```
// The method for finding the Fibonacci number
public static long fib(long n)
{
  if ((n==0)||(n==1))  // Stopping condition
    return 1;
  else  // Reduction and recursive calls
    return fib(n-1) + fib(n-2);
}
}
```

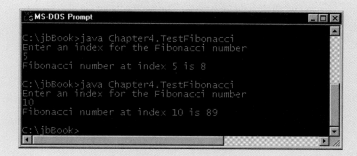

Figure 4.10 *The program prompts the user to enter an index for the Fibonacci number and then displays the number at that index.*

Example Review

The implementation of the method is, in fact, very simple and straightforward. The solution is slightly more difficult if you do not use recursion. For a hint on computing Fibonacci numbers using iterations, see Exercise 4.8.

The computer does much work behind the scenes that is not shown in the program. Figure 4.11 shows successive recursive calls for evaluating `fib(5)`. The original method, `fib(5)`, makes two recursive calls—`fib(4)` and `fib(3)`—and then returns `fib(4)+fib(3)`. But in what order are these methods called? In Java, the operands are evaluated from left to right. In Figure 4.11, the upper-left corner labels show the order in which methods are called.

As shown in Figure 4.11, there are many duplicated recursive calls. For instance, `fib(3)` is called two times, `fib(2)` is called three times, and `fib(1)` is called two times. In general, computing `fib(n)` requires twice as many recursive calls as you need for computing `fib(n-1)`. As you try larger index values, the number of calls substantially increases.

Besides the large number of recursive calls, the computer requires more time and space to run recursive methods. See Exercise 4.8 for a more efficient method.

Each time a method is invoked, the system stores parameters, local variables, and system registers in a certain kind of space known as a *stack*. When a method calls another method, the caller's stack space is kept intact, and new space is

continues

127

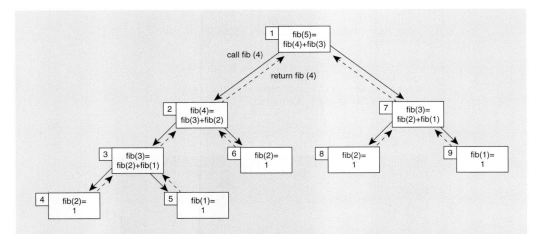

Figure 4.11 *Invoking* fib(5) *engenders recursive calls to* fib().

created to handle the new method call. When a method finishes its work and returns to its caller, its associated space is released. The use of stack space for recursive calls is shown in Figure 4.12.

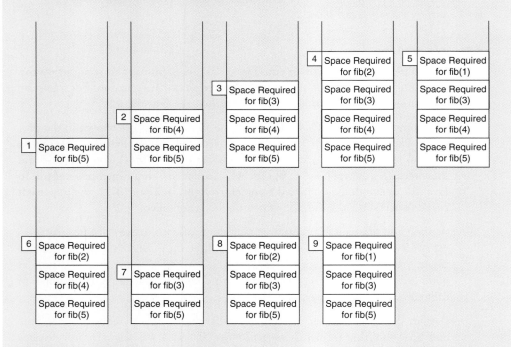

Figure 4.12 *When* fib(5) *is being executed, the* fib() *method is called recursively, causing memory space to dynamically change.*

You have seen a recursive method with a return value. Now, here is an example of a recursive method with a return type of `void`.

Example 4.7 Solving the Towers of Hanoi Problem

This example finds a solution for the Towers of Hanoi problem. The problem involves moving a specified number of disks of a distinct size from one tower to another while observing the following rules:

- There are *n* disks labeled 1, 2, 3, . . . *n*, and three towers labeled A, B, and C.
- No disk can be on top of a smaller disk at any time.
- Initially, all disks are placed on tower A.
- Only one disk can be moved at a time, and this disk must be the top disk of a tower.

The objective of the problem is to move all disks from A to B with the assistance of C. For example, if you have three disks, as shown in Figure 4.13, the following steps will move all of the disks from A to B:

1. Move disk 1 from A to B.
2. Move disk 2 from A to C.
3. Move disk 1 from B to C.
4. Move disk 3 from A to B.
5. Move disk 1 from C to A.
6. Move disk 2 from C to B.
7. Move disk 1 from A to B.

continues

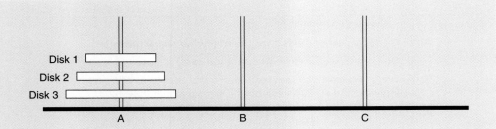

Figure 4.13   *The goal of the Towers of Hanoi problem is to move disks from tower A to tower B without breaking the rules.*

In the case of three disks, you could find the solution manually. However, the problem is quite complex for a larger number of disks—even for four. Fortunately, the problem has an inherently recursive nature, which leads to a straightforward recursive solution.

The base case for the problem is n=1. If n=1, you could simply move the disk from A to B. When n>1, you could split the original problem into the following three subproblems and solve them sequentially:

1. Move the first n-1 disks from A to C with the assistance of tower B.

2. Move disk n from A to B.

3. Move n-1 disks from C to B with the assistance of tower A.

The following method moves *n* disks from the fromTower to the toTower with the assistance of the auxTower:

```
void moveDisks(int n, char fromTower, char toTower, char auxTower)
```

The algorithm for the method is described below:

```
if (n==1) // Stopping condition
  Move disk 1 from the fromTower to the toTower;
else
{
  moveDisks(n-1, fromTower, auxTower, toTower);
  Move disk n from the fromTower to the toTower;
  moveDisks(n-1, auxTower, toTower, fromTower);
}
```

The sample run of the following program appears in Figure 4.14.

```
// TowersOfHanoi.java: Find solutions for the Towers of Hanoi problem
package Chapter4;

import Chapter2.MyInput;

public class TowersOfHanoi
{
  // Main method
  public static void main(String[] args)
  {
    // Read number of disks, n
    System.out.println("Enter number of disks");
```

```
        int n = MyInput.readInt();

        // Find the solution recursively
        System.out.println("The moves are:");
        moveDisks(n, 'A', 'B', 'C');
    }

    // The method for finding the solution to move n disks
    // from fromTower to toTower with auxTower
    public static void moveDisks(int n, char fromTower,
      char toTower, char auxTower)
    {
      if (n==1) // Stopping condition
        System.out.println("Move disk " + n + " from " +
          fromTower+" to " + toTower);
      else
      {
        moveDisks(n-1, fromTower, auxTower, toTower);
        System.out.println("Move disk " + n + " from " +
          fromTower + " to " + toTower);
        moveDisks(n-1, auxTower, toTower, fromTower);
      }
    }
}
```

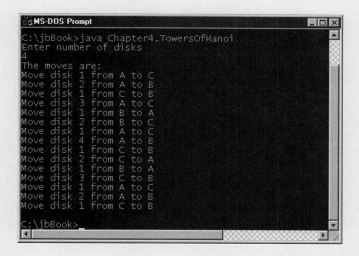

Figure 4.14   *The program prompts the user to enter the number of disks and then displays the steps that must be followed to solve the Towers of Hanoi problem.*

Example Review

This problem is inherently recursive. Using recursion enables us to find a natural, simple solution. Without recursion the problem would be difficult to solve.

Consider tracing the program for n=3. The successive recursive calls are shown in Figure 4.15. As you can see, writing the program is easier than tracing the

continues

recursive calls. The system uses stacks to trace the calls behind the scenes. To some extent, recursion provides a level of abstraction that hides iterations and other details from the user.

The `fib()` method in the previous example returns a value to its caller, but the `moveDisks()` method in this example does not return any value to its caller.

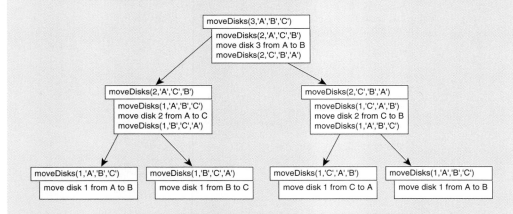

Figure 4.15   *Invoking* `moveDisks(3, 'A', 'B', 'C')` *spawns calls to* `moveDisks()` *recursively.*

Recursion Versus Iteration (Optional)

Recursion is an alternative form of program control. It is essentially repetition without a loop control. When you use loops, you specify a loop body. The repetition of the loop body is controlled by the loop control structure. In recursion, the method itself is called repeatedly. The successive recursive calls are handled behind the scenes by the system. There is always a decision structure to control the repetition.

Recursion carries substantial overhead. Each time the program calls a method, the system must assign space for all of the method's local variables and parameters. This can consume considerable memory, and extra time is required to manage the additional space.

Any problem that can be solved recursively can be solved nonrecursively with iterations. Recursion has many negative aspects—it uses up too much time and too much memory. This being so, why use it? In some cases, using recursion enables you to specify a clear, simple solution that would otherwise be difficult to obtain.

The decision whether to use recursion or iteration should be based on the nature of the problem you are trying to solve and your understanding of the problem. The rule of thumb is to use recursion or iteration to develop an intuitive solution that naturally mirrors the problem. If an iterative solution is obvious, use it. It will generally be more efficient than the recursive option.

> ■ TIP
> If you are concerned about the performance of your program, avoid using recursion because it takes more time and consumes more memory than iteration.

> ■ CAUTION
> Your recursive program could run out of memory, causing a runtime error. In Chapter 11, "Exception Handling," you learn how to handle errors so that the program terminates gracefully when there is a stack overflow.

JBuilder Menu Commands

The main menu contains commands similar to those of other Windows applications. The File menu contains commands for opening, creating, saving, and closing files, for printing files, and for exiting JBuilder. The Edit menu contains the standard Windows commands for editing text, such as Undo, Redo, Cut, Copy, Paste, and Delete. In this section, you will learn how to use the commands in the Search, View, Project, and Run menus.

The Search Commands

You can use the commands in the Search menu to find and/or replace text in source code, to search text in multiple files in the source paths, to position the cursor at a specific line, and to browse code symbols. The Search menu is shown in Figure 4.16.

Figure 4.16   *The Search menu contains commands for searching and replacing text in the source file.*

To find a text in the current Content pane, choose the Find command to display the Find Text dialog box, as shown in Figure 4.17. Use this dialog box to specify the text you want to locate and set options that affect the search.

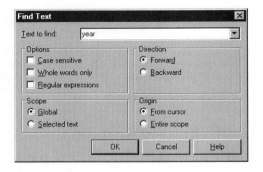

Figure 4.17   *The Find Text dialog box lets you specify a text and set search options, such as direction, scope, and origin, as well as case-sensitive, whole-word, and regular-expression searches.*

To replace a text in the current Content pane, choose the Replace command to display the Replace Text dialog box, as shown in Figure 4.18. Use this dialog box to specify the text you want to locate and another text with which to replace the located text.

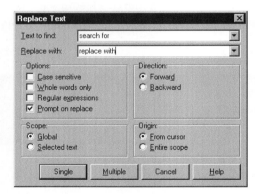

Figure 4.18   *The Replace Text dialog box lets you specify a text to find and the text to replace.*

The Search Again command repeats the last search, replace, or incremental search.

The Incremental Search command moves cursor directly to the next occurrence of text that you type. When you are performing an incremental search, the Content pane status line reads "Searching For:" and displays each letter you have typed. Press Enter or Escape to cancel incremental search.

Occasionally, you want to search a text in multiple files. JBuilder enables you to use the Find in Source Path command to search a string in all the .java files in the specified source path, as shown in Figure 4.19.

Figure 4.19   *The Find in Source Path dialog box lets you specify a text to search in the source path.*

The Go to Line Number command enables you set the cursor directly at a specified line number, as shown in Figure 4.20.

Figure 4.20   *You can set the cursor directly in the source code in the Go to Line Number dialog box.*

The Browse Symbol command displays the Browse Goto dialog box, as shown in Figure 4.21. Use this dialog box to browse a specific class, package, or interface.

Figure 4.21   *The Browse Symbol command dialog box lets you browse a class, package, or interface.*

The View Commands

The View menu (see Figure 4.22) contains commands for displaying or hiding Navigation Pane, Structure Pane, Message View, Toolbar, Command Line, Status Bar, and for viewing loaded classes, the execution log, and breakpoints.

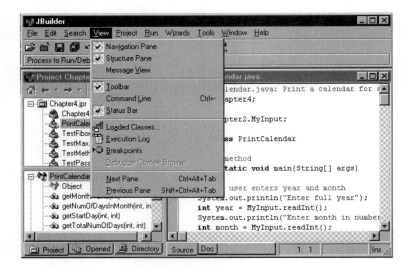

Figure 4.22   *The View menu commands control the display of various IDE information windows.*

The Loaded Classes window (see Figure 4.23) displays a list of all the classes associated with the class currently being debugged.

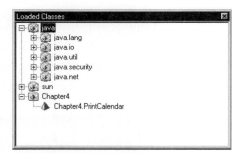

Figure 4.23   *The Loaded Classes window displays a list of loaded classes for the program.*

The Execution Log window (see Figure 4.24) displays all the command-line messages and errors that a program displays during execution or debugging when the Console I/O option is set to Send output to Execution Log on the Run/Debug page of the project properties dialog box.

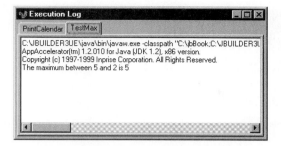

Figure 4.24 *The Execution Log window displays execution information for each program executed.*

The Project Commands

The Project menu (see Figure 4.25) contains the commands for compiling the project, adding files, displaying default or current project properties dialog boxes. The Make command compiles any .java files in the selected node that have outdated or nonexistent .class files. It also compiles the imported programs that have outdated or nonexistent .class files.

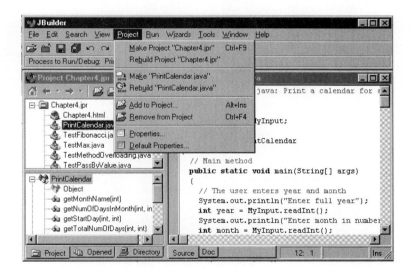

Figure 4.25 *The Project menu contains the commands for processing and managing projects.*

The selected node can be a project, package, or .java file. Making a package or project includes all the .java files in the package or project, including those in nested packages.

The imported files that are checked and compiled include all recursively imported files (that is, imported files of imported files) except for files in stable packages that are not part of the project.

The Rebuild command compiles all .java files in the selected node, regardless of whether their .class files are outdated. It also compiles the imported files upon which the node depends, regardless of whether their .class files are outdated.

TIP
Once you have done the initial compiling, Make is faster than Rebuild.

The Run Commands

The Run menu (see Figure 4.26) contains the commands used for running and debugging your applications or applets from the IDE. The Debugging commands will be introduced in the section "Debugging in JBuilder" in Chapter 6, "Arrays and Strings."

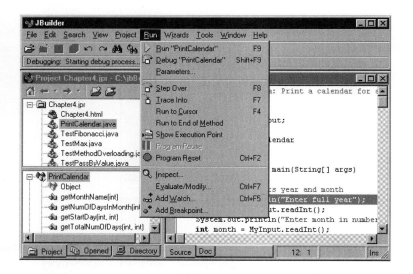

Figure 4.26   *The Run menu contains the commands for running and debugging programs.*

Chapter Summary

One of the central goals in software engineering is to make programs modular and reusable. Java provides many constructs that enable you to achieve this goal. The method is one such powerful construct.

In this chapter, you have learned how to write reusable methods. You now know how to create a method with a method specification, the interface that specifies how the method can be used, and a method body that defines what the method does.

You have also learned how to call a method by passing actual parameters that replace the formal parameters in the method specification. The arguments that are passed to a method should have the same number, type, and order as the parameters in the method definition. Outside of the method, the actual values of the primitive parameters—which are passed by the value— are not affected by the method call.

In addition, you learned that a method can be overloaded. For example, two methods can have the same name as long as their method parameter profiles differ.

You are now familiar with the "divide and conquer" strategy. The best way to develop and maintain a large program is to divide it into several subproblems, each of which is more manageable than the original problem. Subproblems are written in Java as classes and methods.

You learned the techniques needed to write recursive methods. Recursion is an alternative form of program control. It can be used to specify simple, clear solutions for inherently recursive problems that would otherwise be difficult to solve.

This chapter also discussed the Search, View, Project, and Run Commands in the Search, View, Project, and Run menus.

Chapter Review

4.1. What is the purpose of using a method? How do you declare a method? How do you invoke a method?

4.2. What is a return type of a main method?

4.3. What would be wrong if you did not write a return statement in a non-void method? Can you have a return statement in a void method, such as the following:

```java
public static void main(String[] args)
{
  int i;
  while (true)
  {
    i = MyInput.readInt();
    if (i == 0) return;
    System.out.println("i = "+i);
  }
}
```

4.4. What is method overloading? Can you define two methods that have the same name but different parameter types? Can you define two methods in a class that have identical method names and parameter profiles with different return value types or different modifiers?

4.5. How do you pass actual parameters to a method? Can the actual parameter have the same name as its formal parameter?

4.6. What is pass by value? Show the result of the following method call:

```java
public class Test
{
  public static void main(String[] args)
  {
    int max = 0;
    max(1, 2, max);
    System.out.println(max);
  }

  public static void max(int value1, int value2, int max)
  {
    if (value1 > value2)
      max = value1;
    else
      max = value2;
  }
}
```

4.7. A call for the method with a void return type is always a statement itself, but a call for the method with a non-void return type is always a component of an expression. Is the statement true or false?

4.8. In many other languages, you can define methods inside a method. Can you define a method inside a method in Java?

4.9. For each of the following, decide whether a void method or a non-void method is the most appropriate implementation:

■ Computing a sales commission given the sales amount and the commission rate.

■ Printing a calendar for a month.

■ Computing a square root.

■ Testing whether a number is even and returning true if it is.

■ Printing a message for a specified number of times.

4.10. Does the `return` statement in the following method cause syntax errors?

```java
public static void main(String[] args)
{
  int max = 0;
  if (max != 0)
    System.out.println(max);
  else
    return;
}
```

4.11. What is a recursive method?

4.12. Describe the characteristics of recursive methods.

4.13. Show the printout of the following program:

```
public class Test
{
  public static void main(String[] args)
  {
    int sum = xMethod(5);
    System.out.println("Sum is "+sum);
  }

  public static int xMethod(int n)
  {
    if (n==1)
      return 1;
    else
      return n + xMethod(n-1);
  }
}
```

Programming Exercises

4.1. Write a method to find the ceiling of a double value, and write a method to find its floor. The ceiling of a number d is the smallest integer greater than or equal to d. The floor of a number d is the largest integer less than or equal to d. For example, the ceiling of 5.4 is 6, and the floor of 5.4 is 5.

4.2. Write a method to compute the sum of the digits in an integer. Use the following method declaration:

```
public static int sumDigits(long n)
```

For example, sumDigits(234) returns 2+3+4=9.

Hint: Use the % operator to extract digit and use the / operator to remove the extracted digit. For instance, 234%10 = 4 and 234/10 = 23. Use a loop to extract and remove the digit repeatedly until all the digits are extracted.

4.3. Write a method to compute future investment value at a given interest rate for a specified number of years. The future investment is determined using the following formula:

```
futureInvestmentValue = investmentAmount x
    (1 + interestRate)
```
$$futureInvestmentValue = investmentAmount \times (1 + interestRate)^{years}$$

Use the flowing method declaration:

```
public static double futureInvestmentValue(
  double investmentAmount, double interestRate, int years)
```

For example, futureInvestmentValue(10000, 0.05, 5) returns 12762.82.

Hint: Use the Math.pow(a, b) method to compute a raised to the power of b.

4.4. Write a method to convert Celsius to Fahrenheit using the following declaration:

```
public static double celsToFahr(double cels)
```

Write a program that uses a for loop and calls the celsToFahr method in order to result in the following output:

```
Cels. Temp.      Fahr. Temp.
_____  _____
40.00            104.00
39.00            102.20
38.00            100.40
37.00            98.60
36.00            96.80
35.00            95.00
34.00            93.20
33.00            91.40
32.00            89.60
31.00            87.80
```

4.5. Write a program to print the following table using the sqrt() method from Example 4.4.

```
RealNumber       SquareRoot
_____  _____
0                0.0000
2                1.4142
4                2.0000
6                2.4495
8                2.8284
10               3.1623
12               3.4641
14               3.7417
16               4.0000
18               4.2426
20               4.4721
```

4.6. Write a program to meet the following requirements:

- Declare a method to determine whether an integer is a prime number. Use the flowing method declaration:

```
public static boolean isPrime(int num)
```

An integer is a *prime number* if its only divisor is 1 or itself. For example, isPrime(11) returns true and isPrime(9) returns false.

- Use the isPrime method to find all the prime numbers between 1 and 100, and display every ten prime numbers on a row as follows:

1 2 3 5 7 11 13 17 19 23

29 31 37 41 47 53 59 61 67

71 73 79 83 89 97

4.7. Write a recursive method that will compute factorials. The factorial of a natural number is defined as follows:

```
factorial(0) = 1;
factorial(n) = factorial(n-1)*n; for n>0
```

4.8. Write a nonrecursive method to compute Fibonacci numbers.

Hint: To compute `fib(n)` without recursion, you need to obtain `fib(n-2)` and `fib(n-1)` first. Let `f1` and `f2` denote the two preceding Fibonacci numbers. The current Fibonacci number would then be `f1+f2`. The algorithm can be described as follows:

```
f1 = 0; // For fib(0)
f2 = 1; // For fib(1)
for (int i=1; i<=n; i++)
{
  currentFib = f1+f2;
  f1 = f2;
  f2 = currentFib;
}

// After the loop, currentFib is fib(n)
```

4.9. Modify Example 4.7 so that the program finds the number of moves needed to move n disks from tower A to B.

4.10. Write a recursive method for the greatest common divisor (GCD). Given two positive integers, the GCD is the largest integer that divides them both. `GCD(m, n)` can be defined as follows:

■ `GCD(m, n)` is n if n is less than or equal to m and n divides m.

■ `GCD(m, n)` is `GCD(n, m)` if m is less than n.

■ `GCD(m, n)` is `GCD(n, m%n)`, otherwise.

PART II

OBJECT-ORIENTED PROGRAMMING

In Part I, "Fundamentals of Java Programming," you learned how to write simple Java applications using primitive data types, control structures, and methods. These are the usual features available in conventional programming languages. Java is a class-centric object-oriented programming language that uses abstraction, encapsulation, inheritance, and polymorphism to provide great flexibility, modularity, and reusability for developing software. In this part of the book, you will learn how to define classes, extend, and work with classes and their instances.

CHAPTER 5

Programming with Objects and Classes

Objectives

- Understand objects and classes and the relationship between them.
- Learn how to define a class and how to create an object of the class.
- Understand the roles of constructors and modifiers.
- Learn how to pass objects to methods.
- Understand instance and class variables.
- Understand instance and class methods.
- Understand the scope of variables.
- Learn how to use packages.
- Understand the organization of the Java API.
- Become familiar with the Math class.
- Know to generate program templates using the wizards in the JBuilder Object Gallery.

Introduction

Programming in procedural languages like C, Pascal, BASIC, Ada, and COBOL involves choosing data structures, designing algorithms, and translating algorithms into code. Object-oriented languages like Java combine the power of conventional languages with an added dimension that provides such benefits as abstraction, encapsulation, reusability, and inheritance.

In procedural programming, data and operations on the data are separate—a methodology that requires sending data to procedures and functions. Object-oriented programming (OOP), in contrast, places data and operations pertaining to the data within a single data structure. Since data and operations are part of the same entity, this approach solves many of the problems inherent in procedural programming. Object-oriented programming organizes programs in a way that more closely models the real world, where all objects have both attributes and activities associated with them. Programming in Java involves thinking in terms of objects; a Java program can be viewed as a collection of cooperating objects.

This chapter introduces the fundamentals of object-oriented programming: declaring classes, creating objects, manipulating objects, and making objects work together.

Objects and Classes

Object-oriented programming involves programming using objects. *Object* is a broad term that stands for many things. A student, a desk, a circle, and even a mortgage loan, to cite but a few examples, can all be viewed as objects. Certain properties define an object, and certain behaviors define what it does. These properties are known as *data fields*, and the object's behaviors are defined by *methods*. Figure 5.1 shows a diagram of an object with its data fields and methods.

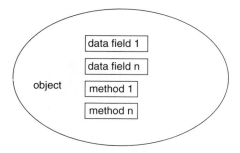

Figure 5.1   *An object contains data and methods.*

A `Circle` object has a data field `radius`, which is the property that characterizes a circle. One behavior of a circle is that its area can be computed. A `Circle` object is shown in Figure 5.2.

Classes are structures that define objects. In a Java class, data are used to describe properties and methods to define behaviors. A class for an object contains a collection of method and data definitions. The following is an example of the class for a circle:

```
class Circle
{
  double radius = 1.0;

  double findArea()
  {
    return radius*radius*3.14159;
  }
}
```

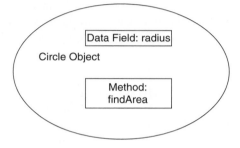

Figure 5.2   *A* Circle *object contains the* radius *data field and the* findArea *method.*

This class is different from all of the other classes you have seen thus far. The Circle class does not have a main method, nor does it extend java.applet.Applet. Therefore, you cannot run this class; it is merely a definition used to declare and create Circle objects. For convenience, the class that contains the main() method will be referred to as the *main class* in this book.

Declaring and Creating Objects

A class is a blueprint that defines what an object's data and methods will be. An object is an instance of a class. You can create many instances of a class (see Figure 5.3). The relationship between classes and objects is analogous to the one between apple pie recipes and apple pies. You can make as many apple pies as you want from a single recipe.

Creating an instance is referred to as *instantiation*. In order to declare an object, you must use a variable to represent it (this is similar to declaring a variable for a primitive data type). The syntax for declaring an object is as follows:

```
ClassName objectName;
```

The following statement declares the variable myCircle to be an instance of the Circle class:

```
Circle myCircle;
```

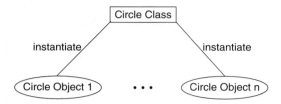

Figure 5.3   *A class can have many different objects.*

Creating an object of a class is called *creating an instance of the class*. An object is a variable that has a class type. To create variables of a primitive data type, you would simply declare them, as is done in the following line:

```
int i;
```

This statement creates a variable and allocates memory space for i.

However, for object variables, declaring and creating are two separate steps. The declaration of an object simply associates the object with a class, making it an instance of that class. The declaration does not create the object. To actually create myCircle, you would need to use the operator new in order to tell the computer to create an object for myCircle and allocate memory space for it. The syntax for creating an object is as follows:

```
objectName = new ClassName();
```

For example, the following statement creates an object, myCircle, and allocates memory for it:

```
myCircle = new Circle();
```

You can combine the declaration and instantiation together in one statement by using the following syntax:

```
ClassName objectName = new ClassName();
```

Here is an example of creating and instantiating myCircle in one step:

```
Circle myCircle = new Circle();
```

After an object is created, it can access its data and methods by using the following dot notation:

objectName.data—References an object's data

objectName.method—References an object's method

For example, myCircle.radius indicates what the radius of myCircle is, and myCircle.findArea() returns the area of myCircle.

NOTE

You can create an anonymous object without explicitly assigning it to a variable. Here is an example:

```
new Circle();
```

The above statement creates an anonymous Circle object. You cannot access the contents of an anonymous object, since there is no explicit reference to the object. Anonymous objects are used in Chapter 8, "Getting Started with Graphics Programming."

Example 5.1 Using Objects

The program in this example creates a `Circle` object from the `Circle` class and uses the data and method in the object. The output of the program is shown in Figure 5.4.

```java
// TestCircle.java: Demonstrate creating and using an object
package Chapter5;

public class TestCircle
{
  // Main method
  public static void main(String[] args)
  {
    Circle myCircle = new Circle();  // Create a Circle object
      System.out.println("The area of the circle of radius "
        + myCircle.radius + " is " + myCircle.findArea());
  }
}

// Define a circle
class Circle
{
  double radius = 1.0;

  // Find the area of this circle
  double findArea()
  {
    return radius*radius*3.14159;
  }
}
```

Figure 5.4   *This program creates a* Circle *object and displays its* radius *and* area.

continues

Example Review

The program contains two classes. The first class, TestCircle, is the main class. Its sole purpose is to test the second class, Circle. Every time you run the program, the Java runtime system invokes its main() method in the main class.

The main class contains the main() method that creates an object of the Circle class and prints its radius and area. The Circle class contains the findArea() method and the radius data field.

To write the findArea() method in a procedural programming language such as Pascal, you would pass radius as argument to the method. But in the object-oriented programming, radius and findArea() are defined in the same class. The radius is a data member in the Circle class, which is accessible by the findArea() method. In the procedural programming languages, data and method are separated, but in the object-oriented programming language, data and methods are defined together in a class.

The findArea() method is an instance method, which is always invoked by an instance in which the radius is specified.

There are many ways to write Java programs. For instance, as shown below, you can combine the two classes in the example into one.

```java
package Chapter5;

public class TestCircle
{
  double radius = 1.0;

  // Find the area of this circle
  double findArea()
  {
    return radius*radius*3.14159;
  }

  // Main method
  public static void main(String[] args)
  {
    // Create a Circle object
    TestCircle myCircle = new TestCircle();
    System.out.println("The area of the circle of radius "
      + myCircle.radius + " is " + myCircle.findArea());
  }
}
```

In this revised program, radius and findArea() are members of the TestCircle class. Since TestCircle contains a main method, it can be executed by the Java interpreter. The main method creates myCircle to be an instance of TestCircle and displays radius and finds area in myCircle.

> ■■■ **NOTE**
>
> The creation of variables of primitive type is implied when the variables are declared. However, declaration and the creation of objects are separate tasks. The compiler allocates memory space for the variables of primitive type when they are declared, but does not allocate space for objects when they are declared.

> ■■■ **CAUTION**
>
> You must always create an object before manipulating it. Manipulating an object that has not been created would cause a `NullPointer` exception.

> ■■■ **NOTE**
>
> The default value of a data field is `null` for object type, `0` for numerical type, `false` for `boolean` type, and `'\u0000'` for `char` type. For example, if `radius` is not initialized in the `Circle` class, Java assigns a default value of `0` to `radius`. However, Java assigns no default value to a local variable inside a method. The following code is erroneous because x is not defined:
>
> ```
> class Test
> {
>   public static void main(String[] args)
>   {
>     int x;
>     System.out.println("x is " + x);
>   }
> }
> ```

Constructors

One problem with the `Circle` class that was just discussed is that all of the objects created from it have the same radius (1.0). Wouldn't it be more useful to create circles with radii of varied lengths? Java enables you to define a special method in the class—known as the *constructor*—that will initialize an object's data. You can use a constructor to assign an initial radius when you are creating an object.

The constructor has exactly the same name as the class it comes from. Constructors can be overloaded, making it easier to construct objects with different kinds of initial data values. Let's see what happens when the following constructors are added to the `Circle` class:

```
Circle(double r)
{
  radius = r;
}

Circle()
{
  radius = 1.0;
}
```

When creating a new `Circle` object that has a radius of 5.0, you can use the following, which assigns 5.0 to `myCircle.radius`:

```
myCircle = new Circle(5.0);
```

If you create a circle using the following statement, the second constructor is used, which assigns the default radius 1.0 to `myCircle.radius`:

```
myCircle = new Circle();
```

NOTE

Constructors are special methods that do not require a return type—not even void.

Now you know why the object is created using the syntax `ClassName()`. This syntax is used to call a constructor. If the class has no constructors, a default constructor (one that takes no arguments) is used, which will not initialize your object's data. If you don't use constructors, all of your objects will be the same initially.

Example 5.2 Using Constructors

In this example, a program is written that will use constructors in the `Circle` class to create two different objects. The output of the program is shown in Figure 5.5.

```java
// TestCircleWithConstructors.java: Demonstrate constructors
package Chapter5;

public class TestCircleWithConstructors
{
  // Main method
  public static void main(String[] args)
  {
    // Create a Circle with radius 5.0
    Circle myCircle = new Circle(5.0);
    System.out.println("The area of the circle of radius "
      + myCircle.radius + " is " + myCircle.findArea());

    // Create a Circle with default radius
    Circle yourCircle = new Circle();
    System.out.println("The area of the circle of radius "
      + yourCircle.radius + " is " + yourCircle.findArea());
  }
}

// Circle with two constructors
class Circle
{
  double radius;

  // Default constructor
  Circle()
  {
    radius = 1.0;
  }
```

```
            // Construct a circle with a specified radius
            Circle(double r)
            {
              radius = r;
            }

            // Find area of this circle
            double findArea()
            {
              return radius*radius*3.14159;
            }
        }
```

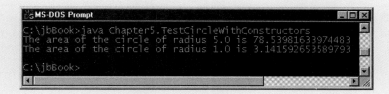

Figure 5.5   *The program constructs two circles of radii 5 and 1, and displays their radii and areas.*

Example Review

The new `Circle` class has two constructors. You can specify a radius or use the default radius to create a `Circle` object. In this example, two objects were created. The constructor `Circle(5.0)` was used to create `myCircle` with a radius of 5.0, and the constructor `Circle()` was used to create `yourCircle` with a default radius of 1.0.

These two objects (`myCircle` and `yourCircle`) have different data but share the same methods. Therefore, you can compute their respective areas by using the `findArea()` method.

NOTE

The `Circle` class in this example has the same name as the `Circle` class in the previous example. Since both files are in the same package, you would get a compilation error in JBuilder indicating the duplication of the Circle class in the project. To avoid getting this error, comment the source code or remove one file from the project.

Modifiers

Java provides modifiers to control access to data, methods, and classes. The following are frequently used modifiers:

- **static**—Defines data and methods. It represents class-wide information that is shared by all instances of the class. It is discussed in more detail in the sections "Instance Variables and Class Variables" and "Instance Methods and Class Methods," later in this chapter.

■ **public**—Defines classes, methods, and data in such a way that all programs can access them.

■ **private**—Defines methods and data in such a way that they can be accessed by the declaring class, but not by any other classes.

NOTE

The modifiers `static` and `private` apply solely to variables or to methods. If `public` or `private` is not used, then by default, the classes, methods, and data are accessible to any class in the same package.

CAUTION

The variables associated with modifiers are members of the class, not local variables inside the methods. Using modifiers inside a method body would cause a compilation error.

More modifiers are described in Chapter 7, "Class Inheritance." Appendix D, "Java Modifiers," contains a table that summarizes all Java modifiers.

Example 5.3 Using the *private* Modifier

In this example, private data are used for the radius to prevent clients from modifying the radius of a `Circle` object. A method, `getRadius()`, is added so that clients can retrieve the radius. A method of this kind is sometimes referred to as a *getter* for obtaining private data value. The output is the same as in the previous example (see Figure 5.5).

```
// TestCircleWithPrivateModifier.java: Demonstrate private modifier
package Chapter5;

public class TestCircleWithPrivateModifier
{
  // Main method
  public static void main(String[] args)
  {
    // Create a Circle with radius 5.0
    Circle myCircle = new Circle(5.0);
    System.out.println("The area of the circle of radius "
      + myCircle.getRadius() + " is " + myCircle.findArea());

    // Create a Circle with default radius
    Circle yourCircle = new Circle();
    System.out.println("The area of the circle of radius "
      + yourCircle.getRadius() + " is " + yourCircle.findArea());
  }
}

// Declare class Circle with constructors and private data
class Circle
{
  private double radius;
```

```
        // Default constructor
        public Circle()
        {
          radius = 1.0;
        }

        // Construct a circle with a specified radius
        public Circle(double r)
        {
          radius = r;
        }

        // Getter method for radius
        public double getRadius()
        {
          return radius;
        }

        // Find the circle area
        public double findArea()
        {
          return radius*radius*Math.PI;
        }
      }
```

Example Review

If a client program is allowed to change the radius in a circle object, programming errors might occur that would make bugs difficult to detect. In this example, the `private` modifier in the data declaration is used to prevent the client program from changing the circle's properties. Therefore, the data in the object can never be changed after its creation.

If you want to access private data from the object, you can provide a getter method to retrieve the data, such as `getRadius()`.

Private data can only be accessed within their defining class. You cannot use `myCircle.radius` in the client program. A compilation error would occur if you attempted to access private data from a client.

Passing Objects to Methods

Just as you can pass the value of variables to methods, you can also pass objects to methods as actual parameters. The following example passes the `myCircle` object as an argument to the method `printCircle()`:

```
class TestPassingObject
{
  public static void main(String[] args)
  {
    Circle myCircle = new Circle(5.0);
    printCircle(myCircle);
  }

  public static void printCircle(Circle c)
  {
```

```
      System.out.println("The area of the circle of radius "
        + c.getRadius() + " is " + c.findArea());
  }
}
```

There are important differences between passing a value of variables of primitive data types and passing objects.

Passing a variable of a primitive type means that the value of the variable is passed to a formal parameter. Changing the value of the local parameter inside the method does not affect the value of a variable that is outside of the method.

Passing an object means that the reference of the object is passed to the formal parameter. Any changes to the local object that occur inside the method body will affect the original object that was passed as the argument. In programming terminology, this is referred to as *passing by reference*.

You will see the difference in the following example.

Example 5.4 Passing Objects as Arguments

In this example, a program is written to pass a `Circle` object to the method `colorCircle()`, which changes the color of the `Circle` object. The output of the program is shown in Figure 5.6.

```java
// TestPassingObject.java: Demonstrate passing objects in methods
package Chapter5;

public class TestPassingObject
{
  // Main method
  public static void main(String[] args)
  {
    Circle myCircle = new Circle(5.0, "white");
    printCircle(myCircle);
    colorCircle(myCircle, "black");
    printCircle(myCircle);
  }

  // Change the color in the circle c
  public static void colorCircle(Circle c, String color)
  {
    c.color = color;
  }

  // Print circle information
  public static void printCircle(Circle c)
  {
    System.out.println("The area of the circle of radius "
      + c.getRadius() + " is " + c.findArea());
    System.out.println("The color of the circle is "
      + c.color);
  }
}

// Circle with a new data field: color
class Circle
{
  private double radius;
  String color;
```

```
  // Default constructor
  public Circle()
  {
    radius = 1.0;
    color = "white";
  }

  // Construct a circle with specified radius and color
  public Circle(double r, String c)
  {
    radius = r;
    color = c;
  }

  // Get radius
  public double getRadius()
  {
    return radius;
  }

  // Find circle area
  public double findArea()
  {
    return radius*radius*Math.PI;
  }
}
```

```
C:\jbBook>java Chapter5.TestPassingObject
The area of the circle of radius 5.0 is 78.53981633974483
The color of the circle is white
The area of the circle of radius 5.0 is 78.53981633974483
The color of the circle is black

C:\jbBook>
```

Figure 5.6 *The program passes circle objects as parameters to the method* printCircle(), *which displays the radius and the area.*

Example Review

The data field radius is private, so it cannot be changed by an assignment like the one that follows:

```
myCircle.radius = newRadius;
```

However, the data field color can be changed by the following assignment statement:

```
myCircle.color = newColor;
```

In the main() method, a "white" object, myCircle, is created with a radius of 5.0. The method colorCircle() is then called with the argument myCircle and a new color, "black". This call changes the color field in the myCircle object to "black" because the object's reference (and not a copy of it) was passed to the

continues

159

method, and that made it possible for the method to change the color value in the object myCircle.

You should use the private modifier for color to prevent the user from accidentally changing the color field. If the color field is private, can it be changed safely? Yes, you can declare a method in the Circle class to set a new color. This is referred to as a *setter* method. See the following example.

Example 5.5 Changing Data in a Private Field Using a Setter Method

In this example, a program is written to demonstrate a safe way to change the data in an object. The output of the program is shown in Figure 5.7.

```java
// TestChangePrivateData.java: Modify a private data using a
// setter method
package Chapter5;

public class TestChangePrivateData
{
  // Main method
  public static void main(String[] args)
  {
    Circle myCircle = new Circle(5.0, "white");
    printCircle(myCircle);
    myCircle.setColor("black");  // Modify color field in myCircle
    printCircle(myCircle);
  }

  // Print circle information
  public static void printCircle(Circle c)
  {
    System.out.println("The area of the circle of radius "
      + c.getRadius() + " is " + c.findArea());
    System.out.println("The color of the circle is "
      + c.getColor());
  }
}

// Circle class with a setter method for color
class Circle
{
  private double radius;
  private String color;

  // Default constructor
  public Circle()
  {
    radius = 1.0;
    color = "white";
  }

  // Construct a circle with a specified radius
  public Circle(double r)
  {
    radius = r;
  }
```

```
        // Construct a circle with radius and color
        public Circle(double r, String c)
        {
          radius = r;
          color = c;
        }

        // Getter method for radius
        public double getRadius()
        {
          return radius;
        }

        // Getter method for color
        public String getColor()
        {
          return color;
        }

        // Setter method for color
        public void setColor(String color)
        {
          this.color = color;
        }

        // Find circle area
        public double findArea()
        {
          return radius*radius*Math.PI;
        }
}
```

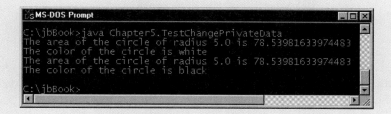

Figure 5.7 *The program views and changes the private data in the object by calling the methods in the object.*

Example Review

The Circle class in this example defines the setter method, setColor(), which allows you to change the color of the object. This method is sometimes referred to as a *setter*. A setter is always a void type method, while a getter has a return type.

This example demonstrates that you can protect the data from mistakes by using a private modifier and providing a setter to change the data safely.

TIP

Provide getters and setters to the clients only if necessary. Avoid using too many getters and setters in a class.

Instance Variables and Class Variables

The variables `radius` and `color` in the `Circle` class in Example 5.5 are known as *instance variables*. Instance variables belong to each instance of the class; they are not shared among objects of the same class. For example, suppose that you create the following objects:

```
Circle myCircle = new Circle();
Circle yourCircle = new Circle();
```

The data in `myCircle` is independent of the data in `yourCircle`, and is in different memory locations (see Figure 5.8). Changes made to `myCircle`'s data do not affect `yourCircle`'s data, and vice versa.

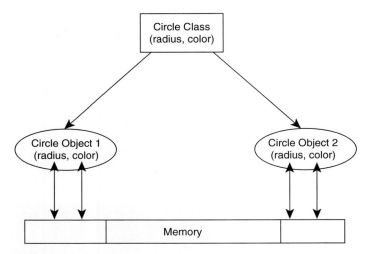

Figure 5.8   *The instance variables, which belong to the instances, have memory storage independent of one other.*

If you want the instances of a class to share data, you can use *class variables*. Class variables store values for the variables in a common memory location (see Figure 5.9). Because of this common location, all objects of the same class are affected if one object changes the value of a class variable.

To declare a class variable, put the modifier `static` in the variable declaration. Suppose that you want to add weight to circles. Assuming that all circles have the same weight, you can define the class variable as follows:

```
static double weight;
```

Here is an example that shows you the effect of using instance variables and class variables.

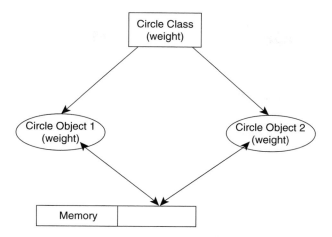

Figure 5.9   *The class variables are shared by all of the instances of the same class.*

Example 5.6 Testing Instance and Class Variables

The program in this example shows you how to use instance and class variables, and illustrates the effects of using them. For this program, assume that all of the Circle objects are of the same weight. Thus, weight is defined as a class variable. By default, the weight is 1.0.

This program creates two circles (myCircle and yourCircle). You will see the effect of using instance and class variables after changing data in the circles. The output of the program is shown in Figure 5.10.

```java
// TestInstanceAndClassVariable.java: Demonstrate using instance and
// class variables
package Chapter5;

public class TestInstanceAndClassVariable
{
  // Main method
  public static void main(String[] args)
  {
    // Create and display myCircle
    Circle myCircle = new Circle(4.0, "white", 5.0);
    System.out.print("myCircle:");
    printCircle(myCircle);

    // Create and display yourCircle
    Circle yourCircle = new Circle(5.0, "black", 3.0);
    System.out.print("yourCircle:");
    printCircle(yourCircle);

    // Change the weight in myCircle
    myCircle.weight = 15.5;

    // Display myCircle and yourCircle
    System.out.print("myCircle:");
```

continues

```
      printCircle(myCircle);
      System.out.print("yourCircle:");
      printCircle(yourCircle);
    }

    // Print circle information
    public static void printCircle(Circle c)
    {
      System.out.println("radius (" + c.getRadius() +
        "), color (" + c.color +") and weight (" + c.weight + ")");
    }
}

// Circle.java: Circle class with instance and class variables
package Chapter5;

public class Circle
{
  private double radius;
  String color;
  static double weight;  // Class variable

  // Default constructor
  public Circle()
  {
    radius = 1.0;
    color = "white";
    weight = 1.0;
  }

  // Construct a circle with a specified radius
  public Circle(double r)
  {
    radius = r;
  }

  // Construct a circle with radius and color
  public Circle(double r, String c)
  {
    radius = r;
    color = c;
  }

  // Construct a circle with specified radius, color, and weight
  public Circle(double r, String c, double w)
  {
    radius = r;
    color = c;
    weight = w;
  }

  // Getter method for radius
  public double getRadius()
  {
    return radius;
  }

  // Getter method for color
  public String getColor()
  {
    return color;
  }
```

```
   // Setter method for color
   public void setColor(String color)
   {
     this.color = color;
   }

   // Find circle area
   public double findArea()
   {
     return radius*radius*Math.PI;
   }
}
```

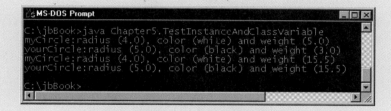

```
MS-DOS Prompt                                         _ □ ✕

C:\jbBook>java Chapter5.TestInstanceAndClassVariable
myCircle:radius (4.0), color (white) and weight (5.0)
yourCircle:radius (5.0), color (black) and weight (3.0)
myCircle:radius (4.0), color (white) and weight (15.5)
yourCircle:radius (5.0), color (black) and weight (15.5)

C:\jbBook>
```

Figure 5.10 *The program uses the instance variables* radius *and* color *as well as the class variable* weight. *All of the objects have the same* weight.

Example Review

What is Math.PI used in the findArea() method? If you followed the Java naming conventions introduced in the section " Programming Style and Documentation" of Chapter 2, "Java Building Elements," you will immediately recognize that PI is a constant and Math is a class name. The Math class comes with the Java system. PI is a constant for π that is defined in the Math class. The Math class is introduced in the section "The Math Class" later in this chapter.

Note that Math.PI was used to access PI, and that c.color in the printCircle() method in this example is used to access color. Math is the class name, and c is an object of the Circle class. To access a constant like PI, you can use either the ClassName.CONSTANTNAME or the objectName.CONSTANTNAME. To access an instance variable like radius, you need to use objectName.variableName.

The Circle class will be used in Chapter 7, "Class Inheritance." To make it accessible by classes from a different package, you need to make this class public. Since Java does not allow more than one public class in a source file, you need to put these two classes in separate files.

▬▬ **TIP**

You should define a constant as static data that can be shared by all class objects. Do not change the value of a constant.

Variables that describe common properties of objects should be declared as class variables.

Instance Methods and Class Methods

Instance methods belong to instances. These methods can only be applied after the instances are created. They are called by the following:

```
objectName.methodName();
```

The methods defined in the `Circle` class are instance methods. Java supports class methods as well as class variables. Class methods can be called without creating an instance of the class. To define class methods, put the modifier `static` in the method declaration as follows:

```
static returnValueType staticMethod();
```

Examples of class methods are the `readDouble()` and the `readInt()` in the class `MyInput`.

Class methods are called by one of the following syntax:

```
ClassName.methodName();
objectName.methodName();
```

For example, `MyInput.readInt()` is a call that reads an integer from the keyboard. `MyInput` is a class, not an object.

TIP

A method that does not use instance variables can be defined as a class method. This method can be invoked without creating an object of the class.

TIP

I recommend that you invoke static variables and methods using ClassName.variable and ClassName.method. This improves readability because the reader can easily recognize the static and class variables.

The Scope of Variables

The *scope of a variable* determines where the variable can be referenced in a program. In general, the scope of a variable is within the block where the variable is declared. You can declare a variable only once in a block. But you can declare the same variable multiple times in different blocks. For example, x is defined twice in the following program:

```
class Foo
{
  int x = 0;
  int y = 0;
```

```
    Foo()
    {
    }

    void p()
    {
      int x = 1;
      System.out.println("x = " + x);
      System.out.println("y = " + y);
    }
  }
```

What is the printout for `f.p()`, in which `f` is an instance of `Foo`? To answer this question, you need to understand the scope rules that determine how a variable is accessed. The following Java scope rules are based on blocks:

- The scope of a variable is the block in which it is declared. Therefore, a variable declared in block B can be accessed in block B or in an inner block nested inside block B.

- If a variable x that was originally declared in block B is declared again in a block nested inside block B (block C), the scope of x that is declared in block B excludes the inner block (C).

Therefore, the printout for `f.p()` is 1 (for x) and 0 (for y), based on the following reasons:

- x is declared again in the method `p()` with an initial value of 1.

- y is declared outside the method `p()`, but is accessible inside it.

TIP

As demonstrated in the example, it is easy to make mistakes. Therefore, to avoid confusion, do not declare the same variable names.

CAUTION

Do not declare a variable inside a block and then use it outside the block. Here is an example of a common mistake:

```
for (int i=0; i<10; i++)
{
}

int j = i;
```

The last statement would cause an error because variable `i` is not defined outside of the `for` loop.

■■■ NOTE
A variable declared in a method is referred to as a *local variable*. You cannot declare a local variable twice in a method even if the variable is declared in nested blocks. For example, the following code would cause a compilation error because x is declared in the for loop body block, which is nested inside the method body block where another x is declared.

```
public void xMethod()
{
  int x = 1;
  int y = 1;

  for (int i = 1; i<10; i++)
  {
    int x = 0;
    x += i;
  }
}
```

Case Studies

By now you have formed some ideas about objects and classes and their programming features. Object-oriented programming is centered on objects; it is particularly involved with getting objects to work together. OOP provides abstraction and encapsulation. You can create the Circle object and find the area of the circle without knowing how the area is computed. The object might have many other data and methods.

The detail of the implementation is encapsulated and hidden from the client. This is referred to as *class abstraction*. You can draw upon many real-life examples to illustrate the OOP concept.

Consider building a computer system, for example. Your personal computer consists of many components, such as a CPU, CD-ROM, floppy disk, motherboard, and fan. Each component can be viewed as an object that has properties and methods. To get them to work together, all you need to know is how each component is used and how it interacts with the others. You don't need to know how it works internally. The internal implementation is encapsulated and hidden from you. You can build a computer without knowing how a component is implemented.

This precisely mirrors the object-oriented approach. Each component can be viewed as an object of the class for the component. For example, you might have a class that models all kinds of fans for use on a computer with properties like fan size, speed, and so on, and with methods, such as start, stop, and so on. A specific fan is an instance of this class with specific property values.

Consider paying a mortgage, for another example. A specific mortgage can be viewed as an object of a mortgage class. Interest rate, loan amount, and loan period are its data properties, and computing monthly payments and total payments are its methods. When you buy a house, a mortgage object is created by instantiating the class with your mortgage interest rate, loan amount, and loan period. You can then easily find the monthly payment and total payment of your loan using the mortgage methods.

Examples 5.7 and 5.8 are case studies of designing classes.

Example 5.7 Using the Mortgage Class

In this example, a mortgage class named Mortgage is created with the following data fields and methods:

Data field:

double interest: Represent interest rate.

int year: Represent loan period.

double loan: Represent loan amount.

Methods:

public double monthlyPay()

Return the monthly payment of the loan.

public double totalPay()

Return the total payment of the loan.

The Mortgage class is given below, followed by a test program. Figure 5.11 shows the output of a sample run of the program.

```java
// Mortgage.java: Encapsulate mortgage information
package Chapter5;

public class Mortgage
{
  private double interest;
  private int year;
  private double loan;

  // Construct a mortgage with specified interest rate, year and
  // loan amount
  public Mortgage(double i, int y, double l)
  {
    interest = i/1200.0;
    year = y;
    loan = l;
  }

  // Getter method for interest
  public double getInterest()
  {
    return interest;
  }
```

continues

```
                  // Getter method for year
                  public double getYear()
                  {
                    return year;
                  }

                  // Getter method for loan
                  public double getLoan()
                  {
                    return loan;
                  }

                  // Find monthly pay
                  public double monthlyPay()
                  {
                    return loan*interest/(1-(Math.pow(1/(1+interest),year*12)));
                  }

                  // Find total pay
                  public double totalPay()
                  {
                    return monthlyPay()*year*12;
                  }
                }

                // TestMortgageClass.java: Demonstrate using the Mortgage class
                package Chapter5;

                import Chapter2.MyInput;

                public class TestMortgageClass
                {
                  // Main method
                  public static void main(String[] args)
                  {
                    // Enter interet rate
                    System.out.println(
                      "Enter yearly interest rate, for example 8.25: ");
                    double interestRate = MyInput.readDouble();

                    // Enter years
                    System.out.println(
                      "Enter number of years as an integer, for example 5: ");
                    int year = MyInput.readInt();

                    // Enter loan amount
                    System.out.println(
                      "Enter loan amount, for example 120000.95: ");
                    double loan = MyInput.readDouble();

                    // Create Mortgage object
                    Mortgage m = new Mortgage(interestRate, year, loan);

                    // Display results
                    System.out.println("The monthly pay is " + m.monthlyPay());
                    System.out.println("The total paid is " + m.totalPay());
                  }
                }
```

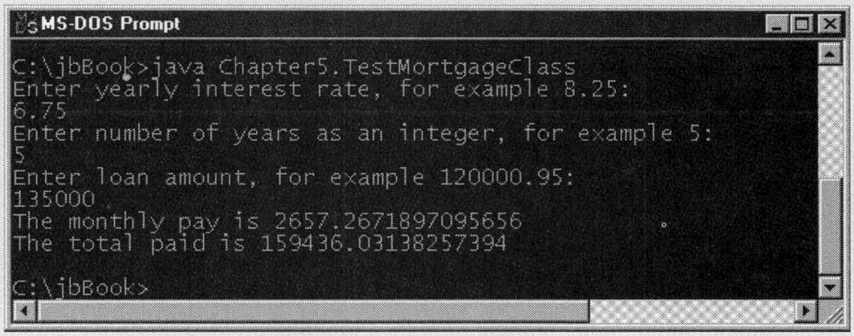

Figure 5.11   *The program creates a* Mortgage *instance with the interest rate, year, and loan amount, and displays monthly payment and total payment by invoking the methods of the instance.*

Example Review

The Mortgage class contains a constructor, three getters, and the methods for finding monthly payment and total payment. You can construct a Mortgage object by using three parameters: interest rate, payment years, and loan amount. The three getters, getInterest(), getYear(), and getLoan(), return interest rate, payment years, and loan amount, respectively.

The main() class reads interest rate, payment period (in years), and loan amount; creates a Mortgage object; and then obtains the monthly payment and total payment using the instance methods in the Mortgage class.

Since the Mortgage class will be used later in Chapter 10, "Applets and Advanced Graphics," this class is declared public and stored in a separate file.

Example 5.8 Using the Rational Class

In this example, a class for rational numbers is defined. The class provides constructors and addition, subtraction, multiplication, and division methods.

A rational number is a number with a numerator and a denominator in the form a/b, where a is the numerator and b is the denominator—for example, 1/3, 3/4, and 10/4.

A rational number cannot have a denominator of 0, but a numerator of 0 is fine. Every integer a is equivalent to a rational number a/1. Rational numbers are used in exact computations involving fractions; for example, 1/3 = 0.33333.... This number cannot be precisely represented in floating-point format using data type double or float. To obtain the exact result, you should use rational numbers.

There are many equivalent rational numbers; for example, 1/3 = 2/6 = 3/9 = 4/12. For convenience, 1/3 is used in this example to represent all rational

continues

numbers that are equivalent to 1/3. The numerator and the denominator of 1/3 have no common divisors except 1, so 1/3 is said to be in lowest terms.

To reduce a rational to its lowest terms, you need to find the greatest common divisor, or GCD, of the absolute values of its numerator and denominator, then divide both numerator and denominator by this value. Here is the classic Euclidean algorithm for finding the GCD of two `int` values `n` and `d`.

```
t1 = Math.abs(n); t2 = Math.abs(d); // Get absolute value of n and d;
r = t1 % t2; // r is the remainder of t1 divided by t2;
while (r != 0)
{
  t1 = t2;
  t2 = r;
  r = t1 % t2;
}

// When r is 0, t2 is the greatest common divisor between t1 and t2
return t2;
```

Based upon the foregoing analysis, the following data and methods are needed in the `Rational` class:

Data field:

`int numerator`: Represent the numerator of the rational number.

`int denominator`: Represent the denominator of the rational number.

Methods:

`public Rational add(Rational secondRational)`

Return the addition of this rational with another.

`public Rational subtract(Rational secondRational)`

Return the subtraction of this rational with another.

`public Rational multiply(Rational secondRational)`

Return the multiplication of this rational with another.

`public Rational divide(Rational secondRational)`

Return the division of this rational with another.

The `Rational` class is presented, followed by a test program. Figure 5.12 shows a sample run of the program.

```
// Rational.java: Define a rational number and its associated
// operations such as add, subtract, multiply, and divide
package Chapter5;

public class Rational
{
  // Data fields for numerator and denominator
  private long numerator = 0;
  private long denominator = 1;
```

```
// Default constructor
public Rational()
{
  numerator = 0;
  denominator = 1;
}

// Construct a rational with specified numerator and denominator
public Rational(long n, long d)
{
  long k = gcd(n,d);
  numerator = n/k;
  denominator = d/k;
}

// Find GCD of two numbers
private long gcd(long n, long d)
{
  long t1 = Math.abs(n);
  long t2 = Math.abs(d);
  long remainder = t1%t2;

  while (remainder != 0)
  {
    t1 = t2;
    t2 = remainder;
    remainder = t1%t2;
  }

  return t2;
}

// Getter method for numerator
public long getNumerator()
{
  return numerator;
}

public long getDenominator()
{
  return denominator;
}

// Add a rational number to this rational
public Rational add(Rational secondRational)
{
  long n = numerator*secondRational.getDenominator() +
    denominator*secondRational.getNumerator();
  long d = denominator*secondRational.getDenominator();
  return new Rational(n, d);
}

// Subtract a rational number from this rational
public Rational subtract(Rational secondRational)
{
  long n = numerator*secondRational.getDenominator()
    - denominator*secondRational.getNumerator();
  long d = denominator*secondRational.getDenominator();
  return new Rational(n, d);
}
```

continues

```
    // Multiply a rational number to this rational
    public Rational multiply(Rational secondRational)
    {
      long n = numerator*secondRational.getNumerator();
      long d = denominator*secondRational.getDenominator();
      return new Rational(n, d);
    }

    // Divide a rational number from this rational
    public Rational divide(Rational secondRational)
    {
      long n = numerator*secondRational.getDenominator();
      long d = denominator*secondRational.numerator;
      return new Rational(n, d);
    }

    // Override the toString() method
    public String toString()
    {
      return numerator + "/" + denominator;
    }
}

// TestRationalClass.java: Demonstrate using the Rational class
package Chapter5;

public class TestRationalClass
{
  // Main method
  public static void main(String[] args)
  {
    // Create and initialize two rational numbers r1 and r2.
    Rational r1 = new Rational(4,2);
    Rational r2 = new Rational(2,3);

    // Display results
    System.out.println(r1.toString() + " + " + r2.toString() +
      " = " + (r1.add(r2)).toString());
    System.out.println(r1.toString() + " - " + r2.toString() +
      " = " + (r1.subtract(r2)).toString());
    System.out.println(r1.toString() + " * " + r2.toString() +
      " = " + (r1.multiply(r2)).toString());
    System.out.println(r1.toString() + " / " + r2.toString() +
      " = " + (r1.divide(r2)).toString());
  }
}
```

Figure 5.12   *The program creates two instances of the* Rational *class and displays their addition, subtraction, multiplication, and division by invoking the instance methods.*

Example Review

The main class creates two rational numbers, r1 and r2, and displays the results of r1+r2, r1-r2, r1*r2, and r1/r2.

The rational number is encapsulated in a Rational object. Internally, a rational number is represented in its lowest terms; in other words, the greatest common divisor between the numerator and the denominator is 1.

The gcd() method is private; it is not intended for client use. The gcd() method is only for internal use by the Rational class.

The abs(x) method is defined in the Math class that returns the absolute value of x.

The expression r1+r2 is called in the form of r1.add(r2), in which add (which is a method in the object r1) returns the following:

```
(r1.numerator*r2.denominator+r1.denominator*r1.numerator)/
(r1.denominator*r2.denominator).
```

The numerator data field of the object r1 is r1.numerator, and the denominator data field of object r1 is r1.denominator.

The return value of r1 + r2 is a new Rational object.

The r.toString() method returns a string representing the rational number r in the form numerator/denominator.

When you are dividing rational numbers, what happens if the divisor is zero? In this example, the program would terminate with a runtime error. You need to make sure this does not occur when you are using the division method. In Chapter 11, "Exception Handling," you will learn to deal with the zero divisor case for a Rational object.

Packages

A *package* is a collection of classes. It provides a convenient way to organize classes. You can put the classes you develop into packages for distribution to other people. Think of packages as libraries to be shared by many users.

All the classes developed in this text are organized into packages, each of which groups the classes in one chapter. The Java language itself comes with a rich set of packages that you can use to build applications. You used the java.awt package in Chapter 1, "Introduction to Java and JBuilder 3," and you will learn more about Java system predefined packages in the section "Java Application Programmer Interface," later in this chapter.

In this section, you will learn about Java package-naming conventions, creating packages, and using packages.

Package-Naming Conventions

Packages are hierarchical, and you can have packages within packages. For example, `java.awt.Button` indicates that `Button` is a class in the package `awt` and that `awt` is a package within the package `java`. You can use levels of nesting to ensure the uniqueness of package names.

Choosing unique names is important because your package might be used on the Internet by other programs. Java designers recommend that you use your Internet domain name in reverse order as a package prefix. This avoids naming conflicts because Internet domain names are unique. Suppose you want to create a package named `mypackage.io` on a host machine with the Internet domain name `liangy.ipfw.indiana.edu`. To follow the naming convention, you would name the entire package `edu.indiana.ipfw.liangy.mypackage.io`.

Java expects one-to-one mapping of the package name and the file system directory structure. For the package named `edu.indiana.ipfw.liangy.mypackage.io`, you must create a directory as shown in Figure 5.13. In other words, a package is actually a directory that contains the bytecode of the classes.

Figure 5.13   *The package* `edu.indiana.ipfw.liangy.mypackge.io` *is mapped to a directory structure in the file system.*

The *CLASSPATH* Environment Variable

The `edu` directory does not have to be the root directory. In order for Java to know where your package is in the file system, you must modify the environment variable `CLASSPATH` so that it points to the directory in which your package resides. For example, the following line adds `c:\edu\ipfw\indiana\liangy` to `CLASSPATH`.

    CLASSPATH=.;%CLASSPATH%;c:\edu\ipfw\indiana\liangy;

The period (.) indicating that the current directory is always in `CLASSPATH`. `%CLASSPATH%` refers to the existing `CLASSPATH`. The directory `c:\edu\ipfw\indiana\liangy` is in `CLASSPATH` so that you can use the package `mypackage.io` in the program.

You can add as many directories as necessary in `CLASSPATH`. The order in which the directories are specified is the order in which the classes are searched. If you have two classes of the same name in different directories, Java uses the first one it finds.

The `CLASSPATH` variable is set differently in Windows 95, Windows 98, Windows NT, and UNIX, as follows:

■ **Windows 95 and Windows 98**—Edit **autoexec.bat** using a text editor, such as Microsoft Notepad.

- **Windows NT**—Go to the Start button and choose Control Panel, select the System icon, then create or modify CLASSPATH in the environment.

- **UNIX**—Use the setenv command to set CLASSPATH, such as

    ```
    setenv CLASSPATH .:/home/edu/indiana/ipfw/liangy
    ```

    You can insert this line into the .cshrc file, so that the CLASSPATH variable is automatically set when you log on.

TIP

You must restart the system for the CLASSPATH variable to take effect on Windows 95 and Windows 98. On Windows NT, however, the settings are stored permanently and affect any new command-line windows, but not existing command-line windows.

NOTE

If a package is rarely used and you do not want it to be in the CLASSPATH permanently, include the class path in the javac and java interpreter as follows:

```
javac -classpath c:\edu\ipfw\indiana\liangy sourcecode.java
java -classpath c:\edu\ipfw\indiana\liangy javaclass
```

Putting Classes into Packages

Every class in Java belongs to a package. The class is added to the package when it is compiled. All the classes that you have used so far in this chapter are placed in the c:\jbBook\Chapter5 directory when the Java source programs are compiled, since the Output root directory is c:\jbBook and each program begins with the statement

```
package Chapter5;
```

The class must be defined as public for it to be accessed by a program in other packages.

To use a class from a package in your program, you should add an import statement to the top of the program. Here is an example:

```
import Chapter2.MyInput;
```

If you have many classes to use from the same package, you can use the asterisk (*) to indicate use of all classes in the package. For example:

```
import Chapter2.*;
```

This statement imports all the classes in the Chapter2 package.

NOTE

This book places all the classes in the projects under the output directory c:\jbBook. If you need to use a package that is not in the output directory, you can add it to the library in the Path page of the Project Properties dialog box.

Java Application Programmer Interface

The Java Application Programmer interface—Java 2 API—consists of numerous classes and interfaces that are grouped into 15 core packages, such as `java.lang`, `java.awt`, `java.event`, `javax.swing`, `java.applet`, `java.util`, `java.io`, and `java.net`. These classes provide an interface that allows Java programs to interact with the system.

- **`java.lang`**—Contains core Java classes (such as `Object`, `String`, `System`, `Math`, `Number`, `Character`, `Boolean`, `Byte`, `Short`, `Integer`, `Long`, `Float`, and `Double`). This package is implicitly imported to every Java program.

- **`java.awt`**—Contains classes for drawing geometrical objects, managing component layout, and creating peer-based (so-called heavyweight) components, such as windows, frames, panels, menus, buttons, fonts, lists, and many others.

- **`java.awt.event`**—Contains classes for handling events in graphics programming.

- **`javax.swing`**—Contains the lightweight graphic user interface components.

- **`java.applet`**—Contains classes for supporting applets.

- **`java.io`**—Contains classes for input and output streams and files.

- **`java.util`**—Contains many utilities, such as date, calendar, locale, system properties, vectors, hashing, and stacks.

- **`java.text`**—Contains classes for formatting information, such as date and time, in a number of formatting styles based on a language, country, and culture.

- **`java.net`**—Contains classes for supporting network communications.

The `java.lang` is the most fundamental package supporting basic operations. Many of the popular classes in `java.lang` are introduced later in the book. See the following chapters for information on them:

- Chapter 6, "Arrays and Strings," introduces classes `java.lang.String`, `java.lang.StringBuffer`, and `java.util.StringTokenizer` for storing and processing strings.

- Chapter 7, "Class Inheritance," covers the numeric wrapper classes, such as `Integer`, and `Double` in the `java.lang` package.

- Chapter 8, "Getting Started with Graphics Programming," and Chapter 9, "Creating User Interfaces," introduce `java.awt`, `java.awt.event` and `javax.swing`, which are used for drawing geometrical objects, responding to mouse movements and keyboard entries, and designing graphical user interfaces.

- Chapter 10, "Applets and Advanced Graphics," introduces `java.applet`, which is used to program Java applets.

- Chapter 11, "Exception Handling," discusses using the `java.lang.Throwable` class and its subclasses for exception handling.

- Chapter 12, "Internationalization," introduces `java.util.Date`, `java.util.Calendar`, and `java.text.DateFormat` for processing and formatting date and time based on locales.

- Chapter 13, "Multithreading," focuses on the `java.lang.Thread` class and the `java.lang.Runnable` interface, which are used for multithreading.

- Chapter 14, "Multimedia," addresses the use of multimedia by several classes from `java.awt` and `java.applet`.

- Chapter 15, "Input and Output," discusses the use of `java.io` by input and output streams.

- Chapter 16, "Networking," discusses using `java.net` for network programming.

NOTE

After you understand the concept of programming, the most important lesson in Java is learning how to use the API to develop useful programs. The core Java API is introduced in the coming chapters.

The *Math* Class

The `Math` class contains the methods needed to perform basic mathematical functions. Two useful constants, `PI` and `E` (the base of natural logarithms), are provided in the `Math` class. You have already used `Math.PI` to obtain the π value instead of again declaring that value in the program. The constants are `double` values. Most methods operate on `double` parameters and return `double` values. The methods in the `Math` class can be categorized as trigonometric methods, exponent methods, and miscellaneous methods.

NOTE

I strongly recommend that you browse through the class definitions for each new class you learn. You can get the class definition from JBuilder Help, or by choosing Search, Browse Symbol to type a fully qualified class name, such as `java.lang.Math`, to view its documentation in the Content pane of the App-Browser. You may also use the JDK command **javap** to display the members of a class in a DOS window, as shown in Figure 5.14.

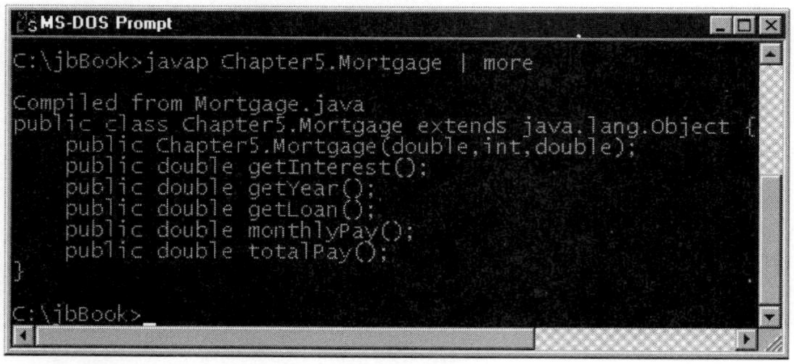

Figure 5.14   *You can display the contents of a class using the javap command at the DOS prompt.*

Trigonometric Methods

The Math class contains the following trigonometric methods, among many others:

```
public static double sin(double a)
public static double cos(double a)
public static double tan(double a)
public static double asin(double a)
public static double acos(double a)
public static double atan(double a)
```

Each method has a single double parameter, and its return type is double. For example, Math.sin(Math.PI) returns the trigonometric sine of π.

Exponent Methods

There are four methods related to exponents in the Math class:

```
public static double exp(double a)
// Return e raised to the power of a

public static double log(double a)
// Return the natural logarithm of a

public static double pow(double a, double b)
// Return a raised to the power of b

public static double sqrt(double a)
// Return the square root of a
```

You used the Math.pow() method in the mortgage calculation program. Note that the parameter in the Math.sqrt() method must not be negative.

The *min()*, *max()*, *abs()*, and *random()* Methods

Other useful methods in the Math class are the min() and max() methods, the abs() method, and the random generator random().

The min() and max() functions return the minimum and maximum numbers between two numbers (int, long, float, or double). For example, max(3.4, 5.0) returns 5.0, and min(3, 2) returns 2.

The abs() function returns the absolute value of the number (int, long, float, and double). For example, abs(-3.03) returns 3.03.

The Math class also has a powerful method, random(), which generates a random double floating-point number between 0 and 1.

NOTE

All methods and data in the Math class are static. They are class methods and class variables. Most methods operate on double parameters and return a double value.

TIP

Occasionally, you want to prohibit the user from creating an instance for a class. For example, there is no reason to create an instance from the Math class because all of the data and methods are of classwide information. One solution is to define a dummy private constructor in the class. The Math class has a private constructor, as follows:

```
private Math() { };
```

Therefore, the Math class cannot be instantiated.

JBuilder Object Gallery

JBuilder provides numerous wizards for generating templates that you can use to speed your development of applications, applets, beans, dialogs, classes, HTML files, and so on. The wizards are contained in the Object Gallery (see Figure 1.22), which is accessible by clicking File, New from the menu bar. In Chapter 8, "Getting Started with Graphics Programming," you will learn how to use the Application Wizard to generate the class templates for your application, and in Chapter 10, "Applets and Advanced Graphics," you will learn how to use the Applet Wizard to generate applets.

To create a Java program, you can use the Class Wizard. Here are the steps in creating a new class named Test.java in project Chapter 5.

1. With the AppBrowser for Chapter5 focused, choose File, New to display the Object Gallery, as shown in Figure 1.22.

2. Click the Class icon to bring up the New Java File Wizard, as shown in Figure 5.15.

3. Type Test in the Class Name field and check the options Public and Generate parameterless constructor. Click OK to close the wizard. You will see Test.java created in the project, as shown in Figure 5.16.

NOTE

The generated code uses the "New line" coding style because you selected "New line" on the Code Style page of the Chapter5.jpr properties dialog box.

Figure 5.15   *The New Java File Wizard helps to generate a Java class.*

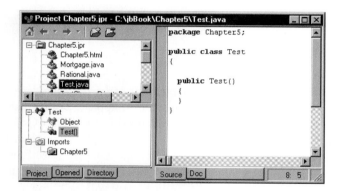

Figure 5.16   *Test.java was created by the New Java File Wizard.*

Chapter Summary

In this chapter, you learned how to program using objects and classes. You learned how to define classes, create objects, and use objects. You also learned about modifiers, instance variables, class variables, instance methods, and class methods.

A class is a template for objects. It defines the generic properties of objects and provides methods to manipulate them.

An object is an instance of a class. It is declared in the same way as a primitive type variable. You use the new operator to create an object, and you use the dot (.) operator to access members of that object.

A constructor is a special method that is called when an object is created. Constructors can be overloaded. I recommend that you provide a constructor for each class so that an instance of the class is properly initialized (although it is legal to write a class without constructors).

Modifiers specify how the class, method, and data are accessed. You learned about `public`, `private`, and `static` modifiers. A `public` class, method, or item of data is accessible to all clients. A `private` method or item of data is only visible inside the class. You should make instance data `private`. You can provide a getter method to enable clients to see the data. A class variable or a class method is defined using the keyword `static`.

Objects are passed to methods using pass by reference. Any changes to the object inside the method affect the object that is passed as the argument.

An instance *variable* is a variable that belongs to the instance of a class. Its use is associated with individual objects. A *class variable* is a variable shared by all objects of the same class.

An instance *method* is a method that belongs to the instance of a class. Its use is associated with individual objects. A *class method* is a method that is called without using instances.

A package is a structure for organizing classes. Java 2 API has numerous classes and interfaces that are organized into 15 core packages. Programming in Java essentially consists of using these classes to build your projects.

The `Math` class contains methods that perform trigonometric functions (`sin`, `cos`, `tag`, `acos`, `asin`, `atan`), exponent functions (`exp`, `log`, `pow`, `sqrt`), and some miscellaneous functions (`min`, `max`, `abs`, `random`). All of these methods operate on `double` values; `min`, `max`, and `abs` can also operate on `int`, `long`, `float`, and `double`.

You learned how to create classes using the JBuilder New Class Wizard.

Chapter Review

5.1. Describe the relationship between an object and its defining class. How do you declare a class? How do you declare an object? How do you create an object? How do you declare and create an object in one statement?

5.2. What are the differences between constructors and methods?

5.3. List the modifiers that you learned in this chapter and describe their purposes.

5.4. Describe pass by reference and pass by value. Show the output of the following program:

```java
package Chapter5;

public class Test
{
  public static void main(String[] args)
  {
    Count myCount = new Count();
    int times = 0;

    for (int i=0; i<100; i++)
      increment(myCount, times);

    System.out.println("count is " + myCount.count);
    System.out.println("times is " + times);
  }

  public static void increment(Count c, int times)
  {
    c.count++;
    times++;
  }
}

class Count
{
  public int count;

  Count(int c)
  {
    count = c;
  }

  Count()
  {
    count = 1;
  }
}
```

5.5. Suppose that the class Foo is defined as follows:

```java
package Chapter5;

public class Foo
{
  int i;
  static String s;

  void imethod()
  {
  }

  static void smethod()
  {
  }
}
```

Let f be an instance of Foo. Are the following statements correct?

```
System.out.println(f.i);
System.out.println(f.s);
f.imethod();
f.smethod();
System.out.println(Foo.i);
System.out.println(Foo.s);
Foo.imethod();
Foo.smethod();
```

5.6. What is the output of the following program?

```
package Chapter5;

public class Foo
{
  static int i = 0;
  static int j = 0;

  public static void main(String[] args)
  {
    int i = 2;
    int k = 3;

    {
      int j = 3;
      System.out.println("i + j is " + i+j);
    }

    k = i + j;
    System.out.println("k is "+k);
    System.out.println("j is "+j);
  }
}
```

5.7. What is wrong with the following program?

```
package Chapter5;

public class ShowErrors
{
  public static void main(String[] args)
  {
    int i;
    int j;

    j = MyInput.readInt();
    if (j > 3)
      System.out.println(i+4);
  }
}
```

5.8. What is wrong with the following program?

```
package Chapter5;

public class ShowErrors
{
  public static void main(String[] args)
  {
    for (int i=0; i<10; i++);
      System.out.println(i+4);
  }
}
```

5.9. Describe a package and its relationship with classes.

5.10. What is the recommended naming convention for creating your own packages?

5.11. Your packages can be stored in any directory or subdirectory. How does the compiler know where to find the packages?

Programming Exercises

5.1. Rewrite the `Rational` class with the following additional methods:

```
public boolean lessThan(Rational r)
// Return true if this Rational is < r

public boolean greaterThan(Rational r)
// Return true if this Rational is > r

public boolean equal(Rational r)
// Return true if this Rational is = r

public boolean lessThanOrEqual(Rational r)
// Return true if this Rational is <= r

public boolean greaterThanOrEqual(Rational r)
// Return true if this Rational is >= r

static Rational max(Rational r1, Rational r2)
// Return the larger one
```

Write a client program to test the new `Rational` class.

5.2. Write a program that will compute the following summation series using the `Rational` class from Example 5.8.

```
1/1 + 1/2 + 1/3 +...+ 1/n
1/1 + 1/2 + 1/2² +...+ 1/2ⁿ
```

$$1/1 + 1/2 + 1/3 + \ldots + 1/n$$
$$1/1 + 1/2 + 1/2^2 + \ldots + 1/2^n$$

5.3. Write a class named `Rectangle` to encapsulate rectangles. The private data fields are `width`, `height`, and `color`. Use `double` for width and height, and `String` for color. The methods are `getWidth()`, `getHeight()`, `getColor()`, and `findArea()`. Suppose that all rectangles have the same color. Use a class variable for color.

```
package Chapter5;

public class Rectangle
{
  private double width, height;
  static String color;

  public Rectangle(double w, double h, String c)
  {
  }

  public double getWidth()
  {
  }
```

```
    public double getHeight()
    {
    }

    public String getColor()
    {
    }

    public double findArea()
    {
    }
}
```

Write a client program to test the class Rectangle. In the client program, create two Rectangle objects. Assign any widths and heights to the two objects. Assign the first object the color red and the second yellow. Display both objects' properties and find their areas.

ARRAYS AND STRINGS

Objectives

- ⚇ Understand the concept of arrays.

- ⚇ Learn the steps involved in using arrays—declaring, creating, initializing, and processing.

- ⚇ Become familiar with sorting and search algorithms.

- ⚇ Use objects as array elements.

- ⚇ Become familiar with the copy array utility.

- ⚇ Learn how to use multidimensional arrays.

- ⚇ Recognize the difference between arrays and strings.

- ⚇ Become familiar with the `String` class, the `StringBuffer` class, and the `StringTokenizer` class.

- ⚇ Know how to use command-line arguments.

- ⚇ Use the JBuilder debugger.

Introduction

In earlier chapters, you studied examples in which values were overwritten during the execution of a program. In those examples, such as Example 3.4 in Chapter 3, "Control Structures," you did not need to worry about storing former values. However, in some cases, you will have to store a large number of values in memory during the execution of a program. For example, suppose that you want to sort a group of numbers. They must all be stored in memory because later you will have to compare each number with all of the other numbers.

To store numbers requires declaring variables in the program. It is practically impossible to declare variables for each number. You need an efficient, organized approach. Java and all other high-level languages provide a data structure, *array*, which stores a collection of the same types of data. Java treats these arrays as objects.

Strings and arrays are based on similar concepts. A string is a sequence of characters. In many languages, strings are treated as arrays of characters. But in Java, a *string* is used very differently from an array object.

Declaring and Creating Arrays

To use arrays in the program, you need to declare arrays and the type of elements that can be stored in them. Here is the syntax to declare an array:

```
datatype[] arrayName;
```

or

```
datatype arrayName[];
```

The following code is an example of this syntax:

```
double[] myList;
```

or

```
double myList[];
```

NOTE

The style `datatype[] arrayName` is preferred. The style `datatype arrayName[]` comes from the C language and was adopted in Java to accommodate C programmers.

Since a Java array is an object, the declaration does not allocate any space in memory for the array. You cannot assign elements to the array unless it is already created.

After an array is declared, you can use the `new` operator to create the array with the following syntax:

```
arrayName = new datatype[arraySize];
```

Declaration and creation can be combined in one statement, as follows:

```
datatype[] arrayName = new datatype[arraySize];
```

or

```
datatype arrayName[] = new datatype[arraySize];
```

Here is an example of such a statement:

```
double[] myList = new double[10];
```

This statement creates an array of 10 elements of `double` type, as shown in Figure 6.1. The array size must be given to specify the number of elements that can be stored in the array when allocating space for the array. After the array is created, its size cannot be changed.

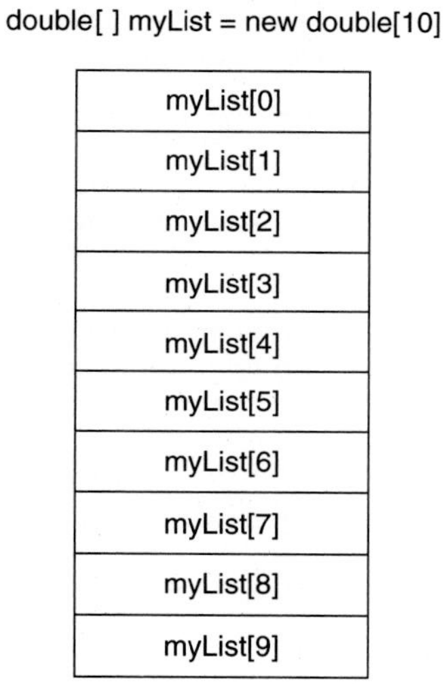

double[ ] myList = new double[10]

| myList[0] |
| myList[1] |
| myList[2] |
| myList[3] |
| myList[4] |
| myList[5] |
| myList[6] |
| myList[7] |
| myList[8] |
| myList[9] |

Figure 6.1   *The array* `myList` *has 10 elements of* `double` *type and integer indices from 0 to 9.*

Initializing and Processing Arrays

When arrays are created, the elements are assigned the default value of `0` for the numeric primitive data type variables, `'\u0000'` for `char` variables, `false` for `boolean` variables, and `null` for object variables. The array elements are accessed through the index. The array indices are from `0` to `arraySize-1`. In the example in Figure 6.1, `myList` holds 10 `double` values and the indices are from `0` to `9`.

Each element in the array is represented using the following syntax:

```
arrayName[index];
```

For example, `myList[9]` represents the last element in the array `myList`.

In Java, an array index is always an integer that starts with 0. In many other languages, such as Ada and Pascal, the index can be an integer or another type of value.

▮▮▮ CAUTION
Some languages use parentheses to reference an array element, as in myList(9). But Java uses brackets, as in myList[9].

After an array is created, you can enter values into array elements. For example, see the following loop:

```
for (int i = 0; i < myList.length; i++)
  myList[i] = (double)i;
```

In this example, myList.length returns the array size (10) for myList.

▮▮▮ NOTE
The size of an array is denoted by arrayObject.length. After an array is created, the length data field is assigned a value that denotes the number of elements in the array.

The word length is a data field belonging to an array object, not to a method. Therefore, using length() would result in an error.

Java has a shorthand notation that creates an array object and initializes it at the same time. The following is an example of its syntax at work:

```
double[] myList = {1.9, 2.9, 3.4, 3.5};
```

This statement creates the array myList, which consists of four elements. Therefore, myList.length is 4 and myList[0] is 1.9. Note that the new operator was not used in the syntax.

When processing array elements, you will often use a for loop for the following reasons:

■ All of the elements in the array are of the same type and have the same properties. They are even processed in the same fashion—by repeatedly using a loop.

■ Since the size of the array is known, it is natural to use a for loop.

Example 6.1 Assigning Grades

In this example, a program is written that will read student scores (int) from the keyboard, get the best score, and then assign grades based on the following scheme:

Grade is A if score is >= best–10;

Grade is B if score is >= best–20;

Grade is C if score is >= best–30;

Grade is D if score is >= best–40;

Grade is F otherwise.

The program prompts the user to enter the total number of students. It then prompts the user to enter all of the scores. Finally, it displays the grades.

The output of a sample run of the program is shown in Figure 6.2.

```java
// AssigningGrade.java: Assign grade
package Chapter6;

import Chapter2.MyInput;

public class AssigningGrade
{
  // Main method
  public static void main(String[] args)
  {
    int numOfStudents; // The number of students
    int[] scores; // Array scores
    int best = 0; // The best score
    char grade; // The grade

    // Get number of students
    System.out.println("Please enter number of students");
    numOfStudents = MyInput.readInt();

    // Create array scores
    scores = new int[numOfStudents];

    // Read scores and find the best score
    System.out.println("Please enter scores");
    for (int i=0; i<scores.length; i++)
    {
      scores[i] = MyInput.readInt();
      if (scores[i] > best)
        best = scores[i];
    }

    // Assign and display grades
    for (int i=0; i<scores.length; i++)
    {
      if (scores[i] >= best - 10)
        grade = 'A';
      else if (scores[i] >= best - 20)
        grade = 'B';
      else if (scores[i] >= best - 30)
        grade = 'C';
      else if (scores[i] >= best - 40)
        grade = 'D';
      else
        grade = 'F';
```

continues

```
                    System.out.println("Student "+i+" score is "+scores[i]+
                        " and grade is " + grade);
                }
            }
        }
```

```
MS-DOS Prompt                                              _ □ ✕

C:\jbBook>java Chapter6.AssigningGrade
Please enter number of students
4
Please enter scores
40
50
60
70
Student 0 score is 40 and grade is C
Student 1 score is 50 and grade is B
Student 2 score is 60 and grade is A
Student 3 score is 70 and grade is A

C:\jbBook>_
```

Figure 6.2   *The program receives the number of students and their scores and then assigns grades.*

Example Review

Array scores[] is declared in order to store scores. At the time this array is declared, the size of the array is undetermined. After the user enters the number of students into numOfStudents, an array with a size of numOfStudents is created.

The array is not needed to find the best score. It is needed, however, to keep all of the scores so that grades can be assigned later on, and it is needed when scores are printed along with the students' grades.

CAUTION

Accessing an array out of bounds is a common programming error. To avoid it, make sure that you do not use an index beyond arrayObject.length-1.

Programmers often mistakenly reference the first element in an array with index 1, so that the index of the tenth element becomes 10. This is called the *off-by-one error*.

Sorting Arrays

Sorting is a common task in computer programming. It would be used, for example, if you wanted to display the grades from the previous example in alphabetical order. There are many algorithms used for sorting. In this section, a simple, intuitive sorting algorithm, *selection sort*, is introduced.

Suppose that you want to sort a list in nondescending order. Selection sort finds the largest number in the list and places it last. It then finds the largest number remaining and places it last, and so on until the remaining list contains a single number.

Consider the following list:

2 9 5 4 8 1 6

If you had selected 9 (the largest number) and swapped it with 6 (the last in the list), the new list would be:

2 6 5 4 8 1 9

Since the number 9 would then be placed in the correct position in the list, it would no longer need to be considered. You could apply selection sort to the remaining numbers in the list as follows:

2 6 5 4 8 1

From the remaining list, you would select 8 and swap it with 1. The new list would be:

2 6 5 4 1 8

Since the number 8 would then be placed in the correct position in the list, it would no longer need to be considered. If you continued in the same process, eventually the entire list would be sorted.

The algorithm could be described as follows:

```
for (int i=list.length-1; i>=1; i—)
{
  select the largest element in list[1..i];
  swap the largest with list[i], if necessary;
  //list[i] is in place. The next iteration apply on list[1..i-1]
}
```

The code is given in the following example. The selectionSort() method in this program works only for a list of double values. In Chapter 7, "Class Inheritance," you will learn the techniques for writing a generic method that will sort elements of any type in a list.

Example 6.2 Using Arrays in Sorting

In this example, the selectionSort() method is used to write a program that will sort a list of double floating-point numbers. The output of the program is shown in Figure 6.3.

```
// TestSelectionSort.java: Sort numbers using selection sort
package Chapter6;

public class TestSelectionSort
{
```

continues

```java
      // Main method
      public static void main(String[] args)
      {
        // Initialize the list
        double[] myList = {5.0, 4.4, 1.9, 2.9, 3.4, 3.5};

        // Print the original list
        System.out.println("My list before sort is: ");
        printList(myList);

        // Sort the list
        selectionSort(myList);

        // Print the sorted list
        System.out.println("My list after sort is: ");
        printList(myList);
      }

      // The method for printing numbers
      static void printList(double[] list)
      {
        for (int i=0; i<list.length; i++)
          System.out.println(list[i]);
      }

      // The method for sorting the numbers
      static void selectionSort(double[] list)
      {
        double currentMax;
        int currentMaxIndex;

        for (int i=list.length-1; i>=1; i—)
        {
          // Find the maximum in the list[0..i]
          currentMax = list[i];
          currentMaxIndex = i;

          for (int j=i-1; j>=0; j—)
          {
            if (currentMax < list[j])
            {
              currentMax = list[j];
              currentMaxIndex = j;
            }
          }

          // Swap list[i] with list[currentMaxIndex] if necessary;
          if (currentMaxIndex != i)
          {
            list[currentMaxIndex] = list[i];
            list[i] = currentMax;
          }
        }
      }
    }
```

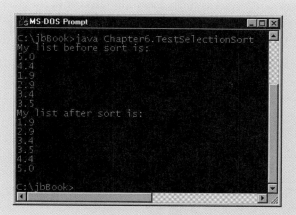

Figure 6.3 *The program invokes* `selectionSort()` *in order to sort a list of* `double` *values.*

Example Review

An array `myList` of length 6 was created. Its initial values are listed in the following single statement:

```
double[] myList = {5.0, 4.4, 1.9, 2.9, 3.4, 3.5};
```

The `selectionSort(double[] list)` method sorts any array of double elements. The method is implemented with a nested `for` loop. The outer loop (with the loop control variable `i`) is iterated in order to find the largest element in the list—which ranges from `list[0]` to `list[i]`—and to exchange it with the current last element, `list[i]`.

The variable `i` is initially `list.length-1`. After each iteration of the outer loop, `list[i]` is in the right place. Eventually, all the elements are put in the right place; therefore, the whole list is sorted.

Searching Arrays

Searching is the process of looking for a particular element in the array—for example, discovering whether a particular score is included in a list of scores. Searching, like sorting, is a common task in computer programming. There are many algorithms and data structures devoted to searching. In this section, two widely used approaches are discussed, *linear search* and *binary search*.

The Linear Search Approach

The linear search approach compares the key element, `key`, with each element in the array `list[]`. The method continues to do so until the key matches an element in the list or the list is exhausted without a match being found. If a match is made, the linear search returns the index of the element in the array that matches the key. If no match is found, the search returns -1. The algorithm can be simply described as follows:

```
for (int i=0; i<list.length; i++)
{
  if (key == list[i])
    return i;
}

return -1;
```

The following example demonstrates a linear search.

Example 6.3 Testing Linear Search

In this example, a program is written that will implement and test the linear search method. The program creates a random array of 10 elements of int type and then displays it. The program prompts the user to enter a key for testing linear search. The output of a sample run of the program is shown in Figure 6.4.

```
// TestLinearSearch.java: Search for a number in a list
package Chapter6;

import Chapter2.MyInput;

public class TestLinearSearch
{
  // Main method
  public static void main(String[] args)
  {
    int[] list = new int[10];

    // Create the list randomly and display it
    System.out.print("The list is  ");
    for (int i=0; i<list.length; i++)
    {
      list[i] = (int)(Math.random()*10);
      System.out.print(list[i]+"  ");
    }
    System.out.println(" ");

    // Prompt the user to enter a key
    System.out.print("Enter a key  ");
    int key = MyInput.readInt();
    int index = linearSearch(key, list);
    if (index != -1)
      System.out.println("The key is found in index "+index);
    else
      System.out.println("The key is not found in the list");
  }

  // The method for finding a key in the list
  public static int linearSearch(int key, int[] list)
  {
    for (int i=0; i<list.length; i++)
```

6.9. What does the following program do?

```
public class Test
{
  public static void main(String[] args)
  {
    Rational[] r = {new Rational(2,3), new Rational(-1, 3),
                    new Rational(3,5)};
    double[] d = new double[r.length];

    for (int i=0; i<r.length; i++)
      d[i] = r[i].getNumerator() / r[i].getDenominator();
  }
}
```

6.10. Use the `arraycopy()` method to copy the following array to a target array t.

```
Circle[] source = {new Circle(3), new Circle(4), new Circle(5)};
```

6.11. Declare and create a 4×5 int matrix.

6.12. Suppose that s1 and s2 are two strings. Which of the following statements or expressions are incorrect?

```
String s = new String("new string");
```

```
String s3 = s1 + s2;
```

```
String s3 = s1 - s2;
```

```
s1 == s2;
```

```
s1 >= s2;
```

```
s1.compareTo(s2);
```

```
int i = s1.length();
```

```
char c = s1(0);
```

```
char c = s1.charAt(s1.length());
```

6.13. Declare a `StringTokenizer` for a string s with slash (/) and backslash (\) as delimiters.

6.14. What is the output of the following program?

```
import java.util.StringTokenizer;

class TestStringTokenizer
{
  public static void main(String[] args)
  {
    //create a string and string tokenizer
    String s = "I/am\learning Java.";
    StringTokenizer st = new StringTokenizer(s, "/\.");

    //retrieve and display tokens
    while (st.hasMoreTokens())
      System.out.print(st.nextToken()+" ");
  }
}
```

Programming Exercises

6.1. Write a program that will read 10 integers and display them in reverse order.

6.2. Use recursion to rewrite the selection sort used in Example 6.2.

6.3. Use iterations to rewrite the binary search used in Example 6.4.

6.4. Write a program that meets the following requirements:

■ Create a class for students. The class must contain the student's name (`String`), ID (`int`), and status (`int`). The status indicates the student's class standing: `1` for freshman, `2` for sophomore, `3` for junior, and `4` for senior.

■ Create 20 students whose names are Name1, Name2, and so on to Name20, and whose IDs and status are assigned randomly.

■ Find all juniors and print their names and IDs.

6.5. Write a program that meets the following requirements:

■ Write a method that will multiply two `int` square matrices. The method is declared as follows:

```
public static int[][] multiply(int[][] m1, int[][] m2)
```

The algorithm for matrix multiplication can be described as follows:

```
for (int i=0; i<m.length; i++)
  for (int j=0; j<m.length; j++)
  {
    c[i][j] = 0;
    for (int k=0; k<m.length; k++)
      c[i][j] = c[i][j] + m1[i][k]*m2[k][j];
  }
}
```

■ Write a main method in the same class to test the method.

6.6. Write a sort method using the bubble-sort algorithm. The bubble-sort algorithm makes several passes through the array. On each pass, neighboring pairs are compared successively. If a pair is in decreasing order, its values are swapped; otherwise, the values remain unchanged. The technique is called a bubble sort or sinking sort because the smaller values gradually "bubble" their way to the top and the larger values sink to the bottom.

The algorithm can be described as follows:

```
boolean changed = true;
do
{
  changed = false;
  for (int j=0; j<list.length-1; j++)
    if (list[j] > list[j+1])
    {
```

```
        swap list[j] with list[j+1];
        changed = true;
    }
}
while (changed);
```

Clearly, the list is in increasing order when the loop terminates. It is easy to show that the do loop executes at most list.length -1 times.

6.7. Write a program that meets the following requirements:

■ Write a method that will check whether a string is a palindrome: a string that reads the same forward and backward.

■ Write a program that will take a string from a command-line argument to check whether it is a palindrome.

6.8. Write a program similar to the one in Example 6.10. Instead of using integers, use rationals. You will need to use the StringTokenizer class to retrieve numerators and denominators.

6.9. Rewrite Example 3.7, "Finding Sales Amount," using the binary search approach. Since the sales amount is between 1 and COMMISSION_SOUGHT/0.08, you can use a binary search to improve Example 3.7.

CHAPTER 7

CLASS INHERITANCE

Objectives

- ℮ Understand the concept of class inheritance and the relationship between superclasses and subclasses.

- ℮ Create new classes from existing classes.

- ℮ Learn to use two keywords: `super` and `this`.

- ℮ Learn to use three modifiers: `protected`, `final`, and `abstract`.

- ℮ Understand polymorphism and object casting.

- ℮ Become familiar with the numerical wrapper classes.

- ℮ Design abstract classes in generic programming.

- ℮ Become familiar with class-design guidelines.

- ℮ Understand the concept of interfaces.

- ℮ Know inner classes.

- ℮ Know how to use the Implement Interface Wizard and Override Methods Wizard in JBuilder.

Introduction

With object-oriented programming, you can derive new classes from existing classes. This is called *inheritance*. In Chapter 1, "Introduction to Java," you created the `WelcomeApplet` applet by deriving it from the `Applet` class. Inheritance is an important and powerful concept in Java. In fact, every class you define in Java is inherited from an existing class, either explicitly or implicitly. The `Circle` class, for instance, is derived implicitly from the class `Object`.

This chapter introduces the concept of inheritance. Specifically, it discusses superclasses and subclasses, the use of the keywords `super` and `this`, the `protected` modifier, the `final` modifier, the `abstract` modifier, polymorphism, casting objects, class-design guidelines, wrapper classes, the interface, and inner classes.

Superclasses and Subclasses

In Java terminology, an existing class is called a *superclass*. A class derived from the superclass is called a *subclass*. Sometimes a superclass is referred to as a *parent class* or a *base class*, and a subclass is referred to as a *child class*, an *extended class*, or a *derived class*. You can reuse or change the methods of superclasses, and you can add new data and new methods in subclasses. In general, subclasses have more functionality than their superclasses.

NOTE

Contrary to conventional interpretation, a subclass is not a subset of its super-class. In fact, a subclass usually contains more functions and more detailed information than its superclass.

Example 7.1 Demonstrating Inheritance

To demonstrate inheritance, this example creates a new class for `Cylinder` from `Circle`. The `Cylinder` class inherits all the data and methods from the `Circle` class. In addition, it has a new data field, `length`, and a new method, `findVolume()`.

The relationship of these two classes is shown in Figure 7.1.

The `Cylinder` class can be declared as follows:

```
// Cylinder.java: Class definition for describing Cylinder
package Chapter7;

public class Cylinder extends Chapter5.Circle
{
  private double length;
```

```
   // Default constructor
   public Cylinder()
   {
     super();
     length = 1.0;
   }

   // Construct a cylinder with specified radius and length
   public Cylinder(double r, double l)
   {
     super(r);
     length = l;
   }

   // Getter method for length
   public double getLength()
   {
     return length;
   }

   // Find cylinder volume
   public double findVolume()
   {
     return findArea()*length;
   }
}
```

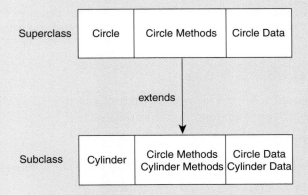

Figure 7.1 *The* Cylinder *class inherits data and methods from the* Circle *class and extends the* Circle *class with its own data and methods.*

Example Review

The Cylinder class extends the Circle class defined in Example 5.6, "Testing Instance and Class Variables," in Chapter 5, "Programming with Objects and Classes."

The reserved word extends tells the compiler that the Cylinder class is derived from the Circle class, thus inheriting data and methods from Circle.

The keyword super is used in the constructors. This keyword is discussed in the next section.

Using the Keyword *super*

The keyword `super` refers to the superclass of the class in which `super` appears. This keyword can be used in two ways:

- To call a superclass constructor.
- To call a superclass method.

Calling Superclass Constructors

The syntax to call a superclass constructor is

```
super(parameters);
```

In the `Cylinder` class, for example, `super()` and `super(r)` are used to call the constructors from the `Circle` class to initialize the radius. The component `super()` must appear in the first line of the constructor and is the only way to invoke a superclass's constructor.

CAUTION

Java requires the `super()` statement to appear first in the constructor, even before data fields.

It also requires using the keyword `super` to call the superclass's constructor. Invoking a superclass constructor's name in a subclass causes a syntax error.

Calling Superclass Methods

The keyword `super` can be used to reference a method other than the constructor in the superclass. The syntax looks like this:

```
super.method(parameters);
```

You could rewrite the `findVolume()` method in the `Cylinder` class as follows:

```
double findVolume()
{
  return super.findArea()*length;
}
```

It is not necessary to put `super` before `findArea()` in this case, however, because `findArea()` is a method in the `Circle` class and can be accessed in the `Cylinder` class. Nevertheless, in some cases the keyword `super` is needed.

The following two examples demonstrate the use of inheritance and the `super` keyword.

Example 7.2 Testing Inheritance

This example shows a program that creates a `Cylinder` object and explores the relationship between the `Cylinder` and `Circle` classes by accessing the data and methods (`radius`, `findArea()`) defined in the `Circle` class and the data and methods (`length`, `findVolume()`) defined in the `Cylinder` class. The output of the program is shown in Figure 7.2.

```
package Chapter7;

public class TestCylinder
{
  public static void main(String[] args)
  {
    // Create a Cylinder object and display its properties
    Cylinder myCylinder = new Cylinder(5.0, 2.0);
    System.out.println("The length is " + myCylinder.getLength());
    System.out.println("The radius is " + myCylinder.getRadius());
    System.out.println("The volume of the cylinder is " +
      myCylinder.findVolume());
    System.out.println("The area of the circle is " +
      myCylinder.findArea());
  }
}
```

Figure 7.2   *The program creates a* `Cylinder` *object and accesses the data and methods defined in the* `Circle` *class and the* `Cylinder` *class.*

Example Review

Since this program uses the `Cylinder` class, you should have compiled the program in Example 7.1 before compiling this program. The `Cylinder` class extends all the functionality of the `Circle` class. Since the `myCylinder` object inherits all the data and methods in `Circle`, it can access the `getRadius()` and `findArea()` methods defined in the `Circle` class.

A subclass cannot call a superclass's constructor without using the `super` keyword. If you replace `super()` with `Circle()` in the `Cylinder` class, you would get a compilation error.

Overriding Methods

The subclass inherits methods from the superclass. Sometimes, it is necessary for the subclass to modify the methods defined in the superclass. This is referred to as *method overriding*.

Example 7.3 Overriding the Methods in the Superclass

In this example, the `Cylinder` class defined in Example 7.1 is modified to override the `findArea()` method in the `Circle` class. The `findArea()` method in the `Circle` class is for computing the area of a circle, while the `findArea()` method in the `Cylinder` class computes the surface area of a cylinder. The output of the program is shown in Figure 7.3.

```java
// TestOverrideMethods.java: Test the Cylinder class that overrides
// its superclass's methods
package Chapter7;

public class TestOverrideMethods
{
  public static void main(String[] args)
  {
    Cylinder myCylinder = new Cylinder(5.0, 2.0);
    System.out.println("The surface area of the cylinder is "+
      myCylinder.findArea());
    System.out.println("The volume of the cylinder is "+
      myCylinder.findVolume());
  }
}

// New cylinder class that overrides the findArea() method defined in
// the circle class
class Cylinder extends Chapter5.Circle
{
  private double length;

  // Default constructor
  public Cylinder()
  {
    super();
    length = 1.0;
  }

  // Construct a cylinder with specified radius and length
  public Cylinder(double r, double l)
  {
    super(r);
    length = 1;
  }

  // Getter method for length
  public double getLength()
  {
    return length;
  }

  // Find cylinder surface area
  public double findArea()
  {
    return 2*super.findArea()+(2*getRadius()*Math.PI)*length;
  }
}
```

```
        // Find cylinder volume
        public double findVolume()
        {
          return super.findArea()*length;
        }
    }
```

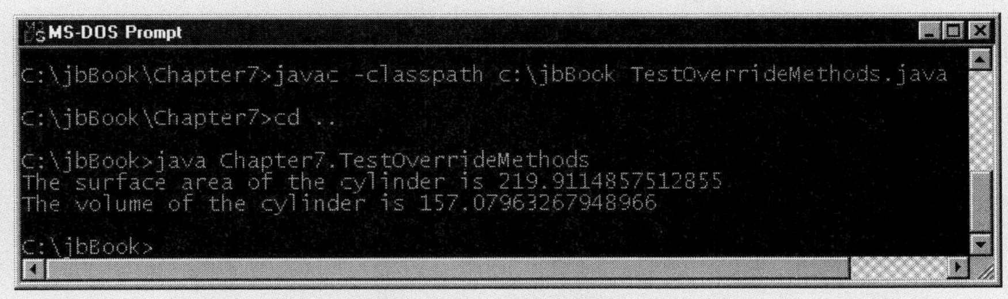

```
MS-DOS Prompt                                              _ □ ✕

C:\jbBook\Chapter7>javac -classpath c:\jbBook TestOverrideMethods.java

C:\jbBook\Chapter7>cd ..

C:\jbBook>java Chapter7.TestOverrideMethods
The surface area of the cylinder is 219.9114857512855
The volume of the cylinder is 157.07963267948966

C:\jbBook>
```

Figure 7.3 *The* Cylinder *class overrides the* findArea() *method defined in the* Circle *class.*

Example Review

The example demonstrates that you can modify a method in the superclass (Circle) and can use super to invoke a method in the superclass. The findArea() method is defined in the Circle class and modified in the Cylinder class. A Cylinder object can use both methods. To use the findArea() method in the Circle class, a Cylinder object must invoke super.findArea().

A subclass of the Cylinder class can no longer access the findArea() method defined in the Circle class because the findArea() method is redefined in the Cylinder class.

NOTE
You will get a compilation error in JBuilder indicating duplicate definition of the Cylinder class, because the Cylinder class was defined both in Example 7.1 and in Example 7.3. To avoid getting this compilation error when using the Make command in JBuilder IDE, compile and run the program from the DOS window.

The Keyword *this*

The keyword super is used to reference superclasses. Occasionally, you need to reference the current class. Java provides another keyword, this, for referencing the current object. The use of the this keyword is analogous to the use of super.

You can use this in the constructor. For example, you can redefine the Circle class as follows:

```
public class Circle
{
  private double radius;
```

```
        public Circle(double radius)
        {
          this.radius = radius;
        }

        public Circle()
        {
          this(1.0);
        }

        public double findArea()
        {
          return radius*radius*Math.PI;
        }
   }
```

The line this.radius = radius means "assign argument radius to the object's data field radius." Here, this means "this object." The line this(1.0) invokes the constructor with a double value argument in the class.

NOTE

Java requires the this() statement to appear first in the constructor, even before data fields.

You don't need to use the this keyword in the Circle class declaration. However, it can be useful in certain cases discussed later in this book; for instance, you can use new Thread(this) to create a thread for this object, as described in Chapter 13, "Multithreading."

The *protected, final,* and *abstract* Modifiers

You have already used the modifiers static, private, and public. Three new modifiers will now be introduced: protected, final, and abstract. These three modifiers are used with respect to class inheritance.

The *protected* Modifier

The protected modifier can be applied on data and methods in a class. A protected data or a protected method in a public class can be accessed by any class in the same package or its subclasses, even if the subclasses are in a different package.

Suppose class C1 contains a protected data named x in package p1, as shown in Figure 7.4. Consider the following scenarios:

1. If class C2 in package p2 is a subclass of C1, then x is accessible in C2, since x can be accessed by any subclass of C1.

2. If class C3 in package p1 contains an instance of C1 named c1, then x is visible in c1, since C3 and C1 are in the same package.

3. If class C4 in package p2 contains an instance of C1 named c1, then x is not visible in c1, because C4 and C1 are in different packages.

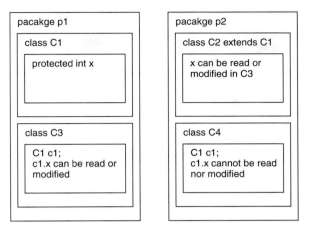

Figure 7.4 *The* protected *modifier can be used to prevent a non-subclass in a different package from accessing the class's data and methods.*

The *final* Modifier

You have already seen the final modifier used in declaring constants. Occasionally, you want to prevent classes from being extended. You can use the final modifier to indicate that a class is final and cannot be a parent class. The Math class introduced in Chapter 5 is a final class.

You also can define a method to be final; a final method can no longer be modified by its subclasses.

The *abstract* Modifier

In the inheritance hierarchy, classes *become* more specific and concrete *with each new subclass*. If you move from a subclass back up to a superclass, the classes become more general and less specific. When designing classes, a superclass should have features that are shared by subclasses. Sometimes a superclass is so abstract that it cannot have any specific instances. These classes are called *abstract classes* and are declared using the abstract modifier.

Abstract classes are like regular classes with data and methods, but you cannot create instances of abstract classes using the new operator. Abstract classes always contain abstract methods. An *abstract method* is a method signature without implementation. Its implementation is provided by its subclasses. For example, you can design an abstract class for all geometric objects as follows:

```java
// GeometricObject.java: The abstract GeometricObject class
package Chapter7;

public abstract class GeometricObject
{
  protected String color;
  protected double weight;

  // Default construct
  protected GeometricObject()
  {
    color = "white";
    weight = 1.0;
  }

  // Construct a geometric object
  protected GeometricObject(String c, double w)
  {
    color = c;
    weight = w;
  }

  // Getter method for color
  public String getColor()
  {
    return color;
  }

  // Getter method for weight
  public double getWeight()
  {
    return weight;
  }

  // Abstract method
  public abstract double findArea();

  // Abstract method
  public abstract double findPerimeter();
}
```

This abstract class provides the common features (data and methods) for geometric objects. Because you don't know how to compute areas and perimeters of geometric objects, findArea() and findPerimeter() are defined as abstract methods. These methods are implemented in the subclasses. For example, you can make Circle a subclass of GeometricObject. The possible implementation of the Circle class is as follows:

```java
// Circle.java: The circle class that extends GeometricObject
package Chapter7;

public class Circle extends GeometricObject
{
  protected double radius;

  // Default constructor
  public Circle()
  {
    this(1.0, 1.0, "white");
  }
}
```

```java
  // Construct circle with specified radius
  public Circle(double r)
  {
    super("white", 1.0);
    radius = r;
  }

  // Construct a circle with specified radius, weight, and color
  public Circle(double r, double w, String c)
  {
    super(c, w);
    radius = r;
  }

  // Getter method for radius
  public double getRadius()
  {
    return radius;
  }

  // Find circle area
  public double findArea()
  {
    return radius*radius*Math.PI;
  }

  // Find circle perimeter
  public double findPerimeter()
  {
    return 2*radius*Math.PI;
  }

  // Override the toString() method defined in the Object class
  public String toString()
  {
    return "Circle radius = " + radius;
  }
}
```

Since the data field `radius` is protected, it can be referenced by any subclass of `Circle`.

For another example, you can make `Rectangle` a subclass of `GeometricObject`. The possible implementation of the `Rectangle` class is as follows:

```java
// Rectangle.java: The Rectangle class that extends GeometricObject
package Chapter7;

public class Rectangle extends GeometricObject
{
  protected double width;
  protected double height;

  // Default constructor
  public Rectangle()
  {
    this(1.0, 1.0, 1.0, "white");
  }

  // Construct a rectangle with specified width and height
  public Rectangle(double width, double height)
  {
    this.width = width;
    this.height = height;
  }
```

```
// Construct a rectangle with specified width, height, weight, and
// color
public Rectangle(double width, double height, double w, String c)
{
  super(c, w);
  this.width = width;
  this.height = height;
}

// Getter method for radius
public double getWidth()
{
  return width;
}

// Find rectangle area
public double findArea()
{
  return width*height;
}

// Find rectangle perimeter
public double findPerimeter()
{
  return 2*(width + height);
}

// Override the toString() method defined in the Object class
public String toString()
{
  return "Rectangle width " + width + " and height " + height;
}
}
```

TIP

Use abstract classes to generalize common properties and methods of sub-classes. Use abstract methods to define the common methods that must be implemented in subclasses.

CAUTION

An abstract method cannot be contained in a nonabstract class. All abstract methods must be implemented in a nonabstract subclass extended from an abstract class, even if they are not used in the subclass.

Polymorphism

Polymorphism is a Greek word meaning many forms. In Java, polymorphism refers to the ability to determine at runtime which code to run given multiple methods with the same name but different operations. There are many forms of polymorphism in Java. For instance, method overloading is a form of polymorphism. Java VM determines which overloaded method to invoke based on the number and types of parameters passed to that method. Another form of polymorphism involves invoking the same methods defined in different classes. Usually, a method defined in a superclass is overridden in its subclasses. Which method in a subclass is invoked depends on the type of the object and determined at runtime.

In the previous section, you created the `Circle` class and the `Rectangle` class. The method `findArea()` and `findPerimeter()` defined in the `GeometricObject` class are overridden in the `Circle` class and in the `Rectangle` class. Suppose you create an array of `GeometricObject` as follows:

```
GeometricObject[] geoObject = new GeometricObject[2];
```

Now create a new circle and a rectangle and assign them to `geoObject[0]` and `geoObject[1]`, as follows:

```
geoObject[0] = new Circle();
geoObject[1] = new Rectangle();
```

The following loop displays the area and the perimeter of the geometric objects in the array:

```
for (int i=0; i<2; i++)
{
  System.out.println("The area of object " + i + " is "
    + geoObject[i].findArea());
  System.out.println("The perimeter of object " + i + " is "
    + geoObject[i].findPerimeter());
}
```

Since `geoObject[0]` is a circle, the `findArea()` method and the `findPeremiter()` method implemented in the `Circle` class are used for `geoObject[0].findArea()` and `geoObject[0].findPerimeter()`. Since `geoObject[1]` is a rectangle, the `findArea()` method and the `findPeremiter()` method implemented in the `Rectangle` class are used for `geoObject[1].findArea()` and `geoObject[1].findPerimeter()`. Which of these methods are invoked is dynamically determined at runtime, depending on the type of the object.

Casting Objects

You have already used the casting operator to convert variables of one primitive type to another. Similarly, casting also can be used to convert an object of one class type to another within an inheritance hierarchy. In the previous section, the statement

```
geoObject[0] = new Circle();
```

is known as *implicit casting*, which assigns a circle to a variable of `GeometricObject` type.

To perform an explicit casting, use a syntax similar to the one used for casting among primitive data types. Enclose the target object type in parentheses and place it before the object to be cast. Here is an example:

```
Circle myCircle = (Circle)myCylinder;
Cylinder myCylinder = (Cylinder)myCircle;
```

The first statement converts myCylinder to its superclass variable myCircle; the second converts myCircle to its subclass variable myCylinder.

It is always possible to convert an instance of a subclass to an instance of a superclass, simply because an instance of a subclass is also an instance of its superclass. For example, an apple is an instance of the Apple class, which is a subclass of the Fruit class. An applet is a always fruit. Therefore, you can always assign an applet to a variable of the Fruit class. For this reason, explicit casting can be omitted for this class. Thus,

```
Circle myCircle = myCylinder;
```

is equivalent to

```
Circle myCircle = (Circle)myCylinder;
```

When converting an instance of a superclass to an instance of its subclass, explicit casting must be used to confirm your intention to the compiler with the (SubclassName) cast notation. For the casting to be successful, you must make sure that the object to be cast is an instance of the subclass. If the superclass object is not an instance of the subclass, a runtime exception occurs. For example, an instance of the Fruit class cannot be cast into an instance of the Apple class, if the fruit is an orange. It is good practice, therefore, to ensure that the object is an instance of another object before attempting a casting. This can be accomplished by using the instanceof operator. For example, consider the following code:

```
Circle myCircle = new Circle();
if (myCircle instanceof Cylinder)
{
  // Perform casting if myCircle is an instance of Cylinder
  Cylinder myCylinder = (Cylinder)myCircle;
  ...
}
```

You may be wondering how myCircle could become an instance of the Cylinder class and why it is necessary to perform casting. There are some cases in which a superclass becomes an instance of a subclass. To fully explore the properties and functions, you need to cast the object to its subclass. This is shown in the following example.

Example 7.4 Casting Objects

Suppose you have an array of geometric objects; some are circles, and some are cylinders. This example shows a program that uses implicit casting to assign circles and cylinders to the array; it then uses explicit casting to access data and methods in the objects when processing the array. The output of a sample run of the program is shown in Figure 7.5.

```
// TestCasting.java: Demonstrate using object casting
package Chapter7;
```

```
public class TestCasting
{
  // Main method
  public static void main(String[] args)
  {
    // Create geoObject array with two objects and initialize it
    GeometricObject[] geoObject = new GeometricObject[2];
    geoObject[0] = new Circle(5.0, 2.0, "white");
    geoObject[1] = new Cylinder(5.0, 2.0, "black", 4.0);

    // Display properties of the objects
    for (int i=0; i<2; i++)
    {
      if (geoObject[i] instanceof Cylinder)
      {
        System.out.println("Object is cylinder");
        System.out.println("Cylinder volume is " +
          ((Cylinder)geoObject[i]).findVolume());
      }
      else if (geoObject[i] instanceof Circle)
      {
        System.out.println("Object is circle");
        System.out.println("Circle area is "+
          ((Circle)geoObject[i]).findArea());
      }
    }
  }
}

// The new cylinder class that extends the circle class
class Cylinder extends Circle
{
  private double length;

  // Default constructor
  public Cylinder()
  {
    super();
    length = 1.0;
  }

  // Construct a cylinder with specified radius, and length
  public Cylinder(double r, double l)
  {
    this(r, 1.0, "white", l);
  }

  // Construct a cylinder with specified radius, weight, color, and
  // length
  public Cylinder(double r, double w, String c, double l)
  {
    super(r, w, c);
    length = l;
  }

  // Getter method for length
  public double getLength()
  {
    return length;
  }
```

continues

249

```
  // Find cylinder volume
  public double findVolume()
  {
    return super.findArea()*length;
  }
}
```

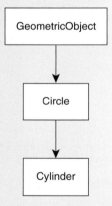

Figure 7.5   *The program creates an array of objects of* GeometricObject *type and casts the objects to subclasses of* GeometricObject *in order to use the data and methods defined in the subclasses* Circle *and* Cylinder.

Example Review

The program concerns three classes: GeometricObject, Circle, and Cylinder. Their inheritance hierarchy is shown in Figure 7.6.

```
┌─────────────────┐
│ GeometricObject │
└─────────────────┘
         │
         ▼
    ┌────────┐
    │ Circle │
    └────────┘
         │
         ▼
   ┌──────────┐
   │ Cylinder │
   └──────────┘
```

Figure 7.6   Cylinder *is a subclass of* Circle, *and* Circle *is a subclass of* GeometricObject.

Casting can only be done when the source object is an instance of the target class. The program uses the instanceof operator to ensure that the source object is an instance of the target class before performing a casting.

The program uses implicit casting to assign a Circle object to geoObject[0] and a Cylinder object to geoObject[1]. The reason for this casting is to store the Circle object and the Cylinder object in the geoObject array.

In the for loop, the cylinder volume is displayed if the object is a cylinder; the circle area of the object is displayed if the object is a circle.

Note that the order in the `if` statement is significant. If it is reversed (for example, testing whether the object is an instance of `Circle` first), then the cylinder will never be cast into `Cylinder` because `Cylinder` is an instance of `Circle`. Try to run the program with the following `if` statement and observe the effect.

```
if (geoObject[i] instanceof Circle)
{
  System.out.println("Object is circle");
  System.out.println("Circle area is " +
    ((Circle)geoObject[i]).findArea());
}
else if (geoObject[i] instanceof Cylinder)
{
  System.out.println("Object is cylinder");
  System.out.println("Cylinder volume is  " +
    ((Cylinder)geoObject[i]).findVolume());
}
```

NOTE

Explicit casting from geoObject[i] to `Cylinder` is necessary. The reason for casting to `Cylinder` is to use the `findVolume()` method, which is available only in the `Cylinder` class. However, explicit casting from geoObject[i] to `Circle` is not necessary, because the `findArea()` method is defined in the `GeometricObject` class and overridden in the `Circle` class. By means of polymorphism, the `findArea()` method of the `Circle` is invoked if the geometric object is a circle.

TIP

I recommend that you use the `instanceof` operator to ensure that the source object is an instance of the target class before performing a casting.

The *Object* Class

Every class in Java is descended from the `java.lang.Object` class. If no inheritance is specified when a class is defined, the superclass of the class is `Object`. Classes like `Rational`, `Mortgage`, and `GeometricObject` are implicitly the child classes of `Object` (as are all the main classes you have seen in this book so far). It is important to be familiar with the methods provided by the `Object` class so that you can use them in your classes. Three useful instance methods in the `Object` class are:

- `public boolean equals(Object object)`
- `public String toString()`
- `public Object clone()`

The *equals()* Method

The `equals()` method tests whether two objects are equal. The syntax for using `equals()` is as follows:

```
object1.equals(object2);
```

The components `object1` and `object2` are of the same class.

The default implementation of the `equals()` method in the `Object` class is as follows:

```
public boolean equals(Object obj)
{
  return (this == obj);
}
```

Thus, using the `equals()` method is equivalent to the `==` operator in the `Object` class, but it is really intended for the subclasses of the `Object` class to modify the `equals()` method to test whether two objects of the same class have the same contents.

You have already used the `equals()` method to compare two strings in Chapter 6, "Arrays and Strings." The `equals()` method in the `String` class is inherited from the `Object` class and is modified in the `String` class to test whether the contents of two strings are identical.

NOTE

The `==` comparison operator is used for comparing two primitive data type values, or for determining whether two objects have the same references. The `equals()` method is intended to test whether two objects have the same contents, provided that it is modified in the defining class of the objects. The `==` operator is stronger than the `equals()` method.

The *toString()* Method

The `object.toString()` method returns a string that represents the value of this object. By default, it returns a string consisting of a class name of which the object is an instance, the at sign (@), and a number representing the object. For example, consider the following code:

```
Cylinder myCylinder = new MyCylinder(5.0, 2.0);
System.out.println(myCylinder.toString());
```

This code displays something like `Cylinder@15037e5`. This message is not very helpful and not informative. Usually you should overwrite the `toString()` method so that it returns a digestible string representation of the object. For example, you can override the `toString()` method in the `Cylinder` class:

```
public String toString()
{
  return "Cylinder length = " + length;
}
```

Then, `System.out.println(myCylinder.toString())` displays something like the following:

```
Cylinder length = 2
```

Alternatively, you could write `System.out.println(myCylinder)` instead of
`System.out.println(myCylinder.toString())`. The Java compiler automatically translates `myCylinder` into a string by invoking its `toString()` method
when it is used in the `print` method.

The *clone()* Method

When you need to make a copy of an object, you would attempt to use the assignment statement, as follows:

```
newObject = someObject;
```

This statement does not create a duplicate object. It simply assigns the reference of
`someObject` to `newObject`. To create a new object with separate memory space, you
need to use the `clone()` method:

```
newObject = someObject.clone();
```

This statement copies `someObject` to a new memory location and assigns the reference of the new object to `newObject`.

━━ NOTE
Some objects cannot be cloned. To make an object clonable, the class of the
object must implement the `java.lang.Clonable` interface. Interfaces are introduced in the section "Interfaces," in this chapter.

━━ NOTE
The `Object` class also contains the `wait()` and `notify()` methods to control
threads, which are used in Chapter 13, "Multithreading."

Processing Primitive Type Values as Objects

Primitive data types are not used as objects in Java, because the primitive data values are heavily used and treating primitive data types as objects would have slowed
the language's performance, due to the overhead of processing objects. However,
many Java methods require the use of objects as arguments. Java offers a convenient way to wrap a primitive data type into an object (for example, wrapping `int`
into the class `Integer`). The corresponding class is called a *wrapper class* in Java terminology.

By using wrapper objects instead of a primitive data type variable, you can take ad-
vantage of generic programming. An example of generic programming is given in
Example 7.5, "Design Abstract Classes," and Example 7.6, "Extending Abstract
Classes."

Wrapper classes provide constructors, constants, and conversion methods for manipulating various data types. Java provides `Boolean`, `Character`, `Double`, `Float`, `Byte`, `Short`, `Integer`, and `Long` wrappers for primitive data types. All the wrapper classes are grouped in the `java.lang` package.

NOTE

The wrapper class name for a primitive type is the same as the primitive data type name with the first letter capitalized. The exception are `Integer` and `Character`.

The next section discusses numeric wrapper classes, specifically the `Integer` and `Double` classes. For more detailed information about wrapper classes, refer to the Java API documentation in JBuilder Help.

The *Number* Class and Its Subclasses

Because numeric wrapper classes (`Byte`, `Double`, `Float`, `Integer`, `Long`, `Short`) are very similar, their common methods are generalized in an abstract superclass named `Number`. The `Number` class defines abstract methods to convert the represented numeric value to `byte`, `double`, `float`, `int`, `long`, and `short`. These methods are implemented in the subclasses of `Number`:

■ `public byte byteValue()`

   This returns the number as a `byte`.

■ `public short shortValue()`

   This returns the number as a `short`.

■ `public int intValue()`

   This returns the number as an `int`.

■ `public long longValue()`

   This returns the number as a `long`.

■ `public float floatValue()`

   This returns the number as a `float`.

■ `public double doubleValue()`

   This returns the number as a `double`.

Numeric Wrapper Class Constructors

You can construct a numeric wrapper object either from a primitive data type value or from a string representing the numeric value. The constructors are:

```
public Integer(int value)
public Integer(String s)
public Double(double value)
public Double(String s)
```

For example:

```
Double doubleObject = new Double(5.0);
```

or

```
Double doubleObject = new Double("5.0");
```

This constructs a wrapper object for Double value 5.0.

```
Integer integerObject = new Integer(5);
```

or equivalently

```
Integer integerObject = new Integer("5");
```

This constructs a wrapper object for Integer value 5.

Numeric Wrapper Class Constants

Each numerical wrapper class has constants: MAX_VALUE and MIN_VALUE. MAX_VALUE represents the maximum value of the corresponding primitive data type. For Byte, Short, Integer, and Long, MIN_VALUE represents the minimum byte, short, int, and long value. For Float and Double, MIN_VALUE represents the minimum *positive* float and double value. The following statements, for example, display the maximum integer (2,147,483,647), minimum positive float (1.4E-45), and maximum double floating-point number (1.79769313486231570e+308d).

```
System.out.println("The maximum integer is " + Integer.MAX_VALUE);
System.out.println("The minimum positive float is " +
   Float.MIN_VALUE);
System.out.println(
   "The maximum double precision floating-point number is " +
   Double.MAX_VALUE);
```

Conversion Methods

Each numeric wrapper class implements the abstract methods doubleValue(), floatValue(), intValue(), longValue(), and shortValue(), which are defined in the Number class. It also overrides the toString() and equals() method defined in the Object class.

For example:

```
long l = doubleObject.longValue();
```

This converts doubleObject's double value to a long variable l.

```
int i = integerObject.intValue();
```

This assigns the int value of integerObject to i.

```
double d = 5.9;
Double doubleObject = new Double(d);
String s = doubleObject.toString();
```

This converts double d to a string s.

The *valueOf()*, *parseInt()* and *parseDouble()* Methods

The numeric wrapper classes have a useful static method `valueOf(String s)`. This method creates a new object, initialized to the value represented by the specified string. For example:

```
Double doubleObject = Double.valueOf("12.4");
Integer integerObject = Integer.valueOf("12");
```

The `Integer` wrapper class has some methods that are not available in `Double`. The `parseInt()` method, for example, is only available in integer wrappers `Integer` and `Long`, but not in `Double` or `Float`.

```
public static int parseInt(String s, int radix)
```

This returns the integer value represented in the string s with the specified `radix`. If `radix` is omitted, base 10 is assumed.

Since JDK 1.2, the `Double` class supports a static method `parseDouble()` with following signature for converting a numeric string into a double value.

```
public static double parseDouble(String s)
```

Class-Design Guidelines

The key to object-oriented programming is to model the application in terms of cooperative objects. Carefully designed classes are critical when developing projects. There are many levels of abstractions in system design. You have learned method abstraction and have applied it to the development of large programs. Methods are means of grouping statements. Classes extend abstraction to a higher level and provide a means of grouping methods. Classes do more than just group methods, however; they also contain data fields. Methods and data fields together describe the properties and behaviors of classes.

The power of classes is further extended by inheritance. Inheritance enables a class to extend existing classes without knowing the details of the existing classes. In developing a Java program, you apply class abstraction to decompose the problem into a set of related classes, and apply method abstraction to design classes.

The following are some guidelines for designing classes:

- A class should use the `private` modifier to hide its data from direct access by clients. This prevents the clients from damaging the data. A class also should hide methods not intended for client use. The `gcd()` method in the `Rational` class is private, for example, because it is only for internal use within the class. Getter and setter methods are used to provide clients with access to hidden data—but only to hidden data you want the client to see or to modify.

- A property that is shared by all the instances of the class should be declared as a class property. For example, the `MAX_VALUE` constant is shared by all the objects of the `Integer` class, therefore, it is declared as a class variable. A method that is not dependent on a specific instance should be declared as a class method. For instance, the parseInt() method in the Integer class is not tied to a specific instance of the Integer class, therefore, it is declared as a class method. The class properties and methods are denoted using the static modifier.

■ A class should describe a single entity or a set of similar operations. You can use a class for students, for example, but do not combine students and staff in the same class. Since the Math class provides mathematical operations, it is natural to group the mathematical methods in one class. A single entity with too many responsibilities can be broken into several classes to separate responsibilities. The String class, StringBuffer class, and StringTokenizer class all deal with strings, for example, but they have different responsibilities.

■ Group common data fields and operations shared by other classes into a superclass. Sometimes this will be an abstract class. For example, the classes Integer, Long, Float, and Double share many common data fields and operations, which are grouped into the abstract class Number. Use inheritance to model the is-a relationship. A student or faculty member is a person, for example, so Student can be designed as a subclass of Person.

■ Follow standard Java programming style. Choose informative names for classes, data fields, and methods. Always place data declarations before constructors, and place constructors before methods. Always provide a constructor and initialize variables to avoid programming errors.

Case Studies (Optional)

This section presents a case study on designing classes for matrix operations. Operations like addition and multiplication are similar for all types of matrices except that their element types differ. As a result, you can design a superclass that describes the common operations shared by all types of matrices regardless of their element types, and create subclasses tailored to a specific type of matrix. Example 7.5 gives the superclass named GenericMatrix, and Example 7.6 presents two subclasses named IntegerMatrix and RationalMatrix that extend GenericMatrix for handling integer matrix operations and rational matrix operations.

Example 7.5 Designing Abstract Classes

This example gives a generic class for matrix arithmetic. The class implements matrix addition and multiplication common for all types of matrices. You will use the Integer matrix and the Rational matrix to test this generic class in Example 7.6.

continues

The generic class named GenericMatrix is created with the following data fields and methods:

Data field:

Object[][] matrix: Data representation for this matrix.

Methods:

public Object[][] addMatrix(Object[][] secondMatrix)

Add secondMatrix with this matrix.

public Object[][] multiplyMatrix(Object[][] secondMatrix)

Multiply secondMatrix with this matrix.

public abstract Object add(Object o1, Object o2);

Abstract method for adding two elements of the matrices.

public abstract Object multiply(Object o1, Object o2);

Abstract method for multiplying two elements of the matrices.

public abstract Object zero();

Abstract method for defining zero for the matrix element.

public static void displayMatrix(Object[][] m)

Display a matrix.

```java
// GenericMatrix.java: Define a matrix and its associated
// operations such as add and multiply
package Chapter7;

public abstract class GenericMatrix
{
  // Representation of a matrix using a two-dimensional array
  private Object[][] matrix;

  // Construct a matrix
  public GenericMatrix(Object[][] matrix)
  {
    this.matrix = matrix;
  }

  // Add two matrices
  public Object[][] addMatrix(Object[][] secondMatrix)
  {
    // Create a result matrix
    Object[][] result =
      new Object[matrix.length][matrix[0].length];

    // Check bounds of the two matrices
    if ((matrix.length != secondMatrix.length) ||
        (matrix[0].length != secondMatrix.length))
    {
      System.out.println(
```

```
        "The matrices do not have the same size");
      System.exit(0);
    }

    // Perform addition
    for (int i=0; i<result.length; i++)
      for (int j=0; j<result[i].length; j++)
        result[i][j] = add(matrix[i][j], secondMatrix[i][j]);

    return result;
  }

  // Multiply two matrices
  public Object[][] multiplyMatrix(Object[][] secondMatrix)
  {
    // Create result matrix
    Object[][] result =
      new Object[matrix.length][secondMatrix[0].length];

    // Check bounds
    if (matrix[0].length != secondMatrix.length)
    {
      System.out.println("Bounds error");
      System.exit(0);
    }

    // Perform multiplication of two matrices
    for (int i=0; i<result.length; i++)
      for (int j=0; j<result[0].length; j++)
    {
      result[i][j] = zero();

      for (int k=0; k<matrix[0].length; k++)
      {
        result[i][j] = add(result[i][j],
          multiply(this.matrix[i][k], secondMatrix[k][j]));
      }
    }

    return result;
  }

  // Abstract method for adding two elements of the matrices
  public abstract Object add(Object o1, Object o2);

  // Abstract method for multiplying two elements of the matrices
  public abstract Object multiply(Object o1, Object o2);

  // Abstract method for defining zero for the matrix element
  public abstract Object zero();

  // Display a matrix
  public static void displayMatrix(Object[][] m)
  {
    for (int i=0; i<m.length; i++)
    {
      for (int j=0; j<m[0].length; j++)
        System.out.print(m[i][j].toString()+"  ");
      System.out.print('\n');
    }
  }
}
```

continues

Example Review

Because the element type in the matrix is not specified, the program doesn't know how to add or multiply two matrix elements or what the zero value is for the element (for example, 0 for `int` or 0/1 for `Rational`). Therefore, `add()`, `multiply()`, and `zero()` are defined as abstract methods. They are implemented in the subclasses in which the matrix element type is specified.

The matrix element type is `Object`. This enables you to use an object of any class, as long as you can implement the abstract `add()`, `multiply()`, and `zero()` methods.

The `addMatrix()` and `multiplyMatrix()` methods are concrete methods, defined and implemented in this generic class. They are ready to use as long as the `add()`, `multiply()`, and `zero()` methods are implemented.

The `displayMatrix()` method displays the matrix on the console. The `toString()` method is used to display the element.

The `addMatrix()` and `multiplyMatrix()` methods check the bounds of the matrices before performing operations. If the two matrices have incompatible bounds, the program terminates.

NOTE

The parameters of the `add()`, `multiply()`, and `zero()` methods are of the `Object` type; thus, you can pass any object type to these methods. This is another form of polymorphism in object-oriented programming, known as generic programming. Generic programming enables a method to operate on arguments of generic types, making the method reusable with multiple types.

Example 7.6 Extending Abstract Classes

This example gives two programs that utilize the `GenericMatrix` class for integer matrix arithmetic and rational matrix arithmetic.

The following program creates two integer matrices and performs addition and multiplication operations. The output of the program is shown in Figure 7.7.

```
// TestIntegerMatrix.java: Test matrix operations involving
// Integer values
package Chapter7;

public class TestIntegerMatrix
{
  // Main method
  public static void main(String[] args)
  {
    // Create Integer arrays m1, m2
    Integer[][] m1 = new Integer[4][4];
    Integer[][] m2 = new Integer[4][4];
```

```java
      // Intialize Integer arrays m1 and m2
      for (int i=0; i<m1.length; i++)
        for (int j=0; j<m1[0].length; j++)
        {
          m1[i][j] = new Integer(i);
        }

      for (int i=0; i<m2.length; i++)
        for (int j=0; j<m2[0].length; j++)
        {
          m2[i][j] = new Integer(i+j);
        }

      // Create an instance of IntegerMatrix
      IntegerMatrix im1 = new IntegerMatrix(m1);

      // Perform integer matrix addition, and multiplication
      Object[][] m3 = im1.addMatrix((Object[][])m2);
      Object[][] m4 = im1.multiplyMatrix(m2);

      // Display m1, m2, m3, m4
      System.out.println("m1 is ...");
      IntegerMatrix.displayMatrix(m1);
      System.out.println("m2 is ...");
      IntegerMatrix.displayMatrix(m2);
      System.out.println("m1+m2 is ...");
      IntegerMatrix.displayMatrix(m3);
      System.out.println("m1*m2 is ...");
      IntegerMatrix.displayMatrix(m4);
  }
}

// Declare IntegerMatrix derived from GenericMatrix
class IntegerMatrix extends GenericMatrix
{
  // Construct an IntegerMatrix
  public IntegerMatrix(Integer[][] m)
  {
    super(m);
  }

  // Implement the add method for adding two matrix elements
  public Object add(Object o1, Object o2)
  {
    Integer i1 = (Integer)o1;
    Integer i2 = (Integer)o2;
    return new Integer(i1.intValue() + i2.intValue());
  }

  // Implement the multiply method for multiplying two matrix
  // elements
  public Object multiply(Object o1, Object o2)
  {
    Integer i1 = (Integer)o1;
    Integer i2 = (Integer)o2;
    return new Integer(i1.intValue() * i2.intValue());
  }
```

continues

261

```
                         // Implement the zero method to specify zero for Integer
                         public Object zero()
                         {
                           return new Integer(0);
                         }
                     }
```

Figure 7.7 *The program creates two* int *matrices and performs addition and multiplication on them.*

This program creates two rational matrices and performs addition and multiplication operations. The output of the program is shown in Figure 7.8.

```
// TestRationalMatrix.java: Test matrix operations involving
// Rational values
package Chapter7;

import Chapter5.Rational;

public class TestRationalMatrix
{
  // Main method
  public static void main(String[] args)
  {
    // Declare Rational arrays m1, m2
    Rational[][] m1 = new Rational[4][4];
    Rational[][] m2 = new Rational[4][4];

    // Initialize Rational arrays m1 and m2
    for (int i=0; i<m1.length; i++)
      for (int j=0; j<m1[0].length; j++)
      {
        m1[i][j] = new Rational(i,i+1);
        m2[i][j] = new Rational(i,i+1);
      }
```

```
      // Create RationalMatrix instance rm1
      RationalMatrix rm1 = new RationalMatrix(m1);

      // Perform Rational matrix addition, and multiplication
      Object[][] m3 = rm1.addMatrix(m2);
      Object[][] m4 = rm1.multiplyMatrix(m2);

      // Display m1, m2, m3, m4
      System.out.println("m1 is ...");
      RationalMatrix.displayMatrix(m1);
      System.out.println("m2 is ...");
      RationalMatrix.displayMatrix(m2);
      System.out.println("m1+m2 is ...");
      RationalMatrix.displayMatrix(m3);
      System.out.println("m1*m2 is ...");
      RationalMatrix.displayMatrix(m4);
   }
}

// Declare RationalMatrix derived from GenericMatrix
class RationalMatrix extends GenericMatrix
{
   // Construct a RationalMatrix for a given Ratonal array
   public RationalMatrix(Rational[][] m1)
   {
      super(m1);
   }

   // Implement the add method for adding two rational elements
   public Object add(Object o1, Object o2)
   {
      Rational r1 = (Rational)o1;
      Rational r2 = (Rational)o2;
      return r1.add(r2);
   }

   // Implement the multiply method for multiplying two rational
   // elements
   public Object multiply(Object o1, Object o2)
   {
      Rational r1 = (Rational)o1;
      Rational r2 = (Rational)o2;
      return r1.multiply(r2);
   }

   // Implement the zero method to specify zero for Rational
   public Object zero()
   {
      return new Rational(0,1);
   }
}
```

continues

263

Figure 7.8   *The program creates two matrices of rational numbers and performs addition and multiplication on them.*

Example Review

`IntegerMatrix` and `RationalMatrix` are concrete subclasses of `GenericMatrix` for integer matrix arithmetic. They extend the `GenericMatrix` class and implement the `add()`, `multiply()`, and `zero()` methods.

Casting the object from type `Object` to type `Integer` in the `IntegerMatrix` class is necessary because the program needs to use the `intValue()` method for integer addition and multiplication, which are not available in `Object`. For the same reason, similar casting is necessary from type `Object` to type `Rational` in the `RationalMatrix` class.

The `TestIntegerMatrix` program creates and initializes two matrices: `m1` and `m2`. The result of adding them is stored in `m3`, and the result of multiplying them is stored in `m4`. The `TestRationalMatrix` program performs similar operations.

The statement

```
IntegerMatrix im1 = new IntegerMatrix(m1);
```

in `IntegerMatrix` creates `im1` as an instance of `IntegerMatrix` for matrix `m1`, so you can use `im1.addMatrix(m2)` and `im1.multiplyMatrix(m2)` to perform matrix addition and multiplication for `m1` and `m2`. The variable `rm1` was created for the same reason in `RationalMatrix`.

Interfaces

You create a subclass by extending a superclass. Can a subclass extend multiple classes? Java does not allow multiple inheritance, instead you can use interfaces to circumvent the single inheritance restriction. With interfaces, you can obtain the effect of multiple inheritance.

An interface is treated like a special class in Java. Each interface is compiled into a separate bytecode file, just like a regular class. You cannot create an instance for the interface. In most cases, however, you use an interface the same way you use an abstract class. For example, you can use an interface as a data type for a variable, as the result of casting, and so on.

The structure of a Java interface is similar to that of an abstract class in that you can have data and methods. The data, however, must be constants, and the methods can only have declarations without implementation in an interface. The syntax to declare an interface is as follows:

```
modifier interface InterfaceName
{
  // Constants declarations;
  // Methods signatures;
}
```

Suppose you want to design a generic sort method to sort elements. The elements can be an array of objects, such as students, circles, and cylinders. Because compare methods are different for different types of objects, you need to define a generic compare method to determine the order of two objects. Then you can tailor the method to comparing students, circles, and cylinders. For example, you can use student ID as the key for comparing students, radius as the key for comparing circles, and volume as the key for comparing cylinders. Here is how you would use an interface to define a generic compareTo() method:

```
// CompareObject.java: Interface for comparing objects
package Chapter7;

public interface CompareObject
{
  public static final int LESS = -1;
  public static final int EQUAL = 0;
  public static final int GREATER = 1;

  public int compareTo(CompareObject otherObject);
}
```

The compareTo() method determines the order of objects a and b of the CompareObject type. The method a.compareTo(b) returns a value of CompareObject.LESS (-1) if a is less than b; a value of CompareObject.EQUAL (0) if a is equal to b; or a value of CompareObject.GREATER (1) if a is greater than b.

A generic sort method for an array of CompareObject objects can be declared in a class named Sort:

```
// Sort.java: Sort objects
package Chapter7;

public class Sort
{
  // Sort an array of objects using the selection sort approach
  public static void sort(CompareObject[] object)
  {
    CompareObject currentMax;
    int currentMaxIndex;

    for (int i=object.length-1; i>=1; i—)
    {
      // Find the maximum in the object[0..i]
      currentMax = object[i];
      currentMaxIndex = i;
      for (int j=i-1; j>=0; j—)
      {
        if (currentMax.compareTo(object[j]) == -1)
        {
          currentMax = object[j];
          currentMaxIndex = j;
        }
      }

      // Swap list[i] with o[currentMaxIndex] if necessary;
      if (currentMaxIndex != i)
      {
        object[currentMaxIndex] = object[i];
        object[i] = currentMax;
      }
    }
  }
}
```

The Sort class contains the static method named sort. This method is based on the same algorithm as Example 6.2, "Using Arrays in Sorting" (see Chapter 6), except that here the order of two elements is determined by the compareTo() method defined in the CompareObject interface.

To use the sort() method for an array of objects of a specific type, you need to implement the CompareObject interface for that type. The following example demonstrates how to use the interface.

Example 7.7 Using Interfaces

In this example, a program is written to use the generic sorting method to sort an array of circles in increasing order of radius and an array of cylinders in increasing order of volume. The output of the program is shown in Figure 7.9.

```
// TestSortCircleCylinder.java: Using the CompareObject interface
// and the generic sort class to sort circles and cylinders
package Chapter7;

public class TestSortCircleCylinder
{
  // Main method
  public static void main(String[] args)
  {
```

```
        // Create an array of circles
        CompareCircle[] circle = new CompareCircle[10];
        for (int i=0; i<circle.length; i++)
          circle[i] = new CompareCircle(100*Math.random(), 1.0, "white");

        // Sort an array of circles
        Sort.sort(circle);

        // Display sorted circles
        System.out.println("Sorted circles");
        printObject(circle);

        // Create an array of cylinders
        CompareCylinder[] cylinder = new CompareCylinder[10];
        for (int i=0; i<cylinder.length; i++)
          cylinder[i] = new CompareCylinder(
            100*Math.random(), 1.0, "white", 100*Math.random());

        // Sort an array of cylinders
        Sort.sort(cylinder);

        // Display sorted cylinders
        System.out.println("Sorted cylinders");
        printObject(cylinder);
      }

      // Print cylinders
      public static void printObject(Object[] object)
      {
        for (int i=0; i<object.length; i++)
          System.out.println(object[i]);
      }
    }

// CompareCircle is a subclass of Circle, which implements the
// CompareObject interface
class CompareCircle extends Circle implements CompareObject
{
      // Construct a CompareCircle with specified radius, weight, and
      // color
      public CompareCircle(double r, double w, String c)
      {
        super(r, w, c);
      }

      // Implement the compare method defined in CompareObject
      public int compareTo(CompareObject otherObject)
      {
        Circle circle = (Circle)otherObject;
        if (getRadius() < circle.getRadius())
          return LESS;
        else if (getRadius() == circle.getRadius())
          return EQUAL;
        else return GREATER;
      }
    }

// CompareCylinder is a subclass of Cylinder, which implements the
// CompareObject interface
class CompareCylinder extends Cylinder implements CompareObject
{
```

continues

```
                    // Construct a CompareCylinder with radius, weight, and color
                    CompareCylinder(double r, double w, String c, double l)
                    {
                      super(r, w, c, l);
                    }

                    // Implement the compare method defined in CompareObject
                    public int compareTo(CompareObject otherObject)
                    {
                      Cylinder c = (Cylinder) otherObject;
                      if (findVolume() < c.findVolume())
                        return LESS;
                      else if (findVolume() == c.findVolume())
                        return EQUAL;
                      else return GREATER;
                    }

                    // Override the toString method defined in the Object class
                    public String toString()
                    {
                      return "Cylinder volume = " + findVolume();
                    }
                  }
```

Figure 7.9   *The program sorts a list of* Circle *objects by their radii and a list of* Cylinder *objects by their volumes.*

Example Review

The sort() method can be used to sort a list of any objects of the CompareObject type. Any object whose class implements the CompareObject interface is an instance of the CompareObject type. The example creates the classes CompareCircle and CompareCylinder in order to utilize the generic sorting method. The relationship of the class hierarchy is shown in Figure 7.10.

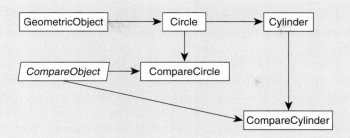

Figure 7.10   *The* CompareCircle *class extends* Circle *and implements* CompareObject; Com-pareCylinder *extends* Cylinder *and implements* CompareObject.

■■■ **NOTE**
This book uses a rectangular box to denote a class and a parallelogram box to denote an interface in the class hierarchy diagram, as in Figure 7.10.

The common functionality is to compare objects in this example, but the compareTo() methods are different for different types of objects. Therefore, the interface CompareObject is used to generalize common functionality and leave the detail for the subclasses to implement.

The keyword implements in the CompareCircle class indicates that CompareCircle inherits all the data from the interface CompareObject and implements the methods in the interface.

The CompareCircle class implements the compareTo() method for comparing the radii of two circles, and the CompareCylinder class implements the compareTo() method for comparing the cylinders based on their volumes.

An interface provides another form of generic programming. It would be difficult to use a generic sort() method to sort all types of objects without using an interface in this example, because multiple inheritance is necessary to inherit the CompareObject class and an object's class, such as Circle or Cylinder.

Suppose you add the compareTo() method in the GeometricObject class. You can define a sort() method as follows:

```
public static void sort(GeometricObject[] list)
```

this new sort() method can be used to sort a list of circles, a list of cylinders, or a list of rectangles, provided that the classes Circle, Cylinder, and Rectangle implement the compareTo() method defined in the GeometricObject class. See Exercise 7.7. There is no need to use the CompareObject interface. This sort() method, however, can only be used to sort instances of the GeometricObject class.

continues

The `Object` class contains the `equals()` method, which is intended for the subclasses of the `Object` class to override for comparing whether the contents of the objects are the same. Suppose the `Object` class contains the `compareTo()` method as defined in the `CompareObject` interface, the new `sort()` method can be used to compare a list of *any* objects. Whether a `compareTo()` method should be included in the `Object` class is debatable. Since the `compareTo()` method is not defined in the `Object` class, the `CompareObject` interface is created to enable a generic `sort()` method to sort a list of the `CompareObject` instances.

CAUTION

Defining an interface is similar to defining an abstract class. There are a few differences, however:

- In an interface, the data must be constants; an abstract class can have all types of data.

- Each method in an interface only has a signature without implementation; an abstract class can have concrete methods.

- No abstract modifier appears in an interface; you must put the abstract modifier before an abstract method in an abstract class.

TIP

Abstract classes and interfaces can both be used to achieve generic programming. Use interfaces if multiple inheritance is needed. Use abstract classes if single inheritance is sufficient. Generally, using an abstract class is simpler than using an interface, but interfaces are more flexible than abstract classes.

Using the Implement Interface Wizard

Often you create a class that implements an interface. JBuilder provides the Implement Interface Wizard, which can be used to create an interface framework with no coding. The framework contains all the methods in the interface. You need to write the code that implements each method.

Suppose you want to implement the `CompareObject` interface in a test program named **Test.java**. Here are the steps in using the Implement Interface Wizard:

1. With the AppBrowser for Chapter7.jpr selected, create Test.java using the New Java File Wizard (see Figure 5.15). The new Java file Test.java is shown in Figure 7.11.

2. Choose Wizards, Implement Interface from the main menu bar to display the Implement Interface Wizard, as shown in Figure 7.12.

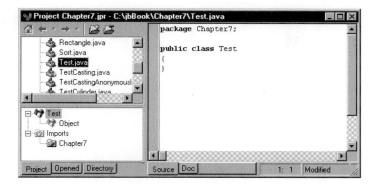

Figure 7.11   *Test.java is shown in the Content pane before the Implement Interface Wizard is applied.*

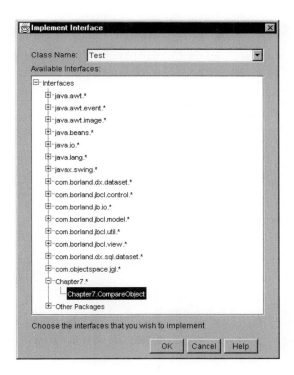

Figure 7.12   *The Implement Interface Wizard enables you to choose an interface from all the interfaces available in the source path and the library.*

3. Expand the node titled Chapter7 and select `CompareObject`. Click OK to close the wizard. JBuilder generated the code to implement the `CompareObject` interface in Test.java, as shown in Figure 7.13.

Figure 7.13   *Test.java is as shown in the Content pane after the Implement Interface Wizard is applied.*

Using the Override Methods Wizard

JBuilder also provides the Override Methods Wizard, which enables you to select a method in a superclass for modification in the subclass. This inserts the method signature at the end of the source code of the subclass. You need to write the code in the method body that overrides it.

Suppose you want to override the `toString()` method of the `Object` class in Test.java. Here are the steps in using the Overrides Methods Wizard:

1. Select Test.java in the Navigation pane, as shown in Figure 7.13.

2. Choose Wizards, Override Methods from the main menu bar to display the Override Inherited Methods Wizard, as shown in Figure 7.14. You will see that all the superclasses of Test are listed in the wizard.

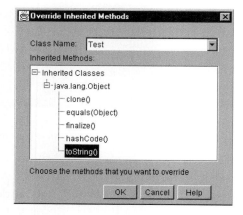

Figure 7.14   *The Override Methods Wizard lists all the superclasses and you can choose a method from a superclass to override.*

3. Expand the node titled `java.lang.Object` and select the `toString()` method. Click OK to close the wizard. JBuilder generated the signature for `toString()`, as shown in Figure 7.15.

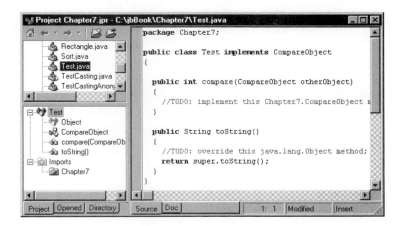

Figure 7.15   *Test.java is shown in the Content pane after the Override Methods Wizard is applied to override the* `toString()` *method.*

Inner Classes

An *inner class*, or *nested class*, is a class defined within the scope of another class. Here is an example of an inner class:

```
// ShowInnerClass.java: Demonstrate using inner classes
package Chapter7;

public class ShowInnerClass
{
  private int data;

  // A method
  public void m()
  {
    // Do something
    InnerClass instance = new InnerClass();
  }

  // An inner class
  class InnerClass
  {
    // A method in the inner class
    public void mi()
    {
      // Directly reference data and method defined in its outer class
      data++;
      m();
    }
  }
}
```

273

The class `InnerClass` is defined inside `ShowInnerClass`. This inner class is just like any regular class, with the following features:

- An inner class can reference the data and methods defined in the outer class in which it nests, so you do not need to pass the reference of the outer class to the constructor of the inner class.

- Inner classes can make programs simple and concise. As you will see, Example 10.8, "The TicTacToe Game," the program is shorter and leaner using inner classes.

- An inner class is only for supporting the work of its containing outer class and is compiled into a class named *OutClassName*`$`*InnerClassName*`.class`. For example, the inner class `InnerClass` in `ShowInnerClass` is compiled into `ShowInnerClass$InnerClass.class`.

NOTE

The inner class can be further shortened with the use of an anonymous inner class. An anonymous inner class is an inner class without a name. An anonymous inner class combines declaring an inner class and creating an instance of the class in one step. Many Java development tools use inner classes to generate adapters for handling events. Event-driven programming is introduced in Chapter 8, "Getting Started with Graphics Programming."

Chapter Summary

In this chapter, you learned about inheritance, an important and powerful concept in object-oriented programming. You can immediately see the benefits of inheritance in Java graphics programming, exception handling, internationalization, multithreading, multimedia, I/O, network programming, and every Java program that inherits and extends existing classes.

You learned how to create a subclass from a superclass by adding new fields and methods. You also can override the methods in the superclass. The keywords `super` and `this` are used to reference the superclass and the subclass, respectively.

You learned to use the `protected` modifier to allow data and methods to be accessed by its subclasses, even if the subclasses are in different packages.

You learned how to use the `final` modifier to prevent changes to a class, method, or variable. A final class cannot be extended. A `final` method cannot be overridden. A `final` variable is a constant.

You learned how to use the `abstract` modifier to design generic superclasses. An abstract class cannot be instantiated. An abstract method contains only the method description without implementation. Its implementation is provided by subclasses.

You learned how to process numeric values as objects. Because most Java methods require the use of objects as arguments, Java provides wrapper classes that model primitive data types as objects. You can take advantage of generic programming by using wrapper objects instead of a primitive data type variable.

You learned how to use an interface to enable multiple inheritance. An interface cannot be instantiated. A subclass can only extend one superclass, but it can implement many interfaces to achieve multiple inheritance.

You learned how to use the Implement Interface Wizard to create a framework for implementing interfaces, and how to use the Override Methods Wizard to modify methods in the superclasses.

Chapter Review

7.1. Describe the following terms: inheritance, superclass, subclass, the keywords `super` and `this`, the modifiers `protected`, `final` and `abstract`, casting objects, and interface.

7.2. Suppose you create a new `Cylinder` class by extending the `Circle` class as follows. Identify the problems in the following classes:

```
package Chapter7;

public class Circle
{
  private double radius;

  public Circle(double radius)
  {
    radius = radius;
  }

  public double getRadius()
  {
    return radius;
  }

  public double findArea()
  {
    return radius*radius*Math.PI;
  }
}

class Cylinder
{
  private double length;

  Cylinder(double radius, double length)
  {
    Circle(radius);
    length = length;
  }

  //find the surface area for the cylinder
  public double findArea()
  {
    return findArea()*length;
  }
}
```

7.3. Indicate true or false for the following statements:

- A protected data or method can be accessed by any class in the same package.
- A protected data or method can be accessed by any class in different packages.
- A protected data or method can be accessed by its subclass in any package.
- A final class can have instances.
- An abstract class can have instances.
- A final class can be extended.
- An abstract class can be extended.
- A final method can be overridden.
- You can always successfully cast a subclass to a superclass.
- You can always successfully cast a superclass to a subclass.
- An interface can be a separate unit and can be compiled into a bytecode file.
- The order in which modifiers appear before a class or a method is important.

7.4. Given the assumption

```
Circle circle = new Circle(1);
Cylinder cylinder = new Cylinder(1,1);
```

are the following Boolean expressions true or false?

```
(circle instanceof Cylinder)
(cylinder instanceof Circle)
```

7.5. Are the following statements correct?

```
Cylinder cylinder = new Cylinder(1,1);
Circle circle = cylinder;
```

7.6. Are the following statements correct?

```
Cylinder cylinder = new Cylinder(1,1);
Circle circle = (Circle)cylinder;
```

7.7. Describe the difference between method overloading and method overriding.

7.8. Does every class have a `toString()` method and an `equals()` method? Where do they come from? How are they used?

7.9. Describe primitive-type wrapper classes. Why do you need these wrapper classes?

7.10. Are the following statements correct?

```
Integer i = new Integer("23");
Integer i = new Integer(23);
Integer i = Integer.valueOf("23");
Integer i = Integer.parseInt("23",8);
Double d = new Double();
Double d = Double.valueOf("23.45");
int i = (Integer.valueOf("23")).intValue();
double d = (Double.valueOf("23.4")).doubleValue();
int i = (Double.valueOf("23.4")).intValue();
String s = (Double.valueOf("23.4")).toString();
```

7.11. Can an inner class be used in a class other than the class in which the inner class nests?

7.12. What modifier should you use on a class so that a class in the same package can access it but a class in a different package cannot access it?

7.13. What modifier should you use so that a class in a different package cannot access the class, but its subclasses in any package can access it?

7.14. Which of the following class definitions defines a legal abstract class?

a.

```
class A
{
  abstract void unfinished()
  {     }
}
```

b.

```
class A
{
  abstract void unfinished();
}
```

c.

```
abstract class A
{
  abstract void unfinished();
}
```

d.

```
public class abstract A
{
  abstract void unfinished();
}
```

7.15. Which of the following is a correct interface?

a.

```
interface A
{
  void print() { };
}
```

b.

```
abstract interface A
{
  print();
}
```

c.

```
abstract interface A
{
  abstract void print() { };
}
```

d.

```
interface A
{
  void print();
}
```

Programming Exercises

7.1. Write a subclass for `Triangle` that extends `GeometricObject`. The class `Triangle` is defined as follows:

```
package Chapter7;

public class Triangle extends GeometricObject
{
  private double side1, side2, side3;

  // Construct a Triangle with the specified sides
  public Triangle(double side1, double side2, double side3);

  // Implement the abstract method findArea in GeometricObject
  public double findArea();

  // Implement the abstract method findPerimeter in
  // GeometricObject
  public double findPerimeter();
}
```

7.2. Create a new class named `NewRational` that extends `java.lang.Number`. The new class contains all the data fields, constructors, and methods defined in the `Rational` class in Example 5.8, "Using the Rational Class." Additionally it must implement the abstract methods defined in the `Number` class. The outline of the `NewRational` class is as follows:

```
public class MyRational extends Number
{
  private int numerator = 0;
  private int denominator = 1;

  public byte byteValue()
  {
    //TODO: override this java.lang.Number method;
  }
```

```
    public double doubleValue()
    {
      //TODO: implement this java.lang.Number abstract method;
    }

    public float floatValue()
    {
      //TODO: implement this java.lang.Number abstract method;
    }

    public int intValue()
    {
      //TODO: implement this java.lang.Number abstract method;
    }

    public long longValue()
    {
      //TODO: implement this java.lang.Number abstract method;
    }

    // other methods and constructor from the Rational class
  }
```

7.3. Modify Example 7.5 to add the following two methods for performing scalar arithmetic with matrix:

```
// Add k with each element in this.matrix
public Object[][] addScalar(Object k);

// Multiply k with each element in this.matrix
public Object[][] multiplyScalar(Object k);
```

Write a client program to test the new methods with `double` type.

7.4. Write a project to meet the following requirements:

■ Write a generic class for vector arithmetic. The following is the outline of the class structure:

```
abstract class GenericVector
{
  Object[] vector;

  // Constructor
  public GenericVector(Object[] vector);

  // Vector addition, return is a new vector. For example,
  // (1, 2, 3) + (1, 2, 3) = (2, 4, 6)
  public Object[] addVector(Object[] vector);

  // Vector multiplication, return is a scalar value.
  // For example,
  // (1, 2, 3) * (1, 2, 3) = 1*1 + 2*2 + 3*3 = 11
  public Object multiplyVector(Object[] vector);

  public abstract Object add(Object o1, Object o2);

  public abstract Object multiply(Object o1, Object o2);

  public abstract Object zero();

  public static void displayVector(Object[] m);
}
```

■ Write a class for `Double` vectors and `Rational` vectors, extending the abstract vector class.

■ Write a client program to test the `Double` and `Rational` vector classes.

7.5. Use an inner class to rewrite Example 5.5, "Changing Data in a Private Field Using a Setter." Make the `Circle` class an inner class.

7.6. Create a class named `CompareRectangle` that extends `Rectangle` and implements `CompareObject`. Implement the `compareTo()` method to compare the rectangles on their areas. Write a test class to sort a list of `CompareRectangle` objects.

7.7. Create a project that meets the following requirements:

■ Add an abstract method `compareTo()` in the `GeometricObject` class as follows:

```
public int compareTo(GeometricObject geoObject)
```

■ Rewrite the `Sort` class with a new `sort()` method signature as follows:

```
public static void sort(GeometricObject[] list)
```

■ Rewrite the `Circle` class that extends the `GeometricObject` class and compare the circles on their sizes.

■ Rewrite the `Cylinder` class that extends the `GeometricObject` class and compare cylinders on their volumes.

■ Write a test class to sort a list of circles and a list of cylinders using the `Sort.sort()` method.

PART III

GRAPHICS PROGRAMMING

In Part II, "Object-Oriented Programming," you learned the basics of object-oriented programming. The design of the API for Java graphics programming is an excellent example of how the object-oriented principle is applied. In this part of the book you will learn the architecture of Java graphics programming API and use the user interface components to develop graphics applications and applets.

GETTING STARTED
WITH GRAPHICS PROGRAMMING

Objectives

- ℮ Describe the Java graphics programming class hierarchy.

- ℮ Understand the concept of event-driven programming.

- ℮ Become familiar with the Java event delegation model: event registration, listening, and handling.

- ℮ Use frames, panels, and simple UI components.

- ℮ Understand the role of layout managers.

- ℮ Use `FlowLayout`, `GridLayout`, and `BorderLayout` managers.

- ℮ Become familiar with the methods: `repaint()`, `update()`, `paint()`, and `paintComponent()`.

- ℮ Become familiar with the classes `Color`, `Font`, and `FontMetrics`.

- ℮ Be able to use the drawing methods in the `Graphics` class.

- ℮ Know to use the Application Wizard to create Java applications in JBuilder.

Introduction

Until now, you have only used text-based input and output. You used `MyInput.readInt()` and `MyInput.readDouble()` to read numbers from the keyboard, and `System.out.println()` to display results on the console. This is the old-fashioned way to program. Today's client/server and Web-based applications use a graphical user interface known as GUI (pronounced gooee).

When Java was introduced, the graphics components were bundled in a library called the *Abstract Window Toolkit,* or *AWT.* For each platform on which Java runs, the AWT components are automatically mapped to the platform-specific components through their respective agents, known as *peers.* AWT is fine for developing simple GUI applications, but not for developing comprehensive GUI projects. Besides, AWT is prone to platform-specific bugs, because its peer-based approach relies heavily on the underlying platform. With the release of Java 2, the AWT user interface components were replaced by a more robust, versatile, and flexible set of a library known as the *Swing components.* Most Swing components are painted directly on canvases using Java code, the exception being the components that are subclasses of `java.awt.Window` or `java.awt.Panel`, which must be drawn using native GUI on a specific platform. Swing components are less dependent on the target platform and use less resource of the native GUI. For this reason, Swing components that don't rely on native GUI are referred to as *lightweight components,* and AWT components are referred to as *heavyweight components.* Although AWT components are still supported in Java 2, I recommend that you learn to program with the Swing components, because the AWT user interface components will eventually fade away.

Java provides a rich set of classes to help you build graphical user interfaces. You can use various GUI-building classes—frames, panels, labels, buttons, text fields, text areas, combo boxes, check boxes, radio buttons, menus, scroll bars, scroll panes, tabbed panes—to construct user interfaces. This chapter introduces the basics of Java graphics programming. Specifically, it discusses GUI components and their relationships, event-driven programming, and two top-level components: `JFrame` and `JPanel`. This chapter gives examples of the use of layout managers to place user interface components (`JButtons`, `JTextField`, and so on) in `JFrame` and `JPanel`. Finally, it introduces the `Graphics` class for drawing geometric figures, such as lines, rectangles, ovals, arcs, and polygons.

NOTE

The Swing components do not replace all of the AWT classes. They only replace the AWT user interface components, namely, `Button`, `TextField`, `TextArea`, etc. The AWT helper classes, `Graphics`, `Color`, `Font`, `FontMetrics`, and `LayoutManager`, remain unchanged. In addition, the Swing components use the AWT event model.

The Java Graphics Class Hierarchy

The design of Java graphics programming API is an excellent example of the use of classes, inheritances, and interfaces. The graphics API contains the essential classes listed below. Their hierarchical relationship is shown in Figure 8.1.

- **Component**—This is a superclass of all user interface classes.

- **Container**—This is used to group components. A container can be embedded in another container. A layout manager is used to position and place the components in the desired location and style in a container. Examples of containers are frames and panels.

- **JComponent**—This is a superclass of all the lightweight Swing components, which are drawn directly on canvases using Java code, rather than using native GUI on specific platforms. Its subclasses, such as JButton, JCheckBox, JMenu, JRadioButton, JLabel, JList, JTextField, JTextArea, and JScrollPane, are the basic elements for constructing the GUI.

- **Window**—The Window class can be used to create a top-level window; however, Window's subclasses—JFrame and JDialog—are often used instead.

- **JFrame**—This is a window that is not contained inside another window. JFrame is the basis that contains other Swing user interface components in Java graphical applications.

- **JDialog**—This is a popup window that is generally used as a temporary window to receive additional information from the user or to provide notification that an event has occurred.

- **JApplet**—This is a subclass of Applet. You must extend JApplet to create any Swing-based Java applets.

- **JPanel**—This is an invisible container that holds user interface components. You can place panels inside panels and in a frame in Java applications or in an applet in Java applets. JPanel can also be used as a canvas to draw graphics.

- **Graphics**—This is an abstract class that provides a graphical context for drawing strings, lines, and shapes.

- **Color**—This deals with the colors of graphics components. For example, you can specify background or foreground colors in a component, such as JFrame and JPanel, or you can specify colors of lines, shapes, and strings in drawings.

- **Font**—This is used to draw strings in Graphics. For example, you can specify the font type (SansSerif), style (bold), and size (24 points) for a string.

- **FontMetrics**—This is an abstract class that is used to get the properties of the fonts used in drawings.

The JFrame, JApplet, JDialog, and JComponent classes and their subclasses are grouped in the package javax.swing. All the other classes in Figure 8.1 are grouped in the package java.awt. Most Swing components are named with the prefix J. The Swing version of Button, for example, is called JButton to distinguish it from its original AWT counterpart.

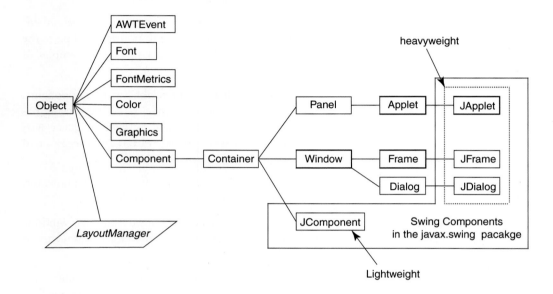

Figure 8.1   *Java graphics programming utilizes the classes shown in this hierarchical diagram.*

NOTE
Swing is a comprehensive solution to developing enterprise GUI applications. There are over 250 classes in Swing. Figure 8.2 illustrates just some of them. The components listed in the dotted rectangle are not covered in the text, since this book is intended to serve only as an introduction to Java graphics programming using Swing. For more detailed coverage of Swing components, including the model-view architecture, look and feel, and advanced components, please refer to my *Rapid Java Application Development Using JBuilder 3*, published by Prentice-Hall.

CAUTION
Do not mix Swing user interface components, such as JButton, with AWT user interface components, such as Button. Do not place JButton in java.awt.Panel; likewise do not place Button in javax.swing.JPanel. Mixing them may cause problems.

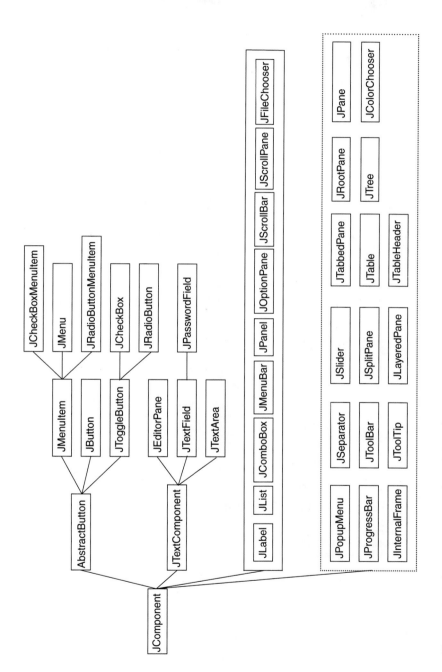

Figure 8.2   *The JComponent and its subclasses are the basic elements for building graphical user interface.*

To create a user interface, you need to create a frame or an applet to hold other user interface components. Figure 8.3 provides examples of possible user interface layouts in a frame and in an applet, respectively.

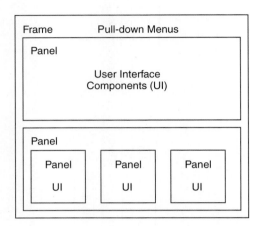
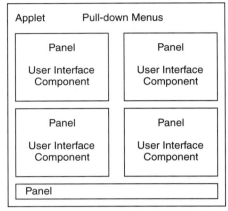

Figure 8.3 *A frame or an applet can contain menus, panels, and user interface components. Panels are used to group user interface components. Panels can contain other panels.*

Creating a Frame

The first thing you want to do with graphics programming is to display a window. Java has a class named `java.awt.Window` that can be used to create a window, but often its subclass `JFrame` is used. The following program creates a frame:

```
// MyFrame.java: Display a frame
package Chapter8;

import javax.swing.*;

public class MyFrame
{
  public static void main(String[] args)
  {
    JFrame frame = new JFrame("Test Frame");
    frame.setSize(400, 300);
    frame.setVisible(true);
  }
}
```

Because `JFrame` is in the package `javax.swing`, the statement `import javax.swing.*` makes all classes from the `javax.swing` package—including `JFrame`—available for use in the `MyFrame` class.

You can use the following two constructors to create a `JFrame` object.

```
JFrame frame = new JFrame(String title);
```

This declares and creates a `JFrame` object `frame` with a specified title.

```
JFrame frame = new JFrame();
```

This declares and creates a JFrame object frame that is untitled.

The frame is not displayed until the frame.setVisible(true) method is applied. frame.setSize(400, 300) specifies that the frame is 400 pixels wide and 300 pixels high. If the setSize() method is not used, the frame will be sized at 0 by 0 pixels, and nothing will be seen except the title bar. The setSize() and setVisible() methods are both defined in the Component class, and therefore are inherited by the JFrame class. Later you will see that these methods are also useful in many other subclasses of Component.

When you run the program MyFrame, the following window will be displayed on-screen (see Figure 8.4).

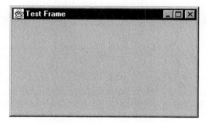

Figure 8.4 *The program creates and displays a frame with the title Test Frame.*

Suppose that you want to terminate the program. Ordinarily, you would click the Window Close button on the upper-right corner or click the upper-left corner to reveal a menu and select Close from it. The window is closed, but the program is still running because you did not tell it to stop when the window is closed. The following section introduces event-handling so that you can tell the program to exit when the window is closed.

NOTE
In Windows 95/98 and Windows NT, you can stop the program by pressing Ctrl+C at the DOS prompt window. With UNIX, you need to use the kill command to kill the process for the program.

Event-Driven Programming

Until this chapter, the programs were object-oriented, but executed in a procedural order. You used decision and loop statements to control the flow of execution, but the program dictated the flow of execution. Java graphics programming is event-driven. In event-driven programming, the codes are executed when events are activated. This section introduces the Java event model.

Event and Event Source

When you run Java graphics programs, the program interacts with the user and the events drive the execution of the program. An *event* can be defined as a type of signal to the program that something has happened. Events are generated by external user actions, such as mouse movements, mouse button clicks, and keystrokes, or by the operating system, such as a timer. The program can choose to respond to or ignore an event.

The GUI component on which the event is generated is called a *source object*. For example, clicking a button triggers an event. The button is the source object. The source object can be obtained by using the getSource() method on the event. Every event is a subclass of the java.util.EventObject class. Various types of events deal with user component actions, mouse movements, and keystrokes. The hierarchical relationship of the graphics events used in this book is shown in Figure 8.5.

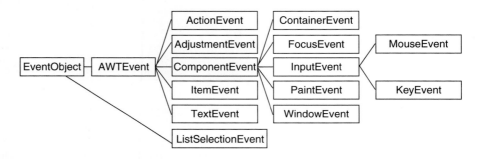

Figure 8.5 *An event is an object of one of the classes in the diagram.*

Event classes contain whatever data values are pertinent to the particular event type. For example, the KeyEvent class defines all key constants, such as VK_DOWN (for down-arrow key), and methods, such as getKeyChar() (returns character associated with the event).

■ **NOTE**
All the event classes in Figure 8.5 are included in the java.awt.event package except for the ListSelectionEvent, which is in the javax.swing.event package. Although the AWT events were originally designed for AWT components, many Swing components can fire them.

Table 8.1 lists external user action, source object, and event type generated.

■ **NOTE**
If a component can generate an event, any subclass of the component can generate the same type of event. For example, every GUI component can generate MouseEvent, KeyEvent, FocusEvent, and ComponentEvent, since Component is the superclass of all GUI components.

TABLE 8.1   User Action, Source Object, and Event Type

User Action	Source Object	Event Type Generated
Clicked on a button	JButton	ActionEvent
Changed text	JTextComponent	TextEvent
Pressed return on a text field	JTextField	ActionEvent
Selected a new item	JComboBox	ItemEvent, ActionEvent
Select item(s)	JList	ListSelectionEvent
Checked a box	JCheckBox	ItemEvent, ActionEvent
Checked a box	JRadioButton	ItemEvent, ActionEvent
Selected a menu item	JMenuItem	ActionEvent
Moved the scroll bar	JScrollBar	AdjustmentEvent
Window opened, closed, iconified, deiconified, or closing	Window	WindowEvent
Component added or removed from the container	Container	ContainerEvent
Component moved, resized, hidden, or shown	Component	ComponentEvent
Component gained or lost focus	Component	FocusEvent
Key released or pressed	Component	KeyEvent
Mouse movement	Component	MouseEvent

Event Registration, Listening, and Handling

Java uses a delegation-based model for event handling: An external user action on a source object triggers an event. An object interested in the event receives the event. Such an object is called a *listener*. Not all objects can receive events. To become a listener, the object must be registered as a listener by the source object. The source object maintains a list of listeners and notifies all the registered listeners by invoking the event-handling method, known as *handler*, on the listener object to respond to the event, as shown in Figure 8.6.

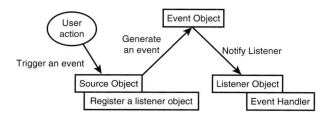

Figure 8.6   *An event is triggered by user actions on the source object, and the source object generates the event object and invokes the handler of the listener object to process the event.*

Here is an example: If a JFrame object is interested in the external events on a JButton source object, the JFrame object must register with the JButton object. The registration is done by invoking a method from the JButton object to declare that the JFrame object is a listener for the JButton object. When you click the button, the JButton object generates an ActionEvent event and notifies the listener by invoking a standard method to handle the event.

NOTE

A source object and a listener object may be the same. A source object may have many listeners. If so, it maintains a queue for all of them.

Registration methods are dependent on the event type. For ActionEvent, the method is addActionListener. In general, the method is named addXListener for XEvent.

For the system to invoke the handler on a listener, the listener must implement the standard handler. The handler is defined in the corresponding event listener interface. Java provides a listener interface for every type of graphics event. For example, the corresponding listener interface for ActionEvent is ActionListener; each listener for ActionEvent should implement the ActionListener interface.

Table 8.2 lists event types, the corresponding listener interface, and the methods defined in the listener interface.

TABLE 8.2   Events, Event Listeners, and Listener Methods

Event Class	Listener Interface	Listener Methods (Handlers)
ActionEvent	ActionListener	actionPerformed(ActionEvent e)
ItemEvent	ItemListener	itemStateChanged(ItemEvent e)
WindowEvent	WindowListener	windowClosing(WindowEvent e)
		windowOpened(WindowEvent e)
		windowIconified(WindowEvent e)
		windowDeiconified(WindowEvent e)
		windowClosed(WindowEvent e)
		windowActivated(WindowEvent e)
		windowDeactivated(WindowEvent e)
ContainerEvent	ContainerListener	componentAdded(ContainerEvent e)
		componentRemoved(ContainerEvent e)
ComponentEvent	ComponentListener	componentMoved(ComponentEvent e)
		componentHidden(ComponentEvent e)
		componentResized(ComponentEvent e)
		componentShown(ComponentEvent e)

Event Class	Listener Interface	Listener Methods (Handlers)
FocusEvent	FocusListener	focusGained(FocusEvent e)
		focusLost(FocusEvent e)
TextEvent	TextListener	textValueChanged(TextEvent e)
KeyEvent	KeyListener	keyPressed(KeyEvent e)
		keyReleased(KeyEvent e)
		keyTyped(KeyEvent e)
MouseEvent	MouseListener	mousePressed(MouseEvent e)
		mouseReleased(MouseEvent e)
		mouseEntered(MouseEvent e)
		mouseExited(MouseEvent e)
		mouseClicked(MouseEvent e)
	MouseMotionListener	mouseDragged(MouseEvent e)
		mouseMoved(MouseEvent e)
AdjustmentEvent	AdjustmentListener	adjustmentValueChanged
		(AdjustmentEvent e)

NOTE

In general, the listener interface is named *X*Listener for *X*Event, except for MouseMotionListener.

Handling Events

A listener object must implement the corresponding listener interface. A listener for a JButton source object, for example, must implement the ActionListener interface. The ActionListener interface contains the actionPerformed(ActionEvent e) method. This method must be implemented in the listener class. Upon receiving the notification, the method is executed to handle the event.

An event object is passed to the handling method. The event object contains information pertinent to the event type. You can get useful data values from the event object for processing the event. For example, for an event object e of the MouseEvent type, you can use e.getX() and e.getY() to obtain the mouse pointer location; in the ActionEvent, you can use e.getSource() to obtain the source object in order to determine whether it is a button, a check box, a radio button, or a menu item.

Here are three examples that use event handling: the first is for the WindowEvent, the second for the MouseEvent, and the last for the ActionEvent.

Example 8.1   Creating a Centered Frame with Exit Handling

This example creates a new frame class that extends the JFrame class with exit handling and a new method for centering the frame. The program displays the frame in the center of the screen when it starts and exits when the window is closing.

Since the closing window event is the WindowEvent type, and its corresponding listener interface is WindowListener, the program must implement the WindowListener interface.

By default, a frame is displayed at the upper-left corner of the screen. To display a frame at a specified location, you can use the setLocation(x, y) method in the JFrame class. This method places the upper-left corner of a frame at location (x, y).

To center a frame on the screen, you need to know the width and height of the screen and the frame in order to determine the frame's upper-left coordinates. The screen width and height can be obtained by using the java.awt.Toolkit class, as follows:

```
Dimension screenSize = Toolkit.getDefaultToolkit().getScreenSize();
int screenWidth = screenSize.width;
int screenHeight = screenSize.height;
```

Therefore, the upper-left x and y coordinates of the frame frame are:

```
Dimension frameSize = frame.getSize();
int x = (screenWidth - frameSize.width)/2;
int y = (screenHeight - frameSize.height)/2;
```

The java.awt.Dimension class encapsulates the width and height of a component (in integer precision) in a single object.

The new frame class MyFrameWithExitHandling is:

```
// MyFrameWithExitHandling.java: Define a new frame with exit
// capability and the center() method
package Chapter8;

import java.awt.*;
import java.awt.event.*;
import javax.swing.JFrame;

public class MyFrameWithExitHandling extends JFrame
  implements WindowListener
{
  // Main method
  public static void main(String[] args)
  {
    MyFrameWithExitHandling frame =
      new MyFrameWithExitHandling("Test Frame");
    frame.setSize(200, 200);
    frame.center();
    frame.setVisible(true);
  }
```

```java
  // Default constructor
  public MyFrameWithExitHandling()
  {
    super();
    addWindowListener(this);  // Register listener
  }

  // Constructor a frame with a title
  public MyFrameWithExitHandling(String title)
  {
    super(title);
    addWindowListener(this); // Register listener
  }

  // Center the frame
  public void center()
  {
    // Get the screen dimension
    Dimension screenSize =
      Toolkit.getDefaultToolkit().getScreenSize();
    int screenWidth = screenSize.width;
    int screenHeight = screenSize.height;

    // Get the frame dimension
    Dimension frameSize = this.getSize();
    int x = (screenWidth - frameSize.width)/2;
    int y = (screenHeight - frameSize.height)/2;

    // Determine the location of the left corner of the frame
    if (x < 0)
    {
      x = 0;
      frameSize.width = screenWidth;
    }

    if (y < 0)
    {
      y = 0;
      frameSize.height = screenHeight;
    }

    // Set the frame to the specified location
    this.setLocation(x, y);
  }

  // Handler for window closed event
  public void windowClosed(WindowEvent event)
  {
  }

  // Handler for window deiconified event
  public void windowDeiconified(WindowEvent event)
  {
  }

  // Handler for window iconified event
  public void windowIconified(WindowEvent event)
  {
  }
```

continues

```
        // Handler for window activated event
        public void windowActivated(WindowEvent event)
        {
        }

        // Handler for window deactivated event
        public void windowDeactivated(WindowEvent event)
        {
        }

        // Handler for window opened event
        public void windowOpened(WindowEvent event)
        {
        }

        // Handler for window closing event
        public void windowClosing(WindowEvent event)
        {
          dispose();
          System.exit(0);
        }
    }
```

Example Review

The main method creates a JFrame instance, sets the window size for the frame using setSize(), centers the frame on the screen using the center() method, and makes it visible using setVisible(true). The frame will not be shown without setVisible(true).

The WindowEvent can be generated by the Window class or by any subclass of Window. Since JFrame is a subclass of Window, it can generate WindowEvent.

MyFrameWithExitHandling extends JFrame and implements WindowListener. The WindowListener interface defines several abstract methods (windowActivated, windowClosed, windowClosing, windowDeactivated, windowDeiconified, windowIconified, windowOpened) for handling the window events when the window is activated, closed, closing, deactivated, deiconified, iconified, or opened.

When a window event such as activation occurs, the windowActivated() method is triggered. You should implement the windowActivated() method with a concrete response if you want the event to be processed.

Because all the methods in the WindowListener interface are abstract, you must implement them all even if your program does not care about some of the events. In MyFrameWithExitHandling, all the window event handlers are implemented, although only the windowClosing() handler is needed. When the window is in the process of closing, the event triggers the windowClosing() method to execute. System.exit(0) terminates the program.

For an object to receive event notification, it must register as an event listener. addWindowListener(this) registers the object of MyFrameWithExitHandling as a window event listener so that the object can receive notification about the window event. MyFrameWithExitHandling is both a listener and a source object.

The `dispose()` method disposes the frame object when the object is no longer needed.

The `center()` method is defined in `MyFrameWithExitHandling`. Invoking this method causes the frame to appear in the center of the screen. This method uses the `java.awt.Toolkit` to obtain platform-dependent information, such as the screen dimension in this example. The `java.awt.Dimension` encapsulates the width and height of a component.

TIP

For all Java graphics applications, you can simply extend the `MyFrameWith-ExitHandling` class to inherit `JFrame` with exit handling and the `center()` method.

Example 8.2 Handling Simple Mouse Events

This example shows a program to create a frame and display a solid square at the mouse pointer when the mouse is pressed. The output of the program is shown in Figure 8.7.

```
// TestMouseEvent.java: Display a filled square at the mouse pointer
// when the mouse is pressed
package Chapter8;

import java.awt.event.*;
import javax.swing.*;
import java.awt.*;

public class TestMouseEvent extends MyFrameWithExitHandling
  implements MouseListener
{
  private int x, y = 0; // x, y coordinates

  // Default constructor
  public TestMouseEvent()
  {
    setTitle("TestMouseEvent");
    addMouseListener(this); // Register listener
  }

  // Main method
  public static void main(String[] args)
  {
    TestMouseEvent frame = new TestMouseEvent();
    frame.setSize(200, 200);
    frame.setVisible(true);
  }

  // When the mouse is pressed, the mouse pointer location
  // will be stored in (x, y)
  public void mousePressed(MouseEvent e)
```

continues

```
  {
    // Get (x, y) coordinates using getX() and getY() methods
    x = e.getX();
    y = e.getY();
    repaint();
  }

  public void mouseClicked(MouseEvent e)
  {
  }

  public void mouseEntered(MouseEvent e)
  {
  }

  public void mouseExited(MouseEvent e)
  {
  }

  public void mouseReleased(MouseEvent e)
  {
  }

  // Draw a small solid square around the point (x, y)
  public void paint(Graphics g)
  {
    g.fillRect(x-5, y-5, 10, 10);
  }
}
```

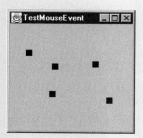

Figure 8.7   *When the mouse button is pressed, a solid square appears that surrounds the area where the mouse pointed.*

Example Review

This program extends `MyFrameWithExitHandling`. For all Java graphics applications throughout the book, you can extend the `MyFrameWithExitHandling` class to inherit `JFrame` with exiting capability without rewriting the same code.

Pressing a mouse button triggers a mouse event (`MouseEvent`) and causes the system to invoke the `mousePressed()` method. This method obtains the mouse-pointer location by using the `e.getX()` and `e.getY()` methods.

The `repaint()` method, defined in the `Component` class, is invoked in the `mousePressed()` method. Invoking `repaint()` causes the `paint()` method to be called. The `paint()` and `repaint()` methods will be further discussed later in this chapter in the section "The `repaint()`, `update()`, `paint()`, and `paintComponent()` Methods."

The `paint()` method displays graphics on the frame. The `paint()` method is defined in the `Component` class. You should always override it to tell the system what you want to paint.

The `g.fillRect()` method is in the `Graphics` class to display a filled rectangle. The parameters in `fillRect()` specify where the rectangle is drawn. Drawing various geometric shapes is introduced in the section "Drawing Geometric Figures," later in this chapter.

TIP

To debug event-driven programs, you can insert a breakpoint at a statement in a handling method that you want to trace. For example, if you want to trace the `mousePressed()` handler, insert a breakpoint at the first line in this method. When the mouse is pressed, the `mousePressed()` handler is invoked, and the program pauses at the breakpoint, as shown in Figure 8.8.

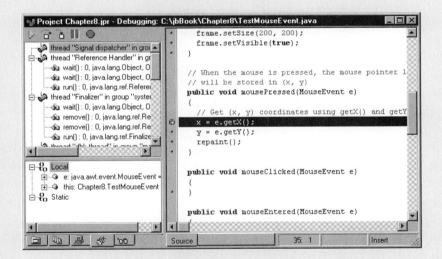

Figure 8.8 *The program pauses at the breakpoint in the* `mousePressed()` *handler.*

NOTE

Although the example draws graphics directly on the frame, this is actually not a good practice. Frame is designed as a container to hold other UI components. Graphics should be drawn on a panel. Panels will be introduced in the section "Using Panels" later in this chapter.

Example 8.3 Handling Simple Action Events

This example presents a program to display a Close button in the window. You can terminate the program by clicking the Close button in the window or on the title bar. Figure 8.9 shows the output of the program.

```java
// TestActionEvent.java: Create a Close button in the frame
package Chapter8;

import javax.swing.*;
import java.awt.*;
import java.awt.event.*;

public class TestActionEvent extends MyFrameWithExitHandling
  implements ActionListener
{
  // Create an object for "Close" button
  private JButton jbtClose = new JButton("Close");

  // Default constructor
  public TestActionEvent()
  {
    // Set the window title
    setTitle("TestActionEvent");

    // Set FlowLayout manager to arrange the components
    // inside the frame
    getContentPane().setLayout(new FlowLayout());

    // Add button to the frame
    getContentPane().add(jbtClose);

    // Register listener
    jbtClose.addActionListener(this);
  }

  // Main method
  public static void main(String[] args)
  {
    TestActionEvent frame = new TestActionEvent();
    frame.setSize(100, 80);
    frame.setVisible(true);
  }

  // This method will be invoked when a button is clicked.
  public void actionPerformed(ActionEvent e)
  {
    if (e.getSource() == jbtClose)
      System.exit(0);
  }
}
```

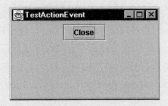

Figure 8.9 *You can close the program by clicking the Close button inside the frame or the Close button on the title bar.*

Example Review

The JFrame uses a content pane, which is a container to hold UI components inside the frame. The method getContentPane() returns the content pane. The statement getContentPane().setLayout(new FlowLayout()) specifies that the components in the content pane are arranged using the FlowLayout style. By default, the Content pane of JFrame uses BorderLayout.

FlowLayout is one of the layout management styles discussed in the next section, "Layout Managers." The layout manager tells the system how to lay out the components in the container. The FlowLayout manager places the components in the container from left to right and row by row.

The statement new FlowLayout() creates an anonymous object of the FlowLayout class, since this object is not directly referenced in the program. However, the statement jbtClose = new JButton("Close") creates a JButton object named jbtClose, because jbtClose needs to be referenced in the program.

The getContentPane().add(jbtClose) method adds the button jbtClose into the frame. JButton is a user interface component whose use is further discussed in Chapter 9, "Creating User Interfaces."

The statement jbtClose.addActionListener(this) registers this (referring to TestActionEvent) to listen to ActionEvent on jbtClose.

Clicking the Close button causes the actionPerformed() to be invoked. The e.getSource() method returns the source object.

■■■■ CAUTION

Missing listener registration is a common mistake with event handling. If the system doesn't notify the listener, the listener cannot act on the events.

Adapters and Anonymous Inner Classes (Optional)

As shown in Figure 8.6, The Java event model is flexible, allowing modifications and variations. One useful variation of the model is to create an adapter for handling events. The adapter is registered as the listener for the source object. When an event occurs, the source object notifies the adapter. The adapter either handles the event or delegates the handling to another object, referred to as the *target object*, as shown in Figure 8.10.

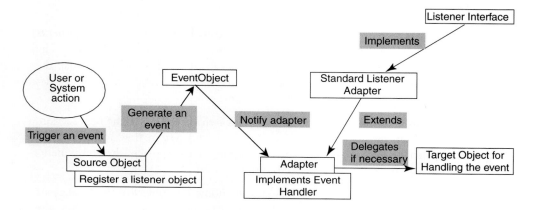

Figure 8.10   *The adapter listens for events and either handles the event or delegates handling to the target object.*

The adapter class should implement the listener interface for the listener it intends to listen, or extend a convenience adapter class for a listener interface. Java provides a convenience adapter class for each listener interface with multiple handlers. The convenience adapter is a simple implementation of the listener interface, containing empty methods for each method defined in the interface. The convenience adapter class is named XAdapter for XListener. For example, MouseListener's corresponding adapter is MouseAdapter. The ActionListener interface does not have a convenience adapter because it contains only one handler (actionPerformed).

Using the adapter, you can rewrite Example 8.2 as follows:

```
// TestMouseEventUsingStandardAdapter.java:
// Using standard adapter
package Chapter8;

import java.awt.event.*;
import javax.swing.*;
import java.awt.*;
```

```
public class TestMouseEventUsingStandardAdapter
  extends MyFrameWithExitHandling
{
  int x, y = 0; // x, y coordinates

  // Default constructor
  public TestMouseEventUsingStandardAdapter()
  {
    setTitle("TestMouseEventUsingStandardAdapter");

    // Register adapter as a listener
    addMouseListener(new StandardMouseAdapter(this));
  }

  // Main method
  public static void main(String[] args)
  {
    TestMouseEventUsingStandardAdapter frame =
      new TestMouseEventUsingStandardAdapter();
    frame.setSize(200, 200);
    frame.setVisible(true);
  }

  // Draw a small solid square around the point (x, y)
  public void paint(Graphics g)
  {
    g.fillRect(x-5, y-5, 10, 10);
  }

  // The real handler for the mousePressed event
  public void processMousePressed(MouseEvent e)
  {
    // Get (x, y) coordinates using getX() and getY() methods
    x = e.getX();
    y = e.getY();
    repaint();
  }
}

// Standard adapter
class StandardMouseAdapter extends MouseAdapter
{
  TestMouseEventUsingStandardAdapter adaptee;

  StandardMouseAdapter(TestMouseEventUsingStandardAdapter adaptee)
  {
    this.adaptee = adaptee;
  }

  // Delegate it to the handler to the adaptee
  public void mousePressed(MouseEvent e)
  {
    adaptee.processMousePressed(e);
  }
}
```

The adapter StandardMouseAdapter serves as an intermediary class interposed between an event source and the target. The reference of the target object is passed to the adapter, since the adapter has to invoke the method in the target object for handling the event. You can shorten the program by implementing Standard-MouseAdapter as an inner class inside the target class, as follows:

```java
// TestMouseEventUsingInnerClass.java: Display a filled square at the
//    mouse pointer
// when the mouse is pressed (Using event adapters)
package Chapter8;

import java.awt.event.*;
import javax.swing.*;
import java.awt.*;

public class TestMouseEventUsingInnerClass
  extends MyFrameWithExitHandling
{
  int x, y = 0; // x, y coordinates

  // Default constructor
  public TestMouseEventUsingInnerClass()
  {
    setTitle("TestMouseEventUsingInnerClass");

    // Register adapter as a listener
    addMouseListener(new InnerClassMouseAdapter());
  }

  // Main method
  public static void main(String[] args)
  {
    TestMouseEventUsingInnerClass frame =
      new TestMouseEventUsingInnerClass();
    frame.setSize(200, 200);
    frame.setVisible(true);
  }

  // Draw a small solid square around the point (x, y)
  public void paint(Graphics g)
  {
    g.fillRect(x-5, y-5, 10, 10);
  }

  // The real handler for the mousePressed event
  public void processMousePressed(MouseEvent e)
  {
    // Get (x, y) coordinates using getX() and getY() methods
    x = e.getX();
    y = e.getY();
    repaint();
  }

  class InnerClassMouseAdapter extends MouseAdapter
  {
    // Delegate it to the handler to the parent class
    public void mousePressed(MouseEvent e)
    {
      processMousePressed(e);
    }
  }
}
```

The program can be further shortened with the use of an anonymous inner class. An *anonymous inner class* is an inner class without a name. An anonymous inner class combines declaring an inner class and creating an instance of the class in one step, as shown in the following code.

```java
// TestMouseEventUsingAnonymousInnerClass.java:
// Using anonymous inner class for event adapter
package Chapter8;

import java.awt.event.*;
import javax.swing.*;
import java.awt.*;

public class TestMouseEventUsingAnonymousInnerClass
  extends MyFrameWithExitHandling
{
  int x, y = 0; // x, y coordinates

  // Default constructor
  public TestMouseEventUsingAnonymousInnerClass()
  {
    setTitle("TestMouseEventUsingAnonymousInnerClass");

    // Register adapter as a listener
    addMouseListener(new MouseAdapter()
    {
      // Delegate it to the handler to the parent class
      public void mousePressed(MouseEvent e)
      {
        processMousePressed(e);
      }
    });
  }

  // Main method
  public static void main(String[] args)
  {
    TestMouseEventUsingAnonymousInnerClass frame =
      new TestMouseEventUsingAnonymousInnerClass();
    frame.setSize(200, 200);
    frame.setVisible(true);
  }

  // Draw a small solid square around the point (x, y)
  public void paint(Graphics g)
  {
    g.fillRect(x-5, y-5, 10, 10);
  }

  // The real handler for the mousePressed event
  public void processMousePressed(MouseEvent e)
  {
    // Get (x, y) coordinates using getX() and getY() methods
    x = e.getX();
    y = e.getY();
    repaint();
  }
}
```

NOTE

Adapters are convenient in some situations, but they are not really needed when creating code manually. For this reason, I designated this section as optional. The examples are all developed without using adapters. Nonetheless, adapters are very useful for automatically associating listener objects with source objects in Java builder tools like JBuilder. For more information on adapters and using adapters in JBuilder, please refer to my *Rapid Java Application Development Using JBuilder 3*.

Layout Managers

In many other windowing systems, the user interface components are often arranged by using hard-coded pixel measurements. For example, put a button at location (10, 10) in the window. Using hard-coded pixel measurements, the user interface may look fine on one system but be unusable on another. Java's layout managers provide a level of abstraction to automatically map your user interface on all windowing systems.

The Java GUI components are placed in containers. Each container has a layout manager to arrange the GUI components within the container. Note that in Example 8.3, you did not specify where to place the Close button in the frame. Java knows where to put it because the layout manager works behind the scenes to place the components in the correct locations. The five basic layout managers are FlowLayout, GridLayout, GridBagLayout, BorderLayout, and CardLayout. These classes implement the LayoutManager interface.

Layout managers are set in a container, such as JFrame, JPanel, or JApplet. Here is the syntax to set the layout manager:

```
container.setLayout(new specificLayout());
```

To add a component to the container, use the add() method. To remove a component from the container, use the remove() method. The following statement adds jbtClose to the container.

```
container.add(jbtClose);
```

The next few sections introduce the FlowLayout, GridLayout, and BorderLayout managers. The CardLayout and GridBagLayout are introduced in Chapter 10, "Applets and Advanced Graphics."

FlowLayout

FlowLayout is the simplest layout manager. The components are arranged in the container from left to right in the order in which they were added. When one row is filled, a new row is started. You can specify the way the components are aligned by using one of three constants: FlowLayout.RIGHT, FlowLayout.CENTER, and FlowLayout.LEFT. You can also specify the gap between components in pixels. FlowLayout has three constructors:

■ public FlowLayout(int align, int hGap, int vGap)

This constructs a new FlowLayout with the specified alignment, horizontal gap, and vertical gap. The gaps are the distances in pixels between components.

■ public FlowLayout(int alignment)

This constructs a new FlowLayout with a specified alignment and a default gap of five pixels horizontally and vertically.

■ public FlowLayout()

This constructs a new FlowLayout with a default center alignment and a default gap of five pixels horizontally and vertically.

Example 8.4 Testing the *FlowLayout* Manager

This example enables a program to arrange components in a frame by using the FlowLayout manager with a specified alignment and horizontal and vertical gaps. The program uses the following simple code to arrange 10 buttons in a frame. The output is shown in Figure 8.11.

```java
// ShowFlowLayout.java: Demonstrate using FlowLayout
package Chapter8;

import javax.swing.JButton;
import java.awt.Container;
import java.awt.FlowLayout;

public class ShowFlowLayout extends MyFrameWithExitHandling
{
  // Default constructor
  public ShowFlowLayout()
  {
    // Get the content pane of the frame
    Container container = getContentPane();

    // Set FlowLayout, aligned left with horizontal gap 10
    // and vertical gap 20 between components
    container.setLayout(new FlowLayout(FlowLayout.LEFT, 10, 20));

    // Add buttons to the frame
    for (int i=1; i<=10; i++)
      container.add(new JButton("Component " + i));
  }

  // Main method
  public static void main(String[] args)
  {
    ShowFlowLayout frame = new ShowFlowLayout();
    frame.setTitle("Show FlowLayout");
    frame.setSize(200, 200);
    frame.setVisible(true);
  }
}
```

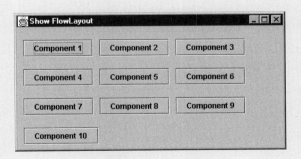

Figure 8.11   *The* FlowLayout *manager is used to add components to fill in the rows in the container one after another.*

continues

Example Review

If you resize the frame, the components are automatically rearranged to fit in the new window.

If you replace the `setLayout` statement with `setLayout(new FlowLayout (FlowLayout.LEFT, 0, 0))`, you will see all the buttons left-aligned with no gaps.

An anonymous object `new FlowLayout()` was created in the program. The `setLayout(new FlowLayout())` is equivalent to the following code:

```
FlowLayout layout = new FlowLayout();
setLayout(layout);
```

This code creates an explicit reference to the object `layout` of the `FlowLayout` class. The explicit reference is not necessary, because the object is not directly referenced in the program.

CAUTION

Don't forget to put the `new` operator before `LayoutManager` when setting a layout style—for example, `setLayout(new FlowLayout())`.

GridLayout

The `GridLayout` manager arranges components in a grid (matrix) formation with the number of rows and columns defined by the constructor. The components are placed in the grid from left to right starting with the first row, then the second, and so on, in the order in which they are added. The `GridLayout` manager has three constructors:

- `public GridLayout(int rows, int columns, int hGap, int vGap)`

  This constructs a new `GridLayout` with the specified number of rows and columns, along with specified horizontal and vertical gaps between components in the container.

- `public GridLayout(int rows, int columns)`

  This constructs a new `GridLayout` with the specified number of rows and columns. The horizontal and vertical gap is zero.

- `public GridLayout()`

  This constructs a new `GridLayout` with one column per component in a single row.

You can specify the number of rows and columns in the grid. The basic rule is given below:

- The number of rows or the number of columns can be zero, but not both. If one is zero and the other is nonzero, the nonzero dimension is fixed, and the zero dimension is determined dynamically by the layout manager. For example, if you specify zero rows and three columns for a grid that has ten components, GridLayout creates three fixed columns of four rows, with the last row containing one component. If you specify three rows and zero columns for a grid that has ten components, GridLayout creates three fixed rows of four columns, with the last row containing two components.

■ If both the number of rows and the number of columns are nonzero, the number of rows is the dominant parameter; that is, the number of rows is fixed, and the layout manager dynamically calculates the number of columns. For example, if you specify three rows and three columns for a grid that has ten components, GridLayout creates three fixed rows of four columns, with the last row containing two components.

Example 8.5 Testing the *GridLayout* Manager

This example presents a program to arrange components on a frame with GridLayout. The program gives the following code to arrange ten buttons in a grid of four rows and three columns. Its output is shown in Figure 8.12.

```java
// ShowGridLayout.java: Demonstrate using GridLayout
package Chapter8;

import java.awt.GridLayout;
import java.awt.Container;
import javax.swing.JButton;

public class ShowGridLayout extends MyFrameWithExitHandling
{
  // Default constructor
  public ShowGridLayout()
  {
    // Get the content pane of the frame
    Container container = getContentPane();

    // Set GridLayout, 4 rows, 3 columns, and gaps 5 between
    // components horizontally and vertically
    container.setLayout(new GridLayout(4, 3, 5, 5));

    // Add buttons to the frame
    for (int i=1; i<=10; i++)
      container.add(new JButton("Component "+i));
  }

  // Main method
  public static void main(String[] args)
  {
    ShowGridLayout frame = new ShowGridLayout();
    frame.setTitle("Show GridLayout");
    frame.setSize(200, 200);
    frame.setVisible(true);
  }
}
```

continues

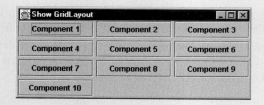

Figure 8.12   *The* GridLayout *manager divides the container into grids, then the components are added to fill in the cells row by row.*

Example Review

If you resize the frame, the layout of the buttons remains unchanged (that is, the number of rows and columns does not change, and the gaps don't change either).

All components in the layout are given equal size in GridLayout.

Replacing the setLayout statement with setLayout(new GridLayout(3, 10)) would yield three rows and *four* columns, with the last row containing two components. The columns parameter is ignored if the rows parameter is nonzero. The actual number of columns is calculated by the layout manager.

NOTE

In FlowLayout and GridLayout, the order in which the components are put into the container is important. It determines the order of the components in the container.

BorderLayout

The BorderLayout manager divides the window into five areas: East, South, West, North, and Center. Components are added to a BorderLayout by using add(Component, index), where index is a constant BorderLayout.EAST, BorderLayout.SOUTH, Border-Layout.WEST, BorderLayout.NORTH, or BorderLayout.CENTER. You can use one of the following two constructors to create a new BorderLayout:

- public BorderLayout(int hGap, int vGap)

  This constructs a new BorderLayout with the specified horizontal and vertical gaps between the components.

- public BorderLayout()

  This constructs a new BorderLayout without horizontal or vertical gaps.

The components are laid out according to their preferred sizes and the constraints of the container's size. The north and south components can stretch horizontally; the east and west components can stretch vertically; the center component can stretch both horizontally and vertically to fill any empty space.

Example 8.6 Testing the *BorderLayout* Manager

This example enables a program to place five buttons in the window by using the BorderLayout manager. The program presents the following code to place East, South, West, North, and Center buttons in the frame by using BorderLayout. The output of the program is shown in Figure 8.13.

```java
// ShowBorderLayout.java: Demonstrate using BorderLayout
package Chapter8;

import java.awt.Container;
import java.awt.BorderLayout;
import javax.swing.JButton;

public class ShowBorderLayout extends MyFrameWithExitHandling
{
  // Default constructor
  public ShowBorderLayout()
  {
    // Get the content pane of the frame
    Container container = getContentPane();

    // Set BorderLayout with horizontal gap 5 and vertical gap 10
    container.setLayout(new BorderLayout(5, 10));

    // Add buttons to the frame
    container.add(new JButton("East"), BorderLayout.EAST);
    container.add(new JButton("South"), BorderLayout.SOUTH);
    container.add(new JButton("West"), BorderLayout.WEST);
    container.add(new JButton("North"), BorderLayout.NORTH);
    container.add(new JButton("Center"), BorderLayout.CENTER);
  }

  // Main method
  public static void main(String[] args)
  {
    ShowBorderLayout frame = new ShowBorderLayout();
    frame.setTitle("Show BorderLayout");
    frame.pack();
    frame.setVisible(true);
  }
}
```

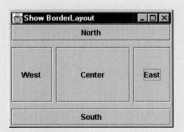

Figure 8.13   BorderLayout *divides the container into five areas, each of which can hold a component.*

continues

Example Review

The buttons are added to the frame. Note that the add() method for BorderLayout is different from FlowLayout and GridLayout. When using BorderLayout, you specify where to put the components.

It is unnecessary to place components to occupy all the areas. If you remove the East button from the program and rerun it, you will see that the center stretches rightward to occupy the East area.

NOTE

For convenience, BorderLayout interprets the absence of an index specification as BorderLayout.CENTER. For example, add(component) is the same as add(Component, BorderLayout.CENTER).

TIP

Always explicitly set a layout style for a container, even though BorderLayout is used by default for the content pane of a JFrame.

Using Panels as Containers

Suppose that you want to place ten buttons and a text field on a frame. The buttons are placed in grid formation, but the text field is placed on a separate row. It is difficult to achieve the desired look by placing all the components into a single container. With Java graphics programming, you can divide a window into panels. The panels act as smaller containers for grouping user interface components. You can add the buttons in one panel, and then add the panel to the frame.

The Swing version of panel is JPanel. The constructor in the JPanel class is simply JPanel(). To add a button to the panel p, for instance, you can use:

```
JPanel p = new JPanel();
p.add(new JButton("ButtonName"));
```

By default, JPanel uses FlowLayout. Panels can be placed inside a frame or inside another panel. The following statement places panel p into frame f:

```
f.getContentPane().add(p);
```

NOTE

To add a component to a JFrame, you actually add it to the content pane of the JFrame. To add a component to a panel, you add it directly to the panel using the add() method.

Example 8.7   Testing Panels

This example uses panels to organize components. The program creates a panel to hold ten buttons labeled 0, 1, 2, and so on to 9, using the GridLayout manager. The panel is placed in the frame by using the BorderLayout manager. The number is displayed in the text field when a number button is clicked. The output is shown in Figure 8.14.

```java
// TestPanels.java: Use panels to group components
package Chapter8;

import java.awt.*;
import java.awt.event.*;
import javax.swing.*;

public class TestPanels extends MyFrameWithExitHandling
  implements ActionListener
{
  // Declare a text field to display a selected number
  private JTextField jtfNum;

  // Create an array of buttons
  private JButton jbtNum[] = new JButton[10];

  // Default constructor
  public TestPanels()
  {
    // Get the content pane of the frame
    Container container = getContentPane();

    // Set BorderLayout for the frame
    container.setLayout(new BorderLayout());

    // Create panel p for the buttons and set GridLayout
    JPanel p = new JPanel();
    p.setLayout(new GridLayout(3, 4));

    // Add buttons to the panel and register listener for each button
    for (int i=0; i<=9; i++)
    {
      p.add(jbtNum[i] = new JButton(" "+i));
      jbtNum[i].addActionListener(this);
    }

    // Create a new text field
    jtfNum = new JTextField();

    // Add the panel and the text field to the frame
    container.add(p, BorderLayout.CENTER);
    container.add(jtfNum, BorderLayout.SOUTH);
  }

  // Main method
  public static void main(String[] args)
  {
    TestPanels frame = new TestPanels();
    frame.setTitle("TestPanels");
    frame.setSize(200,250);
    frame.setVisible(true);
  }
```

continues

```
    // Handler for button actions
    public void actionPerformed(ActionEvent e)
    {
      String actionCommand = e.getActionCommand();
      if (e.getSource() instanceof JButton)
        jtfNum.setText(actionCommand);
    }
}
```

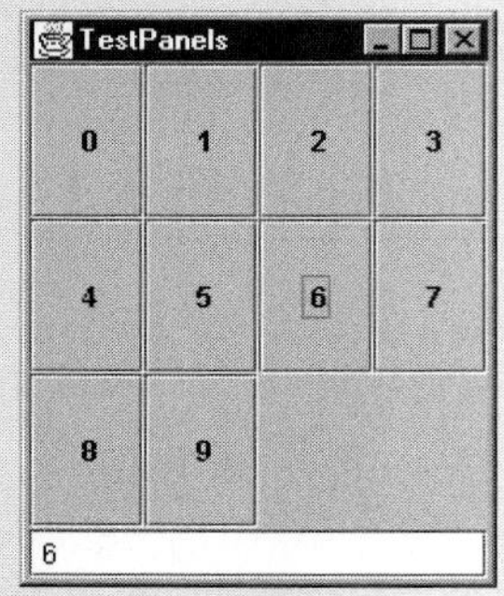

Figure 8.14   *The program uses a panel to group the buttons labeled 0 through 9 and displays the button label on a text field when the button is clicked.*

Example Review

JPanel p is used to group the number buttons by using the GridLayout manager. The program places panel p in the center of the frame and a text field below the panel.

The statement jtfNum = new JTextField() creates an instance of JTextField. Text field is a GUI component that can be used for user input as well as for displaying values. Text fields will be introduced in Chapter 9, "Creating User Interfaces."

Clicking a button triggers the actionPerformed() method to display the label of the button in the text field. If you resize the window, you will see that the button size change, but all the components will remain in the same relative positions.

Using Panels to Draw Graphics

Panels are invisible and are used as small containers to group components in order to achieve a desired layout look. Another important use of JPanel is for drawing graphics.

To draw on a panel, you need to create a new class that extends JPanel and override the paintComponent() method to tell the panel how to draw graphics. You can then display strings, draw geometric shapes, and view images on the panel. Although you can display strings in a frame or directly in an applet, it is recommended that you use JPanel to draw messages and shapes and to show images; this way your drawing does not interfere with other components.

Example 8.8 Drawing on Panels

This example presents a program to create a subclass of JPanel that will display a message. You can use the mouse to move the message. The message moves as the mouse drags and is always displayed at the mouse point. The output of the program is shown in Figure 8.15.

```java
// PanelDrawingDemo.java: Draw on a JPanel
package Chapter8;

import java.awt.*;
import java.awt.event.*;
import javax.swing.*;

public class PanelDrawingDemo extends MyFrameWithExitHandling
{
  // Default constructor
  public PanelDrawingDemo()
  {
    // Create a PaintPanel instance for drawing a message
    PaintPanel p = new PaintPanel("Welcome to Java");

    // Place a drawing panel in the frame
    getContentPane().setLayout(new BorderLayout());
    getContentPane().add(p);
  }

  // Main method
  public static void main(String[] args)
  {
    PanelDrawingDemo frame = new PanelDrawingDemo();
    frame.setTitle("Panel Drawing Demo");
    frame.setSize(300,200);
    frame.setVisible(true);
  }

  // PaintPanel draws a message. This class is defined as inner class
  class PaintPanel extends JPanel implements MouseMotionListener
  {
    private String message;
    private int x = 10;
    private int y = 10;

    // Construct a panel to draw string s
    public PaintPanel(String s)
    {
      message = s;
      this.addMouseMotionListener(this);
      repaint();
    }
```

continues

315

```
                    // Tell the panel how to draw things
                    public void paintComponent(Graphics g)
                    {
                      // It is necessary to invoke this method to clear the viewing
                      // area
                      super.paintComponent(g);

                      // Draw the message at (x, y)
                      g.drawString(message, x, y);
                    }

                    public void mouseMoved(MouseEvent e)
                    {
                    }

                    // Handler for mouse dragged event
                    public void mouseDragged(MouseEvent e)
                    {
                      // Get the new location and repaint the screen
                      x = e.getX();
                      y = e.getY();
                      repaint();
                    }
                  }
                }
```

Figure 8.15   *The program displays "Welcome to Java" on a panel placed in a frame.*

Example Review

The class `PaintPanel` extends `JPanel` and implements `MouseMotionListener`. The `PaintPanel` class is used to display a message. The message is passed to `PaintPanel` through the constructor when creating an object of `PaintPanel`.

The `MouseMotionListener` interface contains two handlers, `mouseMoved()` and `mouseDragged()`, for handling mouse-motion events. When you move the mouse with the button pressed, the `mouseDragged()` method is invoked to repaint the viewing area and display the message at the mouse point.

In Example 8.2, "Handling Simple Mouse Events," you used the `fillRect()` method in the `Graphics` class to display a solid square on a frame. In Example 1.2, "Writing a Simple Applet," you also used the `drawString()` method to display a string on an applet. In this example, the `drawString()` method draws on the panel. The `drawString(s, x, y)` method draws a string s whose left end of the baseline starts at (x, y).

The Swing components use the paintComponent() method to draw things. The paintComponent() method is invoked to paint the graphics context. Invoking super.paintComponent() is necessary to clear the viewing area before a new drawing is displayed. If this method is not invoked, the previous drawings will not be cleared.

The repaint() method is defined in the Component class. Invoking repaint() causes paintComponent() method to be called.

The *repaint(), update(), paint(),* and *paintComponent()* Methods

In Java graphics programming, drawings are painted in graphics mode. The repaint(), update(), paint(), and paintComponent() methods cause strings, lines, figures, and images to be displayed on frames, applets, and panels. It is important to understand the roles of these methods.

The update(), paint(), and paintComponent() methods take a Graphics object as a parameter. The paintings are drawn on this object. The Java system automatically creates a default graphics context, an object of the Graphics class, and passes it to these three methods. This object is local to these methods and cannot be used outside of them.

The repaint(), update(), and paint() methods are defined in the Component class, and are modified in the JComponent class. The repaint() method is invoked to refresh the viewing area. Typically, you call it if you have new things to display. Never override this method. It calls the update() method. In the Component class, the update() method first clears the viewing area and then invokes the paint() method. Sometimes, clearing the entire viewing area is not needed, and repeated erasing and painting causes flickering. For this reason, the update() method was modified in the JComponent to invoke the paint() method directly to avoid clearing the viewing area. In many cases, however, the background needs to be cleared before repainting, so the Swing component introduces the paintComponent() method that clears the background before repainting. The technique known as *double buffering* is implemented with all the Swing components to eliminate flickering. This technique is particularly useful for displaying a sequence of images. From now on, all the paintings will be displayed on Swing components like JPanel.

NOTE

For Swing lightweight components, always use the paintComponent() method rather than the paint() method. If you draw things directly on a heavy weight component like JFrame, as in Example 8.2, you should use the paint() method. The paintComponent() method and the paint() method should never be invoked directly. It is invoked either by the update() method as a result of calling the repaint() method or by the Java system when your viewing area changes.

■■■ NOTE

The `repaint()` method lodges a request to update the viewing area and returns immediately. Its effect is asynchronous, and if several requests are outstanding, it is likely that only the last `paintComponent()` or `paint()` will be done.

■■■ CAUTION

The `paintComponent()` and `paint()` methods are for drawing strings, geometric figures, and images. They are not for displaying user interface components. UI components are displayed in the container using the `setVisible()` method.

The *Color* Class

You can set colors for GUI components by using the `java.awt.Color` class. Colors are made of red, green, and blue components, each of which is represented by a byte value to describe its intensity, ranging from 0 (darkest shade) to 255 (lightest shade). This is commonly known as the RGB model.

The syntax to create a `Color` object is

```
Color color = new Color(r, g, b);
```

in which r, g, and b specify a color by its red, green, and blue components; for example:

```
Color color = new Color(128, 100, 100);
```

You can use the `setBackground(Color c)` and `setForeground(Color c)` methods to set a component's background and foreground colors.

Here is an example of setting the background by using `Color c`:

```
JPanel myPanel = new JPanel();
myPanel.setBackground(c);
```

Alternatively, you can use one of the 13 standard colors (`black`, `blue`, `cyan`, `darkGray`, `gray`, `green`, `lightGray`, `magenta`, `orange`, `pink`, `red`, `white`, `yellow`) defined as constants in `java.awt.Color`. For example, you can use the following code to display a message that uses yellow:

```
JPanel myPanel = new JPanel();
myPanel.setBackground(Color.yellow);
```

■■■ NOTE

The standard color names are constants, but they are named as variables, with lowercase first for the first word, and uppercase for the first letters of subsequent words. Thus the color names violate the Java naming convention.

Drawing Geometric Figures

This section introduces you to drawing in the Graphics context. Java provides a set of methods in the Graphics class that makes it easy to draw geometric figures. These methods are contained in the Graphics class.

All the drawing methods have arguments that specify the locations of the subjects to be drawn. The Java coordinate system has x in the horizontal axis and y in the vertical axis, with the origin (0, 0) at the upper-left corner of the screen. The x coordinate increases to the right, and the y coordinate increases downward. All measurements in Java are made in pixels, as shown in Figure 8.16.

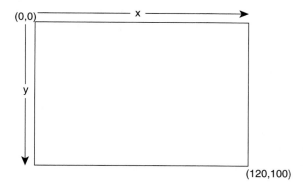

Figure 8.16   *The Java graphics coordinate system is measured in pixels, with* (0, 0) *at its upper-left corner.*

To draw geometric figures, you must either override the paintComponent() method or create a Graphics object and draw graphics there. In many cases, it is easier to draw graphics by overriding paintComponent() in a subclass of JPanel. In some cases, however, you must create your own Graphics object to draw graphics by using the getGraphics() method. You will learn when and how to use the getGraphics() method in Example 10.6, "Handling a Complex Mouse Event," in Chapter 10.

The paintComponent() method takes a Graphics object as an argument. The Graphics object contains a collection of settings, such as fonts and colors. You can set fonts and colors for drawing text, shapes, and images.

The *Font* and *FontMetrics* Classes

You can set the font for the subjects you draw and use font metrics to measure font size. Fonts and font metrics are encapsulated in two AWT classes: Font and FontMetrics.

Whatever font is current will be used in the subsequent drawing. To set a font, you need to create a Font object from the Font class. The syntax is:

```
Font myFont = new Font(name, style, size);
```

You can choose a font name from SansSerif, Serif, Monospaced, Dialog, or DialogInput, and choose a style from Font.PLAIN, Font.BOLD, and Font.ITALIC. The styles can be combined. For example, consider the following code:

```
Font myFont = new Font("SansSerif ", Font.BOLD, 16);
Font myFont = new Font("Serif", Font.BOLD+Font.ITALIC, 12);
```

You can use FontMetrics to compute the exact length and width of a string, which is helpful for measuring a string's size in order to display it in the right position. For example, with the help of the FontMetrics class you can center strings in the viewing area. A FontMetrics is measured by the following attributes (see Figure 8.17):

■ **Leading**—Pronounced *ledding*, this is the amount of space between lines of text.

■ **Ascent**—This is the height of a character, from the baseline to the top.

■ **Descent**—This is the distance from the baseline to the bottom of a descending character, such as *j*, *y*, and *g*.

■ **Height**—This is the sum of leading, ascent, and descent.

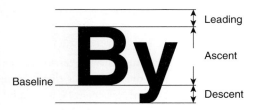

Figure 8.17   *The* FontMetrics *class can be used to determine the font properties of characters.*

To get a FontMetrics object for a specific font, use

```
g.getFontMetrics(Font f); or
g.getFontMetrics(); // Get FontMetrics for current font
```

You can use the following instance methods to obtain font information.

```
public int getAscent()

public int getDescent()

public int getLeading()

public int getHeight()

public int stringWidth(String str)
```

Example 8.9 Using *FontMetrics*

This example presents a program to display "Welcome to Java" in SansSerif 20-point bold, centered in the frame. The output of the program is shown in Figure 8.18.

```java
// TestFontMetrics.java: Draw a message at the center of a panel
package Chapter8;

import java.awt.Font;
import java.awt.FontMetrics;
import java.awt.Graphics;
import javax.swing.JPanel;

public class TestFontMetrics extends MyFrameWithExitHandling
{
  // Main method
  public static void main(String[] args)
  {
    TestFontMetrics frame = new TestFontMetrics();
    frame.setSize(300, 200);
    frame.setTitle("TestFontMetrics");
    frame.setVisible(true);
  }

  // Default constructor
  public TestFontMetrics()
  {
    MessagePanel messagePanel = new MessagePanel("Welcome to Java");
    messagePanel.setCentered(true);
    getContentPane().add(messagePanel);
  }
}

// MessagePanel.java: Display a message on a JPanel
package Chapter8;

import java.awt.Font;
import java.awt.FontMetrics;
import java.awt.Dimension;
import java.awt.Graphics;
import javax.swing.JPanel;

public class MessagePanel extends JPanel
{
  private String message = "Welcome to Java"; // Message to display

  // (x, y) coordinates where the message is displayed
  private int xCoordinate = 20;
  private int yCoordinate = 20;

  // Indicating whether the message is displayed in the center
  private boolean centered;

  // font used to display message
  private Font font = new Font("SansSerif", Font.BOLD, 20);
```

continues

```
// Default constructor
public MessagePanel()
{
  repaint();
}

// Contructor with a message parameter
public MessagePanel(String message)
{
  this.message = message;
  repaint();
}

public String getMessage()
{
  return message;
}

public void setMessage(String message)
{
  this.message = message;
}

public int getXCoordinate()
{
  return xCoordinate;
}

public void setXCoordinate(int x)
{
  this.xCoordinate = x;
}

public int getYCoordinate()
{
  return yCoordinate;
}

public void setYCoordinate(int y)
{
  this.yCoordinate = y;
}

public Font getFont()
{
  return font;
}

public void setFont(Font font)
{
  this.font = font;
}

public boolean isCentered()
{
  return centered;
}

public void setCentered(boolean centered)
{
  this.centered = centered;
}
```

```
public void paintComponent(Graphics g)
{
  super.paintComponent(g);

  if (centered)
  {
    // Get font metrics for the font
    FontMetrics fm = g.getFontMetrics(font);

    // Find the center location to display
    int w = fm.stringWidth(message);  // Get the string width
    int h = fm.getAscent(); // Get the string height
    xCoordinate = (getSize().width-w)/2;
    yCoordinate = (getSize().height+h)/2;
  }

  g.drawString(message, xCoordinate, yCoordinate);
}

public Dimension getPreferredSize()
{
  return new Dimension(200, 100);
}

public Dimension getMinimumSize()
{
  return new Dimension(200, 100);
}
}
```

Figure 8.18   *The program uses the* FontMetrics *class to measure the string width and height and displays them at the center of the frame.*

Example Review

The example contains two classes: TestFontMetrics and MessagePanel. TestFontMetrics creates an instance of MessagePanel to display a message at the center of the panel. TestFontMetrics and MessagePanel are stored in separate files, because MessagePanel is public and will be used by classes in other packages.

The MessagePanel class has the properties: message, xCoordinate, yCoordinate, and centered. xCoordinate and yCoordinate specify where the message is displayed if centered is false. If centered is true, the message is displayed at the center of the panel.

continues

The statement `Font f = new Font("SansSerif", Font.BOLD, 20)` creates a new font with the specified style and size. `g.setFont(f)` sets font for g. The statement `FontMetrics fm = g.getFontMetrics(f)` obtains a FontMetrics instance for font f.

The `getSize()` method defined in the Component class returns the size of this component in the form of a Dimension object. The `height` field of the Dimension object contains the component's height, and the `width` field of the Dimension object contains its width.

Since the `centered` property is set to `true`, the message is displayed in the center of the panel. Resizing the frame results in the message always being displayed in the center of the panel.

The `getPreferredSize()` method defined in Component is overridden in `MessagePanel` to specify a preferred size for the layout manager to consider when laying out a `MessagePanel` object.

Drawing Lines

You can draw a straight line by using the following method:

```
drawLine(x1, y1, x2, y2);
```

The components `(x1, y1)` and `(x2, y2)` are the starting and ending points of the line, as shown in Figure 8.19.

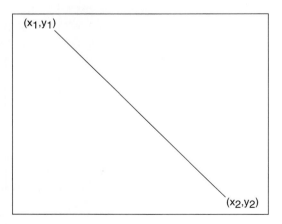

Figure 8.19   *The* `drawLine()` *method draws a line between two specified points.*

Drawing Rectangles

Java provides six methods for drawing rectangles in outline or filled with color. You can draw plain rectangles, rounded rectangles, or 3D rectangles.

To draw a plain rectangle, use:

```
drawRect(x, y, w, h);
```

To draw a rectangle filled with color, use the code:

```
fillRect(x, y, w, h);
```

The component x, y is the upper-left corner of the rectangle, and w and h are the width and height of the rectangle (see Figure 8.20).

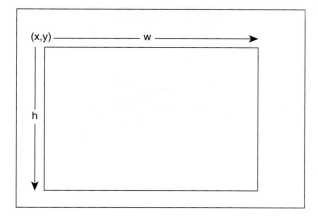

Figure 8.20   *The* drawRect() *method draws a rectangle with specified upper-left corner* (x, y), *width, and height.*

To draw a rounded rectangle, use the following code:

```
drawRoundRect(x, y, w, h, aw, ah);
```

To draw a rounded rectangle filled with color, use this code:

```
fillRoundRect(x, y, w, h, aw, ah);
```

The components x, y, w, and h are the same as in the drawRect() method, the parameter aw is the horizontal diameter of the arcs at the corner, and ah is the vertical diameter of the arcs at the corner (see Figure 8.21).

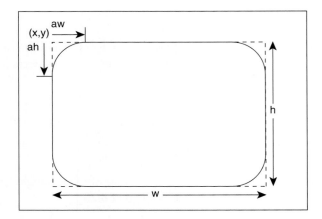

Figure 8.21   *The* drawRoundRect() *method draws a rounded-corner rectangle.*

To draw a 3D rectangle, use

```
draw3DRect(x, y, w, h, raised);
```

in which x, y, w, and h are the same as in drawRect(). The last parameter, a Boolean value, indicates whether the rectangle is raised or indented from the surface.

The example given below demonstrates these methods. The output is shown in Figure 8.22.

```
import java.awt.*;
import javax.swing.JPanel;
public class TestRect extends MyFrameWithExitHandling
{
  public TestRect ();
  { setTitle("Show Rectangles");
    getContentPane() .add(new RectPanel());
  }

  public static void main(string[] args)
  { TestRect frame = new TestRect();
    frame.setSize(300,250);
    frame.setVisible(true);
  }
}

class RectPanel extends jPanel
{
  public void paintComponent(Graphics g)
  { super.paintComponent(g);
    g.drawRect(30,30,100,100); // Draw a rectangle
    g.drawRoundRect(140, 30, 100, 60, 30);
    g.setColor(Color.yellow); // Set new color
    g.fill3DRect(30, 140, 100, 100, true);
  }
}
```

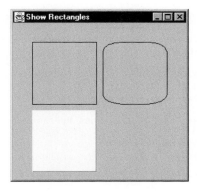

Figure 8.22 *The program draws a rectangle, a rounded rectangle, and a 3D rectangle.*

Ovals

You can use `drawOval()` or `fillOval()` to draw an oval in outline or filled solid. In Java, the oval is drawn based on its bounding rectangle; therefore, give the parameters as if you were drawing a rectangle.

Here is the syntax for drawing an oval:

```
drawOval(x, y, w, h);
```

To draw a filled oval, use the following code:

```
fillOval(x, y, w, h);
```

The parameters x and y indicate the top-left corner of the bounding rectangle, and w and h indicate the width and height, respectively, of the bounding rectangle, as shown in Figure 8.23.

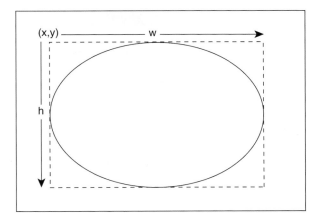

Figure 8.23 *The* `drawOval()` *method draws an oval based on its bounding rectangle.*

Here is an example of how to draw ovals, with the output in Figure 8.24:

```java
// TestOvals.java: Demonstrate drawing ovals
package Chapter8;

import java.awt.Color;
import java.awt.Graphics;
import javax.swing.JPanel;

public class TestOvals extends MyFrameWithExitHandling
{
  // Default constructor
  public TestOvals()
  {
    setTitle("Show Ovals");
    getContentPane().add(new OvalsPanel());
  }

  // Main method
  public static void main(String[] args)
  {
    TestOvals frame = new TestOvals();
    frame.setSize(250, 250);
    frame.setVisible(true);
  }
}

// The class for drawing the ovals on a panel
class OvalsPanel extends JPanel
{
  public void paintComponent(Graphics g)
  {
    super.paintComponents(g);

    g.drawOval(10, 30, 100, 60);
    g.drawOval(130, 30, 60, 60);
    g.setColor(Color.yellow);
    g.fillOval(10, 130, 100, 60);
  }
}
```

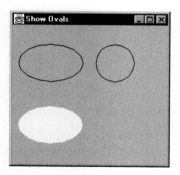

Figure 8.24   *The program draws an oval, a circle, and a filled oval.*

Arcs

Like an oval, an arc is drawn based on its bounding rectangle. An arc is conceived as part of an oval. The syntax to draw or fill an arc is as follows:

```
drawArc(x, y, w, h, angle1, angle2);

fillArc(x, y, w, h, angle1, angle2);
```

The parameters x, y, w, and h are the same as in the drawOval() method; the parameter angle1 is the starting angle; angle2 is the spanning angle (that is, the ending angle is angle1+angle2). Angles are measured in degrees and follow the usual mathematical conventions (that is, 0 degrees is at 3 o'clock, and positive angles indicate counterclockwise rotation; see Figure 8.25).

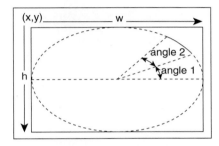

Figure 8.25   *The* drawArc() *method draws an arc based on an oval with specified angles.*

The following is an example of how to draw arcs; the output is shown in Figure 8.26.

```java
// TestArcs.java: Demonstrate drawing arcs
package Chapter8;

import java.awt.Color;
import java.awt.Graphics;
import javax.swing.JPanel;

public class TestArcs extends MyFrameWithExitHandling
{
  // Default constructor
  public TestArcs()
  {
    setTitle("Show Arcs");
    getContentPane().add(new ArcsPanel());
  }

  // Main method
  public static void main(String[] args)
  {
    TestArcs frame = new TestArcs();
    frame.setSize(250, 300);
    frame.setVisible(true);
  }
}
```

```
// The class for drawing arcs on a panel
class ArcsPanel extends JPanel
{
  public void paintComponent(Graphics g)
  {
    super.paintComponent(g);

    g.drawArc(10, 30, 100, 60, 20, 120); // Draw an arc
    g.setColor(Color.yellow); // Set new color
    g.fillArc(10, 150, 100, 60, 120, 300); // Draw another arc
  }
}
```

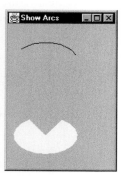

Figure 8.26   *The program draws an arc and a filled arc.*

Polygons

The `Polygon` class encapsulates a description of a closed, two-dimensional region within a coordinate space. This region is bounded by an arbitrary number of line segments, each of which is one side (or edge) of the polygon. Internally, a polygon comprises a list of (x, y) coordinate pairs in which each pair defines a vertex of the polygon, and two successive pairs are the endpoints of a line that is a side of the polygon. The first and final pairs of (x, y) points are joined by a line segment that closes the polygon.

Java provides you with two ways to draw polygons; one uses the direct method, the other uses the `Polygon` object.

The direct method draws a polygon by specifying all the points in the `drawPolygon()` method. The syntax is as follows:

```
drawPolygon(x, y, n);

fillPolygon(x, y, n);
```

Parameters x and y are arrays of x-coordinates and y-coordinates, and n indicates the number of points. For example:

```
int x[] = {40, 70, 60, 45, 20};
int y[] = {20, 40, 80, 45, 60};
g.drawPolygon(x, y, x.length);
g.fillPolygon(x, y, x.length);
```

The drawing method opens the polygon by drawing lines between point (x[i], y[i]) and point (x[i+1], y[i+1]) for i = 0, ... , length-1; it closes the polygon by drawing a line between the first point and the last point (see Figure 8.27).

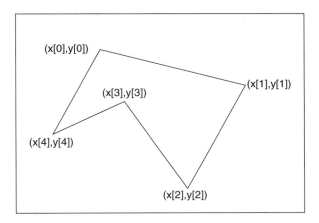

Figure 8.27   *The* drawPolygon() *method draws a polygon with specified points.*

You can also draw a polygon by creating a Polygon object, adding points to it, and finally displaying it. To create a Polygon object, use

```
Polygon poly = new Polygon();
```

or

```
Polygon poly = new Polygon(x, y, n);
```

Parameters x, y, and n are the same as in the previous drawPolygon() method. Here is an example of how to draw a polygon in Graphics g:

```
Polygon poly = new Polygon();
poly.addPoint(20,30);
poly.addPoint(40,40);
poly.addPoint(50,50);
g.drawPolygon(poly);
```

The addPoint() method adds a point to the polygon. The drawPolygon() method also takes a Polygon object as a parameter.

Here is an example of how to draw a polygon, with the output in Figure 8.28:

```
// TestPolygon.java: Demonstrate drawing polygons
package Chapter8;

import java.awt.Graphics;
import java.awt.Polygon;
import javax.swing.JPanel;
```

```java
public class TestPolygons extends MyFrameWithExitHandling
{
  // Default constructor
  public TestPolygons()
  {
    setTitle("Show Polygons");
    getContentPane().add(new PolygonsPanel());
  }

  // Main method
  public static void main(String[] args)
  {
    TestPolygons frame = new TestPolygons();
    frame.setSize(200,250);
    frame.setVisible(true);
  }
}

// Draw a polygon on the panel
class PolygonsPanel extends JPanel
{
  public void paintComponent(Graphics g)
  {
    super.paintComponent(g);

    // Create a Polygon object
    Polygon poly = new Polygon();

    // Add points to the polygon
    poly.addPoint(10, 30);
    poly.addPoint(60, 45);
    poly.addPoint(35, 55);
    poly.addPoint(90, 85);
    poly.addPoint(100, 155);
    poly.addPoint(50, 155);

    // Draw the polygon
    g.drawPolygon(poly);
  }
}
```

Figure 8.28   *The program draws a polygon by using the* drawPolygon() *method.*

> **NOTE**
> Prior to JDK 1.1, a polygon was a sequence of lines that were not necessarily closed. But in JDK 1.1, a polygon is always closed. Nevertheless, you can draw a nonclosed polygon using the `drawPolyline(int[] x, int[] y, int nPoints)` method, which draws a sequence of connected lines defined by arrays of x and y coordinates. The figure is not closed if the first point differs from the last point.

Case Studies

This case study presents an example of combining various drawing methods and trigonometric methods to draw a clock showing the current time in a frame. To draw a clock, you need to draw the circle and three hands for second, minute, and hour. To draw a hand, you need to specify the two ends of the line. As shown in Figure 8.29, one end is the center of the clock at (xCenter, yCenter), and the other end, at (xEnd, yEnd), is determined by the following formula:

```
xEnd = xCenter + handLength × sin(τ)
yEnd = yCenter - handLength × cos(τ)
```

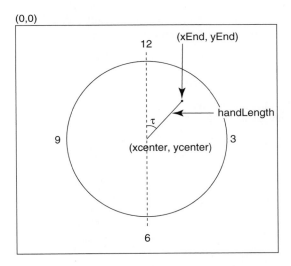

Figure 8.29 *The endpoint of a clock hand can be determined given the spanning angle, the hand length, and the center point.*

The angle τ is in radians. Let `second`, `minute`, and `hour` denote the current second, minute, and hour.

The angle for the second hand is

```
second × (2π/60)
```

The angle for the minute hand is

```
(minute + second/60)×(2π/60)
```

The angle for the hour hand is

```
(hour + minute/60 + second/(60×60))) × (2π/12)
```

For simplicity, you can omit the seconds when computing the angles of the minute hand and the hour hand, since the seconds are very small and can be neglected. Therefore the end points for the second hand, minute hand, and hour hand can be computed as

```
xSecond = xCenter + secondHandLength × sin(second × (2π/60))
ySecond = yCenter - secondHandLength × cos(second × (2π/60))
xMinute = xCenter + minuteHandLength × sin(minute × (2π/60))
yMinute = yCenter - minuteHandLength × cos(minute × (2π/60))
xHour = xCenter + hourHandLength × sin((hour + minute/60)(2π/60)))
yHour = yCenter - hourHandLength × cos((hour + minute/60) ×
        (2π/60)))
```

Example 8.10 Drawing a Clock

This example presents a program that displays a clock based on the specified hour, minute, and second. The hour, minute, and second are passed to the program as command-line arguments like this:

```
java DisplayClock hour minute second
```

The program is given next, and its output is shown in Figure 8.30.

```java
// DisplayClock.java: Display a clock in a panel
package Chapter8;

import java.awt.*;
import java.util.*;
import java.text.*;
import javax.swing.*;

public class DisplayClock extends MyFrameWithExitHandling
{
  // Main method with three auguments:
  // args[0]: hour
  // args[1]: minute
  // args[2]: second
  public static void main(String[] args)
  {
    // Declare hour, minute, and second values
    int hour = 0;
    int minute = 0;
    int second = 0;

    // Check usage and get hour, minute, second
    if (args.length > 3)
    {
      System.out.println(
        "Usage: java DisplayClock hour minute second");
```

```
        System.exit(0);
      }
      else if (args.length == 3)
      {
        hour = new Integer(args[0]).intValue();
        minute = new Integer(args[1]).intValue();
        second = new Integer(args[2]).intValue();
      }
      else if (args.length == 2)
      {
        hour = new Integer(args[0]).intValue();
        minute = new Integer(args[1]).intValue();
      }
      else if (args.length == 1)
      {
        hour = new Integer(args[0]).intValue();
      }

      // Create a frame to hold the clock
      DisplayClock frame = new DisplayClock();
      frame.setTitle("Display Clock");
      frame.getContentPane().add(new DrawClock(hour, minute, second));
      frame.setSize(300, 350);
      frame.setVisible(true);
  }
}

// DrawClock.java: Display a clock in JPanel
package Chapter8;

import java.awt.*;
import java.util.*;
import java.text.*;
import javax.swing.*;

public class DrawClock extends JPanel
{
  private int hour;
  private int minute;
  private int second;
  protected int xCenter, yCenter;
  protected int clockRadius;

  // Construct a clock panel
  public DrawClock(int hour, int minute, int second)
  {
    this.hour = hour;
    this.minute = minute;
    this.second = second;
  }

  // Draw the clock
  public void paintComponent(Graphics g)
  {
    super.paintComponent(g);

    // Initialize clock parameters
    clockRadius =
      (int)(Math.min(getSize().width, getSize().height)*0.7*0.5);
    xCenter = (getSize().width)/2;
    yCenter = (getSize().height)/2;
```

continues

335

```java
      // Draw circle
      g.setColor(Color.black);
      g.drawOval(xCenter - clockRadius,yCenter - clockRadius,
        2*clockRadius, 2*clockRadius);
      g.drawString("12",xCenter-5, yCenter-clockRadius);
      g.drawString("9",xCenter-clockRadius-10,yCenter+3);
      g.drawString("3",xCenter+clockRadius,yCenter+3);
      g.drawString("6",xCenter-3,yCenter+clockRadius+10);

      // Draw second hand
      int sLength = (int)(clockRadius*0.9);
      int xSecond =
        (int)(xCenter + sLength*Math.sin(second*(2*Math.PI/60)));
      int ySecond =
        (int)(yCenter - sLength*Math.cos(second*(2*Math.PI/60)));
      g.setColor(Color.red);
      g.drawLine(xCenter, yCenter, xSecond, ySecond);

      // Draw minute hand
      int mLength = (int)(clockRadius*0.75);
      int xMinute =
        (int)(xCenter + mLength*Math.sin(minute*(2*Math.PI/60)));
      int yMinute =
        (int)(yCenter - mLength*Math.cos(minute*(2*Math.PI/60)));
      g.setColor(Color.blue);
      g.drawLine(xCenter, yCenter, xMinute, yMinute);

      // Draw hour hand
      int hLength = (int)(clockRadius*0.6);
      int xHour = (int)(xCenter +
        hLength*Math.sin((hour+minute/60.0)*(2*Math.PI/12)));
      int yHour = (int)(yCenter -
        hLength*Math.cos((hour+minute/60.0)*(2*Math.PI/12)));
      g.setColor(Color.green);
      g.drawLine(xCenter, yCenter, xHour, yHour);

      // Display current time in string
      g.setColor(Color.red);
      String time = "Hour: " + hour + " Minute: " + minute +
        " Second: " + second;
      FontMetrics fm = g.getFontMetrics();
      g.drawString(time, (getSize().width -
        fm.stringWidth(time))/2, yCenter+clockRadius+30);
    }
  }
```

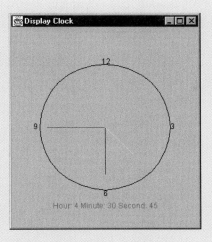

Figure 8.30   *The program displays a clock to show the time with the specified hour, minute, and second.*

Example Review

The `DisplayClock` class obtains command-line arguments for hour, minute, and second, and uses this information to create an instance of `DrawClock`. `DrawClock` is responsible for drawing the clock on a panel.

This program enables the clock size to adjust as the frame resizes. Every time you resize the window, `paintComponent()` is automatically called to paint the new window. The `paintComponent()` method displays the clock in proportion to the window size.

The numeric time (consisting of hour, minute, and second) is displayed below the clock. The program uses font metrics to determine the size of the time string and display it in the center.

Creating Java Applications Using the Application Wizard (Optional)

The Application Wizard is often used to create applications in JBuilder. The Application Wizard creates an application consisting of two files and adds them to the existing project. If no project is open, JBuilder runs the Project Wizard first before it runs the Application Wizard.

In this section, you will use the Application Wizard develop the same program for handling mouse events as in Example 8.2.

Here are the steps to complete the project:

1. With the AppBrowser for Chapter8.jpr selected, choose File, New to display the Object Gallery, as shown in Figure 1.22.

2. Click the Application icon to bring up the Application Wizard, as shown in Figure 8.31.

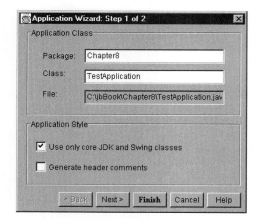

Figure 8.31   *The Application Wizard's Step 1 of 2 dialog box prompts you to enter a package name and an application main class name.*

3. Type TestApplication in the Class field of the Application Wizard's Step 1 of 2, check the option "Use only core JDK and Swing classes," and click Next to display the Application Wizard's Step 2 of 2, as shown in Figure 8.32.

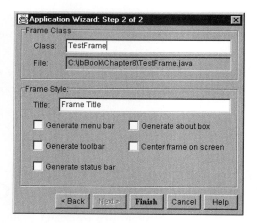

Figure 8.32   *The Application Wizard's Step 2 of 2 dialog box prompts you to enter the frame class name and specify frame style.*

4. Type TestFrame in the Class name and click Finish.

The Application Wizard created the following two files:

■ TestApplication.java, referred to as the *application class*.

■ TestFrame.java, referred to as the *frame class*.

These two files are shown as follows:

```java
// TestApplication.java: Generated by the Application Wizard
package Chapter8;

import javax.swing.UIManager;

public class TestApplication
{
  boolean packFrame = false;

  // Construct the application
  public TestApplication()
  {
    TestFrame frame = new TestFrame();

    // Validate frames that have preset sizes
    // Pack frames that have useful preferred size info,
    // e.g. from their layout
    if (packFrame)
      frame.pack();
    else
      frame.validate();
    frame.setVisible(true);
  }

  // Main method
  public static void main(String[] args)
  {
    try
    {
      UIManager.setLookAndFeel
        (UIManager.getSystemLookAndFeelClassName());
    }
    catch(Exception e)
    {
    }
    new TestApplication();
  }
}

// TestFrame.java: Generated by the Application Wizard
package Chapter8;

import java.awt.*;
import java.awt.event.*;
import javax.swing.*;

public class TestFrame extends JFrame
{
  BorderLayout borderLayout1 = new BorderLayout();

  // Construct the frame
  public TestFrame()
  {
    enableEvents(AWTEvent.WINDOW_EVENT_MASK);
    try
    {
      jbInit();
    }
    catch(Exception e)
    {
      e.printStackTrace();
    }
  }
```

```
    // Component initialization
    private void jbInit() throws Exception
    {
      this.getContentPane().setLayout(borderLayout1);
      this.setSize(new Dimension(400, 300));
      this.setTitle("Frame Title");
    }

    // Overriden so we can exit on System Close
    protected void processWindowEvent(WindowEvent e)
    {
      super.processWindowEvent(e);
      if(e.getID() == WindowEvent.WINDOW_CLOSING)
      {
        System.exit(0);
      }
    }
  }
```

The Java interpreter executes the project starting from the application class. The frame class creates the user interface and performs the actual operations.

The Application Class

The application class contains a constructor and a main method, as shown in Figure 8.33. The constructor creates an instance for the frame class and makes it visible. The main() method is invoked by the Java interpreter to start the application class. Usually you do not need to change any code in the Application class.

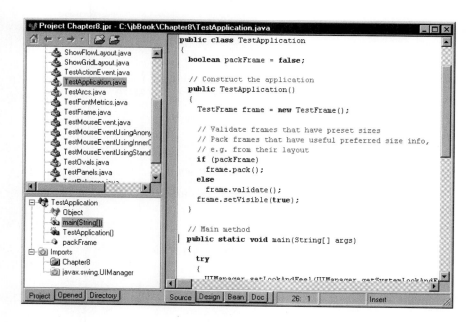

Figure 8.33 *The application class contains a main method and a constructor.*

■■■ NOTE

The main() method also invokes the setLookAndFeel() method in the javax.swing.UIManager class to set the GUI look and feel. Java supports three standard styles of look and feel: Windows, Motif, and Metal. The getSystemLookAndFeelClassName() method returns the name of the LookAndFeel class that implements the native system's look and feel if there is one; otherwise the name of the default cross platform LookAndFeel class is returned.

The Frame Class

You need to modify the frame class to write the right code for the project. Before you modify the frame class, take a look at its contents. Highlighting TestFrame.java in the Navigation pane displays the structure of the source code in the Structure pane and the source code itself in the Content pane (see Figure 8.34).

Figure 8.34 *The frame class contains the code that creates user interface and carries out actual operations.*

The package statement in the first line indicates that the program's bytecode file will be stored in the c:\jbBook\Chapter8 directory. The import statements import standard Java packages and packages supplied with JBuilder. You can import additional packages if needed when you modify the code in the frame class. You can browse the imported classes in the AppBrowser by clicking the class in the Structure pane. For example, To browse JFrame, as shown in Figure 8.35, click JFrame in the Structure pane.

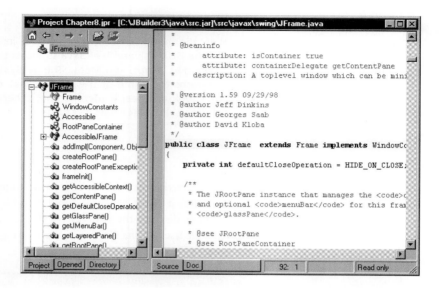

Figure 8.35   *You can browse the Java files you imported to your class in the AppBrowser.*

The `TestFrame` class extends `JFrame`. `TestFrame` has a method `jbInit()` and a constructor. The `jbInit()` method sets the frame's initial size, title, and the layout style. You also can modify or add new code in this method. The constructor simply invokes the `jbInit()` method.

The `processWindowEvent()` method is automatically generated by the Application Wizard. This method is defined in `java.awt.Window`, which is a superclass of `JFrame`. It is invoked when a `WindowEvent` occurs. In `TestFrame`, the `processWindow-Event()` method invokes the same method defined in its superclass and exits the program when the window is closing. Using the `processWindowEvent()` method to exit the program is an alternative to using the `MyFrameWithExitHandling` class.

If you ran the program now, you would see a blank frame.

Modifying the Code in the Frame Class

By now you know the files generated by the Application Wizard as well as their contents. The Application Wizard cannot generate everything you need in the project. To make the program work, you need to modify the `TestFrame` class as follows:

1. Use the Implement Interface Wizard to implement the `MouseListener` interface.

    1.1. Highlight TestFrame.java in the Navigation pane. Choose Wizard, Implement Interface to display the Implement Interface Wizard, as shown in Figure 8.36.

1.2. Expand the node `java.awt.event` to select `MouseListener`. Click OK to let JBuilder generate the code for implementing the `MouseListener`.

1.3. Implement the `mousePressed()` method:

```
public void mousePressed(MouseEvent e)
{
  // TODO: implement this java.awt.event.MouseListener
  // method;
  x = e.getX();
  y = e.getY();
  repaint();
}
```

2. Add the following declaration in the program:

```
private int x, y = 0;
```

3. Add the following line in the `jbInit()` method to register the frame as a listener for mouse events:

```
addMouseListener(this);
```

4. Implement the `paint()` method:

```
public void paint(Graphics g)
{
  // TODO: override this java.awt.Component method;
  g.fillRect(x-5, y-5, 10, 10);
}
```

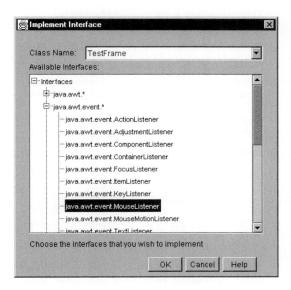

Figure 8.36 *Use the Implement Interface Wizard to create the framework for implementing the MouseListener interface.*

The modified `TestFrame` is shown as follows:

```
// TestFrame.java: Modified TestFrame
package Chapter8;

import java.awt.*;
import java.awt.event.*;
import javax.swing.*;

public class TestFrame extends JFrame implements MouseListener
{
  private int x, y = 0;

  BorderLayout borderLayout1 = new BorderLayout();

  // Construct the frame
  public TestFrame()
  {
    enableEvents(AWTEvent.WINDOW_EVENT_MASK);
    try
    {
      jbInit();
    }
    catch(Exception e)
    {
      e.printStackTrace();
    }
  }

  // Component initialization
  private void jbInit() throws Exception
  {
    this.getContentPane().setLayout(borderLayout1);
    this.setSize(new Dimension(400, 300));
    this.setTitle("Frame Title");

    addMouseListener(this); // Register listener
  }

  // Overriden so we can exit on System Close
  protected void processWindowEvent(WindowEvent e)
  {
    super.processWindowEvent(e);
    if(e.getID() == WindowEvent.WINDOW_CLOSING)
    {
      System.exit(0);
    }
  }

  public void mouseClicked(MouseEvent e)
  {
    // TODO: implement this java.awt.event.MouseListener method;
  }

  public void mousePressed(MouseEvent e)
  {
    // TODO: implement this java.awt.event.MouseListener method;
    x = e.getX();
    y = e.getY();
    repaint();
  }
```

```
      public void mouseReleased(MouseEvent e)
      {
        // TODO: implement this java.awt.event.MouseListener method;
      }

      public void mouseEntered(MouseEvent e)
      {
        // TODO: implement this java.awt.event.MouseListener method;
      }

      public void mouseExited(MouseEvent e)
      {
        // TODO: implement this java.awt.event.MouseListener method;
      }

      public void paint(Graphics g)
      {
        // TODO: override this java.awt.Component method;
        g.fillRect(x-5, y-5, 10, 10);
      }
    }
```

Chapter Summary

In this chapter, you learned Java graphics programming using the container classes, UI component classes, and helper classes.

The container classes, `JFrame`, `JPanel`, and `JApplet`, are used to contain other components. The UI component classes, `JButton`, `JTextField`, `JTextArea`, `JComboBox`, `JList`, `JRadioButton`, and `JMenu`, are subclasses of `JComponent`. They are used to facilitate user interaction. These classes are referred to as Swing UI components and are grouped in the `javax.swing` package.

The helper classes, `Graphics`, `Color`, `Font`, `FontMetrics`, `Dimension`, and `LayoutManager`, are used by components and containers to draw and place objects. These classes are grouped in the `java.awt` package.

Java graphics programming is event-driven. The code is executed upon when events are activated. An event is generated by user actions, such as mouse movements, keystrokes, or clicking buttons. Java uses a delegation-based model to register listeners and handle events. External user actions on the source object generate events. The source object notifies listener objects of events by invoking the handlers implemented by the listener class.

Chapter Review

8.1. Describe the Java graphics class hierarchy. Find the `java.awt` package, `java.awt.event` package, and `javax.swing` package from the JDK documentation in JBuilder Help.

8.2. Describe the methods in `Component`, `Frame`, `JFrame`, `JComponent`, and `JPanel`.

8.3. Describe the difference between the original AWT UI components, such as `java.awt.Button`, and the Swing components, such as `javax.swing.JButton`.

8.4. Can a button generate `WindowEvent`? Can a button generate a `MouseEvent`? Can a button generate an `ActionEvent`?

8.5. Determine whether the following statements are true or false.

- ■ You can add a component to a button.

- ■ You can add a button to a frame.

- ■ You can add a frame to a panel.

- ■ You can add a panel to a frame.

- ■ You can add any number of components to a panel, a frame, or an applet.

- ■ You can derive a class from `JPanel`, `JFrame`, or `JApplet`.

8.6. Describe how to register a listener object and how to implement a listener interface.

8.7. Describe the information contained in an `AWTEvent` object and an object of its subclasses. Find the variables, constants, and methods defined in these event classes.

8.8. How do you override a method defined in the listener interface? Do you need to override all the methods defined in the listener interface?

8.9. What is the event type for a mouse movement? What is the event type for getting key input?

8.10. Describe the `paintComponent()` method. Where is it defined? How is it invoked? Can you use the `paintComponent()` method to draw things directly on a frame?

8.11. Why do you need to use the layout managers?

8.12. Can you use the `setTitle()` method in a panel? Is a panel visible?

8.13. Describe `FlowLayout`. How do you create a `FlowLayout` manager? How do you add a component to a `FlowLayout` container? Is the number of components that can be added to a `FlowLayout` container limited?

8.14. Describe `GridLayout`. How do you create a `GridLayout` manager? How do you add a component to a `GridLayout` container? Is the number of components to be added to a `GridLayout` container limited?

8.15. Describe `BorderLayout`. How do you create a `BorderLayout` manager? How do you add a component to a `BorderLayout` container? List the exact names of the five sections in a `BorderLayout`. Can you add multiple components in the same section?

8.16. Suppose that you want to draw a new message below an existing message. Should the x, y coordinate increase or decrease?

8.17. How do you set colors and fonts in a graphics context? How do you find the current color and font style?

8.18. Describe the drawing methods for lines, rectangles, ovals, arcs, and polygons.

8.19. What methods do you use to detect mouse movements?

8.20. What methods do you use to obtain an input character from a keyboard event?

8.21. Write a statement to draw the following shapes:

- Draw a thick line from (10, 10) to (70, 30). You must draw several lines next to each other to create the effect of one thick line.

- Draw a rectangle of width 100 and height 50 with the upper-left corner at (10, 10).

- Draw a rounded rectangle of width 100, height 200, corner horizontal diameter 40, and corner vertical diameter 20.

- Draw a circle with radius 30.

- Draw an oval with width 50 and height 100.

- Draw the upper half of a circle with radius 50.

- Draw a polygon connecting the following points: (20, 40), (30, 50), (40, 90), (90, 10), (10, 30).

- Draw a 3D cube like the one in Figure 8.37.

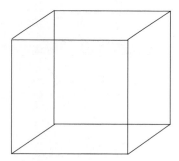

Figure 8.37   *Use the* `drawLine()` *method to draw a 3D cube.*

Programming Exercises

8.1. Write a program to meet the following requirements (see Figure 8.38):

- Create a frame and set its content pane's layout to `FlowLayout`.

- Create two panels and add them to the frame.

- Each panel contains three buttons. The panel uses `FlowLayout`.

- When a button is clicked, display a message indicating that button is clicked on the console.

Figure 8.38   *The first three buttons are placed in one panel, and the remaining three buttons are placed in another panel.*

8.2. Rewrite the preceding program to create the same user interface. Instead of using `FlowLayout` for the frame's content pane, use `BorderLayout`. Place one panel in the south of the content pane and the other panel in the center of the content pane.

8.3. Rewrite the preceding program to create the same user interface. Instead of using `FlowLayout` for the panels, use `GridLayout` of two rows and two columns.

8.4. Rewrite the preceding program to create the same user interface. Instead of creating buttons and panels separately, define a panel class that extends the `JPanel` class. Place three buttons in your panel class, and create three panels from the user-defined panel class.

8.5. Write a program to display the mouse position when the mouse is pressed (see Figure 8.39).

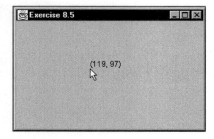

Figure 8.39   *When you click the mouse, the pixel coordinates are shown.*

8.6. Write a program to display a multiplication table in a panel using the drawing methods, as shown in Figure 8.40.

348

Figure 8.40   *The program displays a multiplication table.*

8.7. Write a program to draw the diagram for the function shown below (see Figure 8.41).

(Hint: Create arrays `x[]` and `y[]` for coordinates, and use `drawPolyline` to connect the points.)

```
f(x) = x²;
```

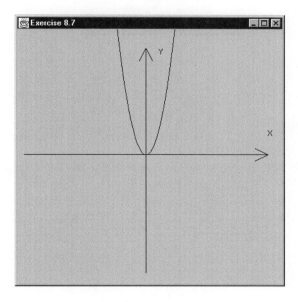

Figure 8.41   *The program draws a diagram for function f(x)= x².*

8.8. Write a generic class to draw the diagram for a function. The class is defined as follows:

```
public abstract class DrawFunction extends JPanel
{
  abstract double f(double x);

  // Draw the function
  public void drawFunction()
  {
  }
}
```

Implement the `drawFunction()` method. Test the class with the following functions:

```
f(x) = x²;
```

```
f(x) = cos(x)+5sin(x);
```

```
f(x) = log(x) + x²;
```

8.9. Write a program to draw a fan with four blades, as shown in Figure 8.42. Draw the circle in blue and the blades in red. (Hints: Use the `fillArc()` method to draw the blades.)

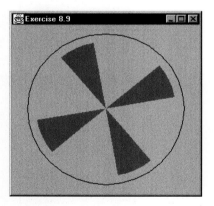

Figure 8.42   *The drawing methods are used to draw a fan with four blades.*

CHAPTER 9

CREATING USER INTERFACES

Objectives

- Become familiar with the JavaBeans concept.

- Know various user interface components: `JButton`, `JLabel`, `JTextField`, `JTextArea`, `JComboBox`, `JList`, `JCheckBox`, `JRadioButton`, `JMenuBar`, `JMenu`, `JMenuItem`, `JCheckBoxMenuItem`, `JRadioButtonMenuItem`, `JScrollBar`, `JScrollPane`, and `JTabbedPane`.

- Create interactive graphical user interfaces using these components.

- Use borders to visually group user interface components.

- Know how to use the message dialog boxes.

- Create multiple windows in an application.

- Implement the listener interface for the user interface components.

Introduction

A graphical user interface (GUI) makes a system easy and fun to use. Creating a GUI requires creativity and knowledge of how GUI components work. Because the GUI components in Java are very flexible, users are able to create an extensive array of different user interfaces.

JBuilder provides tools for visually designing and programming Java classes. This enables you to rapidly assemble the elements of a user interface (UI) for a Java application or applet with minimum coding. Tools, however, cannot do everything. You have to modify the programs they produce. Consequently, before you begin to use the visual tools, it is imperative that you understand the basic concepts of Java graphics programming. Students should finish Chapter 10, "Java Applets and Advanced Graphics," before attempting to use JBuilder's visual tools. Appendix G, "Rapid Java Application Development Using JBuilder," contains an introduction to JBuilder's UI Designer.

This chapter concentrates on the creation of user interfaces. In particular, it discusses the various GUI components that make up a user interface and how to make them work.

JavaBeans

All Swing components are JavaBeans. JavaBeans is a software component architecture that extends the power of the Java language so as to enable well-formed objects to be manipulated visually in a builder tool like JBuilder at design time. Such well-formed objects are referred to as *JavaBeans* or simply *beans*. The classes that define the beans, referred to as *JavaBeans components* or *bean components*, or simply *components*, conform to the JavaBeans component model. The model's requirements are listed below:

- A bean must be a public class.

- A bean must have a public default constructor (one that takes no arguments), although it can have other constructors if needed. For example, a bean named MyBean must either have a constructor with the signature

    ```
    public MyBean();
    ```

    or have no constructors if its superclass has a default constructor.

- A bean must implement the java.io.Serializable or java.io.Externalizable interface to ensure persistent state. JavaBeans can be used in a wide variety of tools, including Lotus, Delphi, MS Visual Basic, and MS Word. When JavaBeans are used in other tools, bean persistence may be required. Some tools need to save the beans and restore them later. Bean persistence ensures that the tools can reconstruct the bean's properties and consistent behaviors to the state they were in when it was saved. For more information on bean persistence and serialization, please refer to my *Rapid Java Application Development Using JBuilder 3*.

■ A bean usually has properties with correctly constructed public accessor methods that enable the properties to be seen and updated visually by a builder tool.

■ A bean may have events with correctly constructed public registration methods that enable the bean to add and remove listeners. If the bean plays a role as the source of events, it must provide registration methods for registering listeners. For example, you can register a listener for ActionEvent using the addActionListener() method of a JButton bean.

The first three requirements must be observed by all beans, and therefore are referred to as *minimum JavaBeans component requirements.* The last two requirements are dependent on implementations. It is possible to write a bean without accessor methods and event registration methods.

A JavaBean component is a special kind of Java class. The relationship of a JavaBean component and a Java class is illustrated in Figure 9.1.

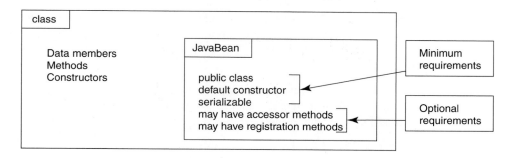

Figure 9.1   *A JavaBean component is a serializable public class with a default constructor.*

The getter method is named get<PropertyName>(), which takes no parameters and returns an object of a type identical to the property type. For example, getContent-Pane() is the getter method for the property contentPane in the JFrame class, which returns an object of the Container type. For a property of the boolean type, the getter method should be named is<PropertyName>(), which returns a boolean value. For example, isVisible() is the getter method for the visible property in the JFrame class, which returns true if the frame is visible.

The setter method is named set<PropertyName>, which takes a single parameter identical to the property type and returns void. For example, setLayout is the setter method for the layout property in the Container class for setting the layout property value.

Once you understand the basics of Java graphics programming, such as containers, layout managers, and event handling, you can learn new components and explore their properties. All but a few Swing components, such as JFrame, JApplet, and JDialog, are subclasses of JComponent. Many Swing component properties are defined in the JComponent class. Here is a list of frequently used properties in JComponent:

- `toolTipText`: The text displayed when the mouse points on the component without clicking. This text is generally used to give the user a tip about the component's function.

- `font`: The font used to display text on the component.

- `background`: The background color of the component.

- `foreground`: The foreground color of the component.

- `doubleBuffered`: Specifies whether the component is painted using double buffering. This is a technique for reducing flickering. In AWT programming, you have to manually implement this technique in the program. With Swing, this capability is automatically supported if the `doubleBuffered` property is set to `true`. By default, it is `true`.

- `border`: Specifies a border of the component. The border types and styles will be introduced in the section "Borders" later in this chapter.

- `preferredSize`: Indicates the ideal size for the component to look best. This property may or may not be considered by the layout manager, depending on its rules. For example, a component uses its preferred size in a container with a `FlowLayout` manager, but its preferred size may be ignored if it is placed in a container with a `GridLayout` manager.

- `minimumSize`: Specifies the minimum size for the component to be useful. For most Swing components, `minimumSize` is the same as `preferredSize`. Layout managers generally respect `minimumSize` rather than `preferredSize`.

- `maximumSize`: Specifies the maximum size the component needs so that the layout manager won't waste space giving it to a component that does not need it. For instance, `BorderLayout` could limit the center component's size to its maximum size, and then either give the space to edge components or limit the size of the outer window when resized.

`font`, `background`, `foreground`, `preferredSize`, `minimumSize`, and `maximumSize` are defined in `java.awt.Component` and inherited in `javax.swing.JComponent`.

The principal benefit of JavaBeans is for use in the Java builder tools for rapid Java application development. As shown in Figure 9.2, you can set the properties of a `JButton` instance in JBuilder's visual designer during design time. See Appendix G for using the visual designer.

UI Designer   Component inspector

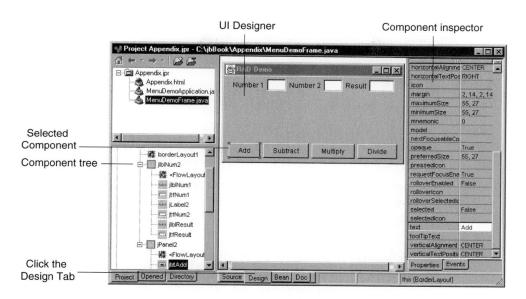

Figure 9.2   *You can set the properties of a JavaBeans instance, such as a* JButton, *during design time.*

Buttons

A *button* is a component that triggers an event when clicked. The Swing version of a button is named JButton. Its default constructor creates an empty button. JButton also has the following constructors:

- public JButton(String text)

  This creates a button labeled with the specified text.

- public JButton(Icon icon)

  This creates a button with the specified icon.

- public JButton(String text, Icon icon)

  This creates a button with the specified text and icon.

An icon is a fixed-size picture; typically it is small and used to decorate components. An icon can be obtained from an image file using the ImageIcon class, such as

```
Icon icon = new ImageIcon("photo.gif");
```

javax.swing.ImageIcon is a subclass of javax.swing.Icon.

NOTE

Java currently supports two image formats: GIF (Graphics Interchange Format) and JPEG (Joint Photographic Experts Group). Image filenames for each of these types end with .gif and .jpg, respectively. If you have a bitmap file, or image files in other formats, you can use image-processing utilities to convert these files into GIF or JPEG format for use in Java.

Since JButton is a subclass of JComponent, all the properties in JComponent can be used in JButton. Additionally, JButton has the following useful properties:

- text: The label on the button. You can set a label using the setText() method.

- icon: The image icon on the button. You can set an icon using the setIcon() method.

- mnemonic: Specifies a shortcut key. You can select the button by pressing the ALT key and the mnemonic key at the same time.

- horizontalAlignment: One of the three values, SwingConstants.LEFT, SwingConstants.CENTER, and SwingConstants.RIGHT, that specify how the label is placed horizontally on a button. The default alignment is SwingConstants.CENTER.

- verticalAlignment: One of the three values, SwingConstants.TOP, SwingConstants.CENTER, and SwingConstants.BOTTOM, that specify how the label is placed vertically on a button. The default alignment is SwingConstants.CENTER.

- horizontalTextPosition: One of the three values, SwingConstants.LEFT, SwingConstants.CENTER, and SwingConstants.RIGHT, that specify the horizontal position of the text relative to the icon. The default alignment is SwingConstants.RIGHT.

- verticalTextPosition: One of the three values, SwingConstants.LEFT, SwingConstants.CENTER, and SwingConstants.RIGHT, that specify the vertical position of the text relative to the icon. The default alignment is SwingConstants.CENTER.

Buttons can generate many types of events, but often you need to respond to an ActionEvent. In order to make a button responsive to the ActionEvent, you must implement the actionPerformed() method in the ActionListener interface. The following code is an example of handling a button event. The code prints out "Button clicked" on the console when the button is clicked.

```
public void actionPerformed(ActionEvent e)
{
  // Make sure the event source is a button.
  if (e.getSource() instanceof JButton)
    System.out.println("Button clicked!");
}
```

Example 9.1 Using Buttons

This example gives a program that displays a message on a panel and uses two buttons, <= and =>, to move the message on the panel to the left or the right. The output of the program is shown in Figure 9.3.

```
// ButtonDemo.java: Use buttons to move message in a panel
package Chapter9;
```

```
        import Chapter8.MyFrameWithExitHandling;
        import Chapter8.MessagePanel;
        import java.awt.*;
        import java.awt.event.ActionListener;
        import java.awt.event.ActionEvent;
        import javax.swing.*;

        public class ButtonDemo extends MyFrameWithExitHandling
          implements ActionListener
        {
          // Declare a panel for displaying message
          private MessagePanel messagePanel;

          // Declare two buttons to move the message left and right
          private JButton jbtLeft, jbtRight;

          // Main method
          public static void main(String[] args)
          {
            ButtonDemo frame = new ButtonDemo();
            frame.pack();
            frame.center();
            frame.setVisible(true);
          }

          public ButtonDemo()
          {
            setTitle("Button Demo");

            // Create a MessagePanel instance and set colors
            messagePanel = new MessagePanel("Welcome to Java");
            messagePanel.setBackground(Color.yellow);

            // Create Panel jpButtons to hold two Buttons "<=" and "right =>"
            JPanel jpButtons = new JPanel();
            jpButtons.setLayout(new FlowLayout());
            jpButtons.add(jbtLeft = new JButton());
            jpButtons.add(jbtRight = new JButton());

            // Set button text
            jbtLeft.setText("<=");
            jbtRight.setText("=>");

            // Set keyboard mnemonics
            jbtLeft.setMnemonic('L');
            jbtRight.setMnemonic('R');

            // Set icons
            //jbtLeft.setIcon(new ImageIcon("images/left.gif"));
            //jbtRight.setIcon(new ImageIcon("images/right.gif"));

            // Set toolTipText on the "<=" and "=>" buttons
            jbtLeft.setToolTipText("Move message to left");
            jbtRight.setToolTipText("Move message to right");

            // Place panels in the frame
            getContentPane().setLayout(new BorderLayout());
            getContentPane().add(messagePanel, BorderLayout.CENTER);
            getContentPane().add(jpButtons, BorderLayout.SOUTH);
```

continues

357

```
                           // Register listeners with the buttons
                           jbtLeft.addActionListener(this);
                           jbtRight.addActionListener(this);
                         }

                         // Handler for button events
                         public void actionPerformed(ActionEvent e)
                         {
                           if (e.getSource() == jbtLeft)
                           {
                             left();
                           }
                           else if (e.getSource() == jbtRight)
                           {
                             right();
                           }
                         }

                         // Move the message in the panel left
                         private void left()
                         {
                           int x = messagePanel.getXCoordinate();
                           if (x > 10)
                           {
                             // Shift the message to the left
                             messagePanel.setXCoordinate(x-10);
                             messagePanel.repaint();
                           }
                         }

                         // Move the message in the panel right
                         private void right()
                         {
                           int x = messagePanel.getXCoordinate();
                           if (x < getSize().width - 20)
                           {
                             // Shift the message to the right
                             messagePanel.setXCoordinate(x+10);
                             messagePanel.repaint();
                           }
                         }
                       }
```

Figure 9.3   *Clicking the <= and => buttons causes the message on the panel to move to left or right, respectively.*

Example Review

The program displays a message on a panel and places two buttons, <= and =>, on a panel below the message panel. The `MessagePanel` class, created in Example 8.9, "Using FontMetrics," displays a message on a panel. When you click a button, the handler, `actionPerformed()`, determines which button is clicked and invokes the `left()` or `right()` method to move the message.

Each button has a tool tip text, which appears when the mouse is set on the button without clicking, as shown in Figure 9.3.

You can set an icon image on the button using the `setIcon()` method. If you replace the `setText()` method with the `setIcon()` method,

```
jbtLeft.setIcon(new ImageIcon("images/left.gif"));
jbtRight.setIcon(new ImageIcon("images/right.gif"));
```

the labels are replaced by the icons, as shown in Figure 9.4. "images/left.gif" is located in "c:\jbBook\Chapter9\images\left.gif" in Windows. Note that the back slash is the Windows file path notation. In Java, the forward slash should be used.

Figure 9.4   *You can set an icon on a* JButton.

If you wish, you can set icons and labels on a button at the same time. By default, the labels and icons are centered horizontally and vertically.

The button can also be accessed using the keyboard mnemonics. Pressing ALT+L is equivalent to clicking the <= button since you set the mnemonics property to 'L' in the left button. If you change the left button text to "Left" and the right button to "Right," the L and R in the captions of these buttons will be underlined, as shown in Figure 9.5.

Figure 9.5   *The buttons can be accessed using the keyboard mnemonics.*

Labels

A *label* is a display area for a short text, an image, or both. It is often used to label other components (usually text fields). As with other components, the layout managers can place labels inside a container. The default constructor of JLabel creates an empty label. Other constructors for JLabel are:

■ public JLabel(String text, int horizontalAlignment)

This creates a label with the specified string and horizontal alignment (SwingConstants.LEFT, SwingConstants.RIGHT, or SwingConstants.CENTER).

■ public JLabel(String text)

This creates a label with a specified text.

■ public JLabel(Icon icon)

This creates a label with an icon.

■ public JLabel(Icon icon, int horizontalAlignment)

This creates a label with the specified image and horizontal alignment.

■ public JLabel(String text, Icon icon, int horizontalAlignment)

This creates a label with the specified text, image, and horizontal alignment.

For example, the following statement creates a label with the string "Interest Rate":

```
JLabel myLabel = new JLabel("Interest Rate");
```

The following statement creates a label with the specified image in the file "images/map.gif":

```
JLabel mapLabel = new JLabel(new ImageIcon("images/map.gif"));
```

JLabel inherits all the properties from JComponent and shares many properties, such as text, icon, horizontalAlignment, and verticalAlignment, with JButton.

Example 9.2 Using Labels

This example gives a program that uses a label as an area for displaying images. There are 52 images in image files named L1.gif, L2.gif, . . . , L52.gif stored in the images directory under c:\jbBook\Chapter9. You can use two buttons, Prior and Next, to browse the images, as shown in Figure 9.6

```
// LabelDemo.java: Use label to display images
package Chapter9;

import Chapter8.MyFrameWithExitHandling;
import java.awt.*;
import java.awt.event.*;
import javax.swing.*;
```

```
public class LabelDemo extends MyFrameWithExitHandling
  implements ActionListener
{
  // Declare an ImageIcon array. There are total 52 images
  private ImageIcon[] imageIcon = new ImageIcon[52];

  // The current image index
  private int currentIndex = 0;

  // Buttons for browsing images
  private JButton jbtPrior, jbtNext;

  // Label for displaying images
  private JLabel jlblImageViewer = new JLabel();

  final int TOTAL_NUMBER_OF_IMAGES = 52;

  // Main Method
  public static void main(String[] args)
  {
    LabelDemo frame = new LabelDemo();
    frame.setSize(500, 500);
    frame.center();
    frame.setVisible(true);
  }

  // Default Constructor
  public LabelDemo()
  {
    setTitle("Label Demo");

    // Load images into imageIcon array
    for (int i=1; i<=52; i++)
    {
      imageIcon[i-1] = new ImageIcon("images/L" + i + ".gif");
    }

    // Show the first image
    jlblImageViewer.setIcon(imageIcon[currentIndex]);

    // Set center alignment
    jlblImageViewer.setHorizontalAlignment(SwingConstants.CENTER);
    //jlblImageViewer.setVerticalAlignment(SwingConstants.CENTER);

    // Panel jpButtons to hold two buttons for browsing images
    JPanel jpButtons = new JPanel();
    jpButtons.add(jbtPrior = new JButton());
    jbtPrior.setIcon(new ImageIcon("images/left.gif"));
    jpButtons.add(jbtNext = new JButton());
    jbtNext.setIcon(new ImageIcon("images/right.gif"));

    // Add jpButton and the label to the frame
    getContentPane().add(jlblImageViewer, BorderLayout.CENTER);
    getContentPane().add(jpButtons, BorderLayout.SOUTH);

    // Register listeners
    jbtPrior.addActionListener(this);
    jbtNext.addActionListener(this);
  }
```

continues

```
        // Handle ActionEvent from buttons
        public void actionPerformed(ActionEvent e)
        {
          if (e.getSource() == jbtPrior)
          {
            // Make sure index is nonnegative
            if (currentIndex == 0) currentIndex = TOTAL_NUMBER_OF_IMAGES;
            currentIndex = (currentIndex - 1)%TOTAL_NUMBER_OF_IMAGES;
            jlblImageViewer.setIcon(imageIcon[currentIndex]);
          }
          else if (e.getSource() == jbtNext)
          {
            currentIndex = (currentIndex + 1)%TOTAL_NUMBER_OF_IMAGES;
            jlblImageViewer.setIcon(imageIcon[currentIndex]);
          }
        }
      }
    }
```

Figure 9.6   *You can use the label to display images.*

Example Review

The images are stored in files L1.gif, L2.gif, . . . , and L52.gif and are loaded to an array of ImageIcon in a for loop.

By default, the icon is centered vertically, but left aligned horizontally. The statement shown below ensures that the image is displayed in the center of the viewing area.

```
jlblImageViewer.setHorizontalAlignment(SwingConstants.CENTER);
```

Text Fields

A *text field* is an input area where the user can type in characters. Text fields are useful because they enable the user to enter variable data, such as a name or a description. The default constructor of JTextField creates an empty text field. Other constructors of JTextField are as follows:

■ `public JTextField(int columns)`

This creates an empty text field with the specified number of columns.

■ `public JTextField(String text)`

This creates a text field initialized with the specified text.

■ `public JTextField(String text, int columns)`

This creates a text field initialized with the specified text and the column size.

In addition to properties like `text` and `horizontalAlignment`, `JTextField` has the following properties:

■ `editable`: A `boolean` property indicating whether the text field can be edited by the user.

■ `columns`: The width of the text field.

`JTextField` can generate `ActionEvent` and `TextEvent`, among many other events. Pressing Enter in a text field triggers the `ActionEvent`. Changing contents in a text field triggers the `TextEvent`.

Here is an example of how to react to an `ActionEvent` on a text field:

```
public void actionPerformed(ActionEvent e)
{
  // Make sure it is a text field
  if (e.getSource() instanceof JTextField)
    // Processing the event
    ...
}
```

Example 9.3 Using Text Fields

This example gives a program that enters two numbers in two text fields and displays their sum in the third text field when you press the Add button. The output of the program is shown in Figure 9.7.

```
// TextFieldDemo.java: Add two numbers in the text fields
package Chapter9;

import Chapter8.MyFrameWithExitHandling;
import java.awt.*;
import java.awt.event.*;
import javax.swing.*;

public class TextFieldDemo extends MyFrameWithExitHandling
  implements ActionListener
{
  // Declare three text fields
  private JTextField jtfNum1, jtfNum2, jtfResult;
  private JButton jtbAdd; // Declare "Add" button
```

continues

```
                // Main method
                public static void main(String[] args)
                {
                  TextFieldDemo frame = new TextFieldDemo();
                  frame.pack();
                  frame.center();
                  frame.setVisible(true);
                }

                // Constructor
                public TextFieldDemo()
                {
                  setTitle("TextFieldDemo");
                  setBackground(Color.yellow);
                  setForeground(Color.black);

                  // Use panel p1 to group text fields
                  JPanel p1 = new JPanel();
                  p1.setLayout(new FlowLayout());
                  p1.add(new Label("Number 1"));
                  p1.add(jtfNum1 = new JTextField(3));
                  p1.add(new Label("Number 2"));
                  p1.add(jtfNum2 = new JTextField(3));
                  p1.add(new Label("Result"));
                  p1.add(jtfResult = new JTextField(4));
                  jtfResult.setEditable(false);    // Set jtfResult noneditable

                  // Use panel p2 for the button
                  JPanel p2 = new JPanel();
                  p2.setLayout(new FlowLayout());
                  p2.add(jbtAdd = new JButton("Add"));

                  // Set FlowLayout for the frame and add panels to the frame
                  getContentPane().setLayout(new BorderLayout());
                  getContentPane().add(p1, BorderLayout.CENTER);
                  getContentPane().add(p2, BorderLayout.SOUTH);

                  // Register listener
                  jbtAdd.addActionListener(this);
                }

                // Handle the add operation
                public void actionPerformed(ActionEvent e)
                {
                  if (e.getSource() == jbtAdd)
                  {
                    // Get int values from text fields and use trim() to
                    // trim extraneous space in the text field
                    int num1 = (Integer.parseInt(jtfNum1.getText().trim()));
                    int num2 = (Integer.parseInt(jtfNum2.getText().trim()));
                    int result = num1 + num2;

                    // Set result in TextField jtfResult
                    jtfResult.setText(String.valueOf(result));
                  }
                }
              }
```

Figure 9.7 *The addition of Number 1 and Number 2 shows in the Result when you click the Add button.*

Example Review

The program uses two panels, p1 and p2, to contain the components. Panel p1 is for labels and text fields, and p2 is for the Add button. You can place the button directly in the frame instead of in p2. However, the button will look very long because it stretches to fill in the entire south area of the BorderLayout.

Instead of using the setSize() method to set the size for the frame, this program uses the pack() method, which automatically sizes up the frame according to the size of the components placed in the frame.

The jtfNum1.getText() method returns the text in the text field jtfNum1, and jtfResult.setText(s) sets the specified string into text field jtfResult.

The trim() method is useful for removing blank space from both ends of a string. If you run a program without applying trim() to the string, a runtime exception may occur when the string is converted to an integer.

Using jtfResult.setEditable(false) prevents the user from editing the Result text field. By default, editing is enabled on all text fields.

Text Areas

If you want to let the user enter multiple lines of text, you cannot use JTextField unless you create several of them. The solution is to use JTextArea, which enables the user to enter multiple lines of text.

The default constructor of JTextArea creates an empty text area. Other constructors of JTextArea are:

- ■ `public JTextArea(int rows, int columns)`

  This creates a text area with the specified number of rows and columns.

- ■ `public JTextArea(String text, int rows, int columns)`

  This creates a text area with the specified text and the number of rows and columns specified.

In addition to properties like text, editable, and columns, JTextArea has the following properties:

- **lineWrap:** A `boolean` property indicating whether the line in the text area is automatically wrapped.

- **wrapStyleWord:** A `boolean` property indicating whether the line is wrapped on word or character. The default value is `false`, which indicates that the line is wrapped on character boundaries.

- **rows:** The number of lines in the text area.

- **lineCount:** The number of lines in the text.

- **tabSize:** The number of characters inserted when the Tab key is pressed.

You can use the following methods to insert, append, and replace text:

- `public void insert(String s, int pos)`

  This inserts string s in the specified position in the text area.

- `public void append(String s)`

  This appends string s to the end of the text.

- `public void replaceRange(String s, int start, int end)`

  This replaces partial texts in the range from position `start` to position `end` with string s.

`JTextArea` does not handle scrolling, but you can create a `JScrollPane` object to hold an instance of `JTextArea` and let the `JScrollPane` handle scrolling for `JTextArea`, as follows:

```
// Create a scroll pane to hold text area
JScrollPane scrollPane = new JScrollPane(jta = new JTextArea());
getContentPane().add(scrollPane, BorderLayout.CENTER);
```

`JScrollPane` will be further discussed in the section "Scroll Panes" later in this chapter.

Example 9.4 Using Text Areas

This example gives a program to let the user enter text from a text field and then append it to a text area. A sample run of the program is shown in Figure 9.8.

```
// TextAreaDemo.java: Append text in a text field to the text area
package Chapter9;

import Chapter8.MyFrameWithExitHandling;
import java.awt.*;
import java.awt.event.*;
import javax.swing.*;

public class TextAreaDemo extends MyFrameWithExitHandling
  implements ActionListener
{
  private JTextField jtf;
  private JButton jbt;
  private JTextArea jta;
```

```
      // Main method
      public static void main(String[] args)
      {
        TextAreaDemo frame = new TextAreaDemo();
        frame.pack();
        frame.center();
        frame.setVisible(true);
      }

      // Constructor
      public TextAreaDemo()
      {
        setTitle("Test TextArea");

        // Create panel p to hold the text field and button
        JPanel p = new JPanel();
        p.setLayout(new FlowLayout());
        p.add(jtf = new JTextField(20));
        p.add(jbt = new JButton("Store"));

        // Create a scroll pane to hold text area
        JScrollPane scrollPane = new JScrollPane(jta = new JTextArea());

        // Set lineWrap true
        jta.setLineWrap(true);

        // Set FlowLayout for the frame and add components in it
        getContentPane().setLayout(new BorderLayout());
        getContentPane().add(scrollPane, BorderLayout.CENTER);
        getContentPane().add(p, BorderLayout.SOUTH);

        // Register listeners
        jtf.addActionListener(this);
        jbt.addActionListener(this);
      }

      // ActionEvent handler
      public void actionPerformed(ActionEvent e)
      {
        jta.append(jtf.getText().trim());
      }
    }
```

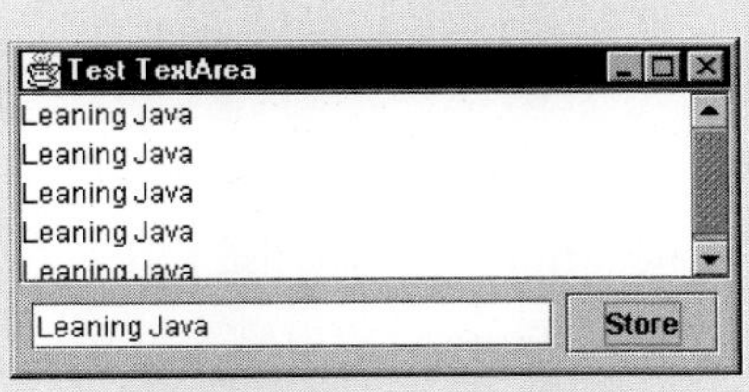

Figure 9.8   *The text in the text field is appended to the text area when you click the Store button.*

Example Review

The program groups the text field and the button in a panel, and places the panel below the text area. The text area is inside a JScrollPane, which provides scrolling functions for the text area. Scroll bars automatically appear if there is

continues

more text than the physical size of the text area, and disappears if the text is deleted and the remaining text does not exceed the text area size.

The `lineWrap` property is set to true so that the line is automatically wrapped when the text cannot fit in one line.

When you click the Store button or press the ENTER key in the text field, the handler, `actionPerformed()`, takes the string from the text field and appends it to the text area, using the `append()` method.

The text area is editable. You can type characters or delete characters directly into it. You also can highlight to select characters in the text area.

Combo Boxes

A *combo box*, also known as *choice*, is a simple list of items from which the user can choose. It is useful in limiting a user's range of choices and avoids the cumbersome validation of data input. You can easily choose and extract the value in a combo box.

To create a `JComboBox`, simply use its default constructor. The following properties are often useful:

- `selectedIndex`: An `int` value indicating the index of the selected item in the combo box.

- `seletedItem`: A selected item whose type is `Object`.

The following methods are useful in operating a `JComboBox` object:

- `public void addItem(Object item)`

  This adds the item of any object into the combo box.

- `public Object getItemAt(int index)`

  This gets an item from the combo box at the specified index.

- `public void removeItem(Object anObject)`

  Removes an item from the item list.

- `public void removeAllItems()`

  Removes all items from the item list.

Here is an example of how to create a combo box and add items to the combo box object:

```
JComboBox jcb = new JComboBox();
jcb.addItem("Item 1");
jcb.addItem("Item 2");
jcb.addItem("Item 3");
```

This creates a `JComboBox` with three items in the combo box.

To get data from a JComboBox menu, you can use getSelectedItem() to return the currently selected item, or you can get the item from the itemStateChanged (ItemEvent e) handler, using the e.getItem() method.

JComboBox can generate ActionEvent and ItemEvent, among many other events. Whenever a new item is selected, JComboBox generates ItemEvent twice, once to deselect the previously selected item, and once to select the currently selected item. JComboBox generates an ActionEvent after generating ItemEvent. To respond to an ItemEvent, you need to implement the itemStateChanged(ItemEvent e) handler for processing a choice. Here is an example of how to get data from the itemStateChanged(ItemEvent e) handler:

```java
public void itemStateChanged(ItemEvent e)
{
  // Make sure the source is a combo box
  if (e.getSource() instanceof JComboBox)
    String s = (String)e.getItem();
}
```

Example 9.5 Using Combo Boxes

This example gives a program that lets users enter their name, department, university, state, and zip code and store the information in a text area. The state is a JComboBox item. Figure 9.9 shows a sample run for the program.

```java
// ComboBoxDemo.java: Use combo box to select values
package Chapter9;

import Chapter8.MyFrameWithExitHandling;
import java.awt.*;
import java.awt.event.*;
import javax.swing.*;

public class ComboBoxDemo extends MyFrameWithExitHandling
  implements ItemListener, ActionListener
{
  private JComboBox jcboState;
  private JTextField jtfName = new JTextField(32);
  private JTextField jtfDepartment = new JTextField(32);
  private JTextField jtfUniversity = new JTextField(20);
  private JTextField jtfZip = new JTextField(5);
  private JTextArea jta = new JTextArea(5, 30);
  private JButton jbtStore = new JButton("Store");
  private String state;

  // Main method
  public static void main(String[] args)
  {
    ComboBoxDemo frame = new ComboBoxDemo();
    frame.pack();
    frame.setVisible(true);
  }
```

continues

369

```java
// Constructor
public ComboBoxDemo()
{
  setTitle("ComboBoxDemo");

  // Panel p1 to hold name field
  JPanel p1 = new JPanel();
  p1.setLayout(new FlowLayout(FlowLayout.LEFT));
  p1.add(new JLabel("Name"));
  p1.add(jtfName);

  // Panel p2 to hold department field
  JPanel p2 = new JPanel();
  p2.setLayout(new FlowLayout(FlowLayout.LEFT));
  p2.add(new JLabel("Department"));
  p2.add(jtfDepartment);

  // Panel p3 to hold university field
  JPanel p3 = new JPanel();
  p3.setLayout(new FlowLayout(FlowLayout.LEFT));
  p3.add(new JLabel("University"));
  p3.add(jtfUniversity);

  // Panel p4 to hold state and zip field
  JPanel p4 = new JPanel();
  p4.setLayout(new FlowLayout(FlowLayout.LEFT));
  p4.add(new JLabel("State"));
  p4.add(jcboState = new JComboBox());
  p4.add(new JLabel("  Zip"));
  p4.add(jtfZip);

  // Initialize choice items
  jcboState.addItem("MA");
  jcboState.addItem("IN");
  jcboState.addItem("OK");
  jcboState.addItem("PA");
  jcboState.setSelectedIndex(1);

  // Panel jpAddress to group p1, p2, p3 and p4
  JPanel jpAddress = new JPanel();
  jpAddress.setLayout(new GridLayout(4,1));
  jpAddress.add(p1);
  jpAddress.add(p2);
  jpAddress.add(p3);
  jpAddress.add(p4);

  // Panel p5 to hold text area and button
  JPanel p5 = new JPanel();
  p5.setLayout(new FlowLayout(FlowLayout.LEFT));
  p5.add(jta);
  p5.add(jbtStore);

  // Add panels to the frame
  getContentPane().setLayout(new BorderLayout());
  getContentPane().add(jpAddress, BorderLayout.CENTER);
  getContentPane().add(p5, BorderLayout.SOUTH);

  // Register listener
  jcboState.addItemListener(this);
  jcboState.addActionListener(this);
  jbtStore.addActionListener(this);
}
```

```
            // Obtain state code
            public void itemStateChanged(ItemEvent e)
            {
              if (e.getSource() instanceof JComboBox)
              {
                state = (String)e.getItem();
                storeToTextArea();
              }
            }

            // Respond to the button action
            public void actionPerformed(ActionEvent e)
            {
              if (e.getSource() == jbtStore)
                storeToTextArea();
            }

            // Store information to the text area
            private void storeToTextArea()
            {
              // Clear text area
              jta.setText(null);

              // Get selected item if needed
              if (state == null)
                state = (String)jcboState.getSelectedItem();

              // Retrieve address information from text field and combo box
              // and append it in the text area
              jta.append(jtfName.getText()+'\n');
              jta.append(jtfDepartment.getText()+'\n');
              jta.append(jtfUniversity.getText()+'\n');
              jta.append(state+", "+jtfZip.getText());
            }
          }
```

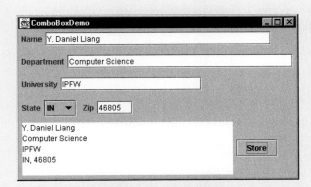

Figure 9.9 *When the Store button is clicked, the name, department, university, state, and zip code are displayed in the text area.*

continues

Example Review

The frame listens to `ActionEvent` for the Store button and `ItemEvent` for the `JComboBox` item, so it implements `ActionListener` and `ItemListener`.

The program uses several panels to organize the user interface. The state field is a choice item with sample values MA, IN, OK, and PA. When the user selects a choice, the handler, `itemStateChanged(ItemEvent e)`, gets the selected item and stores it in the state string.

When the user clicks the Store button, the `actionPerformed()` handler is executed, which invokes the `storeToTextArea()` method to display the address collected from the user input.

When the user selects an item in the combo box, the `ItemStateChanged` handler is executed, which invokes the `storeToTextArea()` method to display the address collected from the user input. You can get the selected item either by using `e.getItem()` in the `itemStateChanged(ItemEvent e)` handler or simply by using `jcboState.getSelectedItem()`.

You can rewrite the program to use `ActionEvent` for handling combo box item selection instead of using the `ItemEvent`, but using `ItemEvent`, you can also get the deselected item if necessary.

Lists

A *list* is a component that performs basically the same function as a combo box, but it enables the user to choose a single value or multiple values. The Swing `JList` is very versatile. Its advanced features are beyond the scope of this book. This section demonstrates selecting string items from a list.

To create a list with a set of strings, use the following constructor:

```
public JList(Object[] stringItems)
```

where `stringItems` is an array of `String`.

The following properties are often useful:

- `selectedIndex`: An int value indicating the index of the selected item in the list.

- `selectedIndices`: An array of int values representing the indices of the selected items in the list.

- `selectedValue`: The first selected value in the list.

- `selectedValues`: An array of objects representing selected values in the list.

- `selectionMode`: One of the three values (SINGLE_SELECTION, SINGLE_INTERVAL_SELECTION, MULTIPLE_INTERVAL_SELECTION) that indicate whether single items, single-interval items, or multiple-interval items can be selected. Single selection allows only one item to be selected. Single-interval selection allows multiple selections, but the selected items must be contiguous. Multiple-interval selection allows the selection of multiple contiguous items. The default value is MULTIPLE_INTERVAL_SELECTION.

■ visibleRowCount: The preferred number of rows in the list that can be displayed without a scroll bar. The default value is 8.

List does not scroll automatically. To make a list scroll, you can create a scroll pane and add the list to the scroll pane. This is the same way you make a text area scrollable.

JList generates javax.swing.event.ListSelectionEvent to notify the listeners of the selections. The listener must implement the valueChanged() handler to process the event. Here is an example of how to get a selected item from the valueChanged(ListSelectionEvent e) handler:

```
public void valueChanged(ListSelectionEvent e)
{
  String selectedItem = (String)jlst.getSelectedValue();
}
```

Example 9.6 Using Lists

This example gives a program that lets users select a country name in a list and display the country's flag in a label. Figure 9.10 shows a sample run for the program.

```
// ListDemo.java: Use list to select a country and display the
// selected country's flag
package Chapter9;

import Chapter8.MyFrameWithExitHandling;
import java.awt.*;
import java.awt.event.*;
import javax.swing.*;
import javax.swing.event.*;

public class ListDemo extends MyFrameWithExitHandling
  implements ListSelectionListener
{
  // Declare an ImageIcon array for the national flags of 9 countries
  private ImageIcon[] imageIcon = new ImageIcon[9];

  // Label for displaying images
  private JLabel jlblImageViewer = new JLabel();

  // The list for selecting countries
  JList jlst;

  // Main Method
  public static void main(String[] args)
  {
    ListDemo frame = new ListDemo();
    frame.setSize(450, 200);
```

continues

373

```
                        frame.setTitle("List Demo");
                        frame.center();
                        frame.setVisible(true);
                    }

                    // Default Constructor
                    public ListDemo()
                    {
                        // Load images into imageIcon array
                        imageIcon[0] = new ImageIcon("images/us.gif");
                        imageIcon[1] = new ImageIcon("images/ca.gif");
                        imageIcon[2] = new ImageIcon("images/uk.gif");
                        imageIcon[3] = new ImageIcon("images/germany.gif");
                        imageIcon[4] = new ImageIcon("images/fr.gif");
                        imageIcon[5] = new ImageIcon("images/denmark.gif");
                        imageIcon[6] = new ImageIcon("images/norway.gif");
                        imageIcon[7] = new ImageIcon("images/china.gif");
                        imageIcon[8] = new ImageIcon("images/india.gif");

                        // Show the first image
                        jlblImageViewer.setIcon(imageIcon[0]);

                        // Set center alignment
                        jlblImageViewer.setHorizontalAlignment(SwingConstants.CENTER);
                        //jlblImageViewer.setVerticalAlignment(SwingConstants.CENTER);

                        // Create a string of country names
                        String[] countries = {"United States of America", "Canada",
                          "United Kingdom", "Germany", "France", "Denmark", "Norway",
                          "China", "India"};

                        // Create a list with the country names
                        jlst = new JList(countries);

                        // Add jpButton and the label to the frame
                        getContentPane().add(jlblImageViewer, BorderLayout.CENTER);
                        getContentPane().add(new JScrollPane(jlst), BorderLayout.WEST);

                        // Register listeners
                        jlst.addListSelectionListener(this);
                    }

                    // Handle list selection
                    public void valueChanged(ListSelectionEvent e)
                    {
                        jlblImageViewer.setIcon(imageIcon[jlst.getSelectedIndex()]);
                    }
                }
```

Figure 9.10   *When the country in the list is selected, a corresponding flag image is displayed in a label.*

Example Review

The frame listens to `ListSelectionEvent` for handling the selection of country names in the list, so it implements `ListSelectionListener`. `ListSelectionEvent` and `ListSelectionListener` are defined in the `javax.swing.event` package, so this package is imported in the program.

The program loads the images of nine countries into an image array and creates a list of the nine countries in the same order as in the image array. Thus the index 0 of the image array corresponds to the first country on the list.

The list is placed in a scroll pane so that you can scroll the list when the number of the items in it exceeds its viewing area.

When the user selects an item in the list, the `valueChanged()` handler is executed, which gets the index of the selected item and sets its corresponding image icon to the label to display the country's flag.

The example constructs a list with a fixed set of strings. If you want to add new items to the list or delete existing items, you have to use the list model. For further discussion of the use of list models, please refer to *Rapid Java Application Development Using JBuilder 3*.

Check Boxes

A *check box* is a component that enables the user to toggle a choice on or off, like a light switch.

To create a check box, use the following constructor:

- ■ `public JCheckBox()`

  This default constructor creates an unselected empty check box.

- ■ `public JCheckBox(String text)`

  This creates an unselected check box with the specified text.

- ■ `public JCheckBox(String text, boolean selected)`

  This creates a check box with a text and specifies whether the check box is initially selected.

- ■ `public JCheckBox(Icon icon)`

  This creates an unselected check box with an icon.

- ■ `public JCheckBox(Icon icon, boolean selected)`

  This creates a check box with an icon and specifies whether the check box is initially selected.

- ■ `public JCheckBox(String text, Icon icon)`

  This creates an unselected check box with an icon and a text.

- public JCheckBox(String text, Icon icon, boolean selected)

    This creates a check box with an icon and a text and specifies whether the check box is initially selected.

In addition to such properties as text, icon, mnemonic, verticalAlignment, horizontalAlignment, horizontalTextPosition, and verticalTextPosition, JCheckBox has the following properties:

- selected: Specifies whether the check box is selected.

JCheckBox can generate ActionEvent and ItemEvent among many other events. The following code shows you how to implement itemStateChanged() to determine whether a box is checked or unchecked in response to an ItemEvent:

```
public void itemStateChanged(ItemEvent e)
{
  // Make sure the source is a JCheckBox
  if (e.getSource() instanceof JCheckBox)
    if (jchk1.isSelected())
      // Process the selection for jchk1;
    if (jchk2.isSelected())
      // Process the selection for jchk2;
}
```

Example 9.7 Using Check Boxes

This example gives a program to display a message in overlapping font styles. The message can be displayed in bold and italic at the same time or displayed in the center of the panel. The output of a sample run of the program is given in Figure 9.11.

```java
// CheckBoxDemo.java: Use check boxes to select one or more choices
package Chapter9;

import Chapter8.MyFrameWithExitHandling;
import Chapter8.MessagePanel;
import java.awt.BorderLayout;
import java.awt.FlowLayout;
import java.awt.Color;
import java.awt.Font;
import java.awt.event.*;
import javax.swing.*;

public class CheckBoxDemo extends MyFrameWithExitHandling
  implements ItemListener
{
  // Declare check boxes
  private JCheckBox jchkCentered, jchkBold, jchkItalic;

  // Declare a panel for displaying message
  private MessagePanel messagePanel;

  // Main method
  public static void main(String[] args)
  {
```

```java
    CheckBoxDemo frame = new CheckBoxDemo();
    frame.pack();
    frame.setVisible(true);
  }

  // Constructor
  public CheckBoxDemo()
  {
    setTitle("Checkbox Demo");

    // Create the message panel
    messagePanel = new MessagePanel();
    messagePanel.setMessage("Welcome to Java!");
    messagePanel.setBackground(Color.yellow);

    // Put three check boxes in panel p
    JPanel p = new JPanel();
    p.setLayout(new FlowLayout());
    p.add(jchkCentered = new JCheckBox("Centered"));
    p.add(jchkBold = new JCheckBox("Bold"));
    p.add(jchkItalic = new JCheckBox("Italic"));

    // Set keyboard mnemonics
    jchkCentered.setMnemonic('C');
    jchkBold.setMnemonic('B');
    jchkItalic.setMnemonic('I');

    // Place messagePanel and p in the frame
    getContentPane().setLayout(new BorderLayout());
    getContentPane().add(messagePanel, BorderLayout.CENTER);
    getContentPane().add(p, BorderLayout.SOUTH);

    // Register listeners on jchkCentered, jchkBold, and jchkItalic
    jchkCentered.addItemListener(this);
    jchkBold.addItemListener(this);
    jchkItalic.addItemListener(this);
  }

  // Handle check box selection
  public void itemStateChanged(ItemEvent e)
  {
    if (e.getSource() instanceof JCheckBox)
    {
      // Determine a font style
      int selectedStyle = 0;
      if (jchkBold.isSelected())
        selectedStyle = selectedStyle+Font.BOLD;
      if (jchkItalic.isSelected())
        selectedStyle = selectedStyle+Font.ITALIC;

      // Set font for the message
      messagePanel.setFont(new Font("Serif", selectedStyle, 20));
      if (jchkCentered.isSelected())
        messagePanel.setCentered(true);
      else
        messagePanel.setCentered(false);

      // Make sure the message is repainted
      messagePanel.repaint();
    }
  }
}
```

continues

377

Figure 9.11   *The program uses three* JCheckBox *components to let the user choose the font style for the message displayed and specify whether the message is centered.*

Example Review

The program displays the message using the MessagePanel class. The check boxes are labeled Centered, Bold, and Italic. The user can toggle on and off to select or deselect these check boxes.

Upon selecting a check box, the handler, itemStateChanged(ItemEvent e), is invoked to determine the state of each check box and combine all the selected fonts. The font styles are int constants: Font.BOLD and Font.ITALIC. Font styles are combined by adding together the selected integers representing the fonts.

The selected property determines whether a check box is selected. The value of this property is synchronized with the display. If it is true, then the check box is selected.

The keyboard mnemonics 'C', 'B', and 'I' are set on the check boxes "Centered," "Bold," and "Italic," respectively. You can select a check box using a mouse gesture or the shortcut keys.

Invoking the methods setFont() and setCentered() in MessagePanel does not repaint the viewing area in the Panel. Thus, you must invoke the repaint() method to refresh the panel.

Radio Buttons

Radio buttons, also known as *option buttons*, enable you to choose one item exclusively from a list of choices. Radio buttons and check boxes are similar in appearance. Check boxes display a square that is either checked or blank, and radio buttons display a circle that is either filled (if selected) or blank (not selected).

The constructors of JRadioButton are similar to the constructors of JCheckBox. Here are the constructors of JRadioButton:

- public JRadioButton()

  This default constructor creates an unselected empty radio button.

■   `public JRadioButton(String text)`

This creates an unselected radio button with the specified text.

■   `public JRadioButton(String text, boolean selected)`

This creates a radio button with a text and specifies whether the radio button is initially selected.

■   `public JRadioButton(Icon icon)`

This creates an unselected radio button with an icon.

■   `public JRadioButton(Icon icon, boolean selected)`

This creates a radio button with an icon and specifies whether the radio button is initially selected.

■   `public JRadioButton(String text, Icon icon)`

This creates an unselected radio button with an icon and a text.

■   `public JRadioButton(String text, Icon icon, boolean selected)`

This creates a radio button with an icon and a text, and specifies whether the radio button is initially selected.

Here is how to create a radio button with a text and an icon:

```
JRadionButton jrb = new JRadioButton("My Radio Button",
  new ImageIcon("imagefile.gif"));
```

Radio buttons are added to a container just like a button. To group the radio buttons, you need to create an instance of `javax.swing.ButtonGroup` and add radio buttons to the instance using the `add()` method as follows:

```
ButtonGroup btg = new ButtonGroup();
btg.add(jrb1);
btg.add(jrb2);
```

This code creates a radio button group so that `jrb1` and `jrb2` are selected mutually exclusively.

`JRadioButton` has such properties as `text`, `icon`, `mnemonic`, `verticalAlignment`, `horizontalAlignment`, `selected`, `horizontalTextPosition`, and `verticalTextPosition`.

`JRadioButton` can generate `ActionEvent` and `ItemEvent` among many other events. The following code shows you how to implement the `itemStateChanged()` handler to determine whether a box is checked or unchecked in response to an `ItemEvent`:

```
public void itemStateChanged(ItemEvent e)
{
  // Make sure the source is a JRadioButton
  if (e.getSource() instanceof JRadioButton)
    if (jrb1.selected())
      // Process the selection for jrb1
    else if (jrb2.isSelected())
      // Process the selection for jrb2
}
```

Example 9.8 Using Radio Buttons

This example gives a program to simulate traffic lights. The program lets the user select one of the three lights: red, yellow, or green. The light is turned on when a radio button is selected, and only one light at a time can be on. No light is on when the program starts. Figure 9.12 contains the output of a sample run of the program.

```java
// RadioButtonDemo.java: Use radio buttons to select a choice
package Chapter9;

import Chapter8.MyFrameWithExitHandling;
import java.awt.*;
import java.awt.event.*;
import javax.swing.*;

public class RadioButtonDemo extends MyFrameWithExitHandling
  implements ItemListener
{
  // Declare radio buttons
  private JRadioButton jrbRed, jrbYellow, jrbGreen;

  // Declare a radio button group
  private ButtonGroup btg = new ButtonGroup();

  // Declare a traffic light display panel
  private Light light;

  // Main method
  public static void main(String[] args)
  {
    RadioButtonDemo frame = new RadioButtonDemo();
    frame.setSize(250, 170);
    frame.setVisible(true);
  }

  // Constructor
  public RadioButtonDemo()
  {
    setTitle("RadioButton Demo");

    // Add traffic light panel to panel p1
    JPanel p1 = new JPanel();
    p1.setSize(200, 200);
    p1.setLayout(new FlowLayout(FlowLayout.CENTER));
    light = new Light();
    light.setSize(40, 90);
    p1.add(light);

    // Put the radio button in Panel p2
    JPanel p2 = new JPanel();
    p2.setLayout(new FlowLayout());
    p2.add(jrbRed = new JRadioButton("Red", false));
    p2.add(jrbYellow = new JRadioButton("Yellow", false));
    p2.add(jrbGreen = new JRadioButton("Green", false));

    // Set keyboard mnemoics
    jrbRed.setMnemonic('R');
    jrbYellow.setMnemonic('Y');
    jrbGreen.setMnemonic('G');
```

```
      // Group radio buttons
      btg.add(jrbRed);
      btg.add(jrbYellow);
      btg.add(jrbGreen);

      // Place p1 and p2 in the frame
      getContentPane().setLayout(new BorderLayout());
      getContentPane().add(p1, BorderLayout.CENTER);
      getContentPane().add(p2, BorderLayout.SOUTH);

      // Register listeners for check boxes
      jrbRed.addItemListener(this);
      jrbYellow.addItemListener(this);
      jrbGreen.addItemListener(this);
  }

  // Handling checkbox events
  public void itemStateChanged(ItemEvent e)
  {
    if (jrbRed.isSelected())
      light.red(); // Set red light
    if (jrbYellow.isSelected())
      light.yellow(); // Set yellow light
    if (jrbGreen.isSelected())
      light.green(); // Set green light
  }
}

// Three traffic lights shown in a panel
class Light extends JPanel
{
  private boolean red;
  private boolean yellow;
  private boolean green;

  public Light()
  {
    red = false;
    yellow = false;
    green = false;
  }

  // Set red light on
  public void red()
  {
    red = true;
    yellow = false;
    green = false;
    repaint();
  }

  // Set yellow light on
  public void yellow()
  {
    red = false;
    yellow = true;
    green = false;
    repaint();
  }
```

continues

```java
// Set green light on
public void green()
{
  red = false;
  yellow = false;
  green = true;
  repaint();
}

// Display lights
public void paintComponent(Graphics g)
{
  super.paintComponent(g);

  if (red)
  {
    g.setColor(Color.red);
    g.fillOval(10, 10, 20, 20);
    g.setColor(Color.black);
    g.drawOval(10, 35, 20, 20);
    g.drawOval(10, 60, 20, 20);
    g.drawRect(5, 5, 30, 80);
  }
  else if (yellow)
  {
    g.setColor(Color.yellow);
    g.fillOval(10, 35, 20, 20);
    g.setColor(Color.black);
    g.drawRect(5, 5, 30, 80);
    g.drawOval(10, 10, 20, 20);
    g.drawOval(10, 60, 20, 20);
  }
  else if (green)
  {
    g.setColor(Color.green);
    g.fillOval(10, 60, 20, 20);
    g.setColor(Color.black);
    g.drawRect(5, 5, 30, 80);
    g.drawOval(10, 10, 20, 20);
    g.drawOval(10, 35, 20, 20);
  }
  else
  {
    g.setColor(Color.black);
    g.drawRect(5, 5, 30, 80);
    g.drawOval(10, 10, 20, 20);
    g.drawOval(10, 35, 20, 20);
    g.drawOval(10, 60, 20, 20);
  }
}

// Set preferred size
public Dimension getPreferredSize()
{
  return new Dimension(40, 90);
}
}
```

Figure 9.12 *The radio buttons are grouped to let you select one color in the group to control traffic lights.*

Example Review

The lights are displayed on a panel. The program groups the radio buttons in a panel and places it below the traffic light panel. The `BorderLayout` is used to arrange these components.

The `Light` class, a subclass of `JPanel`, contains the methods `red()`, `yellow()`, and `green()` to control the traffic lights. For example, use `light.red()` to turn on the red light, where light is an instance of `Light`.

The program creates a `ButtonGroup btg` and puts three `JRadioButton` instances (red, yellow, and green) in the group. When the user checks a box in the group, the handler, `itemStateChanged(ItemEvent e)`, uses the `isSelected()` method to determine which radio button is selected and turns on the corresponding light.

The `getPreferredSize()` method is overridden to set the preferred size to 40 by 90. This is just the right size for displaying traffic lights.

Borders

Borders are one of the interesting new features of Swing components. You can set a border on any object of the `JComponent` class, but often it is useful to set a titled border on a `JPanel` that groups a set of related user interface components.

There are several basic types of borders to choose from. The titled border is very useful. To create a titled border, use the following statement:

```
Border titleBorder = new TitledBorder("A Title");
```

`Border` is the interface for all types of borders. `TitledBorder` is an implementation of `Border` with a title. You can create a desired border using the following properties:

- `title`: The title of the border.
- `titleColor`: The color of the title.
- `titleFont`: The font of the title.
- `titleJustification`: Specifies `Border.LEFT`, `Border.CENTER`, or `Border.RIGHT` for left, center, or right title justification.

- `titlePosition`: One of the six values (`Border.ABOVE_TOP`, `Border.TOP`, `Border.BELOW_TOP`, `Border.ABOVE_BOTTOM`, `Border.BOTTOM`, `Border.BELOW_BOTTOM`) to specify the title position above the border line, on the border line, or below the border line.

- `border`: The `TitledBorder` itself has the `border` property for building composite borders.

Other types of borders can be created using the following classes:

- `BevelBorder`: Creates a 3D-look border that can be lowered or raised. To construct a `BevelBorder`, use the following constructor, which creates a `BevelBorder` with the specified `bevelType` (`BevelBorder.LOWERED` or `Bevel-Border.BevelBorder`):

  ```
  public BevelBorder(int bevelType)
  ```

- `EtchedBorder`: Creates an etched border which can either be etched-in or etched-out. You can use its default constructor to construct an `EtchedBorder` with a lowered border. `EtchedBorder` has a property `etchType` with values `LOWERED` or `RAISED`.

- `LineBorder`: Creates a line border of arbitrary thickness of a single color. To create a `LineBorder`, use the following constructor:

  ```
  public LineBorder(Color c, int thickness)
  ```

- `MatteBorder`: Creates a matte-like border padded with the icon images. To create a `MatteBorder`, use the following constructor:

  ```
  public MatteBorder(Icon tileIcon)
  ```

- `EmptyBorder`: Creates a border with border space, but no drawings. To create an `EmptyBorder`, use the following constructor:

  ```
  public EmptyBorder(int top, int left, int bottom, int right)
  ```

NOTE

All the border classes and interfaces are grouped in the package `javax.swing.border`.

Swing also provides the `javax.swing.BorderFactory` class that contains static methods for creating borders. Some of the static methods are:

```
public static TitledBorder createTitledBorder(String title)

public static Border createLoweredBevelBorder()

public static Border createRaisedBevelBorder()

public static Border createLineBorder(Color color)

public static Border createLineBorder(Color color, int thickness)

public static Border createEtchedBorder()

public static Border createEtchedBorder(Color highlight, Color shadow)
```

```
public static Border createEmptyBorder()

public static MatteBorder createEmptyBorder
  (int top, int left, int bottom, int right)

public static MatteBorder createMatteBorder
  (int top, int left, int bottom, int right, Color color)

public static MatteBorder createMatteBorder
  (int top, int left, int bottom, int right, Icon tileIcon)

public static Border createCompoundBorder
  (Border outsideBorder, Border insideBorder)
```

For example, to create an etched border, use the following statement:

```
Border border = BorderFactory.createEtchedBorder();
```

Example 9.9 Using Borders

This example gives a program that creates and displays various types of borders. You can select a border with or without a title. For a border without a title, you can choose a border style from Lowered Bevel, Raised Bevel, Etched, Line, Matte, or Empty. For a border with a title, you can specify its title position and justification. You can also embed another border into the titled border. Figure 9.13 displays a sample run of the program.

```
// BorderDemo.java: Use borders for JComponent components
package Chapter9;

import Chapter8.MyFrameWithExitHandling;
import Chapter8.MessagePanel;
import java.awt.*;
import java.awt.event.ActionListener;
import java.awt.event.ActionEvent;
import javax.swing.*;
import javax.swing.border.*;

public class BorderDemo extends MyFrameWithExitHandling
   implements ActionListener
{
  // Declare a panel for displaying message
  private MessagePanel messagePanel;

  // A check box for selecting a border with or without a title
  private JCheckBox jchkTitled;

  // Radio buttons for border styles
  private JRadioButton jrbLoweredBevel, jrbRaisedBevel,
    jrbEtched, jrbLine, jrbMatte, jrbEmpty;

  // Radio buttons for titled border options
  private JRadioButton jrbAboveBottom, jrbBottom,
    jrbBelowBottom, jrbAboveTop, jrbTop, jrbBelowTop,
    jrbLeft, jrbCenter, jrbRight;

  // TitledBorder for the message panel
  private TitledBorder messagePanelBorder = new TitledBorder("");
```

continues

```
// Main method
public static void main(String[] args)
{
  BorderDemo frame = new BorderDemo();
  frame.pack();
  frame.setVisible(true);
}

// Constructor
public BorderDemo()
{
  setTitle("Border Demo");

  // Create a MessagePanel instance and set colors
  messagePanel = new MessagePanel
    ("Display the border type");
  messagePanel.setCentered(true);
  messagePanel.setBackground(Color.yellow);
  messagePanel.setBorder(messagePanelBorder);

  // Palce title position radio buttons
  JPanel jpPosition = new JPanel();
  jpPosition.setLayout(new GridLayout(3, 2));
  jpPosition.add(
    jrbAboveBottom = new JRadioButton("ABOVE_BOTTOM"));
  jpPosition.add(jrbAboveTop = new JRadioButton("ABOVE_TOP"));
  jpPosition.add(jrbBottom = new JRadioButton("BOTTOM"));
  jpPosition.add(jrbTop = new JRadioButton("TOP"));
  jpPosition.add(
    jrbBelowBottom = new JRadioButton("BELOW_BOTTOM"));
  jpPosition.add(jrbBelowTop = new JRadioButton("BELOW_TOP"));
  jpPosition.setBorder(new TitledBorder("Position"));

  // Place title justification radio buttons
  JPanel jpJustification = new JPanel();
  jpJustification.setLayout(new GridLayout(3,1));
  jpJustification.add(jrbLeft = new JRadioButton("LEFT"));
  jpJustification.add(jrbCenter = new JRadioButton("CENTER"));
  jpJustification.add(jrbRight = new JRadioButton("RIGHT"));
  jpJustification.setBorder(new TitledBorder("Justification"));

  // Create panel jpTitleOptions to hold jpPosition and
  // jpJustification
  JPanel jpTitleOptions = new JPanel();
  jpTitleOptions.setLayout(new BorderLayout());
  jpTitleOptions.add(jpPosition, BorderLayout.CENTER);
  jpTitleOptions.add(jpJustification, BorderLayout.EAST);

  // Create Panel jpTitle to hold a check box and title position
  // radio buttons, and title justification radio buttons
  JPanel jpTitle = new JPanel();
  jpTitle.setBorder(new TitledBorder("Border Title"));
  jpTitle.setLayout(new BorderLayout());
  jpTitle.add(jchkTitled = new JCheckBox("Titled"),
    BorderLayout.NORTH);
  jpTitle.add(jpTitleOptions, BorderLayout.CENTER);

  // Group radio buttons for title position
  ButtonGroup btgTitlePosition = new ButtonGroup();
  btgTitlePosition.add(jrbAboveBottom);
  btgTitlePosition.add(jrbBottom);
  btgTitlePosition.add(jrbBelowBottom);
```

```
      btgTitlePosition.add(jrbAboveTop);
      btgTitlePosition.add(jrbTop);
      btgTitlePosition.add(jrbBelowTop);

      // Group radio buttons for title justification
      ButtonGroup btgTitleJustification = new ButtonGroup();
      btgTitleJustification.add(jrbLeft);
      btgTitleJustification.add(jrbCenter);
      btgTitleJustification.add(jrbRight);

      // Create Panel jpBorderStyle to hold border style radio buttons
      JPanel jpBorderStyle = new JPanel();
      jpBorderStyle.setBorder(new TitledBorder("Border Style"));
      jpBorderStyle.setLayout(new GridLayout(6, 1));
      jpBorderStyle.add(jrbLoweredBevel =
        new JRadioButton("Lowered Bevel"));
      jpBorderStyle.add(jrbRaisedBevel =
        new JRadioButton("Raised Bevel"));
      jpBorderStyle.add(jrbEtched = new JRadioButton("Etched"));
      jpBorderStyle.add(jrbLine = new JRadioButton("Line"));
      jpBorderStyle.add(jrbMatte = new JRadioButton("Matte"));
      jpBorderStyle.add(jrbEmpty = new JRadioButton("Empty"));

      // Group radio buttons for border styles
      ButtonGroup btgBorderStyle = new ButtonGroup();
      btgBorderStyle.add(jrbLoweredBevel);
      btgBorderStyle.add(jrbRaisedBevel);
      btgBorderStyle.add(jrbEtched);
      btgBorderStyle.add(jrbLine);
      btgBorderStyle.add(jrbMatte);
      btgBorderStyle.add(jrbEmpty);

      // Create Panel jpAllChoices to place jpTitle and jpBorderStyle
      JPanel jpAllChoices = new JPanel();
      jpAllChoices.setLayout(new BorderLayout());
      jpAllChoices.add(jpTitle, BorderLayout.CENTER);
      jpAllChoices.add(jpBorderStyle, BorderLayout.EAST);

      // Place panels in the frame
      getContentPane().setLayout(new BorderLayout());
      getContentPane().add(messagePanel, BorderLayout.CENTER);
      getContentPane().add(jpAllChoices, BorderLayout.SOUTH);

      // Register listeners
      jchkTitled.addActionListener(this);
      jrbAboveBottom.addActionListener(this);
      jrbBottom.addActionListener(this);
      jrbBelowBottom.addActionListener(this);
      jrbAboveTop.addActionListener(this);
      jrbTop.addActionListener(this);
      jrbBelowTop.addActionListener(this);
      jrbLeft.addActionListener(this);
      jrbCenter.addActionListener(this);
      jrbRight.addActionListener(this);
      jrbLoweredBevel.addActionListener(this);
      jrbRaisedBevel.addActionListener(this);
      jrbLine.addActionListener(this);
      jrbEtched.addActionListener(this);
      jrbMatte.addActionListener(this);
      jrbEmpty.addActionListener(this);
    }
```

continues

```java
// Handler for ActionEvents on check box and radio buttons
public void actionPerformed(ActionEvent e)
{
  // Get border style
  Border border = new EmptyBorder(2, 2, 2, 2);

  if (jrbLoweredBevel.isSelected())
  {
    border = new BevelBorder(BevelBorder.LOWERED);
    messagePanel.setMessage("Lowered Bevel Style");
  }
  else if (jrbRaisedBevel.isSelected())
  {
    border = new BevelBorder(BevelBorder.RAISED);
    messagePanel.setMessage("Raised Bevel Style");
  }
  else if (jrbEtched.isSelected())
  {
    border = new EtchedBorder();
    messagePanel.setMessage("Etched Style");
  }
  else if (jrbLine.isSelected())
  {
    border = new LineBorder(Color.black, 5);
    messagePanel.setMessage("Line Style");
  }
  else if (jrbMatte.isSelected())
  {
    border = new MatteBorder(20, 20, 20, 20,
      new ImageIcon("images/swirl.gif"));
    messagePanel.setMessage("Matte Style");
  }
  else if (jrbEmpty.isSelected())
  {
    border = new EmptyBorder(2, 2, 2, 2);
    messagePanel.setMessage("Empty Style");
  }

  if (jchkTitled.isSelected())
  {
    // Get the title position and justification
    int titlePosition = TitledBorder.DEFAULT_POSITION;
    int titleJustification = TitledBorder.DEFAULT_JUSTIFICATION;

    if (jrbAboveBottom.isSelected())
      titlePosition = TitledBorder.ABOVE_BOTTOM;
    else if (jrbBottom.isSelected())
      titlePosition = TitledBorder.BOTTOM;
    else if (jrbBelowBottom.isSelected())
      titlePosition = TitledBorder.BELOW_BOTTOM;
    else if (jrbAboveTop.isSelected())
      titlePosition = TitledBorder.ABOVE_TOP;
    else if (jrbTop.isSelected())
      titlePosition = TitledBorder.TOP;
    else if (jrbBelowTop.isSelected())
      titlePosition = TitledBorder.BELOW_TOP;

    if (jrbLeft.isSelected())
      titleJustification = TitledBorder.LEFT;
    else if (jrbCenter.isSelected())
      titleJustification = TitledBorder.CENTER;
```

```
        else if (jrbRight.isSelected())
          titleJustification = TitledBorder.RIGHT;

        messagePanelBorder = new TitledBorder("A Title");
        messagePanelBorder.setBorder(border);
        messagePanelBorder.setTitlePosition(titlePosition);
        messagePanelBorder.setTitleJustification(titleJustification);
        messagePanelBorder.setTitle("A Title");
        messagePanel.setBorder(messagePanelBorder);
      }
      else
      {
        messagePanel.setBorder(border);
      }
    }
  }
```

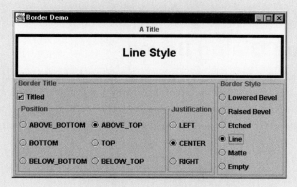

Figure 9.13   *The program demonstrates various types of borders.*

Example Review

This example uses many panels to group UI components to achieve the desired look. Figure 9.13 illustrates the relationship of these panels. The Border Title panel groups all the options for setting title properties. The position options are grouped in the Position Panel. The justification options are grouped in the Justification panel. The Border Style panel groups the radio buttons for choosing Lowered Bevel, Raised Bevel, Etched, Line, Matte, and Empty borders.

The MessagePanel displays the selected border with or without a title, depending on the selection of the title check box. The MessagePanel also displays a message indicating which type of border is being used, depending on the selection of the radio button in the Border Style panel.

The TitledBorder can be mixed with other borders. To do so, simply create an instance of TitledBorder, and use the setBorder() method to embed a new border into the TitledBorder.

The MatteBorder can be used to display icons on the border, as shown in Figure 9.14.

continues

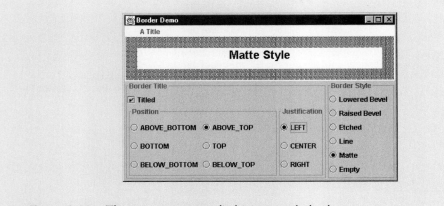

Figure 9.14   *The* `MatteBorder` *can display icons on the border.*

Message Dialog Boxes

A *dialog box* is normally used as a temporary window to receive additional information from the user or to provide notification that some event has occurred. You can build a variety of dialog boxes in Java. This section introduces a simple and frequently used dialog box, known as the *message dialog box*, that displays a message to alert the user, as shown in Figure 9.15.

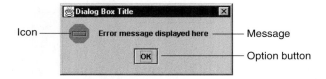

Icon —
Message
Option button

Figure 9.15   *A message dialog box displays a message.*

To display a message dialog box, as shown in Figure 9.15, use the static `showMessageDialog()` method in the `JOptionPane` class:

```
public static void showMessageDialog(Component parentComponent,
                                      Object message,
                                      String title,
                                      int messageType)
```

The `parentComponent` is the parent component of the dialog box, from which the dialog box is launched. The `message` is the object to display. Often you use a string for `message`. The `title` is the title of the dialog box. The `messageType` determines the type of message to be displayed. There are five message types:

```
ERROR_MESSAGE

INFORMATION_MESSAGE

PLAIN_MESSAGE
```

```
WARNING_MESSAGE

QUESTION_MESSAGE
```

Except for PLAIN_MESSAGE, each type has an associated icon. If you wish, you can use the following method to supply your own icon:

```
public static void showMessageDialog(Component parentComponent,
                                     Object message,
                                     String title,
                                     int messageType,
                                     Icon icon)
```

Example 9.10 Using Message Dialogs

This example gives a program that displays student exam grades. The user enters the SSN and the password, then clicks the Find Score button (see Figure 9.16) to show the student name and the grade. If the SSN is incorrect, a message dialog box displays the message SSN not found, as shown in Figure 9.17. If the password is incorrect, a message dialog box displays Password does not match SSN, as shown in Figure 9.18. In either case, the user must click the OK button in the message dialog box to go back to the main frame.

```
// DialogDemo.java: Use message dialog box to select information
package Chapter9;

import Chapter8.MyFrameWithExitHandling;
import java.awt.*;
import java.awt.event.*;
import javax.swing.*;

public class DialogDemo extends MyFrameWithExitHandling
  implements ActionListener
{
  // Create sample student information in arrays
  // with name, SSN, passowrd, and grade
  private String[][] student =
    {
      {"John Willow", "111223333", "a450", "A"},
      {"Jim Brown", "111223334", "b344", "B"},
      {"Bill Beng", "111223335", "33342csa", "C"},
      {"George Wall", "111223336", "343rea2", "D"},
      {"Jill Jones", "111223337", "34g", "E"}
    };

  // Declare text fields for last name, password, full name and score
  private JTextField jtfSSN;
  private JPasswordField jpfPassword;
  private JTextField jtfName;
  private JTextField jtfGrade;
  private JButton jbtFind;

  // Main method
  public static void main(String[] args)
  {
    DialogDemo f = new DialogDemo();
    f.pack();
    f.setVisible(true);
  }
```

continues

```
public DialogDemo()
{
  setTitle("Find The Score");

  // Panel jpLables to hold labels
  JPanel jpLabels = new JPanel();
  jpLabels.setLayout(new GridLayout(4, 1));
  jpLabels.add(new JLabel("Enter SSN"));
  jpLabels.add(new JLabel("Enter Password"));
  jpLabels.add(new JLabel("Name"));
  jpLabels.add(new JLabel("Score"));

  // Panel jpTextFields to hold text fields and password
  JPanel jpTextFields = new JPanel();
  jpTextFields.setLayout(new GridLayout(4, 1));
  jpTextFields.add(jtfSSN = new JTextField(10));
  jpTextFields.add(jpfPassword = new JPasswordField(10));
  jpTextFields.add(jtfName = new JTextField(10));
  jpTextFields.add(jtfGrade = new JTextField(10));

  // Panel p1 for holding jpLables and jpTextFields
  JPanel p1 = new JPanel();
  p1.setLayout(new BorderLayout());
  p1.add(jpLabels, BorderLayout.WEST);
  p1.add(jpTextFields, BorderLayout.CENTER);

  // Panel p2 for holding the Find button
  JPanel p2 = new JPanel();
  p2.setLayout(new FlowLayout(FlowLayout.RIGHT));
  p2.add(jbtFind = new JButton("Find Score"));

  // Place panels into the frame
  getContentPane().setLayout(new BorderLayout());
  getContentPane().add(p1, BorderLayout.CENTER);
  getContentPane().add(p2, BorderLayout.SOUTH);

  // Register listener for jbtFind
  jbtFind.addActionListener(this);
}

public void actionPerformed(ActionEvent e)
{
  // Find the student in the database
  int index = find(jtfSSN.getText().trim(),
    new String(jpfPassword.getPassword()));

  if (index == -1)
  {
    JOptionPane.showMessageDialog(this, "SSN not found",
      "For Your Information", JOptionPane.INFORMATION_MESSAGE);
  }
  else if (index == -2)
  {
    JOptionPane.showMessageDialog(this,
      "Password does not match SSN",
      "For Your Information", JOptionPane.INFORMATION_MESSAGE);
  }
  else
  {
    // Display name and score
    jtfName.setText(student[index][0]);
    jtfGrade.setText(student[index][3]);
  }
}
```

```
// Find the student who matched user name and password
// return the index if found; return -1 if SSN is not in
// the database, and return -2 if password does not match SSN
public int find(String SSN, String pw)
{
  // Find a student who matches SSN and pw
  for (int i=0; i<student.length; i++)
    if (student[i][1].equals(SSN) && student[i][2].equals(pw))
      return i;

  // Determine if the SSN is in the database
  for (int i=0; i<student.length; i++)
    if (student[i][1].equals(SSN))
      return -2;

  // Return -1 since the SSN and pw do not match
  return -1;
  }
}
```

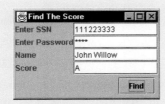

Figure 9.16   *The main frame lets the user enter the SSN and password, and then click the Find button to display the name and score.*

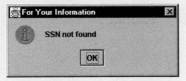

Figure 9.17   *The message box displays the error message* SSN not found.

Figure 9.18   *The message box displays the error message* Password does not match SSN.

Example Review

The message dialog box is *modal*, which means that no other windows can be accessed before the message dialog is dismissed.

continues

The student information is stored in the two-dimensional array student[][]. Each element in the array consists of name, SSN, password, and grade. If the SSN and password match student[i][1] and student[i][2] for some i, the name (student[i][0]) and the grade (grade[i][3]) are displayed in the main frame.

When the program starts, the main frame comes up first, as shown in Figure 9.16. If the user enters a wrong SSN, the message SSN not found appears in the dialog box, as shown in Figure 9.17. If the user enters a correct SSN but a wrong password, the message Password does not match SSN appears in the dialog box, as shown in Figure 9.18. Upon receiving the correct SSN and password, the user's name and grade are displayed in the frame, as shown in Figure 9.16.

The statement

```
JOptionPane.showMessageDialog(this, "SSN not found",
        "For Your Information", JOptionPane.INFORMATION_MESSAGE);
```

displays a message dialog box of the INFORMATION_MESSAGE type with the message "SSN not found" and the title "For Your Information."

The find(SSN, pw) method defined in the main frame returns the index of the student array element that matches the SSN and the password, returns -1 if SSN is not found, and returns -2 if the password does not match the SSN.

The JPasswordField component, a subclass of JTextField, is specifically designed to receive the password. The characters entered in a JPasswordField are echo displayed in * to protect them from being seen by bystanders. To get the password, you need to use the getPassword() method, which returns the password in an array of char, not a string.

Menus

Menus make selection easier and are widely used in window applications. Java provides five classes—JMenuBar, JMenu, JMenuItem, JCheckBoxMenuItem, and JRadioButtonMenuItem—to implement menus.

JMenuBar, the top-level menu component, is used to hold the menus. Menus consist of *menu items* that the user can select (or toggle on or off). Menu items can be an instance of JMenuItem, JCheckBoxMenuItem, or JRadioButtonMenuItem.

The sequence of implementing menus in Java is as follows:

1. Create a menu bar and associate it with a frame.

```
JFrame frame = new JFrame();
frame.setSize(300, 200);
frame.setVisible(true);
JMenuBar jmb = new JMenuBar();
frame.setJMenuBar(jmb);  // Attach a menu bar to a frame
```

This code creates a frame and a menu bar, and sets the menu bar in the frame.

2. Create menus.

Use the following constructor to create a menu:

```
public JMenu(String label)
```

Here is an example of creating menus:

```
JMenu fileMenu = new JMenu("File");
JMenu helpMenu = new JMenu("Help");
jmb.add(fileMenu);
jmb.add(helpMenu);
```

This creates two menus labeled File and Help, as shown in Figure 9.19. The menus will not be seen until they are added to JMenuBar.

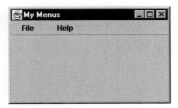

Figure 9.19   *The menu bar appears below the title bar on the frame.*

3. Create menu items and add them to menus.

```
fileMenu.add(new JMenuItem("New"));
fileMenu.add(new JMenuItem("Open"));
fileMenu.addSeparator();
fileMenu.add(new JMenuItem("Print"));
fileMenu.addSeparator();
fileMenu.add(new JMenuItem("Exit"));
```

This code adds the menu items New, Open, a separator bar, Print, another separator bar, and Exit, in this order, to the File menu, as shown in Figure 9.20.

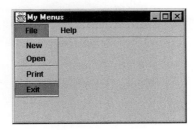

Figure 9.20   *Clicking a menu on the menu bar reveals the items under the menu.*

395

The addSeparator() method adds a separate bar in the menu.

3.1.   Creating submenu items.

You can also embed menus inside menus so that the embedded menus become submenus. Here is an example:

```
JMenu softwareHelpSubMenu = new JMenu("Software");
JMenu hardwareHelpSubMenu = new JMenu("Hardware");
helpMenu.add(softwareHelpSubMenu);
helpMenu.add(hardwareHelpSubMenu);
softwareHelpSubMenu.add(new JMenuItem("Unix"));
softwareHelpSubMenu.add(new JMenuItem("NT"));
softwareHelpSubMenu.add(new JMenuItem("Win95"));
```

This code adds two submenus: softwareHelpMenu and hardwareHelp-Menu in helpMenu. The menu items Unix, NT, and Win95 are added into softwareHelpMenu (see Figure 9.21).

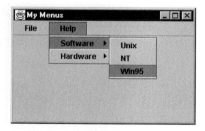

Figure 9.21   *Clicking a menu item reveals the secondary items under the menu item.*

3.2.   Creating check box menu items.

You can also add a JCheckBoxMenuItem to a JMenu. JCheckBoxMenuItem is a subclass of JMenuItem that adds a Boolean state to the JMenuItem, and displays a check when its state is true. You can click the menu item to turn it on and off. The following statement, for instance, adds the check box menu item Check it (see Figure 9.22).

```
helpMenu.add(new JCheckBoxMenuItem("Check it"));
```

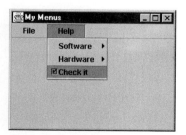

Figure 9.22   *A check box menu item lets you check or uncheck a menu item just like a check box.*

3.3. Creating radio button menu items.

You can also add radio buttons in a menu using the `JRadioButtonMenu-Item` class. This is often useful when you have a group of mutually exclusive choices in the menu. The following statements add a submenu named Color and a set of radio buttons for choosing a color (see Figure 9.23):

```
JMenu colorHelpSubMenu = new JMenu("Color");
helpMenu.add(colorHelpSubMenu);

JRadioButtonMenuItem jrbmiBlue, jrbmiYellow, jrbmiRed;
colorHelpSubMenu.add(jrbmiBlue = new
   JRadioButtonMenuItem("Blue"));
colorHelpSubMenu.add(jrbmiYellow = new
   JRadioButtonMenuItem("Yellow"));
colorHelpSubMenu.add(jrbmiRed = new
   JRadioButtonMenuItem("Red"));

ButtonGroup btg = new ButtonGroup();
btg.add(jrbmiBlue);
btg.add(jrbmiYellow);
btg.add(jrbmiRed);
```

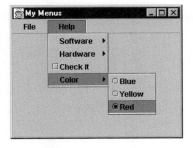

Figure 9.23 *You can use* `JRadioButtonMenuItem` *to choose a mutually exclusive menu choice.*

4. The menu items generate `ActionEvent`. Your program must implement the `actionPerformed()` handler to respond to the menu selection. Here is an example:

```
public void actionPerformed(ActionEvent e)
{
  String actionCommand = e.getActionCommand();

  // Make sure the source is JMenuItem
  if (e.getSource() instanceof JMenuItem)
    if ("New".equals(actionCommand))
      respondeToNew();
}
```

This code executes the method `respondToNew()` when the menu item labeled New is selected.

Image Icons, Keyboard Mnemonics, and Keyboard Accelerators

The menu components JMenu, JMenuItem, JCheckBoxMenuItem, JRadioButtonMenu-Item have the icon and mnemonic properties. Using the code given below, you can set icons for the New and Open menu items and keyboard mnemonics for File, Help, New, and Open:

```
JMenuItem jmiNew, jmiOpen;
fileMenu.add(jmiNew = new JMenuItem("New"));
fileMenu.add(jmiOpen = new JMenuItem("Open"));
jmiNew.setIcon(new ImageIcon("images/new.gif"));
jmiOpen.setIcon(new ImageIcon("images/open.gif"));
helpMenu.setMnemonic('H');
fileMenu.setMnemonic('F');
jmiNew.setMnemonic('N');
jmiOpen.setMnemonic('O');
```

The new icons and mnemonics are shown in Figure 9.24. You can also use JMenu-Item constructors like the ones shown here to construct and set an icon or mnemonic in one statement.

```
public JMenuItem(String label, Icon icon);
```

```
public JMenuItem(String label, int mnemonic);
```

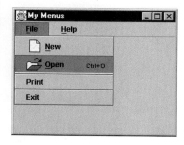

Figure 9.24   *You can set image icons, keyboard mnemonics, and keyboard accelerators in menus.*

To select a menu, press the ALT key and the mnemonic key. For example, press ALT+F to select the File menu. Then press ALT+O to select the Open menu item. Keyboard mnemonics are useful, but they only let you select menu items from the currently open menu. Key accelerators, however, let you select a menu item directly by pressing the CTRL key and the accelerator key. For example, you can attach the accelerator key CTRL+O with the Open menu item using the following code:

```
jmiOpen.setAccelerator(KeyStroke.getKeyStroke
   (KeyEvent.VK_O, ActionEvent.CTRL_MASK));
```

The setAccelerator() method takes an object KeyStroke. The static method getKeyStroke() in the KeyStroke class creates an instance of the key stroke. VK_O is a constant representing the O key, and CTRL_MASK is a constant indicating that the CTRL key is associated with the keystroke.

Example 9.11 Using Menus

This example gives a program that creates a user interface that does arithmetic. The interface contains labels and text fields for Number 1, Number 2, and Result. The Result text field displays the result of the arithmetic operation between Number 1 and Number 2.

The program has four buttons labeled Add, Subtract, Multiply, and Divide. It also creates menus to perform the same operations. The user can choose an operation either from the buttons or from the menu selections. Figure 9.25 contains a sample run for the example.

```java
// MenuDemo.java: Use menus to move message in a panel
package Chapter9;

import Chapter8.MyFrameWithExitHandling;
import java.awt.*;
import java.awt.event.*;
import javax.swing.*;

public class MenuDemo extends MyFrameWithExitHandling
  implements ActionListener
{
  // Text fields for Number 1, Number 2, and Result
  private JTextField jtfNum1, jtfNum2, jtfResult;

  // Buttons "Add", "Subtract", "Multiply" and "Divide"
  private JButton jbtAdd, jbtSub, jbtMul, jbtDiv;

  // Menu items "Add", "Subtract", "Multiply","Divide" and "Close"
  private JMenuItem jmiAdd, jmiSub, jmiMul, jmiDiv, jmiClose;

  // Main Method
  public static void main(String[] args)
  {
    MenuDemo frame = new MenuDemo();
    frame.pack();
    frame.setVisible(true);
  }

  // Default Constructor
  public MenuDemo()
  {
    setTitle("Menu Demo");

    // Create menu bar
    JMenuBar jmb = new JMenuBar();

    // Set menu bar to the frame
    setJMenuBar(jmb);

    // Add menu "Operation" to menu bar
    JMenu operationMenu = new JMenu("Operation");
    operationMenu.setMnemonic('O');
    jmb.add(operationMenu);

    // Add menu "Exit" in menu bar
    JMenu exitMenu = new JMenu("Exit");
    exitMenu.setMnemonic('E');
    jmb.add(exitMenu);
```

continues

```
          // Add menu items with mnemonics to menu "Operation"
          operationMenu.add(jmiAdd= new JMenuItem("Add", 'A'));
          operationMenu.add(jmiSub = new JMenuItem("Subtract", 'S'));
          operationMenu.add(jmiMul = new JMenuItem("Multiply", 'M'));
          operationMenu.add(jmiDiv = new JMenuItem("Divide", 'D'));
          exitMenu.add(jmiClose = new JMenuItem("Close", 'C'));

          // Set keyboard accelerators
          jmiAdd.setAccelerator(
            KeyStroke.getKeyStroke(KeyEvent.VK_A, ActionEvent.CTRL_MASK));
          jmiSub.setAccelerator(
            KeyStroke.getKeyStroke(KeyEvent.VK_S, ActionEvent.CTRL_MASK));
          jmiMul.setAccelerator(
            KeyStroke.getKeyStroke(KeyEvent.VK_M, ActionEvent.CTRL_MASK));
          jmiDiv.setAccelerator(
            KeyStroke.getKeyStroke(KeyEvent.VK_D, ActionEvent.CTRL_MASK));

          // Panel p1 to hold text fields and labels
          JPanel p1 = new JPanel();
          p1.setLayout(new FlowLayout());
          p1.add(new JLabel("Number 1"));
          p1.add(jtfNum1 = new JTextField(3));
          p1.add(new JLabel("Number 2"));
          p1.add(jtfNum2 = new JTextField(3));
          p1.add(new JLabel("Result"));
          p1.add(jtfResult = new JTextField(4));
          jtfResult.setEditable(false);

          // Panel p2 to hold buttons
          JPanel p2 = new JPanel();
          p2.setLayout(new FlowLayout());
          p2.add(jbtAdd = new JButton("Add"));
          p2.add(jbtSub = new JButton("Subtract"));
          p2.add(jbtMul = new JButton("Multiply"));
          p2.add(jbtDiv = new JButton("Divide"));

          // Add panels to the frame
          getContentPane().setLayout(new BorderLayout());
          getContentPane().add(p1, BorderLayout.CENTER);
          getContentPane().add(p2, BorderLayout.SOUTH);

          // Register listeners
          jbtAdd.addActionListener(this);
          jbtSub.addActionListener(this);
          jbtMul.addActionListener(this);
          jbtDiv.addActionListener(this);
          jmiAdd.addActionListener(this);
          jmiSub.addActionListener(this);
          jmiMul.addActionListener(this);
          jmiDiv.addActionListener(this);
          jmiClose.addActionListener(this);
        }

        // Handle ActionEvent from buttons and menu items
        public void actionPerformed(ActionEvent e)
        {
          String actionCommand = e.getActionCommand();

          // Handle button events
          if (e.getSource() instanceof JButton)
          {
            if ("Add".equals(actionCommand))
              calculate('+');
```

```
        else if ("Subtract".equals(actionCommand))
          calculate('-');
        else if ("Multiply".equals(actionCommand))
          calculate('*');
        else if ("Divide".equals(actionCommand))
          calculate('/');
      }
      else if (e.getSource() instanceof JMenuItem)
      {
        // Handling menu item events
        if ("Add".equals(actionCommand))
          calculate('+');
        else if ("Subtract".equals(actionCommand))
          calculate('-');
        else if ("Multiply".equals(actionCommand))
          calculate('*');          else if ("Divide".equals(actionCommand))
          calculate('/');
        else if ("Close".equals(actionCommand))
          System.exit(0);
      }
    }

    // Calculate and show the result in jtfResult
    private void calculate(char operator)
    {
      // Obtain Number 1 and Number 2
      int num1 = (Integer.parseInt(jtfNum1.getText().trim()));
      int num2 = (Integer.parseInt(jtfNum2.getText().trim()));
      int result = 0;

      // Perform selected operation
      switch (operator)
      {
        case '+': result = num1 + num2;
                  break;
        case '-': result = num1 - num2;
                  break;
        case '*': result = num1 * num2;
                  break;
        case '/': result = num1 / num2;
      }

      // Set result in jtfResult
      jtfResult.setText(String.valueOf(result));
    }
  }
```

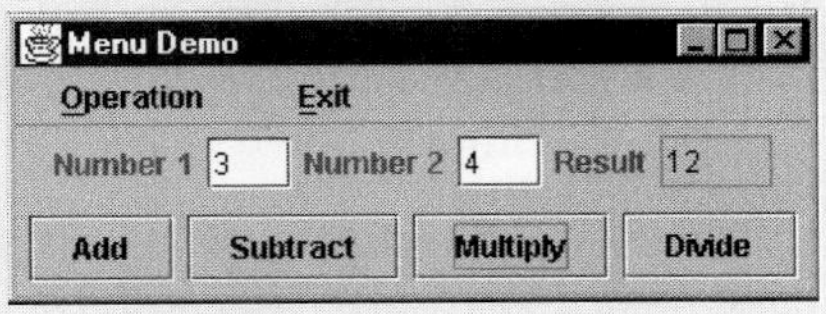

Figure 9.25   *The arithmetic operations can be performed by clicking buttons or by choosing menu items from the Operation menu.*

continues

Example Review

The program creates a menu bar, jmb, which holds two menus: operationMenu and exitMenu. The operationMenu contains four menu items for doing arithmetic: Add, Subtract, Multiply, and Divide. The exitMenu contains the menu item Close for exiting the program. The menu items in the Operation menu are created with keyboard mnemonics and accelerators.

The user enters two numbers in the number fields. If the user chooses an operation from the menu, the result of the operation involving two numbers is displayed in the Result field. The user may also click the buttons to perform the same operation.

The private method calculate(char operator) retrieves operands from the text fields in Number 1 and Number 2, applies the binary operator on the operands, and sets the result in the Result text field.

Creating Multiple Windows

You may occasionally want to create multiple windows in an application. Suppose that your application has two tasks: displaying traffic lights and performing arithmetic calculations. You can design a main frame with two buttons representing the two tasks. When the user clicks one of the buttons, the application opens a new window for performing the specified task. The new windows are called *subwindows,* and the main frame is called the *main window.*

To create a subwindow from an application, you usually need to create a subclass of JFrame that defines the task and tells the new window what to do. You can then create an instance of subclass in the application and launch the new window by setting the frame instance to be visible.

Example 9.12   Creating Multiple Windows

This example creates a main window with two buttons: Simple Calculator and Traffic Lights. When the user clicks Simple Calculator, a new window appears to let the user perform add, subtract, multiply, and divide operations. When the user clicks Traffic Lights, another window appears to display traffic lights.

The Simple Calculator frame named MenuDemo is given in Example 9.11, and the Traffic Lights frame named RadioButtonDemo is given in Example 9.8. They can be directly used in this example without modification.

Figure 9.26 contains the output of a sample run of the program.

```
// MultipleWindowsDemo.java: Use multiple windows in an application
package Chapter9;
```

```java
import Chapter8.MyFrameWithExitHandling;
import java.awt.*;
import java.awt.event.*;
import javax.swing.*;

public class MultipleWindowsDemo
  extends MyFrameWithExitHandling implements ActionListener
{
  // Declare and create a frame: an instance of MenuDemo
  MenuDemo calcFrame = new MenuDemo();

  // Declare and create a frame: an instance of RadioButtonDemo
  RadioButtonDemo lightsFrame = new RadioButtonDemo();

  // Declare two buttons for displaying frames
  private JButton jbtCalc;
  private JButton jbtLights;

  public static void main(String[] args)
  {
    MultipleWindowsDemo frame = new MultipleWindowsDemo();
    frame.pack();
    frame.setVisible(true);
  }

  public MultipleWindowsDemo()
  {
    setTitle("Multiple Windows Demo");

    // Add buttons to the main frame
    getContentPane().setLayout(new FlowLayout());
    getContentPane().add(jbtCalc = new JButton("Simple Calculator"));
    getContentPane().add(jbtLights = new JButton("Traffic Lights"));

    // Register the main frame as listener for the buttons
    jbtCalc.addActionListener(this);
    jbtLights.addActionListener(this);
  }

  public void actionPerformed(ActionEvent e)
  {
    String actionCommand = e.getActionCommand();
    if (e.getSource() instanceof JButton)
      if ("Simple Calculator".equals(actionCommand))
      {
        // Show the MenuDemo frame
        calcFrame.pack();
        calcFrame.setVisible(true);
      }
      else if ("Traffic Lights".equals(actionCommand))
      {
        // Show the traffic light demo frame
        lightsFrame.pack();
        lightsFrame.setVisible(true);
      }
  }
}
```

continues

403

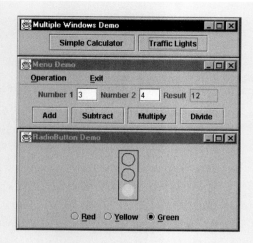

Figure 9.26 *Multiple windows can be displayed simultaneously, as shown in this program.*

Example Review

The program creates `calcFrame` to be an instance of `MenuDemo`, and creates `lightsFrame` to be an instance of `RadioButtonDemo`. The classes `MenuDemo` and `RadioButtonDemo` are given in Examples 9.11 and 9.8, respectively.

The program creates two buttons—Simple Calculator and Traffic Lights—and adds them to the main frame. When a button is clicked, the `ActionEvent` handler determines which source object triggers the event. If the source object is the Simple Calculator button, the window for performing arithmetic calculations is launched with `calcFrame.pack()` and `calcFrame.setVisible(true)`. If the source object is the Traffic Lights button, the window for displaying lights is launched.

Interestingly, the `MenuDemo` class and the `RadioButtonDemo` class are used in this application without any changes. What about the `main()` method in the `MenuDemo` and in the `RadioButtonDemo`? The `main()` method is ignored because the bytecode for `MenuDemo` or `RadioButtonDemo` is not directly invoked by the Java interpreter.

The program has an annoying problem. When you close a subwindow, the whole program exits. This is because the subwindows are the frames that extend `MyFrameWithExitHandling`. How do you close the new windows without terminating the whole program? There are several ways to fix the problem.

One way is to replace `system.exit(0)` in `MyFrameWithExitHandling` with `setVisible(false)`, which in effect closes the subwindow but does not terminate the main frame. The other approach is to change the label of the buttons in the main frame. For example, when you click the Simple Calculator button, the Calculator window appears, and the name of the button changes to Hide Calcu-

404

lator. When you click the Hide Calculator button, the window is closed and the name of the button changes back to Simple Calculator (see Exercise 9.8).

CAUTION

You cannot add an instance of JFrame to a container. For example, adding calcFrame or lightsFrame to the main frame would cause a runtime exception. However, you can create a frame instance and set it to be visible to launch a new window.

Scroll Bars

A *scroll bar* is a control that enables the user to select from a range of values. The scroll bar appears in two styles, *horizontal* and *vertical*, as shown in Figure 9.27.

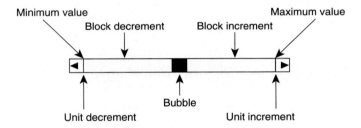

Figure 9.27   *A scroll bar represents a range of values graphically.*

You can use the following constructors to create a scroll bar:

- `public JScrollBar()`

  This constructs a new vertical scroll bar.

- `public JScrollBar(int orientation)`

  This constructs a new scroll bar with the specified orientation (`JScrollBar.HORIZONTAL` or `JScrollBar.VERTICAL`).

- `public JScrollbar(int orientation, int value, int visible, int minimum, int maximum)`

  This constructs a new scroll bar with the specified orientation, initial value, visible bubble size, and minimum and maximum values.

The `JScrollBar` has the following properties.

- `orientation`: Specifies horizontal or vertical style, with `JScrollBar.HORIZONTAL` (0) for horizontal and `JScrollBar.VERTICAL` (1) for vertical.

- **maximum**: The maximum value the scroll bar represents when the bubble reaches to the right end of the scroll bar for horizontal style or to the bottom of the scroll bar for vertical style.

- **minimum**: The minimum value the scroll bar represents when the bubble reaches to the left end of the scroll bar for horizontal style or to the top of the scroll bar for vertical style.

- **visibleAmount**: The relative width of the scroll bar's bubble. The actual width appearing on the screen is determined by the maximum value and the value of `visibleAmount`.

- **value**: Represents the current value of the scroll bar. Normally, a program should change a scroll bar's value by calling the `setValue()` method. The `setValue()` method simultaneously and synchronously sets the minimum, maximum, visible amount and value properties of a scroll bar, so that they are mutually consistent.

- **blockIncrement**: The value that is added (subtracted) when the user activates the block increment (decrement) area of the scroll bar, as shown in Figure 9.27. The `blockIncrement` property, which is new in JDK 1.1, supersedes the `pageIncrement` property used in JDK 1.02.

- **unitIncrement**: The value that is added (subtracted) when the user activates the unit increment (decrement) area of the scroll bar, as shown in Figure 9.27. The `unitIncrement` property, which is new in JDK 1.1, supersedes the `lineIncrement` property used in JDK 1.02.

NOTE

The actual width of the scroll bar's track is `maximum + visibleAmount`. When the scroll bar is set to its maximum value, the left side of the bubble is at `maximum`, and the right side is at `maximum+visibleAmount`.

Normally, the user changes the value of the scroll bar by making a gesture with the mouse. For example, the user can drag the scroll bar's bubble up and down, or click in the scroll bar's unit increment or block increment area. Keyboard gestures can also be mapped to the scroll bar. By convention, the Page Up and Page Down keys are equivalent to clicking in the scroll bar's block increment and block decrement areas.

When the user changes the value of the scroll bar, the scroll bar generates an instance of `AdjustmentEvent`, which is passed to any registered listeners. Any object that wishes to be notified of changes to the scroll bar's value should implement `adjustmentValueChanged()` method in the `AdjustmentListener` interface defined in the package `java.awt.event`.

Example 9.13 Using Scroll Bars

This example uses horizontal and vertical scroll bars to control a message displayed on a panel. You can move the message to the left or the right using the horizontal scroll bar and up and down using the vertical scroll bar. The output of the program is shown in Figure 9.28.

```java
// ScrollBarDemo.java: Use scroll bars to move the message
package Chapter9;

import Chapter8.MyFrameWithExitHandling;
import Chapter8.MessagePanel;
import java.awt.*;
import java.awt.event.*;
import javax.swing.*;

public class ScrollBarDemo extends MyFrameWithExitHandling
  implements AdjustmentListener
{
  // Declare scroll bars
  JScrollBar jscbHort, jscbVert;

  // Declare a MessagePanel
  MessagePanel messagePanel;

  // Main method
  public static void main(String[] args)
  {
    ScrollBarDemo frame = new ScrollBarDemo();
    frame.pack();
    frame.setVisible(true);
  }

  // Constructor
  public ScrollBarDemo()
  {
    setTitle("ScrollBar Demo");

    // Create a vertical scroll bar
    jscbVert = new JScrollBar();
    jscbVert.setOrientation(Adjustable.VERTICAL);

    // Create a horizontal scroll bar
    jscbHort = new JScrollBar();
    jscbHort.setOrientation(Adjustable.HORIZONTAL);

    // Add scroll bars and message panel to the frame
    messagePanel = new MessagePanel("Welcome to Java");
    getContentPane().setLayout(new BorderLayout());
    getContentPane().add(messagePanel, BorderLayout.CENTER);
    getContentPane().add(jscbVert, BorderLayout.EAST);
    getContentPane().add(jscbHort, BorderLayout.SOUTH);

    // Register listener for the scroll bars
    jscbHort.addAdjustmentListener(this);
    jscbVert.addAdjustmentListener(this);
  }

  // Handler for scroll bar adjustment actions
  public void adjustmentValueChanged(AdjustmentEvent e)
  {
```

continues

```
        if (e.getSource() == jscbHort)
        {
          // getValue() and getMaximumValue() return int, but for better
          // precision, use double
          double value = jscbHort.getValue();
          double maximumValue = jscbHort.getMaximum();
          double newX =
            (value*messagePanel.getSize().width/maximumValue);
          messagePanel.setXCoordinate((int)newX);
          messagePanel.repaint();
        }
        else if (e.getSource() == jscbVert)
        {
          // getValue() and getMaximumValue() return int, but for better
          // precision, use double
          double value = jscbVert.getValue();
          double maximumValue = jscbVert.getMaximum();
          double newY =
            (value*messagePanel.getSize().height/maximumValue);
          messagePanel.setYCoordinate((int)newY);
          messagePanel.repaint();
        }
      }
    }
```

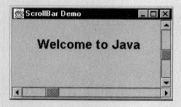

Figure 9.28   *The scroll bars move the message on a panel horizontally and vertically.*

Example Review

The program creates an instance of `MessagePanel` (`messagePanel`) and two scroll bars (`jscbVert` and `jscbHort`). `messagePanel` is placed in the center of the frame; `jscbVert` and `jscbHort` are placed in the east and south sections of the frame, respectively.

You can specify the orientation of the scroll bar in the constructor or use the `setOrientation()` method. By default, the property value is 100 for `maximum`, 0 for `minimum`, 10 for `pageIncrement`, and 10 for `visibleAmount`.

When the user drags the bubble or clicks the increment or decrement unit, the value of the scroll bar changes. An instance of `AdjustmentEvent` is generated and passed to the listener by invoking the `adjustmentValueChanged()` handler. Since there are two scroll bars in the frame, the `e.getSource()` method is used to determine the source of the event. The vertical scroll bar moves the message up and down, and the horizontal bar moves the message to the right and left.

The maximum value of the vertical scroll bar corresponds to the height of the panel, and the maximum value of the horizontal scroll bar corresponds to the width of the panel. The ratio between current value and the maximum of the horizontal scroll bar is the same as the ratio between the x value and the width of the panel. Similarly, the ratio between current value and the maximum of the vertical scroll bar is the same as the ratio between the y value and the height of the panel.

Scroll Panes

Often you need to use a scroll bar to scroll the contents of an object that does not completely fit into the viewing area. JScrollBar can be used for this purpose, but you have to *manually* write the code to implement scrolling with it. JScrollPane is a component that supports *automatically* scrolling without coding. You used it to scroll text area in Example 9.4. In fact, you can use it to scroll any subclass of JComponent.

A JScrollPane can be viewed as a specialized container with a view port that displays the contained component. In addition to horizontal and vertical scroll bars, a JScrollPane can have a column header, a row header, and corners, as shown in Figure 9.29.

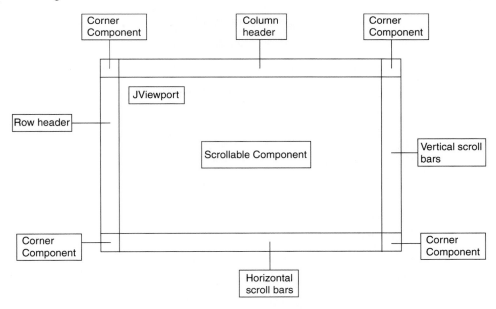

Figure 9.29   *A* JScrollPane *has a view port, optional horizontal and vertical bars, optional column and row headers, and optional corners.*

The view port is an instance of JViewport through which a scrollable component is displayed. When a component is added to a scroll pane, it is actually placed in the scroll pane's view port.

To construct a JScrollPane instance, use the following constructors:

- public JScrollPane()

  This creates an empty scroll pane with a view port and no viewing component where both horizontal and vertical scroll bars appear when needed.

- public JScrollPane(Component view)

  This creates a scroll pane and view port to display the contents of the specified component, where both horizontal and vertical scroll bars appear whenever the component's contents are larger than the view.

- public JScrollPane(Component view, int vsbPolicy, int hsbPolicy)

  This creates a scroll pane that displays the view component in a view port whose view position can be controlled with a pair of scroll bars.

- public JScrollPane(int vsbPolicy, int hsbPolicy)

  This creates an empty scroll pane with specified scroll bar policies.

The constructor always creates a view port regardless of whether the viewing component is specified. The vsbPolicy parameter can be one of the following three values:

JScrollPane.VERTICAL_SCROLLBAR_AS_NEEDED

JScrollPane.VERTICAL_SCROLLBAR_NEVER

JScrollPane.VERTICAL_SCROLLBAR_ALWAYS

The hsbPolicy parameter can be one of the following three values:

JScrollPane.HORIZONTAL_SCROLLBAR_AS_NEEDED

JScrollPane.HORIZONTAL_SCROLLBAR_NEVER

JScrollPane.HORIZONTAL_SCROLLBAR_ALWAYS

The following properties of JScrollPane are often useful:

- horizontalScrollBarPolicy: Determines when the horizontal scroll bar appears in the scroll pane.

- verticalScrollBarPolicy: Determines when the vertical scroll bar appears in the scroll pane.

- viewportView: Specifies the component to be viewed in the view port.

- viewportBorder: Specifies a border around the view port in the scroll pane.

- rowHeaderView: Specifies the row header view component to be used in the scroll pane.

- columnHeaderView: Specifies the column header view component to be used in the scroll pane.

To set a corner component, use the following method:

```
public void setCorner(String key,
                        Component corner)
```

Legal values for the key are the following:

```
JScrollPane.LOWER_LEFT_CORNER

JScrollPane.LOWER_RIGHT_CORNER

JScrollPane.UPPER_LEFT_CORNER

JScrollPane.UPPER_RIGHT_CORNER
```

Example 9.14 Using Scroll Panes

This example uses a scroll pane to browse a large map. The program lets you choose a map from a combo box and display it in the scroll pane, as shown in Figure 9.30.

```java
// ScrollPaneDemo.java: Use scroll pane to view large maps
package Chapter9;

import Chapter8.MyFrameWithExitHandling;
import java.awt.*;
import java.awt.event.*;
import javax.swing.*;
import javax.swing.border.*;

public class ScrollPaneDemo extends MyFrameWithExitHandling
  implements ItemListener
{
  // Create images in labels
  private JLabel lblIndianaMap =
    new JLabel(new ImageIcon("images/indianaMap.gif"));
  private JLabel lblOhioMap =
    new JLabel(new ImageIcon("images/ohioMap.gif"));

  // Declare a scroll pane to scroll map in the labels
  private JScrollPane jspMap;

  // Main method
  public static void main(String[] args)
  {
    ScrollPaneDemo frame = new ScrollPaneDemo();
    frame.setSize(300, 300);
    frame.setVisible(true);
  }

  // Default constructor
  public ScrollPaneDemo()
  {
    setTitle("ScrollPane Demo");

    // Create a scroll pane with northern California map
    jspMap = new JScrollPane(lblIndianaMap);

    // Create a combo box for selecting maps
    JComboBox jcboMap = new JComboBox();
    jcboMap.addItem("Indiana");
    jcboMap.addItem("Ohio");
```

continues

411

```java
      // Panel p to hold combo box
      JPanel p = new JPanel();
      p.setLayout(new BorderLayout());
      p.add(jcboMap);
      p.setBorder(new TitledBorder("Select a map to display"));

      // Set row header, column header and corner header
      jspMap.setColumnHeaderView(
        new JLabel(new ImageIcon("images/horizontalRuler.gif")));
      jspMap.setRowHeaderView(
        new JLabel(new ImageIcon("images/verticalRuler.gif")));
      jspMap.setCorner(JScrollPane.UPPER_LEFT_CORNER,
        new CornerPanel(JScrollPane.UPPER_LEFT_CORNER));
      jspMap.setCorner(ScrollPaneConstants.UPPER_RIGHT_CORNER,
        new CornerPanel(JScrollPane.UPPER_RIGHT_CORNER));
      jspMap.setCorner(JScrollPane.LOWER_RIGHT_CORNER,
        new CornerPanel(JScrollPane.LOWER_RIGHT_CORNER));
      jspMap.setCorner(JScrollPane.LOWER_LEFT_CORNER,
        new CornerPanel(JScrollPane.LOWER_LEFT_CORNER));

      // Add the scroll pane and combo box panel to the frame
      getContentPane().add(jspMap, BorderLayout.CENTER);
      getContentPane().add(p, BorderLayout.SOUTH);

      // Register listener
      jcboMap.addItemListener(this);
    }

    public void itemStateChanged(ItemEvent e)
    {
      String selectedItem = (String)e.getItem();
      if (selectedItem.equals("Indiana"))
      {
        // Set a new view in the view port
        jspMap.setViewportView(lblIndianaMap);
      }
      else if (selectedItem.equals("Ohio"))
      {
        // Set a new view in the view port
        jspMap.setViewportView(lblOhioMap);
      }

      // Revalidate the scroll pane
      jspMap.revalidate();
    }
  }

  // A panel displaying a line used for scroll pane corner
  class CornerPanel extends JPanel implements ScrollPaneConstants
  {
    // Line location
    private String location;

    // Constructor
    public CornerPanel(String location)
    {
      this.location = location;
    }

    // Draw a line depending on the location
    public void paintComponent(Graphics g)
    {
```

```
            super.paintComponents(g);

            if (location == "UPPER_LEFT_CORNER")
              g.drawLine(0, getSize().height, getSize().width, 0);
            else if (location == "UPPER_RIGHT_CORNER")
              g.drawLine(0, 0, getSize().width, getSize().height);
            else if (location == "LOWER_RIGHT_CORNER")
              g.drawLine(0, getSize().height, getSize().width, 0);
            else if (location == "LOWER_LEFT_CORNER")
              g.drawLine(0, 0, getSize().width, getSize().height);
          }
      }
```

Figure 9.30   *The scroll pane can be used to scroll contents automatically.*

Example Review

The program creates a scroll pane to view image maps. The image maps are created using the ImageIcon class and placed in labels. To view an image, the label that contains the image is placed in the scroll pane's view port.

The scroll pane has a main view, a header view, a column view, and four corner views. Each view is a subclass of Component. Since ImageIcon is not a subclass of Component, it cannot be directly used as a view in the scroll pane. Thus the program places an ImageIcon to a label and uses the label as a view.

The CornerPanel is a subclass of JPanel, which is used to display a line. How the line is drawn depends on the location of the corner. The location is a string, passed in as a parameter in the CornerPanel's constructor. Since the CornerPanel class also implements the ScrollPaneConstants interface, the constants indicating the four corners are available in CornerPanel.

Whenever a new map is selected, the label for displaying the map image is set to the scroll pane's view port. The validate() method must be invoked to cause the new image to be displayed. The validate() method causes a container to lay out its subcomponents again after the components it contains have been added to or modified.

Tabbed Panes

JTabbedPane is a useful Swing component that provides a set of mutually exclusive tabs for accessing multiple components. Usually you place the panels inside a JTabbedPane and associate a tab with each panel. JTabbedPane is easy to use, since the selection of the panel is handled automatically by clicking the corresponding tab. You can switch between a group of panels by clicking on a tab with a given title and/or icon.

To construct a JTabbedPane instance, use the following constructors:

- public JTabbedPane()

  Creates an empty tabbed pane.

- public JTabbedPane(int tabPlacement)

  Creates an empty tabbed pane with the specified tab placement of either SwingConstants.TOP, SwingConstants.BOTTOM, SwingConstants.LEFT, or SwingConstants.RIGHT.

You can also use this method to set the tab placement:

```
public void setTabPlacement(int tabPlacement)
```

By default, the tabs are placed at top.

To add a component to a JTabbedPane, use the following add() method:

```
add(Component component, Object constraints)
```

Where component is the component to be displayed when this tab is clicked and constraints can be a title for the tab.

Example 9.15 Using Tabbed Panes

This example uses a tabbed pane with four tabs to display four types of figures: Square, Rectangle, Circle, and Oval. You can select a figure to display by clicking the corresponding tab. You can also use the radio button to specify the tab placement. A sample run of the program is shown in Figure 9.31.

```java
// TabbedPaneDemo.java: Use tabbed pane to select figures
package Chapter9;

import Chapter8.MyFrameWithExitHandling;
import java.awt.*;
import java.awt.event.*;
import javax.swing.*;
import javax.swing.border.TitledBorder;

public class TabbedPaneDemo extends MyFrameWithExitHandling
  implements ItemListener
{
  // Create a tabbed pane to hold figure panels
  private JTabbedPane jtpFigures = new JTabbedPane();
```

```
    // Radio buttons for specifying where tab is placed
    private JRadioButton jrbTop, jrbLeft, jrbRight, jrbBottom;

    // Main method
    public static void main(String[] args)
    {
      TabbedPaneDemo frame = new TabbedPaneDemo();
      frame.setSize(200, 300);
      frame.center();
      frame.setVisible(true);
    }

    // Constructor
    public TabbedPaneDemo()
    {
      setTitle("Tabbed Pane Demo");

      jtpFigures.add(new FigurePanel(FigurePanel.SQUARE), "Square");
      jtpFigures.add(
        new FigurePanel(FigurePanel.RECTANGLE), "Rectangle");
      jtpFigures.add(new FigurePanel(FigurePanel.CIRCLE), "Circle");
      jtpFigures.add(new FigurePanel(FigurePanel.OVAL), "Oval");

      // Panel p to hold radio buttons for specifying tab location
      JPanel p = new JPanel();
      p.add(jrbTop = new JRadioButton("TOP"));
      p.add(jrbLeft = new JRadioButton("LEFT"));
      p.add(jrbRight = new JRadioButton("RIGHT"));
      p.add(jrbBottom = new JRadioButton("BOTTOM"));
      p.setBorder(new TitledBorder("Specify tab location"));

      // Group radio buttons
      ButtonGroup btg = new ButtonGroup();
      btg.add(jrbTop);
      btg.add(jrbLeft);
      btg.add(jrbRight);
      btg.add(jrbBottom);

      // Place tabbed pane and panel p into the frame
      this.getContentPane().add(jtpFigures, BorderLayout.CENTER);
      this.getContentPane().add(p, BorderLayout.SOUTH);

      // Register listeners
      jrbTop.addItemListener(this);
      jrbLeft.addItemListener(this);
      jrbRight.addItemListener(this);
      jrbBottom.addItemListener(this);
    }

    // Handle radio button selection
    public void itemStateChanged(ItemEvent e)
    {
      if (jrbTop.isSelected())
        jtpFigures.setTabPlacement(SwingConstants.TOP);
      else if (jrbLeft.isSelected())
        jtpFigures.setTabPlacement(SwingConstants.LEFT);
      else if (jrbRight.isSelected())
        jtpFigures.setTabPlacement(SwingConstants.RIGHT);
      else if (jrbBottom.isSelected())
        jtpFigures.setTabPlacement(SwingConstants.BOTTOM);
    }
}
```

continues

```java
// The panel for displaying a figure
class FigurePanel extends JPanel
{
  final static int SQUARE = 1;
  final static int RECTANGLE = 2;
  final static int CIRCLE = 3;
  final static int OVAL = 4;
  private int figureType = 1;

  // Constructing a figure panel
  public FigurePanel(int figureType)
  {
    this.figureType = figureType;
  }

  // Drawing a figure on the panel
  public void paintComponent(Graphics g)
  {
    super.paintComponent(g);

    // Get the appropriate size for the figure
    int width = getSize().width;
    int height = getSize().height;
    int side = (int)(0.80*Math.min(width, height));

    switch (figureType)
    {
      case 1:
        g.drawRect((width-side)/2, (height-side)/2, side, side);
        break;
      case 2:
        g.drawRect((int)(0.1*width), (int)(0.1*height),
          (int)(0.8*width), (int)(0.8*height));
        break;
      case 3:
        g.drawOval((width-side)/2, (height-side)/2, side, side);
        break;
      case 4:
        g.drawOval((int)(0.1*width), (int)(0.1*height),
          (int)(0.8*width), (int)(0.8*height));
        break;
    }
  }
}
```

Figure 9.31   *A tabbed pane can be used to access multiple components using tabs.*

Example Review

The program creates a tabbed pane that holds four panels, each of which displays a figure. Each panel is associated with a tab. Tabs are created using the `add()` method and are titled Square, Rectangle, Circle, and Oval.

By default, the tabs are placed at the top of the tabbed pane. You can use the radio buttons to select a different placement, as shown in Figure 9.32.

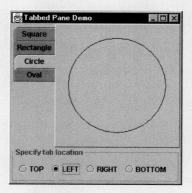

Figure 9.32   *The tabs can be placed at top, bottom, left, or right of the tabbed pane.*

Chapter Summary

In this chapter, you learned how to create graphical user interfaces using `JButton`, `JLabel`, `JTextField`, `JTextArea`, `JComboBox`, `JList`, `JCheckBox`, `JRadioButton`, Border (`TitledBorder`, `BevelBorder`, `LineBorder`, `EtchedBorder`, `MatteBorder`, and `EmptyBorder`), message dialog boxes, `JMenuBar`, `JMenu`, `JMenuItem`, `JCheckBoxMenuItem`, `JRadioButtonMenuItem`, `JScrollBar`, and `JScrollPane`.

`JButton` activates actions. The user expects something to happen when a button is clicked. Clicking a button generates an `ActionEvent` and invokes the listener's `actionPerformed()` method.

`JLabel` is an area for displaying texts or images, or both.

`JTextField` accepts user input into a string. `JTextArea` can accept multiple lines of strings.

`JComboBox` is a simple list of values to choose from. `JList` allows multiple selections. `JCheckBox` is for specifying whether an item is selected or not. `JRadioButton` is similar to `JCheckBox`, but is generally used to select a value exclusively.

A dialog box is used to gather information from the user or show information to the user. This chapter introduced the `showMessageDialog()` method in the `JOptionPane` class, which can be used to display a simple message box.

Menus can be placed in a frame or an applet. A menu bar is used to hold the menus. You must add a menu bar to the frame or applet by using the `setJMenuBar()` method, add menus to the menu bar, and add menu items to the menu.

Scroll bars are the controls for selecting from a range of values. You can use the `JScrollBar` class to create scroll bars, and the `setOrientation()` method to specify horizontal or vertical scroll bars. In most cases, using `JScrollPane` is convenient because it provides automatic scrolling.

`JTabbedPane` can be used to select multiple panels using tabs. The tabs can be placed at the top, left, right, or bottom. Since tab selection is automatically implemented in `JTabbedPane`, clicking a tab causes the associated panel to be displayed.

To handle events generated by buttons, combo boxes, check boxes, radio buttons, menus, or scroll bars, you must register the listener object with the source object and implement the corresponding listener interface.

Since you cannot add an instance of the Window class to a container, a frame cannot be put into a frame. However, you can create a frame and set it to visible to launch a separate window in the program.

Chapter Review

9.1. How do you create a button labeled "OK"? How do you change a label on a button? How do you set an icon in a button?

9.2. How do you create a label named "Address"? How do you change the name on a label? How do you set an icon in a label?

9.3. How do you create a text field with a width of 10 characters and the default text "Welcome to Java"?

9.4. How do you create a text area with 10 rows and 20 columns? How do you insert three lines into the text area? How do you create a scrollable text area?

9.5. How do you create a combo box, add three items into it, and retrieve a selected item?

9.6. How do you create a check box? How do you determine whether a box is checked?

9.7. How do you create a radio button? How do you group the radio buttons together? How do you determine whether a radio button is selected?

9.8. Can you have a border for any subclass of `JComponent`? How do you set a titled border for a panel?

9.9. How do you create the menus File, Edit, View, Insert, Format, and Help, and add the menu items Toolbar, Format Bar, Ruler, Status Bar, and Options to the View menu? (See Figure 9.33.)

9.10. How do you create a vertical scroll bar? What event can a scroll bar generate?

9.11. How do you create a scroll pane to view an image file?

9.12. Describe how to create a simple message dialog box. Describe the message types used in the `JOptionPane` class.

Figure 9.33   *Create a menu like this in WordPad, with menus and menu items.*

9.13. Describe how to create and show multiple frames in an application.

9.14. What is the method to make the layout manager lay out the components in a container again? When should a container be laid out again?

9.15. Suppose you want to display the same component named c into the four corners of a scroll pane named jsp. What is wrong if the following statements are used?

```
jsp.setCorner(JScrollPane.UPPER_LEFT_CORNER, c);
jsp.setCorner(JScrollPane.UPPER_RIGHT_CORNER, c);
jsp.setCorner(JScrollPane.LOWER_RIGHT_CORNER, c);
jsp.setCorner(JScrollPane.LOWER_LEFT_CORNER, c);
```

(Since each corner view is an individual component, you need to create four separate objects.)

Programming Exercises

9.1. Rewrite Example 9.1 to add a group of radio buttons to select background colors. The available colors are red, yellow, white, gray, and green (see Figure 9.34).

Figure 9.34   *The <= and => buttons move the message on the panel, and you can also set the color for the message.*

9.2. Rewrite Example 9.3 to handle double values and perform subtract, multiply, and divide operations in addition to the add operation (see Figure 9.35).

9.3. Write a program to meet the following requirements:

Figure 9.35   *The program performs addition, subtraction, multiplication, and division on double numbers.*

- Create a text field, a text area, and a combo box in a panel using the FlowLayout.

- Create a button labeled Store and place it in a panel using the FlowLayout.

- Place the preceding two panels in a frame.

- The action of the Store button is to retrieve the item from the text field and store it in a text area, or a combo box.

- When an item in the combo box is selected, it is displayed in the text field.

9.4. Write a program to convert Celsius and Fahrenheit temperatures, as shown in Figure 9.36. If you enter a value in the Celsius degree text field and press the Enter key, the Fahrenheit temperature is displayed in the Fahrenheit text field. Likewise, if you enter a value in the Fahrenheit degree text field, the corresponding Celsius degree is displayed in the Celsius text field.

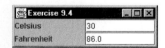

Figure 9.36   *The program converts Celsius to Fahrenheit, and vice versa.*

9.5. Write a program to draw various figures on a panel. The user selects a figure from a radio button. The selected figure is then displayed on the panel (see Figure 9.37).

Figure 9.37   *The program displays lines, rectangles, ovals, arcs, or polygons when you select a shape type.*

9.6. Write a program to calculate the future value of an investment at a given interest rate for a specified number of years. The formula for the calculation is as follows:

futureValue = investmentAmount × (1 + interestRate)^{years}

Use text fields for interest rate, investment amount, and years. Display the future amount in a text field when the user clicks the Calculate button or chooses Calculate from the Operation menu (see Figure 9.38). Show a message dialog box when the user clicks the About menu item from the Help menu.

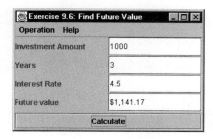

Figure 9.38   *The user enters the investment amount, years, and interest rate to compute future value.*

9.7. Use `JTabbedPane` to write a program that displays maps of the USA, UK, Germany, Canada, China, and India (see Figure 9.39).

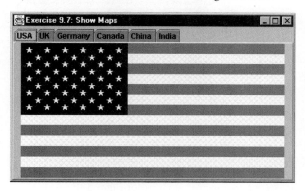

Figure 9.39   *You can show the map by selecting a tab in the tabbed pane.*

9.8. Rewrite Example 9.12, "Creating Multiple Windows," as follows:

■ When the user clicks the Simple Calculator button, the Calculator window appears and the name of the button changes to Hide Calculator. When the user clicks the Hide Calculator button, the window is closed, and the name of the button changes back to Simple Calculator.

■ Modify the function of the Traffic Lights button in the same way as in the preceding item.

9.9. Write a program to use the scroll bars to select the foreground color for a label, as shown in Figure 9.40. Three horizontal scroll bars are used for selecting red, green, and blue components of the color. Use a title border on the panel that holds the scroll bars.

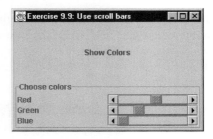

Figure 9.40   *The foreground color changes in the label as you adjust the scroll bars.*

9.10. Write a program to compute sales amount or commission, as shown in Figure 9.41. When the user types a sales amount in the Sales Amount text field and presses the Enter key, the commission is displayed in the Commission text field. Likewise, when the user types a commission, the corresponding sales amount is displayed. The commission rates are the same as in Example 3.7, "Finding Sales Amount." Labels are used to display the commission rates.

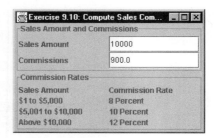

Figure 9.41   *The sales amount and the commission are synchronized. You can compute sales amount given the commission or compute commission given the sales amount.*

9.11. Write a program to set the alignment and text position properties of a button dynamically, as shown in Figure 9.42.

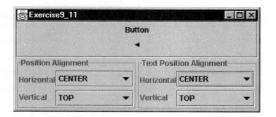

Figure 9.42   *You can dynamically set the alignment and text position properties of a button.*

9.12. Write a program to dynamically set the horizontal alignment and column size properties of a text field, as shown in Figure 9.43.

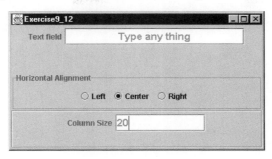

Figure 9.43 *You can dynamically set the horizontal alignment and column size properties of a text field.*

9.13. Write a program that demonstrates the wrapping styles of the text area. The program uses a check box to indicate whether the text area is wrapped. If it is, you need to specify whether it is wrapped by characters or by words, as shown in Figure 9.44.

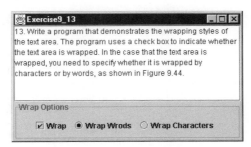

Figure 9.44 *You can dynamically set the options to wrap a text area by characters or by words.*

9.14. Write a program that demonstrates selecting items in a list. The program uses a combo box to specify a selection mode, as shown in Figure 9.45. When you select items, they are displayed in a label below the list.

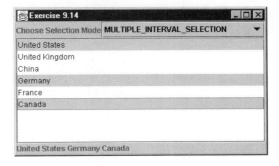

Figure 9.45 *You can choose single selection, single-interval selection, or multiple-interval selection in a list.*

CHAPTER 10

APPLETS AND ADVANCED GRAPHICS

Objectives

- ✪ Understand how the Web browser controls and executes applets.
- ✪ Become familiar with the `init()`, `start()`, `stop()`, and `destroy()` methods in the `Applet` class.
- ✪ Pass parameters to applets from HTML.
- ✪ Create applets using the Applet Wizard.
- ✪ Convert between applications and applets.
- ✪ Write a Java program that can run as an application and as an applet.
- ✪ Handle mouse events and keystrokes.
- ✪ Understand and use `CardLayout` and `GridBagLayout`, or use no layout managers.
- ✪ Deploy Java applications and applets with archived files using the Deployment Wizard.

Introduction

Java's early success was attributed to applets. Applets can run from a Java-enabled Web browser and can bring dynamic interaction and live animation to an otherwise static HTML page. It is safe to say that Java would be nowhere today without applets. They make Java appealing, attractive, and popular.

In this book so far, you have used Java applications in examples that introduce Java programming. Everything you have learned about writing applications, however, also applies to writing applets. Because applets are invoked from a Web page, Java provides special features that enable applets to run from a Web browser.

In this chapter, you will learn how to write Java applets, discover the relationship between applets and the Web browser, and explore the similarities and differences between applications and applets. You also will see more complex examples of handling mouse events and keystrokes, and using advanced layout managers.

The *Applet* Classes

As shown in Chapter 1, "Introduction to Java and JBuilder 3," every Java applet extends the `java.applet.Applet` class. The `Applet` class provides the essential framework that enables your applets to be run by a Web browser. Every Java application has a main method, which is executed when the application starts. Unlike applications, applets do not have a main method. Applets depend on the browser to call the methods. Every applet has a structure like the one that follows:

```
public class MyApplet extends java.applet.Applet
{
  ...
  // Called by the browser when the Web page containing
  // this applet is initially loaded
  public void init()
  {
    ...
  }

  // Called by the browser after the init() method and
  // every time the Web page is visited.
  public void start()
  {
    ...
  }

  // Called by the browser when the page containing this
  // applet becomes inactive.
  public void stop()
  {
    ...
  }

  // Called by the browser when the Web browser exits.
  public void destroy()
  {
    ...
  }
```

426

```
    // Other methods if necessary...
}
```

The browser controls the applets using the `init()`, `start()`, `stop()`, and `destroy()` methods. By default, these methods do nothing. To perform specific functions, they need to be modified in the user's applet so that the browser can call your code properly. Figure 10.1 shows how the browser calls these methods.

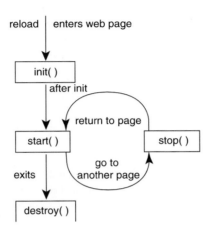

Figure 10.1 *The Web browser controls the applet using the* `init()`, `start()`, `stop()`, *and* `destroy()` *methods.*

The *init()* method

The `init()` method is invoked when the applet is first loaded and again if it is re-loaded.

A subclass of `Applet` should override this method if the subclass has an initialization to perform. Functions usually implemented with this method include creating new threads, loading images, setting up user interface components, and getting parameters from the `<applet>` tag in the HTML page. Chapter 13, "Multithreading," discusses threads in more detail; passing `Applet` parameters is discussed later in this chapter.

The *start()* method

The `start()` method is invoked after the `init()` method. It is also called whenever the applet becomes active again after a period of inactivity. The `start()` method is called, for example, when the user returns to the Web page containing the applet after surfing other pages.

A subclass of `Applet` should override this method if it has any operation that needs to be performed every time the Web page containing the applet is visited. An applet with animation, for example, might want to use the `start()` method to re-sume animation.

The *stop()* method

The `stop()` method is the opposite of the `start()` method. The `start()` method is called when the user moves back to the page containing the applet. The `stop()` method is invoked when the user moves off the page.

A subclass of `Applet` should override this method if it has any operation that needs to be performed each time the Web page containing the applet is no longer visible. When the user leaves the page, any threads the applet has started—but not com-pleted—will continue to run. You should override the `stop()` method to suspend the running threads so that the applet does not take up system resources when it is not active.

The *destroy()* method

The `destroy()` method is invoked when the browser exits normally, to inform the applet that it is no longer needed and should release any resources it has allocated. The `stop()` method is always called before the `destroy()` method.

A subclass of `Applet` should override this method if it has any operation that needs to be performed before it is destroyed. It is usually not necessary to override this method unless you need to release specific resources, such as threads that the applet created.

The *JApplet* Class

The `Applet` class is an AWT class and does not work well with Swing components. To use Swing components in Java applets, you should create a Java applet that ex-tends `javax.swing.JApplet`, which is a subclass of `java.applet.Applet`. `JApplet` in-herits all the methods from the `Applet` class. In addition, it provides support for laying out Swing components.

To add a component to a `JApplet`, you need to add it to the content pane of a `JApplet` instance, which is the same as adding a component to a `JFrame` instance. By default, the content pane of `JApplet` uses `BorderLayout`.

Example 10.1 Using Applets

This example shows an applet that computes mortgages. The applet enables the user to enter the interest rate, the number of years, and the loan amount. Click-ing the Compute button displays the monthly payment and the total payment. The applet and the HTML code containing the applet are provided in the fol-lowing code. Figure 10.2 contains a sample run of the applet.

```java
// MortgageApplet.java: Applet for computing mortgage payments
package Chapter10;

import Chapter5.Mortgage;
import java.awt.*;
import java.awt.event.*;
import javax.swing.*;
import javax.swing.border.TitledBorder;

public class MortgageApplet extends JApplet
  implements ActionListener
{
  // Declare and create text fields for interest rate
  // year, loan amount, monthly payment, and total payment
  private JTextField jtfInterestRate = new JTextField(10);
  private JTextField jtfYear = new JTextField(10);
  private JTextField jtfLoan = new JTextField(10);
  private JTextField jtfMonthlyPay = new JTextField(10);
  private JTextField jtfTotalPay = new JTextField(10);

  // Declare and create a Compute Mortgage button
  private JButton jbtCompute = new JButton("Compute Mortgage");

  // Initialize user interface
  public void init()
  {
    // Set properties on the text fields
    jtfMonthlyPay.setEditable(false);
    jtfTotalPay.setEditable(false);

    // Panel p1 to hold labels and text fields
    JPanel p1 = new JPanel();
    p1.setLayout(new GridLayout(5,2));
    p1.add(new Label("Interest Rate"));
    p1.add(jtfInterestRate);
    p1.add(new Label("Years "));
    p1.add(jtfYear);
    p1.add(new Label("Loan Amount"));
    p1.add(jtfLoan);
    p1.add(new Label("Monthly Payment"));
    p1.add(jtfMonthlyPay);
    p1.add(new Label("Total Payment"));
    p1.add(jtfTotalPay);
    p1.setBorder(new
      TitledBorder("Enter interest rate, year and loan amount"));

    // Panel p2 to hold the button
    JPanel p2 = new JPanel();
    p2.setLayout(new FlowLayout(FlowLayout.RIGHT));
    p2.add(jbtCompute);

    // Add the components to the applet
    getContentPane().add(p1, BorderLayout.CENTER);
    getContentPane().add(p2, BorderLayout.SOUTH);

    // Register listener
    jbtCompute.addActionListener(this);
  }

  // Handler for the "Compute" button
  public void actionPerformed(ActionEvent e)
  {
```

continues

```
                      if (e.getSource() == jbtCompute)
                      {
                        // Get values from text fields
                        double interest =
                          (Double.valueOf(jtfInterestRate.getText())).doubleValue();
                        int year =
                          (Integer.valueOf(jtfYear.getText())).intValue();
                        double loan =
                          (Double.valueOf(jtfLoan.getText())).doubleValue();

                        // Create a mortgage object
                        Mortgage m = new Mortgage(interest, year, loan);

                        // Display monthly payment and total payment
                        jtfMonthlyPay.setText(String.valueOf(m.monthlyPay()));
                        jtfTotalPay.setText(String.valueOf(m.totalPay()));
                      }
                    }
                  }

                  <!-- HTML code, this code is separated from the preceding Java code>
                  <html>
                  <head>
                  <title>Mortgage Applet</title>
                  </head>
                  <body>
                  This is a mortgage calculator, enter your input for interest, year
                  and loan amount, click the "Compute" button, you will get the
                  payment information.<p>
                  <applet
                    code = "Chapter10.MortgageApplet.class"
                    width = 300
                    height = 150
                    alt="You must have a JDK1.2-enabled browser to view the applet">
                  </applet>
                  </body>
                  </html>
```

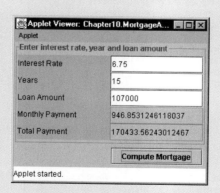

Figure 10.2   *The applet computes the monthly payment and the total payment when provided with the interest rate, number of years, and loan amount.*

Example Review

Unless you use the `public` modifier for the `MortgageApplet`, the Web browser cannot load the applet.

`MortgageApplet` implements `ActionListener` because it listens for button actions.

The `init()` method initializes the user interface. The program overrides this method to create user interface components (labels, text fields, and a button), and places them in the applet.

The only event handler is the Compute button. When it is clicked, the `action-Performed()` method gets the interest rate, year, and loan from the text fields. It then creates a `Mortgage` object to obtain the monthly pay and the total pay. Finally, it displays the monthly and total payments in their respective text fields.

The `Mortgage` class is responsible for computing the payments. This class was discussed in Example 5.7, "Using the `Mortgage` Class" (see Chapter 5, "Programming with Objects and Classes").

The monthly and total payments are not displayed in currency format. To display a number as currency, see Chapter 12, "Internationalization."

Applets are embedded in HTML using the `<applet>` tag, which is discussed in the next section. The `code` parameter specifies the location of the applet byte-code file. The `width` and `height`, both in pixels, specify the initial size of the applet.

The HTML file that invokes the applet should be placed in the directory c:\jbBook. You can create the HTML file by clicking the HTML icon in the Object Gallery (see Figure 1.22).

Suppose the HTML file is named MortgageApplet.html. To run the applet from JBuilder, select MortgageApplet.html in the Navigation pane, right-click the mouse button to display the context menu, and choose Run to run the applet using the Applet Viewer utility.

The *<applet>* HTML Tag

To run applets, you must create an HTML file with the `<applet>` tag to specify the applet bytecode file, the applet viewing area dimension (width and height), and other associated parameters. The syntax of the `<applet>` tag is as follows:

```
<applet
  code=classfilename.class
  width=applet_viewing_width_in_pixels
  height=applet_viewing_height_in_pixels
  [archive=archivefile]
  [codebase=applet_url]
  [vspace=vertical_margin]
```

```
    [hspace=horizontal_margin]
    [align=applet_alignment]
    [alt=alternative_text]
>
<param name=param_name1 value=param_value1>
<param name=param_name2 value=param_value2>
...
<param name=param_name3 value=param_value3>
</applet>
```

The code, width, and height attributes are required; all others are optional. The <param> tag is introduced in the section "Passing Parameters to Applets." The other attributes are described below:

- **archive**—You can use this attribute to instruct the browser to load an archive file that contains all the class files needed to run the applet. The archiving allows the Web browser to load all the classes from a single compressed file only once—thus reducing loading time and improving performance. To learn how to create archives, see the section "Packaging and Deploying Java Projects in JBuilder," later in this chapter.

- **codebase**—If this attribute is not used, the Web browser loads the applet from the directory in which the HTML page is located. If your applet is located in a different directory from the HTML page, you must specify the applet_url for the browser to load the applet. This attribute enables you to load the class from anywhere on the Internet. The classes used by the applet are dynamically loaded when needed.

- **vspace** and **hspace**—These two attributes specify the size in pixels of the blank margin to leave around the applet vertically and horizontally.

- **align**—This attribute specifies how the applet will be aligned in the browser. One of nine values is used: left, right, top, texttop, middle, absmiddle, baseline, bottom, and absbottom.

- **alt**—This attribute specifies the text to be displayed in case the browser cannot run Java.

NOTE

The W3 consortium (**www.w3.org**) has introduced the <object> tag to replace the <applet> tag. The <object> tag has more options and is more versatile than the <applet> tag. This book will continue to use the <applet> tag, since not all Web browsers support the <object> tag at this time.

Running Applets in the Java Plug-In (Optional)

When Java was first introduced in 1995, the only Web browser for viewing Java applets was the HotJava browser by Sun. Netscape quickly updated Navigator 2 to support JDK 1.0. Microsoft followed suit to support JDK 1.0 in Internet Explorer 3. As Java rapidly evolves, browser vendors are falling behind in their efforts to keep up with Java updates. Consequently, it may not be possible to view your Java applets on certain Web browsers. To address this problem, Sun introduced Java Plug-In technology, which enables browsers to install the Java Plug-In and view your applets consistently on any platform.

To use the Java Plug-In, you have to convert your simple HTML file to a rather complex HTML file using the Java Plug-in HTML Converter supplied by Java-Soft. The converter can be downloaded from

www.javasoft.com/products/plugin/1.2/converter.html

in a compressed file named **htmlconv12.zip**. To install it, unzip it and save it in a directory. To use the converter, change the directory to where the HTMLConvert.class is located and type

`java HTMLConverter`

at the DOS prompt to display a window titled "Java Plug-in HTML Converter," as shown in Figure 10.3. Check the One File radio button, specify the simple HTML file with the `<applet>` tag in the text field followed after the label "One File," and select an appropriate conversion template in the Template File text field, as shown in Figure 10.3.

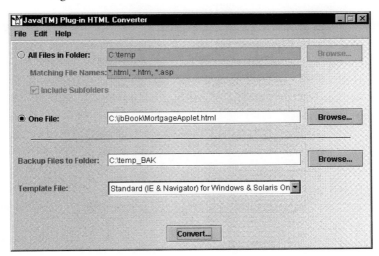

Figure 10.3   *You need to use the HTML converter to translate a simple HTML file to one that uses the Java Plug-In.*

Press the Convert button to generate a new HTML file. The generated file contains the script that prompts you to download and install the Java Plug-In if it is not installed on your machine. You can run it from Netscape or Internet Explorer. Figures 10.4 and 10.5 show sample outputs of the MortgageApplet running on Netscape and Internet Explorer.

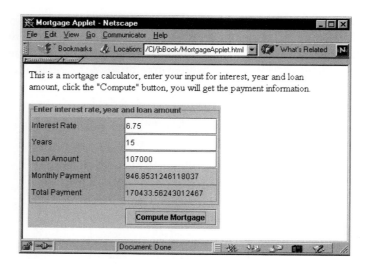

Figure 10.4   *The MortgageApplet runs on Netscape using the Java Plug-In.*

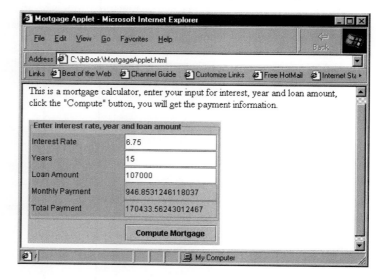

Figure 10.5   *The MortgageApplet runs on Internet Explorer using the Java Plug-In.*

TIP

Using the Java Plug-In is somewhat inconvenient, because you have to use the converter to generate an HTML file. If your applet does not use any Java 2 features except the Swing components, as in all the examples presented so far in this text, you can view your applets from Netscape or Internet Explorer. To enable Netscape or Internet Explorer to display Java applets with Swing components, install swingall.jar in Netscape or Internet Explorer as follows:

■ For Netscape, add swingall.jar in the \Netscape\Communicator\Program\ Java\Classes directory.

■ For Internet Explorer, add swingall.jar in the classpath. On Windows 95 or Windows 98, you need to insert the following line in the autoexec.bat file:

```
set classpath=%classpath%;c:\swingall.jar
```

On Windows NT, you must add it to classpath on the Environment variable page in the System dialog box.

NOTE

swingall.jar is a Java archive file that contains all the classes for Swing components. Java archive files will be introduced later in this chapter. Swing components are built into Java VM in Java 2, but they can also be used in JDK 1.1.7 or JDK 1.1.8 as separate add-ons. JavaSoft provides swingall.jar for using Swing components as add-ons in JDK 1.1.7 or JDK 1.1.8, which can be downloaded from **www.javasoft.com/products/jfc/download.html#standard**

Passing Parameters to Applets

In Chapter 6, "Arrays and Strings," you learned how to pass parameters to Java applications from a command line. The parameters were entered when using the Java interpreter and were passed as an array of strings to the main() method. When the application starts, the main() method can use these arguments. There is no main() method in an applet, however, and applets are not run from the command line by the Java interpreter.

How, then, can applets accept arguments? In this section, you will learn how to pass parameters to Java applets.

To be passed to an applet, parameters must be declared before the applet starts, and must be read by the applet when it is initialized. Parameters are declared using the <param> tag in the HTML file. The <param> tag must be embedded in the <applet> tag, and has no end tag. The syntax for the <param> tag is as follows:

```
<param name=parametername value=parametervalue>
```

This tag specifies a parameter and its corresponding value.

NOTE

There is no comma separating the parameter name from the parameter value in the HTML code.

Suppose you want to write an applet to display a message. The message is passed as a parameter. In addition, you want the message to be displayed at a specific location. The start location of the message is also passed as a parameter in two values, x coordinate and y coordinate. Assume the applet is named DisplayMessage.class. The parameters and their values are listed in Table 10.1.

TABLE 10.1   Parameter Names and Values for `DisplayMessage.class`

Parameter Name	Parameter Value
MESSAGE	"Welcome to Java"
X	20
Y	30

The HTML source file might look like this:

```
<html>
<head>
<title>Passing Parameters to Java Applets</title>
</head>
<body>
This applet gets a message from the HTML page and displays it.
<p>
<applet
  code = "Chapter10.DisplayMessage.class"
  width = 200
  height = 50
  alt="You must have a JDK 1.2-enabled browser to view the applet"
>
<param name=MESSAGE value="Welcome to Java">
<param name=X value=20>
<param name=Y value=30>
</applet>
</body>
</html>
```

To read the parameter from the applet, use the following method defined in the `Applet` class:

```
public String getParameter("parametername");
```

This returns the value of the specified parameter.

Example 10.2 Passing Parameters to Java Applets

This example shows an applet that displays a message at a specified location. The message and the location (x, y) are obtained from the HTML source. The program creates a Java source file named **DisplayMessage.java**, as shown below. The output of a sample run is shown in Figure 10.6.

```
// DisplayMessage.java: Display a message on a panel in the applet
package Chapter10;

import javax.swing.*;
import Chapter8.MessagePanel;

public class DisplayMessage extends JApplet
{
  private String message = "A defualt message"; // Message to display
  private int x = 20; // Default x coordinate
  private int y = 20; // Default y coordinate
```

```
      // Initialize the applet
      public void init()
      {
        // Get parameter values from the HTML file
        message = getParameter("MESSAGE");
        x = Integer.parseInt(getParameter("X"));
        y = Integer.parseInt(getParameter("Y"));

        // Create a message panel
        MessagePanel messagePanel = new MessagePanel(message);
        messagePanel.setXCoordinate(x);
        messagePanel.setYCoordinate(y);

        // Add the message panel to the applet
        getContentPane().add(messagePanel);
      }
    }
```

Figure 10.6   *The applet displays the message* Welcome to Java *passed from the HTML page.*

Example Review

The program gets the parameter values from the HTML in the `init()` method. The values are strings obtained using the `getParameter()` method. Because x and y are `int`, the program uses `Integer.parseInt(string)` to convert a digital string into an `int` value.

If you change Welcome to Java to Welcome to HTML in the HTML file and reload the HTML file in the Web browser, you should see Welcome to HTML displayed. Similarly, x and y values can be changed to display the message in the desired location.

Creating a New Java Applet Using the Applet Wizard

This section shows you how to use the Applet Wizard to create Java applets. Suppose you write an applet, as in Example 10.2, "Passing Parameters to Java Applets." The example displays a message on the applet at a specified location. The message and location are passed as parameters using the <param> tag in HTML. You can use the Applet Wizard to generate the class templates for your applets.

The Applet Wizard uses three dialog boxes to collect applet information from the user, and it generates two files: an HTML file and an applet file. You can modify these two files if necessary to make them work for your project.

The following steps create template files for a new applet:

1. With the AppBrowser for Chapter10.jpr focused, choose File, New to display the Object Gallery. Click the Applet icon to open the Applet Wizard.

2. JBuilder starts Applet Wizard (Step 1 of 3) to configure your applet (see Figure 10.7).

   2.1. Edit the Package field to Chapter10 and the Class field to DisplayMessageApplet, as shown in Figure 10.7. Do not edit the File field. Editing the Package field and the Class field automatically changes the File field.

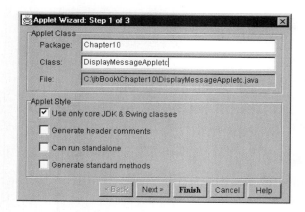

Figure 10.7   *Applet Wizard Step 1 of 3 prompts you to enter the package name, the applet class name, and other optional information.*

   2.2. Check the option "Use only core JDK and Swing classes."

   2.3. Click Next. You will see Step 2 of 3 of the Applet Wizard, as shown in Figure 10.8.

3. Complete Step 2 of 3 in the Applet Wizard. This step enables you to define parameters in the HTML file to be passed to your applets. Each parameter is defined in one line. The Name column specifies the name in the <param> tag. The Variable column specifies the variable for the parameter in the program. The Type column specifies the variable type in the program. The Default column specifies the value of the parameter passed from the HTML file. The Description column gives an explanatory description of the parameter.

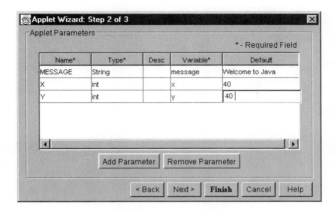

Figure 10.8   *Applet Wizard Step 2 of 3 enables you to enter HTML parameters to be passed to the applet.*

3.1.   Add three parameters in the window, as shown in Figure 10.8. Click the Add Parameter button to start a new parameter line when adding a new parameter.

3.2.   Click Next. You will see Step 3 of 3 of the Applet Wizard, as shown in Figure 10.9.

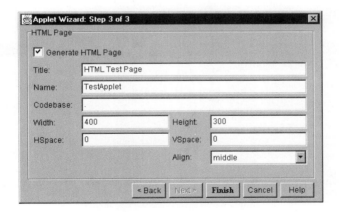

Figure 10.9   *Applet Wizard Step 3 of 3 enables you to specify the applet viewing-area size and other properties for the HTML page.*

4.   Complete Step 3 of 3 in the Applet Wizard. This step gives you the option to generate an HTML file for the applet.

4.1.   Check the Generate HTML Page option. If you check it, the Applet Wizard will generate an HTML file. If you don't check it, you have to create an HTML file manually for this applet. If you checked it, you can specify the width and height of the applet viewing area.

4.2. Fill in the other fields, as shown in Figure 10.9.

4.3. Click Finish.

The Applet Wizard generates two files: DisplayMessageApplet.html and DisplayMessageApplet.java. The source code for DisplayMessageApplet.html is shown in the content pane of the AppBrowser in Figure 10.10. The source code for DisplayMessageApplet.java is shown in Figure 10.11.

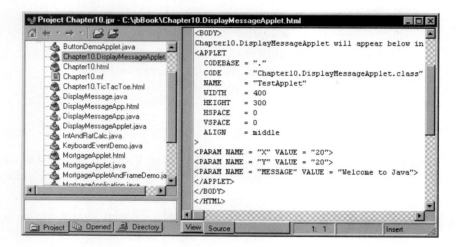

Figure 10.10   *The source code of DisplayMessageApplet.html is shown in the AppBrowser.*

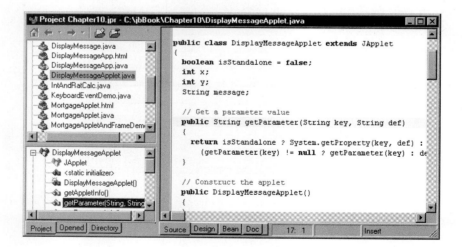

Figure 10.11   *The source code of DisplayMessageApplet.java is shown in the AppBrowser.*

Modifying the Generated Applet Class

Although the Application Wizard generates two .java files, the Applet Wizard generates just one. In this example, the file is DisplayMessageApplet.java. The `DisplayMessageApplet` class contains a constructor and five methods: `getAppletInfo()`, `getParameter()`, `getParameterInfo()`, `init()`, and `jbInit()`. The constructor is useful if you want to run the applet as a standalone application. Because you unchecked the standalone option in Step 1 of 3 of the Applet Wizard, however, it generates an empty body for the constructor.

The methods `getAppletInfo()`, `getParameterInfo()`, and `init()` are defined in the `java.applet.Applet` class and are overridden in `DisplayMessageApplet` with concrete contents. The `jbInit()` method initializes the applet user interface; it is called by the `init()` method. The `getParameter()` method in this class has the same method name as the `getParameter()` method in the `Applet` class. The two methods have different signatures, however. The `getParameter()` method in `DisplayMessageApplet` returns a default value if the parameter does not exist in the HTML file.

NOTE

You can have more methods and varying implementations of the methods if you check certain options in Step 1 of 3 of the Applet Wizard.

The variables message, x, and y are generated because you declared them in Step 2 of 3 of the Applet Wizard, when specifying the HTML parameters.

To complete the program, add the code for creating an instance of `MessagePanel`, set the appropriate instance properties, and place the instance in the applet. The complete code is shown below (the highlighted lines indicate code manually edited):

```
// DisplayMessageApplet.java: Generated from the Applet Wizard
package Chapter10;

import java.awt.*;
import java.awt.event.*;
import java.applet.*;
import javax.swing.*;
import Chapter8.MessagePanel;

public class DisplayMessageApplet extends JApplet
{
  boolean isStandalone = false;
  int x;
  int y;
  String message;

  // Get a parameter value
  public String getParameter(String key, String def)
  {
    return isStandalone ? System.getProperty(key, def) :
      (getParameter(key) != null ? getParameter(key) : def);
  }
```

```
// Construct the applet
public DisplayMessageApplet()
{
}

// Initialize the applet
public void init()
{
  try { x = Integer.parseInt(this.getParameter("X", "20")); }
  catch (Exception e) { e.printStackTrace(); }

  try { y = Integer.parseInt(this.getParameter("Y", "20")); }
  catch (Exception e) { e.printStackTrace(); }

  try { message = this.getParameter("MESSAGE", "Welcome to Java");
  }
  catch (Exception e) { e.printStackTrace(); }

  try
  {
    jbInit();
  }
  catch(Exception e)
  {
    e.printStackTrace();
  }
}

// Component initialization
private void jbInit() throws Exception
{
  this.setSize(new Dimension(400,300));
  MessagePanel messagePanel = new MessagePanel(message);
  messagePanel.setXCoordinate(x);
  messagePanel.setYCoordinate(y);
  getContentPane().add(messagePanel, BorderLayout.CENTER);
  messagePanel.repaint();
}

// Get Applet information
public String getAppletInfo()
{
  return "Applet Information";
}

// Get parameter info
public String[][] getParameterInfo()
{
  String[][] pinfo =
  {
    {"X", "int", ""},
    {"Y", "int", ""},
    {"MESSAGE", "String", ""},
  };
  return pinfo;
}

// static initializer for setting look & feel
static
{
  try
  {
    UIManager.setLookAndFeel
      (UIManager.getSystemLookAndFeelClassName());
```

```
        }
        catch (Exception e) {}
      }
    }
```

You can run the program by highlighting DisplayMessageApplet.html and then choosing Run, Run Applet in "DisplayMessageApplet.html".

Conversions between Applications and Applets

The `JFrame` class and `JApplet` class have a lot in common despite some differences. Since they are both subclasses of the `Container` class. Therefore, all their user interface components, layout managers, and event-handling features are the same. Applications, however, are invoked by the Java interpreter, and applets are invoked by the Web browser. In this section, you will learn how to convert between applets and applications.

Applets can generally be converted to applications. Here are the steps in the conversion:

1. Eliminate the HTML page that invokes the applet. If the applet gets parameters from the HTML page, you can handle them from the command line.

2. Derive the main class named `NewClass`, for instance, from `JFrame` or `MyFrameWithExitHandling` instead of from `JApplet`.

3. Write a constructor in the new class to contain the code in the `init()` and `start()` methods.

4. Place the codes from the `stop()` and `destroy()` methods in the `window-Closing()` method that handles the window-closing event.

5. Add a main method as follows:

```
public static void main()
{
  NewClass frame = new NewClass();

  // width and height are from the <applet> tag
  frame.resize(width, height);
  frame.setVisible(true);
}
```

6. Because applets do not have title bars, you can add a title for the window using the `setTitle()` method.

NOTE

When using frames in applications, specify an initial size in width and height using the `setSize()` method. You can resize the frame after it is displayed. With applets, the viewing area is fixed on a Web page by the `width` and `height` values in the `<applet>` tag.

Example 10.3 Converting Applets into Applications

This example converts the Java applet `MortgageApplet` (from Example 10.1) to a Java application and displays the frame in the center of the screen. The following is the program, and its output is shown in Figure 10.12.

```java
// MortgageApplication.java:
// Application for computing mortgage payments
package Chapter10;

import Chapter5.Mortgage;
import Chapter8.MyFrameWithExitHandling;
import java.awt.*;
import java.awt.event.*;
import javax.swing.*;
import javax.swing.border.TitledBorder;

public class MortgageApplication extends MyFrameWithExitHandling
  implements ActionListener
{
  // Declare and create text fields for interest rate
  // year, loan amount, monthly payment, and total payment
  private JTextField jtfInterestRate = new JTextField(10);
  private JTextField jtfYear = new JTextField(10);
  private JTextField jtfLoan = new JTextField(10);
  private JTextField jtfMonthlyPay = new JTextField(10);
  private JTextField jtfTotalPay = new JTextField(10);

  // Add a main method
  public static void main(String[] args)
  {
    MortgageApplication frame =
      new MortgageApplication();
    frame.setSize(400, 200);
    frame.setTitle("Mortgage Application");
    frame.center();
    frame.setVisible(true);
  }

  // Declare and create a Compute Mortgage button
  private JButton jbtCompute = new JButton("Compute Mortgage");

  // Constructor (replacing the init() method in the applet
  public MortgageApplication()
  {
    // Set properties on the text fields
    jtfMonthlyPay.setEditable(false);
    jtfTotalPay.setEditable(false);

    // Panel p1 to hold labels and text fields
    JPanel p1 = new JPanel();
    p1.setLayout(new GridLayout(5,2));
    p1.add(new Label("Interest Rate"));
    p1.add(jtfInterestRate);
    p1.add(new Label("Years "));
    p1.add(jtfYear);
    p1.add(new Label("Loan Amount"));
    p1.add(jtfLoan);
    p1.add(new Label("Monthly Payment"));
    p1.add(jtfMonthlyPay);
    p1.add(new Label("Total Payment"));
    p1.add(jtfTotalPay);
```

```
      p1.setBorder(new
        TitledBorder("Enter interest rate, year and loan amount"));

      // Panel p2 to hold the button
      JPanel p2 = new JPanel();
      p2.setLayout(new FlowLayout(FlowLayout.RIGHT));
      p2.add(jbtCompute);

      // Add the components to the applet
      getContentPane().add(p1, BorderLayout.CENTER);
      getContentPane().add(p2, BorderLayout.SOUTH);

      // Register listener
      jbtCompute.addActionListener(this);
    }

    // Handler for the "Compute" button
    public void actionPerformed(ActionEvent e)
    {
      if (e.getSource() == jbtCompute)
      {
        // Get values from text fields
        double interest =
          (Double.valueOf(jtfInterestRate.getText())).doubleValue();
        int year =
          (Integer.valueOf(jtfYear.getText())).intValue();
        double loan =
          (Double.valueOf(jtfLoan.getText())).doubleValue();

        // Create a mortgage object
        Mortgage m = new Mortgage(interest, year, loan);

        // Display monthly payment and total payment
        jtfMonthlyPay.setText(String.valueOf(m.monthlyPay()));
        jtfTotalPay.setText(String.valueOf(m.totalPay()));
      }
    }
  }
```

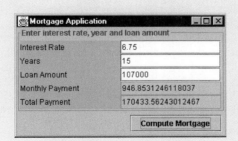

Figure 10.12 *The program is the same as Example 10.1 except that it is written as an application.*

Example Review

The program extends MyFrameWithExitHandling, a subclass of JFrame with exit handling, instead of extending JApplet.

continues

445

The program uses a constructor to initialize the user interface instead of using the init() method. The setTitle() method is used to set a title for the frame in the constructor.

The program creates a main method to start the program by the Java interpreter.

In Chapter 1, you learned that certain limitations are imposed on applets for security reasons. For example, they are not allowed to access local files. If the conversion from application to applet does not violate the security constraints imposed on applets, you can perform the following steps to convert an application to an applet:

1. Create an HTML page with the <applet> tag that invokes the applet. If command-line parameters are used in the application, add them in the <applet> tag and get the parameters using getParameter() in the init() method.

2. Derive the main class from JApplet instead of from JFrame or from MyFrameWithExitHandling.

3. Replace the application's constructor by the init() method.

4. Eliminate the main() method. The main() method usually contains the method to create and display the frame. The applet is automatically displayed in the size specified by the width and height in the <applet> tag. This step is optional. The main() method will simply be ignored if you leave it intact.

5. Because applets do not have title bars, eliminate the setTitle() method (if it is in the application).

Example 10.4 Converting Applications into Applets

This example converts the Java application MenuDemo, which performs arithmetic operations using buttons and menus (Example 9.10, "Using Menus," from Chapter 9, "Creating User Interfaces"), into a Java applet.

The following Java applet AppletMenuDemo is converted from the application MenuDemo. A sample run of this applet is shown in Figure 10.13.

```
// AppletMenuDemo.java: Using menus in an applet
package Chapter10;

import Chapter8.MyFrameWithExitHandling;
import java.awt.*;
import java.awt.event.*;
import javax.swing.*;

public class AppletMenuDemo extends JApplet
  implements ActionListener
{
  // Text fields for Number 1, Number 2, and Result
  private JTextField jtfNum1, jtfNum2, jtfResult;
```

```java
// Buttons "Add", "Subtract", "Multiply" and "Divide"
private JButton jbtAdd, jbtSub, jbtMul, jbtDiv;

// Menu items "Add", "Subtract", "Multiply","Divide" and "Close"
private JMenuItem jmiAdd, jmiSub, jmiMul, jmiDiv, jmiClose;

// Initialize the applet
public void init()
{
  // Create menu bar
  JMenuBar jmb = new JMenuBar();

  // Add menu "Operation" to menu bar
  JMenu operationMenu = new JMenu("Operation");
  operationMenu.setMnemonic('O');
  jmb.add(operationMenu);

  // Add menu "Exit" in menu bar
  JMenu exitMenu = new JMenu("Exit");
  exitMenu.setMnemonic('E');
  jmb.add(exitMenu);

  // Add menu items with mnemonics to menu "Operation"
  operationMenu.add(jmiAdd= new JMenuItem("Add", 'A'));
  operationMenu.add(jmiSub = new JMenuItem("Subtract", 'S'));
  operationMenu.add(jmiMul = new JMenuItem("Multiply", 'M'));
  operationMenu.add(jmiDiv = new JMenuItem("Divide", 'D'));
  exitMenu.add(jmiClose = new JMenuItem("Close", 'C'));

  // Set keyboard accelerators
  jmiAdd.setAccelerator(
    KeyStroke.getKeyStroke(KeyEvent.VK_A, ActionEvent.CTRL_MASK));
  jmiSub.setAccelerator(
    KeyStroke.getKeyStroke(KeyEvent.VK_S, ActionEvent.CTRL_MASK));
  jmiMul.setAccelerator(
    KeyStroke.getKeyStroke(KeyEvent.VK_M, ActionEvent.CTRL_MASK));
  jmiDiv.setAccelerator(
    KeyStroke.getKeyStroke(KeyEvent.VK_D, ActionEvent.CTRL_MASK));

  // Panel p1 to hold text fields and labels
  JPanel p1 = new JPanel();
  p1.setLayout(new FlowLayout());
  p1.add(new JLabel("Number 1"));
  p1.add(jtfNum1 = new JTextField(3));
  p1.add(new JLabel("Number 2"));
  p1.add(jtfNum2 = new JTextField(3));
  p1.add(new JLabel("Result"));
  p1.add(jtfResult = new JTextField(4));
  jtfResult.setEditable(false);

  // Panel p2 to hold buttons
  JPanel p2 = new JPanel();
  p2.setLayout(new FlowLayout());
  p2.add(jbtAdd = new JButton("Add"));
  p2.add(jbtSub = new JButton("Subtract"));
  p2.add(jbtMul = new JButton("Multiply"));
  p2.add(jbtDiv = new JButton("Divide"));

  // Add menu bar to the applet
  setJMenuBar(jmb);

  // Add panels to the applet
  getContentPane().add(p1, BorderLayout.CENTER);
  getContentPane().add(p2, BorderLayout.SOUTH);
```

continues

```java
    // Register listeners
    jbtAdd.addActionListener(this);
    jbtSub.addActionListener(this);
    jbtMul.addActionListener(this);
    jbtDiv.addActionListener(this);
    jmiAdd.addActionListener(this);
    jmiSub.addActionListener(this);
    jmiMul.addActionListener(this);
    jmiDiv.addActionListener(this);
    jmiClose.addActionListener(this);
  }

  // Handling ActionEvent from buttons and menu items
  public void actionPerformed(ActionEvent e)
  {
    String actionCommand = e.getActionCommand();

    // Handling button events
    if (e.getSource() instanceof JButton)
    {
      if ("Add".equals(actionCommand))
        calculate('+');
      else if ("Subtract".equals(actionCommand))
        calculate('-');
      else if ("Multiply".equals(actionCommand))
        calculate('*');
      else if ("Divide".equals(actionCommand))
        calculate('/');
    }
    else if (e.getSource() instanceof JMenuItem)
    {
      // Handling menu item events
      if ("Add".equals(actionCommand))
        calculate('+');
      else if ("Subtract".equals(actionCommand))
        calculate('-');
      else if ("Multiply".equals(actionCommand))
        calculate('*');
      else if ("Divide".equals(actionCommand))
        calculate('/');
      else if ("Close".equals(actionCommand))
        System.exit(0);  //Ignored by the Web bro
    }
  }

  // Calculate and show the result in jtfResult
  private void calculate(char operator)
  {
    // Obtain Number 1 and Number 2
    int num1 = (Integer.parseInt(jtfNum1.getText().trim()));
    int num2 = (Integer.parseInt(jtfNum2.getText().trim()));
    int result = 0;

    // Perform selected operation
    switch (operator)
    {
      case '+': result = num1 + num2;
                break;
      case '-': result = num1 - num2;
                break;
      case '*': result = num1 * num2;
                break;
```

```
        case '/': result = num1 / num2;
      }

      // Set result in jtfResult
      jtfResult.setText(String.valueOf(result));
    }
  }
```

Example Review

The following changes are made to convert the `MenuDemo` application to `AppletMenuDemo`:

1. Extend `JApplet` instead of `MyFrameWithExitHandling`.

2. Replace the constructor with the `init()` method and eliminate the `setTitle()` method.

3. Create an HTML file to run the applet.

Menus can only be used with applications in AWT programming. In Swing, menus can be used in both applications and applets.

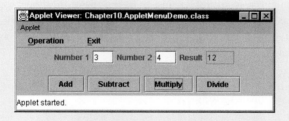

Figure 10.13   *The* `AppletMenuDemo` *class demonstrates the use of menus in an applet.*

Running a Program as an Applet and an Application

You can implement a main method in an applet to run the applet as an application or to run it as an applet using the same program. This feature has both theoretical and practical implications. Theoretically, it blurs the difference between applets and applications. You can write a class that is both an applet and application. Practically, it is convenient to be able to run a program in two ways.

It is not difficult to write such types of programs on your own. Suppose you have an applet named `TestApplet`. To enable it to run as an application, all you need to do is add a main method in the applet with the implementation as follows:

```
public static void main(String[] args)
{
  // Create a frame
  MyFrameWithExitHandling frame = new MyFrameWithExitHandling(
    "Running a program as applet and frame");
```

```
          // Create an instance of TestApplet
          TestApplet applet = new TestApplet();

          // Add the applet instance to the frame
          frame.getContentPane().add(applet, BorderLayout.CENTER);

          // Invoke init() and start()
          applet.init();
          applet.start();

          // Display the frame
          frame.setSize(300, 300);
          frame.setVisible(true);
        }
```

Since the JApplet class is a subclass of Component, it can be placed in a frame. You can invoke the init() and start() methods of the applet to run a JApplet object in an application.

Example 10.5 Running a Program as an Applet and as an Application

This example modifies the DisplayMessage applet in Example 10.2 to enable it to run both as an applet and as an application. The program is identical to DisplayMessage except that a new main method and a variable named isStandalone are added to indicate whether it is running as an applet or as an application.

```java
// DisplayMessageApp.java:
// The program can run as an applet or application
package Chapter10;

import javax.swing.*;
import java.awt.BorderLayout;
import Chapter8.MessagePanel;
import Chapter8.MyFrameWithExitHandling;

public class DisplayMessageApp extends JApplet
{
  private String message = "A default message"; // Message to display
  private int x = 20; // Default x coordinate
  private int y = 20; // Default y coordinate

  // Determine if it is application
  private boolean isStandalone = false;

  // Initialize the applet
  public void init()
  {
    if (!isStandalone)
    {
      // Get parameter values from the HTML file
      message = getParameter("MESSAGE");
      x = Integer.parseInt(getParameter("X"));
      y = Integer.parseInt(getParameter("Y"));
    }
```

```
      // Create a message panel
      MessagePanel messagePanel = new MessagePanel(message);
      messagePanel.setXCoordinate(x);
      messagePanel.setYCoordinate(y);

      // Add the message panel to the applet
      getContentPane().add(messagePanel);
   }

   // Main method with three auguments:
   // args[0]: x coordinate
   // args[1]: y coordinate
   // args[2]: message
   public static void main(String[] args)
   {
      // Create a frame
      MyFrameWithExitHandling frame = new MyFrameWithExitHandling(
        "DisplayMessageApp");

      // Create an instance of the applet
      DisplayMessageApp applet = new DisplayMessageApp();

      // It runs as an application
      applet.isStandalone = true;

      // Get parameters from the command line
      applet.getCommandLineParameters(args);

      // Add the applet instance to the frame
      frame.getContentPane().add(applet, BorderLayout.CENTER);

      // Invoke init() and start()
      applet.init();
      applet.start();

      // Display the frame
      frame.setSize(300, 300);
      frame.setVisible(true);
   }

   // Get command line parameters
   public void getCommandLineParameters(String[] args)
   {
      // Check usage and get x, y and message
      if (args.length != 3)
      {
        System.out.println(
          "Usage: java DisplayMessageApp x y message");
        System.exit(0);
      }
      else
      {
        x = Integer.parseInt(args[0]);
        y = Integer.parseInt(args[1]);
        message = args[2];
      }
   }
}
```

continues

451

Example Review

When you run the program as an applet, the `main()` method is ignored. When you run it as a frame, the `main()` method is invoked.

The `main()` method creates a `JFrame` object `frame` and creates `applet`, an instance of the `JApplet`. The `main()` method then places the applet `applet` into the frame `frame` and invokes the applet's `init()` method. The application runs just like an applet.

The `main()` method sets `isStandalone` true so that it does not attempt to retrieve HTML parameters when the `init()` method is invoked.

The `setVisible(true)` method was invoked *after* the components were added to the applet, and the applet is added to the frame to ensure that the components will be visible. Otherwise, the components will not be shown when the frame starts.

Figure 10.14   *The* `DisplayMessageApp` *class can run as an application and as an applet.*

TIP

When using the Applet Wizard to generate the applet template, you can choose the option "Can run standalone" in the Applet Style to let JBuilder automatically generate the code to enable the applet to run as application.

Mouse Events

A mouse event is generated whenever a mouse is clicked, released, moved, or dragged on a component. The mouse event object captures the nature of the event, such as the number of clicks associated with the event or the location (x and y coordinates) of the mouse. Java provides two listener interfaces, `MouseListener` and `MouseMotionListener`, to handle mouse events. You should implement the `MouseListener` interface to listen for such actions as when the mouse is pressed, released, entered, exited, or clicked, and implement the `MouseMotionListener` interface to listen for such actions as dragging or moving the mouse.

The `MouseEvent` handlers are listed along with the handlers of other events in Table 8.2 in Chapter 8, "Getting Started with Graphics Programming." The following are the handlers:

- The `mouseEntered(MouseEvent e)` and `mouseExit(MouseEvent e)` handlers are invoked when a mouse enters a component or exits the component.

- The `mousePressed(MouseEvent e)` and `mouseReleased(MouseEvent e)` handlers are invoked when a mouse is pressed or released. The `mouseClicked(MouseEvent e)` handler is invoked when a mouse is pressed and then released.

- The `mouseMoved(MouseEvent e)` handler is invoked when the mouse is moved without a button being pressed. The `mouseDragged(MouseEvent e)` handler is invoked when the mouse is moved with a button pressed.

The `Point` class is often used for handling mouse events. The `Point` class encapsulates a point in a plane. The class contains two instance variables, x and y, for coordinates. To create a point object, use the following constructor:

```
Point(int x, int y)
```

This constructs a `Point` object with the specified x and y coordinates.

You can use the `move(int x, int y)` method to move the point to the specified x and y coordinates. You can use the following properties from a `MouseEvent` object when a mouse event occurs:

- `public int getClickCount()`

  This returns the number of mouse clicks associated with the event.

- `public Point getPoint()`

  This returns the x and y coordinates of the event relative to the source component.

- `public int getX()`

  This returns the x coordinate of the event relative to the source component.

- `public int getY()`

  This returns the y coordinate of the event relative to the source component.

Since the `MouseEvent` class inherits `InputEvent`, you can use the methods defined in the `InputEvent` class on a `MouseEvent` object. The following methods in `InputEvent` are often useful for handling mouse events:

■ `public long getWhen()`

This returns the time stamp of when the event occurred.

■ `public boolean isAltDown()`

This returns true if the Alt key is down on the event.

■ `public boolean isControlDown()`

This returns true if the Control key is down on the event.

■ `public boolean isMetaDown()`

This returns true if the right mouse button is pressed.

■ `public boolean isShiftDown()`

This returns true if the Shift key is down on the event.

Example 10.6 Handling Complex Mouse Events

This example shows a program that uses a mouse for drawing. You can use this program to draw anything on a panel by dragging with the left mouse button pressed. You can erase the drawing by dragging with the right button pressed. A sample run of the program is shown in Figure 10.15.

```java
// MouseDrawingDemo.java: Drawing using mouse
package Chapter10;

import Chapter8.MyFrameWithExitHandling;
import java.awt.*;
import javax.swing.*;
import java.awt.event.*;

public class MouseDrawingDemo extends JApplet
{
  // This main method enables the applet to run as an application
  public static void main(String[] args)
  {
    // Create a frame
    MyFrameWithExitHandling frame = new MyFrameWithExitHandling(
      "Mouse Drawing Demo");

    // Create an instance of the applet
    MouseDrawingDemo applet = new MouseDrawingDemo();

    // Add the applet instance to the frame
    frame.getContentPane().add(applet, BorderLayout.CENTER);

    // Invoke init() and start()
    applet.init();
    applet.start();

    // Display the frame
    frame.setSize(300, 300);
    frame.setVisible(true);
  }
```

```java
      // Initialize the applet
      public void init()
      {
        // Create a PaintPanel and add it to the applet
        getContentPane().add(new PaintPanel(), BorderLayout.CENTER);
      }
  }

  // PaintPanel for painting using the mouse
  class PaintPanel extends JPanel
    implements MouseListener, MouseMotionListener
  {
    final int CIRCLESIZE = 20; // Circle diameter used for erasing
    private Point lineStart = new Point(0, 0); // Line start point
    private Graphics g; // Create a Graphics object for drawing

    public PaintPanel()
    {
      // Register listener for the mouse event
      addMouseListener(this);
      addMouseMotionListener(this);
    }

    public void mouseClicked(MouseEvent e)
    {
    }

    public void mouseEntered(MouseEvent e)
    {
    }

    public void mouseExited(MouseEvent e)
    {
    }

    public void mouseReleased(MouseEvent e)
    {
    }

    public void mousePressed(MouseEvent e)
    {
      lineStart.move(e.getX(), e.getY());
    }

    public void mouseDragged(MouseEvent e)
    {
      g = getGraphics(); // Get graphics context

      if (e.isMetaDown()) // Detect right button pressed
      {
        // Erase the drawing using an oval
        g.setColor(getBackground());
        g.fillOval(e.getX() - (CIRCLESIZE/2),
            e.getY() - (CIRCLESIZE/2), CIRCLESIZE, CIRCLESIZE);
      }
      else
      {
        g.setColor(Color.black);
        g.drawLine(lineStart.x, lineStart.y,
          e.getX(), e.getY());
      }
```

continues

```
            lineStart.move(e.getX(), e.getY());

            // Dispose this graphics context
            g.dispose();
        }

        public void mouseMoved(MouseEvent e)
        {
        }
    }
```

Figure 10.15   *The program enables you to use the mouse to draw anything.*

Example Review

The program can run as an application and as an applet. It creates a `PaintPanel` instance to capture mouse movements on the panel. It creates or erases lines by dragging the mouse with the left or right button pressed.

When a button is pressed, the `mousePressed()` handler is invoked. The handler sets the `lineStart` to the current mouse point as the starting point. Drawing begins when the mouse is dragged with the left button pressed. In this case, the `mouseDragged()` handler sets the foreground color to black and draws a line along the path of the mouse movement.

Erasing occurs when the mouse is dragged with the right button pressed. In this case, the `mouseDragged` handler sets the foreground color to the background color and draws an oval filled with the background color at the mouse pointer to erase the area covered by the oval.

The program does not use the `paintComponent(Graphics g)` method. Instead, it uses `getGraphics()` to obtain a `Graphics` instance and draws on this.

Because the `mousePressed()` handler is defined in the `MouseListener` interface and the `mouseDragged()` handler is defined in the `MouseMotionListener` interface, the program implements both interfaces.

The `dispose()` method disposes of the graphics context and releases any system resources it is using. Although the finalization process of the Java runtime system automatically disposes the object after it is no longer used, I recommend that you manually free the associated resources by calling this method rather than relying on a finalization process that may take a long time to run to completion. In this program, a great many `Graphics` objects can be created within a short time. Without manually disposing these objects, the program would run fine, but would consume a lot of memory.

Keyboard Events

Keyboard events are generated whenever a key is pressed. Keyboard events make it possible for users to use the keys to control and perform actions or get input from the keyboard.

A keyboard event object describes the nature of the event (a key is pressed, released, or typed) and the value of the key. To process a keyboard event, use the following handlers from the `KeyListener` interface:

- `public void keyPressed(KeyEvent e)`

  This handler is called when a key is pressed.

- `public void keyReleased(KeyEvent e)`

  This handler is called when a key is released.

- `public void keyTyped(KeyEvent e)`

  This handler is called when a key is pressed and then released.

The keys captured in the event are integers representing Unicode character values, which include alphanumeric characters, function keys, the Tab key, the Enter key, and so on. Every keyboard event has an associated key character or key code, which is returned by the `getKeyChar()` or `getKeyCode()` method in `KeyEvent`, respectively.

Java has defined many constants for normal keys and function keys in the `KeyEvent` class. Table 10.2 shows the most common ones.

TABLE 10.2   Key Constants

Constant	Description
VK_HOME	The Home key
VK_End	The End key
VK_PGUP	The Page Up key
VK_PGDN	The Page Down key
VK_UP	The up-arrow key
VK_DOWN	The down-arrow key
VK_LEFT	The left-arrow key
VK_RIGHT	The right-arrow key
VK_ESCAPE	The Esc key
VK_TAB	The Tab key
VK_BACK_SPACE	The Backspace key
VK_CAPS_LOCK	The Caps Lock key
VK_NUM_LOCK	The Num Lock key
VK_ENTER	The Enter key
VK_F1 to VK_F12	The function keys F1 to F12
VK_0 to VK_9	The number keys from 0 to 9
VK_A to VK_Z	The letter keys from A to Z

Example 10.7 Handling Keyboard Events

This example shows a program that displays a user-input character. The user can move the character up, down, left, and right using arrow keys VK_UP, VK_DOWN, VK_LEFT, and VK_RIGHT. Figure 10.16 contains a sample run of the program.

```java
// KeyboardEventDemo.java: Receive key input
package Chapter10;

import Chapter8.MyFrameWithExitHandling;
import java.awt.*;
import java.awt.event.*;
import javax.swing.*;

public class KeyboardEventDemo extends JApplet
{
  private KeyboardPanel keyboardPanel = new KeyboardPanel();

  // Main method used if run as an application
  public static void main(String[] args)
  {
    // Create a frame
    MyFrameWithExitHandling frame = new MyFrameWithExitHandling(
      "KeyboardEvent Demo");
```

```
    // Create an instance of the applet
    KeyboardEventDemo applet = new KeyboardEventDemo();

    // Add the applet instance to the frame
    frame.getContentPane().add(applet, BorderLayout.CENTER);

    // Invoke init() and start()
    applet.init();
    applet.start();

    // Display the frame
    frame.setSize(300, 300);
    frame.setVisible(true);

    // Set focus on the keyboardPanel
    applet.focus();
  }

  // Initialize UI
  public void init()
  {
    // Add the keyboard panel to accept and display user input
    getContentPane().add(keyboardPanel);

    // Request focus
    focus();
  }

  // Set focus on the panel
  public void focus()
  {
    // It is required for receiving key input
    keyboardPanel.requestFocus();
  }
}

// KeyboardPanel for receiving key input
class KeyboardPanel extends JPanel implements KeyListener
{
  private int x = 100;
  private int y = 100;
  private char keyChar = 'A'; // Default key

  public KeyboardPanel()
  {
    addKeyListener(this); // Register listener
  }

  public void keyReleased(KeyEvent e)
  {
  }

  public void keyTyped(KeyEvent e)
  {
  }

  public void keyPressed(KeyEvent e)
  {
    switch (e.getKeyCode())
    {
```

continues

459

```
            case KeyEvent.VK_DOWN: y += 10; break;
            case KeyEvent.VK_UP: y -= 10; break;
            case KeyEvent.VK_LEFT: x -= 10; break;
            case KeyEvent.VK_RIGHT: x += 10; break;
            default: keyChar = e.getKeyChar();
        }
        repaint();
    }

    // Draw the character
    public void paintComponent(Graphics g)
    {
        super.paintComponent(g);

        g.setFont(new Font("TimesRoman", Font.PLAIN, 24));
        g.drawString(String.valueOf(keyChar), x, y);
    }
}
```

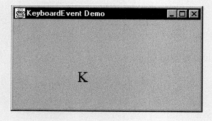

Figure 10.16   The program responds to the keyboard events, displaying a character and moving it up, down, left, and right.

Example Review

When a nonarrow key is pressed, the key is displayed. When an arrow key is pressed, the character moves in the direction indicated by the arrow key.

Because the program gets input from the keyboard, it listens for KeyEvent and implements KeyListener to handle key input.

When a key is pressed, the keyPressed() handler is invoked. The program uses e.getKeyCode() to obtain the int value for the key and e.getKeyChar() to get the character for the key. In fact, (int)e.getKeyChar() is the same as e.getKeyCode().

Only a focused component can receive KeyEvent. When the program runs as an applet, the keyboardPanel component receives focus because it is the last and only component added to the applet. When the program runs as an application, keyboardPanel is not focused, since keyboardPanel is added to the applet, and the applet is placed inside a frame. Thus, you need to set focus to keyboardPanel using the focus() method defined in the KeyboardEventDemo. The focus() method simply sets the focus to keyboardPanel using the requestFocus() method defined in the java.awt.Component class.

Case Studies

You have learned objects, classes, arrays, class inheritance, graphics classes, event-driven programming, and applets from many examples in this chapter and in the preceding chapters. You are now ready to put what you have learned to work in developing comprehensive projects. In this section, you will develop a Java applet that plays the popular game of TicTacToe.

Example 10.8 The TicTacToe Game

This example creates a program for playing TicTacToe. In a TicTacToe game, two players take turns marking a cell in a 3×3 grid with their tokens (X or O). One player is the X and the other is the O. When one player succeeds in placing three tokens in a row on the grid (horizontally, vertically, or diagonally), the game is over and that player wins. A draw (no winner) occurs when all the spaces on the grid are filled with tokens and a win has not been achieved by either player. Figures 10.17 and 10.18 are representative sample runs of the example.

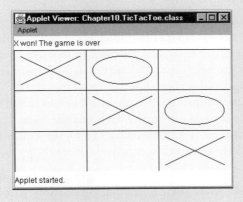

Figure 10.17   *This sample shows that the X player has won.*

All the examples you have seen so far have simple behaviors that are easy to model using classes. The behavior of the TicTacToe game is a bit complex. To create the classes to model the behavior, you need to study and understand the game.

Assume that all the cells are empty initially, and that the first player takes the X token, and the second player the O token. To mark a cell, the player points the mouse to the cell and clicks it. If the cell is empty, the token (X or O) is displayed. If the cell is already filled, the player's action is ignored.

From the preceding description, it is obvious that a cell is a GUI object that handles the mouse-click event and displays tokens. The candidates for such an

continues

461

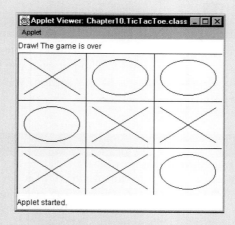

Figure 10.18   *This sample shows a draw with no winner.*

object could be a button or a panel. Panels are more flexible than buttons. The token (X or O) can be drawn on a panel in any size, but can only be displayed as label on a button. Therefore, a panel should be used to model a cell.

Let Cell be a subclass of JPanel. You can declare the 3×3 grid to be an array Cell[][] = new Cell[3][3] that models the game. How do you know the state of the cell (empty, X, or O)? You can simply use a property named token of char type in the Cell class. The Cell class is responsible for drawing the token when an empty cell is clicked, so you need to write the code for listening to the MouseEvent and for painting the shape for tokens X and O. To determine which shape you draw, you can introduce a variable named whoseTurn of char type. Initially, whoseTurn is X, then changes to O, subsequently it changes between X and O whenever a new cell is occupied.

Finally, how do you know whether the game is over, with a winner or without a winner, and who the winner is? You can create a method named isWinning(char token) to check whether a specified token has won, and a method named isFilled() to check whether all the cells are occupied.

Clearly, two classes emerge from the foregoing analysis. One is the Cell class, which handles operations for a single cell; and the other is the TicTacToe class, which plays the whole game and deals with all the cells.

The Cell class has the following data fields and methods:

Data field:

char token: Represent token used in the cell.

Methods:

```
public char getToken()
```

Return the token of the cell.

```
public void setToken(char token)
```

Set the token in the cell.

```
public char getToken()
```

Return the token of the cell.

```
public void paintComponent(Graphics g)
```

Override this method to display the token in the cell.

```
public void mouseClicked(MouseEvent e)
```

Implement this method in the `MouseListener` to handle a mouse click on the cell.

The `TicTacToe` class has the following data fields and methods:

Data field:

`char whoseTurn`: Indicate which player has the turn.

`Cell[][] cell`: Represent the cells.

`JLabel jlblStatus`: A label for displaying game status.

Methods:

```
public void init()
```

Override this method to initialize variables and create UI.

```
public boolean isFilled()
```

Determine if the cells are all filled.

```
public boolean isWinning(char token)
```

Determine if the player with the specified token wins.

The program is given as follows.

```java
// TicTacToe.java: Play the TicTacToe game
package Chapter10;

import java.awt.*;
import Chapter8.MyFrameWithExitHandling;
import java.awt.event.*;
import javax.swing.*;
import javax.swing.border.LineBorder;

public class TicTacToe extends JApplet
{
  // Indicate which player has a turn, initially it is the X player
  private char whoseTurn = 'X';
```

continues

```java
    // Create and initialize cells
    private Cell[][] cell =  new Cell[3][3];

    // Create and initialized a status label
    private JLabel jlblStatus = new JLabel("X's turn playing");

    // Initialize UI
    public void init()
    {
      // Panel p to hold cells
      JPanel p = new JPanel();
      p.setLayout(new GridLayout(3, 3, 0, 0));
      for (int i=0; i<3; i++)
        for (int j=0; j<3; j++)
          p.add(cell[i][j] = new Cell());

      // Set line borders on the cells panel and the status label
      p.setBorder(new LineBorder(Color.red, 1));
      jlblStatus.setBorder(new LineBorder(Color.yellow, 1));

      // Place the panel and the label to the applet
      this.getContentPane().add(p, BorderLayout.CENTER);
      this.getContentPane().add(jlblStatus, BorderLayout.SOUTH);
    }

    // This main method enables the applet to run as an application
    public static void main(String[] args)
    {
      // Create a frame
      MyFrameWithExitHandling frame = new MyFrameWithExitHandling(
        "Tic Tac Toe");

      // Create an instance of the applet
      TicTacToe applet = new TicTacToe();

      // Add the applet instance to the frame
      frame.getContentPane().add(applet, BorderLayout.CENTER);

      // Invoke init() and start()
      applet.init();
      applet.start();

      // Display the frame
      frame.setSize(300, 300);
      frame.setVisible(true);
    }

    // Determine if the cells are all occupied
    public boolean isFilled()
    {
      for (int i=0; i<3; i++)
        for (int j=0; j<3; j++)
          if (cell[i][j].getToken() == ' ')
            return false;

      return true;
    }

    // Determine if the player with the specified token wins
    public boolean isWinning(char token)
    {
      for (int i=0; i<3; i++)
```

```java
      if ((cell[i][0].getToken()==token)
          && (cell[i][1].getToken()==token)
          && (cell[i][2].getToken()==token))
      {
        return true;
      }

    for (int j=0; j<3; j++)
      if ((cell[0][j].getToken()==token)
          && (cell[1][j].getToken()==token)
          && (cell[2][j].getToken()==token))
      {
        return true;
      }

    if ((cell[0][0].getToken()==token)
        && (cell[1][1].getToken()==token)
        && (cell[2][2].getToken()==token))
    {
      return true;
    }

    if ((cell[0][2].getToken()==token)
        && (cell[1][1].getToken()==token)
        && (cell[2][0].getToken()==token))
    {
      return true;
    }

    return false;
  }

  // An inner class for a cell
  public class Cell extends JPanel implements MouseListener
  {
    // Token used for this cell
    private char token = ' ';

    public Cell()
    {
      setBorder(new LineBorder(Color.black, 1)); // Set cell's border
      addMouseListener(this);  // Register listener
    }

    // The getter method for token
    public char getToken()
    {
      return token;
    }

    // The setter method for token
    public void setToken(char c)
    {
      token = c;
      repaint();
    }

    // Paint the cell
    public void paintComponent(Graphics g)
    {
      super.paintComponent(g);
```

continues

465

```
      if (token == 'X')
      {
        g.drawLine(10, 10, getSize().width-10, getSize().height-10);
        g.drawLine(getSize().width-10, 10, 10, getSize().height-10);
      }
      else if (token == 'O')
      {
        g.drawOval(10, 10, getSize().width-20, getSize().height-20);
      }
    }

    // Handle mouse click on a cell
    public void mouseClicked(MouseEvent e)
    {
      if (token == ' ') // If cell is not occupied
      {
        if (whoseTurn == 'X')  // If it is the X player's turn
        {
          setToken('X');  // Set token in the cell
          whoseTurn = 'O';  // Change the turn
          jlblStatus.setText("O's turn");  // Display status
          if (isWinning('X'))
            jlblStatus.setText("X won! The game is over");
          else if (isFilled())
            jlblStatus.setText("Draw! The game is over");
        }
        else if (whoseTurn == 'O') // If it is the O player's turn
        {
          setToken('O'); // Set token in the cell
          whoseTurn = 'X';  // Change the turn
          jlblStatus.setText("X's turn"); // Display status
          if (isWinning('O'))
            jlblStatus.setText("O won! The game is over");
          else if (isFilled())
            jlblStatus.setText("Draw! The game is over");
        }
      }
    }

    public void mousePressed(MouseEvent e)
    {
      // TODO: implement this java.awt.event.MouseListener method;
    }

    public void mouseReleased(MouseEvent e)
    {
      // TODO: implement this java.awt.event.MouseListener method;
    }

    public void mouseEntered(MouseEvent e)
    {
      // TODO: implement this java.awt.event.MouseListener method;
    }

    public void mouseExited(MouseEvent e)
    {
      // TODO: implement this java.awt.event.MouseListener method;
    }
  }
}
```

Example Review

The `TicTacToe` class initializes the user interface with nine cells placed in a panel of `GridLayout`. A label named `jlblStatus` is used to show the status of the game. The variable `whoseTurn` is used to track the next token to be placed in a cell. The methods `isFilled()` and `isWinning()` check the status of the game.

It is worth noting that the `Cell` class is declared as an inner class for `TicTacToe`. This is because the `mouseClicked()` method in `Cell` references variable `whoseTurn` and invokes `isFull` and `won` in the `TicTacToe` class. Since `Cell` is an inner class in `TicTacToe`, it can directly use the variable and methods defined in `TicTacToe`. This approach makes programs simple and concise. If `Cell` were not declared as an inner class of `TicTacToe`, you would have to pass an object of `TicTacToe` to `Cell` for it to use the variables and methods in `TicTacToe`. In Exercise 10.5 you will rewrite the program without using inner class.

The `Cell` class implements `MouseListener` to listen for `MouseEvent`. When a cell is clicked, it draws a shape determined by variable `whoseTurn`, and then checks whether the game has been won or all the cells are occupied.

There is a problem in this program: the user may continue to mark the cells even after the game is over. You will fix this problem in Exercise 10.5.

The *CardLayout* Manager (Optional)

Layout managers arrange components in a container. You have already used the `FlowLayout` manager, `GridLayout` manager, and `BorderLayout` manager. Java has two other layout managers: `CardLayout` and `GridBagLayout`. Java also enables you to directly place components in a specific position without using a layout manager. This section discusses the `CardLayout` manager; the sections that follow it discuss the `GridBagLayout` manager and using no layout manager.

The `CardLayout` manager arranges components in a queue of cards. You can only see one card at a time. To construct a `CardLayout`, use the constructor `CardLayout()`.

Cards are usually placed in a container, such as a panel. Components are placed in the card queue in the order in which they are added. To add a component in the `CardLayout` container, use the following method:

```
public void add(Component component, String name)
```

This adds the specified component to the container. The `String` argument of the method, `name`, gives an explicit identity to the component in the queue.

To make a component visible in the container with `CardLayout`, you can use the following instance methods in the `CardLayout` object:

■ `public void first(Container container)`

This method views the first card in the container.

■ `public void last(Container container)`

This method views the last card in the container.

■ `public void next(Container container)`

This method views the next card in the container.

■ `public void previous(Container container)`

This method views the previous card in the container.

■ `public void show(Container container, String name)`

This method views the component with the specified name in the container. You can use this method to directly display the component.

Example 10.9 Testing *CardLayout* Manager

This example shows a program that creates two panels in a frame. The first panel uses `CardLayout` to hold 15 labels for displaying images. The second panel uses `FlowLayout` to group four buttons named First, Next, Previous, and Last and a combo box labeled `Image`.

These buttons control which image will be shown in the `CardLayout` panel. When the user clicks on the First button, for example, the first image in the `CardLayout` panel appears. The combo box enables the user to directly select an image.

The program follows, and the output of a sample run is shown in Figure 10.19.

```java
// ShowCardLayout.java: Using CardLayout to display images
package Chapter10;

import Chapter8.MyFrameWithExitHandling;
import java.awt.*;
import java.awt.event.*;
import javax.swing.*;

public class ShowCardLayout extends JApplet
  implements ActionListener, ItemListener
{
  private CardLayout queue = new CardLayout();
  private JPanel cardPanel = new JPanel();
  private JButton jbtFirst, jbtNext, jbtPrevious, jbtLast;
  private JComboBox jcboImage;

  public void init()
  {
    // Use CardLayout for cardPanel
    cardPanel.setLayout(queue);
```

```java
  // Add 15 labels for displaying images into cardPanel
  for (int i=1; i<=15; i++)
    cardPanel.add
      (new JLabel(new ImageIcon("images/L"+i+".gif")),
        String.valueOf(i));

  // Panel p to hold buttons and a combo box
  JPanel p = new JPanel();
  p.add(jbtFirst = new JButton("First"));
  p.add(jbtNext = new JButton("Next"));
  p.add(jbtPrevious= new JButton("Previous"));
  p.add(jbtLast = new JButton("Last"));
  p.add(new JLabel("Image"));
  p.add(jcboImage = new JComboBox());

  // Initialize combo box items
  for (int i=1; i<=15; i++)
    jcboImage.addItem(String.valueOf(i));

  // Place panels in the frame
  getContentPane().add(cardPanel, BorderLayout.CENTER);
  getContentPane().add(p, BorderLayout.SOUTH);

  // Register listeners with the source objects
  jbtFirst.addActionListener(this);
  jbtNext.addActionListener(this);
  jbtPrevious.addActionListener(this);
  jbtLast.addActionListener(this);
  jcboImage.addItemListener(this);
}

// This main method enables the applet to run as an application
public static void main(String[] args)
{
  // Create a frame
  MyFrameWithExitHandling frame = new MyFrameWithExitHandling(
    "CardLayout Demo");

  // Create an instance of the applet
  ShowCardLayout applet = new ShowCardLayout();

  // Add the applet instance to the frame
  frame.getContentPane().add(applet, BorderLayout.CENTER);

  // Invoke init() and start()
  applet.init();
  applet.start();

  // Display the frame
  frame.setSize(300, 300);
  frame.setVisible(true);
}

// Handle button actions
public void actionPerformed(ActionEvent e)
{
  String actionCommand = e.getActionCommand();
  if (e.getSource() instanceof JButton)
    if ("First".equals(actionCommand))
      // Show the first component in queue
      queue.first(cardPanel);
```

continues

469

```
                 else if ("Last".equals(actionCommand))
                   // Show the last component in queue
                   queue.last(cardPanel);
                 else if ("Previous".equals(actionCommand))
                   // Show the previous component in queue
                   queue.previous(cardPanel);
                 else if ("Next".equals(actionCommand))
                   // Show the next component in queue
                   queue.next(cardPanel);
             }

             // Handle selection of combo box item
             public void itemStateChanged(ItemEvent e)
             {
               if (e.getSource() == jcboImage)
                 // Show the component at specified index
                 queue.show(cardPanel, (String)e.getItem());
             }
         }
```

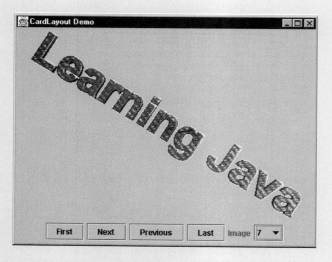

Figure 10.19   *The program shows images in a panel of* CardLayout.

Example Review

The program creates an instance of CardLayout, queue = new CardLayout(). The statement cardPanel.setLayout(queue) sets the cardPanel with the CardLayout; cardPanel is an instance of JPanel. You have used such statements as setLayout(new FlowLayout()) to create anonymous layout object and set the layout for a container, instead of declaring and creating a separate instance of the layout manager, as in this program. The object queue, however, is useful later in the program to show components in cardPanel. You have to use queue.first(cardPanel), for example, to view the first component in cardPanel.

470

The statement `cardPanel.add(new JLabel(new ImageIcon("images/L"+i+".gif"))`, `String.valueOf(i))` adds the image label with identity `String.valueOf(i)`. Later, when the user selects an image with number `i`, this identity `String.valueOf(i)` is used in the `queue.show()` method to view the image with the specified identity.

The *GridBagLayout* Manager (Optional)

The `GridBagLayout` manager is the most flexible and the most complex. It is similar to the `GridLayout` manager in the sense that both layout managers arrange components in a grid. With `GridBagLayout`, however, the components can vary in size and can be added in any order. Thus you can use `GridBagLayout` to create the layout shown in Figure 10.20.

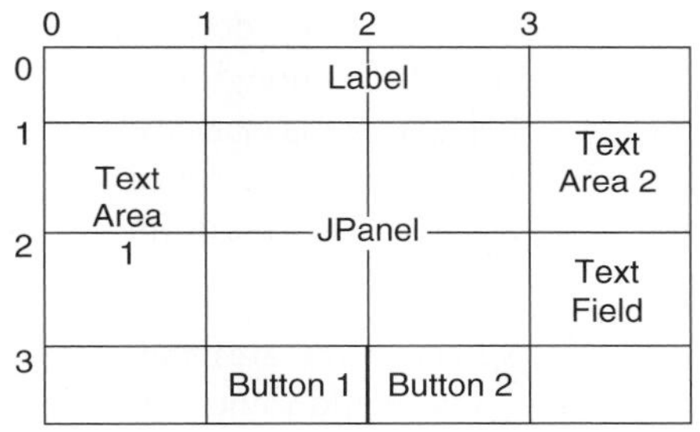

Figure 10.20 *A `GridBagLayout` manager divides the container into cells. A component can occupy several cells.*

The constructor `GridBagLayout()` is used to create a new `GridBagLayout`. In `GridLayout`, the grid size (the number of rows and columns) is specified in the constructor. The size is not specified in `GridBagLayout`.

Each `GridBagLayout` uses a dynamic rectangular grid of cells, with each component occupying one or more cells called its display area. Each component managed by a `GridBagLayout` is associated with a `GridBagConstraints` instance that specifies how the component is laid out within its display area. How a `GridBagLayout` places a set of components depends on each component's `GridBagConstraints` and minimum size, as well as the preferred size of the component's container.

To use a `GridBagLayout` effectively, you must customize the `GridBagConstraints` of one or more of its components. You customize a `GridBagConstraints` object by setting one or more of its instance variables:

- **`gridx`** and **`gridy`**—Specifies the cell at the upper left of the component's display area, where the upper-leftmost cell has address `gridx=0`, `gridy=0`. Note that `gridx` specifies the column in which the component will be placed, and `gridy` specifies the row in which the component will be placed. In Figure 10.20, Button 1 has a `gridx` value of `1` and a `gridy` value of `3`, and Label has a `gridx` value of 0 and a `gridy` value of 0.

- **gridwidth** and **gridheight**—Specifies the number of cells in a row (for gridwidth) or column (for gridheight) in the component's display area. The default value is 1. In Figure 10.20, the panel in the center occupies two columns and two rows, and Text Area 2 occupies one row and one column.

- **weightx** and **weighty**—Specifies the extra space to allocate horizontally and vertically for the component when the window is resized. Unless you specify a weight for at least one component in a row (weightx) and a column (weighty), all the components clump together in the center of their container. This is because when the weight is zero (the default), the GridBagLayout puts any extra space between its grid of cells and the edges of the container. You will see the effect of these parameters in Example 10.10.

- **fill**—Specifies how the component should be resized if the component's viewing area is larger than its current size. Valid values are GridBagConstraints.NONE (the default), GridBagConstraints.HORIZONTAL (makes the component wide enough to fill its display area horizontally, but doesn't change its height), GridBagConstraints.VERTICAL (makes the component tall enough to fill its display area vertically, but doesn't change its width), and GridBagConstraints.BOTH (makes the component completely fill its display area).

- **anchor**—Specifies where in the area the component is placed when it does not fill in the entire area. Valid values are as follows:

GridBagConstraints.CENTER (the default)

GridBagConstraints.NORTH

GridBagConstraints.NORTHEAST

GridBagConstraints.EAST

GridBagConstraints.SOUTHEAST

GridBagConstraints.SOUTH

GridBagConstraints.SOUTHWEST

GridBagConstraints.WEST

GridBagConstraints.NORTHWEST

The fill and anchor parameters deal with how to fill and place the component when the viewing area is larger than the requested area. The fill and anchor parameters are class variables, while gridx, gridy, width, height, weightx, and weighty are instance variables.

Example 10.10 Testing the GridBagLayout **Manager**

This example shows a program that uses the GridBagLayout manager to create a layout for Figure 10.20. The output of the program is shown in Figure 10.21.

```java
// ShowGridBagLayout.java: Using GridBagLayout
package Chapter10;

import Chapter8.MyFrameWithExitHandling;
import java.awt.*;
import java.awt.event.*;
import javax.swing.*;

public class ShowGridBagLayout extends MyFrameWithExitHandling
{
  private JLabel jlbl;
  private JTextArea jta1, jta2;
  private JTextField jtf;
  private JPanel jp;
  private JButton jbt1, jbt2;
  private GridBagLayout gbLayout;
  private GridBagConstraints gbConstraints;

  // Main method
  public static void main(String[] args)
  {
    ShowGridBagLayout frame = new ShowGridBagLayout();
    frame.setSize(350,200);
    frame.setVisible(true);
  }

  // Add a component to the conjtainer
  private void addComp(Component c, GridBagLayout gbLayout,
                       GridBagConstraints gbConstraints,
                       int row, int column, int numRows,
                       int numColumns, int weightx, int weighty)
  {
    // Set parameters
    gbConstraints.gridx = column;
    gbConstraints.gridy = row;
    gbConstraints.gridwidth = numColumns;
    gbConstraints.gridheight = numRows;
    gbConstraints.weightx = weightx;
    gbConstraints.weighty = weighty;

    // Set constraints in the GridBagLayout
    gbLayout.setConstraints(c, gbConstraints);

    // Add component to the conjtainer
    getContentPane().add(c);
  }

  // Constructor
  public ShowGridBagLayout()
  {
    setTitle("Show GridBagLayout");

    // Initialize UI components
    jlbl = new JLabel("Resize the Window and Study GridBagLayout",
                 JLabel.CENTER);
```

continues

```
            jp = new JPanel();
            jta1 = new JTextArea("Text Area", 5, 15 );
            jta2 = new JTextArea("Text Area", 5, 15 );
            jtf = new JTextField("JTextField");
            jbt1 = new JButton("Cancel" );
            jbt2 = new JButton("Ok" );

            // Create GridBagLayout and GridBagConstraints object
            gbLayout = new GridBagLayout();
            gbConstraints = new GridBagConstraints();
            getContentPane().setLayout(gbLayout);

            // Place JLabel to occupy row 0 (the first row)
            gbConstraints.fill = GridBagConstraints.BOTH;
            gbConstraints.anchor = GridBagConstraints.CENTER;
            addComp(jlbl, gbLayout, gbConstraints, 0, 0, 1, 4, 0, 0);

            // Place text area 1 in row 1 and 2, and column 0
            addComp(jta1, gbLayout, gbConstraints, 1, 0, 2, 1, 0, 0);

            // Place Panel in row 1 and 2, and column 1 and 2
            addComp(jp, gbLayout, gbConstraints, 1, 1, 2, 2, 100, 100);
            jp.setBackground(Color.red);

            // Place text area 2 in row 1 and column 3
            addComp(jta2, gbLayout, gbConstraints, 1, 3, 1, 1, 0, 100);

            // Place text field in row 2 and column 3
            addComp(jtf, gbLayout, gbConstraints, 2, 3, 1, 1, 0, 0);

            // Place JButton 1 in row 3 and column 1
            addComp(jbt1, gbLayout, gbConstraints, 3, 1, 1, 1, 0, 0);

            // Place JButton 2 in row 3 and column 2
            addComp(jbt2, gbLayout, gbConstraints, 3, 2, 1, 1, 0, 0);
        }
    }
```

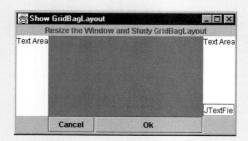

Figure 10.21   *The components are placed in the frame of* GridBagLayout.

Example Review

The program defines the addComp() method to add a component to the GridBagLayout with the specified constraints parameters.

Since the program creates a panel with a weightx of 100 and a weighty of 100, this component has extra space to grow horizontally and vertically up to 100 pixels. If you resize the window, you will see that the panel's viewing area increases or shrinks as the window grows and shrinks.

The program creates the second text area jta2 with `weightx` 0 and `weighty` 100. This text area can grow vertically, but not horizontally, when the window is resized.

The `weightx` and `weighty` for all the other components are 0. Whether the size of these components grows or shrinks depends on the `fill` and `anchor` parameters. The program defines `fill = BOTH` and `anchor = CENTER`.

Because the `fill` and `anchor` parameters are class variables, their values are for all components. Consider this scenario: Suppose you enlarge the window. The panel is expanded, which causes the display area for text area jta1 to increase. Because `fill` is `BOTH` for jta1, jta1 fills in its new display area.

Using No Layout Manager (Optional)

Java enables you to place components in a container without using a layout manager. In this case, the component's instance method `setBounds()` is used to set the component, as follows:

```
public void setBounds(int x, int y, int width, int height);
```

This sets the location and size for the component, as in the example below:

```
JButton jbt = new JButton("Help");
jbt.setBounds(10, 10, 40, 20);
```

The upper-left corner of the Help button is placed at (10, 10); the button width is 40, and the height is 20.

Here are the steps for not using a layout manager:

1. Use the following statement to specify no layout manager:

```
setLayout(null);
```

2. Add the component to the container:

```
add(component);
```

3. Specify the location to place the component, using the `setBounds()` method as follows:

```
JButton jbt = new JButton("Help");
jbt.setBounds(10, 10, 40, 20);
```

Example 10.11 Using No Layout Manager

This example shows a program that places the same components in the same layout as in the preceding example, but without using a layout manager. Figure 10.22 contains the sample output.

```java
// ShowNoLayout.java: Place components without using a layout manager
package Chapter10;

import Chapter8.MyFrameWithExitHandling;
import java.awt.*;
import java.awt.event.*;
import javax.swing.*;

public class ShowNoLayout extends MyFrameWithExitHandling
{
  private JLabel jlbl =
    new JLabel("Resize the Window and Study No Layout",
      JLabel.CENTER);;
  private JTextArea jta1 = new JTextArea("Text Area", 5, 10 );
  private JTextArea jta2 = new JTextArea("Text Area", 5, 10 );
  private JTextField jtf = new JTextField("TextField");
  private JPanel jp = new JPanel();
  private JButton jbt1 = new JButton("Cancel" );
  private JButton jbt2 = new JButton("Ok" );
  private GridBagLayout gbLayout;
  private GridBagConstraints gbConstraints;

  public static void main(String[] args)
  {
    ShowNoLayout frame = new ShowNoLayout();
    frame.setSize(400,200);
    frame.setVisible(true);
  }

  public ShowNoLayout()
  {
    setTitle("Show No Layout");

    // Set background color for the panel
    jp.setBackground(Color.red);

    // Specify no layout manager
    getContentPane().setLayout(null);

    // Add components to frame
    getContentPane().add(jlbl);
    getContentPane().add(jp);
    getContentPane().add(jta1);
    getContentPane().add(jta2);
    getContentPane().add(jtf);
    getContentPane().add(jbt1);
    getContentPane().add(jbt2);

    // Put componets in the right place
    jlbl.setBounds(0, 10, 400, 40);
    jta1.setBounds(0, 50, 100, 100);
    jp.setBounds(100, 50, 200, 100);
    jta2.setBounds(300, 50, 100, 50);
    jtf.setBounds(300, 100, 100, 50);
    jbt1.setBounds(100, 150, 100, 50);
    jbt2.setBounds(200, 150, 100, 50);
  }
}
```

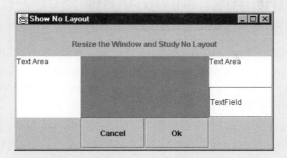

Figure 10.22   *The components are placed in the frame without using a layout manager.*

Example Review

If you run this program on Windows with 640×480 resolution, the layout size is satisfactory. If you run the program on Windows with a higher resolution, the components appear very small and clump together. If you run the program on Windows with a lower resolution, the components cannot be shown in their entirety.

If you resize the window, you will see that the location and size of the components are not changed, as shown in Figure 10.23.

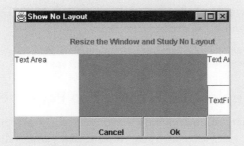

Figure 10.23   *The components' size and positions are fixed with no layout, and can be changed in the frame only with a layout manager.*

■■ **NOTE**

Microsoft Visual J++ 6.0 uses the no-layout approach to generate code in the Form Designer. JBuilder allows you to use FlowLayout, GridLayout, BorderLayout, CardLayout, GridBagLayout, and JBuilder-supplied layout managers in the Visual Designer.

■■ **TIP**

Avoid using the no-layout-manager option to develop platform-independent applications.

---

continues

Packaging and Deploying Java Projects in JBuilder (Optional)

Your project may consist of many classes and supporting files, such as image files and audio files. All of these files have to be provided to the end-users if your programs are to run on their side. For convenience, Java supports an archive file that can group all the project files in a compressed file.

The Java archive file format (JAR) is based on the popular ZIP file format. JAR can be used as a general archiving tool, but transporting Java applications, applets, and their requisite components (.class files, images, and sounds) in a single file was the primary motivation for its development.

This single file can be deployed on an end-user's machine as an application. It also can be downloaded to a browser in a single HTTP transaction, rather than opening a new connection for each piece. This greatly simplifies application deployment and improves the speed with which an applet can be loaded onto a Web page and begin functioning. The JAR format also supports compression, which reduces the size of the file and improves download time still further. Additionally, individual entries in a JAR file can be digitally signed by the applet author to authenticate their origin.

You can create an archive file using the JDK **jar** command or using the JBuilder Deployment Wizard. The following command creates an archive file named MouseDrawingDemo.jar for classes MouseDrawingDemo.class and MyFrameWithExitHandling.class:

```
jar -cf MouseDrawingDemo.jar Chapter10/MouseDrawingDemo.class
    Chapter8/MyFrameWithExitHandling.class
```

Using the Deployment Wizard to Package Projects

With the **jar** command, you have to manually identify the dependent files. JBuilder provides a Deployment Wizard that gathers all the classes on which your program depends into one JAR archive that includes image and audio files.

Let us use the MouseDrawingDemo class in Example 10.6, "Handling Complex Mouse Events," to demonstrate packaging projects. Here are the steps to follow in generating the archive file:

1. Open the Chapter10 project. Make sure that MouseDrawingDemo.java appears in the Navigation pane.

2. Choose Wizards, Deployment Wizards to open the Deployment Wizard, as shown in Figure 10.24. Check "Extract generated manifest file to project." This option adds the new manifest file to your project and displays it in the Navigation pane. This allows you to make additional changes to the manifest file for inclusion in the archive.

3. Check the box for MouseDrawingDemo.java and leave all others unchecked. Choose Compress JAR as archive type and enter C:\jbBook\MouseDraw-

Figure 10.24   *You can use the Deployment Wizard to create an archive file for the project.*

ingDemo.jar in the Output file field. Click Next to let JBuilder automatically identify all the dependent files and display them in Figure 10.25.

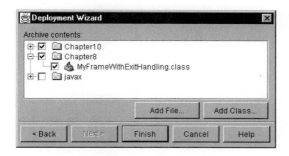

Figure 10.25   *The JBuilder Deployment Wizard finds all the dependent classes needed to run the project.*

4. Assume that the target machine supports Java 2. This means that you don't need to include any Swing components in the archive. Uncheck the box for javax in Figure 10.25. If any files or classes needed to run the project are not shown in Figure 10.25, you can use the Add Class or Add File button to add them.

5. Press Finish to generate the archive file MouseDrawingDemo.jar.

> **NOTE**
>
> You can view the contents of a .JAR file using WinZip32, a popular compression utility for Windows 95 and Windows NT, as shown in Figure 10.26.

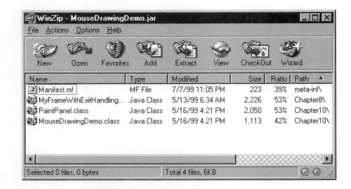

Figure 10.26   You can view the files contained in the archive file using the WinZip utility.

The Manifest File

As shown in Figure 10.26, a manifest file was created with the path name `meta-inf\`. The manifest is a special file that contains information about the files packaged in a JAR file. For instance, the manifest file in Figure 10.26 contains the information shown in Figure 10.27.

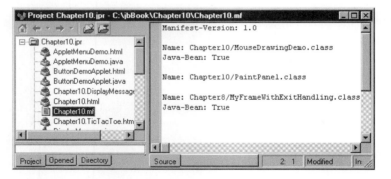

Figure 10.27   *The manifest file is added to the project because you checked the option "Extract generated manifest file to project" in Figure 10.24.*

You can modify the information contained in the manifest file to enable the JAR file to be used for a variety of purposes. For instance, you can add information to specify a main class to run an application using the .jar file.

Running Archived Projects

The Deployment Wizard packages all the class files and dependent resource files into an archive file that can be distributed to the end-user. If the project is a Java application, the user should have a Java Running Environment already installed. If it is not installed, the user can download Java Runtime Environment (JRE) from JavaSoft at **www.javasoft.com/** and install it.

NOTE

The Java Runtime Environment is the minimum standard Java platform for running Java programs. It contains the Java interpreter, Java core classes, and supporting files. The JRE does not contain any of the development tools (such as Applet Viewer or javac) or classes that pertain only to a development environment. The JRE is a subset of JDK.

To run `MouseDrawingDemo` as an application, take the following steps:

1. Update the manifest file to insert an entry for the main class, as shown in Figure 10.28.

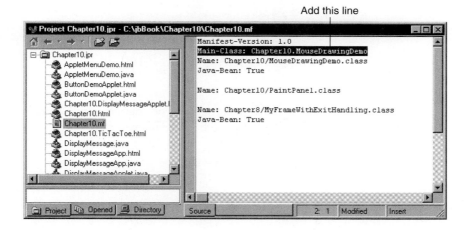

Figure 10.28   *You need to specify a main class in the JAR file to run an application in the JAR file.*

2. Run the Deployment Wizard again and choose Chapter10.mf as Manifest file, as shown in Figure 10.29.

3. Run the .jar file using the java command from the directory that contains MouseDrawingDemo.jar, as follows:

```
java -jar MouseDrawingDemo.jar
```

TIP

You can write an installation procedure that creates the necessary directories and subdirectories on the end-user's computer. The installation can also create an icon that the end-user can use to start the program by double-clicking on it.

To run `MouseDrawingDemo` as an applet, you need to modify the <APPLET> tag in the HTML file to include an ARCHIVE attribute. The ARCHIVE attribute speci-

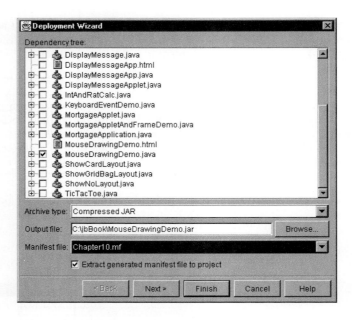

Figure 10.29   *You can specify a manifest file to be added in the JAR file.*

fies the archive file that contains the applet. For example, the HTML file for running the MouseDrawingDemo can be modified as follows:

```
<APPLET
  CODE    = "Chapter10.MouseDrawingDemo.class"
  ARCHIVE = "MouseDrawingDemo.jar"
  WIDTH   = 400
  HEIGHT  = 300
  HSPACE  = 0
  VSPACE  = 0
  ALIGN   = Middle
>
</APPLET>
```

Chapter Summary

In this chapter, you learned about applets and advanced graphics programming using mouse and keyboard events, CardLayout manager, GridBagLayout manager, and using no layout manager. You also learned how to create and use Java archive files to efficiently deploy Java projects.

The Web browser controls and executes applets through the init(), start(), stop(), and destroy() methods in the Applet class. Applets always extend the Applet class and implement these methods if applicable, so they can be run by the Web browser. The applet bytecode must be specified by using the <applet> tag in an HTML file to tell the Web browser where to find the applet. Applets can accept parameters from HTML using the <param> tag. JApplet is a subclass of Applet. You should use it in developing Java applets with Swing components.

Applications and applets are written in much the same way. You can easily convert an applet into an application or an application into an applet. You also can write an applet that has the capability of running as an application.

Two examples and a case study in this chapter demonstrated handling mouse and keyboard events. Mouse events and keyboard events are often useful in graphics programming. Clicking, pressing, or releasing a mouse button generates a `MouseEvent`; dragging or moving a mouse generates a `MouseMotionEvent`. Entering a key generates a `KeyEvent`. The `MouseEvent`, `MouseMotionEvent`, and `KeyEvent` are subclasses of `InputEvent`, which contains several common methods useful in processing mouse and keyboard events.

The `CardLayout` manager arranges components in a queue of cards. You can see one component at a time. To add a component to the container, you need to use `add(component,  string)`. You can see the components using the methods `first(container)`, `last(container)`, `next(container)`, `previous(container)`, or `show(container, string)`. The `show(container, string)` method directly displays the component identified by the string.

The `GridBagLayout` manager gives you the most flexible way to arrange components. It is similar to `GridLayout` in the sense that the components are placed into cells. Unlike `GridLayout`, however, it enables individual components to occupy multiple cells. The components can vary in size and can be placed in any order.

You can place components without using a layout manager. In this case, the components are placed at a hard-coded location. Using this approach, your program might look fine on one machine and be useless on other machines. It is recommended that you use the layout managers to develop a platform-independent graphical user interface.

You also learned how to use the Applet Wizard to create applets and the Deployment Wizard to deploy Java projects.

Chapter Review

10.1. How do you run an applet?

10.2. Describe the `init()`, `start()`, `stop()`, and `destroy()` methods in the `Applet` class.

10.3. Is the `getParameter()` method defined in `Applet`? Is the `paintComponent()` method defined in `Applet`? Find where these methods are originally defined.

10.4. How do you add components to a `JApplet`?

10.5. Describe the `<applet>` HTML tag. How do you pass parameters to an applet?

10.6. Describe the procedure for converting an application to an applet, and vice versa.

10.7. How do you create a frame from an applet?

10.8. Can you place an applet in a frame? Can you place a frame in an applet?

10.9. Describe `CardLayout`. How do you create a `CardLayout`? How do you add a component to a `CardLayout`? How do you show a card in the `CardLayout` container?

10.10. Describe `GridBagLayout`. How do you create a `GridBagLayout`? How do you create a `GridBagConstraints` object? What constraints did you learn in this chapter? Describe their functions. How do you add a component to a `GridBagLayout` container?

10.11. Is the order in which the components are added important for certain layout managers? Which managers?

10.12. Which layout manager allows the components in the container to be moved to other rows when the window is resized?

10.13. Can you place components without using a layout manager? What are the disadvantages of not using a layout manager?

Programming Exercises

10.1. Convert Example 9.7, "Using Radio Buttons," into an applet.

10.2. Rewrite Example 10.2, "Passing Parameters to Java Applets," to display a message with specified color, font, and size. The message, x, y, color, font-name, and fontsize are parameters in the `<applet>` tag, like this:

```
<applet
  code = "Exercise10_2.class"
  width = 200
  height = 50>
  <param name=MESSAGE value="Welcome to Java">
  <param name=X value=40>
  <param name=Y value=50>
  <param name=COLOR value="red">
  <param name=FONTNAME value="Monospaced">
  <param name=FONTSIZE value=20>
You must have a Java-enabled browser to view the applet
</applet>
```

10.3. Rewrite the `MortgageApplet` in Example 10.1, "Using Applets," to enable it to run as an application as well as an applet.

10.4. Write an applet to find a path in a maze, as shown in Figure 10.30. The applet can also run as an application. The maze is represented by an 8×8 board. The path must meet the following conditions:

■ The path is between the upper-left corner cell and the lower-right corner cell in the maze.

■ The applet enables the user to insert or remove a mark on a cell. A path consists of adjacent unmarked cells. Two cells are said to be adjacent if they are horizontal or vertical neighbors, but not diagonal neighbors.

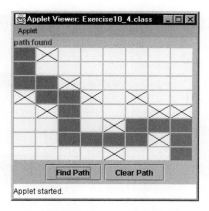

Figure 10.30   *The program finds a path from the upper-left corner to the bottom-right corner.*

■ The path does not contain cells that form a square. The path in Figure 10.31, for example, does not meet this condition. (This condition makes a path easy to identify on the board.)

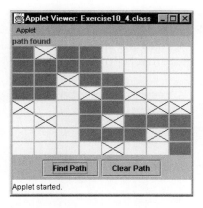

Figure 10.31   *The path does not meet the third condition for this exercise.*

10.5. Rewrite Example 10.8, "The TicTacToe Game," with the following modifications:

■ Declare `Cell` as a standalone class rather than an inner class.

■ When the game is over, the user cannot click to mark empty cells.

10.6. Write an applet that contains two buttons called Simple Calculator and Mortgage. When you click Simple Calculator, a frame for Example 9.9, "Using Menus," appears in a new window so that you can do arithmetic. When you click Mortgage, a frame for Example 10.4 appears in a separate new window so that you can calculate a mortgage (see Figure 10.32).

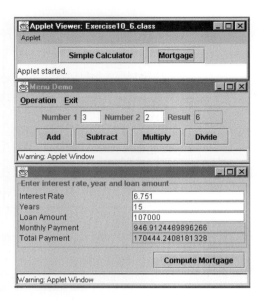

Figure 10.32   *You can show frames in the applets.*

10.7. Use various panels of `FlowLayout`, `GridLayout`, and `BorderLayout` to lay out the following calculator and to implement addition (+), subtraction (−), division (/), square root (sqrt), and modulus (%) functions (see Figure 10.33).

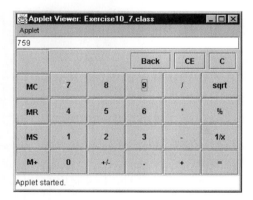

Figure 10.33   *This is a Java implementation of a popular calculator.*

10.8. Use `GridBagLayout` to lay out the preceding calculator.

10.9. Write a program to get character input from the keyboard and put the characters where the mouse points.

10.10. Write an applet to emulate a paint utility. Your program should enable the user to choose options, and draw shapes or get characters from the keyboard based on the selected options (see Figure 10.34). Enable the applet to run as an application.

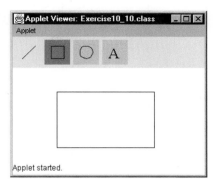

Figure 10.34   *This exercise produces a prototype drawing utility that enables you to draw lines, rectangles, ovals, and characters.*

10.11. Write an applet that does arithmetic on integers and rationals. The program uses two panels in a `CardLayout` manager, one for integer arithmetic and the other for rational arithmetic.

The program provides a menu labeled Operation that has two menu items, Integer and Rational, for selecting the two panels. When the user chooses the Integer menu item from the Operation menu, the integer panel is activated. When the user chooses the Rational menu item, the rational panel is activated (see Figure 10.35).

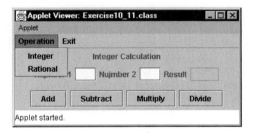

Figure 10.35   *This exercise uses* `CardLayout` *to select panels for performing integer operations or rational number operations.*

10.12. Rewrite the previous example using the tabbed pane instead of the `CardLayout`. (See Figure 10.36)

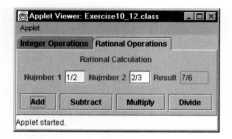

Figure 10.36   *This exercise uses a tabbed pane to select panels for performing integer operations or rational number operations.*

PART IV

DEVELOPING COMPREHENSIVE PROJECTS

This part of the book is devoted to several advanced features of Java programming. In it you will learn how to use these features to develop comprehensive programs. The subjects treated include the use of exception handling to make your programs robust, the use of internationalization support to develop projects for international audiences, the use of multithreading to make your programs more responsive and interactive, the incorporation of sound and images to make your programs user-friendly, the use of input and output to manage and process large quantities of data, and the creation of client/server applications with Java networking support.

CHAPTER 11

EXCEPTION HANDLING

Objectives

- ℮ Understand the concept of exception handling.
- ℮ Become familiar with exception types.
- ℮ Claim exceptions in a method.
- ℮ Throw exceptions in a method.
- ℮ Use the `try-catch` block to handle exceptions.
- ℮ Create your own exception classes.
- ℮ Rethrow exceptions in a `try-catch` block.
- ℮ Use the `finally` clause in a `try-catch` block.
- ℮ Know when to use exceptions.

Introduction

So far you have seen program examples without runtime errors. Runtime errors are unavoidable, even for experienced programmers, and cause *exceptions* in Java: events that occur during the execution of a program and disrupt the normal flow of control.

A program that does not provide the code to handle exceptions may terminate abnormally, causing serious problems. For example, if your program attempts to transfer money from a savings account to a checking account, but because of a runtime error is terminated *after* the money is drawn from the savings account and *before* the money is deposited in the checking account, the customer loses money.

Java provides programmers with the capability to handle runtime errors. With this capability, referred to as *exception handling*, you can develop robust programs for mission-critical computing.

This chapter introduces Java's exception-handling model. The chapter covers exception types, claiming exceptions, throwing exceptions, catching exceptions, creating exception classes, rethrowing exceptions, and the `finally` clause.

Exceptions and Exception Types

Runtime errors occur for various reasons. For example, the user may enter an invalid input, or the program may attempt to open a file that doesn't exist, or the network connection may hang up, or the program may attempt to access an out-of-bounds array element. When a runtime error occurs, Java raises an exception.

Exceptions are handled differently from the events of graphics programming. (In Chapter 8, "Getting Started with Graphics Programming," you learned the events used in graphics programming.) In graphics programming, an *event* may be ignored, but an *exception* cannot be ignored. In graphics programming, a listener must register with the source object. External-user action on the source object generates an event and the source object notifies the listener by invoking the handlers implemented by the listener. If no listener is registered with the source object, the event is ignored. However, when an exception occurs, the program may terminate if no handler can be used to deal with it.

A Java exception is an instance of a class derived from `Throwable`. The `Throwable` class is contained in the `java.lang` package, and subclasses of `Throwable` are contained in various packages. Errors related to graphics programming are included in the `java.awt` package, whereas numeric exceptions are included in the `java.lang` package because they are related to the `java.lang.Number` class. You can create your own exception classes by extending `Throwable` or a subclass of `Throwable`. Figure 11.1 shows some predefined exception classes in Java.

NOTE

The class names `Error`, `Exception`, and `RuntimeException` are somewhat confusing. All the classes are exceptions. `Exception` is just one of these classes, and all the errors discussed here occur at runtime.

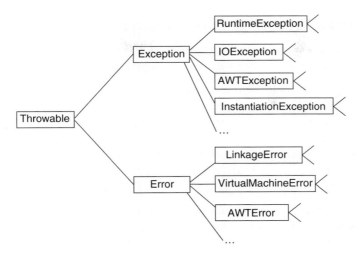

Figure 11.1   *The exceptions are instances of the classes shown in this diagram.*

The Error class describes internal system errors, which rarely occur. If such an error occurs, there is little you can do beyond notifying the user and trying to terminate the program gracefully. Examples of subclasses of Error are LinkageError, VirtualMachineError, and AWTError. Subclasses of LinkageError indicate that a class has some dependency on another class, but that the latter class has incompatibly changed after the compilation of the former class. Subclasses of VirtualMachineError indicate that the Java Virtual Machine is broken or has run out of resources necessary for it to continue operating. AWTError is caused by a fatal error in the graphics programs.

The Exception class describes the errors caused by your program and external circumstances. These errors can be caught and handled by your program. Exception has many subclasses. Examples are RuntimeException, IOException, AWTException, and InstantiationException.

The RuntimeException class describes programming errors such as bad casting, accessing an out-of-bounds array, and numeric errors. Examples of subclasses of RuntimeException are ArithmeticException, NullPointerException, Illegal-ArgumentException, ArrayStoreException, and IndexOutOfBoundsException.

The IOException class describes errors related to input/output operations, such as invalid input, reading past the end of a file, and opening a nonexistent file. Examples of subclasses of IOException are InterruptedIOException, EOFException, and FileNotFoundException.

The AWTException class describes errors caused by graphics operations.

The InstantiationException class describes class instantiation errors. This exception is thrown, for example, if there is an attempt to instantiate an abstract class or an interface.

Understanding Exception Handling

Java's exception-handling model is based on three operations: *claiming an exception*, *throwing an exception*, and *catching an exception*.

In Java, the statement currently being executed belongs to a method: either to `main()` or to a method invoked by another method. The system invokes the `main()` method for a Java application and invokes the `init()` method for a Java applet. In general, every method must state the types of exceptions it can encounter. This process is called *claiming an exception*, which simply tells the compiler what can go wrong.

When a statement causes errors, the method containing the statement creates an exception object and passes it to the system. The exception object contains information about the exception, including its type and the state of the program when the error occurred. This process is called *throwing an exception*.

After a method throws an exception, the Java runtime system begins the process of finding the code to handle the error. The code that handles the error, called the *exception handler*, is found by searching backward through a chain of method calls, starting from the current method. The handler must match the type of exception thrown. If no such handler is found, the program terminates. The process of finding a handler is called *catching an exception*.

Claiming Exceptions

To claim an exception is to tell the compiler what might go wrong during the execution of a method. Because system errors and runtime errors can happen to any code, Java does not require you to claim `Error` and `RuntimeException` in the method. However, all the other exceptions must be explicitly claimed in the method declaration if they are thrown by the method.

To claim an exception in a method, you use the `throws` keyword in the method declaration, as in this example:

```
public void myMethod() throws IOException
```

The `throws` keyword indicates that `myMethod` may throw an `IOException`. If the method may throw multiple exceptions, you can add a list of the exceptions, separated by commas, after `throws`:

```
MethodDeclaration throws Exception1, Exception2,...,ExceptionN
```

Throwing Exceptions

In the method that claims the exception, you can throw an object of that exception if the exception arises. Here is the syntax to throw an exception:

```
throw new TheException();
```

Or if you prefer, you can use this syntax:

```
TheException ex = new TheException();
throw ex;
```

NOTE

The keyword to claim an exception is `throws`, and the keyword to throw an exception is `throw`.

A method can only throw the exceptions claimed in the method declaration or throw `Error`, `RuntimeException`, or subclasses of `Error` and `RuntimeException`. For example, the method cannot throw `IOException` if it is not claimed in the method declaration, but a method can always throw `RuntimeException` or a subclass of it even if it is not claimed by the method.

Example 11.1 Throwing Exceptions

This example demonstrates the throwing of an exception by modifying the `Rational` class defined in Example 5.8, "Using the `Rational` Class" (see Chapter 5, "Programming with Objects and Classes"), so that it can handle the zero denominator exception.

You create a new `Rational` class in the package Chapter 11. The new `Rational` class is the same except that the `divide()` method throws a zero-denominator exception if the client attempts to call the method with a zero denominator. The new `divide()` method is as follows:

```
// Divide a rational number from this rational
public Rational divide(Rational secondRational) throws
  Exception
{
  if (secondRational.getNumerator() == 0)
    throw new Exception("Denominator cannot be zero");

  long n = numerator*secondRational.getDenominator();
  long d = denominator*secondRational.getNumerator();
  return new Rational(n, d);
}
```

Example Review

The original class `Rational` remains intact except for the `divide()` method. The `divide()` method now claims an exception and throws the exception if the divisor is zero.

The `divide()` method claims the exception to be an instance of `Exception` by using `throws Exception` in the method signature. The method throws the exception by using the following statement:

```
throw new Exception("Denominator cannot be zero");
```

Catching Exceptions

You now know how to claim an exception and how to throw an exception. Next, you will learn how to handle exceptions.

When calling a method that explicitly claims an exception, you must use the `try-catch` block to wrap the statement, as shown in the following lines:

```
try
{
  statements;   //statements that may throw exceptions
}
catch (Exception1 ex)
{
  handler for exception1;
}
catch (Exception2 ex)
{
  handler for exception2;
}
...
catch (ExceptionN ex)
{
  handler for exceptionN;
}
```

If no exceptions arise during the execution of the `try` clause, the `catch` clauses are skipped.

If one of the statements inside the `try` block throws an exception, Java skips the re-maining statements and starts to search for a handler for it. If the exception type matches one listed in a `catch` clause, the code in the `catch` clause is executed. If the exception type does not match any exception in the `catch` clauses, Java exits this method, passes the exception to the method that invoked this method, and contin-ues the same process to find a handler. If no handler is found in the chain of the calling method, the program terminates and prints an error message on the con-sole.

Consider the scenario in Figure 11.2. Suppose that an exception occurs in the `try-catch` block that contains a call to `method3`. If the exception type is `Exception3`, it is caught by the `catch` clause for handling exception `ex3`. If the exception type is `Exception2`, it is caught by the `catch` clause for handling exception `ex2`. If the ex-ception type is `Exception1`, it is caught by the `catch` clause for handling exception `ex1` in the `main()` method. If the exception type is not `Exception1`, `Exception2`, or `Exception3`, the program terminates immediately.

If the exception type is `Exception3`, `statement3` is skipped. If the exception type is `Exception2`, `statement2` and `statement3` are skipped. If the exception type is `Exception1`, `statement1`, `statement2`, and `statement3` are skipped.

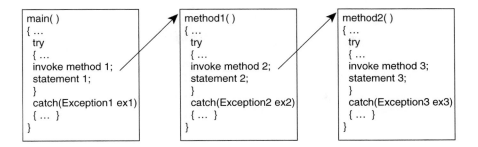

Figure 11.2 *If an exception is not caught in the current method, it is passed to its caller. The process is repeated until the exception is caught or passed to the* main() *method.*

NOTE

If an exception of a subclass of Exception occurs in a graphics program, Java prints the error message on the console, but the program goes back to its user-interface-processing loop to run continuously. The exception is ignored.

The exception object contains valuable information about the exception. This object may use the following instance methods in the java.lang.Throwable class to get the information related to the exception:

- public String getMessage()

  This returns the detailed message of the Throwable object.

- public String toString()

  This returns a short description of the Throwable object, whereas getMessage() returns a detailed message.

- public String getLocalizedMessage()

  This returns a localized description of the Throwable object. Subclasses of Throwable can override this method in order to produce a locale-specific message. For subclasses that do not override this method, the default implementation returns the same result as getMessage().

- public void printStackTrace()

  This prints the Throwable object and its trace information on the console.

NOTE

Several different exception classes can be derived from a common superclass. If a catch clause catches exception objects of a superclass, it can catch all the exception objects of the subclasses of that superclass.

◼◼◼ CAUTION
The order in which the exceptions are specified in a `catch` clause is important. If you fail to specify an exception object of a class before the exception object of the superclass of that class, a compilation error will result.

Example 11.2 Catching Exceptions

This program demonstrates catching exceptions, using the new `Rational` class given in Example 11.1. Figure 11.3 shows the output of a sample run of the program.

```java
// TestRationalException.java: Catch and handle exceptions
package Chapter11;

import Chapter11.Rational;

public class TestRationalException
{
  // Main method
  public static void main(String[] args)
  {
    // Create three rational numbers
    Rational r1 = new Rational(4,2);
    Rational r2 = new Rational(2,3);
    Rational r3 = new Rational(0,1);

    try
    {
      System.out.println(r1+" + "+ r2 +" = "+r1.add(r2));
      System.out.println(r1+" - "+ r2 +" = "+r1.subtract(r2));
      System.out.println(r1+" * "+ r2 +" = "+r1.multiply(r2));
      System.out.println(r1+" / "+ r2 +" = "+r1.divide(r2));
      System.out.println(r1+" / "+ r3 +" = "+r1.divide(r3));
      System.out.println(r1+" + "+ r2 +" = "+r1.add(r2));
    }
    catch(Exception ex)
    {
      System.out.println(ex);
    }

    // Display the result
    System.out.println(r1 + " - " + r2 + " = " + r1.subtract(r2));
  }
}
```

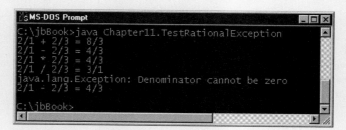

Figure 11.3   *The exception is raised when the divisor is zero.*

498

Example Review

The program creates two `Rational` numbers, `r1` and `r2`, to test numeric methods (`add()`, `subtract()`, `multiply()`, and `divide()`) on rational numbers.

Invoking the `divide()` method with divisor 0 causes the method to throw an exception object. In the `catch` clause, the type of the object `ex` is `Exception`, which matches the object thrown by the `divide()` method. So this exception is caught by the `catch` clause.

The exception handler simply prints a short message, `ex.toString()`, about the exception, using `System.out.println(ex)`.

Note that the execution continues in the event of the zero denominator. If the handlers had not caught the exception, the program would have abruptly terminated.

Example 11.3 Exceptions in GUI Applications

Here Example 9.10, "Using Menus" (in Chapter 9, "Creating User Interfaces"), is used to demonstrate the effect of exceptions in GUI applications. Run the program and enter any number in the Number 1 field and 0 in the Number 2 field; then click the Divide button (see Figure 11.4). You will see nothing in the `Result` field, but an error message appears on the console, as shown in Figure 11.5. The GUI application continues.

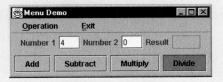

Figure 11.4   *In GUI programs, if an exception of the* `Exception` *class is not caught, it is ignored, and the program continues.*

continues

Figure 11.5   *In GUI programs, if an exception of the* Exception *class is not caught, an error message appears on the console.*

Example Review

If exceptions of the type Exception are not caught when Java graphics programs are running, the error messages are displayed on the console, but the program continues to run.

If you rewrite the calculate() method in the MenuDemo program of Example 9.9 with a try-catch block to catch RuntimeException as follows, the program will display ~~Error~~ in the Result text field in the case of a numerical error. No errors are shown on the console because they are handled in the program.

```
// Calculate and show the result in jtfResult
private void calculate(char operator)
{
  // Obtain Number 1 and Number 2
  int num1 = (Integer.parseInt(jtfNum1.getText().trim()));
  int num2 = (Integer.parseInt(jtfNum2.getText().trim()));
  int result = 0;

  try
  {
    // Perform selected operation
    switch (operator)
    {
      case '+': result = num1 + num2;
              break;
      case '-': result = num1 - num2;
              break;
      case '*': result = num1 * num2;
              break;
      case '/': result = num1 / num2;
    }
```

```
      // Set result in jtfResult
      jtfResult.setText(String.valueOf(result));
    }
    catch (RuntimeException ex)
    {
      jtfResult.setText("Error ");
    }
  }
}
```

Creating Custom Exception Classes

Java provides quite a few exception classes. You should use them whenever possible instead of creating your own exception classes. However, you may run into a problem that cannot be adequately described by these predefined exception classes. In this case, you can create your own exception class, derived from Exception or from a subclass of Exception, such as IOException. This section shows how to create your own exception class.

Example 11.4 Creating Your Own Exception Classes

This program creates 10 accounts and transfers funds among them. If a transaction amount is negative, the program raises a negative-amount exception. If the account's balance is less than the requested transaction amount, an insufficient-funds exception is raised.

The example consists of four classes: Account, NegativeAmountException, InsufficientAmountException, and TestMyException. The Account class provides the information and operations pertaining to the account. NegativeAmountException and InsufficientAmountException are the exception classes dealing with transactions of negative or insufficient amounts. The TestMyException class utilizes all these classes to perform transactions, transferring funds among accounts.

The code for the Account class follows. This class contains two data fields: id (for account ID) and balance (for current balance). The methods for Account are deposit and withdraw. Both methods will throw NegativeAmountException if the transaction amount is negative. The withdraw() method will also throw InsufficientFundException if the current balance is less than the requested transaction amount.

```
// Account.java: The class for describing an account
package Chapter11;

public class Account
{
  // Two data fields in an account
  private int ID;
  private double balance;
```

continues

```
              // Construct an account with specified ID and balance
              public Account(int ID, double balance)
              {
                this.ID = ID;
                this.balance = balance;
              }

              // Getter method for ID
              public int getID()
              {
                return ID;
              }

              // Setter method for balance
              public void setBalance(double balance)
              {
                this.balance = balance;
              }

              // Getter method for balance
              public double getBalance()
              {
                return balance;
              }

              // Deposit an amount to this account
              public void deposit(double amount)
                throws NegativeAmountException
              {
                if (amount < 0)
                  throw new NegativeAmountException
                    (this, amount, "deposit");
                balance = balance + amount;
              }

              // Withdraw an amount from this account
              public void withdraw(double amount)
                throws NegativeAmountException, InsufficientFundException
              {
                if (amount < 0)
                  throw new NegativeAmountException
                    (this, amount, "withdraw");
                if (balance < amount)
                  throw new InsufficientFundException(this, amount);
                balance = balance - amount;
              }
            }
```

The NegativeAmountException exception class follows. It contains information about the attempted transaction type (deposit or withdrawal), the account, and the negative amount passed from the method.

```
        // negative amount exception
        package Chapter11;

        public class NegativeAmountException extends Exception
        {
          // Information to be passed to the handlers
          private Account account;
          private double amount;
          private String transactionType;
```

```
    // Construct an negative amount exception
    public NegativeAmountException(Account account,
                                   double amount,
                                   String transactionType)
    {
      super("Negative amount");
      this.account = account;
      this.amount = amount;
      this.transactionType = transactionType;
    }
  }
```

The InsufficientFundException exception class follows. It contains information about the account and the amount passed from the method.

```
// InsufficientFundException.java: An exception class for describing
// insufficient fund exception
package Chapter11;

public class InsufficientFundException extends Exception
{
  // Information to be passed to the handlers
  private Account account;
  private double amount;

  // Construct an insufficient exception
  public InsufficientFundException(Account account, double amount)
  {
    super("Insufficient amount");
    this.account = account;
    this.amount = amount;
  }

  // Override the "toString" method
  public String toString()
  {
    return "Account balance is " + account.getBalance();
  }
}
```

The TestMyException class follows. It creates 10 accounts with account id 0, 1, and so on, to 9. Each account has an initial balance of $1,000. The program first attempts to deposit −$10 in account 0, raising the negative amount exception. The program then continuously withdraws $9 from account 0. When the balance of account 0 falls below $9, the program begins to withdraw from the next account, and finally terminates when all of the account balances are below $9. The output of the test program is shown in Figure 11.6.

```
// TestMyException.java: Use custom exception classes
package Chapter11;

public class TestMyException
{
  // Main method
  public static void main(String[] args)
  {
```

continues

```
                  // Create 10 accounts with id 0 .. 9 and initial balance 1000
                  Account[] account = new Account[10];
                  for (int i=0; i<10; i++)
                    account[i] = new Account(i, 1000);

                  // Test negative deposit exception
                  try
                  {
                    account[0].deposit(-10);
                  }
                  catch (NegativeAmountException ex)
                  {
                    System.out.println(ex);
                  }

                  // Test negative withdraw exception
                  try
                  {
                    account[0].withdraw(-10);
                  }
                  catch (NegativeAmountException ex)
                  {
                    System.out.println(ex);
                  }
                  catch (InsufficientFundException ex)
                  {
                    System.out.println(ex);
                  }

                  // Keep withdrawing $9 dollars from the accounts
                  for (int j=0; j<10; j++)
                  {
                    boolean enoughFund = true;
                    while (enoughFund)
                    {
                      try
                      {
                        account[j].withdraw(9);
                      }
                      catch (InsufficientFundException ex)
                      {
                        enoughFund = false;
                        System.out.println(ex);
                      }
                      catch (NegativeAmountException ex)
                      {
                        System.out.println(ex);
                      }
                    }
                  }
                }
              }
            }
```

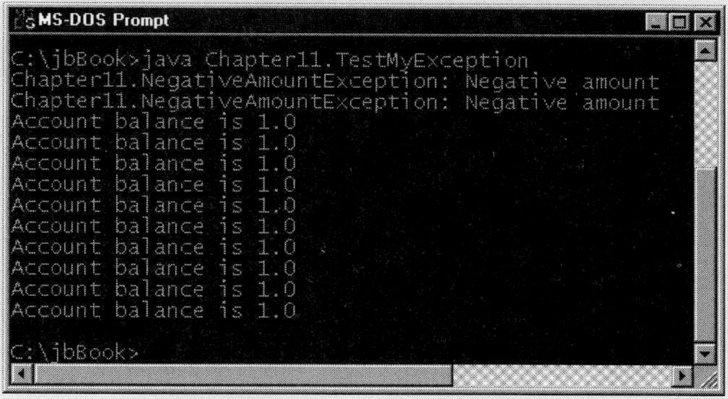

```
MS-DOS Prompt                                    _ □ ×

C:\jbBook>java Chapter11.TestMyException
Chapter11.NegativeAmountException: Negative amount
Chapter11.NegativeAmountException: Negative amount
Account balance is 1.0
Account balance is 1.0
Account balance is 1.0
Account balance is 1.0
Account balance is 1.0
Account balance is 1.0
Account balance is 1.0
Account balance is 1.0
Account balance is 1.0
Account balance is 1.0

C:\jbBook>
```

Figure 11.6 *The TestMyException program tests NegativeAmountException and Insufficient-FundException.*

Example Review

You need to create and save all the programs, either in one combined file or in separate files, then compile the TestMyException class. The Java compiler will compile all the classes on which TestMyException depends. Therefore, the classes Account, NegativeAmountException, and InsufficientFundException will be compiled along with TestMyException.

In the Account class, the deposit() method throws NegativeAmountException if the amount to be deposited is less than 0. The withdraw() method throws a NegativeAmountException if the amount to be withdrawn is less than 0 and throws an InsufficientFundException if the amount to be withdrawn is less than the current balance.

Since the user-defined exception class always extends Exception or a subclass of Exception, both NegativeAmountException and InsufficientFundException extend Exception.

Storing relevant information in the exception object is useful because it enables the handler to retrieve information from the exception object. For example, NegativeAmountException contains the account, the amount, and the transaction type.

The NegativeAmountException occurs when the test program deposits −$10, using account[0].deposit(-10). The NegativeAmountException again occurs when the program withdraws −$10, using account[0].withdraw(-10). The exception handler in the test program displays the first two lines of the output to tell the user that these exceptions have occurred and were caught and properly handled.

continues

The test program then repeatedly withdraws $9 from each account until the account balance is below $9. When the program attempts to withdraw from an account with a balance below $9, an exception is raised and caught by the handler, which displays the account balance.

Note that the test program continues its normal execution after an exception is handled. In the while loop, if the balance of one account is below $9, an exception is raised and handled in the try-catch block; then the program continues to stay in the for loop to withdraw from the next account until the balance of every account is below $9.

Example 11.5 Using Exceptions in Applets

This example demonstrates the use of exceptions in GUI applications. The applet presented here handles account transactions. It displays the account ID and balance, and lets the user deposit to or withdraw from the account. For each transaction, a message is displayed to indicate the status of the transaction: successful or failed. In case of failure, the failure for reason is reported. A sample run of the program is shown in Figure 11.7.

```java
// AccountApplet.java: Use custom exception class
package Chapter11;

import java.awt.*;
import java.awt.event.*;
import javax.swing.*;
import javax.swing.border.*;

public class AccountApplet extends JApplet implements ActionListener
{
  // Declare text fields
  private TextField jtfID, jtfBalance, jtfDeposit, jtfWithdraw;

  // Declare Deposit and Withdraw buttons
  private JButton jbtDeposit, jbtWithdraw;

  // Create an account with initial balance $1000
  private Account account = new Account(1, 1000);

  // Create a label for showing status
  private JLabel jlblStatus = new JLabel();

  // Initialize the applet
  public void init()
  {
    // Panel p1 to group ID and Balance labels and text fields
    JPanel p1 = new JPanel();
    p1.setLayout(new GridLayout(2, 2));
    p1.add(new Label("Accout ID"));
    p1.add(jtfID = new TextField(4));
    p1.add(new Label("Account Balance"));
    p1.add(jtfBalance = new TextField(4));
```

```
        jtfID.setEditable(false);
        jtfBalance.setEditable(false);
        p1.setBorder(new TitledBorder("Display Account Information"));

        // Panel p2 to group deposit amount and Deposit button and
        // withdraw amount and Withdraw button
        JPanel p2 = new JPanel();
        p2.setLayout(new GridLayout(2, 3));
        p2.add(new Label("Deposit"));
        p2.add(jtfDeposit = new TextField(4));
        p2.add(jbtDeposit = new JButton("Deposit"));
        p2.add(new Label("Withdraw"));
        p2.add(jtfWithdraw = new TextField(4));
        p2.add(jbtWithdraw = new JButton("Withdraw"));
        p2.setBorder(new TitledBorder("Deposit or withdraw funds"));

        // Place panels p1, p2, and label in the applet
        this.getContentPane().add(p1, BorderLayout.WEST);
        this.getContentPane().add(p2, BorderLayout.CENTER);
        this.getContentPane().add(jlblStatus, BorderLayout.SOUTH);

        // Refresh ID and Balance fields
        refreshFields();

        // Register listener
        jbtDeposit.addActionListener(this);
        jbtWithdraw.addActionListener(this);
    }

    // Handle ActionEvent
    public void actionPerformed(ActionEvent evt)
    {
        String actionCommand = evt.getActionCommand();
        if (evt.getSource() instanceof JButton)
            if ("Deposit".equals(actionCommand))
            {
                try
                {
                    double depositValue = (Double.valueOf(
                        jtfDeposit.getText().trim())).doubleValue();
                    account.deposit(depositValue);
                    refreshFields();
                    jlblStatus.setText("Transaction Processed");
                }
                catch (NegativeAmountException ex)
                {
                    jlblStatus.setText("Negative Amount");
                }
            }
            else if ("Withdraw".equals(actionCommand))
            {
                try
                {
                    double withdrawValue = (Double.valueOf(
                        jtfWithdraw.getText().trim())).doubleValue();
                    account.withdraw(withdrawValue);
                    refreshFields();
                    jlblStatus.setText("Transaction Processed");
                }
```

continues

507

```
                    catch(NegativeAmountException ex)
                    {
                      jlblStatus.setText("Negative Amount");
                    }
                    catch (InsufficientFundException ex)
                    {
                      jlblStatus.setText("Insufficient Funds");
                    }
                  }
                }

                // Update the display for account balance
                public void refreshFields()
                {
                  jtfID.setText(String.valueOf(account.getID()));
                  jtfBalance.setText(String.valueOf(account.getBalance()));
                }
              }
```

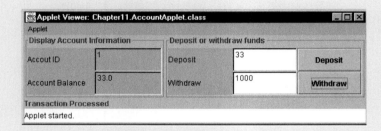

Figure 11.7   *The program lets you deposit and withdraw funds and displays the transaction status on the label.*

Example Review

The program creates an applet with two panels (p1 and p2) and a label to display messages. Panel p1 contains account ID and balance; panel p2 contains the action buttons for depositing and withdrawing funds.

With a click of the Deposit button, the amount in the Deposit text field is added to the balance. With a click of the Withdraw button, the amount in the Withdraw text field is subtracted from the balance.

For each successful transaction, the message Transaction Processed is displayed. For a negative amount, the message Negative Amount is displayed; for insufficient funds, the message Insufficient Funds is displayed.

Rethrowing Exceptions

When an exception occurs in a method, the method exits immediately if it does not catch the exception. If the method is required to perform certain tasks before exiting, you can catch the exception in the method and then rethrow it to the real handler in a structure like this:

```
try
{
  statements;
}
catch(TheException ex)
{
  perform operations before exits;
  throw ex;
}
```

The statement `throw ex` rethrows the exception so that other handlers get a chance to process the exception `ex`.

The *finally* Clause

Occasionally, you may want some code to be executed regardless of whether an exception occurs and is caught. Java has a `finally` clause that you can use to accomplish this objective. The syntax for the `finally` clause might look like this:

```
try
{
  statements;
}
catch(TheException ex)
{
  handling ex;
}
finally
{
  finalStatements;
}
```

The code in the `finally` block is executed under all circumstances, regardless of whether an exception occurs in the `try` block and whether it is caught. Consider three possible cases:

- If no exception arises in the `try` block, `finalStatements` is executed, and the next statement after the `try`-`catch` block is executed.

- If one of the statements causes an exception in the `try` block that is caught in a `catch` clause, the remaining statements in the `try` block are skipped, the `catch` clause is executed, and the `finally` clause is executed. If the `catch` clause does not rethrow an exception, the next statement after the `try`-`catch` block is executed. If it does, the exception is passed to the caller of this method.

- If one of the statements causes an exception that is not caught in any `catch` clause, the remaining statements in the `try` block are skipped, the `finally` clause is executed, and the exception is passed to the caller of this method.

NOTE
The `catch` clause may be omitted when the `finally` clause is used.

Cautions When Using Exceptions

Exception handling separates error-handling code from normal programming tasks, thus making programs easier to read and to modify. Be aware, however, that exception handling usually requires more time and resources because it requires instantiating a new exception object, rolling back the call stack, and propagating the errors to the calling methods.

Exception handling should not be used to replace simple tests. You should test simple exceptions whenever possible, and let exception handling deal with situations that cannot be handled with `if` statements.

Example 11.4 demonstrates the use of exception handling, but it is a bad example in the sense that its implementation is inefficient. Instead of letting the exceptions be caught by the other programs, you could simply check for a negative amount and insufficient balance before calling the `deposit()` and `withdraw()` methods in the test program. This would significantly improve the program's performance.

Example 11.6 Demonstrating Performance Differences With and Without Exception Handling

This example compares the performance of the program in Example 11.4, which uses exception handling, with the performance of the same program without exception handling. Example 11.4 uses exception handlers to process negative amounts and insufficient funds. Here, the program is rewritten without the use of exceptions and the execution time of the two programs is compared. The output of a sample run of the program is shown in Figure 11.8.

```java
package Chapter11;

import java.util.*;

public class UsingNoException
{
  // create 10 accounts with id 0 .. 9 and initial balance 1000
  public static void main(String[] args)
  {
    // create and initialize 10 accounts
    Account[] account = new Account[10];
    for (int i=0; i<10; i++)
      account[i] = new Account(i, 1000);

    // get start time
    long startTime = System.currentTimeMillis();

    // keep withdrawing $9 dollars from the accounts
    for (int j=0; j<10; j++)
    {
      boolean enoughFund = true;
      while (enoughFund)
        try
        {
```

```
        if (account[j].accountBalance() < 9)
        {
          System.out.println("Account balance is "+
            account[j].accountBalance());
          enoughFund = false;
        }
        else
          account[j].withdraw(9);
      }
      catch (InsufficientFundException ex)
      {
        enoughFund = false;
        System.out.println(ex);
      }
      catch (NegativeAmountException ex)
      {
        System.out.println(ex);
      }
    }

    // get end time
    long endTime = System.currentTimeMillis();

    // display elapsed time
    System.out.println("Elapsed time: "+ (endTime - startTime) +
      " Milliseconds");
  }
}
```

To compare the execution time with exception handling, replace the if statement (set in bold in the code) with the following code:

```
account[j].withdraw(9);
```

For convenience, rename the program TestMyExceptionWithTiming. A sample run of the output of the program is shown in Figure 11.9.

Figure 11.8 *The program uses* if *statements to test for negative amounts and insufficient funds.*

continues

Figure 11.9   *Because the program uses exceptions to test for negative amounts and insufficient funds, it takes a little more time.*

Example Review

The `UsingNoException` program uses the `if` statement to check whether the account has a sufficient balance before invoking the `withdraw()` method, whereas the `TestMyExceptionWithTiming` program lets the `catch` block handle the case. The `try-catch` block is required because the program invokes `withdraw()`, which claims two exceptions. Whenever you use a method that claims an exception, the `try-catch` block must be used. However, no exceptions are raised in the `UsingNoException` program because the program uses a simple `if` statement to check the account balance.

You want to see the time spent on the `for` loop, so the program obtains the `startTime` before the `for` loop starts and the `endTime` after the `for` loop finishes.

The static `currentTimeMillis()` method in the `java.lang.System` class is used to obtain the current time in milliseconds. The `System` class provides access to system platform-independent resources, such as forcing garbage collection using the `gc()` method. All the variables and methods in `System` are static. You have already used `System.out` to print messages. The out variable represents the standard output stream, which will be further discussed in Chapter 15, "Input and Output."

The elapsed time is

```
endTime - startTime
```

Note that the elapsed time is not the exact CPU time spent on the loop, and whenever you run the program, you may get a different elapsed time, depending on your system load when the program is executed.

The result of comparing the running times of these two programs clearly shows the performance benefits of not using exceptions. Avoid using exception handling if a simple `if` statement will work instead.

TIP

Do not use exception handling to validate user input. The input can be validated by using simple `if` statements.

Chapter Summary

In this chapter, you learned how Java handles exceptions. When an exception occurs, Java creates an object that contains the information about the exception. This information can be used to handle the exception.

A Java exception is an instance of a class derived from `java.lang.Throwable`. You can create your own exception classes by extending `Throwable` or a subclass of `Throwable`. The Java system provides a number of predefined exception classes, such as `Error`, `Exception`, `RuntimeException`, and `IOException`. You can also define your own exception class.

Exceptions occur during the execution of a method. If a method you are defining might throw a certain exception, you have to claim it, thus telling the compiler what can go wrong. These processes are called *claiming* and *throwing* an exception.

To use a method that claims exceptions, you need to enclose the method call in the `try` clause of a `try-catch` block. When the exception occurs during the execution of the method, the `catch` clause catches and handles it.

Exception handling takes time because it requires instantiating a new exception object. Exceptions are not meant to substitute for simple tests. You should avoid using exception handling if an alternative solution can be found. Using an alternative would significantly improve the performance of the program.

Chapter Review

11.1. Describe the Java `Throwable` class, its subclasses, and the types of exceptions.

11.2. What is the purpose of claiming exceptions? How do you claim an exception, and where? Can you claim multiple exceptions in a method declaration?

11.3. How do you throw an exception? Can you throw multiple exceptions in one `throw` statement?

11.4. What is the keyword `throw` used for? What is the keyword `throws` used for?

11.5. What does the Java runtime system do when an exception occurs?

11.6. How do you catch an exception?

11.7. Does the presence of the `try-catch` block impose overhead when no exception occurs?

11.8. Suppose that `statement2` causes an exception in the following `try-catch` block:

```
try
{
  statement1;
  statement2;
  statement3;
}
catch (Exception1 ex1)
{
}
```

```
catch (Exception2 ex2)
{
}

statement4;
```

Answer the following questions:

■ Will statement3 be executed?

■ If the exception is not caught, will statement4 be executed?

■ If the exception is caught in the catch clause, will statement4 be executed?

■ If the exception is passed to the caller, will statement4 be executed?

11.9. Suppose that statement2 causes an exception in the following try-catch block:

```
try
{
  statement1;
  statement2;
  statement3;
}
catch (Exception1 ex1)
{
}
catch (Exception2 ex2)
{
}
catch (Exception3 ex3)
{
  throw ex3;
}
finally
{
  statement4;
};
statement4;
```

Answer the following questions:

■ Will statement4 be executed?

■ If the exception is of type Exception3, what will happen? Will statement3 be executed? Will statement4 be executed?

11.10. What is wrong in the following program?

```
class TestRationalWithException
{
  public static void main(String[] args)
  {
    Rational r1 = new Rational(4,2);
    Rational r2 = new Rational(2,3);
    Rational r3 = new Rational(0,1);

    try
    {
      System.out.println(
        r1 + " + " + r2 + " = " + r1.add(r2));
```

```
            System.out.println(
                r1 + " - " + r2 + " = " + r1.subtract(r2));
            System.out.println(
                r1 + " * " + r2 + " = " + r1.multiply(r2));
            System.out.println(
                r1 + " + " + r2 + " = " + r1.add(r2));
        }
    }
}
```

11.11. What is displayed on the console when the following program is running?

```
class Test
{
  public static void main(String[] args)
  {
    try
    {
      System.out.println("Welcome to Java");
    }
    finally
    {
      System.out.println("End of the block");
    }
  }
}
```

11.12. What is displayed on the console when the following program is running?

```
class Test
{
  public static void main(String[] args)
  {
    try
    {
      System.out.println("Welcome to Java");
      return;
    }
    finally
    {
      System.out.println("End of the block");
    }
  }
}
```

11.13. What is displayed on the console when the following program is running?

```
class Test
{
  public static void main(String[] args)
  {
    try
    {
      System.out.println("Welcome to Java");
      int i = 0;
      int y = 2/i;
      System.out.println("Welcome to HTML");
    }
    finally
    {
      System.out.println("End of the block");
    }
  }
}
```

11.14. What is displayed on the console when the following program is running?

```
class Test
{
  public static void main(String[] args)
  {
    try
    {
      System.out.println("Welcome to Java");
      int i = 0;
      double y = 2.0/i;
      System.out.println("Welcome to HTML");
    }
    finally
    {
      System.out.println("End of the block");
    }
  }
}
```

11.15. What is displayed on the console when the following program is running?

```
class Test
{
  public static void main(String[] args)
  {
    try
    {
      System.out.println("Welcome to Java");
      int i = 0;
      int y = 2/i;
      System.out.println("Welcome to Java");
    }
    catch (RuntimeException ex)
    {
      System.out.println("Welcome to Java");
    }
    finally
    {
      System.out.println("End of the block");
    }
  }
}
```

11.16. What is displayed on the console when the following program is running?

```
class Test
{
  public static void main(String[] args)
  {
    try
    {
      System.out.println("Welcome to Java");
      int i = 0;
      int y = 2/i;
      System.out.println("Welcome to Java");
    }
    catch (RuntimeException ex)
    {
      System.out.println("Welcome to Java");
    }
```

```
    finally
    {
      System.out.println("End of the block");
    }

    System.out.println("End of the block");
  }
}
```

11.17. What is displayed on the console when the following program is running?

```
class Test
{
  public static void main(String[] args)
  {
    try
    {
      System.out.println("Welcome to Java");
      int i = 0;
      int y = 2/i;
      System.out.println("Welcome to Java");
    }
    finally
    {
      System.out.println("End of the block");
    }

    System.out.println("End of the block");
  }
}
```

In the following questions, assume that the modified `Rational` given in Example 11.1 is used.

11.18. What is wrong with the following code?

```
class Test
{
  public static void main(String[] args)
  {
    try
    {
      Rational r1 = new Rational(3, 4);
      Rational r2   = new Rational(0, 1);
      Rational x = r1.divide(r2);

      int i = 0;
      int y = 2/i;
    }
    catch (Exception ex)
    {
      System.out.println("Rational operation error ");
    }
    catch (RuntimeException ex)
    {
      System.out.println("Integer operation error");
    }
  }
}
```

11.19. What is displayed on the console when the following program is running?

```java
class Test
{
  public static void main(String[] args)
  {
    try
    {
      Rational r1 = new Rational(3, 4);
      Rational r2    = new Rational(0, 1);
      Rational x = r1.divide(r2);

      int i = 0;
      int y = 2/i;
      System.out.println("Welcome to Java");
    }
    catch (RuntimeException ex)
    {
      System.out.println("Integer operation error");
    }
    catch (Exception ex)
    {
      System.out.println("Rational operation error");
    }
  }
}
```

11.20. What is displayed on the console when the following program is running?

```java
class Test
{
  public static void main(String[] args)
  {
    try
    {
      method();
      System.out.println("After the method call");
    }
    catch (RuntimeException ex)
    {
      System.out.println("Integer operation error");
    }
    catch (Exception e)
    {
      System.out.println("Rational operation error");
    }
  }

  static void method() throws Exception
  {
    Rational r1 = new Rational(3, 4);
    Rational r2    = new Rational(0, 1);
    Rational x = r1.divide(r2);

    int i = 0;
    int y = 2/i;
    System.out.println("Welcome to Java");
  }
}
```

11.21. What is displayed on the console when the following program is running?

```
class Test
{
  public static void main(String[] args)
  {
    try
    {
      method();
      System.out.println("After the method call");
    }
    catch (RuntimeException ex)
    {
      System.out.println("Integer operation error");
    }
    catch (Exception ex)
    {
      System.out.println("Rational operation error");
    }
  }

  static void method() throws Exception
  {
    try
    {
      Rational r1 = new Rational(3, 4);
      Rational r2   = new Rational(0, 1);
      Rational x = r1.divide(r2);

      int i = 0;
      int y = 2/i;
      System.out.println("Welcome to Java");
    }
    catch (RuntimeException ex)
    {
      System.out.println("Integer operation error");
    }
    catch (Exception ex)
    {
      System.out.println("Rational operation error");
    }
  }
}
```

11.22. What is displayed on the console when the following program is running?

```
class Test
{
  public static void main(String[] args)
  {
    try
    {
      method();
      System.out.println("After the method call");
    }
    catch (RuntimeException ex)
    {
      System.out.println("Integer operation error");
    }
    catch (Exception ex)
    {
      System.out.println("Rational operation error");
    }
  }
```

```
static void method() throws Exception
{
  try
  {
    Rational r1 = new Rational(3, 4);
    Rational r2   = new Rational(0, 1);
    Rational x = r1.divide(r2);

    int i = 0;
    int y = 2/i;
    System.out.println("Welcome to Java");
  }
  catch (RuntimeException ex)
  {
    System.out.println("Integer operation error");
  }
  catch (Exception ex)
  {
    System.out.println("Rational operation error");
    throw ex;
  }
}
}
```

11.23. If an exception is not caught in a non-GUI application, what will happen? If an exception is not caught in a GUI application, what will happen?

Programming Exercises

11.1. Example 6.10, "Using Command-Line Parameters," in Chapter 6, "Arrays and Strings," is a simple command-line calculator. Note that the program terminates if any operand is non-numeric. Write a program with an exception handler that deals with non-numeric operands; then write another program without using an exception handler to achieve the same objective. Your program should display a message to inform the user of the wrong operand type before exiting (see Figure 11.10).

Figure 11.10   *The program performs arithmetic operations and detects input errors.*

11.2. Example 9.10, "Using Menus," is a GUI calculator. Note that if `Number 1` or `Number 2` were a non-numeric string, the program would display errors on the console. Modify the program with an exception handler to catch `ArithmeticException` (i.e., divided by 0) and `NumberFormatException` (i.e., input is not an integer) and display the errors on a message dialog box.

11.3. Write a program that meets the following requirements:

- Create an array with 100 randomly chosen elements.

- Create a text field to enter an array index and another text field to display the array element at the specified index (see Figure 11.11).

- Create a Show button to cause the array element to be displayed. If the specified index is out-of-bound, display the message Out of Bound.

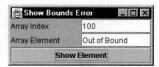

Figure 11.11   *The program displays the array element at the specified index or displays the message* Out of Bound *if the index is out of bounds.*

CHAPTER 12

INTERNATIONALIZATION

Objectives

- Understand the concept of Java's internationalization mechanism.
- Know how to construct a locale with language, country, and variant.
- Process date and time based on locales.
- Display numbers, currencies, and percentages based on locales.
- Use resource bundles.

Introduction

Java is an Internet programming language. The Internet has no boundaries. People who don't understand English may view your applet. What is useful to the English reader may be unusable to the French reader. Many Web sites maintain separate versions of their HTML pages so that readers can choose one written in a language they understand. Since there are so many languages in the world, it would be very difficult to create and maintain enough different versions to meet the needs of clients everywhere. Java comes to the rescue. Java is the first computer language designed from the ground up to support internationalization, which means that it allows your programs to be customized for any number of countries or languages without requiring cumbersome changes to the code.

The following are the major Java features that support internationalization.

■ Java characters use *Unicode*: a 16-bit encoding scheme established by the Unicode Consortium to support the interchange, processing, and display of written texts in the world's diverse languages. Using Unicode encoding makes it easy to write Java programs that manipulate strings in any international language.

■ Java provides the `Locale` class to encapsulate information about a specific locale. A locale determines how locale-sensitive information like date, time, and numbers is displayed and how locale-sensitive operations like sorting strings are performed. The classes for formatting date, time, and numbers and for sorting strings are grouped in the `java.text` package.

■ Java uses the `ResourceBundle` class to separate such locale-specific information as status messages and GUI component labels from the program. The information is stored outside the source code and can be accessed and loaded dynamically at runtime from a `ResourceBundle`, rather than hard-coded into the program.

In this chapter, you will learn how to format date, numbers, currencies, and percentages for different regions, countries, and languages. You will also learn how to use resource bundles to define which images and strings will be used by a component in accordance with the locale and preferences of the user.

Locale

A `Locale` object represents a geographical, political, or cultural region in which a specific language or custom is used. For example, Americans speak English and the Chinese speak Chinese. The conventions for formatting dates, numbers, currencies, and percentages often differ from one country to another. For example, the Chinese use year/month/day for representing date, while Americans use month/day/year. It is important to realize that country alone does not uniquely define a locale. Canadians, for instance, speak either Canadian English or Canadian French, depending on which region of Canada they are in.

To create a `Locale` object, you can use the following constructors in the `java.util.Locale` class.

```
Locale(String language, String country)
Locale(String language, String country, String variant)
```

The `language` should be a valid language code. A valid language code is one of the lowercase, two-letter codes defined by ISO-639. For example, zh stands for Chinese, da for Danish, en for English, de for German, and ko is for Korean. A complete list can be found at a number of sites, including:

http://www.indigo.ie/egt/standards/iso639/

http://www.ics.uci.edu/pub/ietf/http/related/iso639.txt

The country should be a valid ISO country code: that is, an uppercase, two-letter code as defined by ISO-3166. For example, CA stands for Canada, CN for China, DK for Denmark, DE for Germany, and US for the United States. A complete list can be found at a number of sites, including:

ftp://ftp.ripe.net/iso3166-countrycodes

http://userpage.chemie.fu-berlin.de/diverse/doc/ISO_3166.html

Argument `variant` are rarely used and are needed only for exceptional or system-dependent situations to designate information specific to a browser or vendor. For example, the Norwegian language has two sets of spelling rules, the traditional one, called *Bokmål*, and a new one called *Nynorsk*. The locale for traditional spelling would be created as follows.

```
Locale("no", "NO", "B");
```

For convenience, the `Locale` class contains many predefined locale constants. For example, `Locale.CANADA` stands for the country Canada and language English, and `Locale.CANADA_FRENCH` stands for the country Canada and language French.

Java currently supports the locales shown in Table 12.1.

The `Locale` class contains many useful methods (the default locale is used if no locale is specified):

■ `public static Locale getDefault()`

  This method returns the default locale as stored on the machine where the program is running.

■ `public static void setDefault(Locale newLocale)`

  This method sets the default locale.

■ `public String getLanguage()`

  This method returns a lowercase, two-letter language code.

■ `public String getCountry()`

  This method returns an uppercase, two-letter country code.

525

TABLE 12.1   A list of supported locales

Locale	Language	Country
da_DK	Danish	Denmark
de_AT	German	Austria
de_CH	German	Switzerland
el_GR	Greek	Greece
en_CA	English	Canada
en_GB	English	United Kingdom
en_IE	English	Ireland
en_US	English	United States
es_ES	Spanish	Spain
fi_FI	Finnish	Finland
fr_BE	French	Belgium
fr_CA	French	Canada
fr_CH	French	Switzerland
fr_FR	French	France
it_CH	Italian	Switzerland
it_IT	Italian	Italy
ja_JP	Japanese	Japan
ko_KR	Korean	Korea
nl_BE	Dutch	Belgium
nl_NL	Dutch	Netherlands
no_NO	Norwegian (*Nynorsk*)	Norway
no_NO_B	Norwegian (*Bokmål*)	Norway
pt_PT	Portuguese	Portugal
sv_SE	Swedish	Sweden
tr_TR	Turkish	Turkey
zh_CN	Chinese (Simplified)	China
zh_TW	Chinese(Traditional)	Taiwan

■ `public String getVariant()`

This method returns the code for the variant.

■ `public final String getDisplayLanguage()`

This method returns the name of the language for the default locale.

■ `public String getDisplayLanguage(Locale inLocale)`

   This method returns the name of the language for the specified locale.

■ `public final String getDisplayCountry()`

   This method returns the name of the country as expressed in the current locale.

■ `public String getDisplayCountry(Locale inLocale)`

   This method returns the name of the country as expressed in the specified locale.

■ `public final String getDisplayVariant()`

   This method returns the variant code.

■ `public String getDisplayVariant(Locale inLocale)`

   This method returns the variant code for the specified locale.

■ `public String getDisplayName(Locale l)`

   This method returns the name for the locale. For example, the name is `Chinese (China)` for the locale `Locale.CHINA`.

■ `public String getDisplayName()`

   This method returns the name for the default locale.

An operation that requires a `Locale` to perform its task is called *locale-sensitive*. Displaying a number like date or time, for example, is a locale-sensitive operation; the number should be formatted according to the customs and conventions of the user's locale.

Several classes in the Java class libraries contain locale-sensitive methods. For example, `Date`, `Calendar`, `Collator`, `DateFormat`, and `NumberFormat` are locale-sensitive. All locale-sensitive classes contain a static method `getAvailableLocales()`, which returns an array of the locales they support. Here is an example:

```
Locale[] availableLocales = Calendar.getAvailableLocales();
```

returns all locales for which Calendars are installed.

Processing Date and Time

Applications often need to obtain date and time. Java provides a system-independent encapsulation of date and time in the `java.util.Date` class; it also provides `java.util.TimeZone` for dealing with time zones, and `java.util.Calendar` for extracting detailed information from `Date`. Different locales have different conventions for displaying date and time. Should the year, month, or day be displayed first? Should slashes, periods, or colons be used to separate fields of the date? What are the names of the months in the language? The `java.text.DateFormat` class can be used to format date and time in a locale-sensitive way for display to the user.

A `Date` object represents a specific instant in time. The `Calendar` class contains the `get()` method to extract year, month, day, hour, minute, and second. For example, you can use `cal.get(Calendar.YEAR)` to get the year and `cal.get(Calendar.MINUTE)` to get the minute from the `Calendar` object `cal`. Subclasses of `Calendar` interpret a `Date` according to the rules of a specific calendar system. `java.util.GregorianCalendar` is currently supported in Java. Future subclasses may represent other types of calendars used in some parts of the world.

`TimeZone` represents a time zone offset, and also figures out daylight savings. To set a time zone in a `Calendar` object, use the `setTimeZone()` method with a time zone id. For example, `cal.setTimeZone("CST")` sets the time zone to Central Standard Time. To find all the available time zones, use the static method `getAvailableIDs()` in the `TimeZone` class. In general, the international time zone ID is a string in the form of continent/city like Europe/Berlin, Asia/Taipei, and America/Washington.

The `DateFormat` class can be used to format date and time in a number of styles. It supports several standard formatting styles. To format date and time using the `DateFormat` class, simply create an instance of `DateFormat` using one of the following three types of static methods:

- `public static final DateFormat getDateInstance(int dateStyle, Locale aLocale)`

  This method returns the date formatter with the given formatting style for the given locale.

- `public static final DateFormat getTimeInstance(int timeStyle, Locale aLocale)`

  This method returns the time formatter with the given formatting style for the given locale.

- `public static final DateFormat getDateTimeInstance(int dateStyle, int timeStyle, Locale aLocale)`

  This method returns the date/time formatter with the given formatting style for the given locale.

If no arguments are present, the default style or default locale is used. The `dateStyle` and `timeStyle` have to be one of the following constants: FULL, LONG, MEDIUM, and SHORT. The exact result depends on the locale, but generally,

- SHORT is completely numeric, such as 7/24/98 (for date) and 4:49 PM (for time);

- MEDIUM is longer, such as 24-Jul-98 (for date) and 4:52:09 PM (for time);

- LONG is even longer, such as July 24, 1998 (for date) and 4:53:16 PM EST (for time);

- FULL is completely specified, such as Friday, July 24, 1998 (for date) and 4:54:13 o'clock PM EST (for time).

You can use the `getDateTimeInstance()` method to obtain a `DateFormat` object.

```
public static final DateFormat getDateTimeInstance(
   int dateStyle, int timeStyle, Locale aLocale)
```

This gets the date and time formatter with the given formatting styles for the given locale.

The following statements display current time with a specified time zone (CST), formatting style (full date and full time), and locale (US):

```
GregorianCalendar myCal = new GregorianCalendar();
DateFormat myFormat = DateFormat.getDateTimeInstance(
  DateFormat.FULL, DateFormat.FULL, Locale.US);
tz = TimeZone.getTimeZone("CST");
myFormat.setTimeZone(tz);
System.out.println("The local time is "+
  myFormat.format(myCal.getTime()));
```

The date and time formatting subclass, such as `SimpleDateFormat`, enables you to choose any user-defined pattern for date and time formatting. You can use the following constructor to create a `SimpleDateFormat` object, and then use the object to convert a `Date` object into a string with the desired format:

```
public SimpleDateFormat(String pattern)
```

The parameter pattern is a string consisting of characters with special meanings. For example, y means year, M means month, d means day of the month, G is for era designator, h means hours, m means minute of the hour, s means second of the minute, and z means time zone. Therefore, the following code will display a string like "Current time is 1997.11.12 AD at 04:10:18 PST" because the pattern is "yyyy.MM.dd G 'at' hh:mm:ss z."

```
SimpleDateFormat formatter
  = new SimpleDateFormat ("yyyy.MM.dd G 'at' hh:mm:ss z");
Date currentTime = new Date();
String dateString = formatter.format(currentTime);
System.out.println("Current time is " + dateString);
```

The following two examples demonstrate how to display date, time, and calendar based on locales. The first example creates a clock and displays date and time in locale-sensitive format. The second example displays calendars with the names of the days shown in the local language.

Example 12.1 Displaying a Clock

This example presents a program that displays the current clock based on a specified locale and time zone. The language, country, and time zone are passed to the program as parameters. The program can run as an applet or an application. When it runs as an applet, the parameters are passed from HTML tags.

continues

When it runs as an application, the parameters are passed as command-line arguments like this:

```
java CurrentTimeApplet en US CST
```

The program is given next, and its output is shown in Figure 12.1.

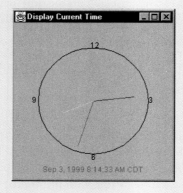

Figure 12.1   *The program displays a clock to show the current time with specified locale and time zone.*

```
// CurrentTimeApplet.java: Display a still clock on the applet
package Chapter12;

import java.awt.*;
import java.util.*;
import javax.swing.*;
import Chapter8.MyFrameWithExitHandling;

public class CurrentTimeApplet extends JApplet
{
  protected Locale locale;
  protected TimeZone tz;
  protected StillClock stillClock;
  private boolean isStandalone = false;

  // Construct the applet
  public CurrentTimeApplet()
  {
  }

  // Initialize the applet
  public void init()
  {
    // Load native fonts. Uncomment the following two statements,
    // if native fonts such as Chinese fonts are not used
    // GraphicsEnvironment ge =
    //   GraphicsEnvironment.getLocalGraphicsEnvironment();
    // ge.getAllFonts();

    if (!isStandalone)
    {
      // Get locale and timezone from HTML
      getHTMLParameters();
    }
```

```java
  // Add the clock to the applet
  createClock();
}

// Create a clock and add it to the applet
public void createClock()
{
  getContentPane().add(stillClock = new StillClock(locale, tz));
}

public void getHTMLParameters()
{
  // Get parameters from the HTML
  String language = getParameter("language");
  String country = getParameter("country");
  String timezone = getParameter("timezone");

  // Set default values if parameters are not given in the HTML
    file
  if (language == null)
    language = "en";

  if (country == null)
    country = "US";

  if (timezone == null)
    timezone = "CST";

  // Set locale and timezone
  locale = new Locale(language, country);
  tz = TimeZone.getTimeZone(timezone);
}

// Main method with three auguments:
// args[0]: language such as en
// args[1]: country such as US
// args[2]: timezone such as CST
public static void main(String[] args)
{
  // Create a frame
  MyFrameWithExitHandling frame = new MyFrameWithExitHandling(
    "Display Current Time");

  // Create an instance of the applet
  CurrentTimeApplet applet = new CurrentTimeApplet();

  // It runs as an application
  applet.isStandalone = true;

  // Get parameters from the command line
  applet.getCommandLineParameters(args);

  // Add the applet instance to the frame
  frame.getContentPane().add(applet, BorderLayout.CENTER);

  // Invoke init() and start()
  applet.init();
  applet.start();
```

continues

531

```
          // Display the frame
          frame.setSize(300, 300);
          frame.setVisible(true);
      }

      // Get command line parameters
      public void getCommandLineParameters(String[] args)
      {
        // Declare locale and timezone with default values
        locale = Locale.getDefault();
        tz = TimeZone.getDefault();

        // Check usage and get language, country and time zone
        if (args.length > 3)
        {
          System.out.println(
            "Usage: java CurrentTimeApplet language country timezone");
          System.exit(0);
        }
        else if (args.length == 3)
        {
          locale = new Locale(args[0], args[1]);
          tz = TimeZone.getTimeZone(args[2]);
        }
        else if (args.length == 2)
        {
          locale = new Locale(args[0], args[1]);
          tz = TimeZone.getDefault();
        }
        else if (args.length == 1)
        {
          System.out.println(
            "Usage: java DisplayTime language country timezone");
          System.exit(0);
        }
        else
        {
          locale = Locale.getDefault();
          tz = TimeZone.getDefault();
        }
      }
  }

  // StillClock.java: Display a clock in JPanel
  package Chapter12;

  import java.awt.*;
  import java.util.*;
  import java.text.*;
  import javax.swing.*;

  public class StillClock extends JPanel
  {
    protected TimeZone tz = TimeZone.getDefault();
    protected int xCenter, yCenter;
    protected int clockRadius;
    protected DateFormat myFormat;

    public StillClock()
    {
    }
```

532

```
public StillClock(Locale locale, TimeZone tz)
{
  setLocale(locale);
  this.tz = tz;
}

// Set timezone using a time zone id such as "CST"
public void setTimeZoneID(String newTimeZoneID)
{
  tz = TimeZone.getTimeZone(newTimeZoneID);
}

public void paintComponent(Graphics g)
{
  super.paintComponent(g);

  // Initialize clock parameters
  clockRadius =
    (int)(Math.min(getSize().width, getSize().height)*0.7*0.5);
  xCenter = (getSize().width)/2;
  yCenter = (getSize().height)/2;

  // Draw circle
  g.setColor(Color.black);
  g.drawOval(xCenter - clockRadius,yCenter - clockRadius,
    2*clockRadius, 2*clockRadius);
  g.drawString("12",xCenter-5, yCenter-clockRadius);
  g.drawString("9",xCenter-clockRadius-10,yCenter+3);
  g.drawString("3",xCenter+clockRadius,yCenter+3);
  g.drawString("6",xCenter-3,yCenter+clockRadius+10);

  // Get current time using GregorianCalendar
  GregorianCalendar cal = new GregorianCalendar(tz);

  // Draw second hand
  int second = (int)cal.get(GregorianCalendar.SECOND);
  int sLength = (int)(clockRadius*0.9);
  int xSecond =
    (int)(xCenter + sLength*Math.sin(second*(2*Math.PI/60)));
  int ySecond =
    (int)(yCenter - sLength*Math.cos(second*(2*Math.PI/60)));
  g.setColor(Color.red);
  g.drawLine(xCenter, yCenter, xSecond, ySecond);

  // Draw minute hand
  int minute = (int)cal.get(GregorianCalendar.MINUTE);
  int mLength = (int)(clockRadius*0.75);
  int xMinute =
    (int)(xCenter + mLength*Math.sin(minute*(2*Math.PI/60)));
  int yMinute =
    (int)(yCenter - mLength*Math.cos(minute*(2*Math.PI/60)));
  g.setColor(Color.blue);
  g.drawLine(xCenter, yCenter, xMinute, yMinute);

  // Draw hour hand
  int hour = (int)cal.get(GregorianCalendar.HOUR_OF_DAY);
  int hLength = (int)(clockRadius*0.6);
  int xHour = (int)(xCenter +
    hLength*Math.sin((hour+minute/60.0)*(2*Math.PI/12)));
```

continues

```
        int yHour = (int)(yCenter -
          hLength*Math.cos((hour+minute/60.0)*(2*Math.PI/12)));
        g.setColor(Color.green);
        g.drawLine(xCenter, yCenter, xHour, yHour);

        // Set display format in specified style, locale and timezone
        myFormat = DateFormat.getDateTimeInstance
          (DateFormat.MEDIUM, DateFormat.LONG, getLocale());
        myFormat.setTimeZone(tz);

        // Display current date
        g.setColor(Color.red);
        String today = myFormat.format(cal.getTime());
        FontMetrics fm = g.getFontMetrics();
        g.drawString(today, (getSize().width -
        fm.stringWidth(today))/2, yCenter+clockRadius+30);
      }
    }
```

Example Review

The program consists of two classes: `CurrentTimeApplet` and `StillClock`. The `CurrentTimeApplet` class can run as an applet or as an application. When it runs as an application. It sets `isStandalone` true so it does not attempt to retrieve HTML parameters.

The program obtains language, country, and time zone as either an HTML parameter or a command-line parameter, and uses this information to create an instance of `StillClock`. `StillClock` is responsible for drawing the clock for the current time. `StillClock` is similar to the `DrawClock` class in Example 8.10, "Drawing a Clock," except that the time (hour, minute, and second) is passed as a parameter to `DrawClock`, but the time in `StillClock` is the current time for the specified locale and time zone.

This program uses the `GregorianCalendar` class to extract the hour, minute, and second from the current time, and the `DateFormat` class to format date and time in a string, with the locale and time zone specified by the user.

The date is displayed below the clock. The program uses font metrics to determine the size of the date/time string and center the display.

The `Component` class has a variable `locale`, which can be accessed through the `getLocale()` and `setLocale()` methods. Since `StillClock` is a `JPanel`, a subclass of `Component`, you can use these methods to work with the locale in `StillClock`.

The variables are purposely declared as protected so that they can be accessed by `StillClock`'s subclasses in later chapters. The `setTimeZoneID()` method defined in `StillClock` is not used here, but it will be used in Example 13.3, "Clock Groups," in Chapter 13, "Multithreading."

The clock is locale-sensitive. If you use the Chinese locale with language (zh) and country (CN), the date and time are displayed in Chinese, as shown in Figure 12.2.

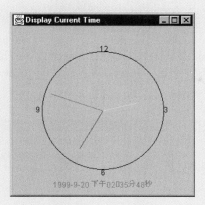

Figure 12.2 *The program displays a clock in the Chinese locale.*

The `CurrentTimeApplet` class is designed for reuse in future chapters. The `createClock()` method is purposely defined to enable creating and adding different types of clocks to the applet in Chapter 14, "Multimedia," by overriding this method.

NOTE

If the right fonts were not installed, empty small boxes will be displayed instead of the characters in the selected language. To install fonts, please refer to JDK documentation on Internationalization. To use Chinese characters, you must have the Chinese fonts installed on your system. If you are interested in Chinese, please refer to www.microsoft.com/msdownload/ieplatform/lang/00000.htm to obtain and install Chinese fonts.

To make Chinese fonts work, you have to uncomment the two statements at the beginning of the `init()` method. These statements, reproduced below, load the native fonts to your program.

```
GraphicsEnvironment ge =
  GraphicsEnvironment.getLocalGraphicsEnvironment();
ge.getAllFonts();
```

The `getAllFonts()` method returns an array of `Font`. Since your program does not directly reference any font, `ge.getAllFonts()` creates an anonymous array of fonts that simply loads the fonts to your program.

Since it takes quite a lot of time and system resource to load these fonts, I recommend commenting these two lines unless you need to use Chinese or other Asian fonts.

Example 12.2 Displaying a Calendar

This example presents a program that displays the calendar based on the specified locale, as shown in Figures 12.3 and 12.4. The user can specify a locale from a combo box that consists of a list of all the available locales supported by the system.

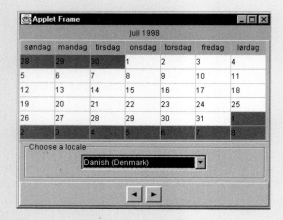

Figure 12.3   *The calendar applet displays the calendar with the Danish locale.*

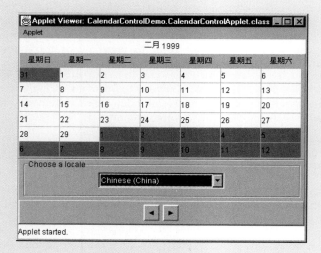

Figure 12.4   *The calendar applet displays the calendar with the Chinese locale.*

```
// CalendarApplet.java: Display a locale-sensitive calendar
package Chapter12;

import java.awt.*;
import java.awt.event.*;
import javax.swing.*;
```

```java
import javax.swing.border.*;
import java.util.*;
import java.text.DateFormat;
import Chapter8.MyFrameWithExitHandling;

public class CalendarApplet extends JApplet
  implements ItemListener, ActionListener
{
  // Create a CalendarPanel for showing calendars
  private CalendarPanel calendarPanel = new CalendarPanel();

  // Combo box for selecting available locales
  private JComboBox jcboLocale = new JComboBox();

  // Declare locales to store available locales
  private Locale locales[] = Calendar.getAvailableLocales();

  // Buttons Prior and Next to displaying prior and next month
  private JButton jbtPrior = new JButton("Prior");
  private JButton jbtNext = new JButton("Next");

  // Initialize the applet
  public void init()
  {
    // Load native fonts. Uncomment the following two statements,
    // if native fonts such as Chinese fonts are not used
    // GraphicsEnvironment ge =
    //   GraphicsEnvironment.getLocalGraphicsEnvironment();
    // ge.getAllFonts();

    // Panel jpLocale to hold the combo box for selecting locales
    JPanel jpLocale = new JPanel();
    jpLocale.setBorder(new TitledBorder("Choose a locale"));
    jpLocale.setLayout(new FlowLayout());
    jpLocale.add(jcboLocale);

    // Initialize the combo box to add locale names
    for (int i=0; i<locales.length; i++)
      jcboLocale.addItem(locales[i].getDisplayName());

    // Panel jpButtons to hold buttons
    JPanel jpButtons = new JPanel();
    jpButtons.setLayout(new FlowLayout());
    jpButtons.add(jbtPrior);
    jpButtons.add(jbtNext);

    // Panel jpCalendar to hold calendarPanel and buttons
    JPanel jpCalendar = new JPanel();
    jpCalendar.setLayout(new BorderLayout());
    jpCalendar.add(calendarPanel, BorderLayout.CENTER);
    jpCalendar.add(jpButtons, BorderLayout.SOUTH);

    // Place jpCalendar and jpLocale to the applet
    this.getContentPane().add(jpCalendar, BorderLayout.CENTER);
    this.getContentPane().add(jpLocale, BorderLayout.SOUTH);

    // Register listeners
    jcboLocale.addItemListener(this);
    jbtPrior.addActionListener(this);
    jbtNext.addActionListener(this);
  }
```

```java
    // Main method
    public static void main(String[] args)
    {
      // Create a frame
      MyFrameWithExitHandling frame = new MyFrameWithExitHandling(
        "Calendar Demo");

      // Create an instance of the applet
      CalendarApplet applet = new CalendarApplet();

      // Add the applet instance to the frame
      frame.getContentPane().add(applet, BorderLayout.CENTER);

      // Invoke init() and start()
      applet.init();
      applet.start();

      // Display the frame
      frame.pack();
      frame.setVisible(true);
    }

    // Handle locale selction
    public void itemStateChanged(ItemEvent e)
    {
      // Set a new locale
      calendarPanel.setLocale(locales[jcboLocale.getSelectedIndex()]);
    }

    // Handle the Prior and Next buttons
    public void actionPerformed(ActionEvent e)
    {
      int currentMonth = calendarPanel.getMonth();

      if (e.getSource() == jbtPrior)
      {
        if (currentMonth==1)
        {
          calendarPanel.setMonth(12);
          calendarPanel.setYear(calendarPanel.getYear()-1);
        }
        else
          calendarPanel.setMonth(currentMonth-1);
      }
      else if (e.getSource() == jbtNext)
      {
        if (currentMonth==12)
        {
          calendarPanel.setMonth(1);
          calendarPanel.setYear(calendarPanel.getYear()+1);
        }
        else
          calendarPanel.setMonth(currentMonth+1);
      }
    }
}

// CalendarPanel.java: Display calendar for a month
package Chapter12;
```

```
import java.awt.*;
import javax.swing.*;
import javax.swing.border.LineBorder;
import java.util.*;
import java.text.*;

public class CalendarPanel extends JPanel
{
  private int month;
  private int year;
  private Locale locale = Locale.getDefault();  // Default locale

  // The header label
  private JLabel jlblHeader = new JLabel(" ", JLabel.CENTER);

  // Labels to display day names and days
  private JLabel[] jlblDay = new JLabel[49];

  // MyCalendar instance
  private MyCalendar calendar = new MyCalendar();

  // Constructor
  public CalendarPanel()
  {
    // Panel jpDays to hold day names and days
    JPanel jpDays = new JPanel();
    jpDays.setLayout(new GridLayout(7, 1));
    for (int i=0; i<49; i++)
    {
      jpDays.add(jlblDay[i] = new JLabel());
      jlblDay[i].setBorder(new LineBorder(Color.black, 1));
      jlblDay[i].setHorizontalAlignment(JLabel.RIGHT);
      jlblDay[i].setVerticalAlignment(JLabel.TOP);
    }

    // Place header and calendar body in the panel
    this.setLayout(new BorderLayout());
    this.add(jlblHeader, BorderLayout.NORTH);
    this.add(jpDays, BorderLayout.CENTER);

    // Set current month, and year
    calendar = new MyCalendar();
    month = calendar.get(Calendar.MONTH)+1;
    year = calendar.get(Calendar.YEAR);

    // Show calendar
    showHeader();
    showDayNames();
    showDays();
  }

  // Update the header based on locale
  private void showHeader()
  {
    SimpleDateFormat sdf = new SimpleDateFormat("MMMM yyyy", locale);
    String header = sdf.format(calendar.getTime());
    jlblHeader.setText(header);
  }
```

continues

```java
// Update the day names based on locale
private void showDayNames()
{
  DateFormatSymbols dfs = new DateFormatSymbols(locale);
  String dayNames[] = dfs.getWeekdays();

  // Set calendar days
  for (int i=0; i<7; i++)
  {
    jlblDay[i].setText(dayNames[i+1]);
    jlblDay[i].setHorizontalAlignment(JLabel.CENTER);
  }
}

// Display days
public void showDays()
{
  // Set the calendar to the first day of the
  // specified month and year
  calendar.set(Calendar.YEAR, year);
  calendar.set(Calendar.MONTH, month-1);
  calendar.set(Calendar.DATE, 1);

  // Get the day of the first day in a month
  int startingDayOfMonth = calendar.get(Calendar.DAY_OF_WEEK);

  // Fill the calendar with the days before this month
  MyCalendar cloneCalendar = (MyCalendar)calendar.clone();
  cloneCalendar.add(Calendar.DATE, -1);
  for (int i=0; i<startingDayOfMonth-1; i++)
  {
    jlblDay[i+7].setForeground(Color.yellow);
    jlblDay[i+7].setText(
      cloneCalendar.daysInMonth()-startingDayOfMonth+2+i+"");
  }

  // Display days of this month
  for (int i=1; i<=calendar.daysInMonth(); i++)
  {
    jlblDay[i-2+startingDayOfMonth+7].setForeground(Color.black);
    jlblDay[i-2+startingDayOfMonth+7].setText(i+"");
  }

  // Fill the calendar with the days after this month
  int j = 1;
  for (int i=calendar.daysInMonth()-1+startingDayOfMonth+7;
    i<49; i++)
  {
    jlblDay[i].setForeground(Color.yellow);
    jlblDay[i].setText(j++ + "");
  }

  showHeader();
}

// Getter method for month
public int getMonth()
{
  return month;
}
```

```java
  // Setter method for month
  public void setMonth(int newMonth)
  {
    month = newMonth;
    showDays();
  }

  // Getter method for year
  public int getYear()
  {
    return year;
  }

  // Setter method for year
  public void setYear(int newYear)
  {
    year = newYear;
    showDays();
  }

  // Set a new locale
  public void setLocale(Locale newLocale)
  {
    locale = newLocale;
    showHeader();
    showDayNames();
  }
}

// MyCalendar.java: A subclass of GregorianCalendar
package Chapter12;

import java.awt.*;
import java.util.*;

public class MyCalendar extends GregorianCalendar
{
  // Find the number of days in a month
  public int daysInMonth()
  {
    switch (get(MONTH))
    {
      case 0: case 2: case 4: case 6: case 7: case 9: case 11:
        return 31;
      case 1: if (isLeapYear(get(YEAR))) return 28;
              else return 29;
      case 3: case 5: case 8: case 10: return 30;
      default: return 0;
    }
  }
}
```

Example Review

When the program starts, the calendar for the current month of the year is displayed. The user can use the Prior and Next buttons to browse the calendar.

The program consists of three classes: CalendarApplet, CalendarPanel, and MyCalendar. MyCalendar is a subclass of GregorianCalendar that has a new

continues

method, `dayInMonth()`, to compute the number of days in a month. Future version of JDK may include this method in `GregorianCalendar`.

`CalendarApplet` creates the user interface and handles the button actions and combo box item selection for locales. The `Calendar.getAvailableLocales()` method is used to find all available locales that have calendars. The `getDisplayName()` method returns the name of each locale, and the locale names are added to the combo box. When the user selects a locale name in the combo box, a new locale is passed to `calendarPanel` and a new calendar is displayed based on the new locale.

`CalendarPanel` is created to control and display the calendar. It displays the month and year in the header, and day names and days in the calendar body. The header and day names are locale-sensitive.

The `showHeader()` method displays the calendar title in a form like "MMMM yyyy." The `SimpleDateFormat` class used in the `showHeader()` method is a subclass of `DateFormat`. `SimpleDateFormat` allows you to customize date format to display the date in various nonstandard styles.

The `showDayNames()` method displays the day names in the calendar. The `DateFormatSymbols` class used in the `showDayNames()` method is a class for encapsulating localizable date-time formatting data, such as the names of the months, the names of the days of the week, and time zone data. You use the `getWeekdays()` method to get an array of day names.

The `showDays()` method displays the days for the specified month in the year. As can be seen in Figure 12.3, the labels before the current month are filled with the last several days of the previous month, and the labels after the current month are filled with the first several days of the next month.

To fill the calendar with the days before the current month, a clone of `calendar`, named `cloneCalendar`, was created to obtain the days for the previous month. `cloneCalendar` is a copy of `calendar` with separate memory space. Thus you can change properties of `cloneCalendar` without corrupting the `calendar` object. The `clone()` method is defined in the `Object` class, which was introduced in Chapter 7, "Class Inheritance." You can clone any object as long as its defining class implements the `Cloneable` interface.

Formatting Numbers

Formatting numbers as currency or percentages is highly locale-dependent. For example, number 5000.50 is displayed as $5,000.50 in US currency, but as 5 000,50 F in French currency.

Formatting numbers is done with the `java.text.NumberFormat` class, which is an abstract base class that provides the methods for formatting and parsing numbers.

`NumberFormat` lets you format and parse numbers for any locale. Your code can be completely independent of the locale conventions for decimal points, thousands-separators, and the particular decimal digits used, or even whether the number format is decimal.

To format a number for the current locale, use one of the factory class methods to get a formatter. Use `getInstance()` or `getNumberInstance()` to get the normal number format. Use `getCurrencyInstance()` to get the currency number format. And use `getPercentInstance()` to get a format for displaying percentages. With this format, a fraction like 0.53 is displayed as 53%.

For example, to display a number in percentages, you can use the following code to create a formatter for the given locale:

```
NumberFormat percForm = NumberFormat.getPercentInstance(locale);
```

You can then use `percForm` to format a number into a string like this:

```
String s = percForm.format(0.075);
```

Conversely, if you want to read a number entered or stored under the conventions of a certain locale, you can use the `parse()` method of a formatter to convert the formatted number into an instance of `java.lang.Number`. The `parse()` method throws a `ParseException` if parsing fails.

You can also control the display of numbers with such methods as `setMinimum-FractionDigits()`. If you want even more control over the format or parsing, or want to give your users more control, you can try casting the `NumberFormat` you get from the factory methods to a `DecimalFormat`, which is a subclass of `NumberFormat`. You can then use the `applyPattern()` method of the `DecimalFormat` class to specify the patterns for displaying the number.

Example 12.3 Formatting Numbers

This example creates a mortgage calculator similar to the one in Example 10.1, "Using Applets." This new mortgage calculator allows the user to choose locales, and displays numbers in locale-sensitive format. As shown in Figure 12.5, the user enters interest rate, years, and loan amount, then presses Show Mortgage to display the interest rate in percentage format, years in normal number format, loan amount, total payment, and monthly payment in currency format.

continues

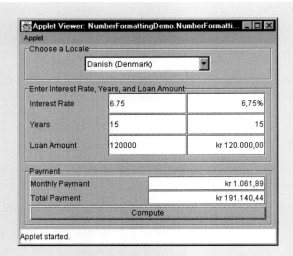

Figure 12.5   *The locale determines the format of the numbers displayed in the mortgage calculator.*

```java
// NumberFormattingDemo.java: Demonstrate formatting numbers
package Chapter12;

import java.awt.*;
import java.awt.event.*;
import javax.swing.*;
import javax.swing.border.*;
import java.util.*;
import java.text.*;
import Chapter8.MyFrameWithExitHandling;

public class NumberFormattingDemo extends JApplet
  implements ItemListener, ActionListener
{
  // Combo box for selecting available locales
  JComboBox jcboLocale = new JComboBox();

  // Text fields for interest rate, year, loan amount,
  JTextField jtfInterestRate = new JTextField(10);
  JTextField jtfYears = new JTextField(10);
  JTextField jtfLoanAmount = new JTextField(10);
  JTextField jtfFormattedInterestRate = new JTextField(10);
  JTextField jtfFormattedYears = new JTextField(10);
  JTextField jtfFormattedLoanAmount = new JTextField(10);

  // Text fields for monthly payment and total payment
  JTextField jtfTotalPay = new JTextField();
  JTextField jtfMonthlyPay = new JTextField();

  // Compute Mortgage button
  JButton jbtCompute = new JButton("Compute Mortgage");

  // Current locale
  Locale locale = Locale.getDefault();

  // Declare locales to store available locales
  Locale locales[] = Calendar.getAvailableLocales();
```

```
// Initialize the combo box
public void initializeComboBox()
{
  // Add locale names to the combo box
  for (int i=0; i<locales.length; i++)
    jcboLocale.addItem(locales[i].getDisplayName());
}

// Initialize the applet
public void init()
{
  // Load native fonts. Uncomment the following two statements,
  // if native fonts such as Chinese fonts are not used
  // GraphicsEnvironment ge =
  //   GraphicsEnvironment.getLocalGraphicsEnvironment();
  // ge.getAllFonts();

  // Panel p1 to hold the combo box for selecting locales
  JPanel p1 = new JPanel();
  p1.setLayout(new FlowLayout());
  p1.add(jcboLocale);
  initializeComboBox();
  p1.setBorder(new TitledBorder("Choose a Locale"));

  // Panel p2 to hold the input
  JPanel p2 = new JPanel();
  p2.setLayout(new GridLayout(3, 3));
  p2.add(new JLabel("Interest Rate"));
  p2.add(jtfInterestRate);
  p2.add(jtfFormattedInterestRate);
  p2.add(new JLabel("Years"));
  p2.add(jtfYears);
  p2.add(jtfFormattedYears);
  p2.add(new JLabel("Loan Amount"));
  p2.add(jtfLoanAmount);
  p2.add(jtfFormattedLoanAmount);
  p2.setBorder(new TitledBorder
    ("Enter Interest Rate, Years, and Loan Amount"));

  // Panel p3 to hold the result
  JPanel p3 = new JPanel();
  p3.setLayout(new GridLayout(2, 2));
  p3.setBorder(new TitledBorder("Payment"));
  p3.add(new JLabel("Monthly Paymant"));
  p3.add(jtfMonthlyPay);
  p3.add(new JLabel("Total Payment"));
  p3.add(jtfTotalPay);

  // Set text field alignment
  jtfFormattedInterestRate.setHorizontalAlignment
    (JTextField.RIGHT);
  jtfFormattedYears.setHorizontalAlignment(JTextField.RIGHT);
  jtfFormattedLoanAmount.setHorizontalAlignment(JTextField.RIGHT);
  jtfTotalPay.setHorizontalAlignment(JTextField.RIGHT);
  jtfMonthlyPay.setHorizontalAlignment(JTextField.RIGHT);

  // Set editable false
  jtfFormattedInterestRate.setEditable(false);
  jtfFormattedYears.setEditable(false);
  jtfFormattedLoanAmount.setEditable(false);
  jtfTotalPay.setEditable(false);
  jtfMonthlyPay.setEditable(false);
```

continues

545

```
    // Panel p4 to hold result payments and a button
    JPanel p4 = new JPanel();
    p4.setLayout(new BorderLayout());
    p4.add(p3, BorderLayout.CENTER);
    p4.add(jbtCompute, BorderLayout.SOUTH);

    // Place panels to the applet
    getContentPane().add(p1, BorderLayout.NORTH);
    getContentPane().add(p2, BorderLayout.CENTER);
    getContentPane().add(p4, BorderLayout.SOUTH);

    // Register listeners
    jcboLocale.addItemListener(this);
    jbtCompute.addActionListener(this);
  }

  // Main method
  public static void main(String[] args)
  {
    // Create a frame
    MyFrameWithExitHandling frame = new MyFrameWithExitHandling(
      "Number Formatting Demo");

    // Create an instance of the applet
    NumberFormattingDemo applet = new NumberFormattingDemo();

    // Add the applet instance to the frame
    frame.getContentPane().add(applet, BorderLayout.CENTER);

    // Invoke init() and start()
    applet.init();
    applet.start();

    // Display the frame
    frame.setSize(300, 300);
    frame.setVisible(true);
  }

  // Handle locale selection
  public void itemStateChanged(ItemEvent e)
  {
    if (e.getSource() == jcboLocale)
    {
      locale = locales[jcboLocale.getSelectedIndex()];
      computeMortgage();
    }
  }

  // Handle button action
  public void actionPerformed(ActionEvent e)
  {
    if (e.getSource() == jbtCompute)
      computeMortgage();
  }

  // Compute payments and display results locale-sensitive format
  private void computeMortgage()
  {
    // Retrieve input from user
    double loan = new Double(jtfLoanAmount.getText()).doubleValue();
    double interestRate =
      new Double(jtfInterestRate.getText()).doubleValue()/1200;
    int years = new Integer(jtfYears.getText()).intValue();
```

546

```
                    // Calculate payments
                    double monthlyPay =
                          loan*interestRate/(1-
                             (Math.pow(1/(1+interestRate),years*12)));
                    double totalPay = monthlyPay*years*12;

                    // Get formatters
                    NumberFormat percForm = NumberFormat.getPercentInstance(locale);
                    NumberFormat currencyForm =
                       NumberFormat.getCurrencyInstance(locale);
                    NumberFormat numberForm = NumberFormat.getNumberInstance(locale);
                    percForm.setMinimumFractionDigits(2);

                    // Display formatted input
                    jtfFormattedInterestRate.setText(
                       percForm.format(interestRate*12));
                    jtfFormattedYears.setText(numberForm.format(years));
                    jtfFormattedLoanAmount.setText(currencyForm.format(loan));

                    // Display results in currency format
                    jtfMonthlyPay.setText(currencyForm.format(monthlyPay));
                    jtfTotalPay.setText(currencyForm.format(totalPay));
                  }
                }
```

Example Review

The `computeMortgage()` method gets the input on interest rate, years, and loan amount from the user, computes monthly payment and total payment, and displays interest in percentage format, years in normal number format, and loan amount, monthly payment and total payment in locale-sensitive format.

The statement `percForm.setMinimumFractionDigits(2)` sets the minimum number of the fractional part to 2. Without this statement, 0.075 would be displayed as 7% rather than 7.5%.

Resource Bundles (Optional)

The `NumberFormattingDemo` in Example 12.3 displays numbers, currencies, and percentages in local customs, but displays all the message strings, titles, and button labels in English. In this section, you will learn how to use resource bundles to localize message strings, titles, button labels, etc.

A *resource bundle* is a Java class file or a text file that provides locale-specific information. This information can be dynamically accessed by Java programs. When your program needs a locale-specific resource—a message string, for example—it can load the string from the resource bundle appropriate for the desired locale. In this way, you can write program code that is largely independent of the user's locale, isolating most, if not all, of the locale-specific information in resource bundles.

With resource bundles, you can write programs that separate the locale-sensitive part of your code from the locale-independent part. The programs can easily handle multiple locales, and can easily be modified later to support even more locales.

The resources are placed inside the classes that extend the `ResourceBundle` class or a subclass of `ResourceBundle`. Resource bundles contain *key/value* pairs. The keys uniquely identify a locale-specific object in the bundle. You can use the key to retrieve the object. `ListResourceBundle` is a convenient subclass of `ResourceBundle`, which is often used to simplify creating resource bundles. Here is an example of a resource bundle that contains four keys using `ListResourceBundle`.

```
// Resource.java: resource file
public class Resource extends java.util.ListResourceBundle
{
  static final Object[][] contents =
  {
    {"nationalFlag", "china.gif"},
    {"nationalAnthem", "china.au"},
    {"nationalColor", Color.red},
    {"annualGrowthRate", new Double(7.8)}
  };

  public Object[][] getContents()
  {
    return contents;
  }
}
```

Keys are case-sensitive strings. In this example, the keys are `nationalFlag`, `nationalAnthem`, `nationalColor`, and `annualGrowthRate`. The values can be any type of `Object`.

If all the resources are strings, they can be placed in a convenient text file with extension .properties. Here is what a typical property file looks like:

```
#Wed Jul 01 07:23:24 EST 1998
nationalFlag=china.gif
nationalAnthem=china.au
```

To retrieve values from a `ResourceBundle` in a program, you first need to create an instance of `ResourceBundle` using one of the following two static methods.

```
public static final ResourceBundle getBundle(String baseName)
    throws MissingResourceException

public static final ResourceBundle getBundle(String baseName,
    Locale locale) throws MissingResourceException
```

The first method returns a `ResourceBundle` for the default locale, and the second method returns a `ResourceBundle` for the specified locale. `baseName` is the base name for a set of classes, each of which describes the information for a given locale. These classes are named in Table 12.2.

For example, Resource_en_BR.class stores resources specific to the UK, Resource_en_US.class stores resources specific to the USA, and Resource_en.class stores resources specific to all the English-speaking countries.

The `getBundle()` method attempts to load the class that matches the specified locale by language, country, and variant, searching the file names in the order shown

TABLE 12.2   Resource bundle naming conventions.

1. BaseName_language_country_variant.class

2. BaseName_language_country.class

3. BaseName_language.class

4. BaseName.class

5. BaseName_language_country_variant.properties

6. BaseName_language_country.properties

7. BaseName_language.properties

8. BaseName.properties

in Table 12.2. The files searched in this order form a *resource chain*. If no file is found in the resource chain, the `getBundel()` method raises a `MissingResource-Exception`.

Once a resource bundle object is created, you can use the `getObject()` method to retrieve the value according to the key. For example,

```
String flagFile = (String)rb.getObject("nationalFlag");
String anthemFile = (String)rb.getObject("nationalAnthem");
Color color = (Color)rb.getObject("nationalColor");
double growthRate =
    (Double)rb.getObject("annualGrowthRate").toDouble();
```

TIP
If the resource value is a string, a convenient `getString()` method can be used to replace the `getObject()` method. The `getString()` method casts the value returned by `getObject` to a string.

What happens if a resource object you are looking for is not defined in the resource bundle? Java employs an intelligent look-up scheme that searches the object in the parent file along the resource chain. This search is repeated in the other parent files in the resource chain until the object is found or all the files are searched. A `MissingResourceException` is raised if the search is unsuccessful.

JBuilder provides a Resource Wizard to help you develop internationalized applications and applets. First you develop the project without worrying about locale. Once the project is done, use the Resource Wizard to create resource bundles to move hard-coded strings to ResourceBundles. JBuilder automatically generates the code for creating a resource bundle object and for retrieving objects from the resource bundle.

Example 12.4 Using Resource Bundles

This example modifies the `NumberFormattingDemo` program in Example 12.3 so that it displays messages, title, and button labels in English, Chinese, and French. You will learn how to use the Resource Wizard that automatically generates the code for handling resources.

To see the development in action, follow the steps below.

1. To keep `NumberFormattingDemo` intact, select NumberFormattingDemo.java in the Navigation pane, and choose File, Save As to save it as ResourceBundleDemo.java in the same folder. Replace all `Number-FormattingDemo` with `ResourceBundleDemo` in ResourceBundleDemo.java and compile the program. The program should run fine.

2. With ResourceBundleDemo.java selected in the Navigation pane, choose Wizards, Resource Strings to display Create ResourceBundle dialog box, as shown in Figure 12.6. You can choose either `ListResourceBundle` or `PropertyResourceBundle`. For simplicity, since all locale-specific resource are strings in this applet, choose PropertyResourceBundle. Click OK to close the dialog box. You will see the Resource Wizard, as shown in Figure 12.7. Note that if the Create ResourceBundle dialog box does not appear as shown in Figure 12.6, click New in the Resource Wizard dialog box to display it.

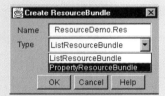

Figure 12.6   *You can choose* `ListResourceBundle` *or* `PropertyResourceBundle` *in the Create ResourceBundle dialog box.*

3. In the Resource Wizard, check "generate key from string value" for Resource Keys. The ResourceBundle Name choice box allows you to choose where the string should be moved. Press Convert to move the string currently displayed in the String field to a `ResourceBundle`. Press Convert All to move the current and all remaining hard-coded strings to a `Resource-Bundle` without further prompting.

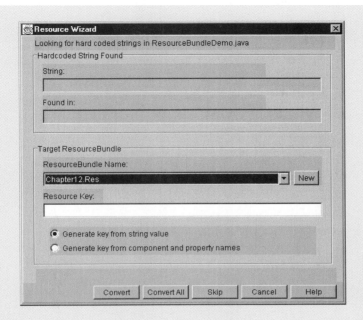

Figure 12.7 *The Resource Wizard automatically generates the resource bundle and the code for retrieving resource.*

4. JBuilder automatically generated the code for creating a resource bundle object and for retrieving resources. To update the locale-sensitive strings, create a method named update() and invoke it in the handler for selecting locales. When locale changes, this method is invoked to update strings.

The source code for ResourceBundleDemo.java is as follows:

```java
// ResourceBundleDemo.java: Demonstrate resource bundle
package Chapter12;

import java.awt.*;
import java.awt.event.*;
import javax.swing.*;
import javax.swing.border.*;
import java.util.*;
import java.text.*;
import Chapter8.MyFrameWithExitHandling;

public class ResourceBundleDemo extends JApplet
  implements ItemListener, ActionListener
{
  // Combo box for selecting available locales
  JComboBox jcboLocale = new JComboBox();
  ResourceBundle res =
    ResourceBundle.getBundle("Chapter12.Res");
```

continues

551

```
      // Create labels
      JLabel jlblInterestRate = new JLabel(res.getString(
        "Interest_Rate"));
      JLabel jlblYears = new JLabel(res.getString("Years"));
      JLabel jlblLoanAmount = new
        JLabel(res.getString("Loan_Amount"));
      JLabel jlblMonthlyPay = new
        JLabel(res.getString("Monthly_Payment"));
      JLabel jlblTotalPay = new JLabel(res.getString(
        "Total_Payment"));

      // Create titled borders
      TitledBorder comboBoxTitle = new TitledBorder
        (res.getString("Choose_a_Locale"));
      TitledBorder inputTitle = new TitledBorder
        (res.getString("Enter_Interest_Rate"));
      TitledBorder paymentTitle = new TitledBorder
        (res.getString("Payment"));

      // Text fields for interest rate, year, loan amount,
      JTextField jtfInterestRate = new JTextField(10);
      JTextField jtfYears = new JTextField(10);
      JTextField jtfLoanAmount = new JTextField(10);
      JTextField jtfFormattedInterestRate = new JTextField(10);
      JTextField jtfFormattedYears = new JTextField(10);
      JTextField jtfFormattedLoanAmount = new JTextField(10);

      // Text fields for monthly payment and total payment
      JTextField jtfTotalPay = new JTextField();
      JTextField jtfMonthlyPay = new JTextField();

      // Compute Mortgage button
      JButton jbtCompute = new JButton(res.getString(
        "Compute_Mortgage"));

      // Current locale
      Locale locale = Locale.getDefault();

      // Declare locales to store available locales
      Locale locales[] = Calendar.getAvailableLocales();

      // Initialize the combo box
      public void initializeComboBox()
      {
        // Add locale names to the combo box
        for (int i=0; i<locales.length; i++)
          jcboLocale.addItem(locales[i].getDisplayName());
      }

      // Initialize the applet
      public void init()
      {
        // Load native fonts. Uncomment the following two
           statements,
        // if native fonts such as Chinese fonts are not used
        // GraphicsEnvironment ge =
        //   GraphicsEnvironment.getLocalGraphicsEnvironment();
        // ge.getAllFonts();

        // Panel p1 to hold the combo box for selecting locales
        JPanel p1 = new JPanel();
        p1.setLayout(new FlowLayout());
```

```
    p1.add(jcboLocale);
    initializeComboBox();
    p1.setBorder(comboBoxTitle);

    // Panel p2 to hold the input for interest rate, years and
    // loan amount
    JPanel p2 = new JPanel();
    p2.setLayout(new GridLayout(3, 3));
    p2.add(jlblInterestRate);
    p2.add(jtfInterestRate);
    p2.add(jtfFormattedInterestRate);
    p2.add(jlblYears);
    p2.add(jtfYears);
    p2.add(jtfFormattedYears);
    p2.add(jlblLoanAmount);
    p2.add(jtfLoanAmount);
    p2.add(jtfFormattedLoanAmount);
    p2.setBorder(inputTitle);

    // Panel p3 to hold the payment
    JPanel p3 = new JPanel();
    p3.setLayout(new GridLayout(2, 2));
    p3.setBorder(paymentTitle);
    p3.add(jlblMonthlyPay);
    p3.add(jtfMonthlyPay);
    p3.add(jlblTotalPay);
    p3.add(jtfTotalPay);

    // Set text field alignment
    jtfFormattedInterestRate.setHorizontalAlignment(
      JTextField.RIGHT);
    jtfFormattedYears.setHorizontalAlignment(
      JTextField.RIGHT);
    jtfFormattedLoanAmount.setHorizontalAlignment(
      JTextField.RIGHT);
    jtfTotalPay.setHorizontalAlignment(JTextField.RIGHT);
    jtfMonthlyPay.setHorizontalAlignment(JTextField.RIGHT);

    // Set editable false
    jtfFormattedInterestRate.setEditable(false);
    jtfFormattedYears.setEditable(false);
    jtfFormattedLoanAmount.setEditable(false);
    jtfTotalPay.setEditable(false);
    jtfMonthlyPay.setEditable(false);

    // Panel p4 to hold result payments and a button
    JPanel p4 = new JPanel();
    p4.setLayout(new BorderLayout());
    p4.add(p3, BorderLayout.CENTER);
    p4.add(jbtCompute, BorderLayout.SOUTH);

    // Place panels to the applet
    getContentPane().add(p1, BorderLayout.NORTH);
    getContentPane().add(p2, BorderLayout.CENTER);
    getContentPane().add(p4, BorderLayout.SOUTH);

    // Register listeners
    jcboLocale.addItemListener(this);
    jbtCompute.addActionListener(this);
  }
```

continues

```java
// Main method
public static void main(String[] args)
{
  // Create an instance of the applet
  ResourceBundleDemo applet = new ResourceBundleDemo();

  // Create a frame with a resource string
  MyFrameWithExitHandling frame = new
    MyFrameWithExitHandling(
    applet.res.getString("Number_Formatting"));

  // Add the applet instance to the frame
  frame.getContentPane().add(applet, BorderLayout.CENTER);

  // Invoke init() and start()
  applet.init();
  applet.start();

  // Display the frame
  frame.setSize(300, 300);
  frame.setVisible(true);
}

// Handle locale selection
public void itemStateChanged(ItemEvent e)
{
  if (e.getSource() == jcboLocale)
  {
    locale = locales[jcboLocale.getSelectedIndex()];

    // Update locale-sensitive strings
    updateStrings();
    computeMortgage();
  }
}

// Handle button action
public void actionPerformed(ActionEvent e)
{
  if (e.getSource() == jbtCompute)
    computeMortgage();
}

// Compute payments and display results locale-sensitive
// format
private void computeMortgage()
{
  // Retrieve input from user
  double loan = new Double(jtfLoanAmount.getText()).
    doubleValue();
  double interestRate =
    new Double(jtfInterestRate.getText()).doubleValue()/1200;
  int years = new Integer(jtfYears.getText()).intValue();

  // Calculate payments
  double monthlyPay =
   loan*interestRate/(1-
     (Math.pow(1/(1+interestRate),years*12)));
  double totalPay = monthlyPay*years*12;

  // Get formatters
  NumberFormat percForm =
    NumberFormat.getPercentInstance(locale);
```

```
            NumberFormat currencyForm =
              NumberFormat.getCurrencyInstance(locale);
            NumberFormat numberForm =
              NumberFormat.getNumberInstance(locale);
            percForm.setMinimumFractionDigits(2);

            // Display formatted input
            jtfFormattedInterestRate.setText(
              percForm.format(interestRate*12));
            jtfFormattedYears.setText(numberForm.format(years));
            jtfFormattedLoanAmount.setText(currencyForm.format(loan));

            // Display results in currency format
            jtfMonthlyPay.setText(currencyForm.format(monthlyPay));
            jtfTotalPay.setText(currencyForm.format(totalPay));
          }

          // Update resource strings
          private void updateStrings()
          {
            res = ResourceBundle.getBundle("Chapter12.Res", locale);
            jlblInterestRate.setText(res.getString("Interest_Rate"));
            jlblYears.setText(res.getString("Years"));
            jlblLoanAmount.setText(res.getString("Loan_Amount"));
            jlblTotalPay.setText(res.getString("Total_Payment"));
            jlblMonthlyPay.setText(res.getString("Monthly_Payment"));
            jbtCompute.setText(res.getString("Compute_Mortgage"));
            comboBoxTitle.setTitle(res.getString("Choose_a_Locale"));
            inputTitle.setTitle(res.getString("Enter_Interest_Rate"));
            paymentTitle.setTitle(res.getString("Payment"));

            // Make sure the new labels are displayed
            repaint();
          }
        }
```

5. The Resource Wizard created a resource bundle file named Res.properties. The content of the file is shown below:

```
# Res.properties
#Thu May 06 07:48:10 EST 1999
Years=Years
Total_Payment=French Total\ Payment
Enter_Interest_Rate=Enter\ Interest\ Rate,\ Years,\ and\ Loan\
Amount
Payment=Payment
Compute_Mortgage=Compute\ Mortgage
Interest_Rate=Interest\ Rate
Number_Formatting=Number\ Formatting\ Demo
Loan_Amount=Loan\ Amount
Choose_a_Locale=Choose\ a\ Locale
Monthly_Payment=Monthly\ Payment
=
```

6. Use Res.properties as a template to create Res_zh.properties and Res_fr.properties for strings in Chinese and in French, as follows:

```
#Res_zh.properties for Chinese language
Choose_a_Locale     = \u9078\u64c7\u570b\u5bb6
Enter_Interest_Rate =
```

continues

555

```
\u8f38\u5165\u5229\u7387,\u5e74\u9650,\u8cb8\u6b3e\u7e3d\u984d
Interest_Rate       =   \u5229\u7387
Years               =   \u5e74\u9650
Loan_Amount         =   \u8cb8\u6b3e\u984d\u5ea6
Payment             =   \u4ed8\u606f
Monthly_Payment     =   \u6708\u4ed8
Total_Payment       =   \u7e3d\u984d
Compute_Mortgage    =   \u8a08\u7b97\u8cb8\u6b3e\u5229\u606f
=


#Res_fr.properties for French language
Years=annees
Total_Payment=reglement total
Enter_Interest_Rate=inscrire le taux d'interet, les annees, et
le montant du pret
Payment=paiement
Compute_Mortgage=Calculer l'hypotheque
Interest_Rate=le taux d'interet
Number_Formatting=demonstration du formatting des chiffres
Loan_Amount=Le montant du pret
Choose_a_Locale=Choisir la localite
Monthly_Payment=versement mensuel
=
```

7. Run the program. Choose the French locale or the Chinese locale; the applet is shown in Figure 12.8.

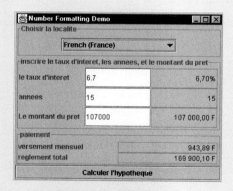

Figure 12.8   *The applet displays the strings in French or in Chinese.*

Example Review

Property resource bundles are implemented as text files with a .properties extension, and are placed in the same location as the class files for the application or applet. `ListResourceBundles` are provided as Java source files. Because they are implemented as Java source code, new and modified `ListResourceBundles` need to be recompiled for deployment. With `PropertyResourceBundles`, there is no need for recompilation when translations are modified or added to the application. `ListResourceBundles` provide considerably better performance than `PropertyResourceBundles`.

If the resource bundle is not found or a resource object is not found in the resource bundle, a `MissingResourceException` is raised. Since `MissingResource-Exception` is a subclass of `RuntimeException`, you do not need to catch the exception explicitly in the code.

If you add new strings, titles, or labels in the source code, you can apply the Resource Wizard again. The Resource Wizard finds the new resources that have not been moved to the resource bundle and moves them to the resource bundle.

This example is the same as Example 12.3 except that the program contains the code for handling resource strings. The `updateString()` method is responsible for displaying locale-sensitive strings. This method is invoked when a new locale is selected in the combo box. The variable `res` of the `ResourceBundle` class is an instance of `ResourceBundleDemo`; thus it cannot be directly used in the `main()` method because the `main()` method is static. To fix the problem, create an applet (as an instance of `ResourceBundleDemo`); you can then reference `res` using `applet.res`.

TIP
To find the Unicode for Asian characters, you can first type the characters in an Asian language (e.g., Chinese, Japanese, Korean) Windows 95/98/NT and save the file, then use the native2ascii utility to convert the characters to Unicode. native2ascii is a JDK utility stored in jbuilder3\java\bin\ directory.

TIP
The code generated by the Resource Wizard is irreversible. I recommend that you save a copy before using the Resource Wizard to convert the program.

Chapter Summary

This chapter introduced the subject of building Java programs that operate correctly for an international audience. You learned how to use the `Locale` object to represent a specific locale, how to localize date and time, and how to display numbers in normal format, currency format, and percentage format. You also learned how to use the Resource Wizard to create resource bundles and move locale-specific strings, titles, and labels to the resource bundles.

Review Questions

12.1. How does Java support international characters in languages like Chinese and Arabic?

12.2. How do you construct a `Locale` object? How do you get all the available locales from a `Calendar` object?

12.3. How do you display current date and time in German?

12.4. How do you format and display numbers and percentages in Chinese?

12.5. How does the `getBundle()` method locate a resource bundle?

12.6. How does the `getObject()` locate a resource?

Programming Exercises

12.1. Develop an applet to display Unicode characters, as shown in Figure 12.9. The user specifies a Unicode in the text field and presses the Enter key to display a sequence of Unicode characters starting with the specified Unicode. The Unicode characters are displayed in a scrollable text area of 20 lines. Each line contains 16 characters following after a Unicode, which is the code for the first character on the line.

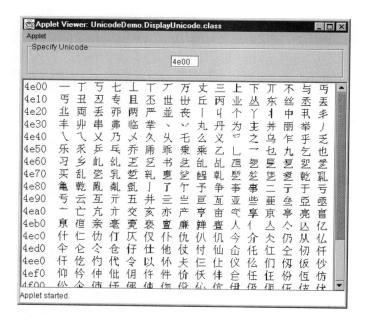

Figure 12.9   *The applet displays the Unicode characters.*

12.2. Modify Example 12.2, "Displaying a Calendar," to localize the labels "Choose a locale" and "Calendar Demo" in French, German, Chinese, or a language of your choice.

12.3. Write a program to display a calendar for a specified month using the `Date`, `Calendar`, and `GregorianCalendar` classes. Your program receives the month and year from the command line. For example:

```
java Exercise12_3 5 1999
```

This displays the calendar shown in Figure 12.10.

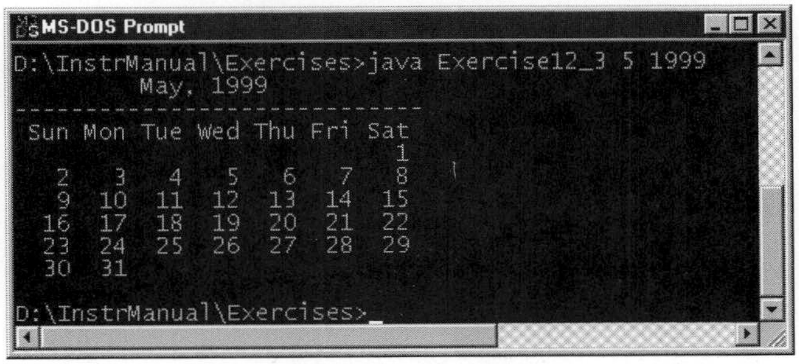

Figure 12.10 *The program displays a calendar for May 1999.*

You also can run the program without the year. In this case, the year is the current year. If you run the program without specifying a month and a year, the month is the current month.

12.4. Write a program to convert US dollars to Canadian dollars, German marks, and British pounds, as shown in Figure 12.11. The user enters the US dollar amount and the conversion rates, and clicks the Convert button to display the converted amount.

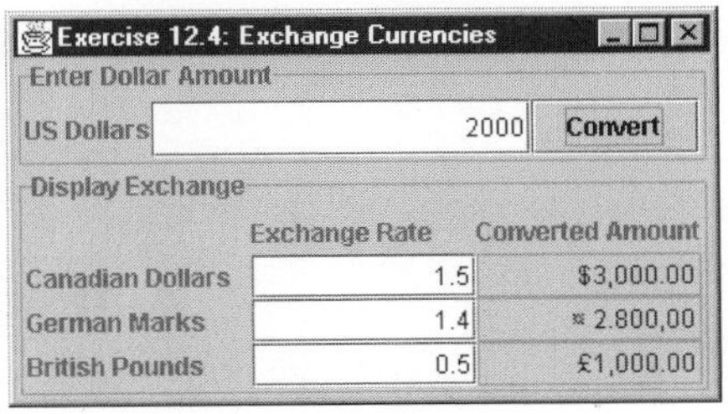

Figure 12.11 *The program converts US dollars to Canadian dollars, German marks, and British pounds.*

12.5. Use a tabbed pane to write a program with two tabs. One, labeled Calendar, displays the calendar, and the other, labeled Clock, displays the current time on a clock (see Figure 12.12).

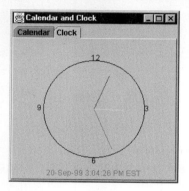

Figure 12.12   *The Calendar tab displays a calendar, and the Clock tab displays a clock.*

MULTITHREADING

Objectives

- ⊘ Understand the concept of multithreading and apply it to developing animation.

- ⊘ Write threads by extending the `Thread` class.

- ⊘ Write threads by implementing the `Runnable` interface in cases of multiple inheritance.

- ⊘ Understand the life-cycle of thread states.

- ⊘ Understand and set thread priorities.

- ⊘ Use thread groups to manage a group of similar threads.

- ⊘ Use thread synchronization to avoid resource conflicts.

Introduction

A *thread* is a flow of execution of a task in a program; it has a beginning and an end. The programs you have seen so far run in a single thread; that is, at any given time, a single statement is being executed. With Java, you can launch multiple threads from a program concurrently. These threads can be executed simultaneously in multiprocessor systems, as shown in Figure 13.1.

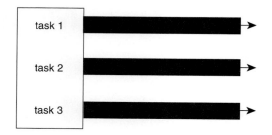

Figure 13.1   *Here, multiple threads run on multiple CPUs.*

In single-processor systems, as shown in Figure 13.2, multiple threads share the CPU time, and the operating system is responsible for scheduling and allocating resources to the threads. This arrangement is practical because the CPU is idle most of the time. It does nothing while the user is entering data, for example.

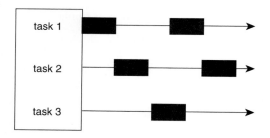

Figure 13.2   *Here, multiple threads share a single CPU.*

Multithreading can make your program more responsive and interactive, as well as enhance performance. For example, a good word processor lets you print or save the file while you are typing. In some cases, multithreaded programs run faster than single-threaded programs even on single-processor systems. In Java, multithreading is particularly useful for animation, because Java is designed to make computer animation easy. Java also provides exceptionally good support for programming with multiple threads of execution, including built-in support for creating threads and for locking resources to prevent conflicts.

You can create threads by extending the Thread class or implementing the Runnable interface. Both Thread and Runnable are defined in the java.lang package. Thread actually implements `Runnable`. In this chapter, you will learn how to use the `Thread` class and the `Runnable` interface to write multithreaded programs.

The *Thread* Class

The `Thread` class contains the constructor `Thread()`, as well as many useful methods that run, start, suspend, resume, interrupt, and stop threads. To create and run a thread, first define a class that extends the `Thread` class. Your thread class must override the `run()` method, which tells the system how the thread will be executed when it runs. You then need a client class that creates an object running on the thread. This object is referred to as a *runnable object*. Figure 13.3 illustrates the structure of a thread class and its client class.

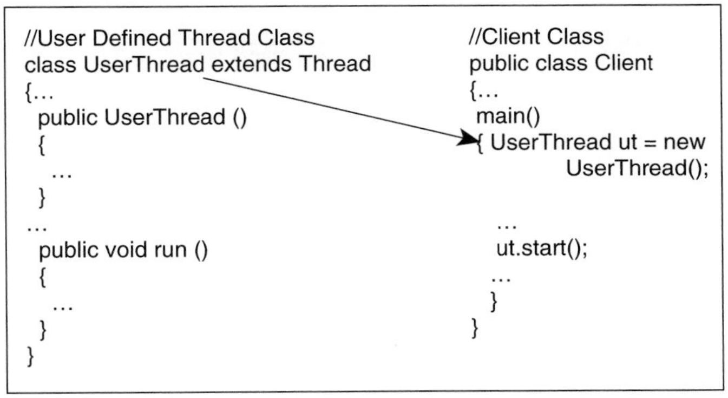

```
//User Defined Thread Class          //Client Class
class UserThread extends Thread       public class Client
{...                                  {...
  public UserThread ()                main()
  {                                   { UserThread ut = new
    ...                                       UserThread();
  }
  ...                                     ...
  public void run ()                      ut.start();
  {                                       ...
    ...                                 }
  }                                   }
}
```

Figure 13.3 *A thread is defined as a subclass of the* `Thread` *class.*

You create a runnable object by using the `Thread()` constructor. The `start()` method tells the system that the thread is ready to run. The constructor and several methods in the `Thread` class are described in the next few paragraphs. The following constructs a new thread:

```
public Thread()
```

Usually, it is called from the client class to create a runnable object. If a user-defined thread class is used, the client program creates a thread by using the user-defined thread class constructor, as shown in Figure 13.3.

The following methods in the `Thread` class are often useful:

■ `public void run()`

   This method is invoked by the Java runtime system to execute the thread. You must override this method and provide the code you want your thread to execute in your thread class. This method is never directly invoked by the runnable object in the program, although it is an instance method of a runnable object.

■ `public void start()`

This method starts the thread, thereby causing the `run()` method to be invoked. This method is called by the runnable object in the client class.

■ `public void stop()`

This method stops the thread. As of Java 2, this method is deprecated because it is known to be inherently unsafe. You should assign `null` to a `Thread` variable to indicate that it is stopped rather than use the `stop()` method.

■ `public void suspend()`

This method suspends the thread. As of Java 2, this method is deprecated because it is known to be deadlock-prone. You should use the `wait()` method along with a `boolean` variable to indicate whether a thread is suspended rather than use the `suspend()` method. An example of implementing the `suspend()` method is introduced in the next section, "The `Runnable` Interface."

■ `public void resume()`

This method resumes the thread. As of Java 2, this method, along with the `suspend()` method, is deprecated because it is deadlock-prone. You should use the `notify()` method along with a `boolean` variable to indicate whether a thread is resumed rather than use the `resume()` method. An example of implementing the `resume()` method will be introduced in the next section, "The `Runnable` Interface."

■ `public static void sleep(long millis) throws InterruptedException`

This method puts the runnable object to sleep for a specified time in milliseconds. Note that `sleep()` is a class method.

■ `public void interrupt()`

This method interrupts the running thread.

■ `public static boolean isInterrupted()`

This method tests to see whether the current thread has been interrupted.

■ `public boolean isAlive()`

This method tests to see whether the thread is currently running.

■ `public void setPriority(int p)`

This method sets priority p (ranging from 1 to 10) for this thread.

The `wait()` and `notify()` methods in the `Object` class are often used with threads.

■ `public final void wait() throws InterruptedException`

This method puts the thread to wait for notification by another thread of a change in this object.

■ `public final void notify()`

This method awakens a single thread that is waiting on this object.

Example 13.1 Using the *Thread* Class to Create and Launch Threads

This program creates and runs the following three threads:

- The first thread prints the letter *a* 100 times.
- The second thread prints the letter *b* 100 times.
- The third thread prints the integers 1 through 100.

The program has three independent tasks. To run them concurrently, the program needs to create a runnable object for each task. Because the first two threads have similar functionality, they can be defined in one thread class.

The program is given here, and its output is shown in Figure 13.4.

```java
// TestThreads.java: Define threads using the Thread class
package Chapter13;

public class TestThreads
{
  // Main method
  public static void main(String[] args)
  {
    // Create threads
    PrintChar printA = new PrintChar('a',100);
    PrintChar printB = new PrintChar('b',100);
    PrintNum  print100 = new PrintNum(100);

    // Start threads
    print100.start();
    printA.start();
    printB.start();
  }
}

// The thread class for printing a specified character
// in specified times
class PrintChar extends Thread
{
  private char charToPrint;  // The character to print
  private int times;  // The times to repeat

  // Construct a thread with specified character and number of
  // times to print the character
  public PrintChar(char c, int t)
  {
    charToPrint = c;
    times = t;
  }

  // Vverride the run() method to tell the system
  // what the thread will do
  public void run()
  {
    for (int i=1; i < times; i++)
      System.out.print(charToPrint);
  }
}
```

continues

```
// The thread class for printing number from 1 to n for a given n
class PrintNum extends Thread
{
  private int lastNum;

  // Construct a thread for print 1, 2, ..., i
  public PrintNum(int n)
  {
    lastNum = n;
  }

  public void run()
  {
    for (int i=1; i <= lastNum; i++)
      System.out.print(" " + i);
  }
}

// The thread class for printing number from 1 to n for a given n
class PrintNum extends Thread
{
  private int lastNum;

  public PrintNum(int i)
  {
    lastNum = i;
  }

  public void run()
  {
    for (int i=1; i <= lastNum; i++)
      System.out.print(" "+i);
  }
}
```

Figure 13.4   *The threads* printA, printB, *and* print100 *are executed simultaneously to display the letter* a *100 times, the letter* b *100 times, and the numbers from 1 to 100.*

Example Review

If you run this program on a multiple CPU system, all three threads will be executing simultaneously. If you run this program on a single CPU system, the three threads will share the CPU and take turns printing letters and numbers on the console.

The program creates thread classes by extending the Thread class. The PrintChar class, derived from the Thread class, overrides the run() method with the print character action. This class provides a framework for printing any single character a given number of times. The runnable objects printA and printB are instances of the user-defined thread class PrintChar.

The PrintNum class overrides the run() method with the print number action. This class provides a framework for printing numbers from 1 to n, for any integer n. The runnable object print100 is an instance of the user-defined thread class printNum.

In the client program, the program creates a thread, printA, for printing the letter *a*; and a thread, printB, for printing the letter *b*. Both are objects of the PrintChar class. The print100 thread object is created from the PrintNum class.

The start() method is invoked to start a thread, which causes the run() method to execute. When the run() method completes, the threads terminate.

NOTE
On some systems, the program may not terminate or print out all the characters and numbers. This problem has nothing to do with your program. It may be an OS problem or a Java Virtual Machine implementation problem. If the program does not seem to terminate, press Ctrl+C to stop it.

The *Runnable* Interface

In the preceding section, you created and ran a thread by declaring a user thread class that extends the Thread class. This approach works well if the user thread class inherits only from the Thread class, but it does not work if the user thread class inherits multiple classes, as in the case of an applet. To inherit multiple classes, you have to implement interfaces. Java provides the Runnable interface as an alternative to the Thread class.

In Example 12.1, "Displaying a Clock," you drew a clock to show the current time in an applet. The clock is not ticking after it is displayed. What can you do to let the clock display a new current time every second? The key to making the clock tick is to repaint the clock every second with a new current time. You could attempt to override the start() method in CurrentTimeApplet with the following code:

```
public void start()
{
  while (true)
  {
    stillClock.repaint();
    try
    {
      Thread.sleep(1000);
    }
```

```
        catch(InterruptedException ex)
        {
        }
      }
    }
```

The `start()` method is called when the applet begins. The infinite loop repaints the clock every 1,000 milliseconds (which equals 1 second). This appears to refresh the clock every second, but if you run the program, the browser hangs up. The problem is that as long as the `while` loop is running, the browser cannot serve any of the other events that may be occurring. Therefore, the `paintComponent()` method is not called. The solution to the problem is to move the `while` loop to another thread, which can be executed in parallel with the `paintComponent()` method.

To create a new thread for the applet, you need to implement the `Runnable` interface in the applet. Here are the implementation guidelines for the `Runnable` interface:

1. Add `implements Runnable` in the applet class declaration:

   ```
   public class MyApplet extends JApplet implements Runnable
   ```

2. Declare a thread in `MyApplet`. For example, the following statement declares a thread instance, `thread`, with the initial value `null`:

   ```
   private Thread thread = null;
   ```

   By default, the initial value is `null`, so assigning `null` in this statement is not necessary.

3. Create a new thread in the applet's `init()` method and start it right away in `MyApplet`:

   ```
   public void init()
   {
     thread = new Thread(this);  // Create a thread
     thread.start();  // Start the thread
   }
   ```

   The `this` argument in the `Thread` constructor is required, which specifies that the run function of `MyApplet` should be called when the thread executes an instance of `MyApplet`.

4. Resume the thread in the applet's `start()` method by invoking `resume()` like this in `MyApplet`:

   ```
   public void start()
   {
     resume();
   }
   ```

   The `resume()` method resumes this thread if it was suspended. The method is ignored if the thread was not suspended. Since the `resume()` method in the `Thread` class has been deprecated, you have to create a new one in the program.

5. Create `resume()` and `suspend()` methods as follows:

```java
public synchronized void resume()
{
  if (suspended)
  {
    suspended = false;
    notify();
  }
}

public synchronized void suspend()
{
  suspended = true;
}
```

The variable `suspended` should be declared as a data member of the class, which indicates the state of the thread. The `synchronized` keyword ensures that the `resume()` and `suspend()` methods are serialized to avoid race conditions that could result in an inconsistent value for the variable `suspended`. The `synchronized` keyword is further discussed in the section titled "Synchronization," later in this chapter.

6. Write the code you want the thread to execute in the `run()` method:

```java
public void run()
{
  while (true)
  {
    stillClock.repaint();

    try
    {
      thread.sleep(1000);
      synchronized (this)
      {
        while (suspended)
          wait();
      }
    }
    catch (InterruptedException ex)
    {
    }
  }
}
```

The `run()` method is invoked by the Java runtime system when the applet starts. The `while` loop invokes the `stillClock.repaint()` method every second if the thread is not suspended. If `suspended` is true, the `wait()` method causes the thread to suspend and wait for notification by the `notify()` method invoked from the `resume()` method. The `repaint()` method runs on the system default thread, which is separate from the thread on which the `while` loop is running. The `synchronized` keyword eliminates potential conflicts that could cause the suspended thread to miss a notification and remain suspended.

7. Override the `stop()` method to suspend the running thread:

```
public void stop()
{
  suspend();
}
```

This code suspends the thread so that it does not consume CPU time while the Web page containing this applet becomes inactive.

8. Override the `destroy()` method to kill the thread:

```
public void destroy()
{
  thread = null;
}
```

This code releases all the resources associated with the thread when the Web browser exits.

Example 13.2 Implementing the *Runnable* Interface in an Applet

The applet presented here displays a clock. To simulate the clock running, a separate thread is used to repaint the clock. The output of the program is shown in Figure 13.5.

```
// ClockApplet.java: Display a running clock on the applet
package Chapter13;

import java.applet.*;
import java.awt.*;
import java.util.*;

public class ClockApplet extends Chapter12.CurrentTimeApplet
  implements Runnable
{
  // Declare a thread for running the clock
  private Thread thread = null;

  // Determine if the thread is suspended
  private boolean suspended = false;

  // Initialize applet
  public void init()
  {
    super.init();

    // Create the thread
    thread = new Thread(this);

    // Start the thread
    thread.start();
  }
```

```
// Implement the start() method to resume the thread
public void start()
{
  resume();
}

// Implement the run() method to dictate what the thread will do
public void run()
{
  while (true)
  {
    // Repaint the clock to display current time
    stillClock.repaint();

    try
    {
      thread.sleep(1000);
      synchronized (this)
      {
        while (suspended)
          wait();
      }
    }
    catch (InterruptedException ex)
    {
    }
  }
}

// Implement the stop method to suspend the thread
public void stop()
{
  suspend();
}

// Destroy the thread
public void destroy()
{
  thread = null;
}

// Resume the suspended thread
public synchronized void resume()
{
  if (suspended)
  {
    suspended = false;
    notify();
  }
}

// Suspend the thread
public synchronized void suspend()
{
  suspended = true;
}
}
```

continues

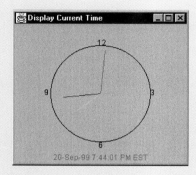

Figure 13.5 *The control of the clock drawing runs a thread separately from the* `paint()` *method that draws the clock.*

Example Review

The `CurrentTimeApplet` class is presented in Example 12.1, "Displaying a Clock," to display the current time. The `ClockApplet` class extends `CurrentTimeApplet` with a control loop running on a separate thread to make the clock tick.

The `run()` method comes from the `Runnable` interface and is modified to specify what the separate thread will do. The `paintComponent()` method is called every second by the `repaint()` method to display the current time.

The `init()`, `start()`, `stop()`, and `destroy()` methods in the `Applet` class are modified for this program to work with the Web browser. The `init()` method is invoked to start the thread when the Web page is loaded. The `stop()` method is invoked to suspend the thread when the Web page containing the applet becomes inactive. The `start()` method is invoked to resume the thread when the Web page containing the applet becomes active. The `destroy()` method is invoked to terminate the thread when the Web browser exits.

The separate thread named `thread` is created and started in the applet's `init()` method:

```
thread = new Thread(this);
thread.start();
```

The `ClockApplet`'s `init()` method calls `super.init()` defined in the `Current-TimeApplet` class, which gets parameters for country, language, and time zone from HTML. Therefore, the `ClockApplet` class can get these parameters from HTML.

The `resume()` method sets the variable `suspended` to `false` and awakens the thread that is waiting on the notification by invoking the `notify()` method. The `suspend()` method sets the variable `suspended` to `true`, which causes the thread to suspend and wait for notification to resume.

> **NOTE**
>
> The `start()` method in `thread.start()` is different from the `start()` method in the applet. The former starts the thread and causes the `run()` method to execute, whereas the latter is executed by the Web browser when the applet starts for the first time or is reactivated.

> **TIP**
>
> Because it is easier and simpler to use the `Thread` class, I recommend that you use it unless your class uses multiple inheritance.

> **CAUTION**
>
> I recommend that you suspend the threads in the applet's `stop()` method so that the applet does not consume CPU time while the Web page is inactive.

Case Studies

The preceding example shows how to implement the `Runnable` interface in an applet. You can implement the `Runnable` interface in any class. The next example shows you how to use the `Runnable` interface in a class other than applets. You will create a new class named `Clock` that extends `StillClock` and implements `Runnable` to make the clock self-running.

Example 13.3 Controlling a Group of Clocks

This program displays three clocks in a group. Each clock has individual Resume and Suspend control buttons. You can also resume or suspend all the clocks by using group-control Resume All and Suspend All buttons. Figure 13.6 contains the output of a sample run of the program.

```java
// ClockGroup.java: Display a group of international clocks
package Chapter13;

import java.awt.*;
import java.awt.event.*;
import java.util.*;
import javax.swing.*;
import Chapter8.MyFrameWithExitHandling;

public class ClockGroup extends JApplet implements ActionListener
{
  // Declare three clock panels
  private ClockPanel clockPanel1, clockPanel2, clockPanel3;
```

continues

```
    // Declare group control buttons
    private JButton jbtResumeAll, jbtSuspendAll;

    // This main method enables the applet to run as an application
    public static void main(String[] args)
    {
      // Create a frame
      MyFrameWithExitHandling frame = new MyFrameWithExitHandling(
        "Clock Group Demo");

      // Create an instance of the applet
      ClockGroup applet = new ClockGroup();

      // Add the applet instance to the frame
      frame.getContentPane().add(applet, BorderLayout.CENTER);

      // Invoke init() and start()
      applet.init();
      applet.start();

      // Display the frame
      frame.setSize(600, 300);
      frame.setVisible(true);
    }

    // Initialize the applet
    public void init()
    {
      // Panel p1 for holding three clocks
      JPanel p1 = new JPanel();
      p1.setLayout(new GridLayout(1, 3));

      // Create a clock for Berlin
      p1.add(clockPanel1 = new ClockPanel());
      clockPanel1.setTitle("Berlin");
      clockPanel1.clock.setTimeZoneID("ECT");
      clockPanel1.clock.setLocale(Locale.GERMAN);

      // Create a clock for San Francisco
      p1.add(clockPanel2 = new ClockPanel());
      clockPanel2.clock.setLocale(Locale.US);
      clockPanel2.clock.setTimeZoneID("PST");
      clockPanel2.setTitle("San Francisco");

      // Create a clock for Taipei
      p1.add(clockPanel3 = new ClockPanel());
      clockPanel3.setTitle("\u6077\u6079");
      clockPanel3.clock.setLocale(Locale.CHINESE);
      clockPanel3.clock.setTimeZoneID("CTT");

      // Panel p2 for holding two group control buttons
      JPanel p2 = new JPanel();
      p2.setLayout(new FlowLayout());
      p2.add(jbtResumeAll = new JButton("Resume All"));
      p2.add(jbtSuspendAll = new JButton("Suspend All"));

      // Add panel p1 and p2 into the applet
      getContentPane().setLayout(new BorderLayout());
      getContentPane().add(p1, BorderLayout.CENTER);
      getContentPane().add(p2, BorderLayout.SOUTH);
```

```
      // Register listeners
      jbtResumeAll.addActionListener(this);
      jbtSuspendAll.addActionListener(this);
    }

    // Handlers for group control buttons
    public void actionPerformed(ActionEvent e)
    {
      if (e.getSource() == jbtResumeAll)
      {
        // Start all clocks
        clockPanel1.resume();
        clockPanel2.resume();
        clockPanel3.resume();
      }
      else if (e.getSource() == jbtSuspendAll)
      {
        // Stop all clocks
        clockPanel1.suspend();
        clockPanel2.suspend();
        clockPanel3.suspend();
      }
    }
  }

  // ClockPanel for holding a header, a clock, and control buttons
  class ClockPanel extends JPanel implements ActionListener
  {
    // Header title of the clock panel
    private JLabel jlblTitle;

    protected Clock clock = null;

    // Individual clock Resume and Suspend control buttons
    private JButton jbtResume, jbtSuspend;

    // Constructor
    public ClockPanel()
    {
      // Panel jpButtons for grouping buttons
      JPanel jpButtons = new JPanel();
      jpButtons.add(jbtResume = new JButton("Resume"));
      jpButtons.add(jbtSuspend = new JButton("Suspend"));

      // Set BorderLayout for the ClockPanel
      setLayout(new BorderLayout());

      // Add title label to the north of the panel
      add(jlblTitle = new JLabel(), BorderLayout.NORTH);
      jlblTitle.setHorizontalAlignment(JLabel.CENTER);

      // Add the clock to the center of the panel
      add(clock = new Clock(), BorderLayout.CENTER);

      // Add jpButtons to the south of the panel
      add(jpButtons, BorderLayout.SOUTH);

      // Register ClockPanel as a listener to the buttons
      jbtResume.addActionListener(this);
      jbtSuspend.addActionListener(this);
    }
```

continues

```java
    // Set label on the title
    public void setTitle(String title)
    {
      jlblTitle.setText(title);
    }

    // Handlers for buttons "Resume" and "Suspend"
    public void actionPerformed(ActionEvent e)
    {
      if (e.getSource() == jbtResume)
      {
        clock.resume();
      }
      else if (e.getSource() == jbtSuspend)
      {
        clock.suspend();
      }
    }

    // Resume the clock
    public void resume()
    {
      if (clock != null) clock.resume();
    }

    // Resume the clock
    public void suspend()
    {
      if (clock != null) clock.suspend();
    }
}

// Clock.java: Show a running clock on the panel
package Chapter13;

import java.util.*;

public class Clock extends Chapter12.StillClock implements Runnable
{
  // Declare a thread for running the clock
  private Thread timer = null;

  // Determine if the thread is suspended
  private boolean suspended = false;

  // Default constructor
  public Clock()
  {
    super();

    // Create the thread
    timer = new Thread(this);

    // Start the thread
    timer.start();
  }

  // Construct a clock with specified locale and time zone
  public Clock(Locale locale, TimeZone tz)
  {
    super(locale, tz);
```

```
      // Create the thread
      timer = new Thread(this);

      // Start the thread
      timer.start();
   }

   // Implement the run() method to dictate what the thread will do
   public void run()
   {
     while (true)
     {
       repaint();
       try
       {
         timer.sleep(1000);
         synchronized (this)
         {
           while (suspended)
             wait();
         }
       }
       catch (InterruptedException ex)
       {
       }
     }
   }

   // Resume the clock
   public synchronized void resume()
   {
     if (suspended)
     {
       suspended = false;
       notify();
     }
   }

   // Suspend the clock
   public synchronized void suspend()
   {
     suspended = true;
   }
}
```

continues

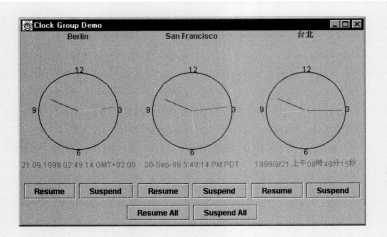

Figure 13.6   *Three clocks run independently with individual control and group control.*

Example Review

The example consists of three classes: ClockGroup, ClockPanel, and Clock. The Clock class extends StillClock and implements Runnable. The repaint() method is invoked each second to call the paintComponent() method defined in StillClock. The paintComponent() method runs on a separate thread to draw a clock on a panel with the new current time.

The ClockPanel contains a title, a clock, and its control buttons, Resume and Suspend. You can use these two buttons to resume or suspend an individual clock.

The ClockGroup class creates and places three clock panels above two group-control buttons, Resume All and Suspend All, in the applet. You can use these two buttons to resume or suspend all the clocks. The three clocks are for Berlin, San Francisco, and Taipei. The title and time displayed in the panel are locale-sensitive. The Unicode "\u6077\u6079" are the Chinese characters for Taipei, and time is automatically displayed in Chinese because you have set the locale for the clock to Locale.CHINESE. If your machine does not support Chinese fonts, you cannot see the Chinese characters.

Thread States

Threads can be in one of five states: new, ready, running, inactive, or finished (see Figure 13.7).

When a thread is newly created, it enters the new state. After a thread is started by calling its start() method, the thread enters the ready state. A ready thread is runnable but may not yet be running. The operating system has to allocate CPU time to it.

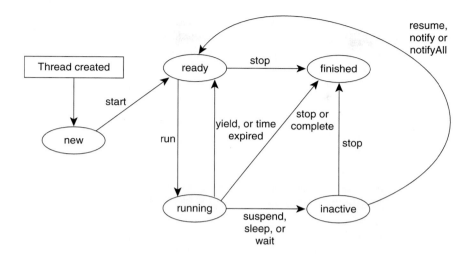

Figure 13.7   *A thread can be in one of five states: new, ready, running, inactive, or finished.*

When the ready thread begins executing, it enters the running state. A running thread may enter the ready state if its given CPU time expires or its `yield()` method is called.

A thread may enter the inactive state for several reasons. It may have invoked the `sleep()`, `wait()`, or `suspend()` method. Some other thread may have invoked its `sleep()` or `suspend()` method. It may be waiting for an I/O operation to finish. An inactive thread may be reactivated when the action inactivating the thread is reversed. For example, if a thread has been put to sleep and the sleep time has expired, the thread is reactivated and enters the ready state.

Finally, a thread is finished if it completes the execution of its `run()` method or if its `stop()` method is invoked.

To find out the state of a thread, you can use the `isAlive()` method. It returns `true` if the thread is in the ready, inactive, or running state; it returns `false` if the thread is new and has not started or if the thread is finished.

Thread Priority

Every thread in Java is assigned a priority. By default, a thread inherits the priority from the thread that spawned it. You can increase or decrease the priority of any thread by using the `setPriority()` method, and you can get the thread's priority by using the `getPriority()` method. Priorities are indicated by numbers ranging from 1 to 10. The `Thread` class has `int` constants `MIN_PRIORITY`, `NORM_PRIORITY`, and `MAX_PRIORITY`, representing 1, 5, and 10, respectively. The priority of the main thread is `Thread.NORM_PRIORITY`.

> ### TIP
>
> The priority numbers may change in a future version of Java. You can mini-mize the impact of any such change by using the constants in the `Thread` class to specify thread priorities.

The Java runtime system always picks the thread with the highest priority that is currently runnable. If several runnable threads have equally high priorities, the CPU is allocated to all of them in a round-robin fashion. A lower-priority thread can run only when no higher-priority threads are currently running.

Example 13.4 Testing Thread Priorities

This program creates three threads named `printA`, `printB`, and `printC` that print the letters *a*, *b*, and *c*, respectively. The program sets priority `NORM_PRIORITY` for `printA`, `NORM_PRIORITY + 1` for `printB`, and `NORM_PRIORITY + 2` for `printC`. Figure 13.8 contains the output of a sample run of the program.

```java
// TestThreadPriority.java: Test thread priorities
package Chapter13;

public class TestThreadPriority
{
  // Main method
  public static void main(String[] args)
  {
    // Create three threads
    PrintChar printA = new PrintChar('a',200);
    PrintChar printB = new PrintChar('b',200);
    PrintChar printC = new PrintChar('c',200);

    // Set thread priorities
    printA.setPriority(Thread.NORM_PRIORITY);
    printB.setPriority(Thread.NORM_PRIORITY+1);
    printC.setPriority(Thread.NORM_PRIORITY+2);

    // Start threads
    printA.start();
    printB.start();
    printC.start();
  }
}
```

Figure 13.8   *The threads* `printA`, `printB`, *and* `printC` *are assigned different priorities.*

Example Review

The `PrintChar` class for repeatedly printing a character in a separate thread was given in Example 13.1.

The three threads are started in this order: `printA`, `printB`, and `printC`. The priority of the threads is `printC`, `printB`, and `printA`, so `printC` will be the first to get CPU time after it is ready to run.

In theory, `printC` should finish first, but the actual execution depends on the system load. You may get different outputs on different systems.

Thread Groups

A *thread group* is a set of threads. Some programs contain quite a few threads with similar functionality. For convenience, you can group them together and perform operations on all the threads in the group. For example, if all the threads belong to a group, you can suspend or resume them at the same time.

The following are the guidelines for using a thread group:

1. Construct a thread group, using the `ThreadGroup` constructor:

   ```
   ThreadGroup g = new ThreadGroup("thread group");
   ```

   This creates a thread group g named `"thread group"`. The name is a string and must be unique.

2. Place a thread in a thread group, using the `Thread` constructor:

   ```
   Thread t = new Thread(g, new ThreadClass(), "This thread");
   ```

   The statement new `ThreadClass()` creates a runnable instance for the `ThreadClass`. You can also add a thread group under another thread group to form a tree in which every thread group except the initial one has a parent.

3. To find out how many threads in a group are currently running, use the `activeCount()` method. The following statement displays the active number of threads in the group g.

   ```
   System.out.println("The number of runnable threads in the group"
     + g.activeCount());
   ```

4. Each thread belongs to a thread group. By default, a newly created thread becomes a member of the current thread group that spawned it. To find which group a thread belongs to, use the `getThreadGroup()` method.

> **NOTE**
> You have to start each thread individually. There is no start() method in ThreadGroup. As of Java 2, the stop(), suspend(), and resume() methods are deprecated. You implemented the stop(), suspend(), and resume() methods in the Thread class. You can also implement them in the ThreadGroup class.

In the next section, you will see an example that uses the ThreadGroup class.

Synchronization

When multiple threads access a shared resource simultaneously, the shared resource may be corrupted. The following example demonstrates the problem.

Example 13.5 Showing Resource Conflict

This program demonstrates the problem of resource conflict. Suppose that you launch 100 threads to transfer money from a savings account to a checking account, and 100 threads to transfer money from the checking account to the savings account, with each thread transferring $1. Assume that the savings account has an initial balance of $10,000 and the checking account has $0. The output of the program is shown in Figure 13.9.

```java
// TestTransferWithoutSync.java: Demonstrate resource conflict
package Chapter13;

import Chapter11.Account;
import Chapter11.NegativeAmountException;
import Chapter11.InsufficientFundException;

public class TestTransferWithoutSync
{
  // Main method
  public static void main(String[] args)
  {
    // Determine if all threads are finished
    boolean done = false;

    // Create a savings account with ID 1 and balance 10000
    Account saving = new Account(1, 10000);

    // Create a checking account with ID 2 and balance 0
    Account checking = new Account(2, 0);

    // Create 100 threads in t1 to transfer money from
    // savings to checking
    Thread t1[] = new Thread[100];

    // Create a thread group g1 for grouping t1's
    ThreadGroup g1 = new ThreadGroup("from savings to checking");

    // Create 100 threads in t2 to transfer money from
    // checking to savings
    Thread t2[] = new Thread[100];
```

```
      // Create a thread group g2 for grouping t2's
      ThreadGroup g2 = new ThreadGroup("from checking to savings");

      // Add t1[i] to g1, and start t1[i]
      for (int i=0; i<100; i++)
      {
        t1[i] = new Thread(g1,
          new TransferThread(saving, checking, 1), "t1");
        t1[i].start();
      }

      // Add t2[i] to g2, and start t2[i]
      for (int i=0; i<100; i++)
      {
        t2[i] = new Thread(g2,
          new TransferThread(checking, saving, 1),"t2");
        t2[i].start();
      }

      // Exit the loop when all threads finished
      while (!done)
        if ((g1.activeCount() == 0) && (g2.activeCount() == 0))
          done = true;

      // Show the balance in the savings and checking accounts
      System.out.println("Savings account balance "+
        saving.getBalance());
      System.out.println("Checking account balance "+
        checking.getBalance());
  }
}

// Define the thread to transfer money between accounts
class TransferThread extends Thread
{
  private Account fromAccount, toAccount;
  private double amount;

  // Construct a thread transferring amount
  // from account s to account c
  public TransferThread(Account s, Account c, double amount)
  {
    fromAccount = s;
    toAccount = c;
    this.amount = amount;
  }

  // Override the run method
  public void run()
  {
    transfer(fromAccount, toAccount, amount);
  }

  // Transfer amount from fromAccount to toAccount
  public void transfer(Account fromAccount,
                       Account toAccount,
                       double amount)
  {
    // Record the balance before transaction for use in recovery
    double fromAccountPriorBalance = fromAccount.getBalance();
    double toAccountPriorBalance = toAccount.getBalance();
```

continues

583

```
                    try
                    {
                      toAccount.deposit(amount);
                      sleep(10);
                      fromAccount.withdraw(amount);
                    }
                    catch (NegativeAmountException ex)
                    {
                      // Reset the balance to the value prior to the exception
                      fromAccount.setBalance(fromAccountPriorBalance);
                      toAccount.setBalance(toAccountPriorBalance);
                    }
                    catch (InsufficientFundException ex)
                    {
                      // Reset the balance to the value prior to the exception
                      fromAccount.setBalance(fromAccountPriorBalance);
                      toAccount.setBalance(toAccountPriorBalance);
                    }
                    catch (InterruptedException ex)
                    {
                    }
                  }
                }
```

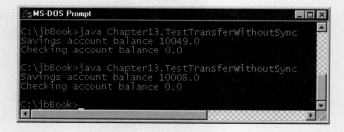

Figure 13.9   *The* TestTransferWithoutSync *program causes data inconsistency.*

Example Review

The program creates an Account object for a savings account with an initial balance of $10,000, and an Account object for a checking account with an initial balance of $0.00. The Account class was given in Example 11.4, "Creating Your Own Exception Classes" (see Chapter 11, "Exception Handling").

The program creates 100 identical threads in array t1 to transfer $1 from the savings account to the checking account, and then creates 100 identical threads to transfer $1 from the checking account to the savings account. The program groups all the threads in t1 in a thread group g1, and then groups all the threads in t2 in a thread group g2 (see Figure 13.10).

The transfer() method is used by all the threads to transfer money from one account to the other.

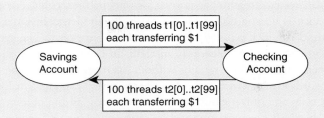

Figure 13.10   *The threads transfer funds between the savings account and the checking account.*

When all the threads finish, the sum of the balances of the two accounts should be 10,000; however, the output is unpredictable. The answers in the sample run are wrong, as shown in Figure 13.9. The sample run demonstrates the data corruption problem caused by unsynchronized threads with access to the same data source.

Interestingly, it is not easy to replicate the problem. The `sleep()` method in the `transfer()` method causes the transfer operation to pause for 10 milliseconds. The `sleep()` method is added deliberately to magnify the data corruption problem, making it easy to see. If you run the program several times, but still do not see the problem, put the `transfer()` method in a `for` loop to run 100 times in the `run()` method. This will dramatically increase the chances for resource conflict.

What caused the error in Example 13.5? Here is a possible scenario:

1. A thread `t1[i]` reads the savings account balances and checking account balances and loses CPU time to a thread `t1[j]`.

2. A thread `t1[j]` reads the savings account balances and checking account balances and completes a transfer.

3. A thread `t1[i]` regains the CPU time and completes a transfer.

The effect of this scenario is that thread `t1[j]` did nothing, because thread `t1[i]` overrides `t1[j]`'s result in Step 3. Obviously, the problem is that `t1[i]` and `t1[j]` access the common resource, causing conflict.

To avoid resource conflict, Java uses the keyword `synchronized` to synchronize method invocation so that only one thread can be in the method at a time. To correct the data corruption problem in the previous example, put the keyword `synchronized` on the `transfer()` method and make `transfer` static, as follows:

```
public static synchronized void transfer(Account saving,
                                          Account checking,
                                          double amount)
```

With the keywords `static synchronized` in the method, the preceding scenario cannot take place. If thread `t1[j]` starts to enter the method and thread `t1[i]` is already there, thread `t1[j]` is blocked until thread `t1[i]` finishes the method.

A synchronized method acquires a lock before it executes. For an instance method, the lock is on the object for which the method was invoked. For a class (static) method, the lock is on all the objects of the same class. The `synchronized` keyword in the `suspend()` and `resume()` methods in Example 13.2 ensures that the variable `suspended` is updated serially without corruption within the object. Adding the keywords `static synchronized` in the `transfer()` method in Example 13.5 ensures that only one object can transfer funds among all the objects in arrays `t1` and `t2`, which avoids the concurrent access of the checking and saving accounts that could corrupt them.

NOTE

In the `run()` method of Example 13.2, a synchronized block was used. A synchronized block obtains the lock in the same way as a synchronized method. If a synchronized block is inside a static method, the lock is associated with the class; if it is inside an instance method, it is associated with the object.

In operating systems and database systems, locks are often used to protect resources exclusively for write or shared read operations. Java does not have the mechanism that lets you lock data.

Chapter Summary

In this chapter, you learned multithreading programming, using the `Thread` class and the `Runnable` interface. You can derive your thread class from the `Thread` class and create a thread instance to run a task on a separate thread. If your class needs to inherit multiple classes, you can implement the `Runnable` interface to simultaneously run multiple tasks in the program.

After a thread object is created, you can use `start()` to start a thread, and use `sleep()` to put a thread to sleep so that other threads can get a chance to run. Since the `stop()`, `suspend()`, and `resume()` methods are deprecated in Java 2, you need to implement these methods to stop, suspend, and resume a thread.

Your thread object never directly invokes the `run()` method. The Java runtime system invokes the `run()` method when it is time to execute the thread. Your class must override the `run()` method to tell the system what the thread will do when it runs.

Threads can be assigned a priority. The Java runtime system always executes the ready thread with the highest priority. You can use a thread group to put relevant threads together for group control. To prevent threads from corrupting a shared resource, you should put the `synchronized` keyword in the method that may cause corruption.

Chapter Review

13.1. Why do you need multithreading capability in applications? How can multiple threads run simultaneously in a single-processor system?

13.2. What are two ways to create threads? When do you use the `Thread` class, and when do you use the `Runnable` interface? What are the differences between the `Thread` class and the `Runnable` interface?

13.3. How do you create a thread and launch a thread object? Which of the following methods are instance methods? Which of them are deprecated in Java 2?

```
run(), start(), stop(), suspend(), resume(), sleep(),
  isInterrupted()
```

13.4. Will the program behave differently if `thread.sleep()` is replaced by `Thread.sleep()` in Example 13.2?

13.5. Describe the life-cycle of a thread object.

13.6. How do you set a priority for a thread? What is the default priority?

13.7. Describe a thread group. How do you create a thread group? Can you control an individual thread in a thread group (suspend, resume, stop, and so on)?

13.8. Give some examples of possible resource corruption when running multiple threads. How do you synchronize conflict threads?

13.9. Why does the following class have a syntax error?

```java
class Test extends Thread
{
  public static void main(String[] args)
  {
    Test t = new Test();
    t.start();
    t.start();
  }

  public void run()
  {
    System.out.println("test");
  }
}
```

13.10. Why does the following class have a syntax error?

```java
import javax.swing.*;

class Test extends JApplet implements Runnable
{
  public void init() throws InterruptedException
  {
    Thread thread = new Thread(this);
    thread.sleep(1000);
  }

  public synchronized void run()
  {
  }
}
```

Programming Exercises

13.1. Write an applet to display a flashing label. Enable it to run as an application.

Hints: To make the label flash, you need to repaint the window alternately with the label and without the label (blank screen). You can use a `boolean` variable to control the alternation.

13.2. Write an applet to display a moving label. The label continuously moves from right to left in the applet's viewing area. When the label disappears from the viewing area, it again begins moving from right to left. The label freezes when the mouse is clicked on the label, and it moves again when the button is released. Enable it to run as an application.

Hints: Repaint the window with a new x coordinate.

13.3. Rewrite Example 13.1, "Using the `Thread` Class to Create and Launch Threads," to display the output on a text area, as shown in Figure 13.11.

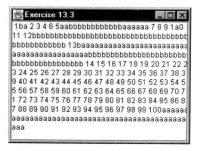

Figure 13.11   *The output from three threads is displayed on a text area.*

13.4. Write a program to launch 100 threads. Each thread is to add 1 to a variable sum. The variable sum is initially zero. You need to pass sum by reference to each thread. In order to pass it by reference, you need to define an `Integer` wrapper object to hold sum. Run the program with and without synchronization to see its effect.

13.5. Write an applet to simulate an elevator going up and down (see Figure 13.12). The buttons on the left indicate the floor where the rider is now located. The rider must first click a button on the left to request that the elevator move to his or her floor. After entering the elevator, the rider clicks a button on the right to request that the elevator go to the specified floor. Enable the applet to run standalone.

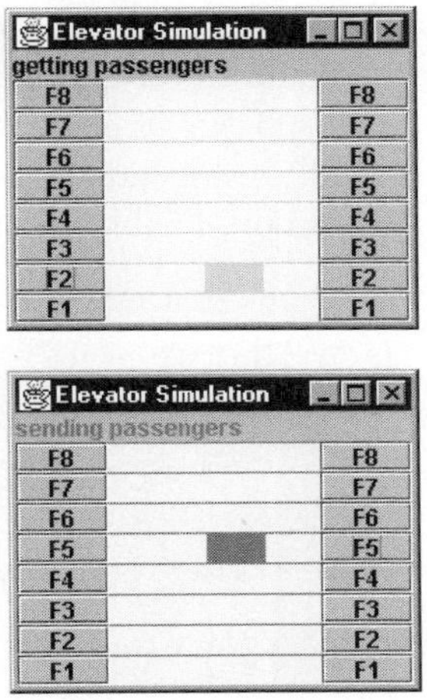

Figure 13.12   *The program simulates elevator operations.*

13.6. Write a Java applet to display a stock index ticker (see Figure 13.13). The stock index information is passed from the <param> tag in the HTML file. Each index has four parameters: Index Name (for example, S&P 500), Current Time (for example, 15:54), the index from the previous day (for example, 919.01), and Change (for example, 4.54). Enable the applet to run standalone.

Use at least five indexes, such as Dow Jones, S & P 500, NASDAQ, NIKKEI, and Gold & Silver Index. Display positive changes in green and negative changes in red. The indexes move from the right to the left in the applet's viewing area. Clicking anywhere on the applet freezes the ticker, and the ticker moves again when the mouse button is released.

Figure 13.13   *The program displays a stock index ticker.*

13.7. Write a Java applet to simulate a running fan, as shown in Figure 13.14. The buttons Start, Stop, and Reverse control the fan. The scroll bar controls the fan speed. Create a subclass of `JPanel` to display the fan. This subclass also contains the methods to suspend and resume the fan, set the fan's speed, and reverse the fan's direction. Enable the applet to run standalone.

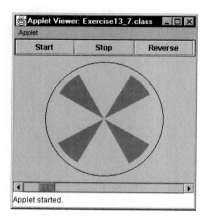

Figure 13.14   *The program simulates a running fan.*

MULTIMEDIA

Objectives

- ❂ Develop multimedia applications with audio and images.
- ❂ Get audio files and play sound in Java applets.
- ❂ Get image files and display graphics in Java applets.
- ❂ Display images and play audio files in Java applications.
- ❂ Use `MediaTracker` to ensure that images are completely loaded before they are displayed.

Introduction

Welcome to the fascinating world of *multimedia*. You have seen computer animation used every day in TV and movies. When surfing the Web, you have seen sites with text, images, sound, animation, and movie clips. These are all examples of multimedia at work.

Multimedia is a broad term that encompasses making, storing, retrieving, transferring, and presenting various types of information, such as text, graphics, pictures, videos, and sound. Multimedia involves a complex weave of communications, electronics, and computer technologies. It is beyond the scope of this book to cover multimedia in great detail. This chapter concentrates on the presentation of multimedia in Java.

Java was designed with multimedia in mind. Most programming languages do not have built-in multimedia capabilities. But Java provides extensive built-in support that enables you to develop powerful multimedia applications easily. Java's multimedia capabilities include animation that uses drawings, audio, and images.

You have already used animation with drawings in simulating a clock. You have also used the image icons in the Swing components. In this chapter, you will learn how to develop Java programs with audio and images.

Playing Audio

Audio is stored in files. There are several formats of audio files. Prior to Java 2, Java was only able to play the format used on UNIX machines. These are sound files in the AU format. With Java 2, you can also play the sound files in WAV, AIFF, MIDI, AU, and RMF format with higher sound quality.

You can play an audio clip in an applet by using the following `play()` method:

```
play(URL url, String filename);
```

This method downloads the audio file from the `url` and plays the audio clip. Nothing happens if the audio file cannot be found.

The URL (Universal Resource Locator) describes the location of a resource on the Internet. Java provides a class that is used to manipulate URLs: `java.net.URL`. Java's security mechanism restricts all files read via a browser to the directory where the HTML file is stored, or to the subdirectory of that location. You can use `getCodeBase()` to get the URL of the applet, or `getDocumentBase()` to get the HTML file that contains the applet. These two methods are defined in the `Applet` class:

```
play(getCodeBase(), "soundfile.au");

play(getDocumentBase(), "soundfile.au");
```

The former method plays the sound file soundfile.au, which is located in the applet's directory. The latter method plays the sound file soundfile.au, which is located in the HTML file's directory.

The play(url, filename) statement downloads the audio file every time you play the audio. If you want to play the audio many times, you can create an *audio clip object* for the file. The audio clip is created once and can be played repeatedly without reloading the file. The following methods can be used to create an audio clip:

```
public AudioClip getAudioClip(URL url);

public AudioClip getAudioClip(URL url, String name);
```

The former requires an absolute URL address for it to specify a sound file; the latter lets you use a relative URL with the filename. The relative URL is obtained using getCodeBase() or getDocumentBase(). For example, the following statement creates an audio clip for the file soundfile.au that is stored in the same directory as the applet that contains the statement.

```
AudioClip ac = getAudioClip(getCodeBase(), "soundfile.au");
```

To manipulate a sound for an audio clip, you can use the instance methods of java.applet.AudioClip shown below:

■ public void play()

Play the clip once. Each time this method is called, the clip is restarted from the beginning.

■ public void loop()

Play the clip repeatedly.

■ public void stop()

Stop playing the clip.

Example 14.1 Incorporating Sound in Applets

This program displays a running clock, as shown in Example 12.1. In addition, the program plays sound files to announce the time at every minute.

```java
// ClockAppletWithAudio.java: Display a running clock on the applet
// with audio
package Chapter14;

import java.applet.*;
import java.awt.*;
import java.util.*;

public class ClockAppletWithAudio extends Chapter12.CurrentTimeApplet
{
  // Declare audio files
  protected AudioClip[] hourAudio = new AudioClip[12];
  protected AudioClip minuteAudio;
  protected AudioClip amAudio;
  protected AudioClip pmAudio;

  // Declare a clock
  ClockWithAudio clock;
```

continues

```java
// Initialize the applet
public void init()
{
  super.init();

  // Create audio clips for pronouncing hours
  for (int i=0; i<12; i++)
    hourAudio[i] = getAudioClip(getCodeBase(),
      "Chapter14/timeaudio/hour"+i+".au");

  // Create audio clips for pronouncing am and pm
  amAudio = getAudioClip(getCodeBase(),
    "Chapter14/timeaudio/am.au");
  pmAudio = getAudioClip(getCodeBase(),
    "Chapter14/timeaudio/pm.au");
}

// Override the createClock method defined in CurrentTimeApplet
public void createClock()
{
  getContentPane().add(clock =
    new ClockWithAudio(locale, tz, this));
}

// Announce the current time at every minute
public void announceTime(int s, int m, int h)
{
  if (s == 0)
  {
    // Announce hour
    hourAudio[h%12].play();

    // Load the minute file
    minuteAudio = getAudioClip(getCodeBase(),
      "Chapter14/timeaudio/minute"+m+".au");

    // Time delay to allow hourAudio play to finish
    try
    {
      Thread.sleep(1500);
    }
    catch(InterruptedException ex)
    {
    }

    // Announce minute
    minuteAudio.play();

    // Time delay to allow minuteAudio play to finish
    try
    {
      Thread.sleep(1500);
    }
    catch(InterruptedException ex)
    {
    }

    // Announce am or pm
    if (h < 12)
      amAudio.play();
```

```
      else
        pmAudio.play();
    }
  }

  // Implement Applet's start method to resume the thread
  public void start()
  {
    clock.resume();
  }

  // Implement Applet's stop method to suspend the thread
  public void stop()
  {
    clock.suspend();
  }
}

// ClockWithAudio.java: Display a clock and announce time
package Chapter14;

import java.awt.*;
import java.util.*;
import java.text.*;

public class ClockWithAudio extends Chapter13.Clock
{
  protected ClockAppletWithAudio applet;

  // Construct a clock with specified locale, timezone, and applet
  public ClockWithAudio(Locale locale, TimeZone tz,
    ClockAppletWithAudio applet)
  {
    // Invoke the Clock class's constructor
    super(locale, tz);

    this.applet = applet;
  }

  // Modify the paintComponent method to play sound
  public void paintComponent(Graphics g)
  {
    // Invoke the paintComponent method in the Clock class
    super.paintComponent(g);

    // Get current time using GregorianCalendar
    GregorianCalendar cal = new GregorianCalendar(tz);

    // Get second, minute and hour
    int s = (int)cal.get(GregorianCalendar.SECOND);
    int m = (int)cal.get(GregorianCalendar.MINUTE);
    int h = (int)cal.get(GregorianCalendar.HOUR_OF_DAY);

    // Announce current time
    applet.announceTime(s, m, h);
  }
}
```

continues

Example Review

This example contains two classes named `ClockAppletWithAudio` and `ClockWithAudio`. The `ClockAppletWithAudio` class extends the `CurrentTimeApplet` class with the capability to announce time. `CurrentTimeApplet` was given in Example 12.1, "Displaying a Clock." The `ClockWithAudio` class extends the `Clock` class and invokes the `announceTime()` method whenever it repaints the clock. The `Clock` class was given in Example 13.3, "Controlling a Group of Clocks."

The `hourAudio` is an array of 12 audio clips that are used to pronounce the 12 hours of the day; the `minuteAudio` is an audio clip used to pronounce the minute in an hour. The `amAudio` pronounces A.M.; the `pmAudio` pronounces P.M.

For example, if the current time is 6:30:00, the applet announces "The time is six-thirty A.M." If the current time is 20:20:00, the applet announces, "The time is eight-twenty P.M." The three audio clips are played in sequence in order to announce a time.

The `init()` method invokes `super.init()` defined in the `CurrentTimeApplet` class, and creates audio clips that pronounce time. `super.init()` gets country, language, and time zone parameters from HTML, and creates and places a clock into the applet.

All of the audio files are stored in the directory `timeaudio`, a subdirectory of the applet's directory. The 12 audio clips used to pronounce the hours are stored in the files **hour0.au**, **hour1.au**, and so on, to **hour11.au**. They are loaded using the following loop:

```
for (int i=0; i<12; i++)
  hourAudio[i] = getAudioClip(getCodeBase(),
    "Chapter14/timeaudio/hour" + i + ".au");
```

Similarly, the `amAudio` clip is stored in the file **am.au**, and the `pmAudio` clip is stored in the file **pm.au**; they are loaded along with the hour clips in the `init()` method.

The program created an array of 12 audio clips to pronounce each hour, but did not create 60 audio clips to pronounce each minute. Instead, the program created and loaded the minute audio clip when needed in the `announceTime()` method. The audio files are very large. Loading all 60 audio clips at once may cause an `OutOfMemoryError` exception.

In the `announceTime()` method, the `sleep()` method is purposely invoked to ensure that one clip finishes before the next clip starts so that the clips do not interfere with each other.

The constructor of `ClockWithAudio` contains an argument pointing to `ClockAppletWithAudio`, which enables the `paintComponent()` method in `ClockWithAudio` to invoke `announceTime()` defined in `ClockAppletWithAudio`. This is a common programming technique whereby an object can reference

596

methods and data from another class. You might declare `ClockWithAudio` as an inner class inside `ClockAppletWithAudio` to avoid passing `ClockAppletWithAudio` as a parameter. That would be fine if `ClockWithAudio` is not reused elsewhere.

The `paintComponent()` method invokes `super.paintComponent()` and `announce-Time()`. `super.paintComponent()` defined in `Clock` draws a clock for the current time. `announceTime(h, m, s)` announces the current hour, minute, and A.M. or P.M. if the second `s` is 0.

▬ NOTE

To get the audio files from JBuilder 3 IDE, you need to add the `codebase` attribute in the HTML file to specify the class code base, as follows:

```
<applet
  codebase = "."
  code = "Chapter14.ClockAppletWithAudio.class"
  width = 200
  height = 220
  alt ="You must have a Java-enabled browser to view the applet">
  <param name=language value=en>
  <param name=country value=US>
  <param name=timezone value=IET>
</applet>
```

Running Audio on a Separate Thread

If you had run the preceding program, you would have noticed that the second hand did not display at the first, second, and third seconds of the minute. This is because `sleep(1500)` is invoked twice in the `announceTime()` method, which takes three seconds to announce the time at the beginning of each minute.

Because of this delay, the `paintComponent()` method does not have time to draw the clock during the first three seconds of each minute. Clearly, the `announce-Time()` method for playing audio interferes with repainting the clock. To avoid the conflict, you should announce the time on a separate thread. This problem is fixed in the next program.

Example 14.2 Announcing the Time on a Separate Thread

To avoid the conflict between painting the clock and announcing the time, the program in this example runs these tasks on separate threads.

```
// ClockAppletWithAudioOnSeparateThread.java:
// Display a running clock on the applet with audio on a separate
// thread
package Chapter14;

import java.applet.*;
```

continues

```
public class ClockAppletWithAudioOnSeparateThread
  extends ClockAppletWithAudio
{
  // Declare a thread for annoucing time
  AnnounceTime announceTime;

  // Initialize the applet
  public void init()
  {
    super.init();
  }

  // Override this method defined in ClockAppletWithAudio
  // to announce the current time at every minute
  public void announceTime(int s, int m, int h)
  {
    // Load the minute file
    minuteAudio = getAudioClip(getCodeBase(),
      "Chapter14/timeaudio/minute" + m + ".au");

    // Announce current time
    if (s == 0)
    {
      if (h < 12)
        announceTime = new AnnounceTime(hourAudio[h%12],
          minuteAudio, amAudio);
      else
        announceTime = new AnnounceTime(hourAudio[h%12],
          minuteAudio, pmAudio);
      announceTime.start();
    }
  }
}

// Define a thread class for announcing time
class AnnounceTime extends Thread
{
  private AudioClip hourAudio, minuteAudio, amPM;

  // Get Audio clips
  public AnnounceTime(AudioClip hourAudio,
                      AudioClip minuteAudio,
                      AudioClip amPM)
  {
    this.hourAudio = hourAudio;
    this.minuteAudio = minuteAudio;
    this.amPM = amPM;
  }

  public void run()
  {
    // Announce hour
    hourAudio.play();

    // Time delay to allow hourAudio play to finish
    // before playing the clip
    try
    {
      Thread.sleep(1500);
    }
```

```
         catch(InterruptedException ex)
         {
         }

         // Announce minute
         minuteAudio.play();

         // Time delay to allow minuteAudio play to finish
         try
         {
           Thread.sleep(1500);
         }
         catch(InterruptedException ex)
         {
         }

         // Announce am or pm
         amPM.play();
     }
   }
```

Example Review

The program extends `ClockAppletWithAudio` with the capability to announce time without interfering with the `paintComponent()` method. The program defines a new thread class, `AnnounceTime`, which is derived from the `Thread` class. This new class plays audio.

To create an instance of the `AnnounceTime` class, you would need to pass three audio clips. These three audio clips are used to announce the hour, the minute, and A.M. or P.M. This instance is created only when s equals 0 at the beginning of each minute.

When running this program, you discover that the audio does not interfere with the clock animation because an instance of `AnnounceTime` starts on a separate thread to announce the current time. This thread is independent of the thread on which the `paintComponent()` method runs.

Displaying Images

In Examples 9.2 and 9.13, "Using Labels" and "Using a Scroll Pane," you used the `ImageIcon` class to create an icon from an image file and the `setIcon()` method to place the image in a UI component. These examples are restricted to Java applications and are not suitable for Java applets, because the image files are directly accessed from the local file system.

To display an image in Java applets, you need to load an image from an Internet source using the `getImage()` method in the `Applet` class. This method returns a `java.awt.Image` object. Here are two versions of the `getImage()` method:

■   `public Image getImage(URL url)`

Load the image from the specified URL.

■ `public Image getImage(URL url, String filename)`

Load the image file from the specified file at the given URL.

NOTE

When the `getImage()` method is invoked, it launches a separate thread to load the image; this enables the program to continue while the image is being retrieved.

Once you have an `Image` instance for the image file, you can create an `ImageIcon` using the following method:

```
ImageIcon imageIcon = new ImageIcon(image);
```

You can now convert Examples 9.2 and 9.13 to Java applets and use the `getImage()` method to load the image files.

Using a label as an area for displaying images is simple and convenient, but you don't have much control over how the image is displayed. A more flexible way to display images is to use the `drawImage()` method of the `Graphics` class on a panel.

Here are four versions of the `drawImage()` method:

■ `drawImage(Image img, int x, int y, Color bgcolor, ImageObserver observer)`

Draw the image in the specified location. Its top-left corner is at (`x`, `y`) in the graphics context's coordinate space. Transparent pixels in the image are drawn in the specified color `bgcolor`. The `observer` is the object on which the image is displayed. The image is cut-off if it is larger than the area it is being drawn on.

■ `drawImage(Image img, int x, int y, ImageObserver observer)`

Same as the previous method except that background color is not specified.

■ `drawImage(Image img, int x, int y, int width, int height, ImageObserver observer)`

Draw a scaled version of the image so that it can fill all of the available space in the specified rectangle.

■ `drawImage(Image img, int x, int y, int width, int height, Color bgcolor, ImageObserver observer)`

Same as the previous method except that a solid background color is provided behind the image being drawn.

Example 14.3 Displaying Images in an Applet

The program in this example will display an image in an applet. The image is stored in a file located in the same directory as the applet. The user enters the filename in a text field and displays the image on a panel. Figure 14.1 contains the output of a sample run of the program.

```java
// DisplayImageApplet.java: Display an image on a panel in the applet
package Chapter14;

import java.awt.*;
import java.awt.event.*;
import javax.swing.*;
import javax.swing.border.LineBorder;

public class DisplayImageApplet extends JApplet
  implements ActionListener
{
  // The panel for displaying the image  private
  private ImagePanel imagePanel = new ImagePanel();

  // The text field for entering the name of the image file
  private JTextField jtfFilename = new JTextField(20);

  // The button for displaying the image
  private JButton jbtShow = new JButton("Show Image");

  // Initialize the applet
  public void init()
  {
    // Panel p1 to hold a text field and a button
    JPanel p1 = new JPanel();
    p1.setLayout(new FlowLayout());
    p1.add(new Label("Image Filename"));
    p1.add(jtfFilename);
    p1.add(jbtShow);

    // Place an ImagePanel object and p1 in the applet
    getContentPane().add(imagePanel, BorderLayout.CENTER);
    getContentPane().add(p1, BorderLayout.SOUTH);

    // Set line border on the image panel
    imagePanel.setBorder(new LineBorder(Color.black, 1));

    // Register listener
    jbtShow.addActionListener(this);
    jtfFilename.addActionListener(this);
  }

  // Handle the ActionEvent
  public void actionPerformed(ActionEvent e)
  {
    if ((e.getSource() instanceof JButton) ||
      (e.getSource() instanceof JTextField))
      displayImage();
  }
```

continues

```
        // Display image on the panel
        private void displayImage()
        {
          // Retrieve image
          Image image = getImage(getCodeBase(),
            jtfFilename.getText().trim());

          // Show image in the panel
          imagePanel.showImage(image);
        }
      }

      // Define the panel for showing an image
      class ImagePanel extends JPanel
      {
        // Image filename
        private String filename;

        // Image instance
        private Image image = null;

        // Default constructor
        public ImagePanel()
        {
        }

        // Set image and show it
        public void showImage(Image image)
        {
          this.image = image;
          repaint();
        }

        // Draw image on the panel
        public void paintComponent(Graphics g)
        {
          super.paintComponent(g);

          if (image != null)
            g.drawImage(image, 0, 0,
              getSize().width, getSize().height, this);
        }
      }
```

Example Review

The image is loaded by using the getImage() method from the file that is in the same directory as the applet. The showImage() method defined in ImagePanel sets the image so that it can be drawn by the paintComponent() method.

The statement g.drawImage(image, 0, 0, getSize().width, getSize().height, this) displays the image in the Graphics context g on the ImagePanel object. You can display the image by entering the filename in the text field, then pressing the Enter key or clicking the Show button. The filename you enter must be located in the same directory as the applet.

ImageObserver is an asynchronous update interface for receiving notifications about image information as the image is constructed. Since the Component class implements ImageObserver, ImagePanel (this) is an instance of ImageObserver.

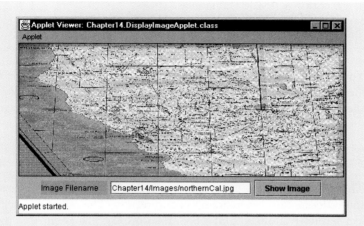

Figure 14.1   *Given the image filename, the applet displays an image.*

Loading Image and Audio Files in Java Applications

The `getImage()` method used in Example 14.3 is defined in the `Applet` class, and thus is only available with the applet. The audio files in Example 14.1 "Incorporating Sound in Applets," are loaded through the URL specified by the `getCodeBase()` method, and thus this method of retrieving audio files is not applicable to Java applications.

When writing Java applications, you can use the `java.lang.Class` class to load an image or an audio file. Whenever the Java VM loads a class or an interface, it creates an instance of a special class named `Class`. The `Class` class provides access to useful information about the class, such as the data fields and method. It also contains the `getResource(filename)` method, which can be used to obtain the URL of a file name in the same directory with the class or in its subdirectory. Thus, this is how you can get the URL of the image or audio file:

```
URL url = this.getClass().getResource(filename);
```

And this is how you can get an audio clip that uses the static method `newAudioClip()` in the `java.applet.Applet`:

```
AudioClip audioClip = Applet.newAudioClip(url);
```

Perhaps you will try to use the `getImage()` method to obtain an `Image` object:

```
Image image = getImage(url);
```

This method would work fine for Java applets, but is not applicable for Java applications. To get an `Image` object from the URL in Java applications, you need to use the `getImage()` method in the `Toolkit` class to create an `Image` object as follows:

```
// Obtain a Toolkit instance
Toolkit toolkit = Toolkit.getDefaultToolkit();

// Get the image from the URL
Image image = toolkit.getImage(url);
```

You used the java.util.Toolkit to get the screen size in Example 8.1, "Creating a Centered Frame with Exit Handling," in order to display the frame in the center of the screen. Another good use of the Toolkit class is to get the image from a URL.

Example 14.4 Using Image and Audio in Applications and in Applets

This program uses the Class class to obtain the URL of the image and audio resource located in the program's class directory. The program enables you to select a country from a combo box, then displays the country's flag image. You can play the selected country's national anthem by clicking the Play Anthem button, as shown in Figure 14.2.

```java
// ResourceLocatorDemo.java: Demonstrate using resource locator to
// load image files and audio files to applets and applications
package Chapter14;

import java.awt.*;
import java.awt.image.*;
import java.awt.event.*;
import javax.swing.*;
import javax.swing.border.*;
import Chapter8.MyFrameWithExitHandling;
import java.net.URL;
import java.applet.*;

public class ResourceLocatorDemo extends JApplet
  implements ActionListener, ItemListener
{
  // Image panel for displaying an image
  private ImagePanel imagePanel = new ImagePanel();

  // Combo box for selecting a country
  private JComboBox jcboCountry = new JComboBox();

  // Button to play an audio
  private JButton jbtPlayAnthem = new JButton("Play Anthem");

  // Selected country
  private String country = "United States of America";

  // Initialize the applet
  public void init()
  {
    // Panel p to hold a label combo box and a button for play audio
    JPanel p = new JPanel();
    p.add(new JLabel("Select a country"));
    p.add(jcboCountry);
    p.add(jbtPlayAnthem);

    // Initialize the combo box
    jcboCountry.addItem("United States of America");
    jcboCountry.addItem("United Kingdom");
```

```
        jcboCountry.addItem("Denmark");
        jcboCountry.addItem("Norway");
        jcboCountry.addItem("China");
        jcboCountry.addItem("India");
        jcboCountry.addItem("Germany");

        // By default, a US flag is displayed
        imagePanel.showImage(createImage("us.gif"));
        imagePanel.setPreferredSize(new Dimension(300, 300));

        // Place p and an image panel in the applet
        getContentPane().add(p, BorderLayout.NORTH);
        getContentPane().add(imagePanel, BorderLayout.CENTER);
        imagePanel.setBorder(new LineBorder(Color.black, 1));

        // Register listener
        jbtPlayAnthem.addActionListener(this);
        jcboCountry.addItemListener(this);
    }

    // Handle ActionEvent
    public void actionPerformed(ActionEvent e)
    {
        // Get the file name
        String filename = null;

        if (country.equals("United States of America"))
            filename = "us.mid";
        else if (country.equals("United Kingdom"))
            filename = "uk.mid";
        else if (country.equals("Denmark"))
            filename = "denmark.mid";
        else if (country.equals("Norway"))
            filename = "norway.mid";
        else if (country.equals("China"))
            filename = "china.mid";
        else if (country.equals("India"))
            filename = "india.mid";
        else if (country.equals("Germany"))
            filename = "germany.mid";

        // Create an audio clip and play it
        createAudioClip(filename).play();
    }

    // Handle ItemEvent
    public void itemStateChanged(ItemEvent e)
    {
        // Get selected country
        country = (String)jcboCountry.getSelectedItem();

        // Get the file name
        String filename = null;

        if (country.equals("United States of America"))
            filename = "us.gif";
        else if (country.equals("United Kingdom"))
            filename = "uk.gif";
        else if (country.equals("Denmark"))
            filename = "denmark.gif";
```

continues

```java
      else if (country.equals("Norway"))
        filename = "norway.gif";
      else if (country.equals("China"))
        filename = "china.gif";
      else if (country.equals("India"))
        filename = "india.gif";
      else if (country.equals("Germany"))
        filename = "germany.gif";

      // Load image from the file and show it on the panel
      imagePanel.showImage(createImage(filename));
    }

    // Create an audio from the specified file
    public AudioClip createAudioClip(String filename)
    {
      // Get the URL for the file name
      URL url = this.getClass().getResource("anthems/" + filename);

      // Return the audio clip
      return Applet.newAudioClip(url);
    }

    // Create an image from the specified file
    public Image createImage(String filename)
    {
      // Get the URL for the file name
      URL url = this.getClass().getResource("images/" + filename);

      // Obtain a Toolkit instance
      Toolkit toolkit = Toolkit.getDefaultToolkit();

      // Return the image
      return toolkit.getImage(url);
    }

    // Main method
    public static void main(String[] args)
    {
      // Create a frame
      MyFrameWithExitHandling frame = new MyFrameWithExitHandling(
        "Flags and Anthems");

      // Create an instance of the applet
      ResourceLocatorDemo applet = new ResourceLocatorDemo();

      // Add the applet instance to the frame
      frame.getContentPane().add(applet, BorderLayout.CENTER);

      // Invoke init() and start()
      applet.init();
      applet.start();

      // Display the frame
      frame.pack();
      frame.setVisible(true);
    }
}
```

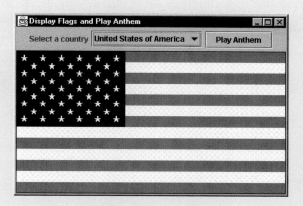

Figure 14.2   *The program displays the flag of the selected country and plays its national anthem.*

Example Review

The program can run as an applet or as an application. Obtaining the URL with the Class class works, not only for standalone applications, but also for Java applets.

The createAudioClip(filename) method obtains the URL instance for the filename and creates an AudioClip for the URL using the newAudioClip static method, a new method introduced in Java 2 that supports playing audio in applications.

Using the getImage() method in the Toolkit class, the createImage(filename) method obtains the URL instance for the filename and creates an Image object.

The program is not efficient if the user repeatedly chooses the same country and plays the same anthem, because a new Image instance is created for every newly selected country, and a new AudioClip instance is created every time an audio is played. To improve efficiency, load the image and audio files once and store them in the memory.

 NOTE
This program uses new features in Java 2 that are not currently supported by Netscape or Internet Explorer. To view the applets in a Web browser, you need to use the Java Plug-In utility.

Displaying a Sequence of Images

In the preceding section, you learned how to display a single image. Now you will learn how to display a sequence of images that will simulate a movie. You can use a control loop to continuously paint the viewing area with different images. As in the clock example, the loop and the paintComponent() method should run on separate threads so that the `paintComponent()` method can execute while the loop controls how the images are drawn. The two images should not be drawn at the same time. The first image should be seen before the next image is drawn.

Example 14.5 Using Image Animation

This example presents a program that will display a sequence of images in order to create a movie. The images are files stored in the `Images` directory that are named **L1.gif**, **L2.gif**, and so on, to **L52.gif**. When you run the program, you will see a phrase entitled "Learning Java" rotate. Figure 14.3 contains the output of a sample run of the program.

```java
// ImageAnimation.java: Display a sequence of images
package Chapter14;

import java.awt.*;
import java.awt.event.*;
import javax.swing.*;
import javax.swing.border.*;

public class ImageAnimation extends JApplet implements ActionListener
{
  private Image imageToDisplay;
  protected Image imageArray[]; // Hold imges
  protected int numOfImages = 52, // Total number of images
                currentImageIndex = 0, // Current image subscript
                sleepTime = 100; // Milliseconds to sleep
  protected int direction = 1; // Image rotating direction

  // Text field for receiving speed
  protected JTextField jtfSpeed = new JTextField(5);

  // Button for requesting reversing direction
  JButton jbtReverse = new JButton("Reverse");

  // Initialize the applet
  public void init()
  {
    // Load the image, the image files are named
    // L1 - L52 in Images directory
    imageArray = new Image[numOfImages];
    for (int i=0; i<imageArray.length; i++ )
    {
      imageArray[i] = getImage(getDocumentBase(),
        "Chapter14/Images/L" + (i+1) + ".gif" );
    }

    // Panel p to hold animation control
    JPanel p = new JPanel();
    p.setLayout(new BorderLayout());
    p.add(new JLabel("Animation speed in millisecond"),
      BorderLayout.WEST);
    p.add(jtfSpeed, BorderLayout.CENTER);
    p.add(jbtReverse, BorderLayout.EAST);

    // Add the image panel and p to the applet
    getContentPane().add(new PlayImage(), BorderLayout.CENTER);
    getContentPane().add(p, BorderLayout.SOUTH);
```

```
    // Register listener
    jtfSpeed.addActionListener(this);
    jbtReverse.addActionListener(this);
}

// Handle ActionEvent
public void actionPerformed(ActionEvent e)
{
  if (e.getSource() == jtfSpeed)
  {
    sleepTime = Integer.parseInt(jtfSpeed.getText());
  }
  else if (e.getSource() == jbtReverse)
  {
    direction = -direction;
  }
}

class PlayImage extends JPanel implements Runnable
{
  private Thread thread = null;

  // Determine the thread status
  protected boolean suspended = false;

  // Constructor
  public PlayImage()
  {
    // Start with the first image
    currentImageIndex = 0;

    // Start the thread
    thread = new Thread(this);
    thread.start();

    // Set line border on the panel
    setBorder(new LineBorder(Color.red, 1));
  }

  public void start()
  {
    resume();
  }

  public void stop()
  {
    suspend();
  }

  public synchronized void resume()
  {
    if (suspended)
    {
      suspended = false;
      notify();
    }
  }
```

continues

```
public synchronized void suspend()
{
  suspended = true;
}

public void destroy()
{
  thread = null;
}

public void run()
{
  while (true)
  {
    imageToDisplay =
      imageArray[currentImageIndex%numOfImages];

    // Make sure currentImageIndex is nonnegative
    if (currentImageIndex == 0) currentImageIndex = numOfImages;
    currentImageIndex = currentImageIndex + direction;
    repaint();

    try
    {
      thread.sleep(sleepTime);
      synchronized (this)
      {
        while (suspended)
          wait();
      }
    }
    catch (InterruptedException ex)
    {
    }
  }
}

// Display an image
public void paintComponent(Graphics g)
{
  super.paintComponent(g);

  if (imageToDisplay != null)
  {
    g.drawImage(imageToDisplay, 0, 0, getSize().width,
      getSize().height, this);
  }
}
}
}
```

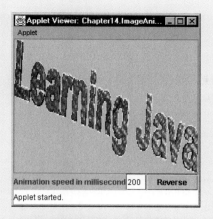

Figure 14.3   *The applet displays a sequence of images.*

Example Review

Fifty-two image files are located in the Images directory, which is a subdirectory of the getDocumentBase() directory. The images in these files are first loaded to imageArray and then painted continuously on the applet on a separate thread.

The image is drawn to occupy the entire applet viewing area in a rectangle. The image is scaled to fill in the area.

The thread for drawing images is created and started in the applet's init() method, and is suspended in the applet's stop() method. Therefore, the images are not displayed when the browser leaves the applet's page. From then on, the thread releases the CPU time when it is not active. When the applet becomes active again, the thread is resumed in the applet's start() method to display images.

continues

You can adjust the sleepTime to control the animation speed by entering a value in milliseconds and clicking the ENTER key for the change to take place.

The display sequence can be reversed by clicking the Reverse button.

You can add a simple function to suspend a running imageThread with a mouse click. You can resume a suspended imageThread with another click. (See Exercises 14.4.)

NOTE

The JComponent class has a property named doubleBuffered. By default, this property is set to true. Double buffering is a technique that reduces animation flickering. It creates a graphics context off-screen and does all the drawings on the off-screen context. When the drawing is complete, it displays the whole context on the real screen. Thus, there is no flickering within the images because all the drawings are displayed at the same time. To see the effect of double buffering, set doubleBuffered property to false. You will see a stunning difference.

Using *MediaTracker*

One problem you would face if you run the preceding example is that the images are only partially displayed when they are first loaded. This occurs because the image has not yet been completely loaded. The problem is particularly annoying when you are downloading the image over a slow modem.

To resolve the problem, Java provides the MediaTracker class to track the status of a number of media objects. The concerned media objects include audio clips as well as images, but currently only images are supported.

You can use MediaTracker to determine whether an image has been completely loaded. To use it, you must first create an instance of MediaTracker for a specific graphics component. The following is an example of creating a MediaTracker:

```
MediaTracker imageTracker = new MediaTracker(this);
```

To enable imageTracker (in order to determine whether the image has been loaded), you need to use the addImage() method to register the image with imageTracker. For example, this statement registers anImage with imageTracker:

```
imageTracker.addImage(Image anImage, int id);
```

The second argument, id, is an integer that controls the priority order in which the images are fetched. Images with a lower id number are loaded in preference to those with a higher id. The id can be used to query imageTracker about the status of the registered image. To query, use the checkID() method. For example, the following method returns true if the image with the id is completely loaded:

```
checkID(id)
```

Otherwise, it returns false.

You can use the waitForID(num) method to force the program to wait until the image registered with the ID num is completely loaded, or you can use the waitForAll() method to wait for all of the registered images to be loaded completely. The following methods block the program until the image is completely loaded:

```
waitForID(int id) throws InterruptedException

waitForAll() throws InterruptedException
```

TIP

To track multiple images as a group, register them with a media tracker using the same ID.

Example 14.6 Using MediaTracker

This example uses MediaTracker to improve upon the preceding example. With MediaTracker, the program's user can make sure that all of the images are fully loaded before they are displayed.

```java
// ImageAnimationUsingMediaTracker.java: Monitor loading images
// using MediaTracker
package Chapter14;

import java.awt.*;
import javax.swing.*;

public class ImageAnimationUsingMediaTracker extends ImageAnimation
{
  private MediaTracker imageTracker = new MediaTracker(this);

  // Initialize the applet
  public void init()
  {
    // Load the image, the image files are named
    // L1 - L52 in Images directory
    imageArray = new Image[numOfImages];
    for (int i=0; i<imageArray.length; i++ )
    {
      imageArray[i] = getImage(getDocumentBase(),
        "Chapter14/Images/L" + (i+1) + ".gif" );

      // Register images with the imageTracker
      imageTracker.addImage(imageArray[i], i);
    }

    // Wait for all the images to be completely loaded
    try
    {
      imageTracker.waitForAll();
    }
    catch (InterruptedException ex)
```

continues

```
        {
          System.out.println(ex);
        }

        // Dispose of imageTracker since it is no longer needed
        imageTracker = null;

        // Panel p to hold animation control
        JPanel p = new JPanel();
        p.setLayout(new BorderLayout());
        p.add(new JLabel("Animation speed in millisecond"),
          BorderLayout.WEST);
        p.add(jtfSpeed, BorderLayout.CENTER);
        p.add(jbtReverse, BorderLayout.EAST);

        // Add the image panel and p to the applet
        getContentPane().add(new PlayImage(), BorderLayout.CENTER);
        getContentPane().add(p, BorderLayout.SOUTH);

        // Register listener
        jtfSpeed.addActionListener(this);
        jbtReverse.addActionListener(this);
    }
}
```

Example Review

The ImageAnimationUsingMediaTracker class extends ImageAnimation, created in Example 14.5. The ImageAnimationUsingMediaTracker uses Media-Tracker to monitor loading images.

The program creates an instance of `MediaTracker`, `imageTracker`, and registers images with `imageTracker` in order to track image loading. The program uses `imageTracker` to ensure that all of the images are completely loaded before they are displayed.

The `waitForAll()` method forces the program to wait for all of the images to be loaded before displaying any of them. Because the program needs to load 52 images, using `waitForAll()` results in a long delay before images are displayed. You should display something while the image is loading to keep the user attentive and/or informed. A simple approach is to use the `showStatus()` method in the `Applet` class to display some information on the Web browser's status bar. Here is an example:

```
showStatus("Please wait while loading images");
```

Put this statement before the `try/catch` block for `waitForAll()` in the program.

The `imageTracker` object is no longer needed after the images are loaded. The statement `imageTracker = null` notifies the garbage collector of the Java runtime system to reclaim the memory space previously occupied by the `imageTracker` object.

You can rewrite this example to enable it to run as an application. See Exercise 14.4.

Chapter Summary

In this chapter, you learned how to play audio and display images in Java multimedia programming. You also learned how to use the `Class` class to load image and audio files and the media tracking mechanism to track loading images.

Audio and images files are accessible through a URL. The `getDocumentBase()` method returns the URL of the HTML file that invokes the applet. The `getCodeBase()` method returns the URL of the applet. The `Class` class can be used to obtain the URL of an image or audio file for Java applications. Since this approach also works for Java applets, it is a good idea to develop programs that can run both as applications and as applets.

The `MediaTracker` class is used to determine whether one image or all of the images are completely loaded. The `MediaTracker` obtains this information in order to ensure that the images will be displayed fully.

Chapter Review

14.1. What types of audio files are used in Java?

14.2. How do you get an audio file? How do you play, repeatedly play, and stop an audio clip?

14.3. The `getAudioClip()` method is defined in the `Applet` class. If you want to use audio in Java applications, what options do you have?

14.4. What is the difference between `getDocumentBase()` and `getCodeBase()`?

14.5. What is the difference between the `getImage()` method in the `Applet` class and the `getImage()` method in the `Toolkit` class?

14.6. How do you get the URL of an image or audio file in Java applications?

14.7. Describe the `drawImage()` method in the `Graphics` class.

14.8. Can you create image icons and use the `setIcon()` method to set an icon in a `JLabel` instance in Java applets?

14.9. Describe the differences between using displaying images in a `JLabel` instance and in a `JPanel` instance.

14.10. How do you get an audio clip in Java applications?

14.11. Why do you use `MediaTracker`? How do you add images to a media tracker? How do you know that an image or all of the images are completely loaded? Can you assign images the same ID in order to register them with a media tracker?

Programming Exercises

14.1. Write an applet to meet the following requirements:

- Get an audio file from the URL of the HTML base code.

- Place three buttons labeled Play, Loop, and Stop, as shown in Figure 14.4.

- If you click the Play button, the audio file is played once. If you click the Loop button, the audio file keeps playing repeatedly. If you click the Stop button, the playing stops.

- The applet can run as an application.

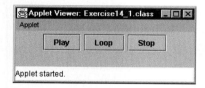

Figure 14.4   *Click Play to play an audio clip once, click Loop to play an audio repeatedly, and click Stop to terminate playing.*

14.2. Modify the elevator program in the fifth exercise in the "Programming Exercises" section of Chapter 13, "Multithreading," by adding sound to the program. When the elevator stops on a floor, announce which floor it is on.

14.3. Sometimes you repaint the entire viewing area on a panel but only a tiny portion of the viewing area is changed. You can improve the performance by only repainting the affected area. To do so, you should not invoke `super.paintComponent(g)` when repainting the panel. Invoking `super.paintComponent(g)` causes the entire viewing area to be cleared. Use this approach to write an applet to display the temperatures of each hour during the last 24 hours in a histogram. Suppose that the temperatures between 50 and 90 degrees Fahrenheit are obtained randomly and are updated every hour. The temperature of the current hour needs to be redisplayed, while others remain unchanged. Use a unique color to highlight the temperature for the current hour (see Figure 14.5).

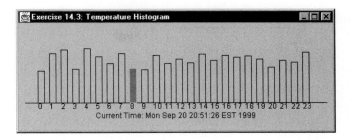

Figure 14.5   *The histogram displays the average temperature of every hour in the last 24 hours.*

14.4. Rewrite Example 14.6, "Using MediaTracker," to add the following new functions:

■ The animation is suspended when the mouse is pressed and resumed when the mouse is released. To implement this feature, add the code in the `PlayImage` inner class of the `ImageAnimation` class to handle the mouse event for `mousePressed` and `mouseReleased` actions.

■ Sound is incorporated into the applet so that it is played while images are displayed.

■ Enable the applet to run standalone.

14.5. Write an applet that will display a digital clock with a large display panel that shows hour, minute, and second. The clock should allow the user to set an alarm. Figure 14.6 shows an example of such a clock. To turn on the alarm, check the Alarm check box. To specify alarm time, click the Set Alarm button to display a new frame, as shown in Figure 14.7. You can set the alarm time in the frame. Enable the applet to run standalone.

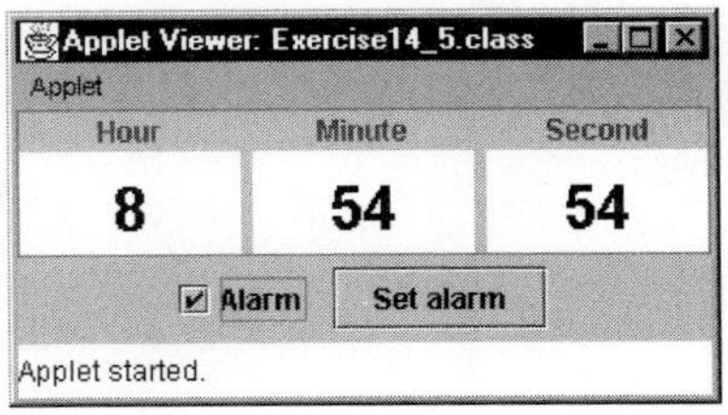

Figure 14.6   *The program displays current hour, minute, and second and enables you to set an alarm.*

Figure 14.7   *You can set alarm time by specifying hour, minute, and second.*

14.6. Create animation using the applet (see Figure 14.8) to meet the following requirements:

■ Allow the user to specify the animation speed. The user can enter the speed in a text field.

■ Get the number of frames and the image filename prefix from the user. For example, if the user enters **n** for the number of the frames and **T** for the image prefix, then the files are **T1**, **T2**, and so on, to **Tn**. Assume that the images are stored in the Images directory, a subdirectory of the applet's directory.

■ Allow the user to specify an audio filename. The audio file is stored in the same directory as the applet. The sound is played while the animation runs.

■ Enable the applet to run standalone.

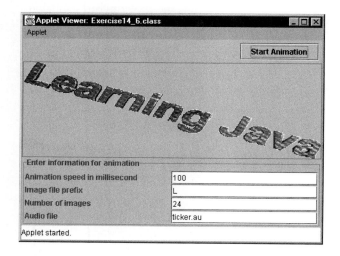

Figure 14.8   *This applet lets the user select image files, audio file, and animation speed.*

14.7. Write an applet that will display a sequence of images for a single image in different sizes. Initially, the viewing area for the image is of 300 width and 300 height. Your program should continuously shrink the viewing area by 10 in width and 10 in height until the viewing area reaches a width of 50 and a height of 50. At that point, the viewing area should continuously enlarge by 1 in width and 1 in height until it reaches a width of 300 and a height of 300. The viewing area should shrink and enlarge (alternately) to create animation for the single image. Enable the applet to run standalone.

14.8. Suppose that the instructor in a Java class asks the students to each write a short paragraph stating their personal objectives in taking the course. Write an applet that introduces the students, giving their photos, names, and paragraphs (see Figure 14.9), along with audio that reads the paragraphs. Your applet should present all of the students, one after the other.

Suppose there are a total of 10 students in the class. Assume that the audio files, named **a1.au**, **a2.au**, and so on, up to **a10.au**, are stored in a subdirectory named `audio` in the applet's directory, and the photo image files named **photo1.gif**, **photo2.gif**, and so on, up to **photo10.gif**, are stored in a subdirectory named `photo` in the applet's directory. Assume that the name and paragraph of each student is passed from the HTML. Here is an example for student **a1**:

```
<param name= "paragraph1"
  value="I am taking the class because I want to
  learn to write cool programs like this!">
<param name= "name1"
  value = "Michael Liang">
```

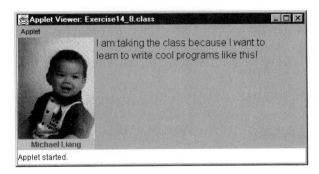

Figure 14.9   *This applet shows the photo, name, and paragraph of each student, one after the other, and reads the paragraph that is currently shown.*

14.9. Rewrite Example 14.4, "Using Image and Audio in Applications and in Applets." Use the resource bundle to retrieve image and audio files. (Hints: When a new country is selected, set an appropriate locale for it. Your program looks for the flag and audio file from the resource file for the corresponding locale.

CHAPTER 15

INPUT AND OUTPUT

Objectives

- Understand input and output streams and learn how to create them.
- Discover the uses of byte and character streams.
- Know how to read from or write to external files using file streams.
- Employ data streams for cross-platform data format compatibility.
- Identify print streams and use them to output data of primitive types in text format.
- Know how to parse text files using `StreamTokenizer`.
- Understand how to use `RandomAccessFile` for both read and write.
- Use `JFileChooser` to display open and save file dialog boxes.
- Become familiar with interactive I/O for input and output on the console.

Introduction

In earlier chapters, you used input and output only on the console. In Chapter 2, "Java Building Elements," you created the `MyInput` class and used `MyInput.readInt()` and `MyInput.readDouble()` to receive data from the console. You used `System.out.print()` to display output on the console. In this chapter, you will learn about many other forms of input and output as well as how these methods work.

In Java, all I/Os are handled in streams. A *stream* is an abstraction of the continuous one-way flow of data. Imagine a swimming pool with pipes that connect it to another pool. Let's consider the water in the first pool as the data and the water in the second pool as your program. The flow of water through the pipes is called a *stream*. If you want input, just open the valve to let water out of the data pool and into the program pool. If you want output, just open the valve to let water out of the program pool and into the data pool.

It's a very simple concept, and a very efficient one. Since Java streams can be applied to any source of data, it is just as easy to input from a keyboard or an output to a console as it is to input from a file or an output to a file. Figure 15.1 shows input and output streams between a program and an external file. Java streams are used liberally. You can even have input and output streams between two programs.

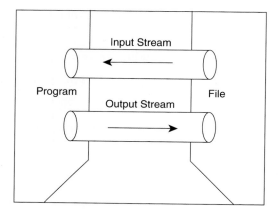

Figure 15.1 *The program receives data through the input stream and sends data through the output stream.*

In general, all streams except random access file streams flow in only one direction; therefore, if you want to input and output, you need two separate stream objects. In Java, streams can be *layered*—that is, connected to one another in pipeline fashion. The output of one stream becomes the input of another stream.

This layering capability makes it possible to filter data along the pipeline of streams so that you can get data in whatever format is desired. For instance, suppose you want to get integers from an external file. You can use a file input stream to get raw data in binary format, then use a data input stream to extract integers from the output of the input stream.

Streams are objects. Stream objects have methods that read and write data and methods that do other useful things, such as flushing the stream, closing the stream, and counting the number of bytes in the stream.

Stream Classes

Java offers many stream classes for processing all kinds of data. Figures 15.2 and 15.3 show the hierarchical relationship of these classes.

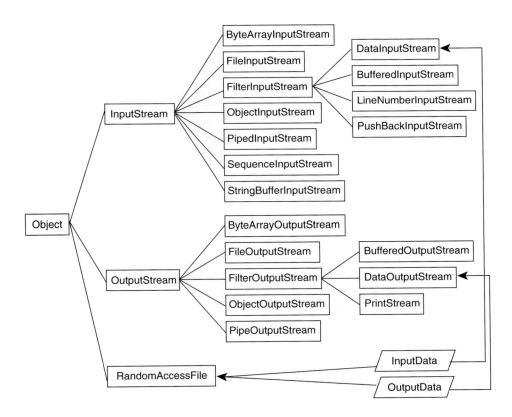

Figure 15.2   InputStream, OutputStream, RandomAccessFile, *and their subclasses deal with streams of bytes.*

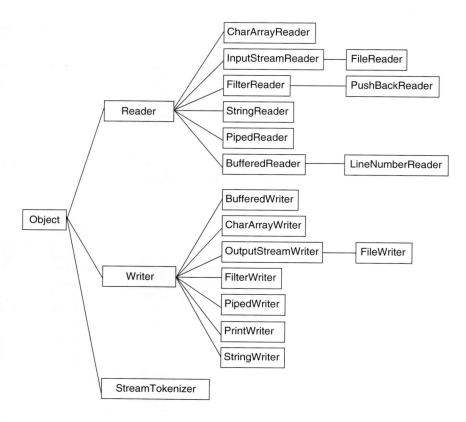

Figure 15.3   `Reader`, `Writer`, `StreamTokenizer`, *and their subclasses are concerned with streams of characters.*

Stream classes can be categorized into two types: *byte streams* and *character streams.* The `InputStream/OutputStream` class is the root of all byte stream classes, and the `Reader/Writer` class is the root of all character stream classes. The subclasses of `InputStream/OutputStream` are analogous to the subclasses of `Reader/Writer`.

Many of these subclasses have similar method signatures, and often you can use them in the same way. The `RandomAccessFile` class extends `Object` and implements the `InputData` and `OutputData` interfaces. This class can be used to open a file that allows both reading and writing. The `StreamTokenizer` class that extends `Object` can be used for parsing text files.

InputStream and Reader

The abstract `InputStream` and `Reader` classes, extending `Object`, are the base classes for all of the input streams of bytes and characters, respectively. These classes and their subclasses are very similar, except that `InputStream` uses bytes for its fundamental unit of information, and `Reader` uses characters. `InputStream` and `Reader` have many methods in common that have identical signatures. Although these methods have similar functionality, `InputStream` is designed to read bytes, and `Reader` is designed to read characters.

The following methods, which are defined in `InputStream`, are often useful.

■ `public abstract int read() throws IOException`

This method reads the next byte and returns its value. The value of the byte is returned as an `int` in the range from 0 to 255. At the end of the stream, it returns `-1`. This method blocks the program from executing until input data is available, the end of the stream is detected, or an exception is thrown. A subclass of `InputStream` must provide an implementation of this method.

■ `public int read(byte[] b) throws IOException`

This method reads `b.length` bytes into array `b`, returns `b.length` if the number of available bytes is more than `b.length`, returns the number of bytes read if the number of available bytes is less than `b.length`, and returns `-1` at the end of the stream.

■ `public void close() throws IOException`

This method closes the input stream.

■ `public void int available() throws IOException`

This method returns the number of bytes that can be read from this input stream without blocking.

■ `public long skip(long n) throws IOException`

This method skips over and discards `n` bytes of data from this input stream. The actual number of bytes skipped is returned.

NOTE

The `read()` method reads a byte from the stream. If no data are available, it blocks the thread from executing the next statement. The thread that invokes the `read()` method is suspended until the data become available.

The `Reader` class contains all of the methods listed previously except `available()`. These methods have the same functionality in `Reader` as in `InputStream`, but they are subject to character stream interpretation. For example, `read()` returns an integer in the range from 0 to 16,383, which represents a Unicode character.

OutputStream and *Writer*

Like `InputStream` and `Reader`, `OutputStream` and `Writer` are counterparts. They are the base classes for all output streams of bytes and characters, respectively. The following instance methods are in both `OutputStream` and `Writer`.

■ `public abstract void write(int b) throws IOException`

This method writes a byte (for `OutputStream`) or a character (for `Writer`).

- ■ `public void write(byte[] b) throws IOException`

  This method writes all bytes in the array b to the output stream (for `OutputStream`) or characters in the array of characters (for `Writer`).

- ■ `public void close() throws IOException`

  This method closes the output stream.

- ■ `public void flush() throws IOException`

  This method flushes the output stream (that is, it sends any buffered data in the stream to their destination).

NOTE

In JDK 1.02, the methods in `OutputStream` do not throw exceptions. But all of the methods in the `OutputStream` class throw an `IOException` in JDK 1.1 and JDK 1.2.

Processing External Files

File streams must be used to read from or write to a disk file. You can use `FileInputStream` or `FileOutputStream` for byte streams, and `FileReader` or `FileWriter` for character streams. To create a file stream, you can use the following constructors:

```
public FileInputStream(String fileNameString)
public FileOutputStream(String fileNameString)
public FileReader(String fileNameString)
public FileWriter(String fileNameString)
```

For example, the following statements create `infile` and `outfile` streams for the input file **in.dat** and the output file **out.dat**, respectively:

```
FileInputStream infile = new FileInputStream("in.dat");
FileOutputStream outfile = new FileOutputStream("out.dat");
```

Note that whenever a filename or a path is used, it is assumed that the host's file-naming conventions are used. For example, a filename with a path on Windows could be **c:\data\in.dat**. If it had a path on UNIX, the same file might be **/username/data/in.dat**.

You can also use a file object to construct a file stream. Consider the following statement:

```
FileInputStream infile = new FileInputStream(new File("in.dat"));
```

The `File` class is intended to provide an abstraction that deals with most of the machine-dependent complexities of files and path names in a machine-independent fashion.

An abstract method, such as `read(byte b)` in `InputStream`, is implemented in `FileInputStream`, and the abstract `write(int b)` method in the `OutputStream` class is implemented in `FileOutputStream`.

Example 15.1 Processing External Files

This example gives a program that uses FileInputStream and FileOutputStream to copy files. The user needs to provide a source file and a target file as command-line arguments. The program copies the source file to the target file and displays the number of bytes in the file. The output of the sample run for the program is shown in Figure 15.4.

```java
// CopyFileUsingByteStream.java: Copy files
package Chapter15;

import java.io.*;

public class CopyFileUsingByteStream
{
  // Main method: args[0] for sourcefile and args[1] for target file
  public static void main(String[] args)
  {
    // Declare input and output file streams
    FileInputStream fis = null;
    FileOutputStream fos = null;

    // Check usage
    if (args.length !=2)
    {
      System.out.println(
        "Usage: java CopyFileUsingByteStream fromfile tofile");
      System.exit(0);
    }

    try
    {
      // Create file input stream
      fis = new FileInputStream(new File(args[0]));

      // Create file output stream if the file does not exist
      File outFile = new File(args[1]);
      if (outFile.exists())
      {
        System.out.println("file " + args[1] + " already exists");
        return;
      }
      else
        fos = new FileOutputStream(args[1]);

      // Display the file size
      System.out.println("The file " + args[0] + " has "+
        fis.available() + " bytes");

      // Continuously read a byte from fis and write it to fos
      int r;
      while ((r = fis.read()) != -1)
        fos.write((byte)r);
    }
    catch (FileNotFoundException ex)
    {
      System.out.println("File not found: " + args[0]);
    }
    catch (IOException ex)
    {
```

continues

```
          System.out.println(ex.getMessage());
        }
        finally
        {
          try
          {
            // Close files
            if (fis != null) fis.close();
            if (fos != null) fos.close();
          }
          catch (IOException ex)
          {
            System.out.println(ex);
          }
        }
      }
    }
```

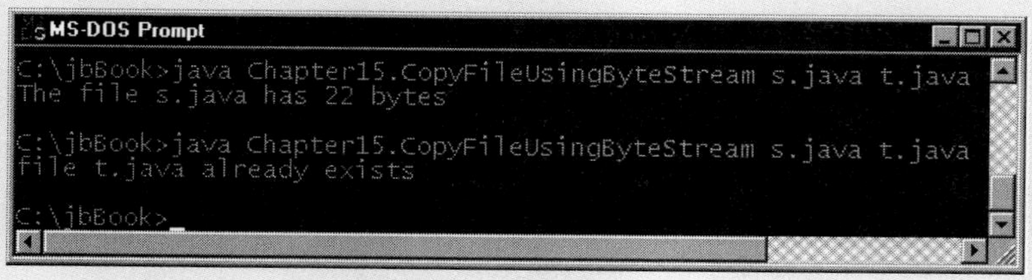

```
MS-DOS Prompt                                         _ □ ✕
C:\jbBook>java Chapter15.CopyFileUsingByteStream s.java t.java
The file s.java has 22 bytes

C:\jbBook>java Chapter15.CopyFileUsingByteStream s.java t.java
file t.java already exists

C:\jbBook>_
```

Figure 15.4   *The program copies a file using byte streams.*

Example Review

The program creates the `fis` and `fos` streams for the input file `args[0]` and the output file `args[1]` (see Figure 15.5).

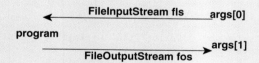

Figure 15.5   *The program uses* `FileInputStream` *to read data from the file and* `FileOutput-` `Stream` *to write data to the file.*

If the input file `args[0]` does not exist, `new FileInputStream(new File(args[0]))` will raise the exception `FileNotFoundException`. By contrast, `new FileOutput-Stream(new File(args[1]))` will always create a file output stream, whether or not the file `args[1]` exists.

To avoid writing in an existing file, the program uses the `exists()` method in the `File` class to determine whether `args[1]` exists. If the file already exists, the user would be notified; otherwise, the file would be created.

The program continuously reads a byte from the `fis` stream and sends it to the `fos` stream until all of the bytes have been read. (The condition (`fis.read() == -1`) signifies the end of a file.)

The program closes any open file streams in the `finally` clause. The statements in the `finally` clause are always executed, whether or not exceptions occur.

The program could be rewritten using `FileReader` and `FileWriter`. The new program would be almost exactly the same. (See Exercise 15.1.)

 TIP
Always close the files when they are not needed. In some cases, programming errors will occur if they are not closed. Files are usually closed in the `finally` clause.

Array Streams

Streams were first used for file input/output in the C language, but Java streams are not limited to this function. You can use array streams to read and write bytes or characters from arrays. These streams include `ByteArrayInputStream`, `CharArrayReader`, `ByteArrayOutputStream`, and `CharArrayWriter`. You can use the following constructors to create array streams:

```
public ByteArrayInputStream(byte[] byteArray)

public ByteArrayOutputStream(byte[] byteArray)

public ByteArrayReader(char[] byteArray)

public ByteArrayWriter(char[] byteArray)
```

For example, the following statements create the byte array input stream `bai` and the character array read stream `car`:

```
byte[] bArray = new byte[2048];
char[] cArray =  new char[2048];
ByteArrayInputStream bai = new ByteArrayInputStream(bArray);
ByteArrayReader car = new ByteArrayReader(cArray);
```

You could now process the streams just as you would process file streams. For example, `bai.read()` reads a byte, and `car.read()` reads a character from the array streams.

Filter Streams

Filter streams are defined as streams that filter bytes or characters for some purpose. The basic input stream provides a read method that can only be used for reading bytes or characters. If you want to read integers, doubles, or strings, you can use a filter class to wrap an input stream. Using a filter class enables you to read integers, doubles, and strings instead of bytes and characters.

When you need to process primitive numeric types, use `FilterInputStream` and `FilterOutputStream` to filter bytes. When you need to process strings, use

BufferedReader and PushbackReader to filter characters. FilterInputStream and FilterOutputStream are abstract classes; their subclasses (listed in Tables 15.1 and 15.2) are often used.

TABLE 15.1 *FilterInputStream* Subclasses

Subclass	Class Usage
DataInputStream	Handles binary formats of all the primitive data types.
BufferedInputStream	Gets data from the buffer and then reads it from the stream if necessary.
LineNumberInputStream	Keeps track of how many lines are read.
PushbackInputStream	Allows single-byte look-ahead. After the byte is looked at, this stream pushes it back to the stream so that the next read can read it.

TABLE 15.2 *FilterOutputStream* Subclasses

Subclass	Class Usage
DataOutputStream	Outputs the binary format of all of the primitive types, which is useful if another program uses the output.
BufferedOutputStream	Outputs to the buffer first and then to the stream if necessary. Programmers can call the flush() method to write the buffer to the stream.
PrintStream	Outputs the Unicode format of all of the primitive types, which is useful if the format is output to the console.

Data Streams

Data streams (DataInputStream and DataOutputStream) read and write Java primitive types in a machine-independent fashion, which enables you to write a data file on one machine and read it on another machine that has a different operating system or file structure.

DataInputStream extends FilterInputStream and implements the DataInput interface. DataOutputStream extends FilterOutputStream and implements the DataOutput interface. The DataInput and DataOutput interfaces are also implemented by the RandomAccessFile class, which is discussed in the section "Random Access Files," later in this chapter.

The following methods are defined in the DataInput interface:

```
public int readByte() throws IOException

public int readShort() throws IOException
```

```
public int readInt() throws IOException

public int readLong() throws IOException

public float readFloat() throws IOException

public double readDouble() throws IOException

public char readChar() throws IOException

public boolean readBoolean() throws IOException

public String readUTF() throws IOException
```

The following methods are defined in the DataOutput interface:

```
public void writeByte(byte b) throws IOException

public void writeShort(short s) throws IOException

public void writeInt(int i) throws IOException

public void writeLong(long l) throws IOException

public void writeFloat(float f) throws IOException

public void writeDouble(double d) throws IOException

public void writeChar(char c) throws IOException

public void writeBoolean(boolean b) throws IOException

public void writeBytes(String l) throws IOException

public void writeChars(String l) throws IOException

public void writeUTF(String l) throws IOException
```

Data streams are often used as wrappers on existing input and output streams to filter data in the original stream.

Here are the data Input and Output stream constructors:

```
public DataInputStream(InputStream instream)
public DataOutputStream(OutputStream outstream)
```

For example, the following statements create data streams. The first statement creates an input stream for file **in.dat**; the second statement creates an output stream for file **out.dat**.

```
DataInputStream infile =
  new DataInputStream(new FileInputStream("in.dat"));
DataOutputStream outfile =
  new DataOutputStream(new FileOutputStream("out.dat"));
```

Example 15.2 Using Data Streams

This example presents a program that creates 10 random integers, stores them in a data file, retrieves data from the file, and then displays the integers on the console. Figure 15.6 contains the output of a sample run of the program.

The program uses a temporary file to store data. The temporary file is named **mytemp.dat**.

```java
// TestDataStreams.java: Create a file, store it in binary form, and
// display it on the console
package Chapter15;

import java.io.*;

public class TestDataStreams
{
  // Main method
  public static void main(String[] args)
  {
    // Declare data input and output streams
    DataInputStream dis = null;
    DataOutputStream dos = null;

    // Construct a temp file
    File tempFile = new File("mytemp.dat");

    // Check if the temp file exists
    if (tempFile.exists())
    {
      System.out.println("The file mytemp.dat already exists,"
        +" delete it, rerun the program");
      System.exit(0);
    }

    // Write data
    try
    {
      // Create data output stream for tempFile
      dos = new DataOutputStream(new
        FileOutputStream(tempFile));
      for (int i=0; i<10; i++)
        dos.writeInt((int)(Math.random()*1000));
    }
    catch (IOException ex)
    {
      System.out.println(ex.getMessage());
    }
    finally
    {
      try
      {
        // Close files
        if (dos != null) dos.close();
      }
      catch (IOException ex)
      {
      }
    }
```

```
        // Read data
        try
        {
          // Create data input stream
          dis = new DataInputStream(new FileInputStream(tempFile));
          for (int i=0; i<10; i++)
            System.out.print("  "+dis.readInt());
        }
        catch (FileNotFoundException ex)
        {
          System.out.println("File not found");
        }
        catch (IOException ex)
        {
          System.out.println(ex.getMessage());
        }
        finally
        {
          try
          {
            // Close files
            if (dis != null) dis.close();
          }
          catch (IOException ex)
          {
            System.out.println(ex);
          }
        }
      }
    }
```

Figure 15.6   *The program creates 10 random numbers and stores them in a file named mytemp.dat. It then reads the data from the file and displays them on the console.*

Example Review

The program creates a DataInputStream object dis wrapped on FileInputStream and creates a DataOutputStream object dos wrapped on FileOutputStream (see Figure 15.7).

continues

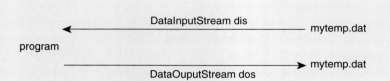

Figure 15.7   *The program uses* DataOutputStream *to write data to a file and* DataInput- Stream *to read the data from the file.*

The program first creates **mytemp.dat** if it does not exist. Then it uses the data output stream to write 10 random integers into **mytemp.dat** and closes the stream.

The program creates a data input stream for **mytemp.dat**, reads integers from it, and displays it.

▬ **NOTE**

The data stored in **mytemp.dat** are in binary format, which is machine-independent and portable. If you need to transport data between different systems, use data input and data output streams.

Print Streams

Since a data output stream outputs a binary representation of data, you cannot view its contents as text. As shown in Figure 15.6, strange symbols are displayed when you attempt to view the **mytemp.dat** file on the console. In Java, you can use print streams to output data into files. These files can be viewed as text.

The PrintStream and PrintWriter classes provide this functionality. You have already used System.out.println() to display data on the console. An instance of PrintStream, out, is defined in the java.lang.System class. PrintStream and PrintWriter have similar method interfaces. PrintStream is deprecated in JDK 1.1, but since the System.out standard output stream is not, you can continue to use it for output to the console.

The constructors for PrintWriter are the following:

```
public PrintWriter(Writer out)

public PrintWriter(Writer out, boolean autoFlush)

public PrintWriter(OutputStream out)

public PrintWriter(OutputStream out, boolean autoFlush)
```

The methods in `PrintWriter` are as follows:

```
public void print(Object o)

public void print(String s)

public void print(char c)

public void print(char[] cArray)

public void print(int i)

public void print(long l)

public void print(float f)

public void print(double d)

public void print(boolean b)
```

You can replace `print` with `println`. The `println()` method, which prints the object, is followed by a new line. When an object is passed to `print` or `println`, the object's `toString()` method converts it to a `String` object.

Example 15.3 Using Print Streams

The program in this example creates 10 random integers and stores them in a text data file. The file can be viewed on the console by using an OS command, such as type on Windows or cat on UNIX. Figure 15.8 contains the output of a sample run of the program.

```java
// TestPrintWriters.java: Create a text file using PrintWriter
package Chapter15;

import java.io.*;

public class TestPrintWriters
{
  // Main method: args[0] is the output file
  public static void main(String[] args)
  {
    // Declare print stream
    PrintWriter pw = null;

    // Check usage
    if (args.length != 1)
    {
      System.out.println("Usage: java TestPrintWriters file");
      System.exit(0);
    }

    File tempFile = new File(args[0]);

    if (tempFile.exists())
    {
      System.out.println("The file " + args[0] +
```

continues

```
                    " already exists, delete it, rerun the program");
                  System.exit(0);
                }

                // Write data
                try
                {
                  // Create data output stream for tempFile
                  pw = new PrintWriter(new FileOutputStream(tempFile), true);
                  for (int i=0; i<10; i++)
                    pw.print(" "+(int)(Math.random()*1000));
                }
                catch (IOException ex)
                {
                  System.out.println(ex.getMessage());
                }
                finally
                {
                  // Close files
                  if (pw != null) pw.close();
                }
              }
            }
```

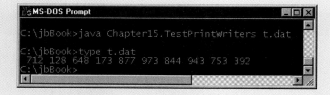

Figure 15.8   *The program creates 10 random numbers and stores them in a text file.*

Example Review

The program creates a print stream `pw` of `PrintWriter`—wrapped in `FileOutputStream`—for output data that are in text format (see Figure 15.9).

Figure 15.9   *The program uses the `PrintWriter` stream, which is wrapped in `FileOutputStream`, to write data in text format.*

The program first creates the file **args[0]** if that file does not already exist. Then it writes 10 random integers into **args[0]** by using the data output stream and closes the stream.

The output in **args[0]** is in text format. The data can be seen by using the `type` command in DOS.

Buffered Streams

Java speeds input and output by means of buffered streams that reduce the number of reads and writes. Buffered streams employ a buffered array of bytes or characters that acts as a cache. In the case of input, the array reads a chunk of bytes or characters into the buffer before the individual bytes or characters are read. In the case of output, the array accumulates a block of bytes or characters before writing the entire block to the output stream.

The use of buffered streams makes it possible for you to read and write a chunk of bytes or characters at a time instead of a single byte or character. The `BufferedInputStream`, `BufferedOutputStream`, `BufferedReader`, and `BufferedWriter` classes provide this functionality.

The following constructors are used to create a buffered stream:

```
public BufferedInputStream(InputStream in)

public BufferedInputStream(InputStream in, int bufferSize)

public BufferedOutputStream(OutputStream in)

public BufferedOutputStream(OutputStream in, int bufferSize)

public BufferedReader(Reader in)

public BufferedReader(Reader in, int bufferSize)

public BufferedWriter(Writer out)

public BufferedWriter(Writer out, int bufferSize)
```

If no buffer size is specified, the default size is 512 bytes or characters. A buffered input stream reads as much data into its buffer as possible in a single read call. By contrast, a buffered output stream calls the write method only when its buffer fills up or when the `flush()` method is called.

The buffered stream classes inherit methods from their superclasses. In addition to using the methods from their superclasses, `BufferedReader` has a `readLine()` method to read a line.

Example 15.4 Displaying a File in a Text Area

This example presents a program that views a file in a text area. When the user enters a filename in a text field and clicks the View button, the file is displayed in a text area. Figure 15.10 contains the output of a sample run of the program.

```
// ViewFile.java: Read a text file and store it in a text area
package Chapter15;

import java.awt.*;
import java.awt.event.*;
```

continues

```java
import java.io.*;
import javax.swing.*;

public class ViewFile extends Chapter8.MyFrameWithExitHandling
  implements ActionListener
{
  // Button to view view
  private JButton jbtView = new JButton("View");

  // Text field to receive file name
  private JTextField jtf = new JTextField(12);

  // Text area to display file
  private JTextArea jta = new JTextArea();

  // Main method
  public static void main(String[] args)
  {
    ViewFile frame = new ViewFile();
    frame.setTitle("View File");
    frame.setSize(400, 300);
    frame.setVisible(true);
  }

  // Constructor
  public ViewFile()
  {
    // Panel p to hold a label, a text field, and a button
    Panel p = new Panel();
    p.setLayout(new BorderLayout());
    p.add(new Label("Filename"), BorderLayout.WEST);
    p.add(jtf, BorderLayout.CENTER);
    jtf.setBackground(Color.yellow);
    jtf.setForeground(Color.red);
    p.add(jbtView, BorderLayout.EAST);

    // Add jta to a scroll pane
    JScrollPane jsp = new JScrollPane(jta);

    // Add jsp and p to the frame
    getContentPane().add(jsp, BorderLayout.CENTER);
    getContentPane().add(p, BorderLayout.SOUTH);

    // Register listener
    jbtView.addActionListener(this);
  }

  // Handle the "View" button
  public void actionPerformed(ActionEvent e)
  {
    if (e.getSource() == jbtView)
      showFile();
  }

  // Display the file in the text area
  private void showFile()
  {
    // Use a BufferedStream to read text from the file
    BufferedReader infile = null;

    // Get file name from the text field
    String filename = jtf.getText().trim();

    String inLine;
```

```
      try
      {
        // Create a buffered stream
        infile = new BufferedReader(new FileReader(filename));

        // Read a line
        inLine = infile.readLine();

        boolean firstLine = true;

        // Append the line to the text area
        while (inLine != null)
        {
          if (firstLine)
          {
            firstLine = false;
            jta.append(inLine);
          }
          else
          {
            jta.append("\n" + inLine);
          }

          inLine = infile.readLine();
        }
      }
      catch (FileNotFoundException ex)
      {
        System.out.println("File not found: " + filename);
      }
      catch (IOException ex)
      {
        System.out.println(ex.getMessage());
      }
      finally
      {
        try
        {
          if (infile != null) infile.close();
        }
        catch (IOException ex)
        {
          System.out.println(ex.getMessage());
        }
      }
    }
  }
}
```

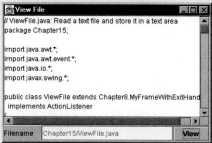

Figure 15.10   *The program displays the specified file in the text area.*

continues

Example Review

The user enters a filename into the Filename text field. When the View button is pressed, the program gets the input filename from the text field, then creates a data input stream. The data is read one line at a time and appended to the text area for display.

The program uses a `BufferedReader` stream to read lines from a buffer. Instead of `BufferedReader` and `Reader` classes, the `BufferedInputStream` and `FileInputStream` can also be used in this example.

You are encouraged to rewrite the program without using buffers and then compare the performance of the two programs. You will see the improvement in performance obtained from using buffers when reading from a large file.

TIP

Typical physical input and output involving I/O devices are extremely slow compared with CPU processing speeds, so you should use buffered input/output streams to improve performance.

Parsing Text Files

It is sometimes necessary to process a text file. The Java source file is an example of a text file. The compiler reads the source file and translates it into bytecode, which is a binary file. Java provides the `StreamTokenizer` class so that you can take an input stream and parse it into words, which are known as *tokens*. The tokens are read one at a time.

To construct an instance of `StreamTokenizer`, you can use `StreamTokenizer(Reader is)` on a given character input stream. The `StreamTokenizer` class contains useful constants, which are listed in the Table 15.3.

TABLE 15.3   *StreamTokenizer* Constants

Constant	Description
TT_WORD	The token is a word.
TT_NUMBER	The token is a number.
TT_EOL	The end of the line has been read.
TT_EOF	The end of the file has been read.

The `StreamTokenizer` class also contains some useful variables, which are listed in Table 15.4.

TABLE 15.4   *StreamTokenizer* Variables

Variable	Description
int ttype	Contains the current token type, which matches one of the constants listed previously.
double nval	Contains the value of the current token if it is a number.
String sval	Contains a string that gives the characters of the current token if it is a word.

Typically, you can use the nextToken() method to retrieve tokens one by one in a loop until TT_EOF is returned. The following method parses the next token from the input stream of a StreamTokenizer:

```
public int nextToken() throws IOException
```

The type of the next token is returned in the ttype field. If ttype == TT_WORD, the token is stored in sval; if ttype == TT_NUMBER, the token is stored in nval.

Example 15.5 Using *StreamTokenizer*

The program in this example demonstrates parsing text files. The program reads a text file containing students' exam scores. Each record in the input file consists of a student's name, two midterm exam scores, and a final exam score. The program reads the fields for each record, computes the total score, and stores the result in a new file. The formula for computing the total score is as follows:

```
total score = midterm1*30% + midterm2*30% + final*40%;
```

Each record in the output file consists of a student's name and total score. Figure 15.11 contains the output of a sample run of the program.

```java
// ParsingTextFile.java: Process text file using StreamTokenizer
package Chapter15;

import java.io.*;

public class ParsingTextFile
{
  // Main method
  public static void main(String[] args)
  {
    // Declare file reader and writer streams
    FileReader frs = null;
    FileWriter fws = null;

    // Declare streamTokenizer
    StreamTokenizer in = null;

    // Declare a print stream
    PrintWriter out = null;
```

continues

```
                    // For input file fields: student name, midterm1,
                    // midterm2, and final exam score
                    String sname = null;
                    double midterm1 = 0;
                    double midterm2 = 0;
                    double finalScore = 0;

                    // Computed total score
                    double total = 0;

                    try
                    {
                      // Create file input and output streams
                      frs = new FileReader("in.dat");
                      fws = new FileWriter("out.dat");

                      // Create a stream tokenizer wrapping file input stream
                      in = new StreamTokenizer(frs);
                      out = new PrintWriter(fws);

                      // Read first token
                      in.nextToken();

                      // Process a record
                      while (in.ttype != in.TT_EOF)
                      {
                        // Get student name
                        if (in.ttype == in.TT_WORD)
                          sname = in.sval;
                        else
                          System.out.println("Bad file format");

                        // Get midterm1
                        if (in.nextToken() == in.TT_NUMBER)
                          midterm1 = in.nval;
                        else
                          System.out.println("Bad file format");

                        // Get midterm2
                        if (in.nextToken() == in.TT_NUMBER)
                          midterm2 = in.nval;
                        else
                          System.out.println("Bad file format");

                        // Get final score
                        if (in.nextToken() == in.TT_NUMBER)
                          finalScore = in.nval;

                        total = midterm1*0.3 + midterm2*0.3 + finalScore*0.4;
                        out.println(sname + " " +total);

                        in.nextToken();
                      }
                    }
                    catch (FileNotFoundException ex)
                    {
                      System.out.println("File not found: in.dat");
                    }
                    catch (IOException ex)
```

```
      {
        System.out.println(ex.getMessage());
      }
      finally
      {
        try
        {
          if (frs != null) frs.close();
          if (fws != null) fws.close();
        }
        catch (IOException ex)
        {
          System.out.println(ex);
        }
      }
    }
  }
```

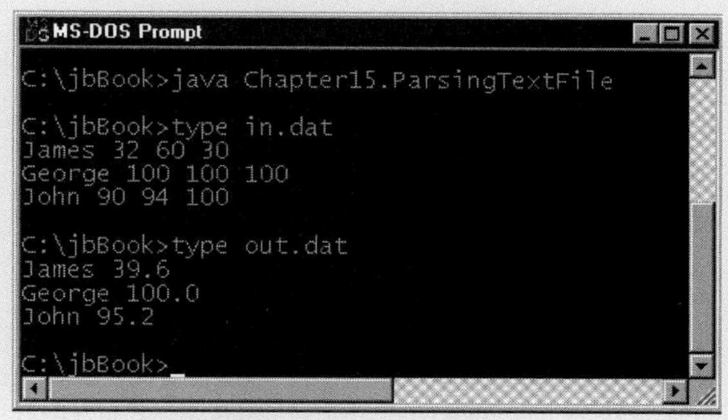

Figure 15.11   *The program uses* StreamTokenizer *to parse the text file into strings and numbers.*

Example Review

Before running this program, make sure you have created the text file **in.dat**. To parse the text file **in.dat**, the program uses StreamTokenizer to wrap a FileReader stream. The nextToken() method is used on a StreamTokenizer object to get one token at a time. The token value is stored in the nval field if the token is numeric, and in the sval field if the token is a string. The token type is stored in the ttype field.

For each record, the program reads the name and the three exam scores and then computes the total score. A FileWriter stream is used to store the name and the total score in the text file **out.dat** (see Figure 15.12).

continues

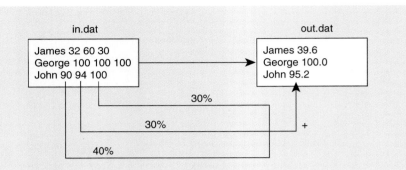

Figure 15.12   *The program reads two midterm scores and a final exam score and then computes a total score.*

Random Access Files

All of the streams you have used so far are known as *read-only* or *write-only* streams. The external files of these streams are sequential files that cannot be updated without creating a new file. It is often necessary to modify files or to insert new records into them. For this reason, Java provides the `RandomAccessFile` class, which allows a file to be read and updated at the same time.

The `RandomAccessFile` class extends `Object` and implements `DataInput` and `DataOutput` interfaces. Because `DataInputStream` implements the `DataInput` interface, and `DataOutputStream` implements the `DataOutput` interface, many methods in `RandomAccessFile` are the same as those in `DataInputStream` and `DataOutputStream`. For example, `readInt()`, `readLong()`, `readDouble()`, `readUTF()`, `writeInt()`, `writeLong()`, `writeDouble()`, and `writeUTF()` can be used in data input streams or data output streams as well as in `RandomAccessFile` streams.

Additionally, `RandomAccessFile` provides the methods listed below to deal with random access.

- `public void seek(long pos) throws IOException`

  This method sets the offset from the beginning of the `RandomAccessFile` stream to where the next read or write occurs.

- `public long getFilePointer() throws IOException`

  This method returns the offset, in bytes, from the beginning of the file to where the next read or write occurs.

- `public long length() throws IOException`

  This method returns the length of the file.

- `public final void writeChar(int v) throws IOException`

  This method writes a character to the file as a two-byte Unicode, with the high byte written first.

■   `public final void writeChars(String s) throws IOException`

This method writes a string to the file as a sequence of characters.

When creating a `RandomAccessFile` stream, you can specify one of two modes (`"r"` or `"rw"`). Mode `"r"` means that the stream is read-only, and mode `"rw"` indicates that it allows both read and write. The following statement creates a new stream, `raf`, that allows the program to read from and write to the file **test.dat**:

```
RandomAccessFile raf = new RandomAccessFile("test.dat", "rw");
```

If **test.dat** already exists, `raf` is created to access it; if **test.dat** does not exist, a new file named **test.dat** is created, and `raf` is created to access it. The method `raf.length()` indicates the number of bytes in **test.dat** at any given time. If you append new data into the file, `raf.length()` increases.

NOTE
When you use `writeChar()` to write a character or use `writeChars()` to write characters, a character occupies two bytes.

TIP
Do not open the file with the `"rw"` mode if the file is not intended to be modified. This will prevent unintentional modifications of the file.

Random access files are often used to process files of records. For convenience, fixed-length records are used in random access files so that a record can be located easily. A record consists of a fixed number of fields. A field can be a string or a primitive data type. A string in a fixed-length record has a maximum size. If a string is smaller than the maximum size, the rest of it is padded with blanks.

Example 15.6 Using Random Access Files

This example presents a program that registers students and displays student information. The user interface consists of a tabbed pane with two tabs: Register Student and View Student. The Register Student tab enables you to store a student in the file, as shown in Figure 15.13. The View Student tab enables you to browse through student information, as shown in Figure 15.14.

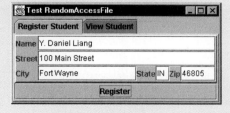

Figure 15.13   *The Register Student tab registers a student.*

continues

645

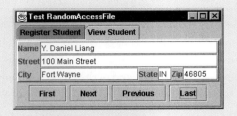

Figure 15.14 *The View Student tab displays student information.*

The program is given as follows:

```
// TestRandomAccessFile.java: Store and read data
// using RandomAccessFile
package Chapter15;

import java.io.*;
import java.awt.*;
import java.awt.event.*;
import javax.swing.*;
import Chapter8.MyFrameWithExitHandling;
import javax.swing.border.*;

public class TestRandomAccessFile extends MyFrameWithExitHandling
{
  // Create a tabbed pane to hold two panels
  private JTabbedPane jtpStudent = new JTabbedPane();

  // Random access file for access the student.dat file
  private RandomAccessFile raf;

  // Main method
  public static void main(String[] args)
  {
    TestRandomAccessFile frame = new TestRandomAccessFile();
    frame.pack();
    frame.setTitle("Test RandomAccessFile");
    frame.setVisible(true);
  }

  // Default constructor
  public TestRandomAccessFile()
  {
    // Open or create a random access file
    try
    {
      raf = new RandomAccessFile("student.dat", "rw");
    }
    catch(IOException ex)
    {
      System.out.print("Error: " + ex);
      System.exit(0);
    }

    // Place buttons in the tabbed pane
    jtpStudent.add(new RegisterStudent(raf), "Register Student");
    jtpStudent.add(new ViewStudent(raf), "View Student");
```

```
      // Add the tabbed pane to the frame
      getContentPane().add(jtpStudent);
  }
}

// Register student panel
class RegisterStudent extends JPanel implements ActionListener
{
  // Button for registering a student
  private JButton jbtRegister;

  // Student information panel
  private StudentPanel studentPanel;

  // Random access file
  private RandomAccessFile raf;

  // Constructor
  public RegisterStudent(RandomAccessFile raf)
  {
    // Pass raf to RegisterStudent Panel
    this.raf = raf;

    // Add studentPanel and jbtRegister in the panel
    setLayout(new BorderLayout());
    add(studentPanel = new StudentPanel(),
      BorderLayout.CENTER);
    add(jbtRegister = new JButton("Register"),
      BorderLayout.SOUTH);

    // Register listener
    jbtRegister.addActionListener(this);
  }

  // Handle button actions
  public void actionPerformed(ActionEvent e)
  {
    if (e.getSource() == jbtRegister)
    {
      Student student = studentPanel.getStudent();

      try
      {
        raf.seek(raf.length());
        student.writeStudent(raf);
      }
      catch(IOException ex)
      {
        System.out.print("Error: " + ex);
      }
    }
  }
}

// View student panel
class ViewStudent extends JPanel implements ActionListener
{
  // Buttons for viewing student information
  private JButton jbtFirst, jbtNext, jbtPrevious, jbtLast;
```

continues

```java
// Random access file
private RandomAccessFile raf = null;

// Current student record
private Student student = new Student();

// Create a student panel
private StudentPanel studentPanel = new StudentPanel();

// File pointer in the random access file
private long lastPos;
private long currentPos;

// Constructor
public ViewStudent(RandomAccessFile raf)
{
  // Pass raf to ViewStudent
  this.raf = raf;

  // Panel p to hold four navigator buttons
  JPanel p = new JPanel();
  p.setLayout(new FlowLayout(FlowLayout.LEFT));
  p.add(jbtFirst = new JButton("First"));
  p.add(jbtNext = new JButton("Next"));
  p.add(jbtPrevious = new JButton("Previous"));
  p.add(jbtLast = new JButton("Last"));

  // Add panel p and studentPanel to ViewPanel
  setLayout(new BorderLayout());
  add(studentPanel, BorderLayout.CENTER);
  add(p, BorderLayout.SOUTH);

  // Register listeners
  jbtFirst.addActionListener(this);
  jbtNext.addActionListener(this);
  jbtPrevious.addActionListener(this);
  jbtLast.addActionListener(this);
}

// Handle navigation button actions
public void actionPerformed(ActionEvent e)
{
  String actionCommand = e.getActionCommand();
  if (e.getSource() instanceof JButton)
  {
    try
    {
      if ("First".equals(actionCommand))
      {
        if (raf.length() > 0)
          retrieve(0);
      }
      else if ("Next".equals(actionCommand))
      {
        currentPos = raf.getFilePointer();
        if (currentPos < raf.length())
          retrieve(currentPos);
      }
      else if ("Previous".equals(actionCommand))
      {
        currentPos = raf.getFilePointer();
        if (currentPos > 0)
          retrieve(currentPos - 2*2*Student.RECORD_SIZE);
      }
```

```
        else if ("Last".equals(actionCommand))
        {
          lastPos = raf.length();
          if (lastPos > 0)
            retrieve(lastPos - 2*Student.RECORD_SIZE);
        }
      }
      catch(IOException ex)
      {
        System.out.print("Error: " + ex);
      }
    }
  }

  // Retrieve a record at specified position
  public void retrieve(long pos)
  {
    try
    {
      raf.seek(pos);
      student.readStudent(raf);
      studentPanel.setStudent(student);
    }
    catch(IOException ex)
    {
      System.out.print("Error: " + ex);
    }
  }
}

// This class contains static methods for reading and writing
// fixed length records
class FixedLengthStringIO
{
  // Read fixed number of characters from a DataInput stream
  public static String readFixedLengthString(int size,
                                             DataInput in)
  throws IOException
  {
    char c[] = new char[size];

    for (int i=0; i<size; i++)
      c[i] = in.readChar();

    return new String(c);
  }

  // Write fixed number of characters (string s with padded spaces)
  // to a DataOutput stream
  public static void writeFixedLengthString(String s, int size,
    DataOutput out) throws IOException
  {
    char cBuffer[] = new char[size];
    s.getChars(0, s.length(), cBuffer, 0);
    for (int i=s.length(); i<cBuffer.length; i++)
      cBuffer[i] = ' ';
    String newS = new String(cBuffer);
    out.writeChars(newS);
  }
}
```

continues

649

```
// StudentPanel.java: Panel for displaying student information
package Chapter15;

import javax.swing.*;
import javax.swing.border.*;
import java.awt.*;

public class StudentPanel extends JPanel
{
  JTextField jtfName = new JTextField(32);
  JTextField jtfStreet = new JTextField(32);
  JTextField jtfCity = new JTextField(20);
  JTextField jtfState = new JTextField(2);
  JTextField jtfZip = new JTextField(5);

  // Constuct a student panel
  public StudentPanel()
  {
    // Set the panel with line border
    setBorder(new BevelBorder(BevelBorder.RAISED));

    // Panel p1 for holding labels Name, Street, and City
    JPanel p1 = new JPanel();
    p1.setLayout(new GridLayout(3, 1));
    p1.add(new JLabel("Name"));
    p1.add(new JLabel("Street"));
    p1.add(new JLabel("City"));

    // Panel jpState for holding state
    JPanel jpState = new JPanel();
    jpState.setLayout(new BorderLayout());
    jpState.add(new JLabel("State"), BorderLayout.WEST);
    jpState.add(jtfState, BorderLayout.CENTER);

    // Panel jpZip for holding zip
    JPanel jpZip = new JPanel();
    jpZip.setLayout(new BorderLayout());
    jpZip.add(new JLabel("Zip"), BorderLayout.WEST);
    jpZip.add(jtfZip, BorderLayout.CENTER);

    // Panel p2 for holding jpState and jpZip
    JPanel p2 = new JPanel();
    p2.setLayout(new BorderLayout());
    p2.add(jpState, BorderLayout.WEST);
    p2.add(jpZip, BorderLayout.CENTER);

    // Panel p3 for holding jtfCity and p2
    JPanel p3 = new JPanel();
    p3.setLayout(new BorderLayout());
    p3.add(jtfCity, BorderLayout.CENTER);
    p3.add(p2, BorderLayout.EAST);

    // Panel p4 for holding jtfName, jtfStreet, and p3
    JPanel p4 = new JPanel();
    p4.setLayout(new GridLayout(3, 1));
    p4.add(jtfName);
    p4.add(jtfStreet);
    p4.add(p3);

    // Place p1 and p4 into StudentPanel
    setLayout(new BorderLayout());
```

```java
      add(p1, BorderLayout.WEST);
      add(p4, BorderLayout.CENTER);
    }

    // Get student information from the text fields
    public Student getStudent()
    {
      return new Student(jtfName.getText().trim(),
                         jtfStreet.getText().trim(),
                         jtfCity.getText().trim(),
                         jtfState.getText().trim(),
                         jtfZip.getText().trim());
    }

    // Set student information on the text fields
    public void setStudent(Student s)
    {
      jtfName.setText(s.getName());
      jtfStreet.setText(s.getStreet());
      jtfCity.setText(s.getCity());
      jtfState.setText(s.getState());
      jtfZip.setText(s.getZip());
    }
}

// Student.java: Student class encapsulates student information
package Chapter15;

import java.io.*;

public class Student
{
  private String name;
  private String street;
  private String city;
  private String state;
  private String zip;

  // Specify the size of five string fields in the record
  final static int NAME_SIZE = 32;
  final static int STREET_SIZE = 32;
  final static int CITY_SIZE = 20;
  final static int STATE_SIZE = 2;
  final static int ZIP_SIZE = 5;

  // the total size of the record in bytes, a Unicode
  // character is 2 bytes size
  final static int RECORD_SIZE =
    (NAME_SIZE + STREET_SIZE + CITY_SIZE + STATE_SIZE + ZIP_SIZE);

  // Default constructor
  public Student()
  {
  }

  // Construct a Student with specified name, street, city, state,
  // and zip
  public Student(String name, String street, String city,
    String state, String zip)
```

continues

651

```
    {
      this.name = name;
      this.street = street;
      this.city = city;
      this.state = state;
      this.zip = zip;
    }

    public String getName()
    {
      return name;
    }

    public String getStreet()
    {
      return street;
    }

    public String getCity()
    {
      return city;
    }

    public String getState()
    {
      return state;
    }

    public String getZip()
    {
      return zip;
    }

    // Write a student to a data output stream
    public void writeStudent(DataOutput out) throws IOException
    {
      FixedLengthStringIO.writeFixedLengthString(
        name, NAME_SIZE, out);
      FixedLengthStringIO.writeFixedLengthString(
        street, STREET_SIZE, out);
      FixedLengthStringIO.writeFixedLengthString(
        city, CITY_SIZE, out);
      FixedLengthStringIO.writeFixedLengthString(
        state, STATE_SIZE, out);
      FixedLengthStringIO.writeFixedLengthString(
        zip, ZIP_SIZE, out);
    }

    // Read a student from data input stream
    public void readStudent(DataInput in) throws IOException
    {
      name = FixedLengthStringIO.readFixedLengthString(
        NAME_SIZE, in);
      street = FixedLengthStringIO.readFixedLengthString(
        STREET_SIZE, in);
      city = FixedLengthStringIO.readFixedLengthString(
        CITY_SIZE, in);
      state = FixedLengthStringIO.readFixedLengthString(
        STATE_SIZE, in);
      zip = FixedLengthStringIO.readFixedLengthString(
        ZIP_SIZE, in);
    }
  }
```

Example Review

A random file, **student.dat**, is created to store student information or is opened if the file already exists. The random file object, raf, is used in both registration and in the viewing part of the program. The user could add a new student record into the file in the Register Student panel and view it immediately in the View Student panel.

Several classes are used in this example. The main class, TestRandomAccessFile, is a subclass of MyFrameWithExitHandling and creates an instance of the RegisterStudent class and an instance of the ViewStudent class. These two instances are added to a tabbed pane with two tabs: Register Student and View Student. When the Register Student tab is clicked, the Registration panel is shown. When the View Student tab is clicked, the Viewing panel is shown.

The RegisterStudent class and the ViewStudent class have many things in common. They both extend the JPanel class, and both use the StudentPanel class, the Student class.

Since the student information panels for registering and viewing student information are identical, the program creates one superclass, StudentPanel, to lay out the labels and text fields, as shown in Figure 15.15. The StudentPanel class also provides the method getStudent() for getting student information from the text fields and the method setStudent() for setting the information to the text fields.

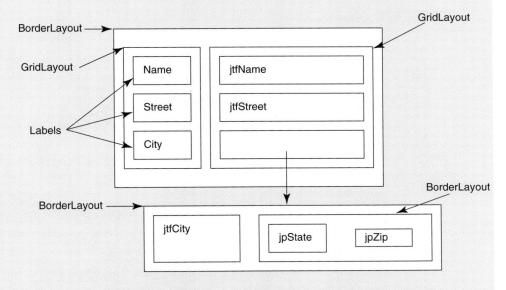

Figure 15.15   *The* StudentPanel *class uses several panels to group components to achieve the desired layout.*

continues

653

The Student class defines the student record structure and provides methods for reading and writing a record into the file. Each field in a student record has a fixed length. The FixedLengthStringIO class defines the methods for reading and writing fixed-length strings.

The size of each field in the student record is fixed. For example, zip code is set to a maximum of five characters. If you entered a zip code of more than five characters by mistake, the ArrayIndexOutofBounds runtime error would occur when the program attempts to write the zip code into the file using the writeFixedLengthString() method defined in the FixedLengthStringIO class.

File Dialogs

Swing provides javax.swing.JFileChooser, which displays a dialog box from which the user can navigate through the file system and select files to load or save, as shown in Figure 15.16.

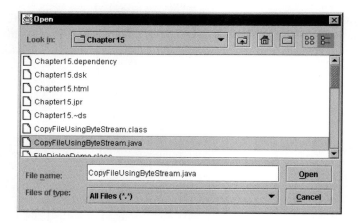

Figure 15.16   *The Swing* JFileChooser *shows files and directories, enabling the user to navigate through the file system visually.*

The file dialog box is modal; when it is displayed, it blocks all other applications until it disappears. The file dialog box can appear in two types: *open* and *save*. The *open type* is for opening a file, and the *save type* is for storing a file.

There are several ways to construct a file dialog box. The simplest is to use the JFileChooser's default constructor.

JFileChooser is a subclass of JComponent. The JFileChooser class has the properties inherited from JComponent. It also has the following useful properties:

■ dialogType: The type of this dialog. Use OPEN_DIALOG when you want to bring up a filechooser that the user can use to open a file. Likewise, use SAVE_DIALOG to let the user choose a file for saving.

■ dialogTitle: The string displayed in the title bar of the dialog box.

■ currentDirectory: The current directory of the file. The type of this property is java.io.File. If you want the current directory to be used, use setCurrentDirectory(new File(".")).

■ selectedFile: The selected file. You can use getSelectedFile() to return the selected file from the dialog box. The type of this property is java.io.File. If you have a default file name that you expect to use, use setSelectedFile(new File(filename)).

■ selectedFiles: A list of selected files if the filechooser is set to allow multiselection. The type of this property is File[].

■ multiSelectionEnabled: A boolean value indicating whether multiple files can be selected. By default, it is false.

To display the dialog box, use the following two methods:

```
public int showOpenDialog(Component parent)

public int showSaveDialog(Component parent)
```

The first method displays an "Open" dialog, and the second method displays a "Save" dialog. Both methods return an int value APPROVE_OPTION or CANCEL_OPTION, which indicates whether the OK button or the Cancel button was clicked.

Example 15.7 Using File Dialogs

This example gives a program that creates a simple notepad using JFileChooser to open and save files. The notepad enables the user to open an existing file, edit the file, and save the note into the current file or a specified file. You can display and edit the file in a text area.

A sample run of the program is shown in Figure 15.17. When you open a file, a file dialog box with the default title "Open" appears on-screen to let you select a file for loading, as shown in Figure 15.16. When you save a file, a file dialog box with the default title "Save" appears to let you select a file for saving, as shown in Figure 15.18. The status label below the text area displays the status of the file operations.

```
// FileDialogDemo.java: Demonstrate using JFileDialog to display
// file dialog boxes for opening and saving files
package Chapter15;
```

continues

```java
import java.awt.*;
import java.awt.event.*;
import java.io.*;
import javax.swing.*;

public class FileDialogDemo extends Chapter8.MyFrameWithExitHandling
  implements ActionListener
{
  // Menu items Open, Save, exit, and About
  private JMenuItem jmiOpen, jmiSave,jmiExit, jmiAbout;

  // Text area for displaying and editing text files
  private JTextArea jta = new JTextArea();

  // Status label for displaying operation status
  private JLabel jlblStatus = new JLabel();

  // File dialog box
  private JFileChooser jFileChooser = new JFileChooser();

  // Main method
  public static void main(String[] args)
  {
    FileDialogDemo frame = new FileDialogDemo();
    frame.setSize(300, 150);
    frame.setVisible(true);
  }

  public FileDialogDemo()
  {
    setTitle("Test JFileChooser");

    // Create a menu bar mb and attach to the frame
    JMenuBar mb = new JMenuBar();
    setJMenuBar(mb);

    // Add a "File" menu in mb
    JMenu fileMenu = new JMenu("File");
    mb.add(fileMenu);

    //add a "Help" menu in mb
    JMenu helpMenu = new JMenu("Help");
    mb.add(helpMenu);

    // Create and add menu items to the menu
    fileMenu.add(jmiOpen = new JMenuItem("Open"));
    fileMenu.add(jmiSave = new JMenuItem("Save"));
    fileMenu.addSeparator();
    fileMenu.add(jmiExit = new JMenuItem("Exit"));
    helpMenu.add(jmiAbout = new JMenuItem("About"));

    // Set default directory to the current directory
    jFileChooser.setCurrentDirectory(new File("."));

    // Set BorderLayout for the frame
    getContentPane().add(new JScrollPane(jta),
      BorderLayout.CENTER);
    getContentPane().add(jlblStatus, BorderLayout.SOUTH);
```

```
      // Register listeners
      jmiOpen.addActionListener(this);
      jmiSave.addActionListener(this);
      jmiAbout.addActionListener(this);
      jmiExit.addActionListener(this);
    }

    // Handle ActionEvent for menu items
    public void actionPerformed(ActionEvent e)
    {
      String actionCommand = e.getActionCommand();

      if (e.getSource() instanceof JMenuItem)
      {
        if ("Open".equals(actionCommand))
          open();
        else if ("Save".equals(actionCommand))
          save();
        else if ("About".equals(actionCommand))
          JOptionPane.showMessageDialog(this,
            "Demonstrate Using File Dialogs",
            "About This Demo",
            JOptionPane.INFORMATION_MESSAGE);
        else if ("Exit".equals(actionCommand))
          System.exit(0);
      }
    }

    // Open file
    private void open()
    {
      if (jFileChooser.showOpenDialog(this) ==
        JFileChooser.APPROVE_OPTION)
      {
        open(jFileChooser.getSelectedFile());
      }
    }

    // Open file with the specified File instance
    private void open(File file)
    {
      try
      {
        // Read from the specified file and store it in jta
        BufferedInputStream in = new BufferedInputStream(
          new FileInputStream(file));
        byte[] b = new byte[in.available()];
        in.read(b, 0, b.length);
        jta.append(new String(b, 0, b.length));
        in.close();

        // Display the status of the Open file operation in jlblStatus
        jlblStatus.setText(file.getName() + " Opened");
      }
      catch (IOException ex)
      {
        jlblStatus.setText("Error opening " + file.getName());
      }
    }
```

continues

657

```
// Save file
private void save()
{
  if (jFileChooser.showSaveDialog(this) ==
    JFileChooser.APPROVE_OPTION)
  {
    save(jFileChooser.getSelectedFile());
  }
}

// Save file with specified File instance
private void save(File file)
{
  try
  {
    // Write the text in jta to the specified file
    BufferedOutputStream out = new BufferedOutputStream(
      new FileOutputStream(file));
    byte[] b = (jta.getText()).getBytes();
    out.write(b, 0, b.length);
    out.close();

    // Display the status of the save file operation in jlblStatus
    jlblStatus.setText(file.getName()  + " Saved ");
  }
  catch (IOException ex)
  {
    jlblStatus.setText("Error saving " + file.getName());
  }
}
```

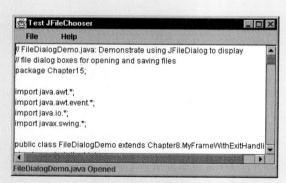

Figure 15.17   *The program enables you to open, save, and edit files.*

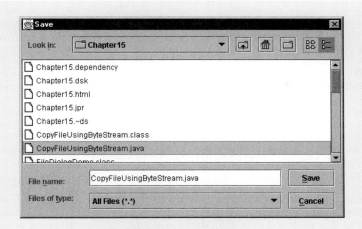

Figure 15.18   *The Save dialog box enables you to save to a new file or an existing file.*

Example Review

The program creates the File and Help menus. The File menu contains the menu commands Open for loading a file, Save for saving a file, and Exit for terminating the program. The Help menu contains the menu command About to display a message about the program, as shown in Figure 15.19.

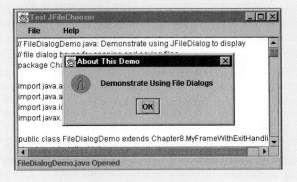

Figure 15.19   *Clicking the About menu item displays a message dialog box.*

An instance jFileChooser of JFileChooser is created for displaying the file dialog box to open and save files. The setCurrentDirectory(new File(".")) method is used to set the current directory to the directory where the class is stored.

The open() method is invoked when the user clicks the Open menu command. The showOpenDialog() method displays an Open dialog box, as shown in Figure 15.17. Upon receiving the selected file, the method open(file) is invoked to load the file to the text area using a BufferedInputStream wrapped on a FileInputStream.

continues

The save() method is invoked when the user clicks the Save menu command. The showSaveDialog() method displays a Save dialog box, as shown in Figure 15.18. Upon receiving the selected file, the method save(file) is invoked to save the contents from the text area to the file using a BufferedOutputStream wrapped on a FileOutputStream.

Interactive Input and Output

There are two types of *interactive I/O*. One involves simple input from the keyboard and simple output in a pure text form. The other involves input from various input devices and output to a graphical environment on frames and applets. The former is referred to as *text interactive I/O*, the latter as *graphical interactive I/O*.

Graphical interactive I/O takes an entirely different approach from text interactive I/O. In the graphical environment, input can be received from an UI component, such as a text field, text area, list, combo box, check box, or radio button. Input can also be received from a keystroke or a mouse movement. Output is usually displayed on the panel, in text fields, or in text areas.

Now turn your attention to text I/O. In all of the previous chapters, you used text input and output with the System class. The System class contains three I/O objects: System.in, System.out, and System.err. The objects in, out, and err are static variables. The variable in is of InputStream type, and out and err are of PrintStream type. These are the basic objects that all Java programmers use to input from the keyboard, output to the screen, and display error messages. Because this class is used in virtually all programs for simple console input and output, they are stored in the java.lang package, which is automatically imported into a class.

To perform console output, you can simply use any of the methods for PrintStream in System.out. Keyboard input is more complicated, however. The MyInput class, which is used for getting int and double from the keyboard, was introduced in the section "Separate Classes" in Chapter 2, "Java Building Elements." In this section, the MyInput class, as well as input for other primitive types and strings, will be described in more detail.

You need to use BufferedReader and StringTokenizer to input from the keyboard. BufferedReader takes the input of the character format of all of the primitive types, such as integer, double, string, and so on. The StringTokenizer class, introduced in Chapter 6, "Arrays and Strings," takes in a string, such as "Welcome to Java", and breaks it into small pieces known as *tokens*.

Tokens are usually separated by spaces (but the programmer can dictate what delimiter is used). StringTokenizer objects are instantiated with the string, and each subsequent call to StringTokenizerObject.nextToken() returns a new token. In order to make input possible, you need to declare these two objects as follows:

```
static private BufferedReader br =
  new BufferedReader(new InputStreamReader(System.in), 1);
static StringTokenizer stok;
```

NOTE

JavaSoft knows that some brands of PCs running Windows 95 are prone to cause input problems if the buffer size for the BufferedReader stream br is not set to 1. Therefore, the buffer size of 1 is purposely chosen in order to eliminate some of the input problems.

Table 15.5 shows the code for reading different primitive data types from the keyboard.

TABLE 15.5   Input and Output of Primitive Types on the Console

Data Type	How to Read It
int	`String str = br.readLine();`
	`stok = new StringTokenizer(str);`
	`int i = Integer.parseInt(stok.nextToken());`
byte	`String str = br.readLine();`
	`stok = new StringTokenizer(str);`
	`int i = Integer.parseInt(stok.nextToken());`
	`byte b = (byte)i;`
short	Same as the preceding entry, except that `byte b = (byte)i` needs to be replaced with `short b = (short)i;`
boolean	`String str = br.readLine();`
	`stok = new StringTokenizer(str);`
	`boolean bo = new Boolean(stok.nextToken()).booleanValue();`
char	`char ch = br.readLine().charAt(0);`
long	`String str = br.readLine(); stok = new StringTokenizer(str);`
	`long lg = Long.parseLong(stok.nextToken());`
float	`String str = br.readLine();`
	`stok = new StringTokenizer(str);`
	`float fl = new Float(stok.nextToken()).floatValue();`
double	`String str = br.readLine();`
	`stok = new StringTokenizer(str);`
	`double db = new Double(stok.nextToken()).doubleValue();`
String	`String str = br.readLine();`

Note that with the previous code, the programmer needs to add an exception handler in the try/catch wraparound because these I/O statements throw IOException.

Piped Streams, String Streams, Pushback Streams, Line-Number Streams, and Object Streams

You have learned many I/O streams in this chapter. Each stream has its intended application. There are several other stream classes that you may find useful. For example, object streams can be used to read or write whole objects from or to files. A brief discussion of these streams follows:

- **Piped streams**—Piped streams can be thought of as the two ends of a pipe that connects two processes. One process sends data out through the pipe, and the other process receives data from the pipe. Piped streams are used in interprocess communication (IPC). Two processes running on separate threads can exchange data. Java provides `PipedInputStream`, `PipedOutputStream`, `PipedReader`, and `PipedWriter` to support piped streams.

- **String streams**—String streams (`StringReader` and `StringWriter`) are exactly like character array streams, except that the source of the string stream is a string, and the destination of the string stream is a string buffer.

- **Pushback streams**—Pushback streams are commonly used in parsers to "push back" a single byte or character in the input stream after reading from the input stream. The pushback stream's purpose is simply to preview the input to determine what to do next. The number of bytes or characters pushed can be specified when the stream is constructed. By default, a single byte or a single character is pushed back. Java provides the classes `PushbackInputStream` and `PushbackReader` to support pushback streams.

- **Line-number streams**—Line-number streams allow you to track the current line number of an input stream. Java provides the `LineNumberReader` class for this purpose. The `LineNumberReader` class is useful for such applications as editors and debuggers. You can use the `getLineNumber()` method to get the current line number of the input and the `getLine()` method to retrieve a line into a string.

- **Object streams**—Thus far, this chapter has covered input and output of bytes, characters, and primitive data types. Object streams enable you to perform input and output at the object level. The `ObjectInputStream` and `ObjectOutputStream` classes provide functionality to support object streams. As discussed in my *Rapid Java Application Development Using JBuilder 3*, object streams are very useful for storing and restoring JavaBeans components in rapid Java application development.

Chapter Summary

In this chapter, you learned about Java input and output. In Java, all I/O is handled in streams. Java offers many stream classes for processing all kinds of data.

Streams can be categorized into two types: byte streams and character streams. The `InputStream` and `OutputStream` classes are the root of all byte stream classes, and the `Reader` and `Writer` classes are the root of all character stream classes. The subclasses of `InputStream` and `OutputStream` are analogous to the subclasses of `Reader` and `Writer`. Many of them have similar method signatures and can be used in the same way.

File streams—`FileInputStream` and `FileOutputStream` for byte streams, and `FileReader` and `FileWriter` for character streams—are used to read from or write data to external files. The data streams `DataInputStream` and `DataOutputStream` read or write Java primitive types in a machine-independent fashion, which enables you to write a data file on one machine and read it on a machine that has a different OS or file structure.

Since a data output stream outputs a binary representation of data, you cannot view its content as text. The `PrintStream` and `PrintWriter` classes allow you to print streams in text format. `System.out`, `System.in`, and `System.err` are examples of `PrintStream` objects.

The `BufferedInputStream`, `BufferedOutputStream`, `BufferedReader`, and `BufferedWriter` classes can be used to speed input and output by reducing the number of reads and writes. Typical physical input/output involving I/O devices is very slow compared with CPU processing, so using buffered I/O can greatly improve performance.

The `StreamTokenizer` class is useful in processing text files. The `StreamTokenizer` class enables you to take an input stream, parse it into tokens, and allow the tokens to be read one at a time.

The `RandomAccessFile` class enables you to read and write data to a file at the same time. You can open a file with the `"r"` mode to indicate that the file is read only, or with the `"rw"` mode to indicate that it is updatable. Since the `RandomAccessFile` class implements `DataInput` and `DataOutput` interfaces, many methods in `RandomAccessFile` are the same as those in `DataInputStream` and `DataOutputStream`.

You can use the `JFileChooser` class to display standard file dialog boxes from which the user can navigate through the file systems and select files to load or save.

Chapter Review

15.1. Which streams must always be used to process external files?

15.2. What type of data is read or written by `InputStream` and `OutputStream`? Can you use `read()` or `write(byte b)` in those streams?

15.3. `InputStream` reads bytes. Why does the `read()` method return an `int` instead of a byte?

15.4. What type of data is read or written by `Reader` and `Writer`? Can you use `read()` or `write(char c)` in those streams?

15.5. What are the differences between byte streams and character streams?

15.6. What type of data is read or written by file streams? Can you use `read()` or `write(byte b)` in file streams?

15.7. How are the data input and output streams used to read and write data?

15.8. What are the differences between `DataOutputStream` and `PrintStream`?

15.9. Answer the following questions regarding `StreamTokenizer`:

- When do you use `StreamTokenizer`?

- How do you read data using `StreamTokenizer`?

- Where is the token stored when you are using the `nextToken()` method?

- How do you find the data type of the token?

15.10. Can you close a `StreamTokenizer`?

15.11. Can `RandomAccessFile` streams read a data file created by `DataOutputStream`?

15.12. Create a `RandomAccessFile` stream for the file **student.dat** to allow the updating of student information in the file. Create a `DataOutputStream` for the file **student.dat**. Describe the differences between these two statements.

15.13. What are the data types for `System.in`, `System.out`, and `System.err`?

15.14. Is `JFileChooser` modal? What is the return type for `getSelectedFile()` and `getSelectedDirectory()`? How do you set the current directory as the default directory for a `JFileChooser` dialog?

15.15. What happens if the file **test.dat** does not exist when you attempt to compile and run the following code?

```
import java.io.*;

class Test
{
  public static void main(String[] args)
  {
    try
    {
      RandomAccessFile raf =
        new RandomAccessFile("test.dat", "r");
      int i = raf.readInt();
    }
    catch(IOException ex)
    {
      System.out.println("IO exception");
    }
  }
}
```

Programming Exercises

15.1. Rewrite Example 15.1, "Processing External Files," using `FileReader` and `FileWriter` streams. Write another program with buffered streams to boost performance. Test the performance of these two programs (one with buffered streams and the other without using buffered streams), as shown in Figure 15.20.

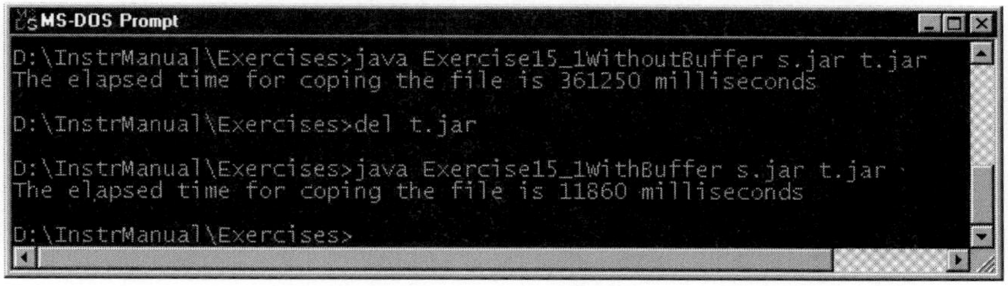

Figure 15.20 *Buffered streams can significantly boost performance.*

15.2. Write a program that will count the number of characters in a file, including blanks, words, and lines. The filename should be passed as a command-line argument, as shown in Figure 15.21.

Figure 15.21 *The program displays the number of characters, words, and lines in the given file.*

15.3. Use `StreamTokenizer` to write a program that will add all of the integers in a data file. Suppose that the integers are delimited by spaces. Display the result on the console. Rewrite the program, assuming this time that the numbers are `double`.

15.4. Rewrite Example 15.5, "Using `StreamTokenizer`," so that it reads a line as a string in a `BufferedReader` stream, and then use `StringTokenizer` to extract the fields.

15.5. Rewrite Example 15.4, "Displaying a File in a Text Area," to enable the user to view the file by opening it from a file open dialog box, as shown in Figure 15.22. A file open dialog box is displayed when the Browse button is clicked. The file is displayed in the text area, and the filename is displayed in the text field, when the OK button is clicked in the file open dialog box. You can also enter the filename in the text field and press the Enter key to display the file in the text area.

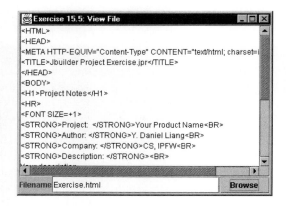

Figure 15.22   *The program enables the user to view a file by selecting it from a file open dialog box.*

15.6. Write a Java application that will display a stock index ticker, as shown in Figure 13.13 for Exercise 13.6. In that exercise, the stock index information is passed from the `<param>` tag in the HTML file.

Your program will get index information from an external text file. The first line in the file contains an integer indicating the number of stock indices given in the file. Each subsequent line should consist of four fields: Index Name, Current Time, Previous Day Index, and Index Change. The fields are separated by the pound sign (#). The file could contain two lines like these:

```
2
"S&P 500"#15:54#919.01#4.54
"NIKKEI"#04:03#1865.17#-7.00
```

15.7. Write a program that will display a histogram on a panel. The histogram should show the occurrence of each letter in a text file, as shown in Figure 15.23. Assume that the letters are not case-sensitive.

■ Place a panel that will display the histogram in the center of the frame.

■ Place a label and a text field in a panel and put the panel in the south side of the frame. The text file will be entered from this text field.

■ Pressing the Enter key on the text field causes the program to count the occurrences of each letter and display the count in a histogram.

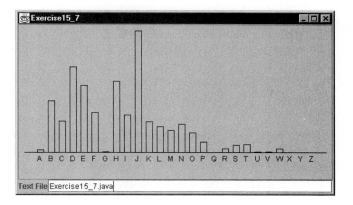

Figure 15.23 *The program displays a histogram that shows the occurrence of each letter in the file.*

15.8. Modify the View Student panel in Example 15.6, "Using Random Access Files," to add an Update button for updating the student record that is displayed, as shown in Figure 15.24. The Tab "View Student" is now changed to "View and Update Student."

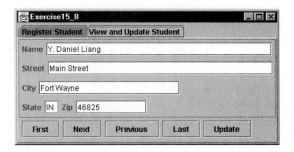

Figure 15.24 *You can browse student records and update the one that is currently displayed.*

16

NETWORKING

Objectives

- Comprehend socket-based communication in Java.
- Understand client/server computing.
- Implement Java networking programs.
- Produce servers for multiple clients.
- Create applets that connect to servers.
- Write programs that will work with Web servers.

Introduction

Network programming is tightly integrated in Java. Java provides *socket-based communication*, which enables programs to communicate through designated sockets. A *socket* is an abstraction that facilitates communication between a server and a client. Java treats socket communication much as it treats I/O operations: A program can read from or write to a socket as easily as it reads from or writes to a file.

Java supports *stream socket* and *datagram socket*. Stream socket uses the Transmission Control Protocol (TCP) for data transmission, and datagram socket uses the User Datagram Protocol (UDP). TCP can detect a lost transmission and resubmit it. Therefore, the transmission is lossless and reliable. UDP, on the other hand, cannot guarantee lossless transmission. Thus, stream sockets are used in most Java programming. The discussion in this chapter is based on stream sockets.

Client/Server Computing

Network programming usually involves a server and one or more clients. The client sends requests to the server, and the server responds to them. The client begins by attempting to establish a connection to the server. The server can accept or deny the connection. After the connection is established, client and server communicate through sockets.

The server must be running when a client starts. The server waits for a connection request from a client. The statements needed to create a server and a client and to exchange data between them are shown in Figure 16.1.

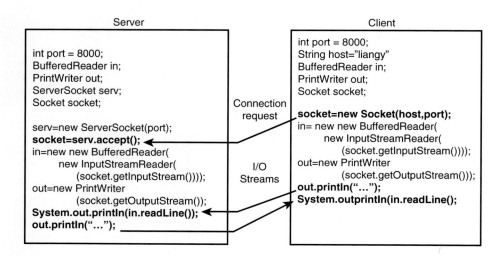

Figure 16.1 *The server uses I/O streams to establish a server socket that facilitates communication between the server and the client.*

To establish a server, you need to create a server socket and attach it to a port, which is where the server listens for connections. The port identifies the TCP service on the socket. Port numbers between 0 and 1023 are reserved for privileged processes. For instance, the e-mail server runs on port 25, and the Web server usually runs on port 80. You can choose any port number that is not currently used by any other process. The following statement creates a server socket s:

```
ServerSocket s = new ServerSocket(port);
```

NOTE

Attempting to create a server socket on a port already in use would cause the `java.net.BindException` runtime exception.

After a server socket is created, the server can use this statement to listen for connections:

```
Socket connectToClient = s.accept();
```

This statement waits until a client connects to the server socket. The client issues this statement to request a connection to a server:

```
Socket connectToServer = new Socket(ServerName, port);
```

This statement opens a socket so that the client program can communicate with the server. *ServerName* is the server's Internet hostname or IP address. The following statement creates a socket at port 8000 on the client machine to connect to the host `liangy.ipfw.edu`:

```
Socket connectToServer = new Socket("liangy.ipfw.edu", 8000);
```

Alternatively, you can use the IP address to create a socket:

```
Socket connectToServer = new Socket("149.164.29.27", 8000)
```

An IP address, such as `149.164.29.27`, consists of four dotted decimal numbers between 0 and 255. It constitutes the unique identity of a computer on the Internet. Since so large a sequence of numbers cannot easily be remembered, they are often mapped to meaningful names called *hostnames*, such as `liangy.ipfw.edu`.

NOTE

There are special servers on the Internet to translate hostnames into IP addresses. These servers are called Domain Name Servers (DNS). The translation is done behind the scenes. When you create a socket with a hostname, the Java Runtime System asks the DNS to translate it into the IP address.

After the server accepts the connection, communication between the server and the client is conducted just as it is for I/O streams. To get an input stream and an output stream, use the `getInputStream()` and `getOutputStream()` methods on a socket object. For example, the following statements create an `InputStream` stream, `isFromServer`, and an `OutputStream` stream, `osToServer`, from the socket `connectToServer`:

```
InputStream isFromServer = connectToServer.getInputStream();
OutputStream osToServer = connectToServer.getOutputStream();
```

The `InputStream` and `OutputStream` streams are used to read or write bytes. You can use `DataInputStream`, `DataOutputStream`, `BufferedReader`, and `PrintWriter` to wrap on the `InputStream`, and `OutputStream` to read or write values of data, such as `int`, `double`, or `String`. For example, the following statements create a `BufferedReader` stream, `isFromClient`, and a `PrintWriter` stream, `osToClient`, for reading and writing primitive data values:

```
BufferedReader isFromClient = new BufferedReader(
  new InputStreamReader(connectToClient.getInputStream()));
PrintWriter osToClient = new PrintWriter(
  connectToClient.getOutputStream(), true);
```

The Boolean `true` is for auto flush, and the `print()` methods flush the output buffer. The server can use `isFromClient.read()` to receive data from the client and `osToClient.write()` to send data to the client.

Example 16.1 A Client/Server Example

This example presents a client program and a server program. The client sends data to a server. The server receives the data, uses them to produce a result, and then sends the result back to the client. The client displays the result on the console. In this example, the data sent from the client are the radius of a circle, and the result produced by the server is the area of the circle (see Figure 16.2).

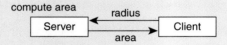

Figure 16.2   *The client sends the radius to the server; the server computes the area and sends it to the client.*

The server program follows. A sample run of the program is shown in Figure 16.3.

```
// Server.java: The server accepts data from the client, processes it
// and returns the result back to the client
package Chapter16;

import java.io.*;
import java.net.*;
import java.util.*;

public class Server
{
  // Main method
  public static void main(String[] args)
  {
    try
```

```
      {
        // Create a server socket
        ServerSocket serverSocket = new ServerSocket(8000);

        // Start listening for connections on the server socket
        Socket connectToClient = serverSocket.accept();

        // Create a buffered reader stream to get data from the client
        BufferedReader isFromClient = new BufferedReader(new
          InputStreamReader(connectToClient.getInputStream()));

        // Create a buffered writer stream to send data to the client
        PrintWriter osToClient = new PrintWriter(
          connectToClient.getOutputStream(), true);

        // Continuously read from the client and process it,
        // and send result back to the client
        while (true)
        {
          // Read a line and create a string tokenizer
          StringTokenizer st = new StringTokenizer
            (isFromClient.readLine());

          // Convert string to double
          double radius = new Double(st.nextToken()).doubleValue();

          // Display radius on console
          System.out.println("radius received from client: "
            +radius);

          // Compute area
          double area = radius*radius*Math.PI;

          // Send the result to the client
          osToClient.println(area);

          // Print the result to the console
          System.out.println("Area found: "+area);
        }
      }
      catch(IOException ex)
      {
        System.err.println(ex);
      }
    }
  }
```

The client program follows. A sample run of the program is shown in Figure 16.4.

```
// Client.java: The client sends the input to the server and receives
// result back from the server
package Chapter16;

import java.io.*;
import java.net.*;
import java.util.*;
import Chapter2.MyInput;
```

continues

```java
public class Client
{
  // Main method
  public static void main(String[] args)
  {
    try
    {
      // Create a socket to connect to the server
      Socket connectToServer = new Socket("localhost",8000);

      // Create a buffered input stream to receive data
      // from the server
      BufferedReader isFromServer = new BufferedReader(
        new InputStreamReader(connectToServer.getInputStream()));

      // Create a buffered output stream to send data to the server
      PrintWriter osToServer =
        new PrintWriter(connectToServer.getOutputStream(), true);

      // Continuously send radius and receive area
      // from the server
      while (true)
      {
        // Read the radius from the keyboard
        System.out.print("Please enter a radius: ");
        double radius = MyInput.readDouble();

        // Send the radius to the server
        osToServer.println(radius);

        // Get area from the server
        StringTokenizer st = new StringTokenizer(
          isFromServer.readLine());

        // Convert string to double
        double area = new Double(
          st.nextToken ()).doubleValue();

        // Print area on the console
        System.out.println("Area received from the server is "
          +area);
      }
    }
    catch (IOException ex)
    {
      System.err.println(ex);
    }
  }
}
```

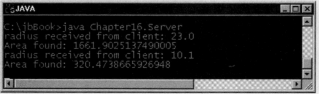

Figure 16.3   *The server receives a radius from the client, computes the area, and sends the area to the client.*

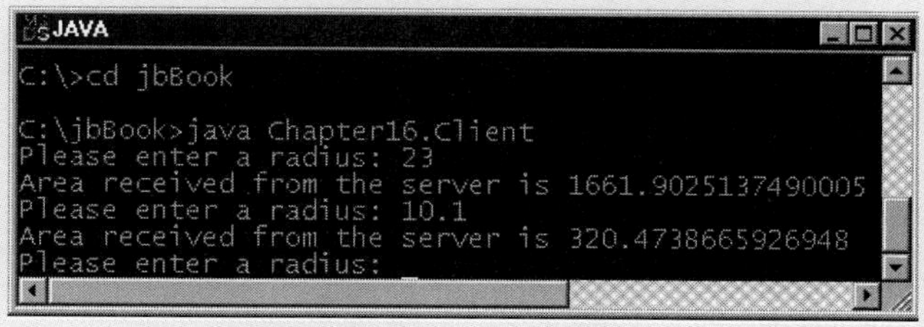

Figure 16.4   *The client sends the radius to the server and receives the area from the server.*

Example Review

You should start the server program first, then start the client program. The client program prompts the user to enter a radius, which is sent to the server. The server computes the area and sends it back to the client. This process is repeated until one of the two programs terminates. To terminate a program, press Ctrl+C on the console if running on Windows, or kill the process if running on UNIX.

The networking classes are in the package `java.net`. This should be imported when writing Java network programs.

The `Server` class creates a `ServerSocket` `serverSocket` and attaches it to port 8000 using the following statement:

```
ServerSocket serverSocket = new ServerSocket(8000);
```

The server then starts to listen for connection requests using the following statement:

```
Socket connectToClient = serverSocket.accept();
```

The server waits until a client requests a connection. After it is connected, the server reads the radius from the client through an input stream, computes the area, and sends the result to the client through an output stream.

Here is the statement the `Client` class uses to create a socket that will request a connection to the server at port 8000:

```
Socket connectToServer = new Socket("localhost", 8000);
```

The hostname `localhost` refers to the machine on which the client is running. If you run the server and the client on different machines, you need to replace `localhost` with the server machine's hostname or IP address. In this example, the server and the client are running on the same machine.

If the server is not running, the client program terminates with an `IOException`. After it is connected, the client gets input and output streams— wrapped by buffered reader and writer streams—in order to receive and send data to the server.

Serving Multiple Clients

It is not at all unusual for multiple clients to connect to a server at the same time. Typically, a server runs constantly on a server computer, and clients from all over the Internet may want to connect to it. You can use threads to handle the server's multiple clients simultaneously. Simply create a thread for each connection. The server should handle the establishment of a connection in the following way:

```
while (true)
{
  Socket connectToClient = serverSocket.accept();
  Thread t = new ThreadClass(connectToClient);
  t.start();
}
```

The server socket can have many connections. Each iteration of the while loop creates a new connection. When the connection is established, a new thread is created to handle communication between the server and the new client; this allows multiple connections to run at the same time.

Example 16.2 Serving Multiple Clients

This example shows how to serve multiple clients simultaneously. For each connection, the server starts a new thread. This thread continuously receives input (the radius of a circle) from a client and sends the result (the area of the circle) back to the client (see Figure 16.5).

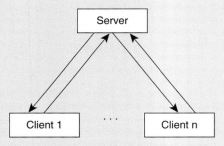

Figure 16.5 *Multithreading enables a server to handle multiple independent clients.*

The new server program follows. A sample run of the server is shown in Figure 16.6, and sample runs of two clients are shown in Figures 16.7 and 16.8.

```
// MultiThreadsServer.java: The server can communicate with
// multiple clients concurrently using the multiple threads
package Chapter16;

import java.io.*;
import java.net.*;
import java.util.*;
```

```java
public class MultiThreadsServer
{
  // Main method
  public static void main(String[] args)
  {
    try
    {
      // Create a server socket
      ServerSocket serverSocket = new ServerSocket(8000);

      // To number a thread
      int i = 0;

      while (true)
      {
        // Listen for a new connection request
        Socket connectToClient = serverSocket.accept();

        // Print the new connect number on the console
        System.out.println("Starting thread "+i);

        // Create a new thread for the connection
        ThreadHandler thread = new ThreadHandler(connectToClient, i);

        // Start the new thread
        thread.start();

        // Increment i to number the next connection
        i++;
      }
    }
    catch(IOException ex)
    {
      System.err.println(ex);
    }
  }
}

// Define the thread class for handling a new connection
class ThreadHandler extends Thread
{
  private Socket connectToClient; // A connected socket
  private int counter; // Number the thread

  // Construct a thread
  public ThreadHandler(Socket socket, int i)
  {
    connectToClient = socket;
    counter = i;
  }

  // Implement the run() method for the thread
  public void run()
  {
    try
    {
      // Create data input and print streams
      BufferedReader isFromClient = new BufferedReader(
        new InputStreamReader(connectToClient.getInputStream()));
      PrintWriter osToClient =
        new PrintWriter(connectToClient.getOutputStream(), true);
```

continues

677

```
                    // Continuously serve the client
                    while (true)
                    {
                      // Receive data from the client in string
                      StringTokenizer st = new StringTokenizer
                        (isFromClient.readLine());

                      // Get radius
                      double radius = new Double(st.nextToken()).doubleValue();
                      System.out.println("radius received from client: "+radius);

                      // Compute area
                      double area = radius*radius*Math.PI;

                      // Send area back to the client
                      osToClient.println(area);
                      System.out.println("Area found: "+area);
                    }
                  }
                  catch(IOException ex)
                  {
                    System.err.println(ex);
                  }
                }
              }
```

Figure 16.6   *The server spawns a thread in order to serve a client.*

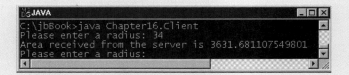

Figure 16.7   *The first client communicates to the server on thread 0.*

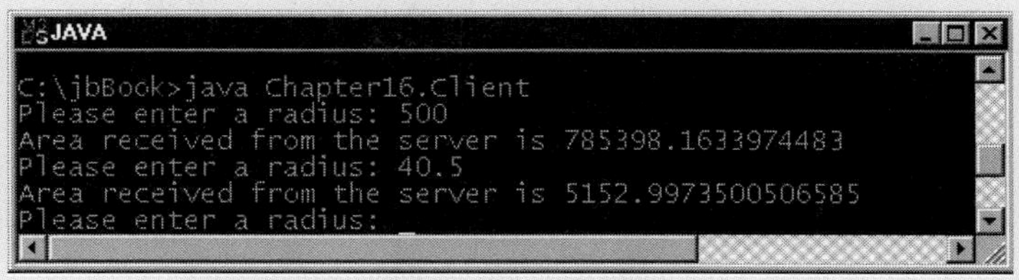

```
JAVA                                                    _ □ ×
C:\jbBook>java Chapter16.Client
Please enter a radius: 500
Area received from the server is 785398.1633974483
Please enter a radius: 40.5
Area received from the server is 5152.9973500506585
Please enter a radius:
```

Figure 16.8   *The second client communicates to the server on thread 1.*

Example Review

The server creates a server socket at port 8000, then waits for a connection. After the connection is established with a client, the server creates a new thread to handle communication with another client, then waits for another connection.

The threads, which run independently of one another, communicate with designated clients. Each thread creates buffered reader and writer streams that receive and send data to the client.

This server accepts an unlimited number of clients. To limit the number of concurrent connections, you can use a thread group to monitor the number of active threads and modify the `while` loop:

```
ThreadGroup g = new ThreadGroup("serving clients");

while (g.activeCount() < maxThreadLimit)
{
  // Listen for a new connection request
  Socket connectToClient = serverSocket.accept();

  // Print the new connect number on the console
  System.out.println("Starting thread " + i);

  // Create a new thread for the connection
  Thread t = new Thread(g, new ThreadHandler(connectToClient, i));

  // Start the new thread
  t.start();

  // Increment i to label the next connection
  i++;
}
```

Windows has a Telnet utility. Telnet can be used to log onto another host and to communicate with other services on the host. Telnet can be used as clients to test the server. This is convenient if you don't have the client program in place.

You can enter the `telnet` command from the DOS prompt to display a Telnet window, as shown in Figure 16.9. In the Telnet window, choose Connect, Remote System to display the Connect dialog box. Enter the server's hostname and port number, and press Connect. You must have the server already running. Here is a sample run with a server running, as shown in Figure 16.10, and with the Telnet session running, as shown in Figure 16.11.

continues

Figure 16.9   *A Telnet client connects to the server on port 8000.*

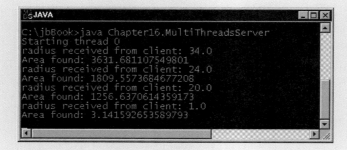

Figure 16.10   *The server receives the radii 34.0, 24.0, 20.0, and 1.0 from the Telnet client and sends the corresponding areas to the client.*

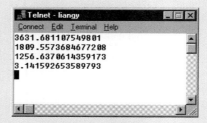

Figure 16.11   *The user enters the radius (not echo printed in the window). The Telnet client sends the radius to the server and receives the area displayed in the Telnet window.*

Applet Clients

Due to security constraints, applets can only connect to the host from which they were loaded. Therefore, the HTML file must be located on the machine on which the server is running. Following is an example of how to use an applet to connect to a server.

Example 16.3 Networking in Applets

This example, which is similar to the one in Example 15.6, "Using Random Access Files," in Chapter 15, "Input and Output," shows how to use an applet to register students. The client collects and sends registration information to the server, which appends the information to a data file using a random access file stream. The server program follows. A sample run of the program is shown in Figure 16.12.

```java
// RegServer.java: The server for the appelt repsonsible for
// writing on the server side
package Chapter16;

import java.io.*;
import java.net.*;
import Chapter15.Student;

public class RegServer
{
  // Main method
  public static void main(String[] args)
  {
    // A random access file
    RandomAccessFile raf = null;

    // Open the local file on the server side
    try
    {
      // Open the file if the file exists, create a new file
      // if the file does not exist
      raf = new RandomAccessFile("student.dat", "rw");
    }
    catch(IOException ex)
    {
      System.out.println("Error: " + ex);
      System.exit(0);
    }

    // Establish server socket
    try
    {
      // Create a server socket
      ServerSocket serverSocket = new ServerSocket(8000);

      // Count the number of threads started
      int count = 1;

      while (true)
      {
        // Connect to a client
        Socket socket = serverSocket.accept();

        // Start a new thread to register a client
        new RegistrationThread(raf, socket, count++).start();
      }
    }
```

continues

681

```java
      catch (IOException ex)
      {
        System.err.println(ex);
      }
    }
  }
}

// Define a thread to process the client registration
class RegistrationThread extends Thread
{
  // The socket to serve a client
  private Socket socket;

  // The file to store the records
  static RandomAccessFile raf = null;

  private int num; // The thread number

  // Buffered reader to get input from the client
  private BufferedReader in;

  // Create a registration thread
  public RegistrationThread(RandomAccessFile raf,
    Socket socket, int num)
  {
    this.raf = raf;
    this.socket = socket;
    this.num = num;

    System.out.println("Thread " + num + " running");

    // Create an input stream to receive data from a client
    try
    {
      in = new BufferedReader
        (new InputStreamReader(socket.getInputStream()));
    }
    catch(IOException ex)
    {
      System.out.println("Error: " + ex);
    }
  }

  public void run()
  {
    String name;
    String street;
    String city;
    String state;
    String zip;

    try
    {
      // Receive data from the client
      name = new String(in.readLine());
      street = new String(in.readLine());
      city = new String(in.readLine());
      state = new String(in.readLine());
      zip = new String(in.readLine());
```

```
            // Display data received
            System.out.println(
              "The following data received from the client");
            System.out.println("name: " + name);
            System.out.println("street: " + street);
            System.out.println("city: " + city);
            System.out.println("state: " + state);
            System.out.println("zip: " + zip);

            // Create a student instance
            Student student = new Student(name, street, city, state, zip);

            writeToFile(student);
          }
          catch (IOException ex)
          {
            System.out.println(ex);
          }
        }

        private synchronized static void writeToFile(Student student)
        {
          try
          {
          // Append it to "student.dat"
          raf.seek(raf.length());
          student.writeStudent(raf);
          }
          catch (IOException ex)
          {
            System.err.println(ex);
          }
        }
      }
```

The applet client follows, and its sample run is shown in Figure 16.13.

```
    // RegClient.java: The applet client for gathering student
    // informationthe and passing it to the server
    package Chapter16;

    import java.io.*;
    import java.net.*;
    import java.awt.BorderLayout;
    import java.awt.event.*;
    import javax.swing.*;
    import Chapter15.StudentPanel;
    import Chapter15.Student;
    import Chapter8.MyFrameWithExitHandling;

    public class RegClient extends JApplet implements ActionListener
    {
      // Button for registering a student in the file
      private JButton jbtRegister = new JButton("Register");

      // Create student information panel
      private StudentPanel studentPanel = new StudentPanel();
```

continues

```
      public void init()
      {
        // Add the student panel and button to the applet
        getContentPane().add(studentPanel, BorderLayout.CENTER);
        getContentPane().add(jbtRegister, BorderLayout.SOUTH);

        // Register listener
        jbtRegister.addActionListener(this);
      }

      // Handle button action
      public void actionPerformed(ActionEvent e)
      {
        if (e.getSource() == jbtRegister)
        {
          try
          {
            // Establish connection with the server
            Socket socket = new Socket("localhost", 8000);

            // Create an output stream to the server
            PrintWriter toServer =
              new PrintWriter(socket.getOutputStream(), true);

            // Get text field
            Student s = studentPanel.getStudent();

            // Get data from text fields and send it to the server
            toServer.println(s.getName());
            toServer.println(s.getStreet());
            toServer.println(s.getCity());
            toServer.println(s.getState());
            toServer.println(s.getZip());
          }
          catch (IOException ex)
          {
            System.err.println(ex);
          }
        }
      }

      // Run the applet as an application
      public static void main(String[] args)
      {
        // Create a frame
        MyFrameWithExitHandling frame = new MyFrameWithExitHandling(
          "Register Student Client");

        // Create an instance of the applet
        RegClient applet = new RegClient();

        // Add the applet instance to the frame
        frame.getContentPane().add(applet, BorderLayout.CENTER);

        // Invoke init() and start()
        applet.init();
        applet.start();

        // Display the frame
        frame.pack();
        frame.setVisible(true);
      }
    }
```

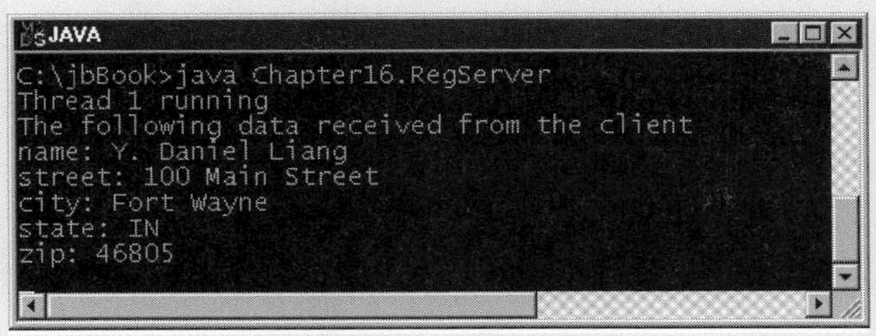

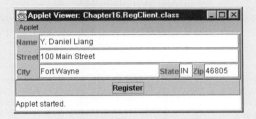

Figure 16.12   *The server receives information (name, street, city, state, and zip code) from the client, and stores it in a file.*

Figure 16.13   *The client gathers the name and address and sends them to the server.*

Example Review

The server handles multiple clients. It waits for a connection request from the client in the `while` loop. After the connection is established, the server creates a thread to serve the client. The server then stays in the `while` loop to listen for the next connection request.

The server passes `raf` (random access file stream), `socket` (connection socket), and `num` (thread number) to the thread. The `num` argument is nonessential. It is only used for identifying the thread. The thread receives student information from the client through the `BufferedReader` stream and appends a student record to **student.dat** using the random access file stream `raf`.

The `StudentPanel` and `Student` classes are defined in Example 15.6. The following statement creates an instance of `Student`:

```
Student s = new Student(name, street, city, state, zip);
```

The following code writes the student record into the file:

```
s.writeStudent(raf);
```

The client is an applet and can run standalone. The data are entered into text fields (name, street, city, state, and zip). When the Register button is clicked, the data from the text fields are collected and sent to the server.

continues

When multiple clients register students simultaneously, data corruption may result. To avoid this, the `writeToFile()` method is synchronized and defined as a static method. Thus, synchronization of this method is at the class level, meaning that only one object of the `RegistrationThread` can execute the `writeToFile()` to write a student to the file at a given time.

Viewing Web Pages

Given its URL, a Web browser can view an HTML page; for example, **http://www.sun.com**. HTTP is the common standard used for communication between Web servers and the Internet. You can open a URL and view a Web page in a Java applet. A URL is a description of a resource location on the Internet. Java provides a class, `java.net.URL`, to manipulate URLs. The following code can be written to create a URL:

```
try
{
  URL location = new URL(URLString);
}
catch(MalformedURLException ex)
{
}
```

This statement, for instance, creates a Java URL object:

```
try
{
  URL location = new URL("http://www.sun.com");
}
catch(MalformedURLException ex)
{
}
```

A `MalformedURLException` is thrown if the URL string has a syntax error. For example, the URL string `"http:/www.sun.com"` would cause the `MalformedURLException` runtime error because two slashes (`//`) are required.

To actually view the contents of an HTML page, you would need to write the following code:

```
AppletContext context = getAppletContext();
context.showDocument(location);
```

The `java.applet.AppletContext` class provides the environment for displaying Web page contents. The `showDocument()` method displays the Web page in the environment.

Example 16.4 Viewing HTML Pages from Java

This example demonstrates an applet that views Web pages. The Web page's URL is entered, the Go button is clicked, and the Web page is displayed (see Figures 16.14 and 16.15).

```java
// ViewingWebPages.java: Access HTML pages through applets
package Chapter16;

import java.net.*;
import java.awt.*;
import java.awt.event.*;
import javax.swing.*;
import java.applet.*;

public class ViewingWebPages extends JApplet implements ActionListener
{
  // Button to display an HTML page on the applet
  private JButton jbtGo = new JButton("Go");

  // Text field for receiving the URL of the HTML page
  private JTextField jtfURL = new JTextField(20);

  // Initialize the applet
  public void init()
  {
    // Add URL text field and Go button
    getContentPane().setLayout(new FlowLayout());
    getContentPane().add(new JLabel("URL"));
    getContentPane().add(jtfURL);
    getContentPane().add(jbtGo);

    // Register listener
    jbtGo.addActionListener(this);
  }

  // Handle the ActionEvent
  public void actionPerformed(ActionEvent evt)
  {
    if (evt.getSource() == jbtGo)
      try
      {
        AppletContext context = getAppletContext();

        // Get the URL from text field
        URL url = new URL(jtfURL.getText());
        context.showDocument(url);
      }
      catch(Exception ex)
      {
        showStatus("Error " + ex);
      }
  }
}
```

continues

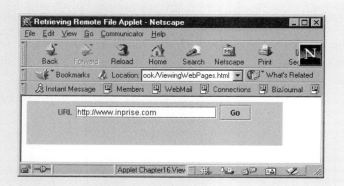

Figure 16.14   *Given a URL, the applet can display a Web page.*

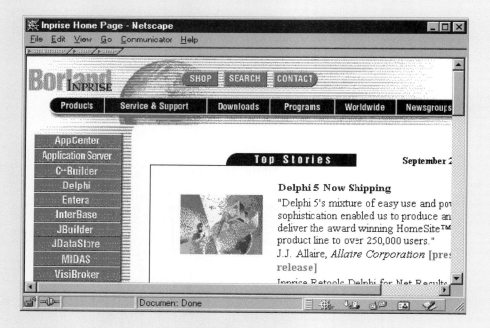

Figure 16.15   *The Web page specified in the applet is displayed in the browser.*

Example Review

When the URL of a publicly available HTML file is entered and the Go button is clicked, a new HTML page is displayed. The page containing the applet becomes the previous page. A user could return to the previous page to enter a new URL and then view the new page.

Anyone using this program would have to run it from a Web browser, not from the Applet Viewer utility.

Retrieving Files from Web Servers

You can display an HTML page from an applet, as shown in the preceding section. But sometimes you need the Web server to give you access to the contents of a file. This access allows you to pass dynamic information from the server to the applet clients or the standalone application clients, as shown in Figure 16.16. The file stored on the server side can be a normal text file or a binary file that is created using `DataOutput` streams. To access the file, you would use the `openStream()` method defined in the URL class to open a stream to the file's URL.

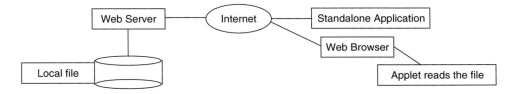

Figure 16.16   *The applet client or application client retrieves files from a Web server.*

The following method opens a connection to the file's URL and returns an `Input-Stream` so that you can read from that connection:

```
public final InputStream openStream() throws IOException
```

For example, the following statements open an input stream for the URL **http://www.ipfw.edu/kt2/liangy/web/java/in.dat** for the file **in.dat**, which is stored on the author's Web server.

```
try
{
  String urlString = "http://www.ipfw.edu/kt2/liangy/web/java/in.dat";
  url = new URL(urlString);
  InputStream is = url.openStream();
}
catch (MalformedURLException ex)
{
  System.out.println("Bad URL : " + url);
}
catch (IOException ex)
{
  System.out.println("IO Error : " + ex.getMessage());
}
```

Example 16.5 Retrieving Remote Data Files

This example, which is similar to Example 15.5, "Using `StreamTokenizer`," in Chapter 15, demonstrates an applet that computes and displays student exam scores.

continues

Rather than reading the file from the local system, this example reads the file from a Web server. The file contains student exam scores. Each record in the input file consists of a student name, two midterm exam scores, and a final exam score. The program reads the fields for each record, computes the total score, and displays the result in a text area. Figure 16.17 contains the output of a sample run of the program.

```java
// RetrievingRemoteFile.java: Retrieve remote files in applets.
// This program can also run as an application.
package Chapter16;

import java.applet.Applet;
import java.awt.*;
import java.io.*;
import java.net.*;
import javax.swing.*;
import Chapter8.MyFrameWithExitHandling;

public class RetrievingRemoteFile extends JApplet
{
  // The author's Web site URL string for the input file
  private String urlString =
    // Get in.dat from a remote host
    "http://www.ipfw.edu/kt2/liangy/web/java/in.dat";
    // Get in.dat from the local file system
    //"file:/C:\\jbBook\\Chapter16\\in.dat";

  // Declare a Java URL object
  private URL url;

  // The StreamTokenizer for parsing input
  private StreamTokenizer in;

  // The fields in the file
  private String sname = null;
  private double midterm1 = 0;
  private double midterm2 = 0;
  private double finalScore = 0;

  // Total score for a student
  private double total = 0;

  // Text area for displaying result
  JTextArea jta = new JTextArea(5, 10);

  // Initialize the applet
  public void init()
  {
    try
    {
      url = new URL(urlString);  // Create a URL
      InputStream is = url.openStream();  // Create a stream

      // Create streamtokenizer
      in = new StreamTokenizer(
        new BufferedReader(new InputStreamReader(is)));
    }
    catch (MalformedURLException ex)
```

```
        {
          System.out.println("Bad URL : " + url);
        }
        catch (IOException ex)
        {
          System.out.println("IO Error : " + ex.getMessage());
        }

        // Create a scroll pane and add text area to the scroll pane
        JScrollPane jsp = new JScrollPane(jta);

        // Add the scroll pane to the applet
        getContentPane().add(jsp);

        try
        {
          // Read first token
          in.nextToken();

          // Process a record
          while (in.ttype != in.TT_EOF)
          {
            // Get student name
            if (in.ttype == in.TT_WORD)
              sname = in.sval;
            else
              System.out.println("Bad file format");

            // Get midterm1
            if (in.nextToken() == in.TT_NUMBER)
              midterm1 = in.nval;
            else
              System.out.println("Bad file format");

            // Get midterm2
            if (in.nextToken() == in.TT_NUMBER)
              midterm2 = in.nval;
            else
              System.out.println("Bad file format");

            // Get final score
            if (in.nextToken() == in.TT_NUMBER)
              finalScore = in.nval;

            // Compute total score
            total = midterm1*0.3 + midterm2*0.3 + finalScore*0.4;

            // Display result
            jta.append(sname + " " + total + '\n');

            // Get the next token
            in.nextToken();
          }
        }
        catch (IOException ex)
        {
          System.out.println("IO Errors " + ex.getMessage());
        }
      }
```

continues

```
        // Run the applet as an application
        public static void main(String[] args)
        {
          // Create a frame
          MyFrameWithExitHandling frame = new MyFrameWithExitHandling(
            "Retrieve Remote File Demo");

          // Create an instance of the applet
          RetrievingRemoteFile applet = new RetrievingRemoteFile();

          // Add the applet instance to the frame
          frame.getContentPane().add(applet, BorderLayout.CENTER);

          // Invoke init() and start()
          applet.init();
          applet.start();

          // Display the frame
          frame.setSize(300, 300);
          frame.setVisible(true);
        }
    }
```

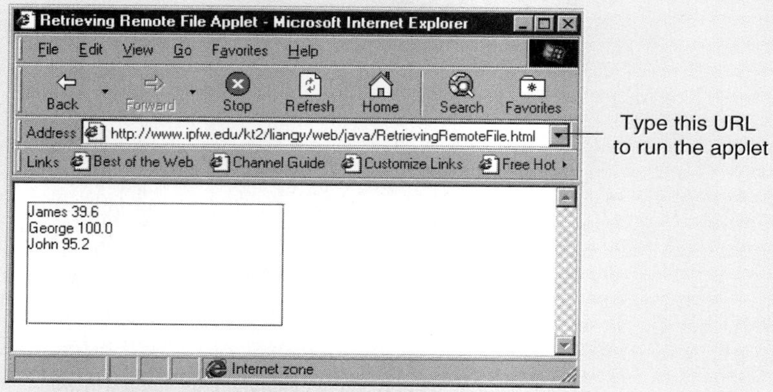

Type this URL
to run the applet

Figure 16.17 *The applet retrieves the file from the Web server and processes it.*

Example Review

This program can run as an applet or an application. In order for it to run as an applet, a user would need to place three files on the Web server:

RetrievingRemoteFile.class
RetrievingRemoteFile.html
in.dat

RetrievingRemoteFile.html can be browsed from any JDK 1.2-aware Web browser.

The `url = new URL(urlString)` statement creates a URL. The `InputStream` `is = url.openStream()` opens an input stream to read the remote file. After the input stream is established, reading data from the remote file is just like reading data locally.

The program uses `StreamTokenizer` to extract a student's name, two midterm exam scores, and the final exam score from the input stream, computes the total score, and displays it on the text area.

For this program to run as an application, you must place the following two files in the same directory:

RetrievingRemoteFile.class

in.dat

TIP

If you have no Internet access when testing this example, place all the files on your local disk and replace the urlString as follows:

```
private String urlString = "file:/C:\\jbBook\\Chapter16\\in.dat";
```

Chapter Summary

In this chapter, you learned how to write client/server applications and programs to work with the Web server. In client/server computing, the server must be running when a client starts. The server waits for a connection request from a client.

To create a server, you must first obtain a server socket using `new ServerSocket(port)`. After a server socket is created, the server can start to listen for connections using the `accept()` method on the server socket. The client requests a connection to a server by using `new socket(ServerName, port)` to create a client socket.

Stream socket communication is very much like input/output streams after the connection between a server and a client is established. The server and the client can communicate through input and output streams using `BufferedReader` and `PrintWriter`.

Often a server must work with multiple clients at the same time. You can use threads to handle the server's multiple clients simultaneously by simply creating a thread for each connection.

Applets are recommended for deploying multiple clients. They can be run anywhere with a single copy of the program. However, because of security restrictions, an applet client can only connect to the server where the applet is loaded.

To get the HTML pages through HTTP, Java programs can directly connect with a Web server. You can use the URL to view a Web page in a Java applet. To retrieve data files on the Web server from applets, you can open a stream on the file's URL on the Web server.

Chapter Review

16.1. How do you create a server socket? What port numbers can be used? What happens if a requested socket number is already in use? Can a port connect to multiple clients?

16.2. What are the differences between a server socket and a client socket?

16.3. How does a client program initiate a connection?

16.4. How does a server accept a connection?

16.5. How are data transferred between a client and a server?

16.6. How do you make a server serve multiple clients?

16.7. Can an application retrieve a file from a remote host? Can an application update a file on a remote host?

Programming Exercises

16.1. Rewrite Example 16.2 using GUI for the server and client rather than console input and output. Display a message in the text area on the server side when the server receives a message from a client, as shown in Figure 16.18. On the client side, you can use a text field to enter the radius, as shown in Figure 16.19.

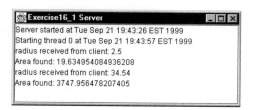

Figure 16.18   *The server receives a radius from a client, computes the area, and sends the area to the client.*

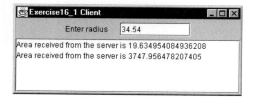

Figure 16.19   *The client sends the radius to the server and receives the area from the server.*

16.2. Write a client/server application. The client should retrieve a file from the Web server. The client can run as an application or an applet—similar to the one in Example 15.4, "Displaying a File in a Text Area"—that includes a text field in which to enter the URL of the filename, a text area in which to show the file, and a button that can be used to submit an action. Also, add a label at the bottom of the frame to indicate the status, such as File loaded successfully or Network connection problem. Figure 16.20 demonstrates an example of viewing the file at http://www.ipfw.edu/kt2/liangy/default.htm located on the Web server. Swing provides a new component named `javax.swing.JEditorPane`, which can be used to render HTML files. For more information, see Chapter 5, "Swing Components," in my *Rapid Java Application Development Using JBuilder 3*.

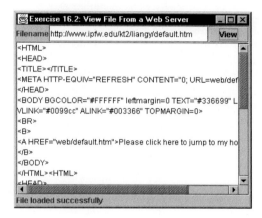

Figure 16.20   *The program displays the contents of a specified file on the Web server.*

16.3. Modify Example 16.3, "Networking in Applets," by adding the following features:

1. Add a View button to the user interface to allow the client to view a record for a specified name. The user will be able to enter a name in the Name field and click the View button to display the record for the student, as shown in Figure 16.21.

2. Limit the concurrent connections to two clients.

3. Display the status of the submission (Successful or Failed) on a label.

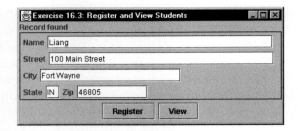

Figure 16.21 *You can view or register students in this applet.*

16.4. Write an applet that will display a stock index ticker—similar to the ones in Exercise 15.6. Ensure that the applet gets the stock index from a file stored on the Web server. Enable the applet to run standalone.

16.5. Write an applet to show the number of visits made to a Web page. The count should be stored on the server side in a file. Every time the page is visited or reloaded, the applet should send a request to the server, and the server should increase the count and send it to the applet. The applet should then display the count in a message, such as You are visitor number: 1000. The server can read or write to the file using a random file access stream.

APPENDIXES

The appendixes cover a mixed bag of topics. Appendix A lists Java keywords. Appendix B gives tables of ASCII characters and their associated codes in decimal and in hex. Appendix C shows the operator precedence. Appendix D summarizes Java modifiers and their usage. Appendix E introduces HTML basics. Appendix F contains information for using the companion CD-ROM. Appendix G demonstrates rapid Java application development using JBuilder. Finally, Appendix H provides a glossary of key terms and their definitions.

APPENDIX A   JAVA KEYWORDS

APPENDIX B   THE ASCII CHARACTER SET

APPENDIX C   OPERATOR PRECEDENCE CHART

APPENDIX D   JAVA MODIFIERS

APPENDIX E   AN HTML TUTORIAL

APPENDIX F   USING THE COMPANION CD-ROM

APPENDIX G   RAPID JAVA APPLICATION DEVELOPMENT USING JBUILDER

APPENDIX H   GLOSSARY

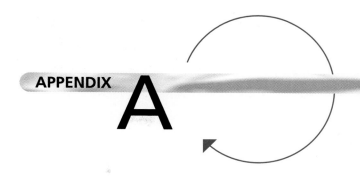
JAVA KEYWORDS

The following 47 keywords are reserved for use by the Java language:

abstract	finally	public
boolean	float	return
break	for	short
byte	goto	static
case	if	super
catch	implements	switch
char	import	synchronized
class	instanceof	this
const	int	throw
continue	interface	throws
default	long	transient
do	native	try
double	new	void
else	package	volatile
extends	private	while
final	protected	

The keywords goto and const are C++ keywords reserved, but not currently used, in Java. This enables Java compilers to identify them and to produce better error messages if they appear in Java programs.

The Boolean literal values true and false are not keywords. Similarly, the null object value is not classified as a keyword. You cannot use them for other purposes, however.

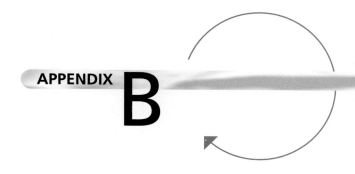

THE ASCII CHARACTER SET

Tables B.1 and B.2 show ASCII characters and their respective decimal and hexadecimal codes. The decimal or hexadecimal code of a character is a combination of its row index and column index. For example, in Table B.1, the letter A is at row 6 and column 5, so its decimal equivalent is 65; in Table B.2, letter A is at row 4 and column 1, so its hexadecimal equivalent is 41.

TABLE B.1   ASCII Character Set in the Decimal Index

	0	1	2	3	4	5	6	7	8	9
0	nul	soh	stx	etx	eot	enq	ack	bel	bs	ht
1	nl	vt	ff	cr	so	si	dle	dc1	dc2	dc3
2	dc4	nak	syn	etb	can	em	sub	esc	fs	gs
3	rs	us	sp	!	"	#	$	%	&	'
4	(	)	*	+	,	-	.	/	0	1
5	2	3	4	5	6	7	8	9	:	;
6	<	=	>	?	@	A	B	C	D	E
7	F	G	H	I	J	K	L	M	N	O
8	P	Q	R	S	T	U	V	W	X	Y
9	Z	[	\	]	^	_	`	a	b	c
10	d	e	f	g	h	i	j	k	l	m
11	n	o	p	q	r	s	t	u	v	w
12	x	y	z	{	|	}	~	del		

TABLE B.2   ASCII Character Set in the Hexadecimal Index

	0	1	2	3	4	5	6	7	8	9	A	B	C	D	E	F
0	nul	soh	stx	etx	eot	enq	ack	bel	bs	ht	nl	vt	ff	cr	so	si
1	dle	dc1	dc2	dc3	dc4	nak	syn	etb	can	em	sub	esc	fs	gs	rs	us
2	sp	!	"	#	$	%	&	'	(	)	*	+	,	-	.	/
3	0	1	2	3	4	5	6	7	8	9	:	;	<	=	>	?
4	@	A	B	C	D	E	F	G	H	I	J	K	L	M	N	O
5	P	Q	R	S	T	U	V	W	X	Y	Z	[	\	]	^	_
6	`	a	b	c	d	e	f	g	h	i	j	k	l	m	n	o
7	p	q	r	s	t	u	v	w	x	y	z	{	|	}	~	del

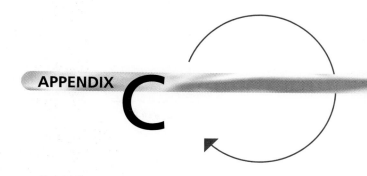

OPERATOR PRECEDENCE CHART

The operators are shown in decreasing order of precedence from top to bottom. Operators in the same group have the same precedence and are executed from left to right.

Operator	Type
()	Parentheses
()	Function call
[]	Array subscript
.	Object member access
++	Prefix increment
--	Prefix decrement
+	Unary plus
-	Unary minus
!	Unary logical negation
(type)	Unary casting
new	Creating object
*	Multiplication
/	Division
%	Integer modulus
+	Addition
-	Subtraction
<	Less than
<=	Less than or equal to
>	Greater than
>=	Greater than or equal to
instanceof	Checking object type
==	Equal comparison
!=	Not equal
&&	Boolean AND
||	Boolean OR
?:	Ternary condition (Conditional expression)

Operator	Type
=	Assignment
+=	Addition assignment
-=	Subtraction assignment
*=	Multiplication assignment
/=	Division assignment
%=	Integer modulus assignment
++	Postfix increment
--	Postfix decrement

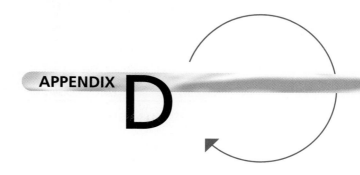

JAVA MODIFIERS

Modifiers are used on classes and class members (methods and data), but the `final` modifier can also be used on local variables in a method. A modifier that can be applied to a class is called a *class modifier*. A modifier that can be applied to a method is called a *method modifier*. A modifier that can be applied to a data field is called a *data modifier*. Some modifiers can be applied to all three entities. The following table gives a summary of the modifiers covered in this book.

Modifier	class	method	data	Explanation
(default)	✓	✓	✓	A class, method, or data field is visible in this package.
public	✓	✓	✓	A class, method, or data field is visible to all the programs in any package.
private		✓	✓	A method or data field is only visible in this class.
protected		✓	✓	A method or data field is visible in this package and in subclasses of this class in any package.
static		✓	✓	Define a class method or a class data field.
final	✓	✓	✓	A final class cannot be extended. A final method cannot be modified in a subclass. A final data field is a constant.
abstract	✓	✓		An abstract class must be extended. An abstract method must be overridden.
synchronized		✓		Only one thread can execute this method at a time.

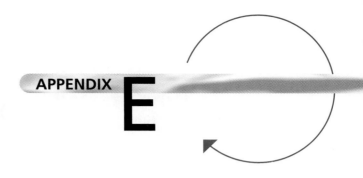

An HTML Tutorial

Java applets are embedded in HTML files. HTML (HyperText Markup Language) is a markup language used to design Web pages for creating and sharing multimedia-enabled, integrated electronic documents over the Internet. HTML allows documents on the Internet to be hyperlinked and presented using fonts and image and line justification appropriate for the systems on which they are displayed. The World Wide Web is a network of static and dynamic documents, including texts, sound, and images. The Internet has been around for more than thirty years, but has only recently become popular. The Web is the major reason for its popularity.

HTML documents are displayed by a program called a *Web browser*. When a document is coded in HTML, a Web browser interprets the HTML to identify the elements of the document and render it. The browser has control over the document's look and feel. At present there is no absolute unifying HTML standards. Different vendors have rushed to introduce their own features interpretable by their proprietary browsers. However, the differences aren't significant. This tutorial introduces some frequently used HTML features that have been adopted by most browsers.

There are many easy-to-use authoring tools for creating Web pages. For example, you may create HTML files using Microsoft Word. The Internet Explorer and Netscape Navigator have simple authoring tools to let you create and edit HTML files. Microsoft FrontPage is a comprehensive and fully loaded tool that enables you to design more sophisticated Web pages. Authoring tools can greatly simplify the task of creating Web pages, but do not support all features of HTML. Since you will probably end up editing the source text produced by the tools, it is imperative to know the basic concept of HTML. In this tutorial, you will learn how to use HTML to create your own Web pages.

Getting Started

Let us begin with an example that demonstrates the structure and syntax of an HTML document.

Example E.1 An HTML Example

The following HTML document displays a message and a list of Web browsers: Netscape, Internet Explorer, and Mosaic. You may use any text editor, such as Microsoft NotePad on Windows, to create HTML documents, as long as it can save the file in ACSII text format.

```
<html>
<head>
<title>My First Web Page</title>
</head>
<body>
<i>Welcome to</i> <b>HTML</b>. Here is a list of popular Web
browsers.
<ul>
  <li>Netscape
  <li>Internet Explorer
  <li>Mosaic
</ul>
<hr size=3>
Created by <A HREF=www.ipfw.edu/kt2/liangy>Y. Daniel Liang</A>.
</body>
</html>
```

Assume that you have created a file named **ExampleE1.html** for this HTML document. You may use any Web browser to view the document. To view it on Internet Explorer, start up your browser, choose Open from the File menu. A popup window opens to accept the filename. Type the full name of the file (including path), or click the Browser button to locate the file. Click OK to load and display the HTML file. Your document should be displayed as shown in Figure E.1.

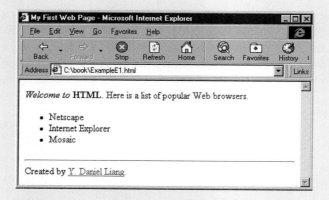

Figure E.1   *The HTML page is rendered by a Web browser.*

What makes *Welcome to* appear in italic in Figure E.1? What makes the document appear in the desired style? HTML is a document-layout and hyperlink-specification language; that is, it tells the Web browser how to display the contents of the document, including text, images, and other media, using instructions called *tags*. The browser interprets the tags and decides how to display or otherwise treat the subsequent contents of the HTML document. Tags are enclosed in brackets; `<html>`, `<i>`, `<b>`, and `</html>` are tags that appear in the preceding HTML example. The first word in a tag, called the *tag name*, describes tag functions. Tags may have additional attributes, sometimes with values after an equals sign, which further define the tag's action. For example, in Example E.1, the attribute size in the tag `<hr>` defines the size of the bar as 3 inches.

Most tags have a *start tag* and a corresponding *end tag*. A tag has a specific effect on the region between the start tag and the end tag. For example, `<b>text</b>` advises the browser to display the word "text" in bold. `<b>` and `</b>` are the start and end tags for displaying boldface text. An end tag is always the start tag's name preceded by a forward slash (/). A few tags do not have end tags. For example, `<hr>`, a tag to draw a line, has no corresponding end tag.

A tag can be embedded inside another tag; for example, all tags are embedded within `<html>` and `</html>`. However, tags cannot overlap; it would be wrong, for instance, to use `<b>bold  and  <i>italic</b></i>`; the correct use should be `<b><i>bold and italic</i></b>`.

The following types of tags are introduced in the upcoming sections:

- **Structure tags**—Define the structure of the documents.

- **Text appearance tags**—Define the appearance of text.

- **Paragraph tags**—Define headings, paragraphs, and line breaks.
- **Font tags**—Specify font sizes and colors.
- **List tags**—Define ordered or unordered lists and definition lists.
- **Table tags**—Define tables.
- **Link tags**—Specify navigation links to other documents.
- **Image tags**—Specify where to get images and how to display images.

Structure Tags

An HTML document begins with the `<html>` tag, which declares that the document is written with HTML. Each document has two parts—*head* and *body*—defined by `<head>` and `<body>` tags, respectively. The head part contains the document title (using the `<title>` tag) and other parameters the browser may use when rendering the document; the body part contains the actual contents of the document. An HTML document may have the following structure:

```
<html>
<head>
<title>My First Web Page</title>
</head>
<body>
<!-- document body-->
</body>
</html>
```

Here the special starting tag `<!--` and ending tag `-->` are used to enclose comments in the HTML documents. The comments are not displayed.

NOTE

Your documents may be displayed properly even if you don't use the `<html>`, `<head>`, `<title>`, and `<body>` tags. However, use of these tags is strongly recommended because they communicate certain information about the properties of a document to the browser; the information they provide is helpful for the effective use of the document.

Text Appearance Tags

HTML provides tags to advise the appearance of text. At present, some text tags have the same effect. For example, `<em>`, `<cite>`, and `<i>` will all display the text in italic. However, a future version of HTML may make these tags distinct. Text tag names are fairly descriptive. Text tags can be classified into two categories: *content-based tags* and *physical tags*.

Content-Based Tags

Content-based tags inform the browser to display the text based on semantic meaning, such as citation, program code, and emphasis. Here is a summary of content-based tags:

- **`<cite>`**—Indicates that the enclosed text is a bibliographic citation, displayed in italic.

- **`<code>`**—Indicates that the enclosed text is a programming code, displayed in monospace font.

- **`<em>`**—Indicates that the enclosed text should be displayed with emphasis, displayed in italic.

- **`<strong>`**—Indicates that the enclosed text should be strongly emphasized, displayed in bold.

- **`<var>`**—Indicates that the enclosed text is a computer variable, displayed in italic.

- **`<address>`**—Indicates that the enclosed text is an address, displayed in italic.

Table E.1 lists the content-based tags and provides examples of their use.

TABLE E.1   Using Content-Based Tags

Tag	Example	Display
`<cite>...</cite>`	`<cite>bibliographic </cite>`	*bibliographic*
`<code>...</code>`	`<code>source code </code>`	source code
`<em>...</em>`	`<em>emphasis</em>`	*emphasis*
`<strong>... </strong>`	`<strong>strongly emphasized</strong>`	**strongly emphasized**
`<var>...</var>`	`<var>programming variable</var>`	*programming variable*
`<address>... </address>`	`<address>Computer Dept</address>`	*Computer Dept*

Physical Tags

Physical tags explicitly ask the browser to display text in bold, italic, or other ways. Following are six commonly used physical tags:

- `<i>` (italic)

- `<b>` (bold)

- `<u>` (underline)

- `<tt>` (monospace)

- `<strike>` (strike-through text)

- `<blink>` (blink)

Table E.2 lists the physical tags and provides examples of their use.

715

TABLE E.2   Using Physical Tags

Tag	Example	Display
`<i>...</i>`	`<i>italic</i>`	*italic*
`<b>...</b>`	`<b>bold</b>`	**bold**
`<u>...</u>`	`<u>underline</u>`	underline
`<tt>...</tt>`	`<tt>monospace</tt>`	monospace
`<strike>...</strike>`	`<strike>strike</strike>`	~~strike~~
`<blink>...</blink>`	`<blink>blink</blink>`	blink (causes it to blink)

Paragraph Style Tags

There are many tags in HTML to deal with paragraph styles. There are six heading tags (`<h1>`, `<h2>`, `<h3>`, `<h4>`, `<h5>`, `<h6>`) for different sizes of headings, a line break tag *(`<br>`)*, a paragraph start tag (`<p>`), a preformat tag (`<pre>`), and a block quote tag (`<blockquote>`).

The six heading tags indicate the highest (`<h1>`) and lowest (`<h6>`) precedence a heading may have in the document. Heading tags may be used with an align attribute to place the heading toward *left*, *center*, or *right*. The default alignment is left. For example, `<h3 align=right>Heading</h3>` tells the browser to right-align the heading.

The line break tag `<br>` tells the browser to start displaying from the next line. This tag has no end tag.

The paragraph start tag `<p>` signals the start of a paragraph. This tag has an optional end tag `</p>`.

The `<pre>` tag and its required end tag (`</pre>`) define the enclosed segment to be displayed in monospaced font by the browser.

The `<blockquote>` tag is used to contain text quoted from another source. The quote will be indented from both left and right.

Example E.2 HTML Source Code Using Structure Tags

The following HTML source code illustrates the use of paragraph tags. The text the code creates is displayed in Figure E.2.

```
<html>
<head>
<title>Demonstrating Paragraph Tags</title>
</head>
```

```
<body>
<!-- Example E.2 -->
<h1 align=right>h1: Heading 1</h1>
<h3 align=center>h3: Heading 3</h3>
<h6 align=left>h6: Heading 6</h6>
<p>
<pre>preformat tag</pre>
<blockquote>
block quote tag
<br>
and line break
</blockquote>
</body>
</html>
```

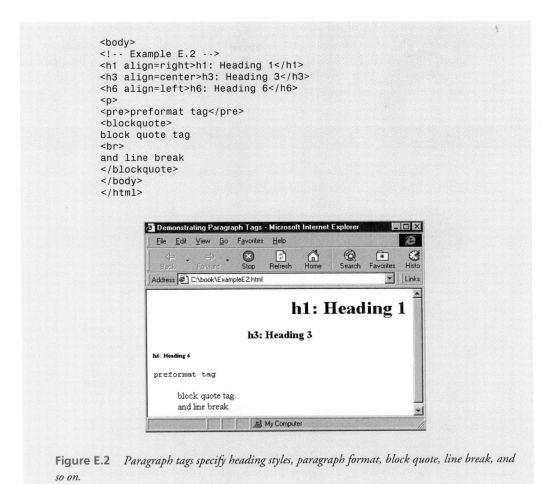

Figure E.2 *Paragraph tags specify heading styles, paragraph format, block quote, line break, and so on.*

Font, Size, and Color Tags

With HTML you can specify font size and colors using font tags. There are two font tags: `<basefont>` and `<font>`.

The `<basefont>` tag is typically placed in the head of an HTML document, where it sets the base font size for the entire document. However, it may appear anywhere in the document, and it may appear many times, each time with a new size attribute. Many browsers use a relative model for sizing fonts, ranging from 1 to 7; the default base font size is 3. Each successive size is 20 percent larger than its predecessor in the range.

The `<font>` tag allows you to specify the size and color of the enclosed text using size and color attributes. The size attribute is the same as the one for `<basefont>` tag. The color attribute sets the color for the enclosed text between `<font>` and

717

</font>. The value of the attribute is a six-digit hex number preceded by a pound sign (#). The first two digits are the red component, the next two digits are the green component, and the last two digits are the blue component. The digits are from 00 to FF. Alternatively, you may set the color by using standard names like red, yellow, blue, or orange.

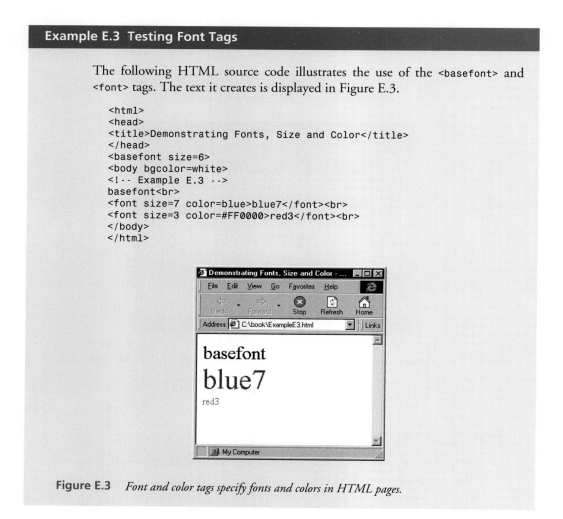

Example E.3 Testing Font Tags

The following HTML source code illustrates the use of the <basefont> and <font> tags. The text it creates is displayed in Figure E.3.

```
<html>
<head>
<title>Demonstrating Fonts, Size and Color</title>
</head>
<basefont size=6>
<body bgcolor=white>
<!-- Example E.3 -->
basefont<br>
<font size=7 color=blue>blue7</font><br>
<font size=3 color=#FF0000>red3</font><br>
</body>
</html>
```

Figure E.3   *Font and color tags specify fonts and colors in HTML pages.*

List Tags

HTML allows you to define three kinds of lists: *ordered lists, unordered lists,* and *definition lists.* You can also build nested lists. Example E.1 contains an unordered list of three Web browsers.

Ordered Lists

Ordered lists label the items they contain. An ordered list is used when the sequence of the listed items is important. For example, chapters are listed in order. An ordered list starts with the tag `<ol>` and ends with `</ol>`, and items are placed in between. Each item begins with an `<li>` tag. The browser automatically numbers list items starting from numeric 1. Instead of using the default numeric numbers for labeling, you may associate the tag `<ol>` with a type attribute. The value of the type determines the style of the label.

- Type value `A` for uppercase letter labels A, B, C, . . .

- Type value `a` for lowercase letter labels a, b, c, . . .

- Type value `I` for capital Roman numerals I, II, III, . . .

- Type value `i` for lowercase Roman numerals i, ii, iii, . . .

- Type value `1` for Arabic numerals 1, 2, 3, . . .

Unordered Lists

When the sequence of the listed items is not important, you may use an unordered list. For example, a list of Web browsers may be given in any order. An unordered list starts with the tag `<ul>` and ends with `</ul>`. Inside, you use `<li>` tags for items. By default, the browser uses bullets to mark each item. You may use `disc`, `circle`, or `square` as type values to indicate the use of markers other than bullets.

Definition Lists

A definition list is used to define terms. The list is enclosed between `<dl>` and `</dl>` tags. Inside the tags are the terms and their definition. The term and definition have leading tags `<dt>` and `<dd>`, respectively. Browsers typically render the term name at the left margin and render the definition below it and indented.

Example E.4 Using Various List Tags

This example illustrates the use of tags for ordered lists, unordered lists, definition lists, and nested lists. The output of the following code is displayed in Figure E.4.

```
<html>
<head>
<title>Demonstrating List Tags</title>
</head>
<body bgcolor=white>
<!-- Example E.4 List Tags -->
<center><b>List Tags</b></center>
An ordered List
```

continues

719

```
<ol type=A>
  <li>Chapter 1: Introduction to Java
  <li>Chapter 2: Java Building Elements
  <li>Chapter 3: Control Structures
</ol>
An unordered List
<ul type=square>
  <li>Apples
  <li>Oranges
  <li>Peaches
</ul>
Definition List
<dl>
   <dt>What is Java?
   <dd>An Internet programming language.
</dl>
</body>
</html>
```

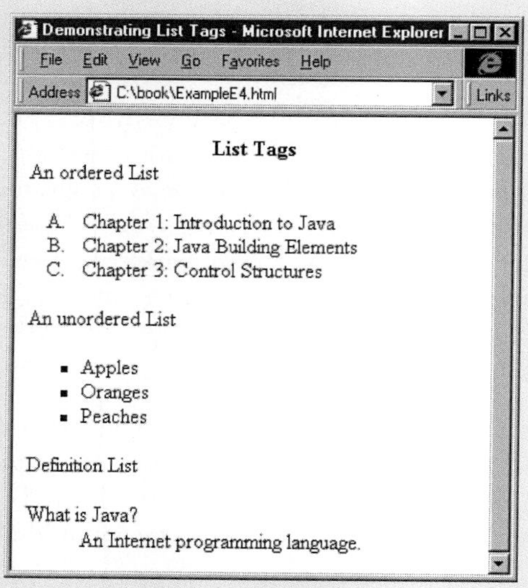

Figure E.4 *HTML list tags can display ordered lists, unordered lists, and definition lists.*

Table Tags

Tables are useful features supported by many browsers. Tables are collections of numbers and words arranged in rows and columns of cells. In HTML, table elements, including data items, row and column headers, and captions, are enclosed between <table> and </table> tags. Several table tags may be used to specify the layout of tables. Each row in the table is wrapped by <tr> and </tr>. Inside the row, data or words in a cell are enclosed by <td> and </td>. You may use <caption>...</caption> to display a caption for the table and <th>...</th> to display column headers.

Table tags may be used with attributes to obtain special effects. Here are some useful attributes:

■ **border**—Can appear in the <table> tag to specify that all cells are surrounded with a border.

■ **align**—Can appear in the <caption>, <tr>, <th>, or <td> tag. If it appears in <caption>, it specifies whether the caption appears above or below the table using values top or bottom. The default is align=top. If it appears in <tr>, <th>, or <td>, align specifies whether the text is aligned to the left, the right, or centered inside the table cell(s).

■ **valign**—Can appear in <tr>, <th>, or <td>. The values of the attribute are top, middle, and bottom to specify whether text is aligned to the top, the bottom, or centered inside the table cell(s).

■ **colspan**—Can appear in any table cell to specify how many columns of the table the cell should span. The default value is 1.

■ **rowspan**—Can appear in any column to specify how many rows of the table the cell should span. The default value is 1.

Example E.5 Illustration of Table Tags

This example creates an HTML table. The output of the code is displayed in Figure E.5.

```
<html>
<head>
<title>Demonstraitng Table Tags</title>
</head>
<body bgcolor=white>
<!— Example E.5 Table Tags —>
<center>Table Tags</center>
<br>
<table border=2>
<caption>This is a Table</caption>
<tr>
  <th>Table heading</th>
  <td>Table data</td>
</tr>
<tr>
  <th valign=bottom>Second row
  <td>Embedded Table
     <table border=3>
     <tr>
       <th>Table heading</th>
       <td align=right>Table data</td>
     </tr>
     </table>
  </td>
</tr>
</table>
</body>
</html>
```

continues

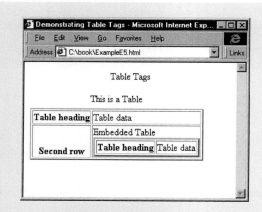

Figure E.5 *Table tags are useful for displaying tables in HTML pages.*

Hyperlink Tags

The true power of HTML lies in its capability to join collections of documents together into a full electronic library of information, and to link documents with other documents over the Internet. This is called *hypertext linking*, which is the key feature that makes the Web appealing and popular. By adding hypertext links, called *anchors*, to your HTML document, you can create a highly intuitive information flow and guide users directly to the information they want. You can link documents on different computers or on the same computer, and can jump within the same document using anchor tags.

Linking Documents on Different Computers

Every document on the Web has a unique address, known as its *Uniform Resource Locator* (URL). To navigate from a source document to a target document, you need to reference the target's URL inside the anchor tags `<a>` and `</a>` using attribute `href`. The following example displays a list of database vendors:

```
<ul>
 <li><a href="http://www.oracle.com">Oracle</a>
 <li><a href="http://www.sybase.com">Sybase</a>
 <li><a href="http://www.informix.com">Informix</a>
</ul>
```

In this example, clicking on Oracle will display the Oracle home page. The URL of Oracle's home page Internet address is **http://www.oracle.com**. The general format of a URL is:

```
method://servername:port/pathname/fullfilename
```

method is the name of the operation that is performed to interpret this URL. The most common methods are `http`, `ftp`, and `file`.

■   `http`—Accesses a page over the network using the HTTP protocol. For example, **http://www.microsoft.com** links to Microsoft's homepage. **http://** can be omitted.

■   `ftp`—Downloads a file using anonymous FTP service from a server, for example: **ftp://hostname/directory/fullfilename**.

■   `file`—Reads a file from the local disk. For example, `file://home/liangy/liangy.html` displays the file **liangy.html** from the directory `/home/liangy` on the local machine.

servername is a computer's unique Internet name or Internet Protocol (IP) numerical address on the network. For example, **www.sun.com** is the hostname of Sun Microsystem's Web server. If a server name is not specified, it is assumed that the file is on the same server.

port is the TCP port number that the Web server is running on. Most Web servers use port number 80 by default.

pathname is optional and indicates the directory under which the file is located.

fullfilename is optional and indicates the target filename. Web servers usually use **index.html** on UNIX and **default.htm** on Windows for a default filename. For example, `<a  href="http://www.oracle.com">Oracle</a>` is equivalent to `<a href="http://www.oracle.com/index.html">Oracle</a>`.

Linking Documents on the Same Computer

To link documents on the same computer, you should use the `file` method rather than the `http` method in the target URL. There are two types of links: *absolute link* and *relative link*.

When linking to a document on a different machine, you must use an absolute link to identify the target document. An absolute link uses a URL to indicate the complete path to the target file.

When you are linking to a document on the same computer, it is better to use a relative link. A relative URL omits method and server name and directories. For instance, assume that the source document is under directory `~liangy/teaching` on the server `sewrk01.ipfw.indiana.edu`. The URL

```
file://sewrk01.ipfw.indiana.edu/~liangy/teaching/teaching.html
```

is equivalent to

```
file://teaching.html
```

Here, `file://` can be omitted. An obvious advantage of using a relative URL is that you can move the entire set of documents to another directory or even another server and never have to change a single link.

Jumping Within the Same Document

HTML offers navigation within the same document. This is helpful for direct browsing of interesting segments of the document.

Example E.6 Navigation Within the Same Document

This example shows a document with three sections. The output of the following code is shown in Figure E.6. When the user clicks Section 1: Introduction on the list, the browser jumps to Section 1 of the document. The name attribute within the <a> tag labels the section. The label is used as a link to the section. This feature is also known as *using bookmarks*.

When you test this example, make the window small so that you can see the effects of jumping to each reference through the link tags.

```
<html>
<head>
<title>Deomonstrating Link Tags</title>
</head>
<body>
<ol>
  <li><a href="#introduction">Section 1: Introduction</a>
  <li><a href="#methodology">Section 2: Methodology</a>
  <li><a href="#summary">Section 3: Summary</a>
</ol>

<h3><a name="introduction"><b>Section 1</b>: Introduction</a></h3>
an introductory paragraph

<h3><a name="methodology"><b>Section 2</b>: Methodology</a></h3>
a paragraph on methodology

<h3><a name="summary"><b>Section 3</b>: Summary</a></h3>
a summary paragraph
</body>
</html>
```

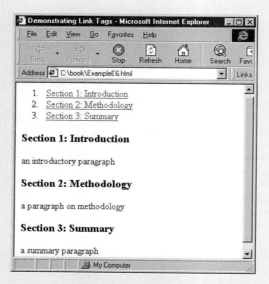

Figure E.6 *Hyperlink tags link documents.*

Embedding Graphics

One of most compelling features of the Web is its ability to embed graphics in a document. You may use graphics for icons, pictures, illustrations, drawings, and so on. Graphics bring a live dimension to your documents. You may use an image as a visual map of hyperlinks. This section introduces the use of *horizontal bar tags* and *image tags*.

Horizontal Bar Tags

The horizontal bar tag (<hr>) is used to display a rule. It is useful to separate sections of your document with horizontal rules. You may associate attributes size, width, and align to achieve the desired effect. You may thicken the rule using the size attribute with values in pixels. The width attribute specifies the length of the bar with values in either absolute number of pixels or extension across a certain percentage of the page. The align attribute specifies whether the bar is left, centered, or right aligned.

Example E.7 Illustration of Horizontal Bar Tags

This example illustrates the use of the size, width, and align attributes in horizontal bar tags. The output of the following code is shown in Figure E.7.

```
<html>
<head>
<title>Demonstrating Horizontal Rules</title>
</head>
<body bgcolor=white>
<! -- Example E.7 Horizontal Rule -- >
<center>Horizontal Rules</center>
<hr size=3 width=80% align=left>
<hr size=2 width=20% align=right noshade>
<hr>
</body>
</html>
```

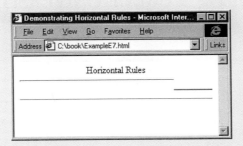

Figure E.7   *Horizontal bar tags are often used to separate contents in documents.*

continues

Image Tags

The image tag, `<img>`, lets you reference and insert images into the current text. The syntax for the tag is:

```
<img src=URL alt=text align = [top ¦ middle ¦ bottom ¦ texttop ]>
```

Most browsers support GIF and JPEG image format. Format is an encoding scheme to store images. The attribute `src` specifies the source of the image. The attribute `alt` specifies an alternative text message to be displayed in case the client's browser cannot display the image. The attribute `alt` is optional; if omitted, no message is displayed. The attribute `align` tells the browser where to place the image.

Example E.8 Illustration of Image Tags

This example creates a document with image tags. The output of the code is shown in Figure E.8.

```
<html>
<head>
<title>Demonstrating Image Tags</title>
</head>
<body bgcolor=white>
<!-- Example E.8 Image Tags -->
<center>Image Tags</center>
<img src="ipfwlogo.gif" align=middle>
</body>
</html>
```

Figure E.8   *Image tags display images in HTML pages.*

More on HTML

This tutorial is not intended to be a complete reference manual on HTML. It does not mention many interesting features, such as *forms* and *frames*. You will find dozens of books on HTML in your local bookstore. *Special Edition Using HTML* by Mark Brown and John Jung, published by QUE, is a comprehensive reference; it covers all the new HTML features supported by Netscape Navigator and Microsoft Internet Explorer. *HTML Quick Reference* by Robert Mullen, also published by QUE, contains all the essential information you need to build Web pages with HTML in 100 pages. Please refer to these and other books for more information. You can also get information on-line at the following Web sites:

- **www.ncsa.uiuc.edu/General/Internet/WWW/HTMLPrimer.html**

- **www.w3.org/pub/WWW/MarkUp/**

- **www.mcli.dist.maricopa.edu/tut/lessons.html**

- **www.netscape.com/assist/net_sites/frames.html**

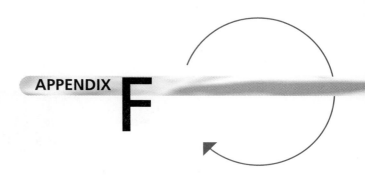

Using the Companion CD-ROM

The companion CD-ROM contains JBuilder 3 University Edition, and the entire source code in the text in jbBook.zip. This appendix covers installing JBuilder 3 University Edition and introduces the use of source code.

Installing JBuilder 3 University Edition

To install JBuilder 3 University Edition on Windows, you need a Pentium 166 MHz or faster processor, a minimum of 64 megabytes of RAM, and at least 180 megabytes of free disk space for typical installation. Here are the steps to install JBuilder 3 University Edition from the companion CD-ROM.

1. Insert the companion CD into your CD-ROM drive. JBuilder 3 installation automatically starts, as shown in Figure F.1. If it does not automatically start, click the CD-ROM drive from the My Computer Folder.

2. The CD contains JBuilder 3 University Edition, JBuilder 3 Enterprise Trial Edition. To install JBuilder 3 University Edition, click JBuilder 3 University to start setup for installing JBuilder 3. The InstallShield wizard will guide you through the setup process. You will see the Welcome dialog box, as shown in Figure F.2.

3. Click Next to display the "Software License Agreement" dialog box, as shown in Figure F.3. Click Yes to accept the license. You will see the Installation Notes dialog box, as shown in Figure F.4.

4. Click Next to display the "Choose Destination Location" dialog box, as shown in Figure F.5. I recommend that you choose the default destination C:\JBuilder3 to match the examples in the text.

5. Click Next to display the "Select Setup Type" dialog box, as shown in Figure F.6. Choose "Typical" to install JBuilder 3 with most common options.

6. Click Next. You will see the "Select Program Folder" dialog box, as shown in Figure F.7.

Figure F.1   *The "Borland JBuilder 3 University Installation" dialog box enables you to choose components from the CD for installation.*

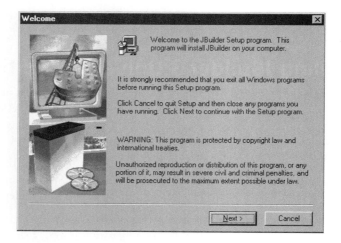

Figure F.2   *The Welcome dialog box reminds you to close all applications before installing JBuilder.*

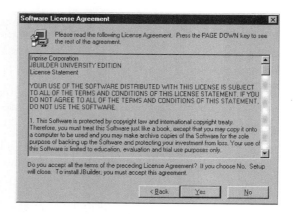

Figure F.3   *The "Software License Agreement" dialog box reveals the licensing terms for using JBuilder 3 University Edition.*

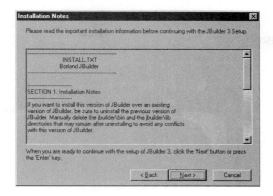

Figure F.4   *The "Installation Notes" dialog box alerts you to some installation issues.*

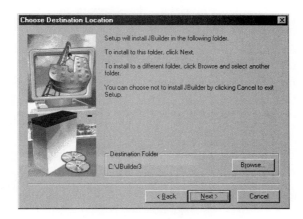

Figure F.5   *The "Choose Destination Location" dialog box enables you to choose a destination direc-tory for the JBuilder files.*

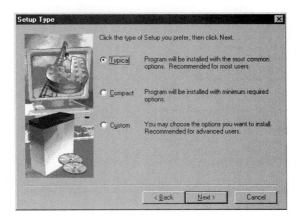

Figure F.6   *The "Select Setup Type" dialog box enables you to choose installation options.*

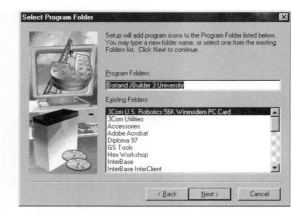

Figure F.7   *The "Select Program Folder" dialog box enables you to specify a name for program folder.*

7. Click Next to display the "Start Copying Files" dialog box, as shown in Figure F.8. Click Next to begin copying files. When it is finished, the "Product Notes" dialog box is displayed, as shown in Figure F.9. Click Next to display the "Setup Completed" dialog box, as shown in Figure F.10. Click Finish to finish installation.

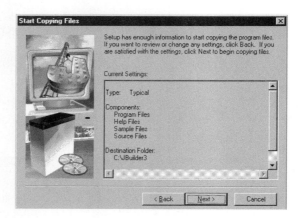

Figure F.8   *The "Start Copying Files" dialog box alerts you that the files will be copied to install JBuilder 3.*

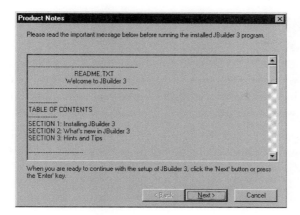

Figure F.9   *The "Products Notes" dialog box displays the product readme file.*

Figure F.10   *The "Setup Completed" dialog box signifies the completion of the installation.*

TIP

The performance of JBuilder and your Java programs can be improved significantly if the Java HotSpot Performance Engine is plugged into JBuilder 3. The Java HotSpot Performance Engine speeds up execution by identifying the "hotspots", the parts of the application where the most time is spent executing bytecode, and accelerating the rate of execution for this performance-critical code. The HotSpot Performance Engine can be downloaded at **www.javasoft.com/products/hotspot/index.html**. To plug HotSpot Performance Engine to JBuilder 3, create a directory named hotspot under the JBuilder3\java\jre\bin and copy jvm.dll to the hotspot directory. When you type C:\JBuilder3\java\bin\java -version, you should see the following message to indicate that the HotSpot Performance Engine is correctly installed.

```
java version "1.2"
HotSpot VM (1.0.1, mixed, build g)
```

733

Using the Examples in the Book

The source code for the examples in the text can be found in the jbBook directory on the CD-ROM in one compressed filename jbBook.zip. You can unpack the files by using an appropriate decompressing utility, such as unzip, gunzip, pkunzip, or WinZip. Your utility must support long filenames. WinZip can be downloaded from **www.winzip.com**.

You should extract the files into the c: directory so that the programs can be run without modifications. For instance, if you are installing the documents using WinZip, enter c: in the Extract to field of the Extract dialog box, as shown in Figure F.11. The folder jbBook and its sub folders like Chapter1, Chapter2, and etc, will be automatically created to hold the files.

Figure F.11 *The WinZip utility unpacks the text examples in the c: directory.*

The files are located and named as follows:

■ The Java source code in Chapter *X* is located in directory jbBook\Chapter*X*.

■ If the example contains a single class, the class name is the filename. For instance, the class name in Example 1.1 is Welcome, thus the filename for this example is Welcome.java.

■ If the example is a Java application with multiple classes, the class that contains the main method determines the filename. For instance, the filename for Example 9.1 is ButtonDemo.java since the main class is ButtonDemo.

■ If the example is a Java applet, the filename is the applet class name. For instance, the filename for Example 10.1 is MortgageApplet.java since the applet class is MortgageApplet.

■ For each applet, the associated HTML file is also provided. The HTML file is named according to the applet name. For instance, the HTML filename for Example 10.1 is MortgageApplet.html because the applet class is MortgageApplet. The HTML files are placed directly in jbBook directory.

734

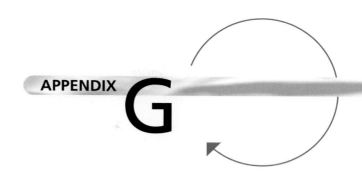

RAPID JAVA APPLICATION
DEVELOPMENT USING JBUILDER

Rapid Application Development, or *RAD*, is a software development technology for developing programs efficiently and effectively. This technology has been successfully implemented in program development tools like Visual Basic, Delphi, Power Builder, and Oracle Developer 2000 among many others. Using a RAD tool, projects can be developed quickly and efficiently with minimum coding. The projects developed with RAD are easy to modify and easy to maintain. The key elements in a RAD tool are the software components: buttons, labels, text fields, text areas, combo boxes, lists, radio buttons, and menus. These components can be visually manipulated and tailored during design time to develop customized programs.

JBuilder provides tools for visually designing and programming Java classes. This enables you to quickly and easily assemble the elements of a user interface (UI) for a Java application or applet. You can construct the UI with various building blocks chosen from the Component palette. The Component palette, as shown in Figure G.1, contains visual components for Rapid Application Development. The components are grouped into nine groups with the tab names Swing, Swing Containers, JBCL, JBCL Containers, AWT, KL Group, and Other. You click a tab to select a group of components. JBuilder has an intelligent click-and-drop capability that enables you to click a button or some other component from the Swing group, then drop it into the user interface. You then set the values of the component properties and attach event-handler code to the component events, telling the program how to respond to UI events.

■■ NOTE
JBuilder's visual designer is available in the Standard Edition, Professional Edition, and Enterprise Edition; it is not available in the University Edition.

JBuilder's visual tools make programming in Java easier and more productive. Since tools cannot do everything, however, you will have to modify the programs

Figure G.1   *The Component palette contains the JavaBeans components for rapid Java application development.*

they produce. This makes it imperative to know the basic concepts of Java graphics programming before starting to use visual tools.

JBuilder's visual tools are designed to work well with class templates created with JBuilder wizards. Use the Application Wizard, the Applet Wizard, and the other wizards in the Object Gallery to create classes to work with the JBuilder visual design tools. Since JBuilder synchronizes visual designing with the source code, any changes you make in the designer are automatically reflected in the source code. Likewise, any changes to the source code that affect the visual interface are also reflected in the visual designer. This synchronization enables you to build Java programs by editing the source code or using the visual designer, whichever is more convenient.

When using visual designers to develop a project, carefully plan the project before implementing it. The major part of the planning involves the design of the user interface. Draw a sketch of the layout that shows all the visible components you plan to use.

Implementation is a two-step process that involves creating user interface and writing code. To create a user interface, click-and-drop the components, such as a JButton and a JLabel, from the Component palette to the frame or applet and set the component's properties through the Component Inspector. Write code to implement event handlers to carry out the actions required by the applications.

This appendix uses Example 9.11, "Using Menus," to demonstrate the use of visual design tools in JBuilder. The example performs addition, subtraction, multiplication, and division using the Add, Subtract, Multiply, and Divide buttons and the menu commands Add, Subtract, Multiply, and Divide from the Operation menu, as shown in Figure 9.25.

The task for completing this application is divided into three phases:

1. Create user interface, as shown in Figure G.2.

2. Implement handlers to carry out actions of the Add, Subtract, Multiply, and Divide buttons.

3. Create and implement menu commands for Add, Subtract, Multiply, and Divide in the Operation menu.

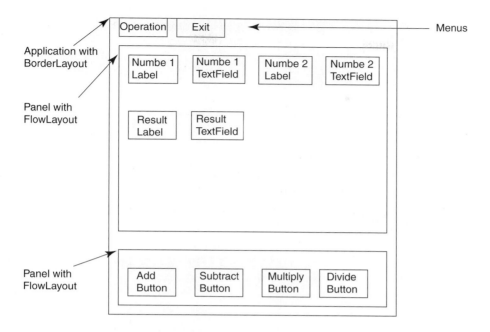

Figure G.2 *The panel containing the labels and text fields is placed in the center of the application, and the panel containing the buttons is placed in the south of the application.*

Phase 1: Creating User Interface

The user interface in Example 9.11 consists of labels and text boxes in a panel with FlowLayout and four buttons in another panel with FlowLayout. The two panels are placed in the frame using BorderLayout (see Figure G.2.) You wrote the code to create the UI in Example 9.11. Now you will learn how to use JBuilder's visual design tools to create the UI interface.

The following are the steps in creating the user interface for Example 9.11.

1. Create the application using the Application Wizard, as follows:

    1.1. Create a new project named AppendixG using the Project Wizard, as shown in Figure G.3. With the AppBrowser for project AppendixG.jpr focused, choose File, New to display the Object Gallery. Double-click the Application icon to start the Application Wizard.

    1.2. Type MenuDemoApplication in the Class field in Step 1 of 2 of the Application Wizard, as shown in Figure G.4. Click Next to display Step 2 of 2 of the Application Wizard.

    1.3. Type MenuDemoFrame in the Class field of Step 2 of 2, as shown in Figure G.5. Check "Generate menu bar." Click Finish to let JBuilder generate MenuDemoApplication.java and MenuDemoFrame.java. The Application Wizard was first introduced in Chapter 8, "Graphics Programming."

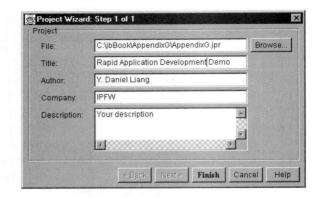

Figure G.3 *Use the Project Wizard to create project AppendixG.*

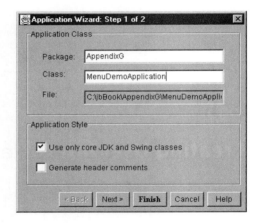

Figure G.4 *Step 1 of 2 of the Application Wizard collects information for generating the application file.*

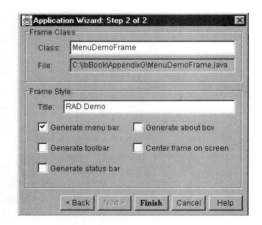

Figure G.5 *Step 2 of 2 of the Application Wizard collects information for generating the frame file.*

2. Start the UI Designer as follows. With MenuDemoFrame.java selected in the Navigation pane, choose the Design tab in the Content pane. You will see the UI Designer appear in the Content pane, as shown in Figure G.6. The Component Tree appears in the Structure pane to display a structured view of all the components in your source file (and their relationships). You can use it to navigate through the components in the UI Designer. You will also see the Inspector window displayed inside the AppBrowser or displayed standalone. The Inspector window is used to inspect and set the values of component properties and to attach methods to component events. Changes made in the Inspector are reflected visually in the UI Designer. When you highlight a component in the Component Tree, an Inspector window for the component is displayed. The component is also highlighted in the UI Designer.

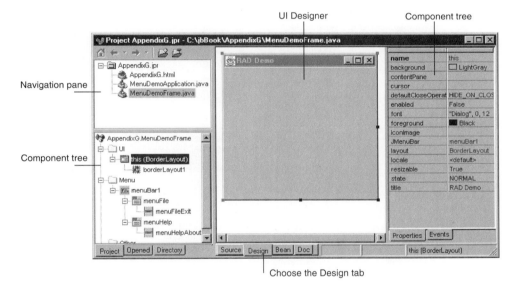

Figure G.6   *The UI Designer, Component Tree, and Component Inspector are shown in the App-Browser.*

TIP
You can specify the appearance of the Inspector window on the AppBrowser page of the IDE options dialog box. The Inspector may be embedded inside the AppBrowser or displayed as a standalone window. You can show or hide it by choosing View, Show Inspector or View, Hide Inspector.

---

3. On the Swing Containers page of the Component palette, click the JPanel icon, then drop it into the center of the UI Designer in the Content pane. JBuilder creates an instance of JPanel named jPanel1. You can see jPanel1 in the Component Tree under the node this, as shown in Figure G.7. jPanel1 will be used to hold the labels and text fields. You can also see the code for creating jPanel1 in the program source code. To see the source code, choose the Source tab in the Content pane, as shown in Figure G.8.

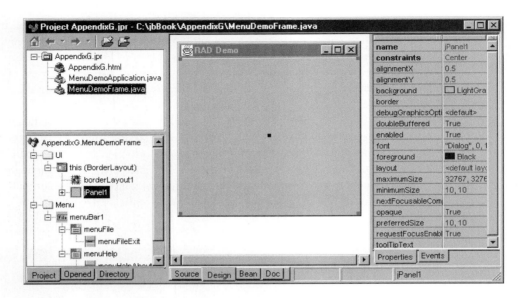

Figure G.7 *The* `javax.swing.JPanel` *was added to the UI Designer to create* `jPanel1`.

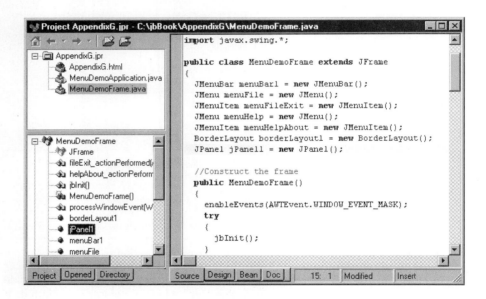

Figure G.8 *The source code is synchronized with the UI Designer.*

4. You need to create a second panel in the frame to hold the action buttons: Add, Subtract, Multiply, and Divide. Here are the steps in creating this panel.

4.1. Select the node this in the Component Tree.

4.2. Click the JPanel icon on the Swing Containers page of the Component palette and drop it to the node this on the Component Tree to create jPanel2. You will see jPanel2 appearing under the node this in the Component Tree, as shown in G.9.

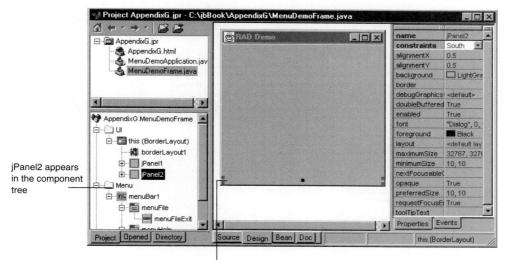

jPanel2 appears in the component tree

jPanel2 appears in the UI Designer

Figure G.9 jPanel2 *was added to the frame.*

5. Set the properties for jPanel1 and jPanel2.

5.1. With jPanel1 selected in the Component Tree, set its layout property to FlowLayout and its constraints to Center in the Inspector window.

5.2. With jPanel2 selected in the Component Tree, set its layout property to FlowLayout and its constraints to South in the Inspector window.

6. Create labels and text fields in jPanel1.

6.1. To create the label Number 1 in jPanel1, click the JLabel icon on the Swing page of the Component palette. Drop it into jPanel1 in the UI Designer. This action creates a label named jLabel1 in jPanel1. In the Inspector for jLabel1, set the text property to Number 1 and change the name property to jlblNum1. You will see Number 1 in the UI Designer and jlblNum1 as the new name for jLable1 in the Component Tree.

6.2. To place a text field in jPanel1, click the JTextField icon in the Swing page, and drop it into jPanel1 after the label Number 1. This action creates a JTextField named jTextField1 in jPanel1. In the Inspector for jTextField1, set the column property to 4, text property to empty, and change the name property to jtfNum1. You will see jtfNum1 as the new name for jTextField1 in the Component Tree.

6.3. Similarly, you can create a label Number 2, a text field for Number 2, a label Result, and a text field for Result in jPanel1, as shown in Figure G.10. Name the labels jlblNum2 and jlblResult and the text fields jtfNum2 and jtfResult. If you want to see all the components on the same row in the panel, adjust the frame size by resetting the size field in the Inspector window for the frame. Don't worry about the look now. When you run the program, you can adjust the frame size.

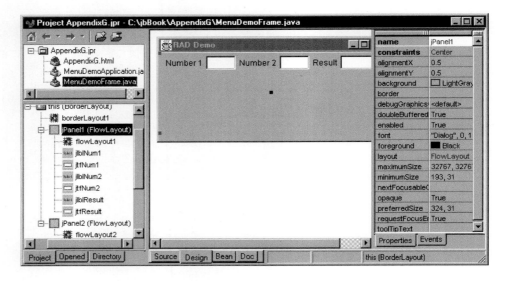

Figure G.10 *The labels and text fields were added to* jPanel1.

7. Create buttons in the panel jPanel2.

7.1. To create the Add button in jPanel2, click the JButton icon in the Swing page of the Component palette and drop it into jPanel2 in the UI Designer. This action creates jButton1 and adds it to jPanel2. In the Inspector for jButton1, set the text property to Add and change the name property to jbtAdd. You will see the button with caption Add in the UI Designer and jbtAdd as the new name for jButton1 in the Component Tree.

■■ TIP

If you don't see the caption Add, click jPanel2 in the Component Tree twice to refresh the UI Designer.

7.2. Other buttons, such as Subtract, Multiply, and Divide, can also be created (see Figure G.11).

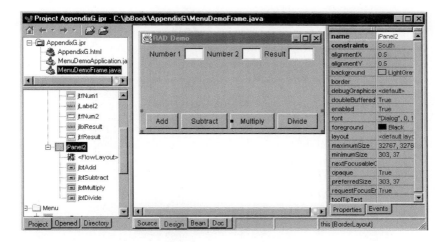

Figure G.11   *The UI components were placed in the panels, and the panels were placed in the frame.*

■■■ CAUTION

For safety, you should save your work frequently by choosing File, Save All to save all the files before proceeding.

■■■ TIP

JBuilder also allows you to change the attributes of the layout manager using the Inspector. If you want to change the attributes in the `FlowLayout` manager in `jPanel2`, select `flowLayout2` under the node `jPanel2` in the Component Tree to display the Inspector for `flowLayout2`, as shown in Figure G.12. You can specify the alignment using the `alignment` property, and set the vertical and horizontal gaps using the `vgap` and `hgap` properties.

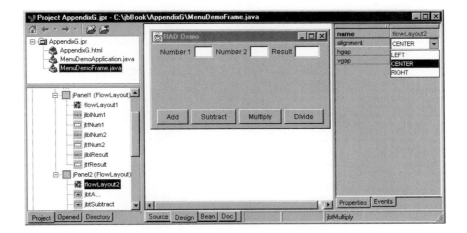

Figure G.12   *You can use the Inspector to change the attributes of the layout manager.*

Phase 2: Implementing Event Handlers

If you run this program now, you will see the user interface on the frame; but you cannot perform any calculations because no code is associated with the action buttons. You can add the code for handling the button actions as follows:

1. Add a handler for the Add button.

    1.1. Switch to the UI Designer (if necessary). Double-click the Add button. JBuilder automatically creates a handler method named `jbtAdd_action-Performed()` in the program. You can see that JBuilder points to the `jbtAdd_actionPerformed()` method in the program source code of the Content pane (see Figure G.13).

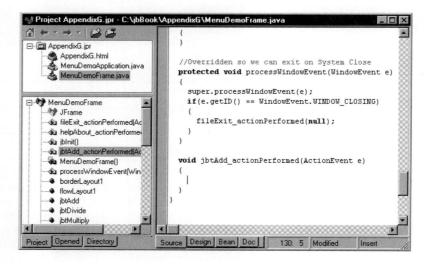

Figure G.13 *JBuilder creates a method for handling button action when the button is clicked on the Designer pane.*

NOTE

You know that the handler for button action is `actionPerformed()`. Why does JBuilder create `jbtAdd_actionPerformed()`? If you browse to the source code in the `jbInit()` method, you will see that JBuilder added an anonymous adapter to handle the Add button action event, as follows:

```
jbtAdd.addActionListener(new java.awt.event.ActionListener()
{
  public void actionPerformed(ActionEvent e)
  {
    jbtAdd_actionPerformed(e);
  }
});
```

You can choose anonymous adapter or standard adapter on the Code Style page of the Project Properties dialog box, as shown in Figure G.14.

Figure G.14 *You can choose anonymous adapter or standard adapter for generating handlers.*

1.2. Add the following code into the `jbtAdd_actionPerformed()` method.

```
add();
```

1.3. Insert a new method `add()` after the `jbtAdd_actionPerformed()` method in the source code, as follows:

```java
private void add()
{
  // Use trim() to trim extraneous space in the text field
  int num1 = Integer.parseInt(jtfNum1.getText().trim());
  int num2 = Integer.parseInt(jtfNum2.getText().trim());
  int result = num1 + num2;

  // Set result in JTextField jtfResult
  jtfResult.setText(String.valueOf(result));
}
```

2. Run the program to see how it works so far. Fix syntax errors if necessary.

The handlers for other buttons can be added similarly. Omit these handlers for the time being and proceed to the next section to learn how to use Menu Designer.

Phase 3: Creating Menus

In this section, you will add a menu bar to perform the same operations as the buttons. Menus can be added using Menu Designer, an easy-to-use tool for designing comprehensive menu interfaces.

The following are the steps in creating menus and implementing menu handlers:

1. Start Menu Designer. Switch to the UI Designer and click menuBar1 under the Menu node on the Component Tree. You will see Menu Designer in the Content pane, as shown in Figure G.15.

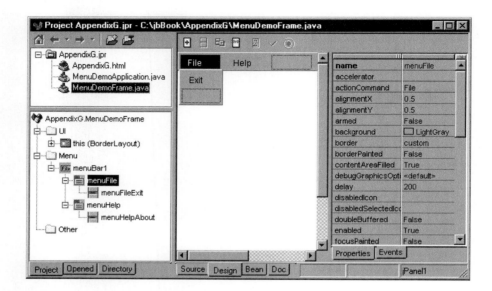

Figure G.15   *The Menu Designer is shown in the Content pane.*

2. The Menu Designer has two default menus, File and Help. They were created automatically because you selected the option "Generate menu bar" in Step 2 of 2 of the Application Wizard (see Figure G.5). This program does not need these menus, so, as shown below, you can delete them.

    2.1. Point the mouse at File, then click the right mouse button to reveal a list of options in a popup menu.

    2.2. Choose Delete from the list to delete the File menu.

    2.3. You can delete the Help menu similarly.

Figure G.16 shows the Menu Designer after File and Help were deleted. Note that File and Help were also removed from the Component Tree.

3. Add an Operation menu and its menu items.

    3.1. Highlight the first menu, type Operation, then press the Enter key.

    3.2. The first menu item under Operation is automatically highlighted. Type Add and press Enter.

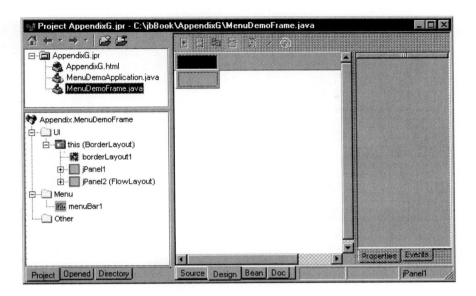

Figure G.16   *The File and Help menus have been deleted from the Menu Designer.*

3.3. The next menu item after Add is highlighted automatically. Type Subtract and press Enter.

3.4. The next menu item after Subtract is highlighted automatically. Type Multiply and press Enter.

3.5. The next menu item after Multiply is highlighted automatically. Type Divide and press Enter.

3.6. Highlight the menu to the right of Operation. Type Exit and press Return.

3.7. Highlight the menu item under Exit. Type Close and press Enter.

The menus are added to the Menu Designer, as shown in Figure G.17. The changes are reflected automatically in the Component Tree and in the source code.

4. Rename the menus. JBuilder creates variables for the menus and menu items you just typed. The variables are `jMenu1` for the Operation menu and `jMenuItem1` for the Add menu. You can change these to more descriptive names.

4.1. Click the Operation menu in either the Component Tree or the Menu Designer to reveal its Inspector window. Change the `name` property to `menuOperation`.

4.2. Similarly, set the menu item names to `jmiAdd`, `jmiSub`, `jmiMul`, and `jmiDiv` for the menu items Add, Subtract, Multiply, and Divide.

4.3. Set the names for Exit and Close to `menuExit` and `jmiClose`.

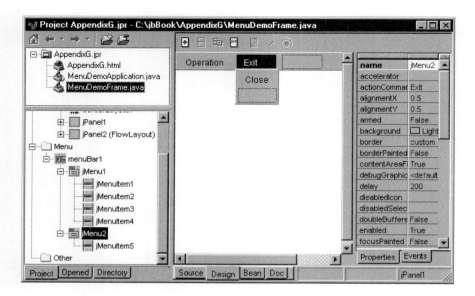

Figure G.17 *The Operation and Exit menus (and their menu items) were created in the Menu Designer.*

5. Implement menu handlers.

5.1. Highlight the menu item `jmiAdd` in the Component Tree to reveal its Inspector window.

5.2. Select the Events tab at the bottom of the Inspector window (see Figure G.18).

5.3. Point the mouse at the `actionPerformed` value field on the right, then press Enter. JBuilder automatically generates a method for handling the Add menu item. You can immediately see the method in the source code.

5.4. Simply add the following statement in the method body:

```
add();
```

Because `add()` was already implemented in the source code, the program is ready to run. Run the program to see how the menus are working. You can complete handlers for the rest of the menu items in a similar manner.

Menu Designer

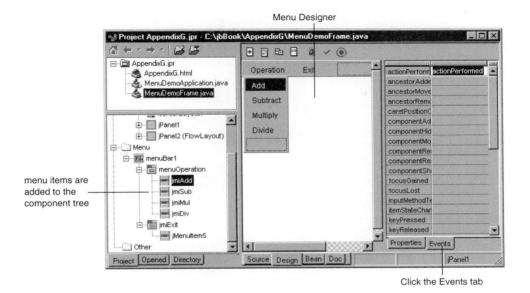

menu items are
added to the
component tree

Click the Events tab

Figure G.18 *Click the Event Tab in the Inspector window to display the event handlers associated with the component.*

NOTE

You can do many other things using the Menu Designer, such as enter separator bars and shortcuts, disable (dim) a menu item or make it checkable, and create submenus. For more information about JBuilder Menu Designer, browse the online user's guide about using JBuilder Menu Designer.

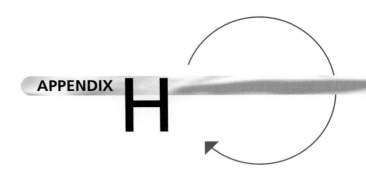

GLOSSARY

This glossary lists and defines the key terms used in *Introduction to Java Programming with JBuilder 3*.

abstract class   When you are designing classes, a superclass should contain common features that are shared by subclasses. Sometimes the superclass is so abstract that it cannot have any specific instances. These classes are called *abstract classes* and are declared using the abstract modifier. Abstract classes are like regular classes with data and methods, but you cannot create instances of abstract classes using the new operator.

abstraction   A technique in software development that hides detailed implementation. Java supports method abstraction and class abstraction. *Method abstraction* is defined as separating the use of a method from its implementation. The client can use a method without knowing how the method is implemented. If you decide to change the implementation, the client program will not be affected. Similarly, class abstraction hides the implementation of the class from the client.

abstract method   A method signature without implementation. Its implementation is provided by its subclasses. An abstract method is denoted with an abstract modifier and must be contained in an abstract class. In a nonabstract subclass extended from an abstract class, all abstract methods must be implemented, even if they are not used in the subclass.

Abstract Window Toolkit (AWT)   The set of components for developing simple graphics applications that were in use before the introduction of Swing components. These components have now been replaced by the Swing components.

accessor method   The getter and setter methods for retrieving and setting private fields in an object.

actual parameter   The value passed to a method when it is invoked. Actual parameters should match formal parameters in type, order, and number.

algorithm   Pseudocode that describes how a problem is solved in terms of the actions to be executed, and specifies the order in which these actions should be executed. Algorithms can help the programmer plan a program before writing it in a programming language.

applet   A special kind of Java program that can run directly from a Web browser or an applet viewer. Various security restrictions are imposed on applets. For example, applets cannot perform input/output operations on a user's system and therefore cannot read or write files or transmit computer viruses.

application   Standalone programs, such as any program written using a high-level language. Applications can be executed from any computer with a Java interpreter. Applications are not subject to the security restrictions imposed on Java applets. An application class must contain a main method.

argument   Same as actual parameter.

array   A container object that stores an indexed sequence of the same types of data. Typically, the individual elements are referenced by an index value. The index is an `int` value starting with 0 for the first element, 1 for the second, and so on.

assignment statement   A simple statement that assigns a value to a variable.

block   A sequence of statements enclosed in braces ({}).

bytecode   The result of compiling Java source code. The bytecode is machine-independent and can run on any machine that has a Java running environment.

casting   The process of converting a primitive data type value into another primitive type or converting an object of one data type into another object type. For example, `(int)3.5` converts 3.5 into an int value and `(Cylinder)c` converts an object `c` into the Cylinder type. In Java, an object of a class can be cast to an instance of another class as long as the latter is a subclass of the first class or, if an interface, implements it.

child class   Same as subclass.

class   An encapsulated collection of data and methods that operate on data. A class may be instantiated to create an object that is an instance of the class.

class hierarchy   A collection of classes organized in terms of superclasses and subclass relationships.

class method   A method that can be invoked without creating an instance of the class. To define class methods, put the modifier `static` in the method declaration.

class variable   A data member declared using the `static` modifier. A class variable is global to a class and to all instances of that class. Class variables are used to communicate between different objects with the same class and to handle global states among these objects.

752

comment   Comments document what a program is and how it is constructed. They are not programming statements and are ignored by the compiler. In Java, comments are preceded by two slashes (//) in a line or enclosed between /* and */ in multiple lines.

compiler   A software program that translates Java source code into bytecode.

constant   A variable declared `final` in Java. Since a class constant is usually shared by all objects of the same class, a class constant is often declared `static`. A local constant is a constant declared inside a method.

constructor   A special method for initializing objects when creating objects using the `new` operator. The constructor has exactly the same name as its defining class. Constructors can be overloaded, making it easier to construct objects with different kinds of initial data values.

data type   Data type is used to define variables. Java supports primitive data types and object data types.

debugging   The process of finding and fixing errors in a program.

declaration   Defines variables, methods, and classes in a program.

default constructor   A constructor that has no parameters. A default constructor is required for a JavaBeans component.

definition   Alternative term for a declaration.

design   To plan how a program can be structured and implemented by coding.

double buffering   A technique to reduce flickering in image animation in Java.

encapsulation   Combining of methods and data into a single data structure. In Java, this is known as a *class*.

event   A signal to the program that something has happened. Events are generated by external user actions, such as mouse movements, mouse button clicks, and keystrokes, or by the operating system, such as a timer. The program can choose to respond to an event or ignore it.

event adapter   A class used to filter event methods and handle only specified ones.

event delegation   In Java event-driven programming, events are assigned to the listener object for processing. This is referred to as event delegation.

event-driven programming   Java graphics programming is event-driven. In event-driven programming, codes are executed upon the activation of events, such as clicking a button or moving the mouse.

event handler   A method in the listener's object that is designed to do some specified processing when a particular event occurs.

event listener   The object that receives and handles the event.

event listener interface   An interface implemented by the listener class to handle the specified events.

event registration   To become a listener, an object must be registered as a listener by the source object. The source object maintains a list of listeners and notifies all the registered listeners when an event occurs.

event source   The object that generates the event.

exception   An unexpected event indicating that a program has failed in some way. Exceptions are represented by exception objects in Java. Exceptions can be handled in a `try/catch` block.

handler   *See* event handler.

`final`   A modifier for classes, data, methods, and local variables. A final class cannot be extended, a final data or local variable is a constant, and a final method cannot be overridden in a subclass.

formal parameter   The parameters defined in the method signature.

getter method   For retrieving private data in a class.

graphical user interface (GUI)   An interface to a program that is implemented using AWT or Swing components, such as frames, buttons, labels, text fields, and so on.

HTML (Hypertext Markup Language)   A script language to design Web pages for creating and sharing multimedia-enabled, integrated electronic documents over the Internet.

identifier   A name of a variable, method, class, interface, or package.

information hiding   A software engineering concept for hiding and protecting an object's internal features and structure.

inheritance   In object-oriented programming, the use of the `extends` keyword to derive new classes from existing classes.

inner class   A class embedded in another class. Inner classes enable you to define small auxiliary objects and pass units of behavior, thus making programs simple and concise.

instance   An object of a class.

instance method   A nonstatic method in a class. Instance methods belong to instances and can only be invoked by them.

instance variable   A nonstatic data member of a class. A copy of an instance method exists in every instance of the class that is created.

instantiation   The process of creating an object of a class.

Integrated Development Environment (IDE)   Software that helps programmers write code efficiently. IDE tools integrate editing, compiling, building, debugging, and online help in one graphical user interface.

interface   An interface is treated like a special class in Java. Each interface is compiled into a separate bytecode file, just like a regular class. You cannot create an instance for an interface. The structure of a Java interface is similar to that of an abstract class in that you can have data and methods. The data, however, must be constants, and the methods can have only declarations without implementation. Single inheritance is the Java restriction wherein a class can inherit from a single superclass. This restriction is eased by use of interface.

interpreter   Software for interpreting and running Java bytecode.

JavaBean   A public class that has a default constructor and is serializable.

Java Development Toolkit (JDK)   Defines the Java API and contains a set of command-line utilities, such as `javac` (compiler) and `java` (interpreter). With Java 2, Sun renamed JDK 1.2 to Java 2 SDK v 1.2. SDK stands for Software Development Toolkit.

Just-in-Time compiler   Capable of compiling each bytecode once, and then reinvoking the compiled code repeatedly when the bytecode is executed.

keyword   A reserved word defined as part of Java language. (See Appendix A, "Java Keywords," for a full list of keywords.)

local variable   A variable defined inside a method definition.

main class   A class that contains a main method.

method   A collection of statements grouped together to perform an operation. *See* class method; instance method.

method overloading   Method overloading means that you can define methods with the same name in a class as long as there is enough difference in their parameter profiles.

method overriding   Method overriding means that you can modify a method in a subclass that was originally defined in a superclass.

modal dialog box   A dialog box that prevents the user from using other windows before it is dismissed.

modifier   A Java keyword that specifies the properties of data, methods, and classes and how they can be used. Examples of modifiers are `public`, `private`, and `static`.

multithreading   The capability of a program to perform several tasks simultaneously within a program.

object   Same as instance.

object-oriented programming (OOP)   An approach to programming that involves organizing objects and their behavior into classes of reusable components.

operator   Operations for primitive data type values. Examples of operators are +, -, *, /, and %.

operator precedence   Defines the order in which operators will be evaluated in an expression.

package   A collection of classes.

parent class   Same as superclass.

pass-by-reference   A term used when an object reference is passed as a method parameter. Any changes to the local object that occur inside the method body will affect the original object that was passed as the argument.

pass-by-value   A term used when a copy of a primitive data type variable is passed as a method parameter. The actual variable outside the method is not affected, regardless of the changes made to the formal parameter inside the method.

primitive data type   The primitive data types are `byte`, `short`, `int`, `long`, `float`, `double`, `boolean`, and `char`.

`private`   A modifier for members of a class. A private member can only be referenced inside the class.

`protected`   A modifier for members of a class. A protected member of a class can be used in the class in which it is declared or any subclass derived from that class.

`public`   A modifier for classes, data, and methods that can be accessed by all programs.

recursive method   A method that invokes itself, directly or indirectly.

reserved word   Same as keyword.

setter method   For updating private data in a class.

signature   The combination of the name of a method and the list of its parameters.

socket   The facilitation of communication between a server and a client.

statement   A unit of code that represents an action or a sequence of actions.

static method   Same as class method.

static variable   Same as class variable.

stream   The continuous one-way flow of data between a sender and receiver.

subclass   A class that inherits from or extends a superclass.

superclass   A class inherited from a subclass.

Swing component   The Swing GUI components are painted directly on canvases using Java code except for components that are subclasses of `java.awt.Window` or `java.awt.Panel`, which must be drawn using native GUI on a specific platform. Swing components are less dependent on the target platform and use less resource of the native GUI. Swing components are more flexible and versatile than their AWT counterparts.

tag   An HTML instruction that tells a Web browser how to display a document. Tags are enclosed in brackets such as `<html>`, `<i>`, `<b>`, and `</html>`.

thread   A flow of execution of a task, with a beginning and an end, in a program.

Unicode   A code system for international characters managed by the Unicode Consortium. Java supports Unicode.

INDEX

Borland® JBuilder™3 University Edition

TO THE MAXIMUM EXTENT PERMITTED BY APPLICABLE LAW, IN NO EVENT SHALL THE PUBLISHER, INPRISE, OR THE PUBLISHER'S OR INPRISE'S SUPPLIERS BE LIABLE FOR ANY SPECIAL, INCIDENTAL, INDIRECT, OR CONSEQUENTIAL DAMAGES WHATSOEVER (INCLUDING, WITHOUT LIMITATION, DAMAGES FOR LOSS OF BUSINESS PROFITS, BUSINESS INTERRUPTION, LOSS OF BUSINESS INFORMATION, OR ANY OTHER PECUNIARY LOSS) ARISING OUT OF THE USE OF OR INABILITY TO USE THE SOFTWARE PRODUCT OR THE PROVISION OF OR FAILURE TO PROVIDE SUPPORT SERVICES, EVEN IF INPRISE HAS BEEN ADVISED OF THE POSSIBILITY OF SUCH DAMAGES. IN ANY CASE, INPRISE'S ENTIRE LIABILITY UNDER ANY PROVISION OF THIS LICENSE AGREEMENT SHALL BE LIMITED TO THE GREATER OF THE AMOUNT ACTUALLY PAID BY YOU FOR THE SOFTWARE PRODUCT OR U.S. $25; PROVIDED, HOWEVER, IF YOU HAVE ENTERED INTO A INPRISE SUPPORT SERVICES AGREEMENT, INPRISE'S ENTIRE LIABILITY REGARDING SUPPORT SERVICES SHALL BE GOVERNED BY THE TERMS OF THAT AGREEMENT. BECAUSE SOME STATES AND JURISDICTIONS DO NOT ALLOW THE EXCLUSION OR LIMITATION OF LIABILITY, THE ABOVE LIMITATION MAY NOT APPLY TO YOU.

HIGH RISK ACTIVITIES

The Software is not fault-tolerant and is not designed, manufactured or intended for use or resale as on-line control equipment in hazardous environments requiring fail-safe performance, such as in the operation of nuclear facilities, aircraft navigation or communication systems, air traffic control, direct life support machines, or weapons systems, in which the failure of the Software could lead directly to death, personal injury, or severe physical or environmental damage ("High Risk Activities"). The Publisher, Inprise, and their suppliers specifically disclaim any express or implied warranty of fitness for High Risk Activities.

U.S. GOVERNMENT RESTRICTED RIGHTS

The Software and documentation are provided with RESTRICTED RIGHTS. Use, duplication, or disclosure by the Government is subject to restrictions as set forth in subparagraphs (c)(1)(ii) of the Rights in Technical Data and Computer Software clause at DFARS 252.227-7013 or subparagraphs (c)(1) and (2) of the Commercial Computer Software-Restricted Rights at 48 CFR 52.227-19, as applicable.

GENERAL PROVISIONS

This License Agreement may only be modified in writing signed by you and an authorized officer of Inprise. If any provision of this License Agreement is found void or unenforceable, the remainder will remain valid and enforceable according to its terms. If any remedy provided is determined to have failed for its essential purpose, all limitations of liability and exclusions of damages set forth in the Limited Warranty shall remain in effect.

This License Agreement shall be construed, interpreted and governed by the laws of the State of California, U.S.A. This License Agreement gives you specific legal rights; you may have others which vary from state to state and from country to country. Inprise reserves all rights not specifically granted in this License Agreement.